Essential Maths

Book 7 Higher

Elmwood Education

First published 2019 by

Elmwood Education Ltd
Unit 5, Mallow Park
Watchmead
Welwyn Garden City
Herts.
AL7 1GX
Tel. 01707 333232

All rights reserved. No part of this publication may be reproduced, stored in a retrieval system, or transmitted, in any form or by any means, electronic, mechanical, photocopying, recording or otherwise, without permission in writing from the publisher or under licence from the Copyright Licensing Agency, 5th Floor, Shackleton House, Hay's Galleria, 4 Battle Bridge Lane, London SE1 2HX.

Any person who commits any unauthorised act in relation to this publication may be liable to criminal prosecution and civil claims for damages.

© Elmwood Education
The moral rights of the authors have been asserted.
Database right Elmwood Education (maker).

ISBN 9781 906 622 725

Typeset and illustrated by Tech-Set Ltd., Gateshead, Tyne and Wear.

CONTENTS

Unit 1 | *Page*
1.1 Whole number arithmetic review | 1
1.2 Decimals | 11
1.3 Using a calculator | 24
    Spot the mistakes 1 | 33
1.4 Rules of algebra | 34
1.5 Negative numbers | 55
    Spot the mistakes 2 | 61
1.6 Applying mathematics 1 | 61
    Unit 1 Mixed Review | 63
    Puzzles and Problems 1 | 67
    Mental Arithmetic 1 | 70
    A long time ago! 1 Napier's rods | 72

Unit 2
2.1 Fractions | 74
2.2 Fractions, decimals, percentages | 84
2.3 Coordinates | 93
2.4 Straight line graphs | 97
    Spot the mistakes 3 | 110
2.5 Area | 111
2.6 Angles | 122
    Spot the mistakes 4 | 132
2.7 Applying mathematics 2 | 136
    Unit 2 Mixed Review | 138
    Puzzles and Problems 2 | 142
    Mental Arithmetic 2 | 144
    A long time ago! 2 The Four Colour Theorem | 146

Unit 3
3.1 Properties of numbers | 147
3.2 Further arithmetic | 161
    Spot the mistakes 5 | 166
3.3 Averages and range | 168
3.4 Displaying and interpreting data | 180
3.5 Probability 1 | 196
    Spot the mistakes 6 | 207
3.6 Applying mathematics 3 | 210
    Unit 3 Mixed Review | 212
    Puzzles and Problems 3 | 216
    Mental Arithmetic 3 | 218
    A long time ago! 3 Pounds, shillings and pence | 219

PREFACE

Essential Maths Book 7 Higher has been written for pupils who are working at the higher end of the ability range.

There is no set path through the book. The book has, however, been split into 6 units. Each unit of work can be used during one half-term with appropriate revision material at the end of the unit. Many topics are reviewed later in the book which is essential for consolidation.

Puzzles activities and mental arithmetic tasks can be found between the units, to be used whenever appropriate. Investigations appear regularly throughout the book. Ideas for discussing and exploring themes from the 'history of mathematics' are included between each pair of units.

No textbook will have the 'right' amount of material for every class.
The authors believe that it is preferable to have too much material rather than too little. There are many opportunities for reasoning and for pupils to start to develop the skills to explain and to justify. Twelve 'Spot the mistakes' sections are included to encourage these aspects.

Very occasionally an exercise is labelled with an 'E'. This suggests that these questions may be particularly demanding. Each topic finishes with consolidation and extension questions to be used as appropriate.

Pupil self-assessment is very important. Regular 'check yourself' sections appear throughout the book. Answers to these parts only are provided at the back of the book for immediate feedback.

The authors are indebted to Sam Hartburn for her invaluable contribution to this book.

Michael White and David Rayner

Unit 4
4.1	Percentages	221
4.2	Proportion and ratio	231
	Spot the mistakes 7	240
4.3	Constructing triangles	243
4.4	Two dimensional shapes	248
4.5	Translation	255
4.6	Reflection	257
4.7	Rotation	265
	Spot the mistakes 8	273
4.8	Applying mathematics 4	277
	Unit 4 Mixed Review	279
	Puzzles and Problems 4	281
	Mental Arithmetic 4	284
	A long time ago! 4 The Königsberg Problem	286

Unit 5
5.1	More algebra	287
5.2	Interpreting graphs	301
	Spot the mistakes 9	307
5.3	Number review	310
5.4	Rounding numbers	320
5.5	Probability 2	328
	Spot the mistakes 10	337
5.6	Applying mathematics 5	339
	Unit 5 Mixed Review	341
	Puzzles and Problems 5	345
	Mental Arithmetic 5	347
	A long time ago! 5 Roman numerals	348

Unit 6
6.1	Metric and imperial units	350
6.2	Angles and constructions	359
6.3	Circles	368
6.4	Three dimensional objects	376
	Spot the mistakes 11	382
6.5	More equations	385
6.6	Sequences	391
	Spot the mistakes 12	404
6.7	Applying mathematics 6	406
	Unit 6 Mixed Review	408

UNIT 1

1.1 Whole number arithmetic review

In section 1.1 you will practise:
- using the place value of digits in whole numbers
- solving problems involving addition, subtraction, multiplication and division

Exercise 1M

1. How many £10 notes are there in £760 000?

2. Answer true or false:
   (a) $7 + 8 + 9 + 10 + 11 = 5 \times 9$
   (b) $1 + 2 + 3 + \ldots\ldots + 14 + 15 = 15 \times 8$
   (c) $\dfrac{(100 - 75) \times 4}{10} = (20\,000 - 19\,000) \div 100$

3. A determined frog is climbing a greasy rope. It takes $8\frac{1}{2}$ seconds to climb up and then half a second to slide down.

   How many complete up and down journeys can he make in three minutes?

4. Micheline has the same number of 10p and 50p coins. The total value of the coins is £9. How many of each coin does she have?

5. I am a 2 digit number. The sum of my digits is 13. The product of my digits is 36.
   What number am I?

6. One subtraction using the digits 2, 3, 4, 5, 6 is $\boxed{642 - 35}$
   (a) Which subtraction using all the digits 2, 3, 4, 5, 6 gives the answer 481?
   (b) Which subtraction using all the digits has the smallest positive answer?

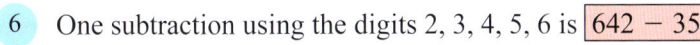

7 Work out the missing numbers.
 (a) 927 + ☐ = 1001 (b) 542 − ☐ = 231 (c) ☐ × 7 = 1645
 (d) ☐ ÷ 9 = 24 (e) ☐ − 950 = 1222 (f) 2000 ÷ ☐ = 50

8 Here are five number cards:

 (a) Use all the cards to make the largest possible *odd* number.
 (b) Use all the cards to make the smallest possible *even* number.

9 (a) Lisa puts a 2 digit whole number into her calculator.
 She multiplies the number by 10.
 Fill in *one* other digit which you know must now be on the calculator.

 (b) Lisa starts again with the same 2 digit number and this time she multiplies it by 1000.
 Fill in all five digits on the calculator this time.

10 Find a number p so that $6 \times p + 8 = 68$.

11 Find a pair of numbers a and b for which $8 \times a + b = 807$.

12 Find a pair of numbers p and q for which $7 \times p + 5 \times q = 7050$.

13 Show how you can use the numbers **63, 100, 2000** and **2** to make the number 2035 by adding and subtracting.

14 Wyatt eats a banana each day for 52 weeks.
Eva eats a banana six times each week for 60 weeks.
How many more bananas does Wyatt eat than Eva?

15 How many spots are there on nine ordinary dice?

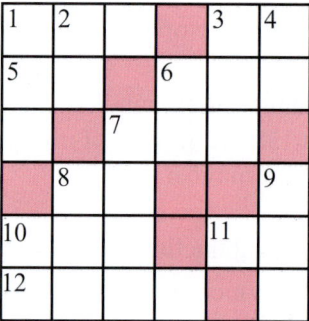

Exercise 2M

Copy and complete the cross number puzzle.

Clues across
 1. 413 − 61
 3. 17 × 4
 5. 3 × 3 × 3 × 3
 6. 9 × 16
 7. Half of 980
 8. 1003 − 985
 10. 472 + 256
 11. 712 − 618
 12. 4006 − 2994

Clues down
 1. 5 × 11 × 7
 2. 17 × 3
 3. 7 + 17 + 117 + 499
 4. 173 − 89
 6. 9 × 12 − 89
 7. 5002 − 121
 8. 28 + 29 + 31 + 32
 9. 9 × 49
 10. (16 × 5) − 9

Exercise 3M

1 Copy and complete the multiplication squares. The numbers outside the square are always 2, 3, 4, 5, 6, 7, 8, 9.

(a)
	8	2	7
5			35
		32	
3	27		
6			

(b)
	4	7	3	8
5				
			42	
2				

(c)
	5	8	2
		28	56
6			
9			

(d)
	4		3
		45		72
		30	
7		35	

(e)
	7		9
24		32	
			18
	42		

(f)
	5	7	
	40		32
3			
6	12		

(g)
	35	40	15
			18
18			27

(h)
		8	
			27
	56		
	40	30	
			36

(i)
		3	
7	42		
	24		
45			72

(j)
18	14		
45		20	
54			48

(k)
		10	16
	24		48
63			72

(l)
		40	
	18		
18		30	42

2 In the next three squares you may have the same number at the top and along the side of the square and some numbers are not used.

(a)
		4		
	56			
			15	
		36		
	14	49		
30			25	

(b)
			18	48
		49		
		9		
	45		40	
16		28		

(c)
	42	28		
	48		64	
15			40	
				81
			24	

Exercise 4M

Work out the following division calculations.

1. 8)2056
2. 5)1025
3. 6)7776
4. 7)5082
5. 3050 ÷ 10
6. 1387 ÷ 1
7. 38 199 ÷ 7
8. 14 032 ÷ 8
9. 31 386 ÷ 6
10. 3490 ÷ 5
11. 28 926 ÷ 9
12. 15 638 ÷ 7

13. Eight tins of pears weigh 3480 g. How much does each tin weigh?

14. 336 children are divided into eight equal teams. How many children are in each team?

15. Books are sold in boxes of 8. How many boxes are needed for 184 books?

16. Cinema tickets cost £6.
How many tickets can be bought for £162?

17. Six crocodiles each laid the same number of eggs.
Altogether there are 138 eggs.
How many eggs did each crocodile lay?

18. Here is a number chain $\rightarrow$ 5 $\boxed{\times 4}$ $\rightarrow$ 20 $\boxed{+12}$ $\rightarrow$ 32 $\boxed{\div 8}$ $\rightarrow$ 4

Find the missing numbers in these chains.

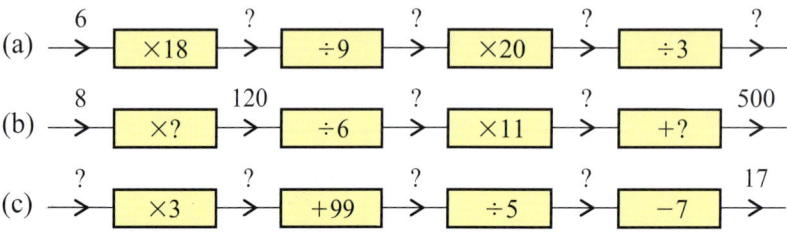

Rounding remainders up or down

(a) How many teams of 5 can you make from 113 people?

Work out 113 ÷ 5.

$$2\ 2 \quad \text{remainder } 3$$
$$5\overline{)1\ 1^13}$$

Here we round *down*. You can make 22 teams and there will be 3 people left over.

(b) An egg box holds 6 eggs. How many boxes do you need for 231 eggs?

Work out 231 ÷ 6.

$$3\ 8 \quad \text{remainder } 3$$
$$6\overline{)2\ 3^51}$$

Here we round *up* because you must use complete boxes. You need 39 boxes altogether.

Exercise 5M

1. Train tickets cost £5. How many tickets can be bought for £88?

2. A car can carry 3 children as passengers.
How many cars are needed to carry 40 children?

3. There are 23 children in a class.
How many teams of 4 can be made?

4 Eggs are packed six in a box. How many boxes do I need for 200 eggs?

5 Tickets cost £6 each and I have £80. How many tickets can I buy?

6 I have 204 plants and one tray takes 8 plants. How many trays do I need?

7 There are 51 children in the dining room and a table seats 6. How many tables are needed to seat all the children?

8 A prize consists of 10 000 one pound coins.
The prize is shared between 7 people.
How many pound coins will each person receive?

9 How many 9p stamps can I buy with a £5 note?

10 Find the missing numbers
(a)   7 1 4 r ☐
     8)5 7 1 4
(b)   5 6 r 4
     7)3 9 ☐
(c)   8 1 2 r 7
     9)7 3 1 ☐

11 In the number pyramids below, each number is found by multiplying the two numbers below it. Copy and complete each number pyramid.

(a)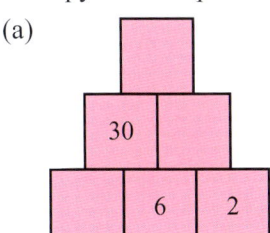

(b)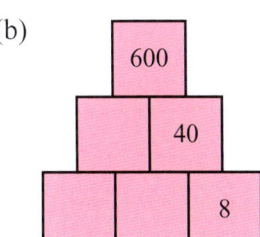

12 The numbers outside the multiplication square are 2, 3, 4, 5, 6, 7, 8, 9. Copy and complete the square.

	?	?	?	?
?	14			21
?			30	
?				12
?	16		48	

13 Tins of spaghetti are packed 8 to a box. How many boxes are needed for 913 tins?

14 Find the missing numbers in these calculations

(a)   ☐ 8 4
     ×   ☐
     ─────────
      7 0 5 6

(b)   ☐ ☐ 8
     ×   ☐
     ─────────
      2 6 4 6

(c)   ☐ ☐ 6
     ×   ☐
     ─────────
      3 6 4 8

(d)   5 3 7
    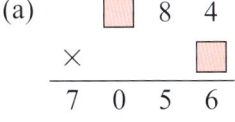

(e)   5 6 4
    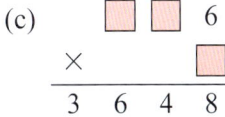

Long multiplication

- Traditional method

```
    35
 ×  41
 ────
    35   (35 × 1)
  1400   (35 × 40)
 ────
  1435
```

- Using grids

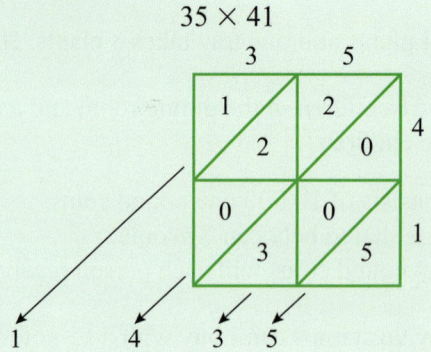

Exercise 6M

Use any method of your choice to work out the following questions.

1. 36 × 27
2. 49 × 24
3. 36 × 25
4. 38 × 44
5. 326 × 15
6. 208 × 24
7. 141 × 27
8. 324 × 213

9. Each week a shop assistant earns £84. How much does he earn in 15 weeks?

10. Gold-plated trees cost €69 each.
    How much would 81 of these trees cost?

11. A film company hires 94 extras to film crowd scenes. They are paid £75 each. What is the total wage bill?

12. If 1222 ÷ 26 = 47, *explain* how you can work out the value of 47 × 26 and write down this value.

13. If 3024 ÷ 48 = 63, write down the value of 48 × 63.

14. A delivery van uses an average of 43 litres of petrol per day. How much does the van use in 14 days?

15 An aircraft holds 174 people. The aircraft was full on every trip for three days. Look at the table opposite and work out how many people the aircraft carried in total over the three days.

Day	Number of trips
Fri	16
Sat	22
Sun	18

16 In a car park there are 25 rows of 42 cars. How many cars are in the car park?

17 How many hours are there in eleven weeks?

18 Fill in the boxes with the digits 2, 3, 4, 5 to make the answer correct.

$$\begin{array}{r} \square\square \\ \times\ \square\square \\ \hline 8\ 4\ 0 \end{array}$$

19 Raima buys 48 chairs for £26 each and 22 tables for £89 each. She then sells 42 of the chairs for £41 each and 16 of the tables for £136 each. How much profit does Raima make?

Long division

With ordinary short division, you divide and find remainders. The method for 'long' division is really the same but you set it out so that the remainders are easier to find.

Work out $864 \div 36$

$$\begin{array}{r} 24 \\ 36\overline{)864} \\ -72\downarrow \\ \hline 144 \\ -144 \\ \hline 0 \end{array}$$

36 into 86 goes 2 times
$2 \times 36 = 72$
$86 - 72 = 14$
bring down 4
36 into 144 goes 4 times

Exercise 7M

Work out. There are no remainders in these questions.

1 $888 \div 24$ **2** $992 \div 32$ **3** $810 \div 18$ **4** $644 \div 46$

5 $1224 \div 51$ **6** $1035 \div 45$ **7** $612 \div 36$ **8** $1769 \div 29$

9 Copy and complete   (a) $\square\square \times 17 = 408$ (b) $11 \times \square\square\square = 3531$

10 A box of 15 golf balls costs 975 pence. How much does each ball cost?

11 There are 23 rooms in a school and each room has 33 chairs. How many chairs are there altogether?

12 Copy and complete this multiplication square.

×	?	11	25
?	?	187	?
?	208	?	400
?	286	?	?

Exercise 8M

There are remainders in some of the divisions.

1 450 ÷ 14 **2** 515 ÷ 15 **3** 851 ÷ 23 **4** 580 ÷ 13

5 775 ÷ 31 **6** 1128 ÷ 24 **7** 830 ÷ 36 **8** 945 ÷ 41

9 A hammer costs £14. How many hammers can be bought with £355?

10 A rugby team has 15 players. How many teams can be made from 187 players?

11 How many 32 cm lengths of string can be cut from 60 metres?

12 A school hall can fit 28 chairs into one row. How many rows are needed to seat 1000 people?

13 Each pack of wooden cubes contains 64 cubes.
How many packs can be filled from 7845 cubes?

14 On average a shop sells 32 chess sets a week.
How many sets are sold in a year?

15 Jars of peaches are packed 18 to a box.
How many boxes do you need for 625 jars?

16 In this multiplication the missing digits are 3, 4, 5, 6.
Find the missing numbers

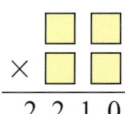

17 The stairs on an escalator move up at a rate of 14 cm per second. How far will the stairs go up in three quarters of a minute?

18 There are 35 offices in a building and each office has 14 phones. The phones are delivered in boxes of 15. How many boxes are needed?

Need more practice with whole number arithmetic?

1. Copy and complete.
   (a) $77 \div \square = 7$
   (b) $\square \div 8 = 6$
   (c) $42 \div \square = 7$
   (d) $54 \div \square = 6$
   (e) $24 \div \square = 12$
   (f) $500 \div \square = 50$
   (g) $\square \div 9 = 9$
   (h) $\square \div 7 = 7$
   (i) $\square \div 7 = 8$
   (j) $40 \div \square = 5$
   (k) $\square \div 8 = 9$
   (l) $30 \div \square = 15$
   (m) $\square \div 7 = 6$
   (n) $200 \div \square = 5$
   (o) $80 \div \square = 10$

2. Here are five number cards:
   (a) Use all the cards to make the smallest number divisible by five.
   (b) Use two of the cards to make a prime number $\square\square$.
   (c) Use three of the cards to make a number which is 426 less than 1000.
   (d) Use three of the cards to make a number which is divisible by three.

Work out

3. 53×26
4. 29×37
5. 412×63
6. 294×38
7. $8\overline{)128}$
8. $9\overline{)729}$
9. $4\overline{)1028}$
10. $8\overline{)1856}$

11. Answer true or false:
    (a) $3 + 4 + 5 + 6 + 7 = 5 \times 5$
    (b) $77 + 78 + 79 = 3 \times 78$

12. A frog drinks 420 ml of water in 7 days.
    How many days will a 24 litre tank of water last?

13. What number, when divided by 8
    and then multiplied by 7, gives an answer of 56?

Work out

14. $286 \div 13$
15. $360 \div 15$
16. $672 \div 21$
17. $621 \div 23$

18. There are 332 children in a school. One coach holds 53 children. How many coaches are needed for a whole school trip?

19. On one day a farmer delivers 42 trays of eggs as shown opposite. How many eggs does he deliver in total?

20. A football team contains 11 players. 283 players turn up for a competition. How many complete teams can be made up?

Extension questions with whole number arithmetic

1.  The length of this rectangle is twice the width.
   The perimeter is 42 cm. Calculate the area of the rectangle.

2. What number, when divided by 14 and then multiplied by 37, gives an answer of 962?

3. Mike knows that 221 × 31 = 6851. Explain how he can use this information to work out 222 × 31.

4. Given that 357 × 101 = 36 057, work out 358 × 101 without multiplying.

5. Use each of the digits 1 to 6.
   Put one digit in each box to make the statement true.

   5 ☐ ☐ × ☐ = 1 ☐ ☐ ☐

6. Find three numbers which multiply together to give 216 and which add up to 19.

   ☐ × ☐ × ☐ = 216   ☐ + ☐ + ☐ = 19

7. A Toyota car uses 9 litres of petrol for every 80 km travelled. Petrol costs 95p per litre. Calculate the cost in £s of travelling 400 km.

8. Copy and complete

   (a) ☐ 7
       ×   5
       ─────
       2 3 ☐

   (b) ☐ ☐ 6
       ×   7
       ─────
       2 2 8 ☐

   (c) ☐ ☐ 3
       ×   8
       ─────
       5 6 2 ☐

9. A special computer costs $220 to hire for 5 minutes.
   How much will it cost to hire this computer for 24 hours?

10. A balloon ride costs £82 in the Summer and £49 in the Winter.

    It costs the balloon company £27 to do each balloon ride. The company does 98 balloon rides in the Summer and makes a profit of £6776 for all the Summer and Winter rides.
    How many balloon rides take place during the Winter?

1.2 Decimals

In section 1.2 you will:

- review decimal place value and adding/subtracting decimals
- learn how to multiply and divide with decimals

Ordering decimals

Consider these three decimals ...

   0.09, 0.101, 0.1.

Which is the correct order from lowest to highest?

> When ordering decimals it is always helpful to write them with the same number of digits after the decimal point.

   0.09 ⟶ 0.090   Empty spaces can be
   0.101 ⟶ 0.101   filled with zeros.
   0.1 ⟶ 0.100

Now we can clearly see the correct order of these decimals from lowest to highest... 0.090, 0.1, 0.101.

Exercise 1M

1. What does the digit 7 in 3.271 represent? And the 2? And the 1?

2. What does the digit 3 in 5.386 represent? And the 6? And the 8?

3. Write the decimal number equivalent to:
   (a) three tenths
   (b) seven hundredths
   (c) eleven hundredths
   (d) four thousandths
   (e) sixteen hundredths
   (f) sixteen thousandths

In questions 4 to 13, arrange the numbers in order of size, smallest first.

4. 0.41, 0.041, 0.14

5. 0.809, 0.81, 0.8

6. 0.006, 0.6, 0.059

7. 0.15, 0.143, 0.2

8. 0.04, 0.14, 0.2, 0.53

9. 1.2, 0.12, 0.21, 1.12

10. 2.3, 2.03, 0.75, 0.08

11. 0.62, 0.26, 0.602, 0.3

12. 0.5, 1.3, 1.03, 1.003

13. 0.79, 0.792, 0.709, 0.97

14 The weights of some butterflies are given below:

0.21 g   0.18 g
0.2 g   0.206 g
0.109 g   0.24 g

Write down these weights in descending order (ie. start with the largest weight).

15 Increase the following numbers by $\frac{1}{100}$:

(a) 11.25   (b) 1.294   (c) 0.382

16 Here are numbers with letters.

(a) Put the numbers in order, smallest first. Write down just the letters.

(b) Finish the sentence using letters and numbers of your own. The numbers must increase from left to right.

B 0.01	M 0.003	S 0.21

T 0.06	I 0.015	R 0.03	H 0.061

A 0.1	Y 0.007	D 0.08

I 0.201	Y 0.2

Adding and subtracting decimals

Remember: *Line up the decimal points*

(a) 2.4 + 3.23

put a zero →
```
  2.40
+ 3.23
------
  5.63
```
↑
(line up the points)

(b) 7 − 2.3

```
  ⁶7̸.¹0
−  2.3
------
  4.7
```
(write 7 as 7.0)

(c) 0.31 + 4 + 11.6

```
   0.31
   4.00
+ 11.60
-------
  15.91
```
(write 4 as 4.00)

Exercise 2M

Work out

1 2.9 + 4.37

2 16.374 + 0.947 + 27

3 81.8 − 29.9

4 6.7 − 4.29

5 2.718 − 1.732

6 12 − 3.74

7 Jack spent £5.15 in the supermarket and £10.99 in the music shop. How much change did he get from £20.

8 Winston was 1.52 m tall and a year later he had grown 9 cm. How tall was he then?

9 Olive has £322.15 in her bank account.
On Monday she goes shopping and buys the items shown in the box opposite. She is also paid £135 which her friend, Alice, owes her.
How much money does she have in her bank account at the end of Monday?

skirt	£42.59
blouse	£23.60
socks	£14.35
food	£32.47

In questions **10** to **15** find the missing digits.

10
```
   5.☐7
+  ☐.5☐
  ─────
   8.91
```

11
```
   6.95
+  ☐.2☐
  ─────
   9.☐1
```

12
```
   ☐.8☐
+  2.☐7
  ─────
   9.03
```

13
```
   ☐.5☐
−  4.☐3
  ─────
   3.73
```

14
```
   4.☐7
+  ☐.9☐
  ─────
   9.03
```

15
```
   3.17☐
−  ☐.4☐8
  ─────
   0.☐48
```

16 I started with 6.658 and then subtracted a number. The answer was 6.648. What number did I subtract?

17 The twelfth term in the sequence 0.3, 1, 1.7… is 8.
What is (a) the thirteenth term (b) the tenth term?

18 Find the missing numbers.

(a) 1.45 → [+0.05] → [×10] → ? → [−9.7] → ? → [+?] → [−0.2] → 11

(b) 0.63 → [−0.04] → ? → [+0.11] → ? → [−0.07] → ? → [+7] → [−?] → 5.2

19 Pieces of timber are used for building houses.
The table opposite shows how much timber is used each week during February.
The total length of timber used in February is 782.5 m.
How much timber was used in week 3?

Week 1	212.65 m
Week 2	169.83 m
Week 3	?
Week 4	275.19 m

20 *Explain* clearly why 1.2 added to 7 is not 1.9.

Multiplying decimals by whole numbers

Method 1

- $7.93 \times 4 \approx 8 \times 4 = 32$ (Estimate first)
  7.93×4
  $7.00 \times 4 = 28.00$
  $0.90 \times 4 = 3.60$
  $0.03 \times 4 = 0.12 +$
  $\overline{31.72}$

- $3.16 \times 6 \approx 3 \times 6 = 18$ (Estimate first)
  3.16×6
  $3.00 \times 6 = 18.00$
  $0.10 \times 6 = 0.60$
  $0.06 \times 6 = 0.36 +$
  $\overline{18.96}$

Method 2

- $7.24 \times 4 \approx 7 \times 4 = 28$ (Estimate first)
  7.24
  $\times4$
  $\overline{28.96}$
  1

- $0.096 \times 9 \approx 0.1 \times 9 = 0.9$ (Estimate first)
  0.096
  $\times9$
  $\overline{0.864}$
  85

> The answer has the same number of figures after the point as there are in the numbers being multiplied.

Exercise 3M

Work out the following. Find an estimate first.

1. 6.13×6
2. 10.22×7
3. 5.34×8
4. 1.29×9

5. 13.6×5
6. 0.074×5
7. 6×2.22
8. 8.4×11

9. Find the cost of 6 golf balls at £1.95 each.

10. A new car tyre costs £29.99.
    What is the total cost of 4 new tyres?

11. Find the total cost of 8 batteries at £1.19 each.

12. If 1 kg of cheese costs £4.59, find the cost of 3 kg.

13 Copy and complete

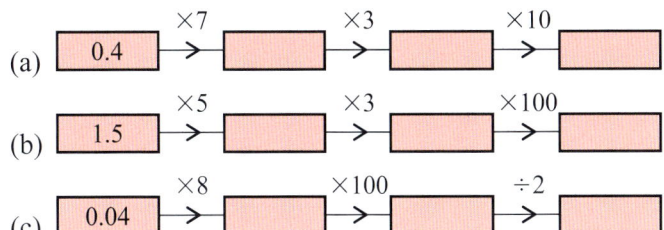

14 Tony can stitch 0.32 m of cloth in one minute. How much can he stitch in 7 minutes?

15
A pair of sandals costs £14.50.
A parcel contains 8 pairs of sandals.
A van contains 1000 parcels full of sandals.
(a) What is the cost of one parcel?
(b) What is the cost of the sandals on the van?

16 Find the cost of 3 tins of beans at £0.64 each, 5 packets of bread sauce at £1.12 each and 2 litres of milk at £1.24 per litre.

17 If £1 is equivalent to $1.35
(a) how many dollars are equivalent to £9?
(b) how many dollars are equivalent to £36?

18 A lady smokes 30 cigarettes a day and a packet of 20 costs £4.30.
How much does she spend on cigarettes in four days?

19 Work out
(a) 0.4 × 3 × 100
(b) 1.7 × 3 × 100
(c) 4.2 × 6 × 1000
(d) 0.6 × 400
(e) 2.3 × 500
(f) 5.3 × 7000

Multiplying decimal numbers

- 5 × 0.3 is the same as 5 × $\frac{3}{10}$. Work out (5 × 3) ÷ 10 = 15 ÷ 10 = 1.5

  4.2 × 0.2 is the same as 4.2 × $\frac{2}{10}$. Work out (4.2 × 2) ÷ 10 = 8.4 ÷ 10 = 0.84

  21.4 × 0.05 is the same as 21.4 × $\frac{5}{100}$. Work out (21.4 × 5) ÷ 100 = 107 ÷ 100 = 1.07

- Quick method:

  When we multiply two decimal numbers together, the answer has the same number of figures to the right of the decimal point as the total number of figures to the right of the decimal point in the question.

(a) 0.3 × 0.4
    (3 × 4 = 12)
So 0.3 × 0.4 = 0.12

(b) 0.7 × 0.05
    (7 × 5 = 35)
So 0.7 × 0.05 = 0.035

Exercise 4M

1. 0.4 × 0.2
2. 0.6 × 0.3
3. 0.8 × 0.2
4. 0.4 × 0.03
5. 0.7 × 3
6. 0.7 × 0.02
7. 0.9 × 0.5
8. 6 × 0.04
9. 0.04 × 0.05
10. 0.7 × 0.7
11. 8 × 0.1
12. 14 × 0.3
13. 15 × 0.03
14. 0.4 × 0.04
15. 0.001 × 0.6
16. 33 × 0.02
17. 1.2 × 0.3
18. 3.2 × 0.2
19. 1.4 × 0.4
20. 2.1 × 0.5

21. If £1 = €1.14, how many euros do Ava and Jack get for £80 when on holiday?

22. Copy and complete
    (a) 6 × 0.2 = ☐
    (b) 0.4 × ☐ = 0.04
    (c) 1.5 × ☐ = 150
    (d) 0.3 × ☐ = 0.06
    (e) 0.1 × ☐ = 0.08
    (f) ☐ × 0.013 = 1.3

23. Work out the area of each shape

    (a)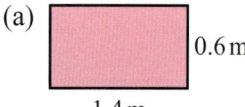
    0.6 m, 1.4 m

    (b)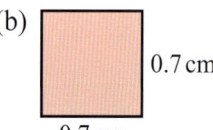
    0.7 cm, 0.7 cm

    (c)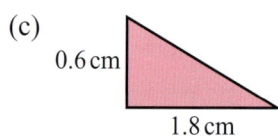
    0.6 cm, 1.8 cm

Exercise 4E

1. If 319 × 7 = 2233, what is the value of 3.19 × 0.7?

2. If 24 × 38 = 912, what is the value of 2.4 × 3.8?

Work out the following

3. 0.33 × 0.2
4. 3.24 × 0.1
5. 8.11 × 0.7
6. 16.2 × 0.8
7. 5.06 × 0.05
8. 30.9 × 0.3
9. 0.2^2
10. 0.4^2

11. Copy and complete the multiplication square.

×	0.1	0.02		
		0.06		24
0.2			0.1	
2.1				
				80

12. Phone cable costs £0.55 per metre.
    Calculate the cost of 2.6 m of cable.

13.

    The length of a rectangle is 1.5 m
    and its perimeter is 4.2 m.
    Find the area of the rectangle.

    1.5 m

14. Work out
    (a) 160 × 0.01
    (b) 1800 × 0.01
    (c) 238 × 0.01
    (d) *Explain* the quickest way to multiply by 0.01.

15. A box of paint brushes costs £8.79.
    How much will 12 boxes cost?

16. Work out
    (a) 3.76 × 2.4
    (b) 7.93 × 0.36
    (c) 82.49 × 3.62

17. A square has a perimeter of 3.64 m.
    Calculate the area of the square.

    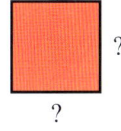
    ?

    ?

Division of decimals by whole numbers

(a) 9.6 ÷ 3

$$\begin{array}{r} 3.2 \\ 3\overline{)9.6} \end{array}$$

(b) 22.48 ÷ 4

$$\begin{array}{r} 5.\;62 \\ 4\overline{)22.^248} \end{array}$$

(c) 7.3 ÷ 4

$$\begin{array}{r} 1.\;8\;2\;5 \\ 4\overline{)7.^33^10^20} \end{array}$$
        ↑ ↑
    Note the extra zeros.

(d) 21.28 ÷ 7

$$\begin{array}{r} 3.0\;4 \\ 7\overline{)21.2^28} \end{array}$$

(e) 312 ÷ 4

$$\begin{array}{r} 0.\;7\;8 \\ 4\overline{)3.^31^32} \end{array}$$

Exercise 5M

1. 49.92 ÷ 8
2. 487.26 ÷ 9
3. 6.7 ÷ 5
4. 0.82 ÷ 4
5. 17 ÷ 5
6. 22 ÷ 8

7. A father shares £4.56 between his three children. How much does each receive?

8. The total bill for a meal for four people is £33.88. How much does each person pay if they each paid the same?

9. If 5 bricks weigh 4.64 kg, find the weight of one brick.

10. How many times will a 9 litre bucket have to be filled and emptied to completely empty a water drum containing 139.5 litres?

11. If 9 cups of coffee cost £8.55, find the cost of 7 cups.

12. Find the answer to the calculation in each box.
    Arrange the answers in order of size, smallest first. What word do you get?

    N: 60 ÷ 100
    E: 0.022 × 1000
    S: 5.5 × 10
    U: 0.006 × 1000
    R: 4000 ÷ 100
    B: 880 ÷ 100
    M: 63 ÷ 9

13. Copy and complete
    (a) 57.8 ÷ 17 = ☐
    (b) 108 ÷ 25 = ☐
    (c) ☐ × 21 = 75.6
    (d) ☐ × 46 = 143.52
    (e) 244.8 ÷ 34 = ☐

14. Copy and complete the cross number puzzle. There are decimal points on some lines.

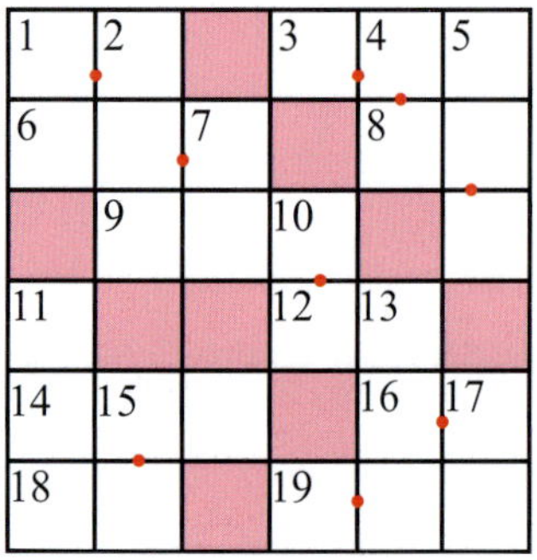

    Clues across
    1. 4 × 1.9
    3. 6.2 ÷ 5
    6. 83.2 ÷ 4
    8. 0.42 × 2 × 50
    9. 348 ÷ 3
    12. 0.95 × 40
    14. 928 + 45
    16. 31.8 ÷ 6
    18. 2004 − 1989
    19. 5.1 ÷ 5

    Clues down
    1. 36.4 + 35.6
    2. 542 + 5 + 54
    4. 7.2 ÷ 3
    5. (85 × 5) ÷ 10
    7. 0.081 × 1000
    10. 31.5 ÷ 5
    11. 200 − (0.9 × 10)
    13. 0.85 × 1000
    15. 60 ÷ 8
    17. 0.0032 × 100 × 100

Dividing by decimals

Dividing by a decimal directly can be awkward at times so using equivalent fractions is useful.

Consider $0.9 \div 0.06$

Write the division as a fraction $\dfrac{0.9}{0.06}$

Multiply the top and bottom by a power of 10 so that both become whole numbers.

$$\dfrac{0.9}{0.06} = \dfrac{90}{6}$$ (×100 top and bottom)

Now work out $90 \div 6$ which equals 15.

$0.9 \div 0.06 = 15$

(a) $8 \div 0.05 = \dfrac{8}{0.05}$

$\dfrac{8}{0.05} = \dfrac{800}{5} = 160$ (×100 top and bottom)

(b) $1.8 \div 0.002 = \dfrac{1.8}{0.002}$

$\dfrac{1.8}{0.002} = \dfrac{1800}{2} = 900$ (×1000 top and bottom)

Exercise 5E

1. Work out the following decimal divisions by completing the equivalent fractions first.

   (a) $\dfrac{0.74}{0.05} = \dfrac{74}{5} = ?$

   (b) $\dfrac{0.6}{0.02} = \dfrac{60}{?} = ?$

   (c) $\dfrac{21.6}{0.04} = \dfrac{?}{4} = ?$

   (d) $\dfrac{1.23}{0.004} = \dfrac{?}{4} = ?$

Work out

2. $12.4 \div 0.2$

3. $2.24 \div 0.08$

4. $153 \div 0.9$

5. $0.72 \div 0.03$

6. $0.08 \div 0.005$

7. $0.885 \div 0.015$

8. A full glass contains 0.04 litres of lemonade. How many glasses can be filled from a bottle containing 2.6 litres of lemonade?

9 There are 3.84 kg of dog food in a packet.
A puppy eats 0.12 kg of dog food for each meal.
How many meals will the puppy get from the
food in this packet?

10 A 50.4 litre barrel of wine is emptied into bottles.
How many 0.7 litre bottles can be completely filled?

11 Copy and complete the division table below:

	÷ 0.1	÷ 0.01	÷ 0.001
12			
0.6			
0.02			
8.9			
6.71			
86.3			

(a) *Describe* what happens when a positive number is divided by a number between 0 and 1.

(b) Make more comments about what you notice when dividing by 0.1, 0.01 and 0.001.

Work out

12 $295.2 \div 1.8$

13 $11.02 \div 0.29$

14 $13.43 \div 0.17$

15 $929.2 \div 4.6$

16 $2.236 \div 0.026$

17 $0.0224 \div 0.0014$

18 How many 0.33 litre cans of drink can be completely filled with 35 litres of drink?

Need more practice with decimals?

1 $11.07 + 15$

2 $18 - 3.7$

3 0.304×100

4 $8.7 \div 5$

5 $11.63 \div 10$

6 $5.1 + 0.51 + 7$

7 1.52×7

8 $11.4 - 8.26$

9 $0.002 \times 10\,000$

10 4.1×300

11 $200 - 5.5$

12 1.7×0.4

13 5.6×0.7

14 $0.79 \div 5$

15 0.3×0.02

16 $28.74 + 19.852$

Copy and complete by finding the missing number.

17 $8.2 + \square = 13$

18 $7.2 \times \square = 0.072$

19 $\square \div 3 = 9.14$

20 $\square - 3.64 = 7.5$

21 $\square \div 11 = 8.2$

22 $\square \times 7 = 24.78$

23 The perimeter of the rectangle shown is 35.2 cm.
Work out the area of the rectangle.

10.2 cm

24 A chocolate cake weighing 1.4 kg is cut into eight equal pieces.
What is the mass of each piece?

25 Sad news of the sparrow that was killed a year ago in Leeuwarden in the Netherlands, in dramatic circumstances. The sparrow flew onto a set on which an attempt at creating a world record of toppled dominoes was being made. The bird knocked over 23 000 dominoes before it was cornered and shot to prevent it causing further mayhem.

It takes an experienced domino technician 5.2 seconds to place each piece in position for the record attempt.
How long will it take to repair the damage caused by the unfortunate sparrow? Give your answer in hours, correct to one decimal place.

Extension questions with decimals

1 Answer true or false
(a) $0.1 \times 0.1 = 0.1$
(b) $0.1 - 0.01 = 0.09$
(c) $0.1 \div 100 = 0.01$
(d) $0.1 > 0.02$
(e) $3.3 - 0.6 = 0.6 - 3.3$
(f) $0.71 = 710 \div 1000$

2 Draw a copy of the cross number puzzle and then fill it in using the clues given.

Clues across
1. $(0.352 \times 10) \times 100$
3. $47.6 \div 7$
5. $(0.9)^2 \times 100$
6. $2 - 0.56$
7. $7^2 + 21^2$
8. 45×0.4
10. $1.6^2 + 4.72$
11. 4.7×20
12. $(1 + 0.01 + 0.002) \times 1000$

Clues down
1. $77 \div 2$
2. 17×0.3
3. $2^7 \times 5$
4. $588 \div 7$
6. 100×0.19
7. $7 \times 7 - (19 \times 0.01)$
8. $600 \div 5$
9. 8.82×5
10. $8 \times 9 - (4 \times 0.25)$

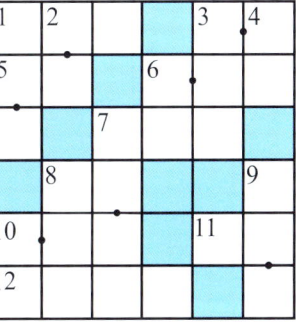

3 The weights of five players in a basketball team are 60.4 kg, 47.8 kg, 71.6 kg, 55 kg and 68.6 kg. Calculate the mean weight of the players.

4 Work out
(a) $0.098 \div 0.002$
(b) $18.92 \div 0.11$
(c) $1.848 \div 0.028$

5 Find the missing numbers

(a) $18 + (4.27 \div \square) = 18.61$

(b) $8 - (\square \times 0.2) = 7.16$

6 A pile of ten 10p coins is 18 mm high. When Izrie emptied her piggy bank she had enough 10p coins to make three towers of height 1.53 m. Work out the value in pounds of the coins which Izrie had saved.

Each empty square contains either a number or an operation (+, −, ×, ÷).
Copy each square and fill in the missing details. The arrows are equals signs.

Designing squares

- Make up your own operator squares starting from a blank grid like the one shown. Try to make your square difficult to solve, but give enough information so that it can be done.

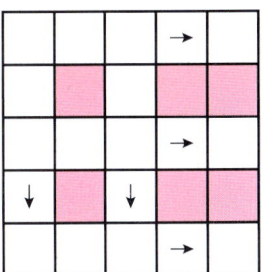

- The grid shown opposite is much more difficult to fill (as you will discover!)

  Try to make up one of these 'super operator' squares.

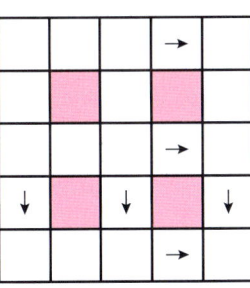

Here is one that works.

10	×	8	→	80
÷		÷		÷
2	×	2	→	4
↓		↓		↓
5	×	4	→	20

CHECK YOURSELF ON SECTIONS 1.1 AND 1.2

1   Using the place value of digits in whole numbers.

Here are four number cards:

(a) Use all the cards to make the largest possible number.
(b) Use all the cards to make the smallest possible number.

2   Solving problems involving addition, subtraction, multiplication and division.

Work out
(a) $(3617 - 1422) \div 5$ (b) 63×37 (c) $1035 \div 23$
(d) How many 8p stamps can I buy with a £5 note?

(e) Tins of paint are packed 9 to a box.
How many boxes are needed for 673 tins?

(f) On average a school needs 87 exercise books a week.
How many books are needed for 38 weeks?

(g) A prize of 470 chocolate bars is shared equally between 18 winners.
How many bars does each winner get and how many are left over?

3 Reviewing decimal place value and adding/subtracting decimals.

(a) Write the numbers in order, smallest first, to make a word.

I	L	N	E	O	R	T	A
0.501	0.3	4	0.034	0.8	0.03	0.5	0.33

(b) Copy and complete the addition square.

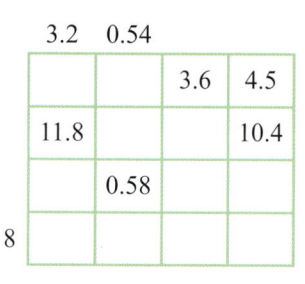

		3.2	0.54
			3.6	4.5
	11.8			10.4
			0.58	
8				

4 Multiplying and dividing with decimals.

Work out

(a) 3.24×7
(b) $21.24 \div 6$
(c) 0.4×0.5
(d) $0.2^2 + 0.01^2$
(e) $3.6 \div 0.05$
(f) $1.802 \div 0.034$

(g) The perimeter of a square is 5.6 m. Work out the area of the square.

1.3 Using a calculator

In section 1.3 you will:

- review the order of operations (BIDMAS)
- use a calculator for fractions
- use brackets on a calculator

Order of operations

Consider the possible answers to this question:
'Work out $5 + 7 \times 3$'

On some calculators, we get: $5 + 7 \times 3$
$= 12 \times 3$ (adding first)
$= 36$

On other calculators, we get: $5 + 7 \times 3$
$= 5 + 21$ (multiplying first)
$= 26$

Both answers seem sensible but if we could get different answers to the same question people around the world would argue over who is correct. Another question comes when there are brackets in a calculation, for example $6 \times (8 - 3)$.

The rule we use is

'work out the brackets first and then multiply or divide before you add or subtract'

The correct answers to the calculations above are

$5 + 7 \times 3 = 26$
$6 \times (8 - 3) = 30$

Later we will work with indices like 5^2 or 4^3. When they are involved the complete rule is shown in the table below.

B rackets	( )	do first	'B'
I ndices	x^y	do next	'I'
D ivision	÷	do this pair next	'D'
M ultiplication	×		'M'
A ddition	+	do this pair next	'A'
S ubtraction	−		'S'

Remember the word 'B I D M A S'.

(a) $40 \div 5 \times 2$
$= 8 \times 2$
$= 16$

(b) $9 + 8 - 7$
$= 17 - 7$
$= 10$

(c) $5 + 2 \times 3$ × before +
$= 5 + 6$
$= 11$

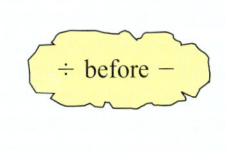

(d) $10 - 8 \div 2$ ÷ before −
$= 10 - 4$
$= 6$

Exercise 1M

Work out the following. Show every step in your working.

1. $5 + 3 \times 2$
2. $4 - 1 \times 3$
3. $7 - 4 \times 3$
4. $2 + 2 \times 5$
5. $9 + 2 \times 6$
6. $13 - 11 \times 1$
7. $7 \times 2 + 3$
8. $9 \times 4 - 12$
9. $2 \times 8 - 7$
10. $4 \times 7 + 2$
11. $13 \times 2 + 4$
12. $8 \times 5 - 15$

13. $6 + 10 \div 5$
14. $7 - 16 \div 8$
15. $8 - 14 \div 7$
16. $5 + 18 \div 6$
17. $14 - 3 \times 2$
18. $6 - 12 \div 4$
19. $20 \div 4 + 2$
20. $15 \div 3 - 7$
21. $24 \div 6 - 8$
22. $30 \div 6 + 9$
23. $8 \div 2 + 9$
24. $28 \div 7 - 4$
25. $13 + 3 \times 13$
26. $9 + 26 \div 13$
27. $10 \times 8 - 70$
28. $96 \div 4 - 4$
29. $36 \div 9 + 1$
30. $1 \times 2 + 3$

31. Copy each calculation and write in the missing number.

(a) $4 \times \square - 7 = 9$
(b) $20 - 3 \times \square = 5$
(c) $24 \div \square - 4 = 4$
(d) $(10 - \square) \times 4 = 36$
(e) $26 - (10 - \square) = 19$
(f) $36 \div (7 - \square) = 6$
(g) $(\square + 7) \times 5 = 65$
(h) $11 - \square \div 2 = 5$
(i) $\square + 7 \times 3 = 30$
(j) $44 + (24 \div \square) = 56$
(k) $(\square \times 7) - 21 = 0$
(l) $48 \div \square + 11 = 17$

(a) $8 + 3 \times 4 - 6$
$= 8 + (3 \times 4) - 6$
$= 8 + 12 - 6$
$= 14$

× and ÷ before + and −

(b) $3 \times 2 - 8 \div 4$
$= (3 \times 2) - (8 \div 4)$
$= 6 - 2$
$= 4$

(c) $\dfrac{8 + 6}{2} = \dfrac{14}{2}$
$= 7$

A horizontal line acts as a bracket.

Notice that we have put brackets in to make the working easier.

Exercise 2M

Evaluate the following. Show every step in your working.

1. $2 + 3 \times 4 + 1$
2. $4 + 8 \times 2 - 10$
3. $7 + 2 \times 2 - 6$
4. $25 - 7 \times 3 + 5$
5. $17 - 3 \times 5 + 9$
6. $11 - 9 \times 1 - 1$
7. $1 + 6 \div 2 + 3$
8. $6 - 28 \div 7 - 2$
9. $8 + 15 \div 3 - 5$
10. $5 - 36 \div 9 + 3$
11. $6 - 24 \div 4 + 0$
12. $8 - 30 \div 6 - 2$
13. $3 \times 4 + 1 \times 6$
14. $4 \times 4 + 14 \div 7$
15. $2 \times 5 + 8 \div 4$
16. $21 \div 3 + 5 \times 4$
17. $10 \div 2 + 1 \times 3$
18. $15 \div 5 + 18 \div 6$
19. $5 \times 5 - 6 \times 4$
20. $2 \times 12 - 4 \div 2$
21. $7 \times 2 - 10 \div 2$

22 $35 \div 7 - 5 \times 1$
23 $36 \div 3 - 1 \times 7$
24 $42 \div 6 - 56 \div 8$
25 $72 \div 9 + 132 \div 11$
26 $19 + 35 \div 5 - 16$
27 $50 - 6 \times 7 + 8$
28 $30 - 9 \times 2 + 40$
29 $4 \times 11 - 28 \div 7$
30 $13 \times 11 - 4 \times 8$

In questions 31 to 54 remember to perform the operation in the brackets first.

31 $3 + (6 \times 8)$
32 $(3 \times 8) + 6$
33 $(8 \div 4) + 9$
34 $3 \times (9 \div 3)$
35 $(5 \times 9) - 17$
36 $10 + (12 \times 8)$
37 $(16 - 7) \times 6$
38 $48 \div (14 - 2)$
39 $64 \div (4 \times 4)$
40 $81 + (9 \times 8)$
41 $67 - (24 \div 3)$
42 $(12 \times 8) + 69$
43 $(6 \times 6) + (7 \times 7)$
44 $(12 \div 3) \times (18 \div 6)$
45 $(5 \times 12) - (3 \times 9)$
46 $(20 - 12) \times (17 - 9)$
47 $100 - (99 \div 3)$
48 $1001 + (57 \times 3)$
49 $(3 \times 4 \times 5) - (72 \div 9)$
50 $(2 \times 5 \times 3) \div (11 - 5)$
51 $\dfrac{15 - 7}{2}$
52 $\dfrac{160}{7 + 3}$
53 $\dfrac{19 + 13}{6 - 2}$
54 $\dfrac{5 \times 7 - 9}{13}$

Indices

Remember BIDMAS: **B** rackets
 I ndex
 D ivide
 M ultiply
 A dd
 S ubtract

$2 \times (8 - 3)^3$
$= 2 \times 5^3$
$= 2 \times 125$
$= 250$

bracket then index then multiply

Exercise 3M

Evaluate the following, showing all your working.

1 2^4
2 3^3
3 0^5
4 $10 + 3^3$
5 $4^2 - 8$
6 $32 - 5^2$
7 $3 + 3^2$
8 8^2
9 5×4^2
10 $3^2 \times 2$
11 62×2^3
12 $5^3 \times 1$
13 $1^4 \times 3^4$
14 $(1 + 1)^3$
15 $(1 + 2)^3$

16. $(5-4)^3$
17. $4 \times (3+1)^2$
18. $(9-5)^4 \div 4$
19. $2 \times (3^2 - 1)$
20. $(5^2 + 5^2) \div 5$
21. $2 \times (6-3)^2$
22. $5 \times (2 \times 1)^3$
23. 3×2^3
24. $20 - 4^2$

Exercise 4M

1. Theo puts some brackets into a calculation as shown below:
   $$36 - (9 \div 3)$$
   He wants the answer to be 9.
   Explain clearly what mistake he has made.

Copy each question and write brackets so that each calculation gives the correct answer.

2. $3 + 4 \times 5 = 35$
3. $6 + 9 \times 7 = 69$
4. $7 \times 2 + 3 = 17$
5. $9 + 12 \times 5 = 105$
6. $6 \times 8 - 2 = 36$
7. $3 \times 8 - 6 = 18$
8. $19 - 6 \times 3 = 39$
9. $27 - 9 \div 3 = 24$
10. $51 \div 3 + 4 = 21$
11. $7 \times 24 - 5 = 133$
12. $6 + 14 \div 2 = 10$
13. $11 + 6 \times 4 = 68$
14. $12 \times 8 - 9 \times 7 = 33$
15. $8 \times 9 - 4 \times 7 = 44$

16. Which calculations below have the brackets in the correct place? For those that do not, write out the sum with the brackets in the correct position.
    (a) $5 \times (6 - 4 \div 2) = 13$
    (b) $(81 \div 9) \times (12 - 4) = 72$
    (c) $(3 + 5) \times (9 - 7) = 16$
    (d) $(16 - 10) \div (18 \div 6) = 2$
    (e) $6 + (7 - 1) \div 2 = 6$
    (f) $(5 + 7) \div 3 \times 0 = 0$

Jumble the numbers

Exercise 4E

Using each number once, find the calculation which gives the correct answer.

For example:

Numbers	Answer	Calculation
5, 3, 6	3	$(6 - 5) \times 3 = 3$

	Numbers			Answer	Calculation		Numbers			Answer	Calculation
1.	2	4	8	6		2.	2	3	5	21	
3.	7	2	3	3		4.	9	2	4	7	
5.	8	4	5	20		6.	20	2	3	6	
7.	7	2	4	30		8.	7	22	6	20	
9.	6	4	3	8		10.	8	40	3	8	
11.	8	36	4	5		12.	7	49	2	14	
13.	21	14	11	24		14.	16	3	9	57	
15.	12	4	16	7		16.	24	42	6	24	
17.	18	5	13	25		18.	40	6	16	4	
19.	7	8	6	50		20.	13	8	4	44	
21.	4	3	9	12		22.	7	9	3	21	
23.	45	4	3	11		24.	121	11	7	77	

25 Make up your own question to try on a friend.
You may use as many numbers as you like.

Using a calculator for fractions

Division can be written with a horizontal line.

$8 \div 2 = \dfrac{8}{2}$ $\qquad (4 + 6) \div 2 = \dfrac{4 + 6}{2}$ $\qquad 4 + 6 \div 2 = 4 + \dfrac{6}{2}$

$12 \div (4 + 2) = \dfrac{12}{4 + 2}$ $\qquad (8 - 3) \div (11 + 2) = \dfrac{8 - 3}{11 + 2}$

The fraction button on a calculator is

Use the arrow keys to move between the numerator and denominator.

Exercise 5M

1 Write the following expressions with a horizontal line.
   (a) $8 + 6 \div 2$
   (b) $10 \div 2 + 4$
   (c) $12 - (8 \div 2)$
   (d) $10 \div (3 + 1)$
   (e) $(12 - 7) \div 2$
   (f) $10 \div 5 - 1$

In questions 2 to 13 use a calculator to find the answer.

2 $\dfrac{8 - 2}{3}$ $\qquad$ 3 $12 - \dfrac{8}{2}$ $\qquad$ 4 $\dfrac{14 - 8}{2}$

5 $\dfrac{8}{4} + 1$ $\qquad$ 6 $\dfrac{8}{3 + 1}$ $\qquad$ 7 $\dfrac{12 - 8}{2}$

8 $\dfrac{16}{1 + 3}$ $\qquad$ 9 $15 + \dfrac{12}{3}$ $\qquad$ 10 $\dfrac{15.48}{1.72}$

11 $\dfrac{8.448}{1.32}$ **12** $2.9 + \dfrac{6.039}{1.83}$ **13** $\dfrac{1.5 \times 1.5}{25}$

14 Emma types $\dfrac{8+4}{4}$ into her calculator which gives 3 as the answer. The correct answer to the sum is 9. Describe what mistake Emma might have made when typing in this sum?

15 Use a calculator to work out

(a) $\dfrac{9.408}{6.72} - 0.28$ (b) $\dfrac{1.9 + 2.953}{2.3}$ (c) $\dfrac{8.7 - 5.622}{1.14} + 2.3$

16 Explain which fraction buttons could be used on a calculator for the sum $(6.6 + 3.4) \div 2.5 + 15 \div 1.5$

Using brackets

For the calculation $14 - (8 \div 2)$ you press

[1] [4] [−] [(] [8] [÷] [2] [)] [=]

The calculation inside the brackets will be done first by the calculator.

Exercise 6M

1 Work out what answer you would get when the buttons are pressed.

(a) [(] [8] [+] [7] [)] [÷] [3] [=]   (b) [1] [8] [−] [(] [5] [×] [2] [)] [=]

(c) [1] [2] [÷] [(] [6] [−] [3] [)] [=]   (d) [9] [÷] [(] [6] [÷] [2] [)] [=]

2 Write down the sequence of buttons you would press to work out the following calculations.

(a) $17 - (4.2 \times 3)$ (b) $\dfrac{28}{2.41 + 4.59}$

Work out

3 $18.41 - (7.2 \times 1.3)$ **4** $11.01 + (2.45 \div 7)$ **5** $(2.38 + 5.6) \div 1.4$

6 $9.6 + (11.2 \div 4)$ **7** $(8.73 \div 3) - 1.4$ **8** $11.7 - (2.6 \times 2.7)$

9 $7.41 - \left(\dfrac{6.44}{1.4}\right)$ **10** $\left(\dfrac{11.39}{1.7}\right) - 2.63$ **11** $\dfrac{28.65}{(1.7 + 0.21)}$

12 $(1.56 + 4.32) \div 2.45$ **13** $3.2 \times (1.9 - 0.74)$ **14** $4.956 \div (1.3 - 0.71)$

15 $(7.77 \div 1.4) \times 1.49$ **16** $(2.67 + 1.2 + 5) \times 1.1$ **17** $23 - (9.2 \times 1.85)$

18 $\dfrac{(8.41 + 0.704)}{1.47}$ **19** $\dfrac{132.43}{8.2 \times 0.95}$ **20** $\dfrac{43.87 - 8.17}{17}$

21 Find three pairs of equivalent expressions.

A $\dfrac{24}{3} - 2$ B $\dfrac{24 - 2}{3}$ C $24 - 2 \div 3$ D $(24 - 2) \div 3$

E $24 - \dfrac{2}{3}$ F $\dfrac{24}{3 - 2}$ G $24 \div (3 - 2)$

22 Write down the sequence of buttons you would press to evaluate the following.

(a) $\dfrac{9 - 3}{4 + 8}$ (b) $\dfrac{30}{8 - 3} + 4 \times 7$

In questions 23 to 44 use the x^2 button where needed and write down all the numbers on your calculator display.

23 $2.6^2 - 1.4$ **24** $8.3^2 \times 1.17$ **25** $7.2^2 \div 6.67$

26 $(1.4 + 2.67)^2$ **27** $(8.41 - 5.7)^2$ **28** $(2.7 \times 1.31)^2$

29 $8.2^2 - (1.4 + 1.73)$ **30** $\dfrac{2.6^2}{(1.3 + 2.99)}$ **31** $4.1^2 - \left(\dfrac{8.7}{3.2}\right)$

32 $\dfrac{(2.7 + 6.04)}{(1.4 + 2.11)}$ **33** $\dfrac{(8.71 - 1.6)}{(2.4 + 9.73)}$ **34** $\left(\dfrac{2.3}{1.4}\right)^2$

35 $9.72^2 - (2.9 \times 2.7)$ **36** $(3.3 + 1.3^2) \times 9$ **37** $(2.7^2 - 2.1) \div 5$

38 $\left(\dfrac{2.84}{7}\right) + \left(\dfrac{7}{11.2}\right)$ **39** $\dfrac{(2.7 \times 8.1)}{(12 - 8.51)}$ **40** $\left(\dfrac{2.3}{1.5}\right) - \left(\dfrac{6.3}{8.9}\right)$

41 $(1.31 + 2.705) - 1.3^2$ **42** $(2.71 - 0.951) \times 5.62$ **43** $\dfrac{(8.5 \times 1.952)}{(7.2 - 5.96)}$

44 $\left(\dfrac{80.7}{30.3}\right) - \left(\dfrac{11.7}{10.2}\right)$

Need more practice with using a calculator?

Work out and write down all the numbers in your calculator display.

1 $\dfrac{5.63}{2.8 - 1.71}$ **2** $\dfrac{11.5}{5.24 + 1.57}$ **3** $\dfrac{8.27}{2.9 \times 1.35}$

4 $\dfrac{3.7 - 2.41}{1.9 + 0.72}$ **5** $\dfrac{8.5 + 9.3}{12.9 - 8.72}$ **6** $\dfrac{0.97 \times 3.85}{1.24 + 4.63}$

7. $14.5 - \left(\dfrac{1.9}{0.7}\right)$

8. $8.41 - 3.2 \times 1.76$

9. $11.62 - \dfrac{6.3}{9.8}$

10. $\dfrac{9.84 \times 0.751}{6.3 \times 0.95}$

11. $5.62 + 1.98 + \dfrac{1.2}{4.5}$

12. $8.5 - \dfrac{8.9}{11.6}$

13. $\dfrac{6.3}{4.2} + \dfrac{8.2}{11.9}$

14. $\dfrac{8.43 + 1.99}{9.6 - 1.73}$

15. $\dfrac{17.6}{8.4} - \dfrac{1.92}{8.41}$

16. $25.1 - 4.2^2$

17. $(9.8 - 4.43)^2$

18. $18.7 - 2.33^2$

19. $8.21^2 + 1.67^2$

20. $9.23^2 - 7.42^2$

21. $16.1 - 1.1^2$

22. $\dfrac{16.1}{4.7} - 1.8^2$

23. $\left(\dfrac{17.2}{9.8} - 1.2\right)^2$

24. $9.9 - 8.3 \times 0.075$

25. $1.21 - \dfrac{9}{14^2}$

26. $3.7^2 + \dfrac{11.4}{1.7}$

27. $\dfrac{11.7 - 3.73}{2.45^2}$

28. You can buy euros at the rate of 1.14 euros to the pound.
    (a) How many euros will you get for £265?
    (b) How many pounds will you get for €700?
    Give your answers to the nearest whole number.

29. A rectangular field measures 115 m by 215 m.
    Work out the area of the field
    (a) in m²　　(b) in hectares (1 hectare = 10 000 m²)

30. A man's heart beats at 70 beats/min. How many times will his heart beat between 03.30 and 23.30 on the same day?

31. The year 2000 is clearly not a prime number but it is a thousand times a prime number. Which, if any, of the years from 2000 to 2010 are prime numbers?

Extension questions with using a calculator

Calculator words

- When you hold a calculator display upside down some numbers appear to form words:　4506　spells 'Gosh'

  0.70　spells 'Old' (ignoring the decimal point)

  Warning
  The letters on some calculators are not so easy to make out. Agree with your teacher which number gives which letter.

Translate this passage using a calculator and the clues below:

'①!' shouted Olag out of the window of his ②. 'I need some ③ / ④ for my dinner. Do you ⑤ them?'
'⑥ did' ⑦ / ⑧ 'I even took off the ⑨ for free. ⑩ / ⑪ / ⑫ they were. The problem is that all the ⑬ were eaten in the ⑭, mostly by ⑮. ⑯ / ⑰ such a ⑱ / ⑲ lately. ⑳ and ㉑ are always ㉒ because of the amount of ㉓ they drink every night'
'㉔ well, he is the ㉕ I suppose' Olag grumbled 'Roast ㉖ again tonight then…'

Clues to passage

1. $(2.37 + 2.53) \div 0.7^2$
2. $(3 \div 40) + 0.0011$
3. $\frac{3}{8} - (39.2 \div 10^4)$
4. $5 \times 12 \times 100 - 7$
5. $(90 \times 80) + (107 \times 5)$
6. $\sqrt{0.01} \times 10$
7. $(68 + 1.23) \div 200$
8. $101^2 - (5 \times 13) - 2$
9. $750^2 + (296\,900 \div 20)$
10. $2^3 \times 5^2 \times 3 + 16.3 + 1.7$
11. $(70\,000 \div 2) + (3 \times 2)$
12. $11\,986 \div 2$
13. $(600^2 - 6640) \div 10$
14. $200^2 - 685$
15. $(0.5^2 \times 0.6)$
16. $\sqrt{289} \times 2$
17. $836.4 \div 17 + 1.8$
18. $30^2 + 18$
19. $5^3 \times 64.6$
20. $(63\,508 \times 5) - 3$
21. $\sqrt{(1160 - 4)}$
22. 1.3803×0.25
23. $(32 \times 10^3) + 8$
24. $2^3 \times 5$
25. $(5^3 \times 2^2 \times 11) + 8$
26. $7 \times 10^7 - 9\,563\,966$

✖ Spot the mistakes 1 ✖

Number calculations

Work through each question below and *explain clearly* what mistakes have been made. Beware – some questions are correctly done.

1.
```
   52
 × 69
 ----
  468
  312
 ----
  780
```
so 52 × 69 = 780

2. $0.6 \times 0.2 = 1.2$

3   A box contains 28 packets when full. What is the least number of boxes needed to hold 1000 packets?

$$28\overline{)100^{16}0} \quad \begin{array}{r} 3\;5\text{ r. }20 \end{array}$$ so 35 boxes are needed.

4
$$\begin{array}{r} 148 \\ \times\;\;\;39 \\ \hline 1332 \\ 4440 \\ \hline 5772 \end{array}$$
so $148 \times 39 = 5772$

5
$$7\overline{)18^47.^56} \quad \begin{array}{r} 2\;5.\;8 \end{array}$$
so $187.6 \div 7 = 25.8$

6   Ruhi buys 1.2 kg of grapes at £4.60 per kg and 3 peppers at £0.67 each. What is the total cost?

$$\begin{array}{r} 460 \\ \times\;\;\;12 \\ \hline 820 \\ 4600 \\ \hline 5420 \end{array}$$
so 4.60×1.2
$= 5.420$
$= £5.42$

0.67×3
$= £2.01$

total cost $= 5.42 + 2.01 = £7.43$

7   $22 \div 0.04 = \dfrac{22}{0.04} = \dfrac{220}{4} = 55$

8   $3 + \dfrac{17}{5} = \dfrac{20}{5} = 4$

9   Mr Avis arranges a trip to the theatre by coach for 83 people. One coach can carry up to 50 people. Each person pays £29 for the coach and theatre ticket. The leftover money is given to charity. How much money is given to charity?

	cost
theatre ticket	£19
1 coach	£322

Each person pays £10 for the coach
total $= 83 \times 10 = £830$
2 coaches $= 2 \times 322 = £644$
charity money $= 830 - 644 = £186$

10   $8 + 12 \div (2 \times 3) = 30$
Are the brackets in the correct place?

1.4 Rules of algebra

In section 1.4 you will learn how to:
- use letters for numbers
- simplify algebraic expressions
- substitute numbers into a formula
- multiply out single brackets
- tackle balance puzzles

Using letters for numbers

Many problems can be solved by using letters instead of numbers. This is called using *algebra*.

Remember: the letters stand for numbers

- Suppose there are N cows in a field. If the farmer puts 3 more cows in the field, there will be $N + 3$ cows in the field.

- $N + 3$ is an expression. An expression is usually a mixture of letters, numbers and signs. An expression has no '=' sign.

- A term is a single number or letter (or a product of numbers or letters), e.g. 3 or N or $3N$.

- Suppose there are y people on a bus. At a bus stop n people get off the bus. There are now $y - n$ people on the bus.

- $y - n$ is an expression.

- If I start with a number N and treble it, I will have $N \times 3$. In algebra the '$\times$' sign is left out and the number is written before the letter so I will have $3N$.

- If I start with a number x then double it and add 4, I will have $2x + 4$.

- $2x + 4$ is an expression.

- $x \div 4$ is written as $\dfrac{x}{4}$

Exercise 1M

Write down an expression for each question below.

1. I start with a number d then take away 9.

2. I start with a number x then double it.

3. I start with a number y then add 25.

4. I start with a number m then divide it by 6.

5. I start with a number k, double it then subtract 8.

6. I start with a number M, treble it then take away 4.

7. I start with a number p and multiply it by 25.

8. I start with a number w, double it then add 15.

9. I start with a number q, multiply it by 10 then subtract 8.

10. I start with a number n, divide it by 3 then add 5.

11. I start with a number b, multiply it by 3 then add 8.

12. I start with a number y, divide it by 8 then subtract 7.

13 I start with a number f, multiply it by 3 then divide it by 10.

14 The perimeter p of this rectangle is
$$p = a + b + a + b$$
This is written as $p = 2a + 2b$

Write down the perimeter p for this triangle.

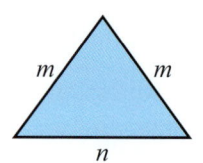

Use algebra to find the perimeter p of each shape in questions **15** to **17**.

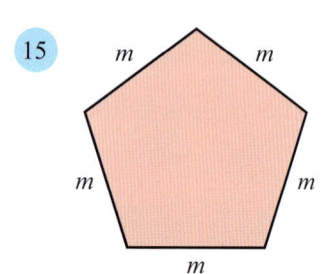

15

16

17

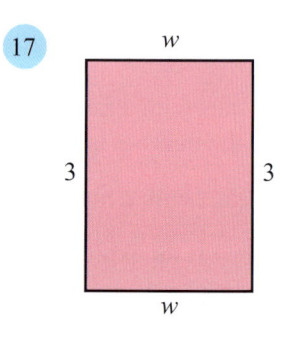

18 Harry says the perimeter of this shape is $mn + 18$.

Explain clearly the mistake that Harry has made.

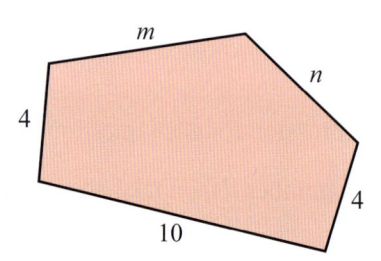

19 Adam says the perimeter of the triangle opposite is $2x + y$.

Jin says the triangle perimeter is $x + y + x$.

What is correct?

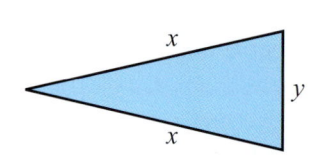

20 Write down an expression for the total area of the two rectangles shown opposite.

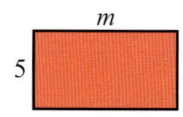

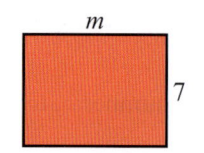

Exercise 2M

In questions ① to ⑩ write down the expression.

1. I start with x, double it and then add y.
2. I start with s, treble it and then take away w.
3. I start with $4x$, take away y and then add 5.
4. I start with n, divide it by 5 and then subtract 3.
5. I subtract f from g and then add n.
6. I start with $2y$, add $3w$ and then take away x.
7. I add together p and q then multiply the total by 4.
8. I start with m then multiply by 6 and add $3n$.
9. I subtract $3p$ from $5q$ then add $4m$.
10. I start with n, double it, divide by 9 and then add 6.

11. A sweet weighs x grams. How many grams do five sweets weigh?

12. A piece of rope is 20 m long. A prisoner ties on an extra piece of rope of length y metres. How long is the entire piece of rope now?

13. Jackie shares N pounds equally between six children. How much money does each child receive?

14. A piece of wood is w cm long. I cut off a piece 9 cm long. What is the length of the remaining piece of wood?

15. Carl has m books. Shalina has 3 times as many books. How many books does Shalina have?

16. On Tuesday there are x people in a cinema. On Saturday there are four times as many people plus another 45. How many people are in the cinema on Saturday?

17. w toffees are shared equally between you and three others. How many toffees do you receive?

18. A bottle contains n millilitres of medicine. 8 doses of medicine are given from the bottle. Each dose is 5 ml.
    (a) How many millilitres of medicine remain in the bottle?
    (b) The remaining medicine is given out in m doses. How many millilitres of medicine is in each new dose?

19 Tania spends £n on magazines. Chris spends £4 more than Tania. Tania says that Chris spends £4n in total. Is Tania correct? Give a reason for your answer.

20 Draw and label a triangle whose perimeter p is given by the formula $p = 2x + 5$.

21 Draw and label a rectangle whose perimeter p is given by the formula $p = 2a + 2b$.

Simplifying algebraic expressions

> **Collecting like terms**
>
> The expression $4a + 3a$ can be simplified to $7a$.
>
> This is because $4a + 3a$ means four a s plus three a s which gives seven a s.
>
> a means $1a$ so $6a - a = 6a - 1a = 5a$
>
> $5x$ and $3x$ are called *like* terms.
>
> $5x$ and $3y$ are called *unlike* terms.
>
> The sum or difference of two terms can only be simplified if the terms are *like* terms.

We can collect like terms.

(a) $5 + n + 2 + 4n = 5n + 7$

(b) $y + 3 + y + 4 + w = w + 2y + 7$

Collect in alphabetical order, with letter terms written before any numbers on their own.

(c) $4x - 4$ cannot be simplified (no like terms)

(d) $5y + x - 5y = x$

Do not write $0y$
Do not write $1x$

(e) Simplify $6x + 4y + 2x - 2y$

$(6x)(+4y)(+2x)(-2y) = 8x + 2y$

$6x$ means $+6x$

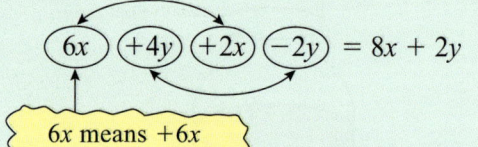

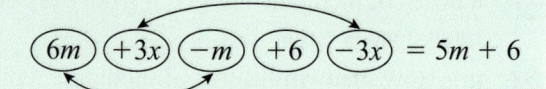

(f) Simplify $6m + 3x - m + 6 - 3x$

$(6m)(+3x)(-m)(+6)(-3x) = 5m + 6$

Exercise 3M

Simplify the following expressions where possible.

1. $3a + 5a$
2. $6y - 5y$
3. $4x + 6$
4. $20t - 8t$
5. $6a - 5$
6. $14h + 16h$
7. $12y - 12$
8. $12y - y$

9. Kosh says that $8n + 3 - n + 6$ simplifies to $8n + 9$.
Explain clearly the mistake that Kosh has made.

10. Write down an expression for the perimeter of each shape below. Collect like terms where possible.

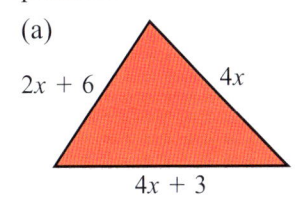

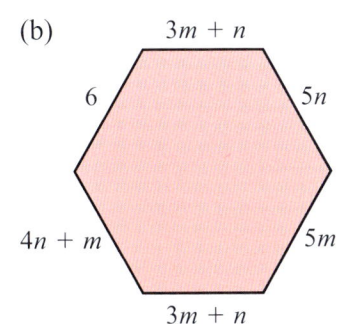

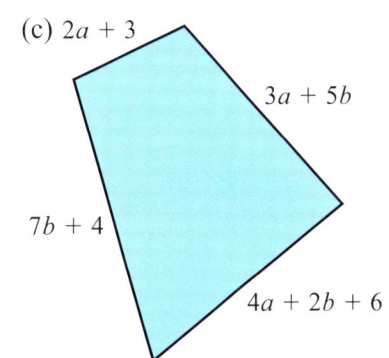

    (a) Triangle with sides $2x + 6$, $4x$, $4x + 3$

    (b) Hexagon with sides $3m + n$, $5n$, $5m$, $3m + n$, $4n + m$, 6

    (c) Quadrilateral with sides $2a + 3$, $3a + 5b$, $4a + 2b + 6$, $7b + 4$

11. Which expressions below are equivalent to $5m + 3n - n - 2 - 3m$?

    A $2m + 2n - 2$ B $8m + 2n - 2$ C $2m + 3n - 2$

Simplify the following expressions as far as possible by collecting like terms.

12. $5x + 9 - 2x - 7$
13. $7p + 9q + 2p - 4q$
14. $7x + 8 + x - 6$
15. $a + 14b + 5a - 4b$
16. $6m + 8 + 6m - 7$
17. $3h + 20 - h + 5$
18. $5m + 2n + 4n + 7m$
19. $8p + 6q - 3q - 2p$
20. $6x + 10 - 6 + 3x$
21. $7x + 3y + x + 6$
22. $8a + 3b - 4a + 4c$
23. $5w + 8 - 3w + w$
24. $8 + 4a + 7 - 2a$
25. $4y + 8 - 5 - 3y$
26. $5c - c + 6a + 8c$
27. $5p + 6q + 4p - 4q$
28. $7m + 9n - 7n + 4$
29. $6x + 8 - x + 9x$

30. Which two expressions below are *equivalent* (this means they give the same answer when the like terms are collected).

    (a) $5x + 3 - 2x + 6y + x$ (b) $3y + 4x + 3y + 6 - 2$ (c) $7 + 4y + 4x + 2y - 3$

31

(rectangle with sides $n - 2$ and $3n + 1$)

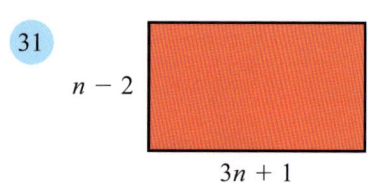

(lengths are in cm)

(a) Draw a rectangle and write on the side lengths so that each side is 5 cm greater than the sides of the rectangle shown opposite.

(b) Write down and simplify an expression for the perimeter of the new rectangle.

32 n^2 does not equal n (try using $n = 3$ to show this!). n^2 and n are unlike terms – they cannot be added together.

$3n^2 + 5n$ cannot be simplified further.

Simplify the following expressions.

(a) $5n^2 + 3n^2$ (b) $4n^2 + 8n - 2n^2$ (c) $8n + 3n^2 + n^2$

(d) $3 + 6n^2 - 1$ (e) $5n + 7n^2 - 2n - 3n^2$ (f) $4n^2 + 2 + 3n^2 + 4n$

(g) $9n - 4 + 2n^2 - 3n$ (h) $7n^2 + 4n - 2n + n^2$ (i) $5n^2 + 6n - 2n^2 - n$

More rules

$a + b = b + a$

$a \times b = b \times a$ ($a \times b$ is written as ab so $ab = ba$)

$a \times a = a^2$

$\dfrac{a}{b} = a \div b$

Exercise 4M

1 (a) Write down any pairs of expressions from below that are equal to each other.

xy $\dfrac{y}{x}$ $x - y$

$\dfrac{x}{y}$ $y - x$ $x + y$

yx $y + x$

(b) For each chosen pair from part (a), write down a pair of values for x and y which show that you are correct.

2 Which expression below is the odd one out?

$n + n + n$ $n \times n \times n$ $3n$ $5n - n - n$

3 (a) Write down any pairs of expressions from below that are equal to each other.

$n + n$		$2 \times n$
$4 - n$	$\frac{n}{4}$	n^2
$n \times n$	$n - 4$	$\frac{4}{n}$

(b) For each chosen pair from part (a), write down a value for n which shows that you are correct.

In questions 4 to 15 write down each statement and say whether it is 'true' or 'false' for all values of the symbols used.

If you are not sure, try different values for the letters

4 $x + x + x = 3x$
5 $xw = wx$
6 $m \times m = 2m$
7 $m + n = n + m$
8 $5y - y = 5$
9 $a \times 5 = 5a$
10 $\frac{x}{2} = \frac{2}{x}$
11 $a \times a \times a = 3a$
12 $a^2 = 2a$
13 $a \div 3 = 3 \div a$
14 $\frac{1}{2}$ of $b = \frac{b}{2}$
15 $3n^2 = (3n)^2$

16 Simplify the following expressions.
(a) $\frac{m}{m}$
(b) $\frac{4a}{4}$
(c) $\frac{n^2}{n}$
(d) $\frac{6x}{x}$

Multiplying terms

(a) Simplify $3b \times 6a$
$3b \times 6a = 3 \times b \times 6 \times a$
$= 3 \times 6 \times b \times a$
$= 18ba$
write in alphabetical order
$= 18ab$

(b) Simplify $xy + 3x + 5yx - 2$
$5yx = 5xy$
so xy and $5yx$ are like terms
$xy + 5yx = xy + 5xy = 6xy$

Answer: $xy + 3x + 5yx - 2$
$= 6xy + 3x - 2$

Exercise 5M

Simplify

1 $4a \times 2b$
2 $5c \times 3d$
3 $6m \times 7n$
4 $3p \times 8q$
5 $9b \times 2a$
6 $2m \times n \times 5p$

7 $7a \times 3b \times 2c$ **8** $4q \times 6r \times p$ **9** $5a \times 3 \times 2b$

10 $4m \times 5 \times 7n$ **11** $m \times m$ **12** $8m \times 4m$

13 $3p \times 3p$ **14** $2a \times 2 \times a$ **15** $3p \times p \times 3p$

16 Use algebra to write down an expression for the area of each rectangle below.

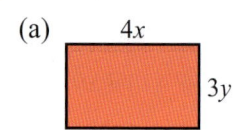

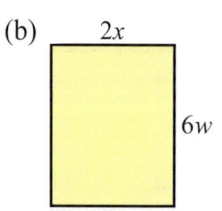

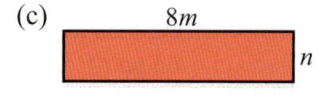

(a) rectangle with sides $4x$ and $3y$

(b) rectangle with sides $2x$ and $6w$

(c) rectangle with sides $8m$ and n

17 Charlie says that $5n \times 7m = 35mn$. Faith says that Charlie is not correct and the answer is $35nm$. Who is correct? Give a reason for your answer.

18 Simplify by collecting like terms.

(a) $pq + qp$ (b) $3xy + 4mn - 2mn + 4yx$

(c) $5m + nm + 3mn - 2m$ (d) $4ab + 3a - 2ba - a + 3ab$

(e) $x + y + xy + 3yx - x + 3xy$ (f) $6cd + 4dc + ab - 2c + 3cd + ba$

(g) $2a + 3ba - a + 5ab - 2ba$ (h) $3q + 4pq - 2q + 3qp + 4$

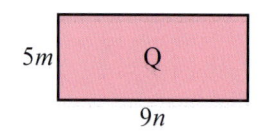

19 Rectangle P with sides $2m$ and $3n$. Rectangle Q with sides $5m$ and $9n$.

Write down an expression for how much greater the area of rectangle Q is compared to the area of rectangle P.

20 What must be added to $6ba$ to give $8ab$?

21 What must be added to $3x + 7yx$ to give $5x + 8xy$?

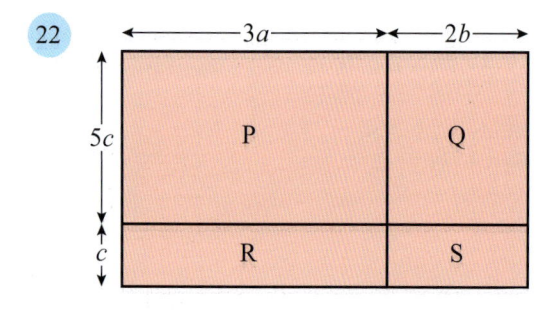

22 Rectangle divided into four parts P, Q, R, S. Top widths $3a$ and $2b$. Left heights $5c$ and c.

Use algebra to write down an expression for the area of each of the following.

(a) P   (b) Q   (c) P + R

(d) S   (e) Q + S   (f) P + Q + R + S

23 Neil multiplies two algebraic terms together and gets the answer $12ab$. Write down all the different pairs of terms that Neil may have used (numbers used must be whole numbers).

24 Write down your own algebraic expression and ask a friend to simplify it.

Investigation – Number walls

Here we have three bricks with a number written inside each one.

A wall is built by putting more bricks on top to form a sort of pyramid.

The number in each of the new bricks is found by adding together the numbers in the two bricks below like this:

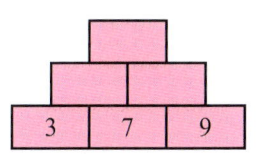

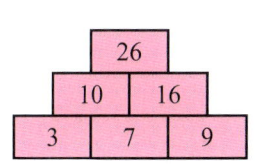

Part A

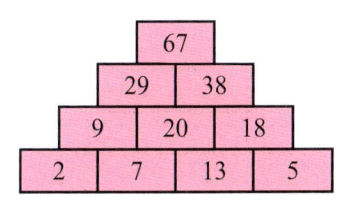

Here is another wall.

1. If you rearrange the numbers at the bottom, does it affect the total at the top?
2. What is the largest total at the top that you can get using the same numbers?
3. What is the smallest total?
4. *How* do you get the largest total?

Part B

1. What happens to the total at the top if the bottom numbers are
   (a) the same? (eg. 5, 5, 5, 5)
   (b) consecutive? (eg. 2, 3, 4, 5)
2. Write down any patterns or rules that you notice.

Part C

1. What happens if you use different numbers at random (eg. 7, 3, 5, 11)?
2. Given 4 numbers at the bottom, can you find a way to predict the top number without finding all the bricks in between?

Part D

Can you find a rule with 3 bricks at the bottom, or 4 bricks? Can algebra help? (Hint: see diagram)

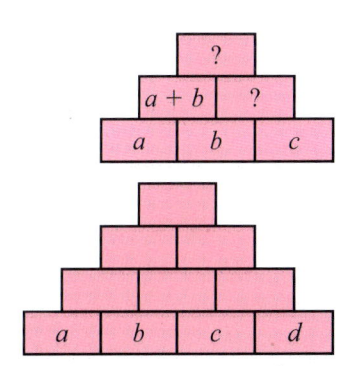

Substituting into a formula

(a) The perimeter p of this shape is given by the formula
$$p = 3a + 2b$$
Find p when $a = 5$ and $b = 4$.
$p = 3a + 2b$
$p = (3 \times 5) + (2 \times 4)$
$p = 15 + 8$
$p = 23$

(b) $h = 4(x + 3)$ Find h when $x = 7$.
(Remember: always work out brackets first)
$h = 4(x + 3)$
$h = 4(7 + 3)$ do brackets first
$h = 4 \times 10$
$h = 40$

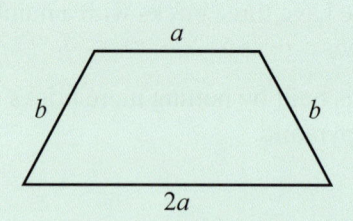

Exercise 6M

1. The perimeter p of this triangle is given by the formula $p = 3x$.
   Find p when $x = 6$.

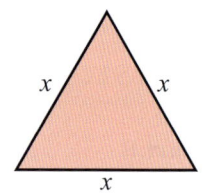

2. The perimeter p of a four-sided shape (quadrilateral) is given by the formula $p = 4w + 17$.
   Find p when $w = 5$.

3. The cost in pounds, C, for hiring a car is given by the formula $C = 2n + 25$ where n is the number of miles travelled.
   Find C when $n = 150$.

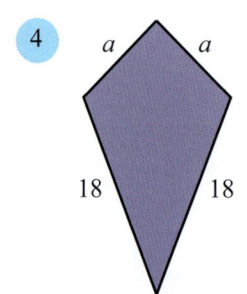

4. A formula for the perimeter p of this kite is given by
   $$p = 2a + 36$$
   Find p when   (a) $a = 7$ (b) $a = 43$ (c) $a = 3.5$

5. A formula to work out the speed v of an object is $v = u + at$.
   Find v when $u = 5$, $a = 10$ and $t = 7$.

6 The cost in pounds, C, for hiring a bike is given by the formula $C = 8d + 12$ where d is the number of days of hire.
Find C when $d = 6$.

7 The perimeter p of a rectangle with sides x and y is given by the formula $p = 2(x + y)$.
Find p when $x = 8$ and $y = 6$.

8 The area A of a shape is given by the formula $A = bh + 16$.
Find A when $b = 7$ and $h = 6$.

In questions **9** to **18** a formula is given. Find the value of the letter required in each case.

9 $h = 18 - 2g$
Find h, when $g = 6$.

10 $w = 4(p + 5)$
Find w, when $p = 3$.

11 $a = \dfrac{b}{3} + 16$
Find a, when $b = 21$.

12 $c = \dfrac{d}{8} + 7$
Find c, when $d = 56$.

13 $y = ab - 8$
Find y, when $a = 8$, $b = 3$.

14 $x = m(9 - n)$
Find x, when $m = 10$, $n = 4$.

15 $n = \dfrac{x}{y} + x$
Find n, when $x = 12$, $y = 4$.

16 $r = \dfrac{5s}{t}$
Find r, when $s = 8$, $t = 10$.

17 $w = \dfrac{x^2 - x}{2}$
Find w, when $x = 5$.

18 $y = mn + m^2$
Find y, when $m = 9$, $n = 3$.

19 Milena runs a dog walking and dog sitting business. She charges £9 for a one hour walk and £12 for a dog sitting session.

(a) Write down a formula for the amount, A, which Milena receives for doing w walks and n sitting sessions.

(b) Find the amount, A, if $w = 12$ and $n = 7$.

20 (a) Write down a formula for the area, A, of the rectangle shown opposite.

(b) Use the formula to work out the value of A when $m = 15$ and $n = 6$.

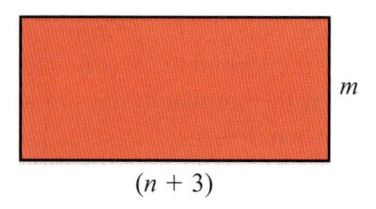

m

$(n + 3)$

Multiply out single brackets

$6(4 + 3) = 6(7) = 6 \times 7 = 42$

We also get the correct answer if the number outside the brackets multiplies each number inside the brackets.

$6(4 + 3) = 6 \times 4 + 6 \times 3 = 24 + 18 = 42$

(a) Multiply out $3(a + b)$
$3(a + b) = 3 \times a + 3 \times b$
$= 3a + 3b$

(b) Multiply out $6(n - 3)$
$6(n - 3) = 6 \times n - 6 \times 3$
$= 6n - 18$

Exercise 7M

1 Multiply out the brackets and match up with the correct answer.

	Question		Answer
(a)	$5(n + 2)$	A	$6n + 18$
(b)	$3(4 - 2n)$	B	$5n + 2$
(c)	$6(n + 3)$	C	$10n + 15$
(d)	$2(4n - 1)$	D	$6n + 3$
(e)	$5(2n + 3)$	E	$5n + 10$
		F	$8n - 2$
		G	$8n - 1$
		H	$12 - 6n$

2 Helina says that $4(3x - 1)$ equals $12x - 1$.
Aaron says that $4(3x - 1)$ equals $12x - 4$.
Explain clearly who is correct and why.

Multiply out the brackets in questions **3** to **23**.

3 $2(x + 3)$ **4** $6(x + 4)$ **5** $3(x + 9)$

6. $5(x + 8)$
7. $4(x - 7)$
8. $2(x - 8)$
9. $9(x - 4)$
10. $6(x - 8)$
11. $4(x + y)$
12. $7(a + b)$
13. $3(m - n)$
14. $5(2x + 3)$
15. $6(4x - 7)$
16. $4(2a + b)$
17. $9(m + 2n)$
18. $4(x + 3y)$
19. $2(4m + n)$
20. $7(5x - 3)$
21. $8(3 - x)$
22. $6(4 - 2x)$
23. $5(3a + 5b)$

24. Josh says that an expression for the area of the rectangle opposite is $(21m - 14)\,\text{cm}^2$.
Rachel says he is not correct.
Explain clearly who is correct.

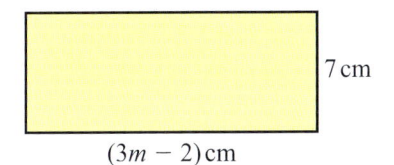

7 cm

$(3m - 2)\,\text{cm}$

'Expand' means 'multiply out'.

(a) Expand $m(n + y)$
$m(n + y) = m \times n + m \times y$
$= mn + my$

(b) Expand $w(w - 3)$
$w(w - 3) = w \times w - 3 \times w$
$= w^2 - 3w$

Exercise 8M

1. $n(5 - 3n) = 5n - 3n = 2n$
Explain clearly why this is not correct.

Expand

2. $p(q + r)$
3. $m(n - p)$
4. $a(b + c)$
5. $a(b - e)$
6. $x(y + 3)$
7. $m(n - 6)$
8. $x(y - 9)$
9. $p(q - 5)$
10. $a(c + 7)$
11. $m(m - 6)$
12. $p(p - 2)$
13. $a(7 - a)$
14. $5(2a + 3)$
15. $9(3m - 2)$
16. $6(4x - 1)$
17. $4(8n + 7)$
18. $b(4 - b)$
19. $2m(m + 3)$
20. $4n(3n + 4)$
21. $5m(2m - 7)$
22. $3x(2 - 5x)$
23. $8m(1 - 4m)$
24. $2x(3x - 2y)$
25. $4m(2n + 6m)$

26 Ian earns £m each week and a weekly bonus of £25. 
   (a) Write down an expression for how much money Ian receives in n weeks.
   (b) Simplify your answer to part (a).
   (c) How much money does Ian receive if $m = 230$ and $n = 6$?

27 The area of triangle P is $2n(3n + 1)$.
   The area of triangle Q is $3n(n + 2)$.
   The area of rectangle R is $4n(2n - 3)$.
   (a) Write down the area of each shape with no brackets.
   (b) Which shape has the largest area when $n = 4$?
       Explain your answer clearly.

> Remove the brackets and simplify $4(2x + 1) + 6(3x + 5)$
>
> Expand the brackets separately: $4(2x + 1) = 8x + 4$ and $+6(3x + 5) = +18x + 30$
>
> Finally, collect the like terms: $8x + 4 + 18x + 30 = 26x + 34$

Exercise 8E

Remove the brackets and simplify

1 $3(x + 2) + 2(x + 4)$
2 $5(x + 3) + 2(x + 3)$
3 $5(x + 2) + 2(x + 1)$
4 $7(x + 2) + 4(x + 5)$
5 $3(2x + 3) + 4(x + 6)$
6 $2(5x + 2) + 3(x + 4)$
7 $4(3x + 5) + 5(2 + 5x)$
8 $6(x + 2) + 4(x - 3)$
9 $6(3 + x) + 2(4x + 1)$
10 $5(2x + 3) + (3x - 7)$
11 $8(2 + 3x) + 5x$
12 $3x + 4(2x + 6)$
13 $3(5x + 2) - 9x$
14 $8 + 7(3x - 1)$
15 $10x + 4(3x + 2)$
16 $4(7x + 4) + 2(3x - 5)$
17 $6(1 + 3x) - 4$
18 $8(2x - 1) + 5(3x + 2)$
19 $7(5x + 3) + x$
20 $4(9x - 6) + 3(4x + 10)$

21 Rectangle A: 5 by $x + 6$
   Rectangle B: 7 by $x + 4$
   Rectangle C: 6 by $2x + 3$

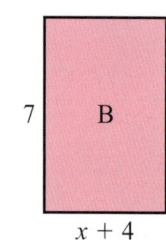

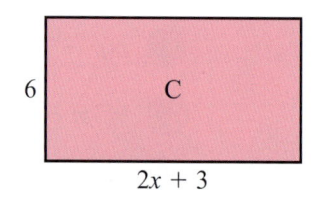

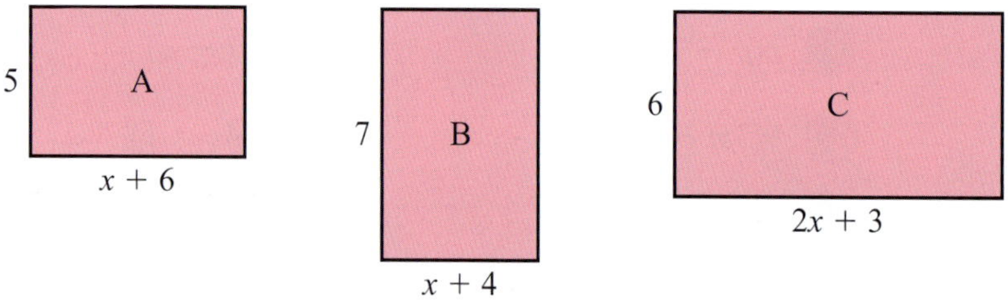

   Find an expression for the total area of the rectangles stated below. Simplify each answer.
   (a) A and B
   (b) A and C
   (c) all three rectangles

22 Write down an expression for the perimeter of this quadrilateral and simplify your answer fully.

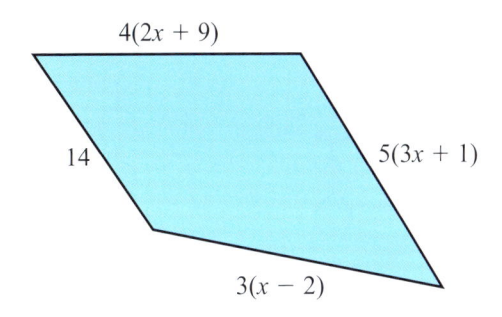

Sides: $4(2x+9)$, 14, $5(3x+1)$, $3(x-2)$

Balance Puzzles

On the balance ◯ and △ represent weights.

Find ◯ if △ = 5 for this balance puzzle.

Clearly for these scales to balance exactly, then ◯ = 10.

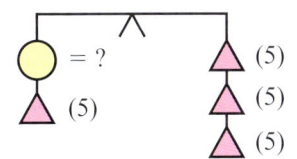

◯ = ?   △ (5)
△ (5)   △ (5)
         △ (5)

Exercise 9M

Copy each diagram and find the value of the required symbol.

1 Find ▢ if △ = 4.

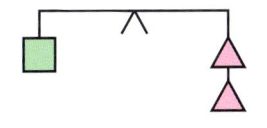

2 Find ◯ if △ = 10.

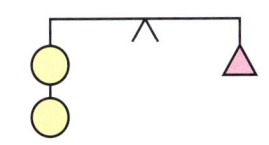

3 Find ◯ if ▢ = 4.

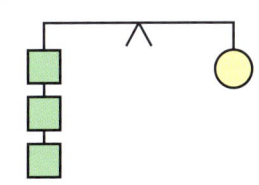

4 Find ▢ if △ = 12.

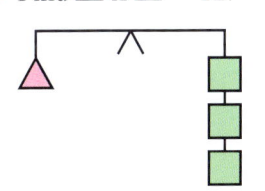

5 Find △ if ▢ = 2.

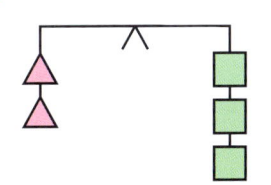

6 Find △ if ◯ = 6.

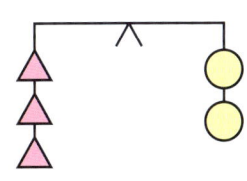

7 Find ▢ if ◯ = 8.

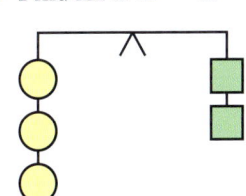

8 Find △ if ▢ = 15.

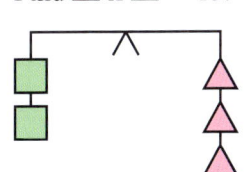

9 Find △ if ◯ = 14.

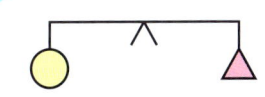

10 Find ⬜ if ◯ = 8.

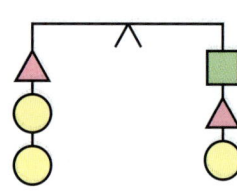

11 Find ◯ if △ = 6.

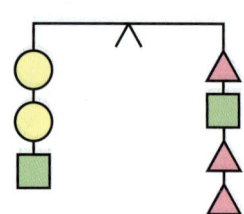

12 Find ◯ if ⬜ = 5.

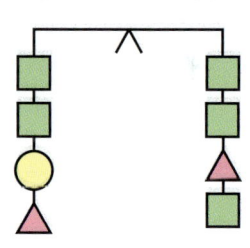

Exercise 9E

Copy each diagram and find the value of the unknown symbols.

1 ◯ = 10, find △ and ⬜.

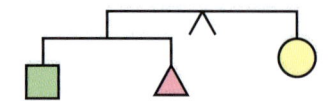

2 △ = 8, find ◯ and ⬜.

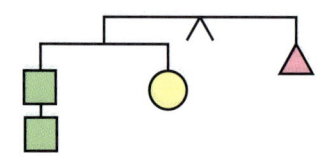

3 ◯ = 8, find ⬜ and △.

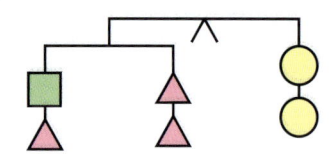

4 ⬜ = 4, find ◯ and △.

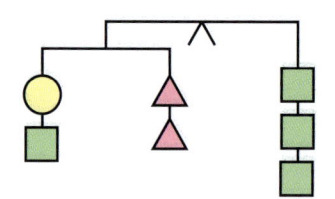

5 △ = 4, find ◯ and ⬜.

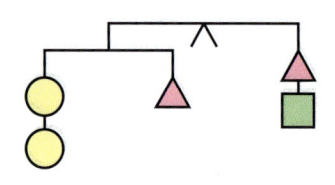

6 ◯ = 10, find △ and ⬜.

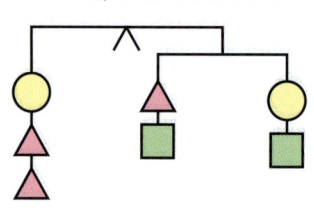

7 △ = 5, find ◯ and ⬜.

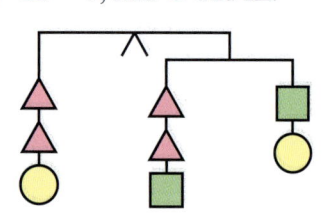

8 ⬜ = 3, find ◯ and △.

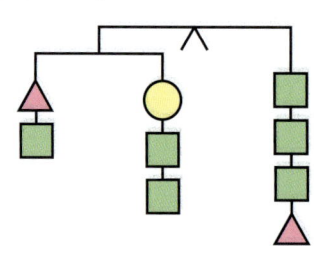

9 □ = 6, find △ and ○.

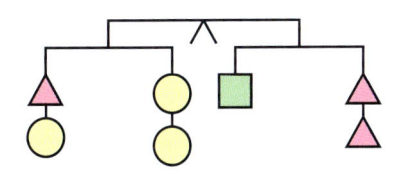

10 ○ = 5, find □ and △.

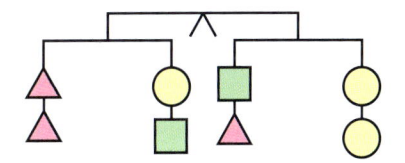

11 △ = 4, find ○ and □.

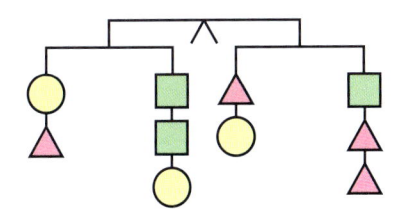

12 ○ = 8, find □ and △.

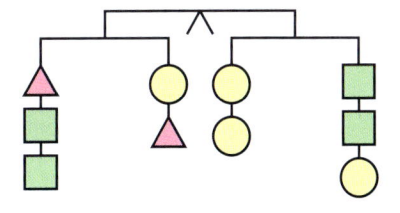

13 □ = 4, find ○ and △.

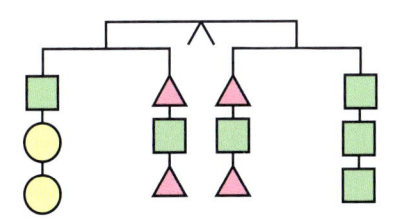

14 ○ = 3, find ⬡.

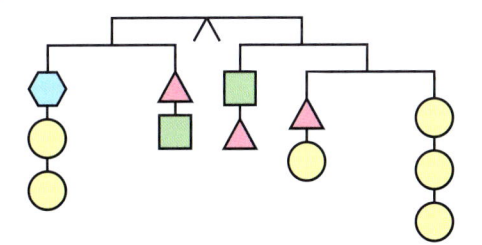

Need more practice with the rules of algebra?

1 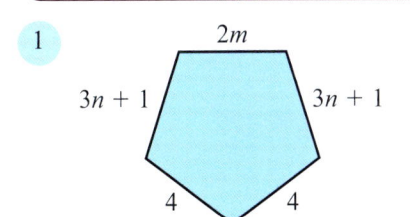 Write down an algebraic expression for the perimeter of this pentagon.

(Pentagon sides: 2m, 3n + 1, 3n + 1, 4, 4)

2 Pair off expressions below which are equivalent:

A $2m + 3n + m + 3$ B $m + 4n + 5 - 2$ C $3m + 3n + 3$ D $6m + 3 + 2m + 3n$

E $m + 4n + 3$ F $4m + 3n + 3$ G $8m + 3n + 3$ H $4m + 5n + 3 - 2n$

3 $p = 7(q - 4)$

Find p when $q = 8$.

4 $y = \dfrac{m}{4}$

Find y when $m = 36$.

5 *Explain* clearly why the value of $b - a$ is usually not the same as the value of $a - b$.

6 Simplify
  (a) $7m \times 4n$
  (b) $4x \times 3y$
  (c) $6n \times 4n$
  (d) $4a \times 5 \times 2b$
  (e) $5mn + 7 - 2nm$
  (f) $3ab + 4a - ba + 2$
  (g) $5ab + 3b + ba - 2b$
  (h) $2n \times 4 \times 4n$
  (i) $2n + 4mn + n - 3nm$

7 The cost in pounds, C, for hiring a boat is given by the formula $C = 6n + 15$ where n is the number of hours of hire. Find C when $n = 8$.

8 $4(2m + 9) = 8m + 36$. Is this correct or not? *Explain* your answer fully.

9 $f = gh + h$
Find f when $g = 5$ and $h = 9$.

10 $k = a(a + b)$
Find k when $a = 8$ and $b = 2$.

11 Expand (multiply out)
  (a) $8(3n + 5)$
  (b) $n(n + 4)$
  (c) $m(2m - 3)$
  (d) $n(9n + 7)$
  (e) $2m(m - n)$
  (f) $3a(5a + 4b)$

Extension questions with the rules of algebra

1 A box contains 48 packets of biscuits.
The weight of a box is v kg.
Several of these boxes are taken to a supermarket.
The supermarket buys 211 packets of biscuits.
Write down an expression for the total weight of these 211 packets.

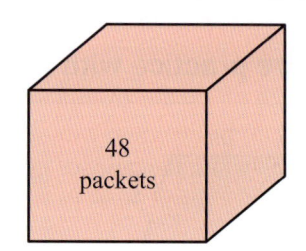

2 The front of a house has a wooden framework as shown.
  (a) Write down an expression for the total length of wood used.
  (b) The back of the house has the same wooden framework. Six identical houses are built. Write down an expression for the total length of wood used for the front and back of the six houses. Write your answer in simplified form.

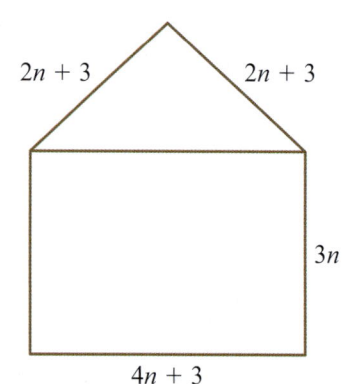

3 $y = a^2 - b^2$

Find y when $a = 8$ and $b = 3$.

4 $a = \dfrac{3b + 2}{4}$

Find a when $b = 6$.

5 Stacia writes $\dfrac{7n}{8} - \dfrac{5n}{8} = \dfrac{2n}{8} = \dfrac{n}{4}$

Is Stacia correct? *Explain* your answer fully.

6 Remove the brackets and simplify
   (a) $4n(2n + 3) + 2n(3n + 5)$
   (b) $5m(3m + 7) + 3m(m - 2)$
   (c) $2y(2y + 9) + y(3y - 4)$
   (d) $7n(4n + 1) - 2n(3n - 7)$

7 Can $x - y$ give the same value as $y - x$? *Explain* your answer fully.

8 Simplify these expressions
   (a) $5n \times 3 \times 2n$
   (b) $7n \times 4n \times 2n$
   (c) $6m \times 3n \times 4n$
   (d) $4m \times 2m \times 5n$
   (e) $\dfrac{5n}{7} - \dfrac{2n}{7}$
   (f) $\dfrac{4m}{9} + \dfrac{m}{9}$
   (g) $\dfrac{m}{4} + \dfrac{3m}{4}$
   (h) $\dfrac{5n}{8} - \dfrac{n}{4}$
   (i) $\dfrac{2m}{5} + \dfrac{2m}{5}$

9 When does $\dfrac{n}{3} = \dfrac{3}{n}$? *Explain* your answer fully.

10 A metal window frame is shown opposite.
   (a) Write down an expression for the total length of metal.
   (b) The total length of metal is actually 640 cm. If a and b are multiples of 10, list all the pairs of possible values for a and b.

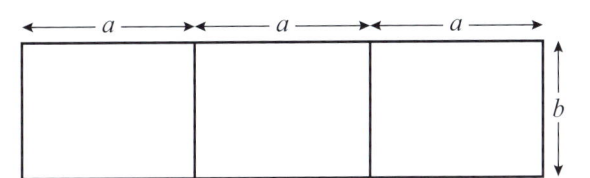

CHECK YOURSELF ON SECTIONS 1.3 AND 1.4

1 Order of operations

Work out
   (a) $8 - 24 \div 4$
   (b) $8 \times 3 - 10 \div 2$
   (c) $\dfrac{6 \times 5 - 6}{8}$
   (d) $(2 + 7 \times 4) \times (21 - 17)$
   (e) Write in brackets to make the sum $5 \times 4 - 1^2$ give the answer 45.

2 Using a calculator for fractions

Use a calculator to work out

(a) $8.15 - \dfrac{6.72}{3.2}$

(b) $\dfrac{4.771 - 1.711}{0.85}$

3 Using brackets on a calculator

Use a calculator to work out

(a) $23.78 - (6.7 + 1.9)$

(b) $31.8 \times (7.19 - 2.3) \times 4$

4 Using letters for numbers

(a) Joe has n mints. He gives six mints to his sister. Write down an expression for how many mints Joe now has.

(b) I start with a number x, multiply it by 5 and then subtract 8. Write down an expression for what I now have.

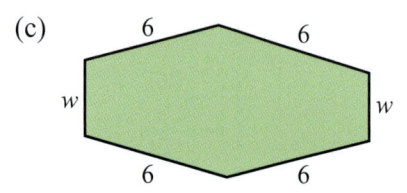

(c) Write down an expression for the perimeter of this shape.

5 Simplifying algebraic expressions

Simplify the following expressions as far as possible

(a) $4m + 3n - 2m + 6n$

(b) $8y - y$

(c) $8p + 6 + 3p - 7p$

(d) $6xy + 3y + y - 2yx$

(e) $4m \times 7n$

(f) $8p \times q \times 4r$

(g) Which two rectangles below have the same area?

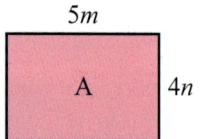

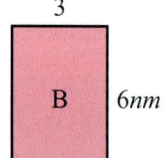

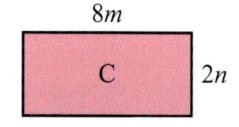

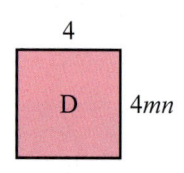

A: $5m$ by $4n$
B: 3 by $6nm$
C: $8m$ by $2n$
D: 4 by $4mn$

6 Substituting numbers into a formula

(a) The cost in pounds, C, for hiring a van is given by the formula $C = 3n + 45$ where n is the number of miles travelled. Find C when $n = 200$.

(b) $y = 3(7 - x)$

Find y when $x = 5$.

(c) $m = \dfrac{n}{6} - 9$

Find m when $n = 72$.

7 Multiplying out single brackets

Expand (multiply out)

(a) $5(x + 7)$ (b) $n(p - 3)$ (c) $x(x + 8)$

(d) Simplify $3(4x + 2) + 6(x + 1)$

(e) Find an expression for the total area of the rectangles shown.

Simplify your answer.

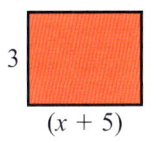

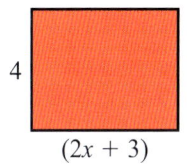

Rectangle 1: height 3, width $(x + 5)$
Rectangle 2: height 4, width $(2x + 3)$

8 Tackling balance puzzles

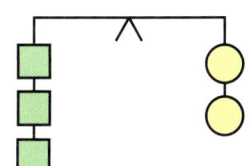

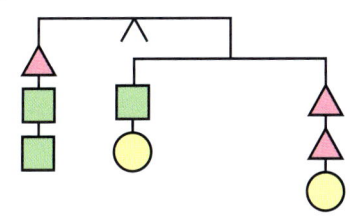

(a) Find ☐ if ○ = 12.

(b) Find ☐ and ○ if △ = 6.

1.5 Negative numbers

In section 1.5 you will:

- add and subtract negative numbers
- multiply and divide negative numbers

Adding and subtracting negative numbers

For adding and subtracting with negative numbers a number line is very useful.

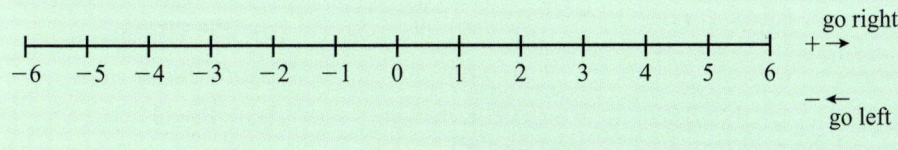

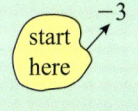

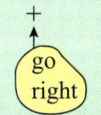

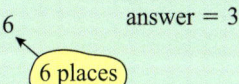

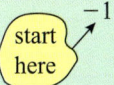

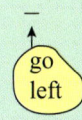

Number line from −6 to 6.

+ → go right
− ← go left

start here, −3, + go right, 6 places, answer = 3

start here, −1, − go left, 4 places, answer = −5

In the sequence of subtractions on the right the numbers in column A go down by one each time. The numbers in column B increase by one each time.

$$\begin{array}{cc} A & B \\ \downarrow & \downarrow \end{array}$$

$$8 - (+3) = 5$$
$$8 - (+2) = 6$$
$$8 - (+1) = 7$$
$$8 - (0) = 8$$
$$8 - (-1) = 9$$
$$8 - (-2) = 10$$
$$8 - (-3) = 11$$

Continue the sequence downwards:

We see that $8 - (-3)$ becomes $8 + 3$.

This always applies when subtracting negative numbers. It is possible to replace *two* signs next to each other by *one* sign as follows:

+	+	=	+
−	−	=	+
−	+	=	−
+	−	=	−

Remember: 'same signs: +'
'different signs: −'

When two signs next to each other have been replaced by one sign in this way, the calculation is completed using the number line as before.

(a) $-3 + (-5)$
$= -3 - 5$
$= -8$

(b) $6 + (-12)$
$= 6 - 12$
$= -6$

(c) $4 - (-3)$
$= 4 + 3$
$= 7$

(d) $5 - (-2) + (-6)$
$= 5 + 2 - 6$
$= 1$

Exercise 1M

1 Work out
(a) $-9 + 3$
(b) $5 - 11$
(c) $-4 - 4$
(d) $7 - 20$
(e) $-6 + 8$
(f) $7 - 3$
(g) $-6 - 5$
(h) $-10 + 6$
(i) $-3 + 3$
(j) $1 - 10$
(k) $-8 + 1$
(l) $-8 - 4$

2 Now work out these
(a) $-3 + 12$
(b) $-7 + 7$
(c) $-6 - 1$
(d) $-5 - 4$
(e) $-10 + 10$
(f) $3 - 15$
(g) $-7 + 8$
(h) $-4 - 1 + 3$
(i) $30 - 60$
(j) $-6 - 14$
(k) $-60 + 20$
(l) $5 - 7 - 2$

3 Now try this
$-4 + 1 - 6 - 3 + 2 + 5 - 3$

4 Work out

(a) $7 + (-3)$ (b) $9 - (-2)$ (c) $4 - 9$ (d) $-5 + 2$
(e) $-4 + (-5)$ (f) $-8 + (-3)$ (g) $10 - 12$ (h) $6 - (-4)$
(i) $12 - (-4)$ (j) $-6 + (-6)$ (k) $-4 - (-4)$ (l) $-5 + (-6)$

5 Copy and complete each number wall below. The number in each box is found by adding the two numbers below it.

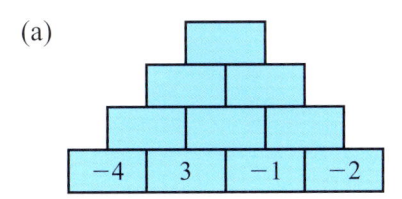

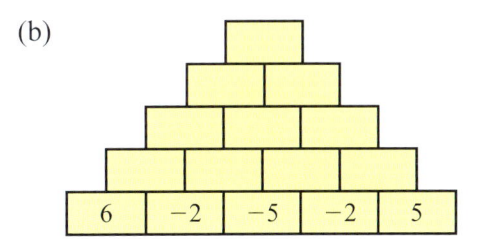

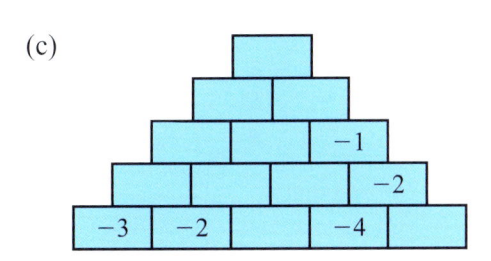

(a) Bottom row: $-4, 3, -1, -2$

(b) Bottom row: $6, -2, -5, -2, 5$

(c) Bottom row: $-3, -2, \square, -4$; next row: $\square, \square, -2$; next row: $\square, -1$

6 Work out

(a) $8 + (-7)$ (b) $-5 + (-1)$ (c) $-2 - (-3)$ (d) $-9 - (-9)$
(e) $8 - 12$ (f) $6 + (-9)$ (g) $-4 - (-3)$ (h) $3 + (-3)$
(i) $-7 - 5$ (j) $6 + (-13)$ (k) $-5 - (-6)$ (l) $3 + (-10)$

7 What is the missing number for each box below?

(a) $\square - (-3) = 7$ (b) $\square + (-4) = 6$ (c) $3 + \square = 1$
(d) $4 - \square = 8$ (e) $\square - 6 = -8$ (f) $8 + \square = -1$

8 Copy and complete the magic squares (ie. you get the same answer when you add up the numbers in any row, column or diagonal).

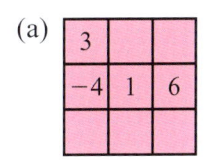

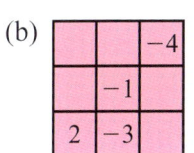

(a) Row 1: $3, \_, \_$; Row 2: $-4, 1, 6$; Row 3: $\_, \_, \_$

(b) Row 1: $\_, \_, -4$; Row 2: $\_, -1, \_$; Row 3: $2, -3, \_$

9 Write down whether each statement below is true or false

(a) $4 + (-6) = -2$ (b) $8 - (-2) = 6$ (c) $-7 - 2 = -9$
(d) $8 - (-4) = 12$ (e) $5 + (-5) = -10$ (f) $2 - (-2) = 0$
(g) $16 + (-3) = 13$ (h) $10 + (-3) = 13$ (i) $-6 - (-8) = -14$

10 Each week a restaurant gets positive and negative ratings. The boxes below show how many of each were received in the month of February.

Week 1: 17, −20
Week 2: 30, ☐
Week 3: 19, −14
Week 4: 26, −32

The overall score for February was −8. What score belongs in the week 2 empty box?

Multiplying and dividing negative numbers

A   B
↓   ↓
$5 \times 3 = 15$
$5 \times 2 = 10$
$5 \times 1 = 5$
$5 \times 0 = 0$

$5 \times -1 = -5$
$5 \times -2 = -10$
$5 \times -3 = -15$

In the sequence of multiplications shown, the numbers in column A go down by one each time. The numbers in column B go down by five each time.

C   D
↓   ↓
$-3 \times 3 = -9$
$-3 \times 2 = -6$
$-3 \times 1 = -3$
$-3 \times 0 = 0$

$-3 \times -1 = 3$
$-3 \times -2 = 6$
$-3 \times -3 = 9$

In this sequence the numbers in column C go down by one each time.

The numbers in column D *increase* by 3 each time.

We see that:

> When a positive number is multiplied by a negative number the answer is negative.

We see that:

> When two negative numbers are multiplied together the answer is positive.

> For division, the rules are the same as for multiplication.

$-4 \times (-6) = 24$
$40 \div (-4) = -10$

$7 \times (-3) = -21$
$-60 \div (-20) = 3$

$-15 \div 3 = -5$
$(-2) \times (-3) \times (-2) = -12$

Exercise 2M

Work out

1 (a) $4 \times (-2)$ (b) $5 \times (-4)$ (c) -3×4 (d) $-2 \times (-3)$
   (e) -6×3 (f) $8 \times (-2)$ (g) $-5 \times (-6)$ (h) -1×7

2 (a) $12 \div (-3)$ (b) $20 \div (-4)$ (c) $-8 \div 2$ (d) $-12 \div (-4)$
   (e) $-18 \div (-6)$ (f) $25 \div (-5)$ (g) $-15 \div 3$ (h) $-30 \div (-10)$

3 (a) $-40 \div 20$ (b) $8 \times (-6)$ (c) $-4 \times (-7)$ (d) $4 \times (-8)$
(e) $-50 \div (-25)$ (f) $24 \div (-8)$ (g) $10 \times (-9)$ (h) $-63 \div (-7)$

4 Write down two negative numbers which multiply together to make 8. Are there any other pairs of negative numbers which will multiply together to make 8? Write them down.

5 What is the missing number for each box below?
(a) $-4 \times \square = -28$ (b) $-6 \times \square = 42$ (c) $32 \div \square = -16$
(d) $-45 \div \square = 5$ (e) $\square \div (-10) = 5$ (f) $\square \div (-9) = -8$
(g) $\square \times (-9) = 108$ (h) $6 \times \square = -90$ (i) $\square \div 7 = -3$

6 Copy and complete the squares below

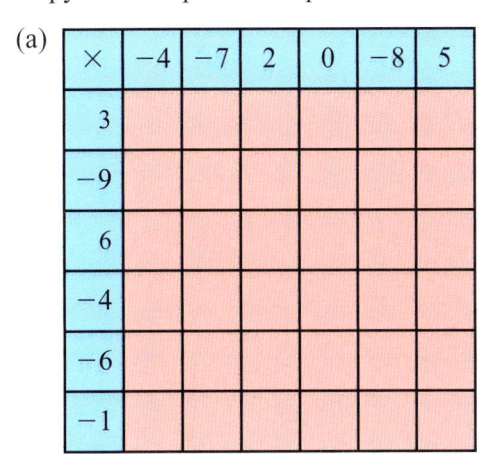

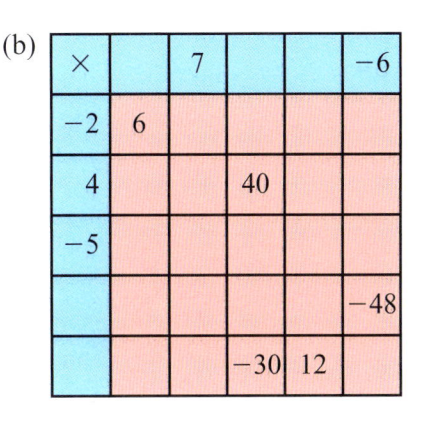

(a)
×	−4	−7	2	0	−8	5
3						
−9						
6						
−4						
−6						
−1						

(b)
×		7		−6
−2	6			
4			40	
−5				
				−48
			−30	12

7 Work out
(a) $(-2) \times (-4) \times (-1)$ (b) $3 \times (-5) \times (-2)$ (c) $(-3)^2$ (d) $(-6)^2$
(e) $4 \times (-2) \times 4$ (f) $(-5) \times (-2) \times (-4)$ (g) $(-1)^2$ (h) $(-2)^3$

Need more practice with negative numbers?

1 Which gives the greater answer? $-7 + 4$ or $-7 - 4$

2 Work out
(a) $8 + (-4)$ (b) $-9 - 2$ (c) $-7 - (-3)$ (d) $5 + (-9)$
(e) $4 - (-2)$ (f) $-6 - 3$ (g) $-1 - 7$ (h) $-4 - (-3)$

3 The acceleration a of a small vehicle is given by the formula $a = 5t + 3$ where t is the time taken.
Find the value of a when (a) $t = -2$ (b) $t = -6$ (c) $t = -10$

4 What is the missing number for each box below?

(a) $-56 \div \square = 8$ (b) $9 \times \square = -36$ (c) $-48 \div \square = -8$

(d) $100 \div \square = -10$ (e) $\square \div 4 = -8$ (f) $\square \times (-6) = 54$

5 Complete the chain, filling in the empty boxes.

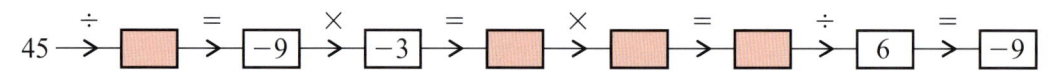

$45 \xrightarrow{\div} \square \xrightarrow{=} \boxed{-9} \xrightarrow{\times} \boxed{-3} \xrightarrow{=} \square \xrightarrow{\times} \square \xrightarrow{=} \square \xrightarrow{\div} \boxed{6} \xrightarrow{=} \boxed{-9}$

6 Work out $-3 + 4 \times 2 - 6 \div 3$

Extension questions with negative numbers

1 Work out

(a) $-3 \times (-5) \times 2$ (b) $9 \times (-4) \times 3$ (c) $-8 \times -4 \div (-2)$

(d) $-50 \div 5 \times (-3)$ (e) $-10 \times (-8) \div (-4)$ (f) $-3 \times 4 \times (-9)$

2 $s = \dfrac{v^2 - u^2}{2a}$ Find the value of s when $v = 8$, $u = -4$, and $a = 0.25$

3 An integer is a positive or negative whole number (or 0).
Write down every possible pair of integers which give a product of -24.

4 Find the two negative numbers m and n such that $m^3 - n^3 = -19$.

5 Work out

(a) $(-5)^2 + (-2)^3$ (b) $(-1)^3 + (-1)^2$ (c) $(-7)^2 - (-2)^2$

(d) $(-1)^3 + (-2)^3 + (-3)^3$ (e) $(-2)^4 + (-4)^2$ (f) $3 \times (-5)^3 + 4 \times (-10)^2$

CHECK YOURSELF ON SECTION 1.5

1 Adding and subtracting negative numbers

Work out

(a) $-6 + 2$ (b) $-3 - 4$ (c) $2 + (-5)$ (d) $-8 - (-6)$

2 Multiplying and dividing negative numbers

Work out

(a) $3 \times (-5)$ (b) $-16 \div (-2)$ (c) $-30 \div 10$ (d) $-8 \times (-4)$

✗ Spot the mistakes 2 ✗

Algebra rules and negative numbers

Work through each question below and *explain clearly* what mistakes have been made. Beware – some questions are correctly done.

1. $3m + 2m^2 = 5m^2$

2. $4mn + 6n - 4n - 2nm = 2mn + 2n$

3. $-5 + 3 = -8$

4. $(-4)^2 = -16$

5. $3(2n + 1) = 6n + 1$

6. $2n^2 + 6n^2 + 4n - n^2 = 7n^2 + 4n$

7. $v = u + at$ Louise uses $u = 6$, $a = 4$ and $t = 3$ to get the answer $v = 6 + 43 = 49$.

8. The formula $S = 180(n - 2)$ gives the sum of the angles in a polygon with n sides. George finds the value of S when $n = 6$. He writes $S = 180(6 - 2) = 180 \times 4 = 720$.

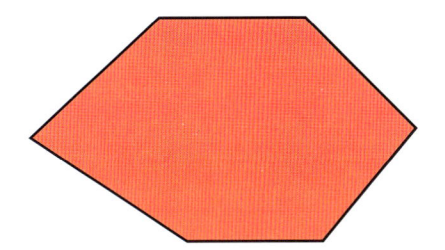

9. Arjun works out $-3 \times 4 - 5$ and gets the answer -7.

10. Tamsin completes a number wall where the number in each box is found by adding the two numbers below it.

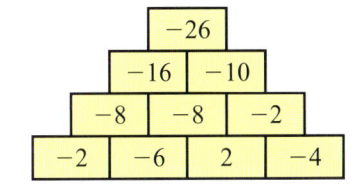

    Number wall (top to bottom):
    - Top: -26
    - Row: -16, -10
    - Row: -8, -8, -2
    - Bottom: -2, -6, 2, -4

1.6 Applying mathematics 1

In section 1.6 you will apply maths in a variety of situations.

1. Numbers are missing on four of these calculator buttons.
   Copy the diagram and write in numbers to make the answer 35.

   [3] [8] [+] [ ] [ ] [−] [ ] [ ] [=] [3] [5]

2. Ronnie has the same number of 10p and 20p coins. The total value of the coins is £6. How many of each coin does he have?

3 Draw a copy of the grid shown. The sum of the numbers in each column ↕ is the same as the sum of the numbers in each diagonal ↗ or ↘.

What number goes in the centre?

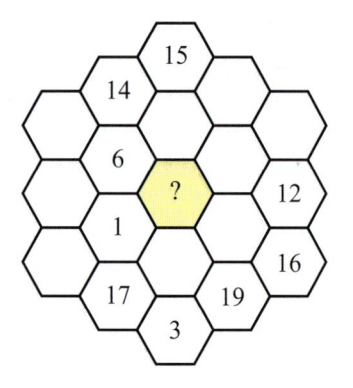

4 In an election 7144 votes were cast for the two candidates. Mr Putin won by 424 votes. How many people voted for Putin?

5 An artist won the Turner art prize by 'carefully' walking across his canvas with bare feet. Unfortunately his prize winning piece was thrown in the bin by the cleaner at his studio. The painting was on sale for £620 000. The cleaner offered to make up for her mistake by paying the artist £20 per week. How many years would it take to pay the full amount?

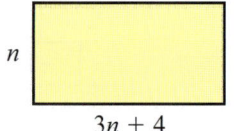

6 Write down an algebraic expression for the difference between the areas of the two rectangles shown.

7 A shopkeeper bought 30 pens at £3.40 each and a number of books costing £8.40 each. In all the shopkeeper spent £312. How many books did the shopkeeper buy?

8 This table shows the approximate weights of coins.

1p	2p	5p	10p	20p
3.6 g	7.2 g	3.2 g	6.5 g	5.0 g

(a) What is the lightest weight with a value of 12p made from these coins?
(b) A group of mixed coins weighs 228 g, of which 48 g is the silver coins. What is the value of the bronze coins?

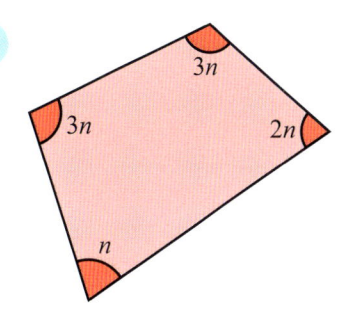

9 All the angles in a quadrilateral add up to 360°.

(a) Write down an algebraic expression for the sum of the angles in this quadrilateral.
(b) Simplify the expression.
(c) Work out the value of n.
(d) Use this value of n to work out the value of $n^2(3n + 1)$.

10 The ingredients for a chocolate cake cost £1.25 and the chef charges £1.10 to make each cake. A shop sells the cakes at £11.99. Calculate the total profit made if 200 cakes are sold.

UNIT 1   MIXED REVIEW

Part one

1 Copy and complete the cross number.

Clues across
1. 311 − 92
4. 275 ÷ 5
6. 70.01 − 3.47
8. 0.069 × 100
9. 188 × 2
11. 4 − 0.31
12. 21^2
14. 67.9 ÷ 7
16. 30 × 25
17. 1.28 × 50

Clues down
1. 38 × 7
2. 13^2
3. 50 × 1.9
5. 32.16 ÷ 6
7. 54.5 × 8
10. 10 003 − 2 007
11. (366 + 254) ÷ 2
12. (9 × 8) − 25
13. 36 ÷ 8
15. 0.37 × 200

2 Copy and complete by finding the missing number.

(a) 5 × ☐ − 6 = 24
(b) 30 − 4 × ☐ = 2
(c) 36 ÷ ☐ + 7 = 11
(d) (12 − ☐) × 4 = 20
(e) 32 − (12 − ☐) = 28
(f) 13 − ☐ ÷ 2 = 7

3 Simplify

(a) $6p + 2q − p + 4q$
(b) $3m + 5 − m − 3$
(c) $3xy + 2y − yx + 6y$

4 Write down an expression for the perimeter of each shape.

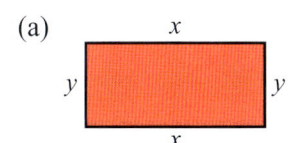

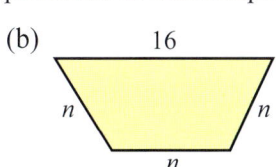

(a)

(b)

5 Draw a shape with a perimeter of $m + 2n$.

6 Which list is arranged in ascending order?
A 0.14, 0.05, 0.062, 0.09
B 0.14, 0.09, 0.062, 0.05
C 0.050, 0.062, 0.09, 0.14
D 0.050, 0.090, 0.14, 0.062

7 The distance s travelled by an object is given by the formula
$$s = \frac{1}{2}t(u + v)$$
Find s when $t = 8$, $u = 3$ and $v = 8$.

8 In number walls each brick is made by adding the two bricks underneath it.

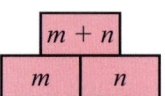

Fill in the missing expressions on these walls

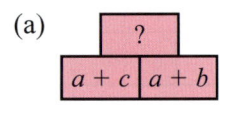

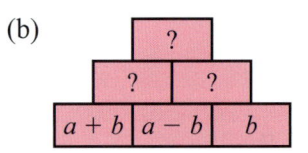

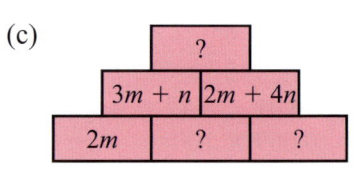

(a) Top: ?; Bottom: $a + c$, $a + b$

(b) Top: ?; Middle: ?, ?; Bottom: $a + b$, $a - b$, b

(c) Top: ?; Middle: $3m + n$, $2m + 4n$; Bottom: $2m$, ?, ?

9 Evaluate, using a calculator

(a) $4.5 + \dfrac{4.48}{1.4}$

(b) $\dfrac{8.94 + 3.66}{3.6}$

(c) $25 - (8.2 \times 1.75)$

(d) $\dfrac{14.24}{9.17 - 4.72}$

(e) $4.956 \div (1.5 - 0.91)$

(f) $\dfrac{28.1 + 0.55}{1.6 + 0.31}$

10 At the end of Year 7 Mark said 'I have now lived for over one million hours'. Work out if Mark was right.

11 Work out
(a) $20 \div (-4)$
(b) $(-5)^2$
(c) $(-3)^3$

12 *Explain* why $4(2n + 3) + 2(3n + 1)$ does *not* equal $14n + 4$.

Part two

1 Copy and complete by writing the missing digits in the boxes.

(a) 5 ☐ 9
   + ☐ 9 ☐
   ─────
     8 5 3

(b) 6 ☐ 1
   − ☐ 7 ☐
   ─────
     4 1 3

(c) 4 ☐ 4
   − ☐ 2 ☐
   ─────
     3 4 5

(d)   ☐ ☐ 9
     ×   6
     ─────
     1 4 3 ☐

(e)   ☐ ☐ 3
     ×   4
     ─────
     2 1 3 ☐

(f)   9 4
     6 ⟌ 5 ☐ 4

(g)   6 5
     7 ⟌ 4 5 ☐

(h)   6 3
     7 ⟌ ☐ 4 1

(i)   5 4
     9 ⟌ 4 ☐ 6

2 In one million seconds which of these would you be able to do?
  (a) Take a term off school.
  (b) Go without sleep for the whole month of July.
  (c) Spend ten days on the beach in France.
  (d) Go to Africa for a year.
  Explain your working.

3 Copy and complete the multiplication squares.

		8	
5	35		40
	8	18	
		54	48
	63		

15			18
	63		28
10			
		40		20
	72		48	

4 Seventeen people pay a total of £7871 for a holiday. They each pay the same amount. Eight of these people pay a total of £1088 to go diving when on holiday. They each pay the same amount. Jenny is one of the people who goes diving. She spends a further £230 whilst on holiday. How much money does Jenny spend in total on everything.

5 Here are six algebra cards.

A: $2n + 1$ B: $4n$ C: $3n$
D: $n + 2n$ E: $2n + 3$ F: $4 - n$

(a) Add the expressions on card B and card E.
(b) Which two cards always have the same value?
(c) Which card has the largest value when $n = 3$.
(d) Add the expressions on all six cards.

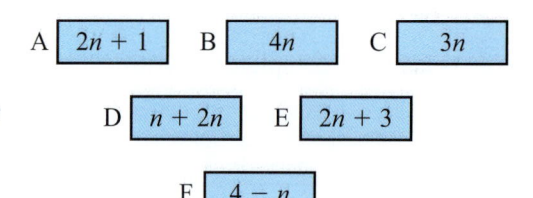

6 Solve the following balance puzzle, writing your answer $x = \ldots$

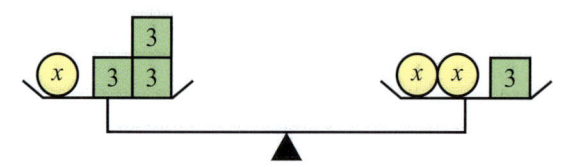

Left side: $x, 3, 3, 3$ (with a 3 on top)
Right side: $x, x, 3$

7 Expand (multiply out)
(a) $5(3m + 2)$ (b) $4(6n - 5)$ (c) $n(4m + n)$

8 In a 'magic square' the sum of the numbers in each row, column and main diagonal is the same. Copy and complete these magic squares.

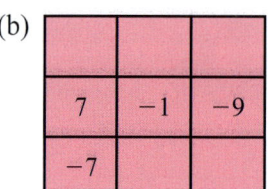

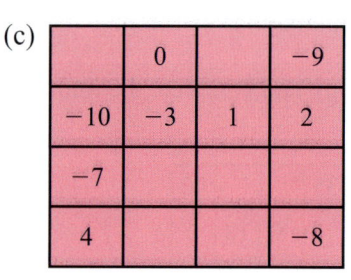

(a) 3×3 grid: top-left -3; middle row: _, 0, -2; bottom row: _, 3, _

(b) 3×3 grid: top row blank; middle row: 7, -1, -9; bottom row: _, -7, _

(c) 4×4 grid:
Row 1: _, 0, _, -9
Row 2: -10, -3, 1, 2
Row 3: -7, _, _, _
Row 4: 4, _, _, -8

9 Leroy says that $0.6 \div 0.03$ equals 0.2
Explain clearly whether Leroy is correct.

10 If n is a number between 0 and 1, which of the following expressions is the larger?

$\frac{2}{n}$ or $\frac{n}{2}$

Explain your answer.

11 $3 + 2 \times 6 - 1 = 29$ *Explain* clearly what mistake has been made with this calculation.

12 Work out $-3 + 2 - 6 - -2 - 4 - -1 - 8 + 6$

Puzzles and Problems 1

1 The totals for the rows and columns are given. Unfortunately some of the totals are hidden by ink blots. Find the values of the letters.

(a)
A	A	A	A	28
A	B	C	A	27
A	C	D	B	30
D	B	B	B	◯
◯	25	30	24	

(b)
A	B	A	B	B	18
B	B	E	C	D	21
A	B	B	A	B	18
C	B	C	B	C	19
E	B	D	E	D	26
27	10	25	23	17	

This one is more difficult.

(c)
A	A	A	A	24
C	A	C	D	13
A	B	B	A	18
B	B	D	C	12
◯	18	15	18	

(d)
A	B	B	A	22
A	A	B	B	22
A	B	A	B	22
B	B	A	B	17
27	17	22	17	

Find the missing digits

2 (a)
```
    3 1 4
  + □ 6 3
  ─────────
    7 □ □
```
(b)
```
    3 5 □
  + □ 2 4
  ─────────
    9 □ 8
```
(c)
```
    □ 5 8
  + 1 4 □
  ─────────
    5 □ 2
```

3 (a)
```
    5 3 6
  + 2 □ 4
  ─────────
    □ 5 □
```
(b)
```
    2 □ 6
  + 3 5 7
  ─────────
    □ 0 3
```
(c)
```
    6 3 4
  + □ 8 □
  ─────────
    9 □ 8
```

4 (a)
```
      3 □
  ×     5
  ───────
    1 8 5
```
(b)
```
      4 □
  ×     9
  ───────
    4 2 3
```
(c)
```
    □ □ 4
  ×     8
  ───────
  2 9 9 2
```

5 (a) □□□ ÷ 7 = 33   (b) □□ × 11 = 143
  (c) 12 × □ = 108   (d) □□□ ÷ 6 = 153

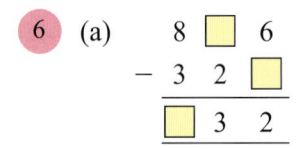

6 (a) $\begin{array}{r} 8\square 6 \\ -\ 3\ 2\ \square \\ \hline \square\ 3\ 2 \end{array}$ (b) $\begin{array}{r} 8\ \square\ 2 \\ -\ \square\ 1\ \square \\ \hline 4\ 1\ 7 \end{array}$ (c) $\begin{array}{r} \square\ 4\ \square \\ -\ 2\ \square\ 8 \\ \hline 3\ 5\ 7 \end{array}$

7 (a) $\square\square \times 8 = 440$ (b) $\square\square \times 11 = 231$
  (c) $400 \div \square = 50$ (d) $\square\square\square \div 6 = 163$

8 (a) $\square\square + 48 = 127$ (b) $\square\square\square - 49 = 463$

  (c) $\begin{array}{r} \square\ 5\ 3 \\ -\ 4\ \square\ 7 \\ \hline 1\ 6\ \square \end{array}$ (d) $\begin{array}{r} 8\ 7\ 5 \\ -\ 5\ 7\ \square \\ \hline \square\ \square\ 6 \end{array}$

9 What is the largest possible number of people in a room if no two people have a birthday in the same month?

10 The letters A, B, C, D, E appear once in every row, every column and each main diagonal of the square. Copy the square and fill in the missing letters.

				B
D				
				E
A	D			

11 Two different numbers on this section of a till receipt are obscured by food stains. What are the two numbers?

◯ tapes at £◯.99 : £87.89

12 King Henry has 9 coins which look identical but in fact one of them is an underweight fake. Describe how he could discover the fake using just two weighings on an ordinary balance.

Divisibility investigation

Below is a quick way to check if a whole number is divisible by 2, 3, 4, 5, 6, 8, 9 or 10.

- number is even → divisible by 2

- sum of the digits is divisible by 3 → divisible by 3

- last two digits are divisible by 4 → divisible by 4

- last digit is 0 or 5 → divisible by 5

- number is even and also divisible by 3 → divisible by 6

- half of the number is divisible by 4 → divisible by 8

- sum of digits is divisible by 9 → divisible by 9

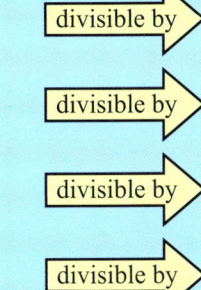

- last digit is 0 → divisible by 10

TASK A Copy and complete the table below, using √'s and ×'s.

Number	\multicolumn{6}{c}{Divisible by}
	2	3	4	5	6	8	9
363	×	√					
224							
459							
155							
168							
865							
360							
2601							

> **TASK B** Is there a test for divisibility by 7?
>
> Test 18228.
> Find the difference between the last 3 digits and the digits at the front: 228 − 18 = 210.
> This difference is divisible by 7. Does this mean that the original number is divisible by 7?
> Using a calculator gives 18228 ÷ 7 = 2604 so the original number is divisible by 7.
>
> Try the same test on these numbers:
> 37177, 8498, 431781, 42329, 39579, 910987.
>
> Now choose some numbers of your own (4, 5 or 6 digit numbers). Check with a calculator. Does the test always work?
>
> **TASK C** Investigate to find out whether or not a similar test works for 'divisibility by 11'.

Mental Arithmetic Practice 1

There are two sets of mental arithmetic questions in this section. Ideally a teacher will read out each question twice, with pupils' books closed. Each test of 25 questions should take about 15–20 minutes.

Test 1

1. What is forty-two divided by seven?
2. What is six hundred and forty seven to the nearest hundred?
3. Write 0.25 as a fraction.
4. Add together seven, nine and fifteen.
5. Change five and a half metres into centimetres.
6. How many thirds make up three whole ones?
7. What is four squared?
8. If seventy-three per cent of the children in a class are girls, what percentage of the class are boys?
9. The side of a square is six metres. What is the area of the square?
10. Write down a factor of 16 which is greater than 5.
11. What is eight thousand five hundred divided by ten?
12. Write down any multiple of eight.
13. What is the remainder when 50 is divided by 8?
14. What is the difference between 2.6 and 6.9?
15. Write down the number that is halfway between twelve and eighteen?
16. At midnight the temperature is minus four degrees celsius. By midday the temperature rises eighteen degrees. What is the temperature at midday?
17. How much change from five pounds would you get after spending three pounds and forty-two pence?
18. How many fourteens are there in two hundred and eighty?

19. Ten per cent of a number is twenty-eight. What is the number?

20. What is the obtuse angle between clock hands showing four o'clock?

21. Add together 11, 12 and 13.

22. True or false: 'All prime numbers are odd numbers'.

23. Write down the square root of 64.

24. Work out $\frac{1}{4}$ plus $\frac{1}{8}$.

25. Find 20% of the sum of 11 and 29.

Test 2

1. Divide 7 into 63.

2. Write the number that is sixteen less than two hundred.

3. Write three-quarters as a decimal.

4. Work out 24 divided by 10 as a decimal.

5. What four coins make 67p?

6. What is the cost of 3 calculators at £5.99 each?

7. Change fifteen centimetres into millimetres.

8. What is the product of 40 and 6?

9. One fifth of a number is 6. What is the number?

10. Subtract the sum of 5 and 9 from 70.

11. Oranges cost 87p for three. What is the cost of one orange?

12. What number is halfway between four and eleven?

13. Write 5:30 p.m. in 24 hour clock time.

14. Two angles in a triangle are seventy-four degrees and sixty degrees. How large is the third angle?

15. The area of a square is 49 cm^2. How long is each side?

16. Ali buys a pen for £1.25 and a drink for 53p. How much change will Ali receive from a twenty pound note?

17. Peaches cost 34p each. What is the cost of 6 peaches?

18. A film starts at twenty minutes to six and lasts for two hours forty-five minutes. At what time does the film finish?

19. What is three-fifths of one hundred?

20. How many millimetres are there in 4 metres?

21. Add together three and minus seven.

22. What is half of 2.5?

23. Take away 50 from 5000.

24. Which is larger: $\frac{2}{5}$ or $\frac{3}{6}$?

25. Find the sum of all the coins from 1p to 20p.

A long time ago! 1

Napier's rods

An early calculator was invented by John Napier in the sixteenth century. It was made of rods which were marked as shown below. Each rod shows the 'times table' for the number at the top.

To multiply two numbers together eg. 678 × 7, place the rods together with 6, 7 and 8 at the top. Place next to the blue rod with the numbers 1 to 10.

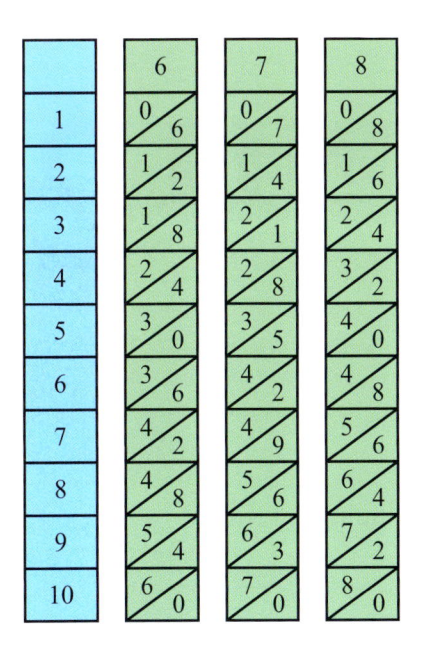

We are multiplying by 7 so look at row 7.
Add the numbers diagonally moving from right to left.

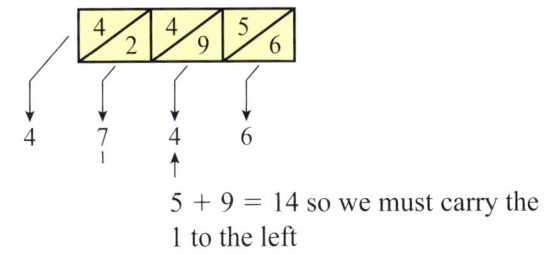

4 7 4 6
  ↑
  1

5 + 9 = 14 so we must carry the
1 to the left

678 × 7 = 4746

Exercise

1. Draw and cut out a set of Napier's rods. Your teacher will tell you how long to make the rectangles.

2. Use your Napier's rods to work out the following.
    (a) 368 × 4
    (b) 427 × 6
    (c) 592 × 7
    (d) 4276 × 9
    (e) 56 392 × 4
    (f) 684 539 × 7
    (g) A builder uses 4965 bricks for each of 8 houses. How many bricks does he use in total?
    (h) The Army has to pay 3 shillings each to 27 483 soldiers. How many shillings in total is this?

3. **RESEARCH:** Find out
    (a) When were Napier's rods most widely used?
    (b) In which kinds of jobs were they used?
    (c) How can Napier's rods be used to multiply by 2 digit numbers?
    (d) Can Napier's rods be used for division?

UNIT 2

2.1 Fractions

In section 2.1 you will:
- review equivalent fractions
- review adding and subtracting fractions (including mixed numbers)
- multiply and divide fractions

Equivalent fractions

In the table given below, pick out all the letters above the fractions which are equivalent to one half $\left(\frac{1}{2}\right)$.

C	Q	E	A	Y	P	R	N	H	F	letters
$\frac{5}{10}$	$\frac{3}{4}$	$\frac{2}{4}$	$\frac{21}{42}$	$\frac{1}{3}$	$\frac{3}{5}$	$\frac{6}{12}$	$\frac{3}{6}$	$\frac{4}{7}$	$\frac{5}{10}$	fractions

The letters are   C,   E,   A,   R,   N,   F

because... $\frac{5}{10}, \frac{2}{4}, \frac{21}{42}, \frac{6}{12}, \frac{3}{6}, \frac{5}{10}$ are all the same as $\frac{1}{2}$.

Numerator and denominator are both divided by the same number.

Now rearrange the letters to make the name of a country.

C,   E,   A,   R,   N,   F   ⟶   FRANCE

Exercise 1M

In questions ① to ④ , find the fractions in the table which are equivalent to the given fraction. Rearrange the letters to make a word using the clue.

1 $\left(\frac{3}{5}, \text{sport}\right)$

T	G	U	F	O	Y	R	A	B	L
$\frac{18}{36}$	$\frac{36}{60}$	$\frac{27}{45}$	$\frac{30}{40}$	$\frac{20}{25}$	$\frac{12}{20}$	$\frac{9}{15}$	$\frac{12}{18}$	$\frac{6}{10}$	$\frac{18}{21}$

2 $\left(\frac{2}{3}, \text{country}\right)$

A	N	E	R	S	B	I	Z	Q	L
$\frac{4}{6}$	$\frac{9}{12}$	$\frac{14}{22}$	$\frac{60}{90}$	$\frac{16}{25}$	$\frac{8}{12}$	$\frac{22}{33}$	$\frac{20}{30}$	$\frac{32}{49}$	$\frac{12}{18}$

3 $\left(\frac{5}{9}, \text{clothing}\right)$ 4 $\left(\frac{3}{4}, \text{fruit}\right)$

T	M	S	R	K	C	E	H	O	I
$\frac{100}{180}$	$\frac{21}{70}$	$\frac{20}{36}$	$\frac{35}{63}$	$\frac{18}{21}$	$\frac{40}{70}$	$\frac{24}{45}$	$\frac{45}{81}$	$\frac{140}{160}$	$\frac{15}{27}$

B	O	P	A	E	I	H	C	R	T
$\frac{6}{7}$	$\frac{12}{16}$	$\frac{33}{44}$	$\frac{6}{8}$	$\frac{6}{9}$	$\frac{30}{40}$	$\frac{18}{25}$	$\frac{15}{20}$	$\frac{36}{48}$	$\frac{9}{12}$

5 Ask your teacher for card. Cut out 24 cards as shown.
On each pair of cards write down two equivalent fractions.

Now play a game with 2, 3 or 4 players using these equivalent fraction cards.

How to play:
- Shuffle the cards, place them face down in a pattern of 6 rows by 4 columns.
- Decide who will go first.
- Each turn requires a player to turn over a pair of cards.
- If the pair of cards are equivalent such as $\frac{1}{5}$ and $\frac{2}{10}$ the player keeps the pair. If the cards are not equivalent turn the cards face down again.
- Try to remember which cards are where!
- If you find a pair you get another go. The player with the most pairs when no cards are left is the winner.

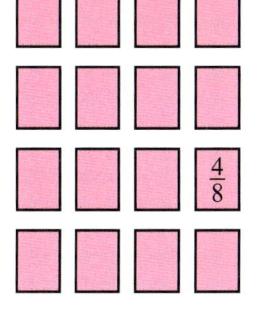

Adding and subtracting fractions

If fractions do not have the same denominator, change them into *equivalent fractions* which do have the same denominator before adding or subtracting.

(a) $\frac{1}{6} + \frac{1}{3}$

$= \frac{1}{6} + \frac{2}{6}$

$= \frac{3}{6} = \frac{1}{2}$

cancel final answer if you can

(b) $\frac{7}{8} - \frac{3}{4}$

$= \frac{7}{8} - \frac{6}{8}$

$= \frac{1}{8}$

(c) $\frac{2}{5} + \frac{3}{7}$

$= \frac{14}{35} + \frac{15}{35}$

$= \frac{29}{35}$

Exercise 2M

Work out

1 $\frac{2}{8} + \frac{3}{8}$ 2 $\frac{5}{7} - \frac{2}{7}$ 3 $\frac{1}{4} - \frac{1}{8}$ 4 $\frac{5}{8} - \frac{1}{2}$

5 $\frac{4}{5} + \frac{1}{10}$ 6 $\frac{7}{20} - \frac{1}{10}$ 7 $\frac{5}{9} - \frac{7}{18}$ 8 $\frac{5}{12} + \frac{1}{3}$ 9 $\frac{19}{40} - \frac{3}{8}$

10

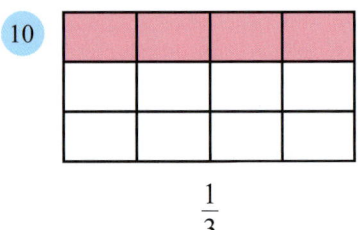

$\frac{1}{3}$ + $\frac{1}{4}$ = $\frac{7}{12}$

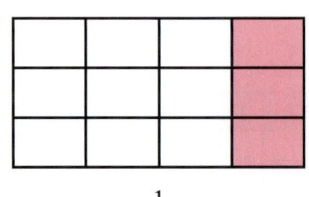

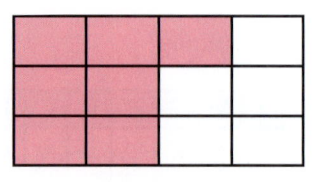

Draw similar diagrams to show that $\frac{2}{3} + \frac{1}{4} = \frac{11}{12}$

Work out

11 $\frac{3}{5} + \frac{1}{4}$ **12** $\frac{3}{4} - \frac{1}{3}$ **13** $\frac{2}{3} - \frac{4}{7}$ **14** $\frac{3}{8} + \frac{2}{5}$ **15** $\frac{9}{10} - \frac{7}{9}$

16 $\frac{5}{6} - \frac{5}{8}$ **17** $\frac{11}{12} - \frac{1}{5}$ **18** $\frac{5}{7} + \frac{2}{9}$ **19** $\frac{4}{9} + \frac{1}{5}$ **20** $\frac{7}{10} - \frac{2}{3}$

21 Ruby goes shopping. She spends $\frac{1}{3}$ of her money on shoes and $\frac{1}{5}$ of her money on shirts.

(a) What fraction of her money has she spent in total?

(b) What fraction of her money does she have left?

22 Find the missing fraction for each box.

(a) $\frac{2}{5} + \square = \frac{11}{15}$ (b) $\frac{9}{10} - \square = \frac{7}{30}$ (c) $\frac{3}{4} - \square = \frac{1}{6}$

23 Work out

(a) $\frac{1}{2} + \frac{1}{3} + \frac{1}{12}$ (b) $\frac{3}{5} + \frac{1}{4} - \frac{7}{10}$ (c) $\frac{5}{6} + \frac{1}{10} - \frac{4}{5}$

Adding and subtracting mixed numbers

Convert mixed numbers into improper fractions before adding or subtracting.

proper fraction ⬇ numerator is less than denominator. examples: $\frac{3}{7}, \frac{17}{59}$

improper fraction ⬇ numerator is larger than denominator. examples: $\frac{4}{3}, \frac{17}{5}$
(often called 'top-heavy' fractions)

mixed number ⬇ contains both a whole number and a fraction. examples: $4\frac{1}{2}, 7\frac{3}{4}$

$1\frac{3}{4} + 2\frac{1}{3} = \frac{7}{4} + \frac{7}{3} = \frac{21}{12} + \frac{28}{12} = \frac{49}{12}$

Convert back to a mixed number at the end.

$\frac{49}{12} = 49 \div 12 = 4\frac{1}{12}$

Exercise 3M

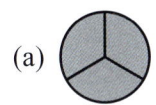

1. Change the following improper fractions to mixed numbers.
   (a) $\frac{8}{3}$ (b) $\frac{13}{7}$ (c) $\frac{12}{5}$ (d) $\frac{17}{9}$ (e) $\frac{73}{10}$

2. How many quarters are there in $7\frac{3}{4}$?

3. Change the mixed numbers to improper fractions.
   (a) $3\frac{1}{4}$ (b) $4\frac{3}{7}$ (c) $2\frac{4}{5}$ (d) $8\frac{1}{5}$ (e) $7\frac{4}{9}$

Work out

4. $1\frac{3}{4} + \frac{1}{3}$
5. $1\frac{4}{5} + \frac{2}{3}$
6. $2\frac{1}{2} - \frac{7}{8}$
7. $3\frac{1}{4} - 1\frac{5}{6}$
8. $2\frac{3}{5} + 1\frac{3}{4}$
9. $3\frac{1}{6} - 1\frac{3}{8}$
10. $4\frac{1}{2} - 2\frac{4}{5}$
11. $2\frac{5}{8} + 1\frac{3}{10}$
12. $3\frac{1}{4} - 1\frac{7}{10}$
13. $4\frac{3}{5} - 2\frac{7}{8}$
14. $3\frac{2}{3} + 1\frac{1}{4}$
15. $5\frac{1}{2} - 3\frac{5}{6}$

16. Find the perimeter of this rectangle.

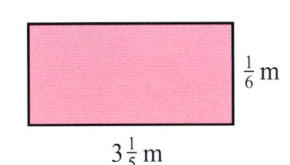

    $\frac{1}{6}$ m

    $3\frac{1}{5}$ m

17 What is one sixth less than seven tenths?

18 $\frac{1}{5}$ of the dogs in a full kennels leave on a Friday and $\frac{1}{6}$ leave on a Saturday.
What fraction of the dogs remain if no new dogs arrive?

19 A baker sells chocolate cakes in slices on a market stall one day. In the morning $5\frac{1}{4}$ cakes are sold and in the afternoon $7\frac{5}{6}$ cakes are sold.
The baker started with 15 cakes. How many cakes are left over?

20 The fraction sum $\frac{1}{3} + \frac{4}{6}$ is made from four different digits and the sum is 1.
Find other fraction sums using four different digits so that the sum is 1.

Multiplying fractions

The red shaded strip is $\frac{1}{4}$ of the rectangle.

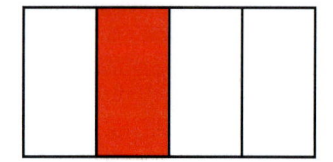

The black section is $\frac{1}{3}$ of $\frac{1}{4}$ of the rectangle.

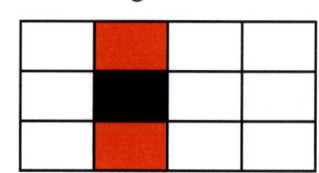

$\frac{1}{3}$ of $\frac{1}{4} = \frac{1}{12}$

$\frac{1}{3} \times \frac{1}{4} = \frac{1}{12}$

(a) $\frac{3}{7} \times \frac{4}{5} = \frac{12}{35}$ multiply the numerators and multiply the denominators

(b) $\frac{3}{4} \times \frac{1}{9} = \frac{\cancel{3}^1}{\cancel{36}_{12}} = \frac{1}{12}$ or $\frac{\cancel{3}^1}{4} \times \frac{1}{\cancel{9}_3} = \frac{1}{12}$ multiply then cancel or cancel then multiply

Exercise 4M

1 Draw a rectangle and use it to show that $\frac{1}{4} \times \frac{1}{5} = \frac{1}{20}$

2 Work out

(a) $\frac{3}{5} \times \frac{4}{7}$ (b) $\frac{5}{8} \times \frac{1}{9}$ (c) $\frac{1}{4}$ of $\frac{1}{9}$ (d) $\frac{1}{10}$ of $\frac{1}{4}$

(e) $\frac{3}{4} \times \frac{2}{9}$ (f) $\frac{1}{5} \times \frac{10}{11}$ (g) $\frac{4}{9}$ of $\frac{1}{8}$ (h) $\frac{2}{3} \times \frac{3}{4}$

(i) $\frac{7}{10}$ of $\frac{2}{21}$ (j) $\frac{7}{8} \times \frac{12}{15}$ (k) $\frac{5}{9} \times \frac{6}{15}$ (l) $\frac{5}{6} \times \frac{4}{5}$

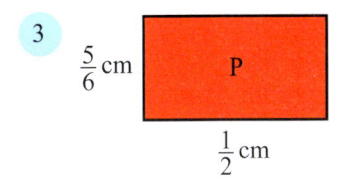

3 Work out the area of:
(a) P (b) Q (c) P and Q

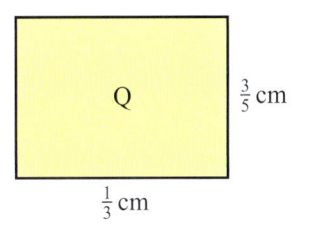

P: $\frac{5}{6}$ cm by $\frac{1}{2}$ cm

Q: $\frac{3}{5}$ cm by $\frac{1}{3}$ cm

4 One day a grocer sells $\frac{4}{5}$ of the strawberries on sale. Mr Jenkins buys $\frac{7}{8}$ of the strawberries sold. What fraction overall of the strawberries on sale did Mr Jenkins buy?

5 Work out
(a) $\frac{4}{5} \times \frac{10}{1}$
(b) $\frac{2}{3} \times \frac{6}{1}$
(c) $\frac{5}{6} \times 18$
(d) $\frac{3}{8} \times 16$
(e) $\frac{9}{10} \times 5$
(f) $\frac{3}{4} \times 2$
(g) $\frac{7}{8} \times 4$
(h) $\frac{3}{20} \times 15$

6 Work out $\frac{1}{3} \times \frac{2}{5} \times \frac{3}{4}$

Exercise 4E

1 Change mixed numbers to improper fraction before multiplying. Work out
(a) $2\frac{1}{2} \times \frac{2}{3}$
(b) $1\frac{1}{3} \times \frac{9}{10}$
(c) $2\frac{1}{4} \times \frac{1}{3}$
(d) $3\frac{2}{3} \times \frac{3}{4}$
(e) $1\frac{1}{4} \times 1\frac{3}{5}$
(f) $2\frac{1}{3} \times 1\frac{3}{7}$
(g) $1\frac{7}{8} \times 2\frac{3}{5}$
(h) $3\frac{1}{2} \times 2\frac{1}{7}$

2 At 8.30 one morning $\frac{5}{8}$ of the cars on a bridge are heading West. $\frac{3}{10}$ of these cars are stuck in a traffic jam. What fraction of all the cars on the bridge are stuck in this traffic jam?

3 Work out
(a) $1\frac{1}{2} \times 2\frac{2}{3} \times 1\frac{3}{4}$
(b) $2\frac{1}{4} \times 3\frac{1}{3} \times 1\frac{4}{5}$
(c) $2\frac{3}{4} \times \frac{8}{9} \times 2\frac{3}{11}$

4 There are 50 Christmas presents under a Christmas tree.
$\frac{3}{5}$ of these presents are for Mr and Mrs Williams.
Mr Williams opens $\frac{4}{5}$ of these presents.
How many presents does Mr Williams open?

5 Simplify

(a) $\dfrac{m}{3} \times \dfrac{n}{4}$ (b) $\dfrac{n}{5} \times \dfrac{n}{5}$ (c) $\dfrac{3n}{7} \times \dfrac{2n}{9}$ (d) $\dfrac{4m}{9} \times \dfrac{6n}{8}$

6 Work out the area of this triangle.

$1\tfrac{3}{7}$ cm, $\tfrac{4}{5}$ cm

7 Work out $\dfrac{3}{4} \times \dfrac{4}{5} \times \dfrac{5}{6} \times \dfrac{6}{7} \times 2\tfrac{4}{5}$

Dividing fractions

3 thirds make a whole one so $1 \div \tfrac{1}{3} = 3$

6 thirds make two whole ones so $2 \div \tfrac{1}{3} = 6$

Consider $1 \div \tfrac{1}{3}$. Turn the second fraction upside down then multiply so $1 \times \tfrac{3}{1} = 3$. This gives the correct answer for $1 \div \tfrac{1}{3}$.

Consider $2 \div \tfrac{1}{3}$. Turn the second fraction upside down then multiply so $2 \times \tfrac{3}{1} = 6$. This gives the correct answer for $2 \div \tfrac{1}{3}$.

Dividing by a fraction method

When dividing by a fraction, turn it upside down then multiply by the first number.

$$\dfrac{2}{3} \div \dfrac{5}{6} = \dfrac{2}{3} \times \dfrac{6}{5} = \dfrac{12}{15} = \dfrac{4}{5}$$

Exercise 5M

1 Copy and complete

(a) $\dfrac{3}{4} \div \dfrac{4}{5}$
$= \dfrac{3}{4} \times \dfrac{\square}{4}$
$= \dfrac{\square}{16}$

(b) $\dfrac{5}{8} \div \dfrac{2}{3}$
$= \dfrac{5}{8} \times \dfrac{\square}{\square}$
$= \dfrac{\square}{\square}$

(c) $\dfrac{7}{10} \div \dfrac{4}{5}$
$= \dfrac{7}{10} \times \dfrac{\square}{\square}$
$= \dfrac{\square}{\square} = \dfrac{\square}{8}$

2 Work out

(a) $\dfrac{3}{8} \div \dfrac{5}{7}$ (b) $\dfrac{5}{9} \div \dfrac{1}{2}$ (c) $\dfrac{5}{6} \div \dfrac{3}{4}$ (d) $\dfrac{9}{10} \div \dfrac{2}{3}$

(e) $\dfrac{3}{10} \div \dfrac{2}{5}$ (f) $\dfrac{4}{5} \div \dfrac{7}{8}$ (g) $\dfrac{1}{4} \div \dfrac{5}{7}$ (h) $\dfrac{1}{6} \div \dfrac{8}{9}$

3. Find the missing fraction for each empty box.

   (a) $\frac{2}{3} \times \boxed{} = \frac{14}{27}$
   (b) $\frac{5}{8} \div \boxed{} = \frac{45}{56}$
   (c) $\frac{3}{4} \times \boxed{} = \frac{3}{14}$

4. A large bottle contains $\frac{9}{10}$ litre of water. A small bottle contains $\frac{3}{8}$ litre of water when full. How many small bottles can be filled completely with the water from the large bottle? *Give your reasons in detail.*

5. Work out $\frac{2}{3} \times \frac{5}{7} \div \frac{10}{11}$

6. A dog has $\frac{1}{8}$ kg of meat added to each meal. Exactly how many meals are covered by $\frac{2}{3}$ kg of meat?

7. The area of this rectangle is $\frac{7}{16}$ cm². What is its width if its length is $\frac{7}{10}$ cm?

   $\frac{7}{10}$ cm

8. Use a diagram to *explain why* $\frac{1}{5} \div 6 = \frac{1}{30}$

9. Work out the value of $\left(\frac{3}{4}\right)^2 \div \left(\frac{3}{2}\right)^2$

$1\frac{1}{4} \div 2\frac{2}{3} = \frac{5}{4} \div \frac{8}{3} = \frac{5}{4} \times \frac{3}{8} = \frac{15}{32}$

Exercise 5E

1. Copy and complete

   (a) $2\frac{1}{2} \div 4\frac{1}{5}$

   $= \frac{5}{2} \div \frac{\boxed{}}{5}$

   $= \frac{5}{2} \times \frac{5}{\boxed{}}$

   $= \frac{25}{\boxed{}}$

   (b) $2\frac{3}{4} \div 1\frac{7}{8}$

   $= \frac{11}{4} \div \frac{\boxed{}}{\boxed{}}$

   $= \frac{11}{4} \times \frac{\boxed{}}{\boxed{}}$

   $= \frac{88}{\boxed{}}$

   $= \frac{22}{\boxed{}}$

   $= 1\frac{7}{\boxed{}}$

   (c) $3\frac{2}{3} \div 1\frac{1}{2}$

   $= \frac{11}{3} \div \frac{\boxed{}}{\boxed{}}$

   $= \frac{11}{3} \times \frac{\boxed{}}{\boxed{}}$

   $= \frac{\boxed{}}{\boxed{}}$

   $= 2\frac{\boxed{}}{\boxed{}}$

2 Work out

(a) $1\frac{3}{4} \div 3\frac{1}{3}$ (b) $4\frac{2}{5} \div 2\frac{3}{4}$ (c) $2\frac{4}{5} \div 4\frac{1}{2}$

(d) $5\frac{2}{3} \div 1\frac{3}{10}$ (e) $4\frac{5}{6} \div 2\frac{7}{10}$ (f) $1\frac{7}{12} \div 2\frac{1}{4}$

3 At a party each person ate $\frac{1}{6}$ of a cake.
How many people ate cake if $5\frac{1}{2}$ cakes were eaten in total?

4 Jamie has $4\frac{1}{2}$ litres of paint in total.
Each tin contains $\frac{3}{8}$ litre of paint.
How many tins of paint does Jamie have?

5 Work out the value of $4\frac{1}{2} \div 1\frac{5}{6} \div 1\frac{4}{7}$

6 Jess runs a race at a steady speed. She completes $\frac{5}{8}$ of the race in $\frac{2}{3}$ of an hour.
How long does she take to complete the whole race?

Need more practice with fractions?

1 Which fractions below are equivalent?

$\frac{6}{15}$ $\frac{14}{35}$ $\frac{10}{25}$ $\frac{12}{45}$ $\frac{22}{55}$

2 Work out

(a) $\frac{3}{8} + \frac{3}{5}$ (b) $\frac{6}{7} - \frac{2}{5}$ (c) $\frac{8}{9} - \frac{1}{4}$ (d) $\frac{1}{3} + \frac{5}{8}$

(e) $\frac{9}{10} - \frac{4}{7}$ (f) $\frac{5}{8} - \frac{2}{9}$ (g) $\frac{1}{4} + \frac{3}{7}$ (h) $\frac{7}{12} - \frac{1}{3}$

3 What fraction of each shape is shaded?

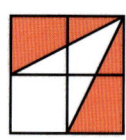

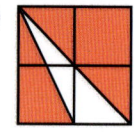

(a)   (b)   (c)

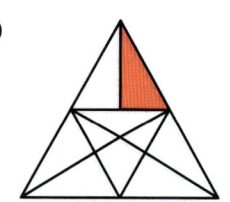

4 $\frac{5}{8} \times \frac{\square}{\square} = \frac{35}{72}$ Write down this calculation with the correct value in each box.

5. Mario has an order for 60 pizzas. If $\frac{5}{12}$ of his pizzas must be vegetarian, how many will be non-vegetarian?

6. A petrol tank in a car holds 56 litres when full. How much *more* petrol can be put into the tank when it is $\frac{3}{8}$ full?

7. Work out
   (a) $\frac{5}{8} \times \frac{4}{9}$
   (b) $\frac{2}{3} \times 10$
   (c) $\frac{8}{9} \div \frac{9}{10}$
   (d) $\frac{3}{5} \div \frac{7}{8}$
   (e) $\frac{1}{9} \div \frac{3}{4}$
   (f) $\frac{6}{7} \times \frac{21}{24}$
   (g) $\frac{5}{8}$ of $\frac{3}{4}$
   (h) $\frac{2}{11} \div \frac{5}{6}$

8. If $\frac{2}{7}$ of a number is 14, what is the number?

Extension questions with fractions

1. Work out
   (a) $3\frac{1}{2} \times 2\frac{4}{5}$
   (b) $3\frac{3}{5} \times 3\frac{1}{3}$
   (c) $5\frac{1}{4} \div 1\frac{7}{8}$
   (d) $2\frac{1}{8} \times \frac{6}{7}$
   (e) $1\frac{1}{3} \div 3\frac{1}{4}$
   (f) $4\frac{2}{3} \div 2\frac{1}{2}$

2. Alma has a bag of 32 sweets. Alma gives $\frac{3}{8}$ of her sweets to her brother Max. Max then gives $\frac{1}{4}$ of his share to a friend and eats the rest. Alma meanwhile eats $\frac{2}{5}$ of her remaining sweets.
   (a) How many sweets does Alma have left at the end?
   (b) How many sweets does Max eat?

3. Mason has a piece of wood $2\frac{1}{10}$ m long. He cuts off a $1\frac{1}{3}$ m piece then a piece $\frac{2}{5}$ m long. How long is the remaining piece of wood?

4. A cylinder is $\frac{1}{2}$ full of water. After 90 ml of water is added the cylinder is $\frac{4}{5}$ full.

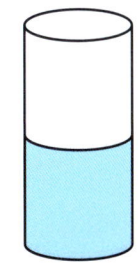

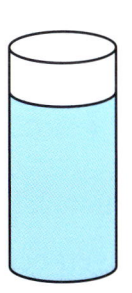

   Calculate the total volume of the cylinder.

5 A pond is $\frac{1}{4}$ full. After a further 4200 gallons of water are pumped in the pond is $\frac{2}{5}$ full.

(a) What is the total volume of the pond?

(b) How many more gallons are required to fill the pond?

6 In her will Granny Sheldrake left $\frac{1}{3}$ of her money to her sister Emily, $\frac{2}{5}$ of her money to her grandson Eric and the rest to her cat, which was to be looked after by Eric. Eric immediately spent $\frac{3}{4}$ of his inheritance on a new car and put the rest in the bank. One day, while driving his new car, he ran over the cat and consequently inherited the cat's share of the money. Eric put this money in the bank. If Emily inherited £45 000, work out

(a) how much money was left to the cat

(b) how much money Eric had in the bank after the cat's 'accident'.

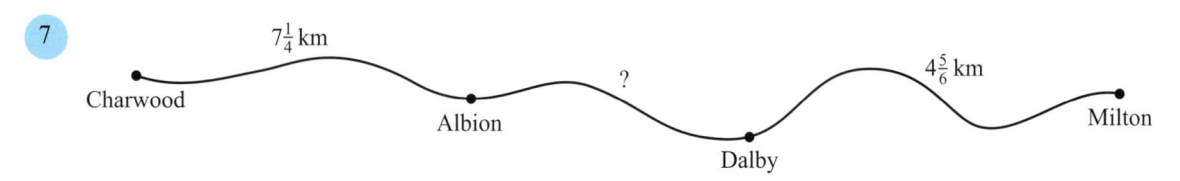

7

Charwood — $7\frac{1}{4}$ km — Albion — ? — Dalby — $4\frac{5}{6}$ km — Milton

The distance from Charwood to Milton is 18 km.
The distance between each pair of villages is shown above.
Work out the distance between Albion and Dalby.

8 Work out a half of ninety-nine and a half.

9 Andy has $\frac{3}{7}$ of a pint of beer in his pint glass.
He asks Tina to pour another half a pint into his glass.
Tina fills Andy's glass up completely.
How much *more* than half a pint does Tina pour into Andy's glass?

10 (a) Draw a 4 × 5 rectangle.
Use different colours to show $\frac{1}{2}, \frac{1}{4}, \frac{1}{5}$ and $\frac{1}{20}$ of the whole rectangle. Parts must not overlap.

(b) Draw a 5 × 6 rectangle. Divide it into three parts using three different fractions, each with numerator 1.

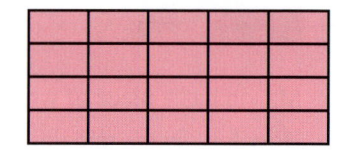

2.2 Fractions, decimals, percentages

In section 2.2 you will:

- convert between fractions, decimals and percentages

Changing fractions to decimals

Convert denominator to 10, 100, etc.

$\frac{1}{5} = \frac{2}{10} = 0.2$ $\quad\quad\quad\quad$ $\frac{1}{25} = \frac{4}{100} = 0.04$ $\quad\quad\quad\quad$ $\frac{9}{20} = \frac{45}{100} = 0.45$

Cancelling fractions can help.

$\frac{12}{16} = \frac{3}{4} = 0.75$ $\quad\quad\quad\quad$ $\frac{60}{240} = \frac{1}{4} = 0.25$

Exercise 1M

Copy and complete the boxes.

1. $\frac{7}{20} = \frac{35}{100} = 0.\square\square$

2. $\frac{3}{20} = \frac{\square}{100} = 0.\square\square$

3. $\frac{4}{5} = \frac{\square}{10} = 0.\square$

4. $\frac{3}{12} = \frac{\square}{4} = 0.\square\square$

5. $\frac{3}{5} = \frac{\square}{10} = 0.\square$

6. $\frac{4}{25} = \frac{\square}{100} = 0.\square\square$

Convert these fractions into decimals.

7. $\frac{11}{20}$ $\quad$ 8. $\frac{2}{5}$ $\quad$ 9. $\frac{7}{25}$ $\quad$ 10. $\frac{27}{36}$ $\quad$ 11. $\frac{17}{20}$

12. $\frac{23}{25}$ $\quad$ 13. $\frac{19}{25}$ $\quad$ 14. $\frac{150}{200}$ $\quad$ 15. $\frac{120}{200}$ $\quad$ 16. $\frac{18}{72}$

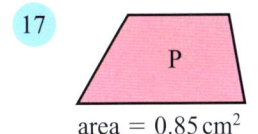

17. By how much is area P greater than area Q?

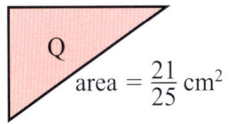

    P area = 0.85 cm²
    Q area = $\frac{21}{25}$ cm²

18. Convert the fractions to decimals and then write the numbers in order of size, smallest first.

    (a) $\frac{8}{20}$, 0.3, $\frac{9}{25}$ $\quad$ (b) $\frac{3}{4}$, $\frac{3}{5}$, 0.7 $\quad$ (c) $\frac{12}{16}$, 0.7, $\frac{4}{5}$ $\quad$ (d) $\frac{1}{5}$, 0.15, $\frac{1}{20}$

19. On a calculator $\frac{1}{9} = 0.1111111$

    Without using a calculator, write down $\frac{1}{900}$ as a decimal.

20 Convert these fractions into decimals.

(a) $\frac{19}{1000}$ (b) $\frac{1}{125}$ (c) $\frac{17}{125}$ (d) $\frac{54}{72}$ (e) $\frac{150}{2000}$

(f) $\frac{7}{250}$ (g) $\frac{19}{76}$ (h) $\frac{89}{500}$ (i) $\frac{36}{3000}$ (j) $\frac{173}{10000}$

Changing decimals into fractions

$0.6 = \frac{6}{10} = \frac{3}{5}$ $\qquad$ $0.27 = \frac{27}{100}$

$0.65 = \frac{65}{100} = \frac{13}{20}$ $\qquad$ $0.04 = \frac{4}{100} = \frac{1}{25}$

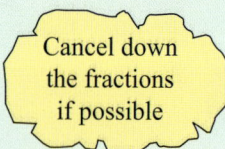

Cancel down the fractions if possible

Exercise 2M

Convert these decimals into fractions

1 0.3 **2** 0.7 **3** 0.01 **4** 0.09 **5** 0.13

6 0.51 **7** 0.69 **8** 0.9 **9** 0.23 **10** 0.37

11 0.89 **12** 2.3 **13** 4.73 **14** 5.01 **15** 6.7

16 Carol and Oscar each have a bar of chocolate. Both bars are the same size.
Carol has eaten 0.85 of her bar and Oscar has eaten $\frac{17}{20}$ of his bar. Who has eaten the most chocolate?

Change these decimals into fractions (cancel down fractions when possible).

17 0.8 **18** 0.05 **19** 0.08 **20** 0.25 **21** 0.24

22 0.02 **23** 0.32 **24** 0.18 **25** 3.2 **26** 6.04

27 7.12 **28** 3.75 **29** 8.6 **30** 2.95 **31** 4.36

32 Cameron weighs 67.8 kg. He loses weight during the next fortnight. He now weighs $66\frac{3}{20}$ kg. How much weight does he lose? Give the answer both as a decimal and a fraction.

Changing fractions and percentages

(a) Percentage to fraction
('per cent' means 'out of 100')

$$60\% = \frac{60}{100} = \frac{3}{5}$$

$$24\% = \frac{24}{100} = \frac{6}{25}$$

$$2\% = \frac{2}{100} = \frac{1}{50}$$

(b) Fraction to percentage
(make the denominator equal to 100)

$$\frac{4}{5} = \frac{80}{100} = 80\%$$

$$\frac{3}{20} = \frac{15}{100} = 15\%$$

$$3\frac{1}{2} = \frac{350}{100} = 350\%$$

- Learn the following:

$$\frac{1}{4} = 25\% \qquad \frac{1}{8} = 12\frac{1}{2}\% \qquad \frac{1}{3} = 33\frac{1}{3}\% \qquad \frac{2}{3} = 66\frac{2}{3}\%$$

Exercise 3M

1. Change these percentages into fractions. Cancel down answers where possible.
   (a) 40%   (b) 7%   (c) 22%   (d) 80%   (e) 5%
   (f) 89%   (g) 10%   (h) 28%   (i) 4%   (j) 35%

2. Copy and complete the following.
   (a) $\frac{9}{20} = \frac{45}{100} = \Box\%$
   (b) $\frac{3}{25} = \frac{\Box}{100} = \Box\%$
   (c) $\frac{19}{50} = \frac{\Box}{100} = \Box\%$

3. Here are some test marks. Change them to percentages.
   (a) $\frac{17}{20}$ (b) $\frac{13}{25}$ (c) $\frac{46}{50}$

4. During one season, José won 85% of his races. What *fraction* of his races did he *not* win?

5. Megan spent 36% of her money on the first day of her holiday. What *fraction* of her money did she have left?

6. Rosa was absent from school for $\frac{1}{25}$ of the Autumn term. What *percentage* of the Autumn term was she absent for?

7 One in five people in Henton own a laptop computer.
What *percentage* of people in Henton do *not* own a laptop?

8 Answer true or false for each of the following statements.

(a) $\frac{2}{3} = 66\frac{2}{3}\%$ (b) $\frac{1}{8} = 18\%$ (c) $\frac{4}{25} = 16\%$

(d) $\frac{1}{3} = 35\%$ (e) $\frac{7}{50} = 14\%$ (f) $\frac{19}{20} = 95\%$

9 Write down which fractions are greater than the given percentage.

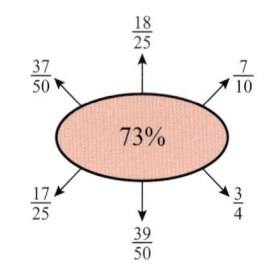

Fractions around 73%: $\frac{18}{25}$, $\frac{37}{50}$, $\frac{7}{10}$, $\frac{17}{25}$, $\frac{39}{50}$, $\frac{3}{4}$

10 Use the symbols <, > or = to copy and complete each statement below.

(a) $\frac{7}{20} \square 0.4$ (b) $0.22 \square \frac{6}{25}$ (c) $32\% \square \frac{16}{50}$

(d) $83\% \square \frac{21}{25}$ (e) $3\frac{1}{4} \square 3.27$ (f) $7\% \square 0.7$

Changing decimals, fractions and percentages

Exercise 4M

1 Change the following decimals into percentages.

(a) 0.37   (b) 0.17   (c) 0.03   (d) 0.4

2 Change these percentages into decimals.

(a) 52%   (b) 80%   (c) 130%   (d) 240%

3 Copy and complete the table.

	fraction	decimal	percentage
(a)		0.3	
(b)			55%
(c)			12%
(d)	$\frac{1}{20}$		
(e)		0.48	
(f)	$\frac{11}{25}$		
(g)			28%

4. Write these numbers in order of size, starting with the smallest.

$$\frac{3}{4}, 0.73, \frac{17}{25}, 70\%, \frac{18}{25}$$

5. Each fraction, decimal or percentage has an equivalent in the list with letters.
Find the letters to make a sentence.

(a) $\boxed{50\%, \frac{1}{4}, 10\%, 0.2, 0.11}$ $\boxed{17\%, 11\%}$ $\boxed{0.75, 99\%, \frac{1}{10}}$ $\boxed{20\%, \frac{1}{4}, \frac{1}{8}, 0.7}$

(b) $\boxed{\frac{7}{10}, 0.8, 45\%, \frac{17}{100}, 0.5, \frac{1}{4}, \frac{10}{25}, 0.11}$ $\boxed{\frac{3}{6}, \frac{4}{16}, 0.05, 80\%}$ $\boxed{\frac{22}{200}, 0.8\ 75\%, 11\%, \frac{8}{10}}$

(c) $\boxed{17\%}$ $\boxed{45\%, 0.25, 75\%}$ $\boxed{0.11, \frac{99}{100}, \frac{4}{10}, \frac{41}{50}, \frac{400}{500}}$ $\boxed{\frac{3}{20}, \frac{2}{16}, \frac{99}{100}, \frac{1}{3}, 0.4, 0.8, \frac{10}{20}, 11\%}$

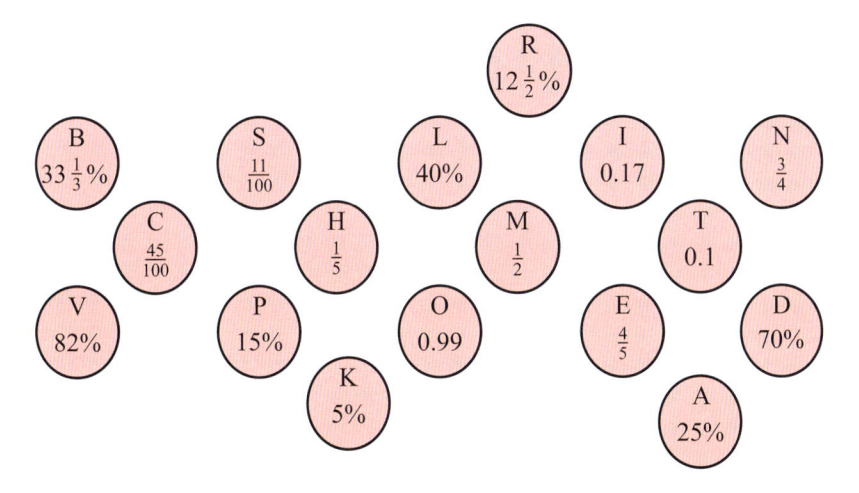

R $12\frac{1}{2}\%$
B $33\frac{1}{3}\%$ S $\frac{11}{100}$ L 40% I 0.17 N $\frac{3}{4}$
C $\frac{45}{100}$ H $\frac{1}{5}$ M $\frac{1}{2}$ T 0.1
V 82% P 15% O 0.99 E $\frac{4}{5}$ D 70%
K 5% A 25%

Need more practice with fractions, decimals, percentages?

1. Which fractions below are equivalent to 0.35?

$$\frac{7}{20} \quad \frac{35}{50} \quad \frac{21}{60} \quad \frac{35}{1000} \quad \frac{3}{25}$$

2. (a) What fraction of the shapes opposite are triangles?
   (b) What percentage of the shapes opposite are circles?

3. *Explain clearly* why we know that $0.6 = 60\%$?

4 Convert these fractions into decimals.

(a) $\dfrac{3}{125}$ (b) $\dfrac{180}{2000}$ (c) $\dfrac{45}{500}$ (d) $\dfrac{48}{64}$ (e) $\dfrac{190}{250}$

5 Write down true or false for each statement below.

(a) $0.3 = 3\%$ (b) $0.55 > \dfrac{13}{20}$ (c) $\dfrac{17}{50} > 0.32$

(d) $\dfrac{9}{40} = 0.225$ (e) $\dfrac{48}{400} < 14\%$ (f) $0.04 < 40\%$

6 $\dfrac{8}{25} = \dfrac{32}{100} = 0.032$ Is this statement correct? If not, identify the mistake.

7

Test A	Test B	Test C	Test D
$\dfrac{13}{25}$	$\dfrac{14}{20}$	$\dfrac{32}{50}$	$\dfrac{13}{20}$

During one term Gina has four maths tests. Work out the difference between her highest test percentage and her lowest test percentage.

Extension questions with fractions, decimals, percentages

1 Write these fractions as percentages.

(a) $\dfrac{73}{250}$ (b) $\dfrac{23}{500}$ (c) $\dfrac{87}{125}$ (d) $\dfrac{59}{2000}$ (e) $\dfrac{119}{125}$

2 Write these numbers in order of size, starting with the smallest.

$$\dfrac{139}{250}, \quad \dfrac{11}{20}, \quad 56\%, \quad \dfrac{21}{40}, \quad \dfrac{412}{800}$$

3

Player	Wins	Games
Alexis	12	20
Hunter	5	8
Arnav	23	40
Shun	15	25

Four people play squash. The table shows the number of wins and games for each player.

(a) Which two players won the same percentage of games?

(b) Who won the greatest percentage of games and by how much more than the next best percentage of wins?

4 300 students out of 450 in total are girls.

Explain clearly why $33\tfrac{1}{3}\%$ of the students are boys.

5 *Explain clearly* how to show that $\dfrac{5}{9} = 0.\dot{5}$

6   The three fractions below match up to three of the recurring decimals shown.
    Write down the recurring decimal which does not match up.

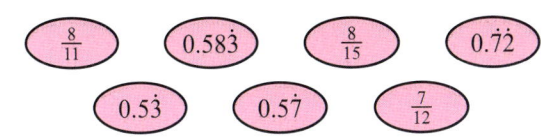

    $\frac{8}{11}$ $0.58\dot{3}$ $\frac{8}{15}$ $0.\dot{7}\dot{2}$

    $0.5\dot{3}$ $0.5\dot{7}$ $\frac{7}{12}$

7   Issy has 61.2% of a bottle of water remaining. She drinks a further $\frac{19}{80}$ of the bottle.
    What percentage of the water is now left over?

Investigation – Escape

In the town of Decford a prison has 10 cells. Each cell has one prisoner in it
and all the cell doors are locked.

- A jailer walks from cell 1 to cell 10 and unlocks each door.
- The jailer returns to the start and locks every second door.
- The jailer returns to the start and changes the state of every
  third door (ie. cells 3, 6, 9). *'Changes the state of a door'*
  means *'lock if unlocked'* or *'unlock if locked'*.
- The jailer repeats the process for every fourth door then fifth
  door, sixth, seventh, eighth, ninth and finally tenth.

(a) How many prisoners can now escape through an unlocked door?
    Write down the cell numbers of those prisoners who can escape.

(b) The prison in the city of Centford has 100 cells. A jailer repeats the above process from
    changing the state of every door then every second door, etc. to changing the state of every
    100th door. How many prisoners can now escape through an unlocked door? Write down the
    cell numbers of those prisoners who can escape. Can you explain *why* these cell doors are
    unlocked at the end?

(c) If the process was repeated for 1000 cells, how many prisoners would be able to escape
    through the unlocked doors?

CHECK YOURSELF ON SECTIONS 2.1 AND 2.2

1   Reviewing equivalent fractions

    Find the missing number to make these fractions equivalent.

    (a) $\frac{1}{6} = \frac{\square}{42}$ (b) $\frac{7}{9} = \frac{28}{\square}$ (c) $\frac{32}{48} = \frac{2}{\square}$

(d) Write down which fractions are equivalent to $\frac{7}{8}$.

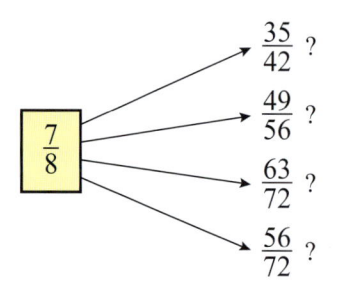

$\frac{7}{8}$ → $\frac{35}{42}$?
→ $\frac{49}{56}$?
→ $\frac{63}{72}$?
→ $\frac{56}{72}$?

(e) Which statement below is true?

A $\frac{15}{35} > \frac{9}{21}$ B $\frac{15}{35} = \frac{9}{21}$ C $\frac{15}{35} < \frac{9}{21}$

2 Adding and subtracting fractions (including mixed numbers)

Work out

(a) $\frac{2}{5} + \frac{3}{7}$ (b) $\frac{3}{4} - \frac{2}{3}$ (c) $3\frac{1}{5} - \frac{7}{8}$ (d) $1\frac{2}{3} + 2\frac{1}{4}$

(e) Josh uses $1\frac{4}{5}$ litres of milk and $\frac{7}{8}$ litre of milk from a full 5 litre churn. How much milk is left in the churn?

3 Multiplying and dividing fractions

Work out

(a) $\frac{9}{10} \times \frac{3}{7}$ (b) $\frac{4}{5} \div \frac{9}{11}$ (c) $1\frac{2}{3} \times 1\frac{1}{5}$ (d) $2\frac{2}{5} \div 1\frac{3}{7}$

(e) Work out the total area of these two rectangles.

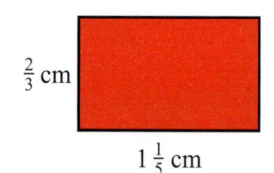

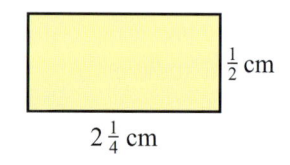

Red rectangle: $\frac{2}{3}$ cm by $1\frac{1}{5}$ cm
Yellow rectangle: $\frac{1}{2}$ cm by $2\frac{1}{4}$ cm

4 Converting between fractions, decimals and percentages

There are four groups of equivalent fractions, decimals and percentages below. Write down each group (beware: there are two odd ones out). For example $\frac{1}{2}$, 0.5, 50% is a group.

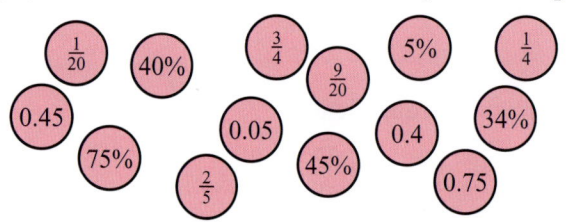

$\frac{1}{20}$, 40%, $\frac{3}{4}$, 5%, $\frac{1}{4}$, $\frac{9}{20}$, 0.45, 0.05, 0.4, 34%, 75%, $\frac{2}{5}$, 45%, 0.75

2.3 Coordinates

In this section you will:
- review coordinates with negative numbers
- solve problems involving shapes

Negative coordinates

The x axis can be extended to the left and the y axis can be extended downwards to include the negative numbers $-1, -2, -3$ etc.

The word 'BACON' can be found using the letters in the following order:

$(2, -2), (2, 3), (-2, -3), (-2, -1), (-1, 2)$

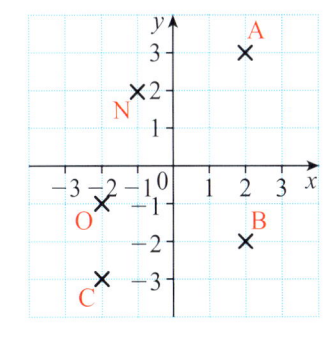

Exercise 1M

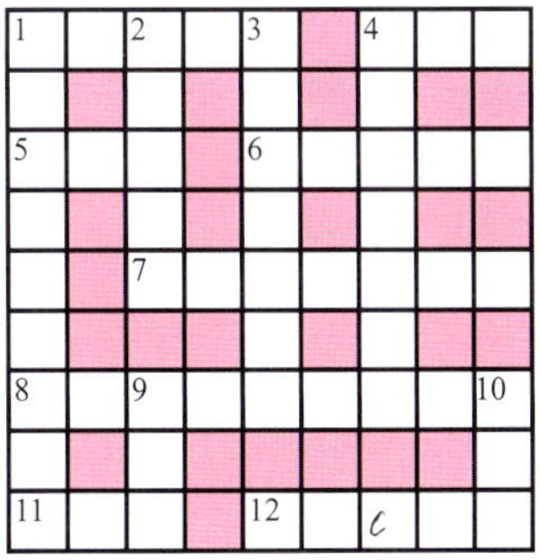

Copy the crossword grid and complete it using the clues below.

The letters are found using coordinates on the grid.

Across
1. $(-3, 4) (-4, -2) (-3, 4) (1, 3) (3, -3)$
4. $(5, 5) (-4, -2) (3, -3)$
5. $(-4, -2) (5, 2) (5, -5)$
6. $(-4, -2) (-3, -4) (3, -3) (-4, -2) (5, -5)$
7. $(2, -2) (3, -3) (-2, 5) (-4, 1) (-3, -4) (2, -2) (1, 3)$
8. $(3, -3) (1, 3) (-3, 4) (-3, -4) (4, 4) (0, 1) (-4, -2)$
   $(0, 1) (2, -2)$
11. German for 'THE'
12. $(-4, 1) (-4, -2) (-2, -2) (5, 2) (0, 1)$

Down
1. $(-3, 4) (5, -5) (-4, -2) (-2, 2) (2, -2) (1, 3)$
   $(3, -3) (1, 3) (2, 5)$
2. $(-3, 4) (-2, 5) (5, -5) (5, 2) (2, -2)$
3. Useful for books
4. Used in mathematics
9. $(-3, 4) (-4, -2) (3, -3)$
10. $(2, -2) (-4, -2) (0, 1)$

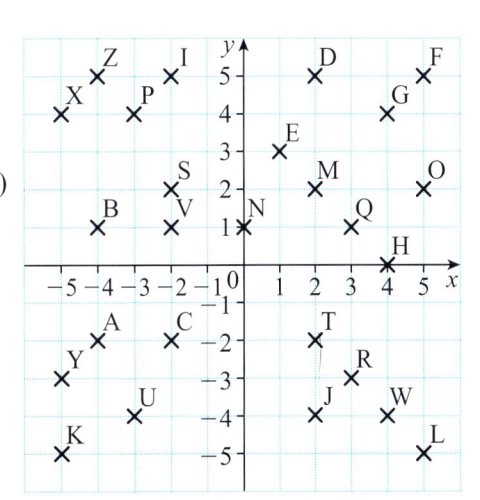

Exercise 2M

Draw some axes on squared paper.
Label the x axis from -10 to 8.
Label the y axis from -10 to 18.

Plot the points below and join them up with a ruler in the order given.

(0, 18) (6, 18) (8, 16) (8, 14) (6, 12)
$(4\frac{1}{2}, 10)$ (4, 8) (4, −2) (2, −4) (2, −9)

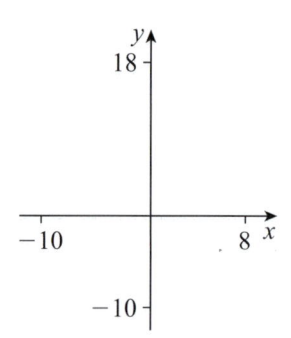

On the same diagram, plot the points below and join them up with a ruler in the order given.
(Do not join the last point in the box above with the first point in the new box)

(−5, −9) (−3, −7) (−3, −5) (−4, −4) (−5, −4) (−6, −3) (−4, −3) (−2, −3) (0, −2)

On the same diagram, plot the points below and join them up with a ruler in the order given.

(−6, −3) (−7, −2) (−6, −1) (−4, −1)

On the same diagram, plot the points below and join them up with a ruler in the order given.

(−6, −1) (−6, 0) (−5, 0)

On the same diagram, plot the points below and join them up with a ruler in the order given.

(−3, 2) (−4, 3) (−5, 3) (−6, 2) (−6, 1) (−5, 0) (−4, 0)
(−3, 1) (−3, 2) (−2, 3) (−1, 3) (0, 2) (0, 1) (−1, 0) (−2, 0) (−3, 1)

On the same diagram, plot the points below and join them up with a ruler in the order given.

(0, 18) (−2, 16) (−3, 14) $\left(-3\frac{1}{2}, 12\right)$ (−4, 10) $\left(-4\frac{1}{2}, 8\right)$
(−5, 6) (−5, 3) $\left(-5, 3\frac{1}{2}\right)$ (−3, 4) (−1, 4) (2, 3) (2, −4)

Draw a ⊕ around the points below, making the circles touch like this ⊕⊕⊕⊕⊕⊕

(−3, −6) (−2, −6) (−1, −6) (0, −6) (1, −6) (2, −6)

Draw a • at (−4, 1) and a • at (−1, 1)

Who am I? Colour me in.

Complete the shape

Two sides of a rectangle are drawn.

Find   (a) the coordinates of the fourth vertex of the rectangle

         (b) the coordinates of the centre of the rectangle.

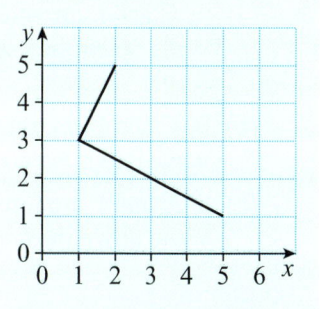

The complete rectangle is shown.

(a) Fourth vertex is at (6, 3)

(b) Centre of rectangle is at $(3\frac{1}{2}, 3)$

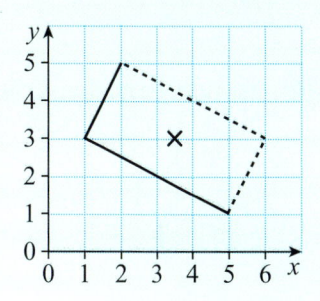

Exercise 3M

1 Draw a grid with values from 0 to 10. Plot the three points given and then find the coordinates of the point which makes a square when the points are joined up.

(a) (1, 2), (1, 5), (4, 5)

(b) (5, 6), (7, 3), (10, 5)

(c) (0, 9), (1, 6), (4, 7)

2 The graph shows several incomplete quadrilaterals.

Copy the diagram and complete the shapes.

Write down the coordinates of the fourth vertex of each shape.

Write down the coordinates of the centre of each shape.

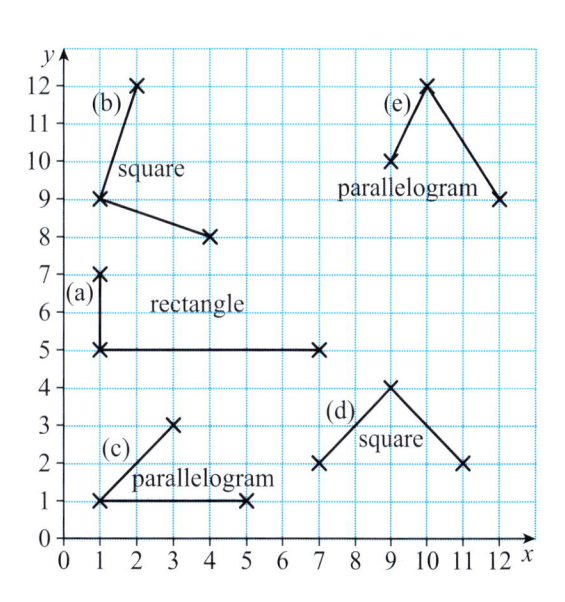

3 Copy the graph shown.

(a) A, B and F are three corners of a square. Write down the coordinates of the other corner.

(b) B, C and D are three corners of another square. Write down the coordinates of the other corner.

(c) D, E and F are three corners of a rectangle. Write down the coordinates of the other corner.

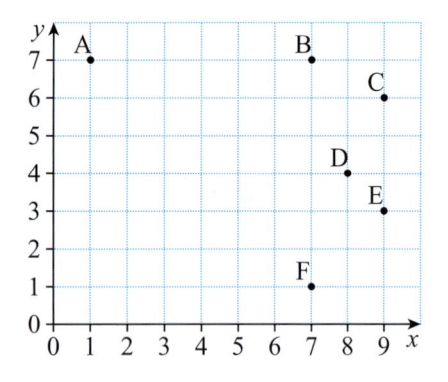

4 You are given the vertices but not the sides of two parallelograms P and Q.

For each parallelogram find *three* possible positions for the fourth vertex.

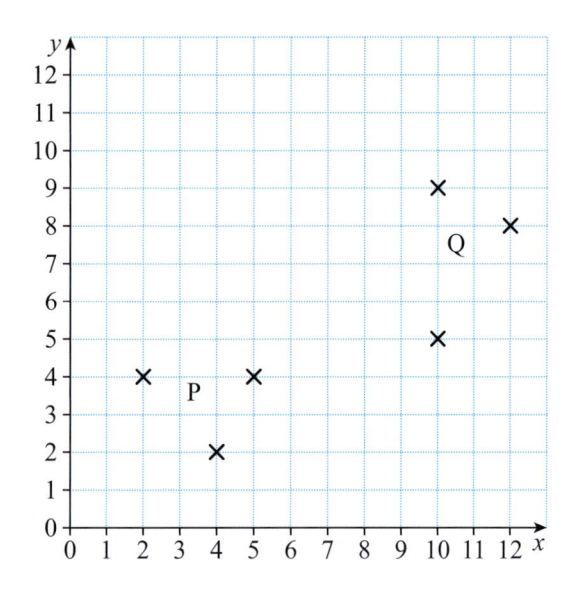

5 Copy the graph shown.

(a) A, B and C are three corners of a square. Write down the coordinates of the other corner.

(b) C, A and D are three corners of another square. Write down the coordinates of the other corner.

(c) B, D and E are three corners of a rectangle. Write down the coordinates of the other corner.

(d) C, F and G are three vertices of a parallelogram. Write down the coordinates of the other vertex.

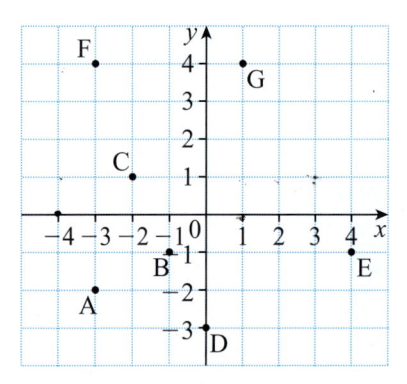

6.

[Graph showing two crosses marking two vertices of isosceles triangle A, at approximately (2, 3) and (4, 5), on axes from 0 to 6 (x) and 0 to 7 (y).]

The crosses mark two vertices of an isosceles triangle A.

Find as many points as you can, with whole number coordinates, for the third vertex of the triangle.

[There are, in fact, 12 possible points for the third vertex. Find as many as you can.]

7. The diagram shows one side of an isosceles triangle B.
   (a) Find *six* possible points, with whole number coordinates, for the third vertex of the triangle.
   (b) Explain how you could find the coordinates of several more positions for the third vertex.

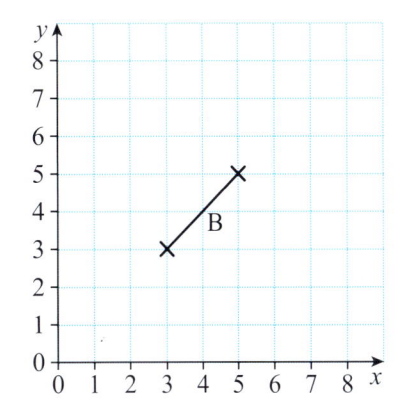

[Graph showing two crosses marking vertices of triangle B, at approximately (3, 3) and (6, 5), on axes from 0 to 8.]

8. (a) Draw a pair of axes with values of x and y from 0 to 12.
   (b) Draw a line from A(2, 0) to B(9, 7).
   (c) Draw a line from C(1, 11) which is perpendicular to AB and meets AB at point D.
   (d) Write down the coordinates of D.
   (e) Draw a line from point E(4, 2) which is perpendicular to BC and meets BC at point F.
   (f) Write down the coordinates of the point where line EF intersects line CD.
   (g) Draw a line through F parallel to AB. Write down the coordinates of the point where this line meets the y axis.

2.4 Straight line graphs

In section 2.4 you will learn about:
- lines which are parallel to the axes
- sloping lines
- drawing straight line graphs
- finding gradients of lines

Lines parallel to the axes

- The points P, Q, R and S have coordinates (4, 4), (4, 3), (4, 2) and (4, 1) and they all lie on a straight line. Since the x coordinate of all the points is 4, we say the *equation* of the line is $x = 4$.
- The points A, B and C have coordinates (1, 3), (2, 3) and (3, 3) and they all lie on a straight line. Since the y coordinate of all the points is 3, we say the *equation* of the line is $y = 3$.

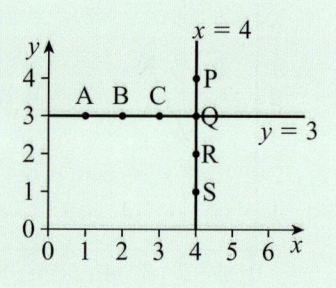

Exercise 1M

1. Write down the equations for the lines marked A, B and C.

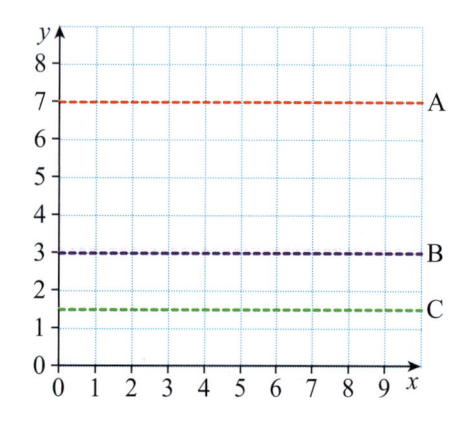

2. Write down the equations for the lines marked P, Q and R.

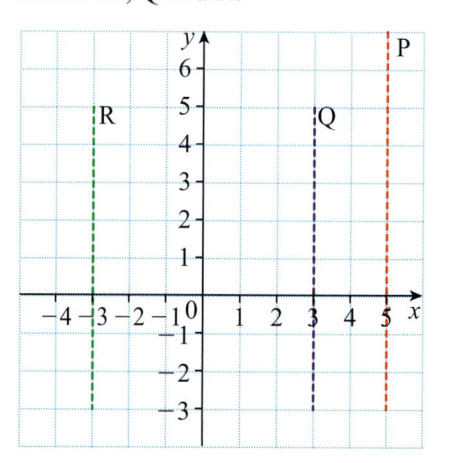

In questions 3 and 4 below there is a red line A, a blue line B and a green line C.

Write down the equations of the lines in each question.

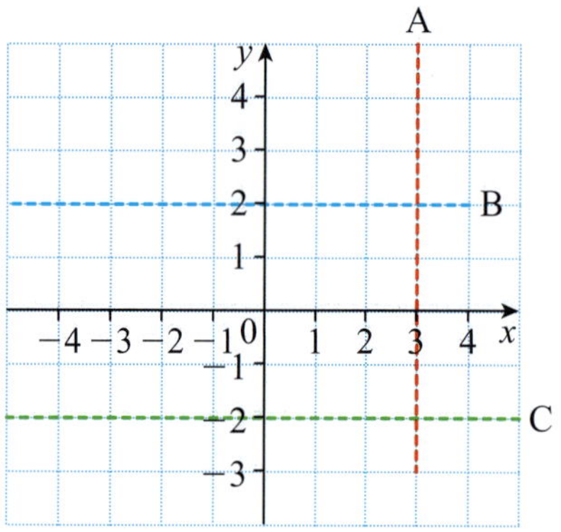

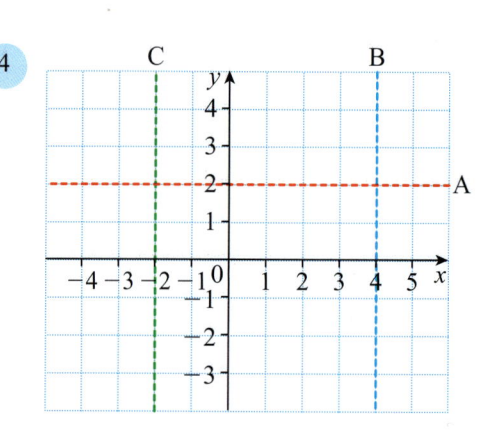

5 On squared paper, draw suitable axes.

(a) Draw the lines $y = 2$ and $x = 3$. At what point do they meet?

(b) Draw the lines $y = 5$ and $x = 1$. At what point do they meet?

(c) Draw the lines $x = 7$ and $y = 3$. At what point do they meet?

6 In the diagram, E and N lie on the line with equation $y = 1$. B and K lie on the line $x = 5$. In parts (a) to (h) find the equation of the line passing through the given points.

(a) A and D
(b) A, B and I
(c) M and P
(d) I and H
(e) L and E
(f) D, K and G
(g) C, M, L and H
(h) P and F

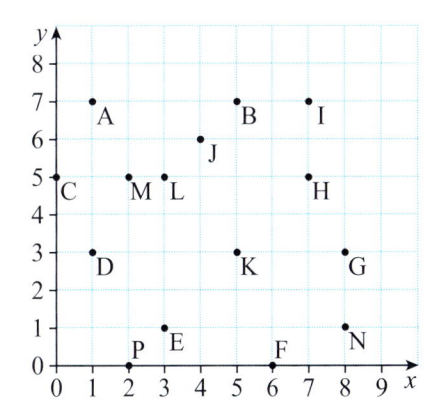

Relating x and y

- The sloping line passes through the following points:
(1, 1), (2, 2), (3, 3), (4, 4), (5, 5).

For each point, the y coordinate is equal to the x coordinate.

The equation of the line is $y = x$ (or $x = y$).

This is the rule for any point on the line.

- This line passes through:
(0, 1), (1, 2), (2, 3), (3, 4), (4, 5).

For each point the y coordinate is one more than the x coordinate.

The equation of the line is $y = x + 1$.

We could also say that the x coordinate is always one less than the y coordinate. The equation of the line could then be written as $x = y - 1$.
[Most mathematicians use the equation beginning '$y = $'.]

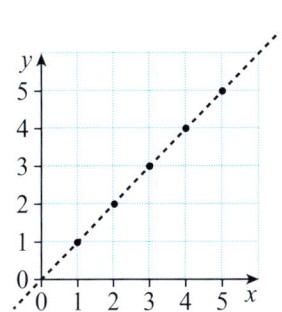

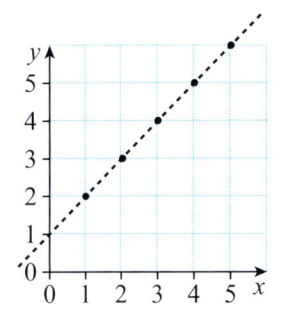

- This line slopes the other way and passes through:
  (0, 5), (1, 4), (2, 3), (3, 2), (4, 1), (5, 0).

  The sum of the x coordinate and the y coordinate is always 5.

  > The equation of the line is $x + y = 5$ (or $y = 5 - x$)

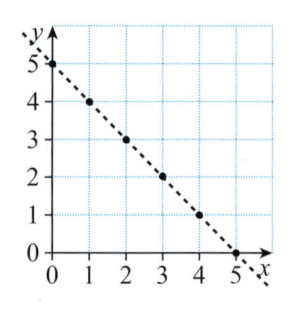

Exercise 1E

For each question write down the coordinates of the points marked. Find the equation of the line through the points.

1.

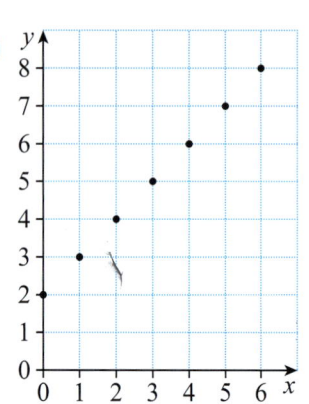

2.

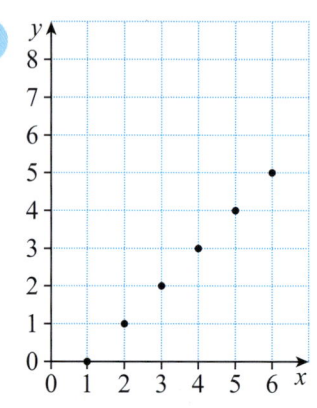

3.

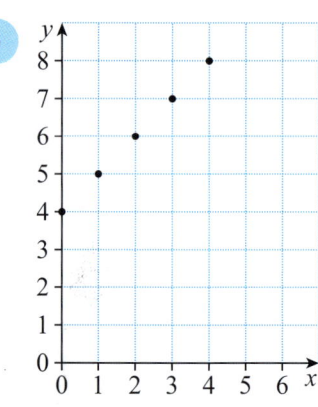

4.

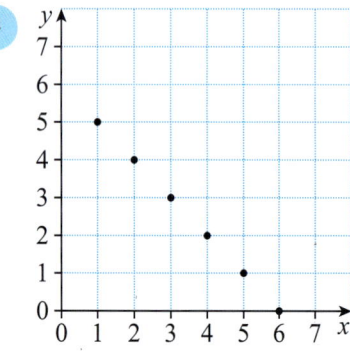

5.

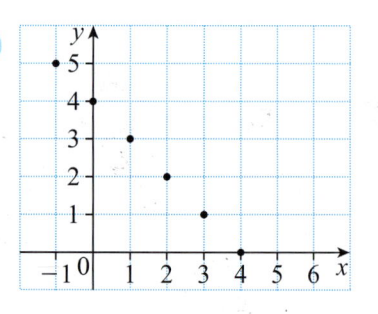

6.

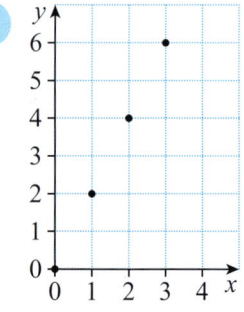

7. Polly says that the equation of the line though the points opposite is $y = 3 - x$.

   Explain clearly the mistake that Polly has made.

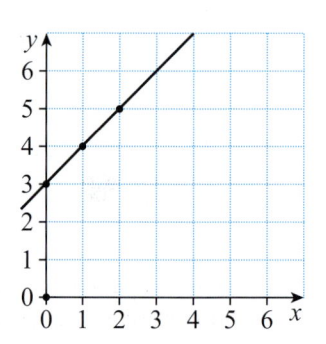

8. Look at the graph. Find the equation for
   (a) line A
   (b) line B
   (c) line C
   (d) line D

9. This is the table of the points on line G.

x	0	2	4	6
y	8	9	10	11

   Find the equation for line G.
   [Hint: It starts $y = \frac{1}{2}x + \ldots$]

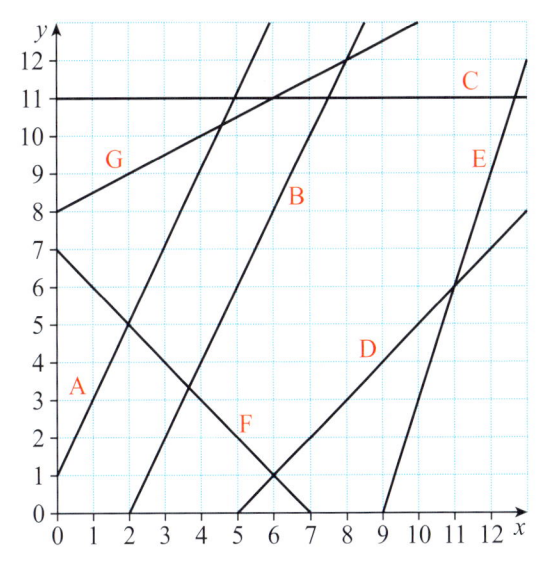

10. This is the table for the points on line E.

x	9	10	11	12
y	0	3	6	9

    Find the equation of line E.

11. Make a table for the points on line F.

x	0	1	2	3
y	7			

    Find the equation of line F.

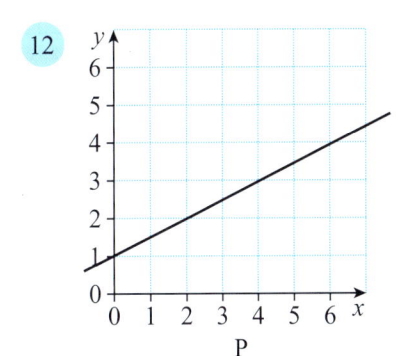

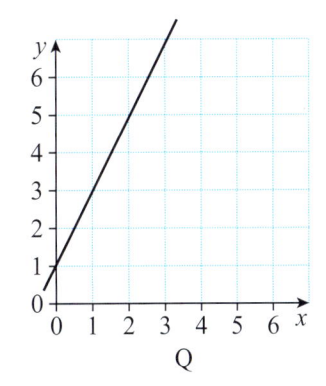

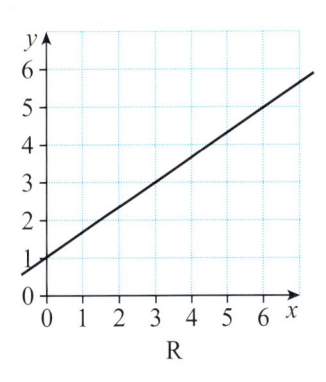

12. Which line above has the equation $y = \frac{1}{2}x + 1$?
    Give reasons for your answer.

Drawing graphs

- The equation of a line is $y = x + 2$. Here is a list of five points on the line: (0, 2), (1, 3), (2, 4), (3, 5), (4, 6)

  The points are plotted on a graph and the line $y = x + 2$ is drawn. Notice that the line extends beyond (0, 2) and (4, 6).

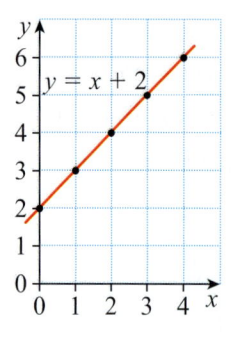

Exercise 2M

1. (a) The equation of a line is $y = x + 3$. Copy and complete a list of points on the line:
   (0, 3) (1, 4) (2, ☐) (3, ☐) (4, ☐)
   (b) Draw x and y axes.
   (c) Plot the points above and draw a line through them. This is the graph of $y = x + 3$.

2. The equation of a line is $y = x + 5$. Copy and complete a list of points on the line:
   (0, 5) (1, 6) (2, ☐) (3, ☐) (4, ☐).
   Draw the graph of $y = x + 5$.

In questions 3 to 6 you are given the equation of a line and a list of points on the line. Fill in the missing numbers and then draw the graph.

3. $y = x - 4$; (0, −4) (1, −3), (2, ☐), (3, ☐), (4, ☐)

4. $y = 2x - 2$; (0, ☐), (2, ☐), (4, ☐)

5. $y = 6 - x$; (1, ☐), (3, ☐), (5, ☐), (6, ☐)

6. $y = 3x + 2$; (0, ☐), (1, ☐), (2, ☐)

7. (a) Draw axes with values of x from 0 to 5 and with values of y from −1 to 7.
   (b) Draw the lines $y = 5 - x$ and $y = 2x - 1$ on the same graph.
   (c) Write down the coordinates of the point where the lines meet.

8. (a) Draw axes with values of x from 0 to 10 and values of y from 0 to 12.
   (b) On the same graph draw the lines
   $y = x + 3$
   $y = \frac{1}{2}x + 3$
   $y = 15 - x$
   (c) Write down the coordinates of the vertices of the triangle formed by the three lines.

Gradients of lines

The gradient of a hill tells you how steep the hill is.
The gradient of a line tells you how steep the line is.
The gradient of a line is how many units the line goes up for each one unit across.

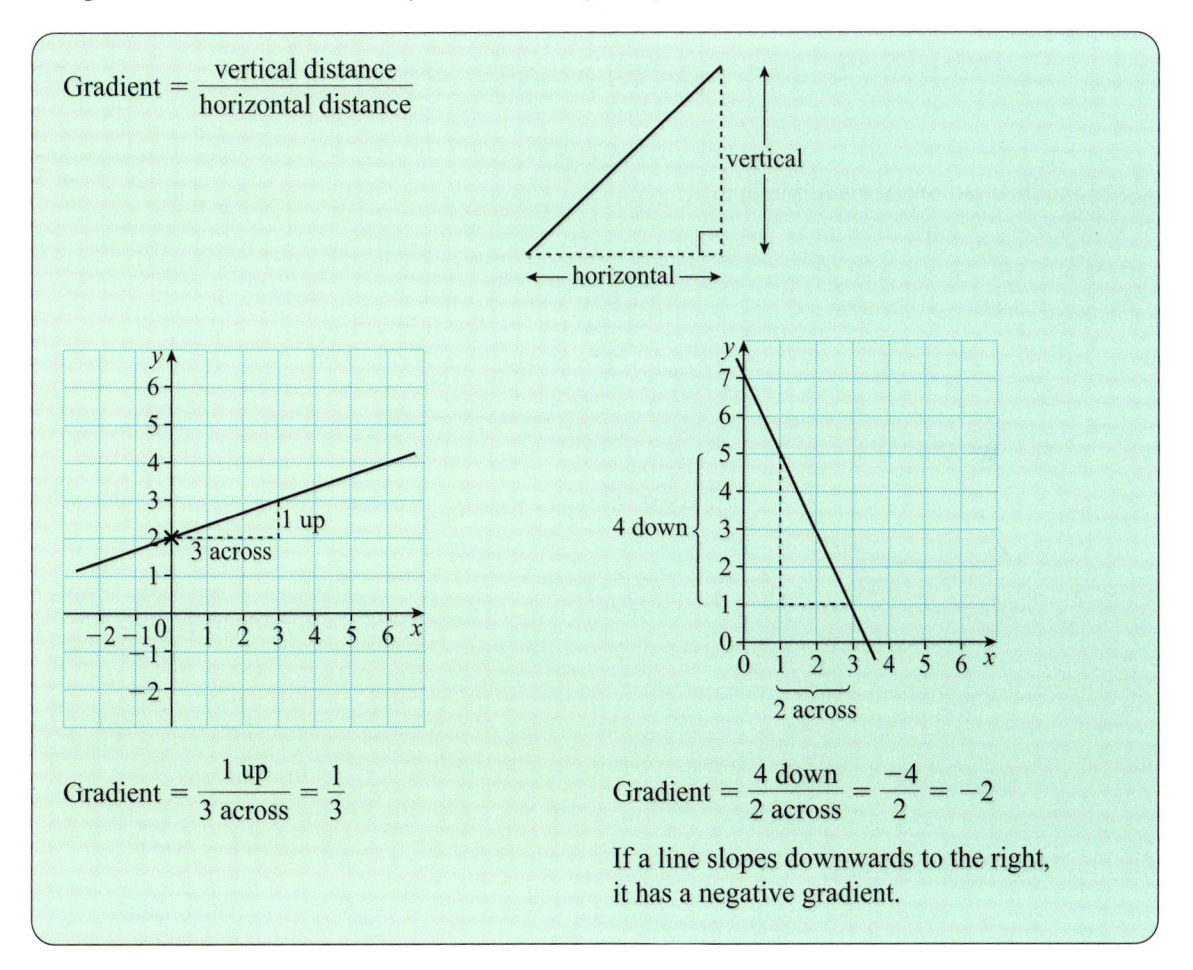

Gradient = $\dfrac{\text{vertical distance}}{\text{horizontal distance}}$

Gradient = $\dfrac{1 \text{ up}}{3 \text{ across}} = \dfrac{1}{3}$

Gradient = $\dfrac{4 \text{ down}}{2 \text{ across}} = \dfrac{-4}{2} = -2$

If a line slopes downwards to the right, it has a negative gradient.

Exercise 3M

Find the gradient of each line.

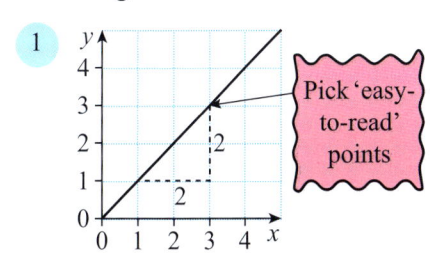

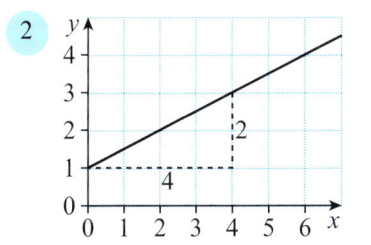

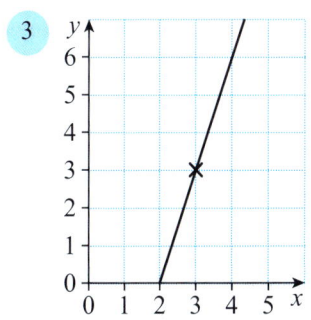

1.

Pick 'easy-to-read' points

2.

3.

4 [graph]

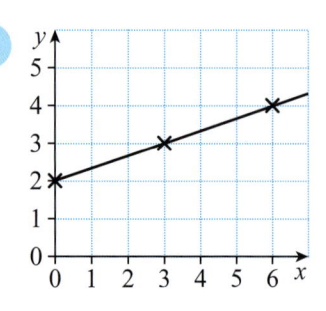

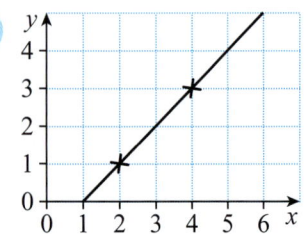

5 [graph]

6 [graph]

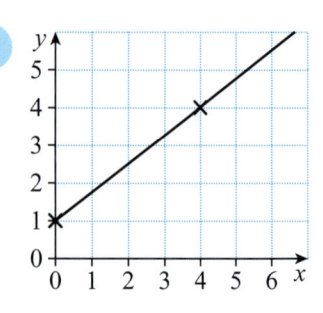

7 Find the gradient of each line below.

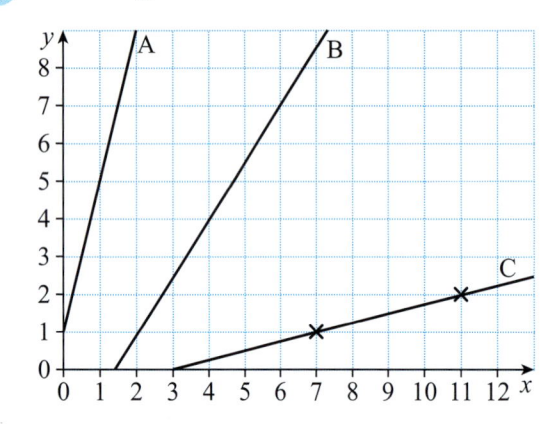

[graph showing lines A, B, C]

8 A line has a gradient of $\frac{1}{2}$. How much does the line go up for every 4 units across?

9 A line has a gradient of $\frac{3}{5}$. How much does the line go up for every 15 units across?

Find the gradient of each line.

10 [graph with "3 down" and "1 across" labels]

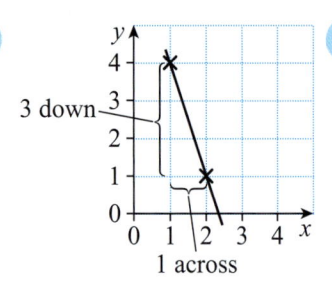

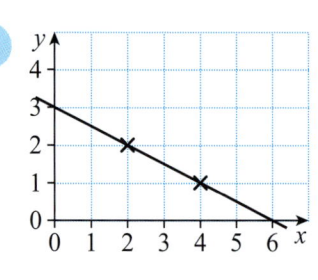

11 [graph]

12 [graph]

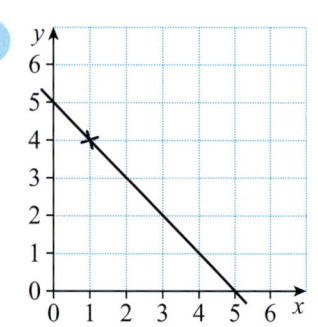

13 *Explain clearly* why each gradient in questions **10** to **12** is negative.

14 Line A has a gradient of $\frac{5}{6}$ and line B has a gradient of $-\frac{6}{7}$. Which line is steeper? Justify your answer.

15 Find the gradient of each line below.

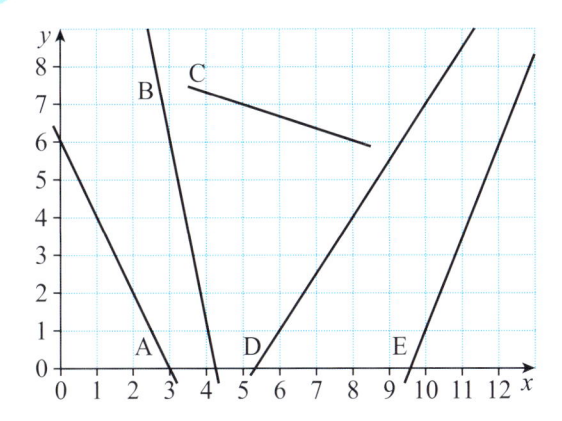

16 Draw axes on squared paper. Draw a line with gradient −4.
Ask a friend to check the gradient.

17 Draw axes on squared paper. Draw a line with gradient $\frac{2}{5}$.
Ask a friend to check the gradient.

Need more practice with coordinates and straight line graphs?

1 Draw axes with both x and y from −5 to 6. Plot the points below and join them up in order.
(a) (2, −4) (−2, −4) (−4, 5) (−3, 6) (−2, 5) (−1, 6) (0, 5) (1, 6) (2, 5) (3, 1) (3, 0)
(4, −$\frac{1}{2}$) (4, −1) (3, −1) (4, −2) (0, −2) (0, −3) (2, −4)

(b) (0, 0) (−1, 1) (0, 2) (1, 1) (2, 2) (3, 1) (2, 0) (1, 1) (0, 0)

(c) (0, −3) (1, −3) (1, −3$\frac{1}{2}$)

(d) (2, 0) (3, 0)

(e) (2, −1) (3, −1)

(f) (−2, 2) (−3, 1$\frac{1}{2}$)(−2, 1)

(g) Put dots at (0, 1) and (2, 1)

2 Calvin says that the equation of the red line shown opposite is $x = 3$.
Explain clearly whether Calvin is correct or not.

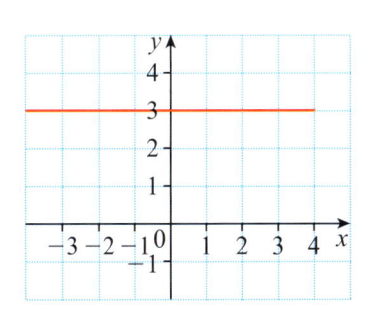

③ Draw x and y axes from 0 to 8.

The equation of a line is $y = 7 - x$.

Copy and complete the list of points below which lie on the line:

(0, 7) (1, 6) (2, ☐) (3, ☐) (4, ☐)

Plot these points then draw a line through them.

④ Draw x and y axes then draw the line $y = 2x + 3$.

⑤ Write down the equations of lines A to D opposite. (Remember to look at the coordinates of the points on each line to find the rule connecting x and y)

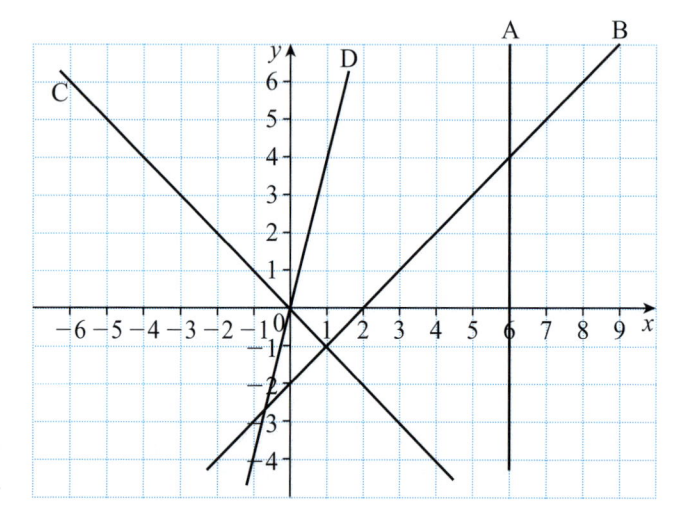

⑥ Line P has a gradient of $-\frac{1}{2}$ and line Q has a gradient of $-\frac{1}{3}$.

Which line is steeper? *Explain* your answer fully.

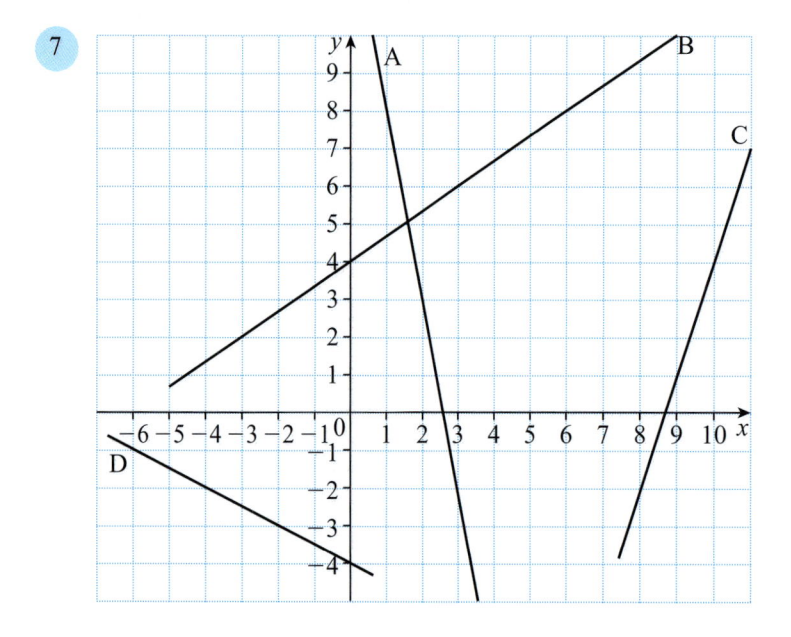

⑦ Work out the gradient of lines A to D opposite.

Extension questions with coordinates and straight line graphs

1. (a) Write down the equations of lines P and Q.
   (b) Write down the gradients of lines P and Q.
   (c) Look at the equation of each line. Does there appear to be any connection with the gradient?

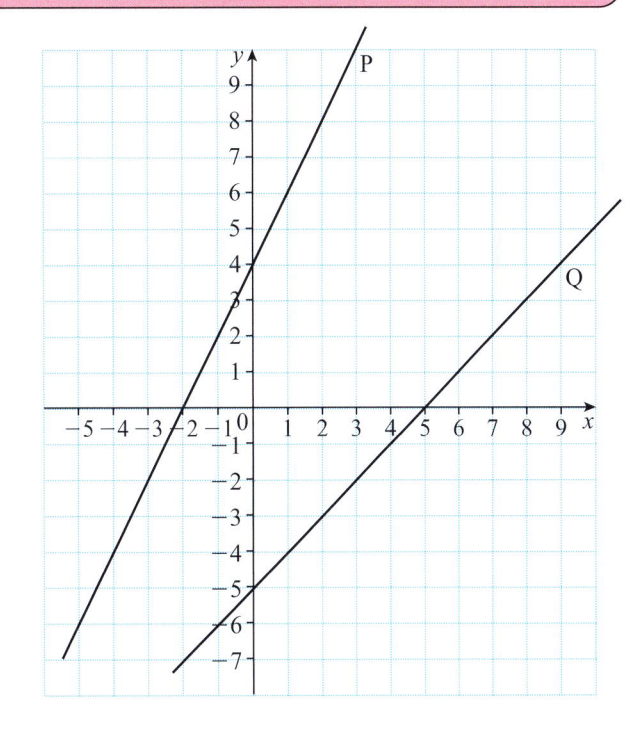

2. Draw x and y axes then any line with a gradient equal to zero. Write down the equation of the line you have drawn.

3. Line A has a gradient of 62%. Line B has a gradient of $-\frac{3}{5}$ and line C has a gradient of $\frac{16}{25}$. Which line is steeper? *Explain* your answer fully.

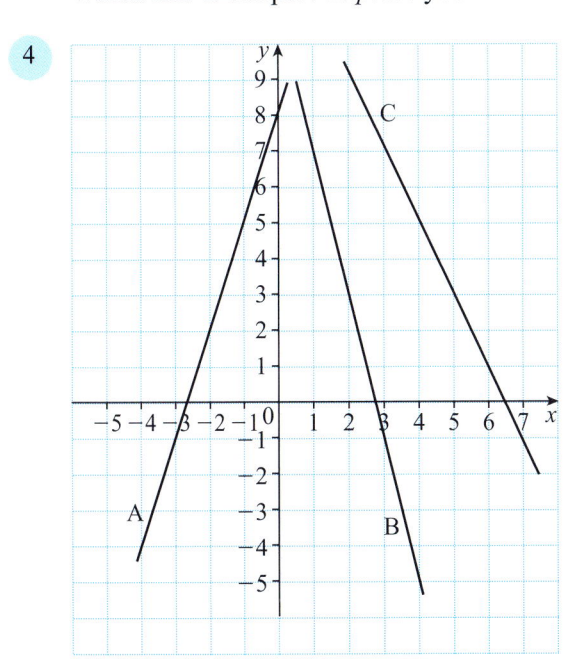

4. (a) Write down the equations and gradients of each line shown opposite.
   (b) Look at your answers to part (a) then write down the gradient of the line $y = 5x - 3$.

5. Draw x and y axes then any line with a gradient equal to 3.
   Write down the equation of the line you have drawn.

6. $y = 4x + 7$ $y = -6x + 2$ $y = -5x + 3$

   Which line above is the steepest? Give a reason for your answer.

7. Draw x and y axes then draw the line $y = \frac{1}{4}x + 3$.
   Confirm that this line has a gradient equal to $\frac{1}{4}$.

8. What is the value of the gradient of the line $x = 3$ shown opposite?

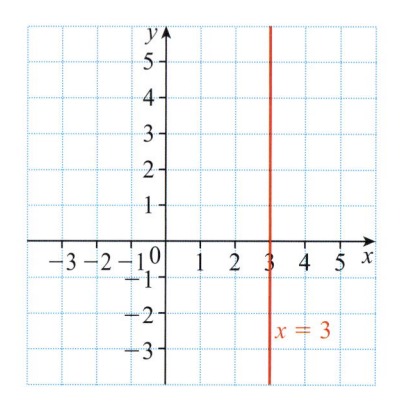

CHECK YOURSELF ON SECTIONS 2.3 AND 2.4

1 Reviewing coordinates with negative numbers

Write down the coordinates of P, Q and R.

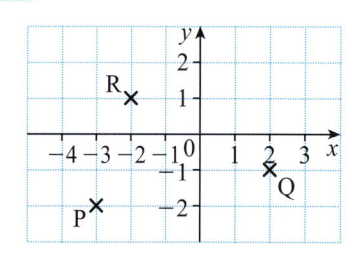

2 Using coordinates to solve problems involving shapes

(a) Points A, D and E are three vertices of a rectangle.
    Write down the coordinates of the other vertex.

(b) C, E and D are three vertices of a square.
    Write down the coordinates of the other vertex.

(c) B, C and E are three vertices of a parallelogram.
    Write down the coordinates of the other vertex.
    (There is more than one answer but you only need to give one.)

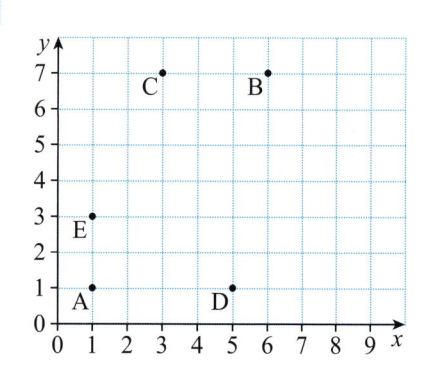

3 Lines parallel to the axes

ABCD is a rectangle.

(a) Write down the coordinates of A.
(b) Write down the equation of line AD.
(c) Write down the equation of line DC.
(d) N is in the middle of the rectangle. What are the coordinates of N?

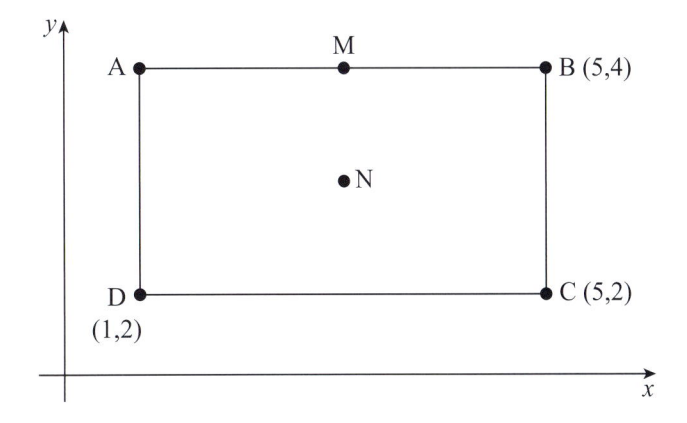

4 Finding the equation of a line and drawing graphs

(a) Which is the equation of line C?
$y = 2x$, $y = x$, $y = x - 2$

(b) Write down the equation of (i) line A (ii) line B

(c) Which of the points below lie on the line $y = x + 1$?
P(4, 5)   Q(6, 5)   R(0, 1)

(d) Fill in the missing numbers for the line $y = 2x - 1$
(0, −1),   (1, ☐),   (2, ☐),   (3, ☐)

(e) Draw the graph of $y = 2x - 1$

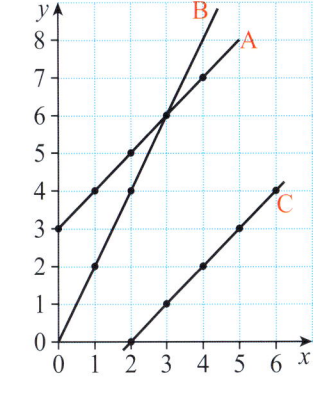

5 Finding gradients of lines

Find the gradient of the line joining:
(a) A and B
(b) A and D
(c) C and D
(d) B and C

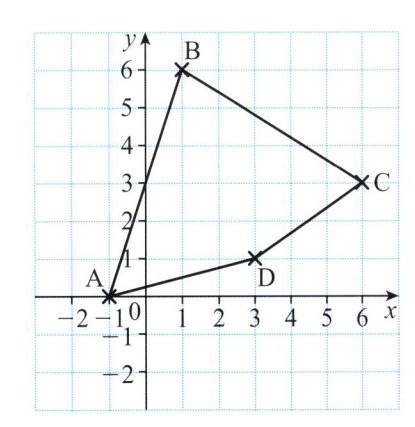

✗ Spot the mistakes 3 ✗

Fractions, decimals, percentages and straight line graphs

Work through each question below and *explain clearly* what mistakes have been made. Beware – some questions are correctly done.

1) $\frac{3}{5} \times \frac{7}{8} = \frac{24}{40} \times \frac{35}{40} = \frac{840}{40} = 21$

2) $6\frac{1}{2} \div 2\frac{1}{3} = 6 \div 2 = 3$ and $\frac{1}{2} \div \frac{1}{3} = \frac{1}{2} \times \frac{3}{1} = \frac{3}{2}$
   so answer $= 3\frac{3}{2} = 4\frac{1}{2}$

3) $19\% = \frac{19}{100} = 0.019$

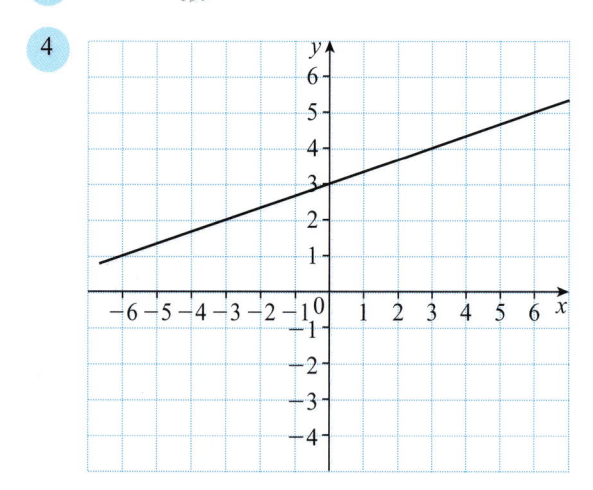

4) The equation of this line is $y = \frac{1}{3}x + 3$

5) $2\frac{5}{6} + 2\frac{1}{4} = \frac{17}{6} + \frac{9}{4} = \frac{68 + 54}{24} = \frac{122}{24} = \frac{61}{12} = 5\frac{1}{12}$

6) $\frac{13}{20} = \frac{52}{100} = 0.52$

7) The gradient of the line opposite is 2.

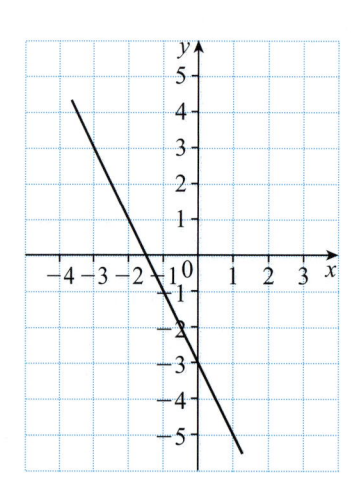

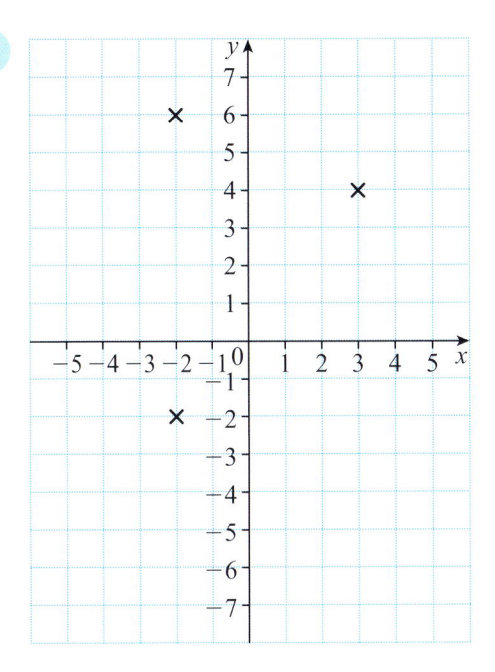

8   The three crosses shown can be joined with the point (3, −4) to form a parallelogram.

9   $3 \times \dfrac{3}{4} = \dfrac{9}{12} = \dfrac{3}{4}$

10 The gradient of the line $y = 1$ is equal to 1.

2.5 Area

In section 2.5 you will review:
- finding areas involving rectangles and triangles
- finding areas of parallelograms and trapeziums

Areas, involving, rectangles

Exercise 1M

1   Find the area of each shape. The lengths are in cm.

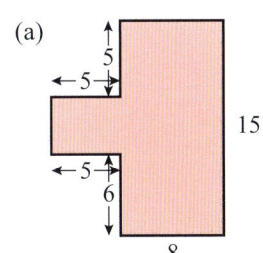

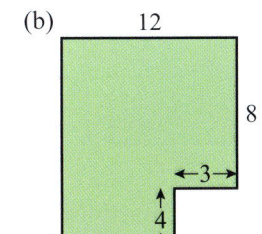

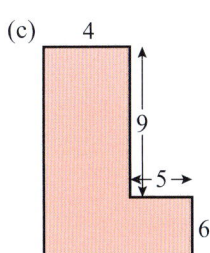

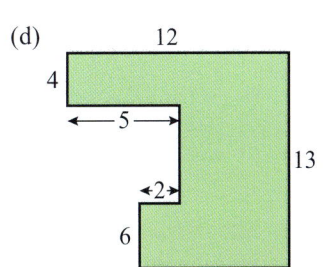

2. A square has an area of 144 cm². Find the perimeter of this square.

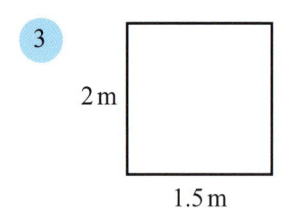

3. (a) Write down the length and width in cm only.
   (b) This wall is to be covered with tiles. Each tile has a length of 20 cm and a width of 10 cm. How many tiles are needed to cover the entire wall?

   (Diagram: rectangle 2 m by 1.5 m)

4. Five identical squares are placed next to each other as shown. Each square has an area of 225 cm². Find the perimeter of the overall rectangle shown.

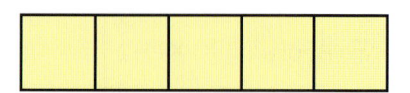

5. A lawn is surrounded by a path which is 1 m wide. Calculate the area of the path.

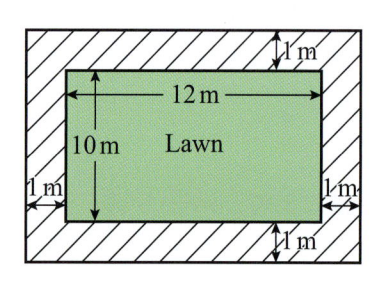

   (Diagram: lawn 12 m by 10 m, path 1 m wide all around)

6. Calculate the area of the pink cross.

   (Diagram: rectangle 90 cm by 50 cm, with 20 cm top strip and 30 cm centre column forming a pink cross)

7. How many panes of glass 35 cm by 25 cm can be cut from a sheet which is 1 metre square?

8. A rectangle has a perimeter of 34 m and a length of 7.5 m. What is its area?

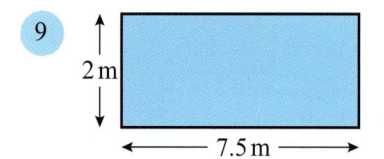

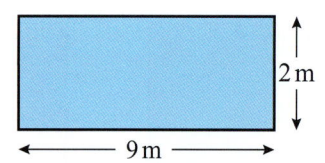

9. (Diagram: two rectangles, 7.5 m by 2 m, and 9 m by 2 m)

   Shahanya wants to paint the two walls shown above. Each tin of paint will cover 11 m². How many tins of paint will she need?

Areas involving triangles

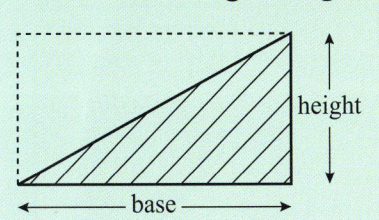

Area of rectangle = base × height

Area of triangle = $\frac{1}{2}$ (area of rectangle)

Area of triangle = $\frac{1}{2}$ (base × height)

Exercise 2M

1 Find the area of each triangle. Lengths are in cm.

(a) 4, 8
(b) 7, 3
(c) 10, 16
(d) 12, 9
(e) 14, 5
(f) 5, 9
(g) 5, 12, 13
(h) 14, 12, 16

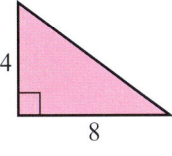

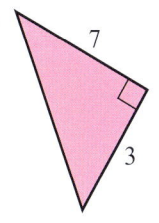

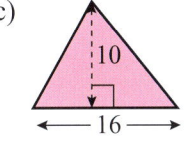

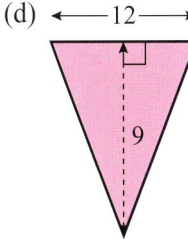

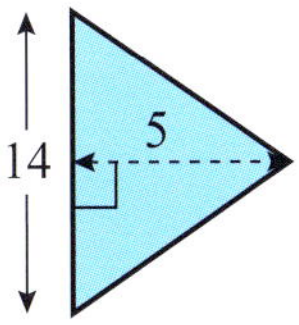

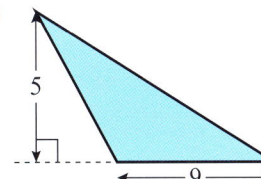

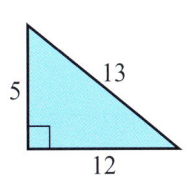

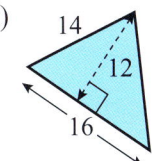

2 Copy and complete this table showing the measurements of triangles.

base	6 cm	8 cm	14 cm		7 cm
height	4 cm			30 cm	
area		36 cm²	140 cm²	90 cm²	105 cm²

3 The base and height of a triangle are equal in length.
How long is the base if the area of the triangle is 128 cm²?

4 Find the area of each triangle. Give each answer in square units.

(a) (b) 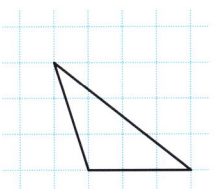 (c) 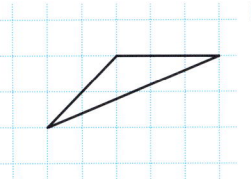 (d)

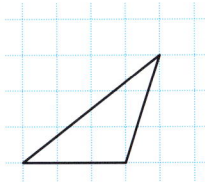

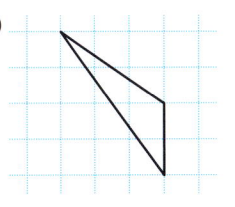

5   Find the total area of each shape. Lengths are in cm.

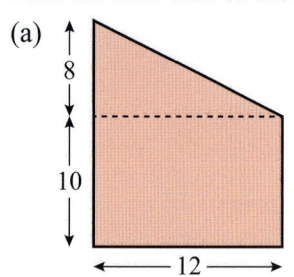

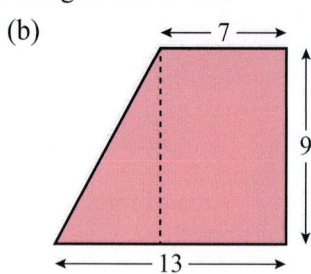

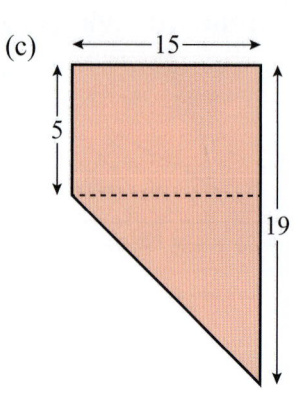

(a) 8, 10, 12

(b) 7, 9, 13

(c) 15, 5, 19

6   Find the total area of each shape. Lengths are in cm.

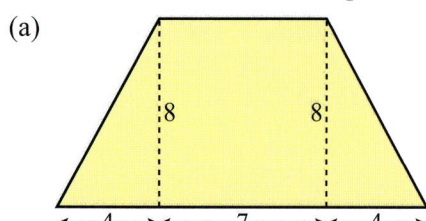

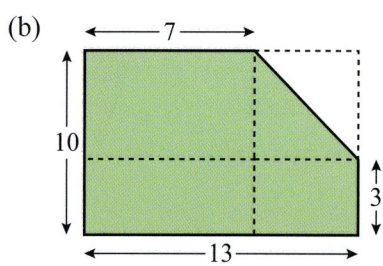

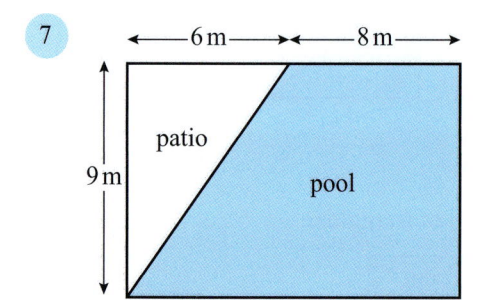

(a) 8, 8, 4, 7, 4

(b) 7, 10, 13, 3

7   Calculate the area of the pool.

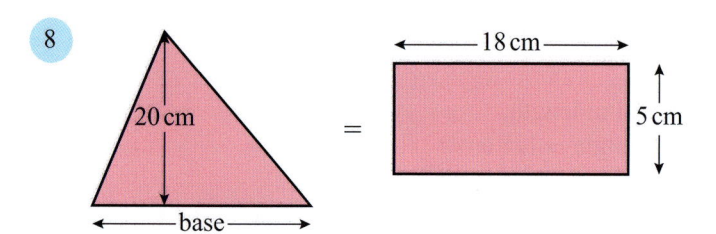

6 m, 8 m, 9 m — patio, pool

8   The area of the triangle is equal to the area of the rectangle. How long is the base of the triangle?

20 cm, base = 18 cm, 5 cm

9   Work out the area of the triangle shown opposite.

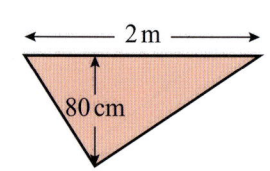

2 m, 80 cm

10 Find the area coloured blue. Lengths are in cm.

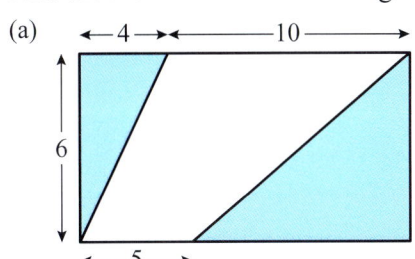

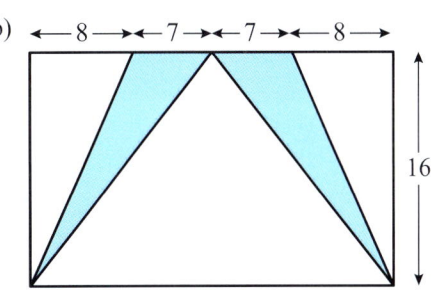

(a) ←4→←—10—→

6

←5→

(b) ←8→←7→←7→←8→

16

Irregular shapes

It is not easy to find the exact area of the triangle shown because we do not know either the length of the base or the height.

We could measure both lengths but this would introduce a small error due to the inevitable inaccuracy of the measuring.

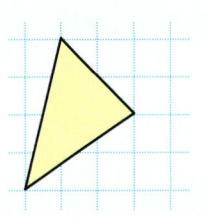

- A good method is to start by drawing a rectangle around the triangle. The corners of the triangle lie either on the sides of the rectangle or at a corner of the rectangle.
  Calculate the area of the rectangle. In this example:
  Area of rectangle = 3 × 4
  $\qquad\qquad\qquad\quad$ = 12 square units

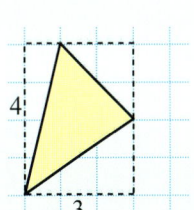

- Now find the areas of the three triangles marked A, B and C. This is easy because the triangles each have a right angle.
  Use the symbol 'ΔA' to mean 'triangle A'

  Area of $\Delta A = \dfrac{4 \times 1}{2} = 2$ square units

  Area of $\Delta B = \dfrac{2 \times 2}{2} = 2$ square units

  Area of $\Delta C = \dfrac{3 \times 2}{2} = 3$ square units

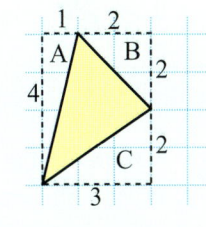

Now we can find the area of the required triangle by subtracting the areas of ΔA, ΔB and ΔC from the area of the rectangle.

Area of yellow triangle = 12 − [2 + 2 + 3]
$\qquad\qquad\qquad\qquad\quad$ = 5 square units

Exercise 2E

1 Find the area of each shape.

(a) 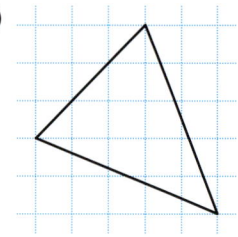 (b) 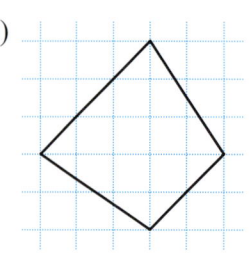 (c)

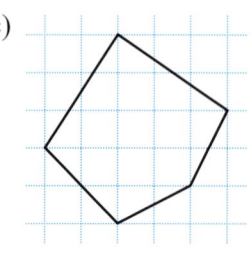

2 For each question, draw two axes from 0 to 6. Plot the points given and join them up in order. Find the area of each shape.

(a) (1, 3), (3, 4), (5, 1)   (b) (5, 1), (2, 4), (4, 6), (6, 5)

3 Do the same as question **2** with the two axes drawn from 0 to 7.

(a) (1, 7), (5, 5), (5, 2), (2, 3)   (b) (0, 3), (3, 7), (7, 2), (3, 2), (1, 1)

4 Do the same as question **2** with the two axes drawn from 0 to 10.

(a) (2, 1), (4, 8), (7, 8), (10, 6), (8, 2), (6, 4)
(b) (0, 2), (2, 4), (0, 8), (9, 7), (10, 2), (6, 4), (4, 1)

5 A triangle and a square are drawn on dotty paper with dots 1 cm apart. What is the area of the shaded region?

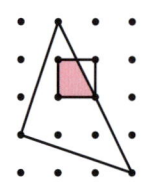

6 A triangle is drawn inside a regular hexagon. What is the area of the triangle as a fraction of the area of the hexagon?

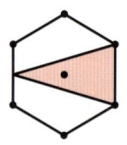

Areas of parallelograms and trapeziums

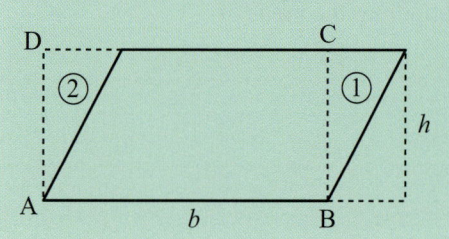

Area of parallelogram
= area of rectangle ABCD + area of Δ1 − area of Δ2
area of Δ1 = area of Δ2

Area of parallelogram = $b \times h$

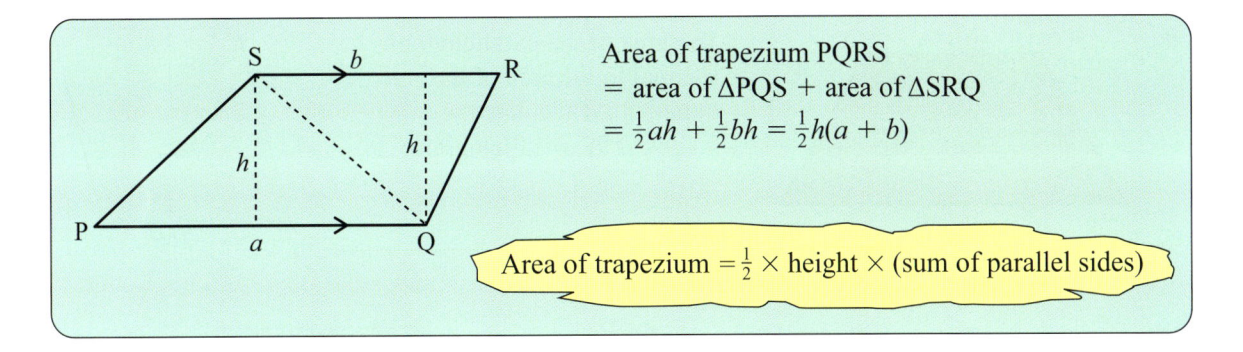

Area of trapezium PQRS
= area of △PQS + area of △SRQ
= $\frac{1}{2}ah + \frac{1}{2}bh = \frac{1}{2}h(a+b)$

Area of trapezium = $\frac{1}{2}$ × height × (sum of parallel sides)

Area of trapezium = $\frac{1}{2}h(a+b)$
= $\frac{1}{2} \times 8 \times (5+12)$
= $4 \times 17 = 68 \text{ cm}^2$

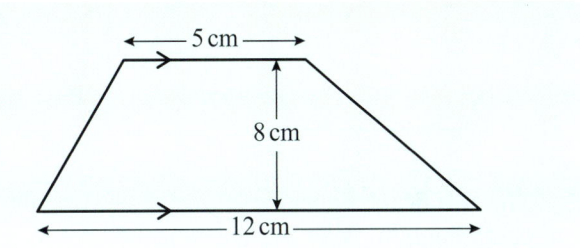

Exercise 3M

Calculate the area of each shape. The lengths are in cm.

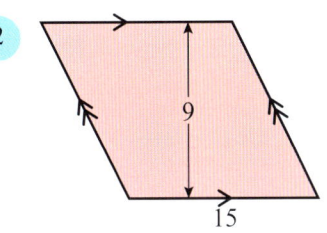

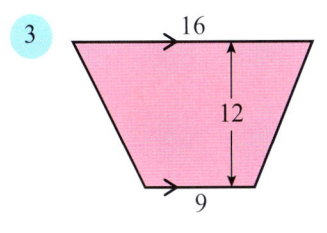

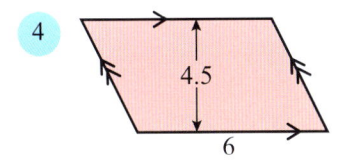

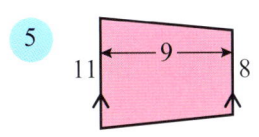

1. [trapezium: parallel sides 8 and 12, height 3]

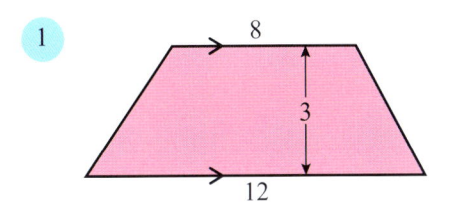

2. [parallelogram: base 15, height 9]

3. [trapezium: parallel sides 16 and 9, height 12]

4. [parallelogram: base 6, height 4.5]

5. [trapezium: parallel sides 9 (top) and 8 (right side shown), with 11 on left — sides 11 and 8, parallel sides separated by 9]

6. [parallelogram: base 8, slant side 5, height 4]

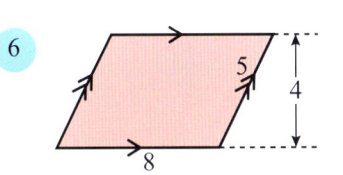

7. A parallelogram has a base of length 16 cm and an area of 72 cm².
   Calculate the height of the parallelogram.

8. A car park is in the shape of the trapezium shown opposite. The car park is to be covered with tarmac at £54 per square metre.
   Work out the total cost of covering this car park with tarmac.

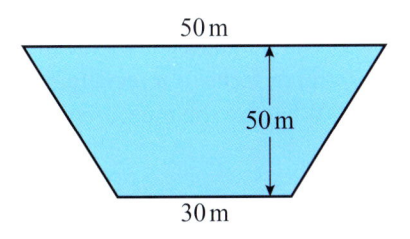

   [trapezium: parallel sides 50 m and 30 m, height 50 m]

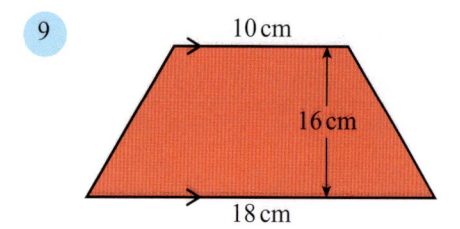

9 The area of the parallelogram is equal to the area of the trapezium. Calculate the height of the parallelogram.

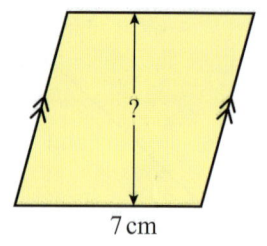

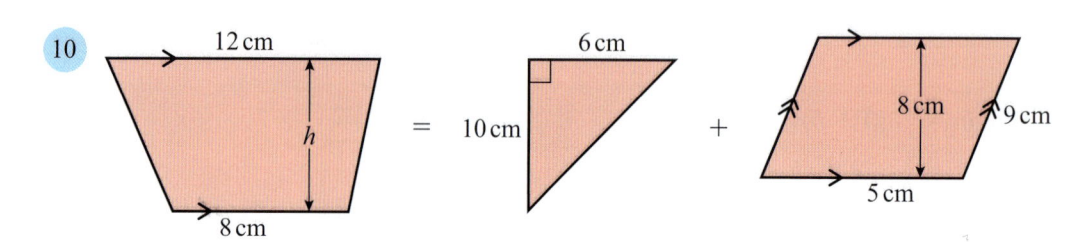

10 The area of the trapezium above is equal to the sum of the areas of the triangle and the parallelogram. Work out the value of h.

Need more practice with areas?

1 Find each area shaded blue. All the lengths are in cm.

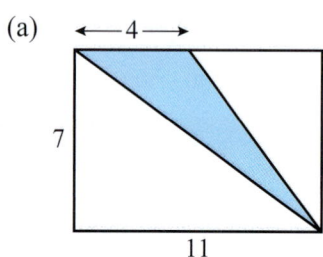

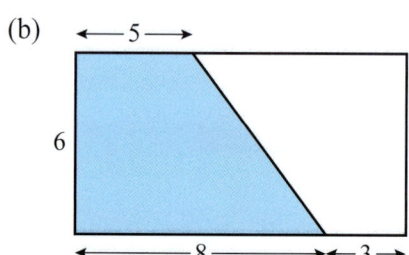

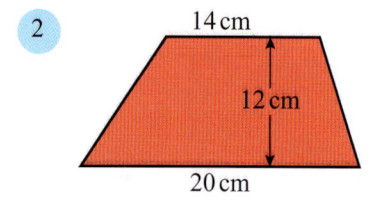

(a)

(b)

2 Work out the area of this trapezium.

3 The diagram shows the areas of three faces of a rectangular box. What are the measurements of the box?

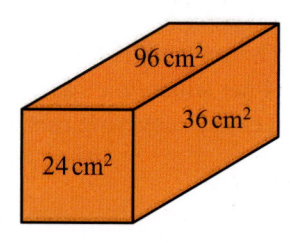

4. A floor measures 5 m by 4 m. It is to be covered by rectangular tiles measuring 80 cm by 50 cm. How many tiles are needed?

5. A picture measures 12 cm by 7 cm. It is surrounded by a border 3 cm wide. What is the area of the border?

6. A path passing through a garden is shown opposite. Find the area of the shaded path.

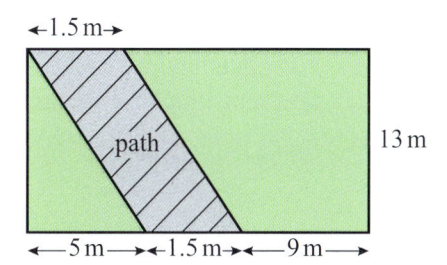

7. How many square centimetres in 1 square metre?

8. A line starts at A and goes along the dotted lines to B. It divides the area of the square into two halves.
   (a) Draw a rectangle like the one on the right and draw a line from C to D which divides the area of the rectangle into two halves.
   (b) Draw a second rectangle and draw a line from C to D which divides the area of the rectangle into two parts so that one part has *twice* the area of the other part.

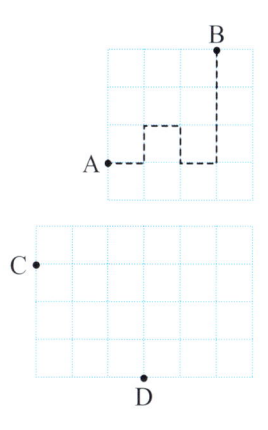

Extension questions with areas

(Note that $10\,000 \text{ m}^2 = 1$ hectare)

1. A rectangular field measures 0.8 km by 500 m. Find the area of the field in hectares.

2. A rectangular field 500 m long has an area of 7 hectares. Calculate the width of the field.

3. A groundsman has enough grass seed to cover 1.5 hectares. A tennis court measures 15 m by 40 m. How many courts can he cover with seed?

4 Farmland is sold at £3500 per hectare. How much would you pay for a piece of farmland in the shape of a right angled triangle with base 500 m and height 320 m?

5 A rectangular field 280 m long has an area of 3.5 hectares. Calculate the perimeter of the field.

6 A waterproofing spray is applied to the outside of the four walls, including the door, and the roof of the garage shown.
  (a) Calculate the total area to be sprayed.
  (b) The spray comes in cans costing £3.95 and each can is enough to cover 4 m². How much will it cost to spray this garage? (Assume you have to buy full cans)

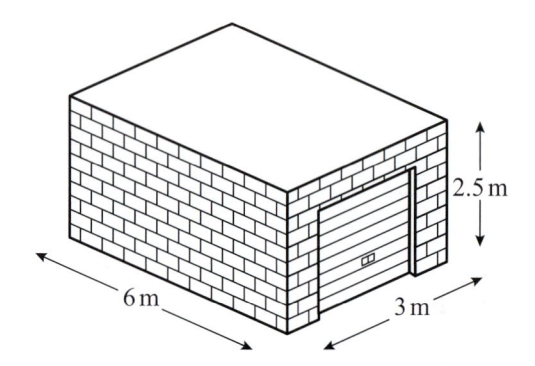

7 A gardener is using moss killer on his lawn. The instructions say that 4 measures of the mosskiller, in water, will treat 10 m² of lawn. The box contains 250 measures and costs £12.50.
Find the area of the lawn and hence the cost of the moss killer required.

8 The pink triangle is drawn inside a rectangle with longer side 12 cm.
  (a) If area of triangle ② = 2 × (area of triangle ①), find the length x.
  (b) If area of triangle ② = 3 × (area of triangle ①), find the length x.

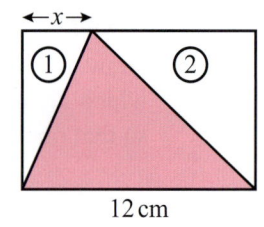

9 A trapezium has a height of 9 cm and an area of 135 cm². Write down the possible lengths of its parallel sides.

10 The field shown is sold at auction for £55,250. Calculate the price *per acre* which was paid.
[1 acre = 4840 square yards]

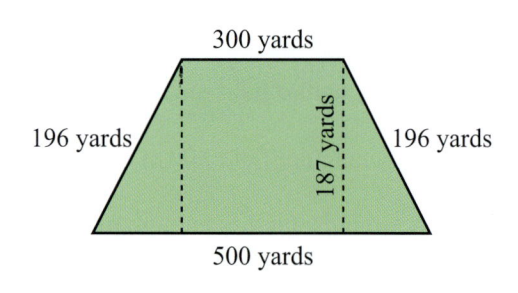

11 A red square is inside a yellow square as shown. All lengths are in cm. Calculate the value of x, giving your answer to the nearest cm.

12 In a recent major survey of children's mathematical ability only 1 in 20 of fifteen year olds gave the correct answer to the following question:

'Find the length of the rectangle if the area is $\frac{1}{3}$ cm^2.'

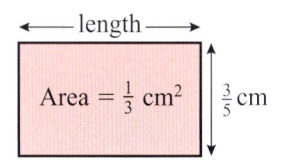

Calculate the length.

Area = $\frac{1}{3}$ cm^2, $\frac{3}{5}$ cm

13 The diagrams show squares A, B, C and D. The sum of the areas of squares A, B, and C is equal to the area of square D.

A 5 cm, B 3 cm, C 7 cm

Calculate the length of the side of square D.

14 Work out the areas of A, B, C, ..., I in the shapes below. The dots are 1 cm apart.

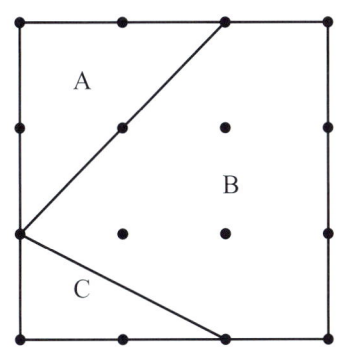

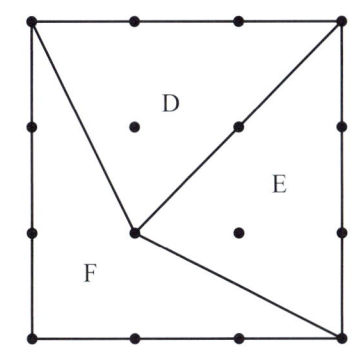

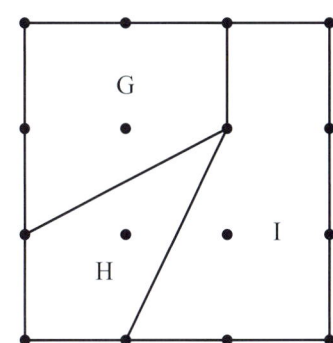

Investigation – area and perimeter

You need squared paper. Each side of the rectangles below must be a whole number.

Part A

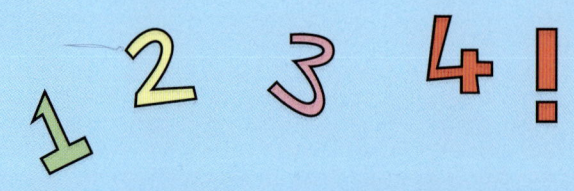

Draw four different rectangles which all have a *perimeter* of 24 cm.

Part B

Draw three different rectangles which all have an *area* of 24 cm².

Part C

Draw at least four rectangles which have a perimeter of 20 cm.
(1) Work out the area of each rectangle.
(2) Which of your rectangles has the largest area?

Part D

The perimeter of a new rectangle is 32 cm.
(1) *Predict* what the sides of the rectangle will be so that it has the largest possible area.
(2) Check by drawing different rectangles to see if your prediction was correct.

Part E

A rectangle has a perimeter of 100 cm. What are the length and width if the rectangle is to have the largest possible area? What is the largest possible area?

2.6 Angles

In section 2.6 you will:

- review basic angle calculations
- calculate angles with parallel lines
- calculate angles in a quadrilateral

Labelling angles

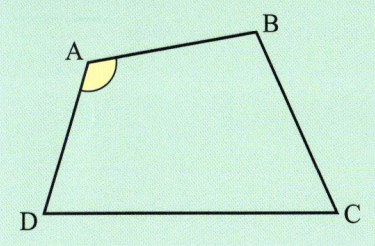

The marked angle is called angle DAB or angle BAD. We write this as DÂB or BÂD. Angles are labelled with capital letters and the middle letter wears a 'hat' to indicate an angle.

Exercise 1M

Measure the following angles with a protractor.

1. BÂC
2. RĈD
3. DÊR
4. EÂB
5. DR̂C
6. BÊA
7. SR̂B
8. AĈB
9. DT̂B
10. CP̂E
11. CD̂E
12. DŜC
13. DĈB
14. ED̂S
15. UD̂Q
16. EĈB

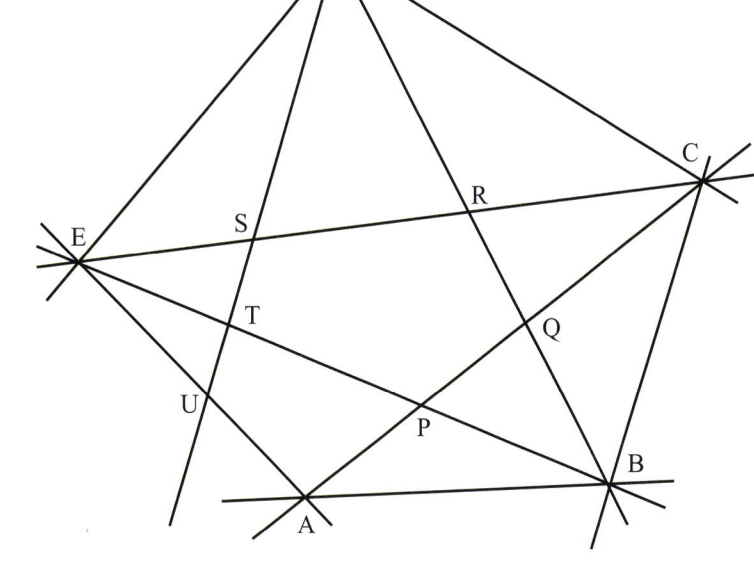

17. Use a protractor to draw the following angles accurately.
    (a) 85°   (b) 48°   (c) 130°   (d) 164°   (e) 18°
    (f) 25°   (g) 210° (h) 156°   (i) 304°   (j) 123°

18. For each angle in question 17, state whether it is acute, obtuse or reflex.

Remember: The angles on a straight line add up to 180°.
The angles at a point add up to 360°.
The angles in a triangle add up to 180°.

Isosceles and equilateral triangles

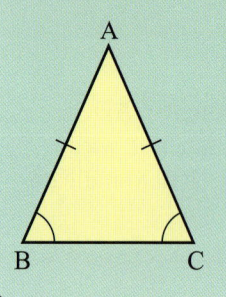

An *isosceles* triangle has two equal sides and two equal angles.

The sides AB and AC are equal (marked with a dash) so angles B̂ and Ĉ are also equal.

An *equilateral* triangle has three equal sides and three equal angles (all 60°).

Find the angles marked with letters.

(a)

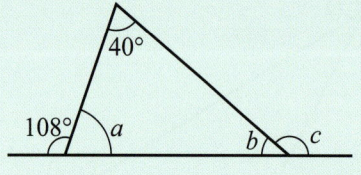

$a = 72°$ (angles on a straight line)
$b + 72° + 40° = 180°$ (angles in a triangle)
$b = 68°$
$c = 112°$ (angles on a straight line)

(b)

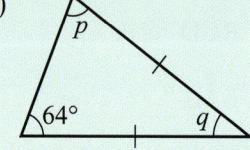

$p = 64°$ (isosceles triangle)
$q + 64° + 64° = 180°$ (angles in a triangle)
$q = 52°$

Exercise 2M

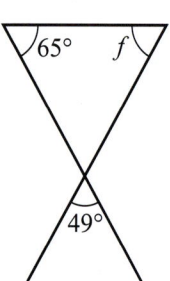

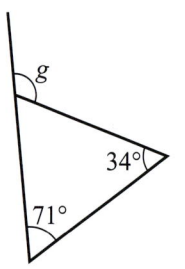

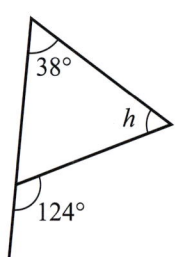

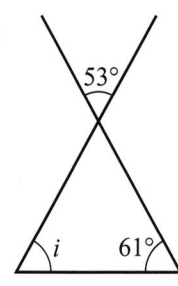

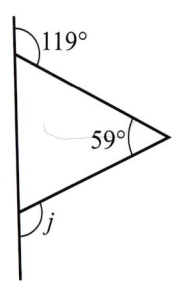

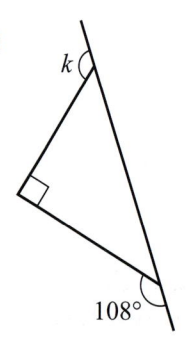

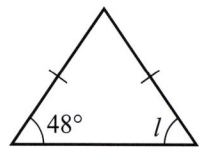

Find the angles marked with letters.

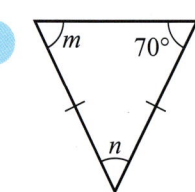

9. [triangle with angles p, p and right angle]

10. [equilateral triangle with angles q, q, q]

11. [isosceles triangle with apex r and 36°]

12. [triangle with t, u, s and exterior 115°]

13. [crossed lines, 76° at top, a at bottom]

14. [triangle with exterior b and 53°]

15. [triangle with 62° at top, d, c at bottom]

16. [triangle with e, exterior 109°, exterior f]

17. [three angles g, g, g on isosceles triangle]

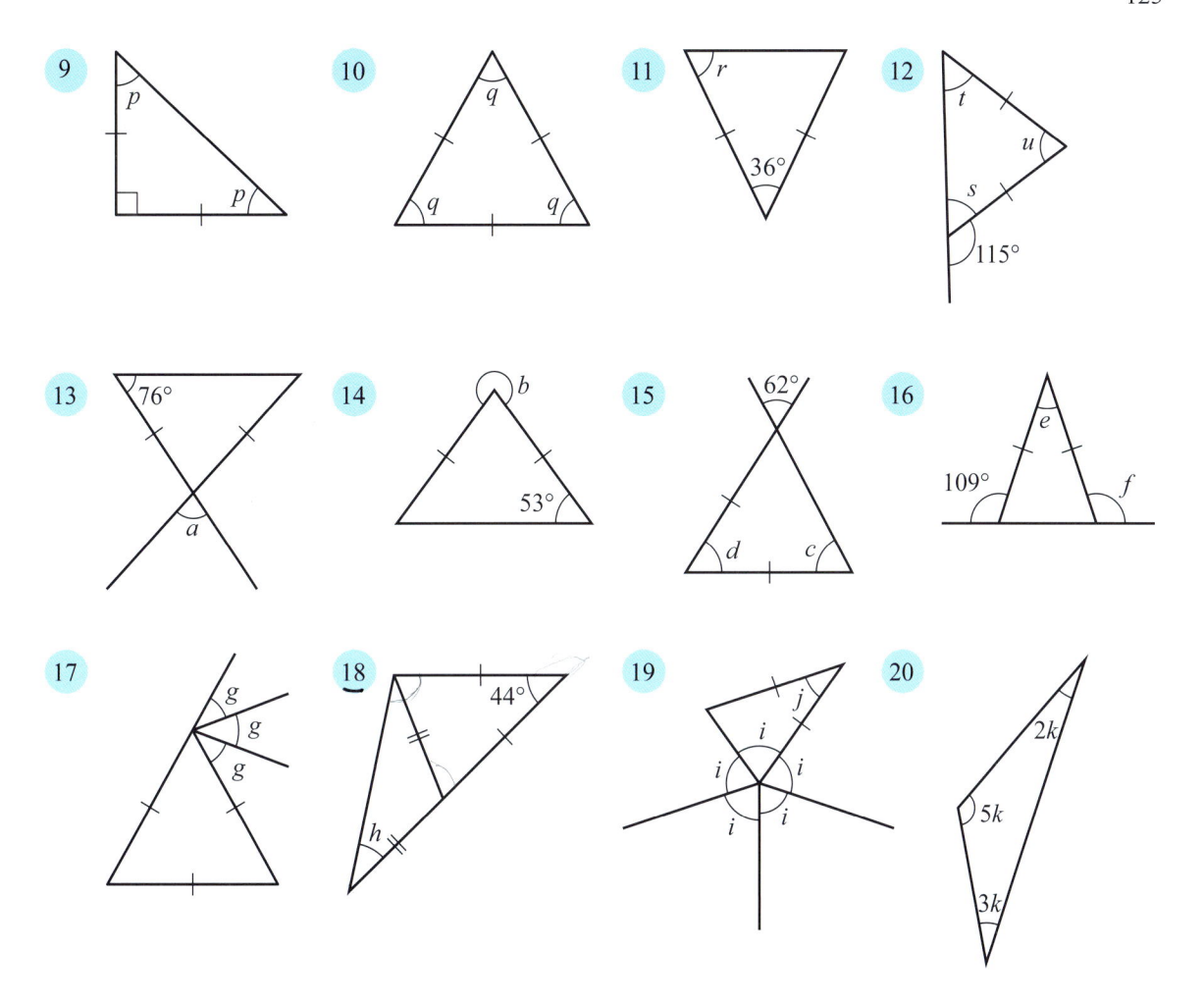

18. [triangle with 44° and h]

19. [five angles i, i, i, i and j about a point]

20. [triangle with angles $2k$, $5k$, $3k$]

21. Julie has laid a patio with triangular slabs as shown below. She has one space to fill (indicated below). She has three slabs remaining. Which slab will fit perfectly into the space? Explain why.

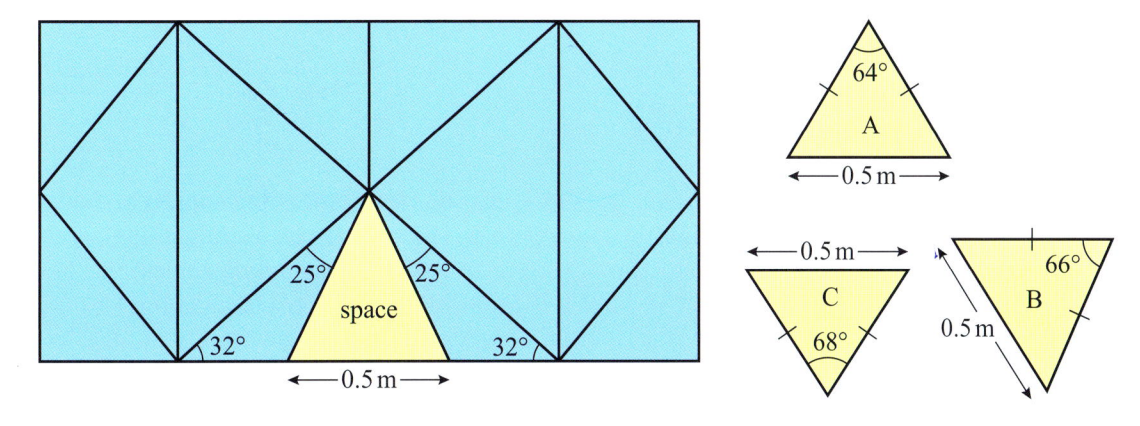

[diagram: space with angles 25°, 25°, 32°, 32°, base 0.5 m]

Slab A: 64°, base 0.5 m
Slab B: 66°, side 0.5 m
Slab C: 68°, top 0.5 m

22. Angle Q in triangle PQR is three times as large as angle P.
What is the size of angle P if angle R is double the size of angle Q?

Angles and parallel lines

In this diagram all the arrow lines are parallel.

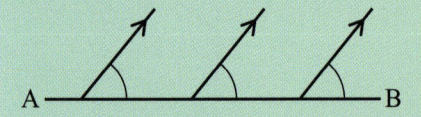

The arrows all make the same angle with the line AB. These angles are called **corresponding** angles.

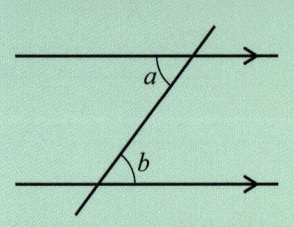

angle a = angle b
These are called *alternate* angles.

Many people think of corresponding angles as 'F' angles.

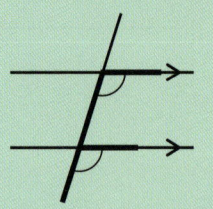

Many people think of alternate angles as 'Z' angles.

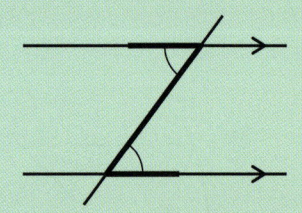

Find the angles marked with letters.

(a)

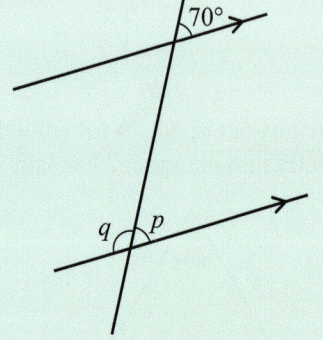

$p = 70°$ (corresponding angles)
$q = 110°$ (angles on a straight line)

(b)

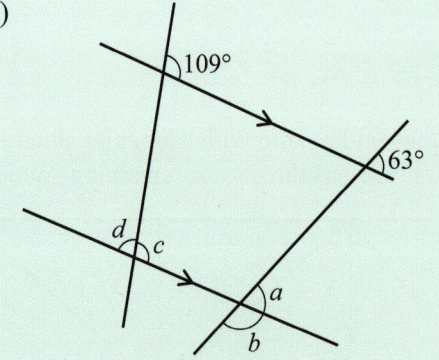

$a = 63°$ (corresponding angles)
$b = 117°$ (angles on a straight line)
$c = 109°$ (corresponding angles)
$d = 71°$ (angles on a straight line)

Exercise 3M

Find the angles marked with letters.

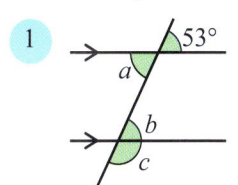

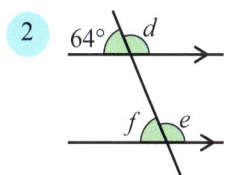

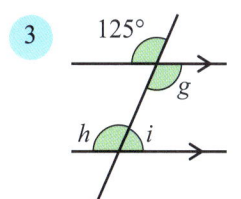

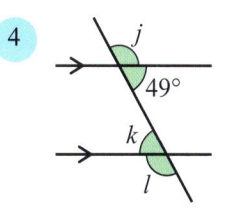

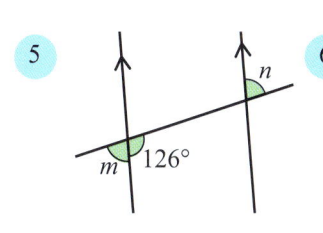

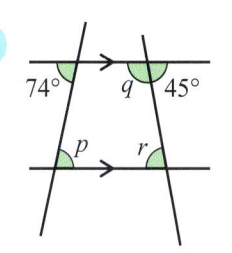

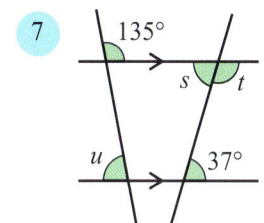

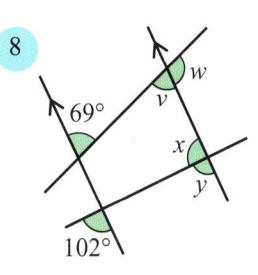

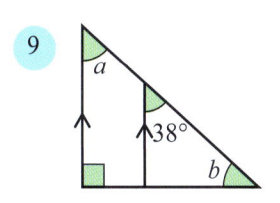

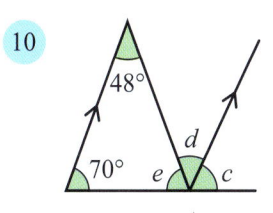

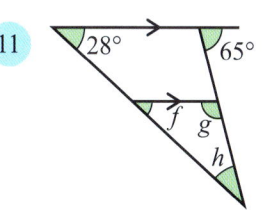

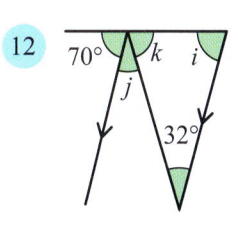

1. (angles with 53°: a, b, c)
2. (angles with 64°: d, e, f)
3. (angles with 125°: g, h, i)
4. (angles with 49°: j, k, l)
5. (angles with 126°: m, n)
6. (angles with 74° and 45°: p, q, r)
7. (angles with 135° and 37°: s, t, u)
8. (angles with 69° and 102°: v, w, x, y)
9. (angles with 38°: a, b)
10. (angles with 48° and 70°: c, d, e)
11. (angles with 28° and 65°: f, g, h)
12. (angles with 70° and 32°: i, j, k)

13. Angle c is one third the size of angle a. What is the size of angle a?

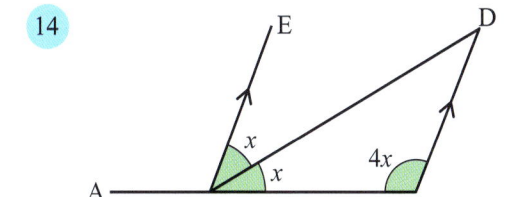

14. Work out the value of x. Give reasons for your answer.

(Triangle ABC with E and D, angles x, x at B and 4x at C)

15. Find the values of m and n opposite. Give full reasons for each answer.

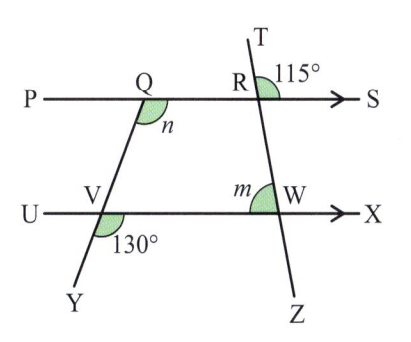

(Diagram with lines PQRS, UVWX, angles 115° at R, 130° at Y, m at W, n at Q)

Angles in a quadrilateral

Draw a quadrilateral of any shape on a piece of paper or card and cut it out. Mark the four angles *a*, *b*, *c* and *d* and tear them off.

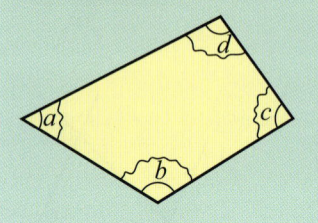

Arrange the four angles about a point.

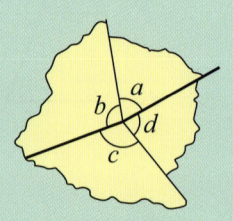

We see that:
The angles in a quadrilateral add up to 360°

Exercise 4M

Find the angles marked with letters.

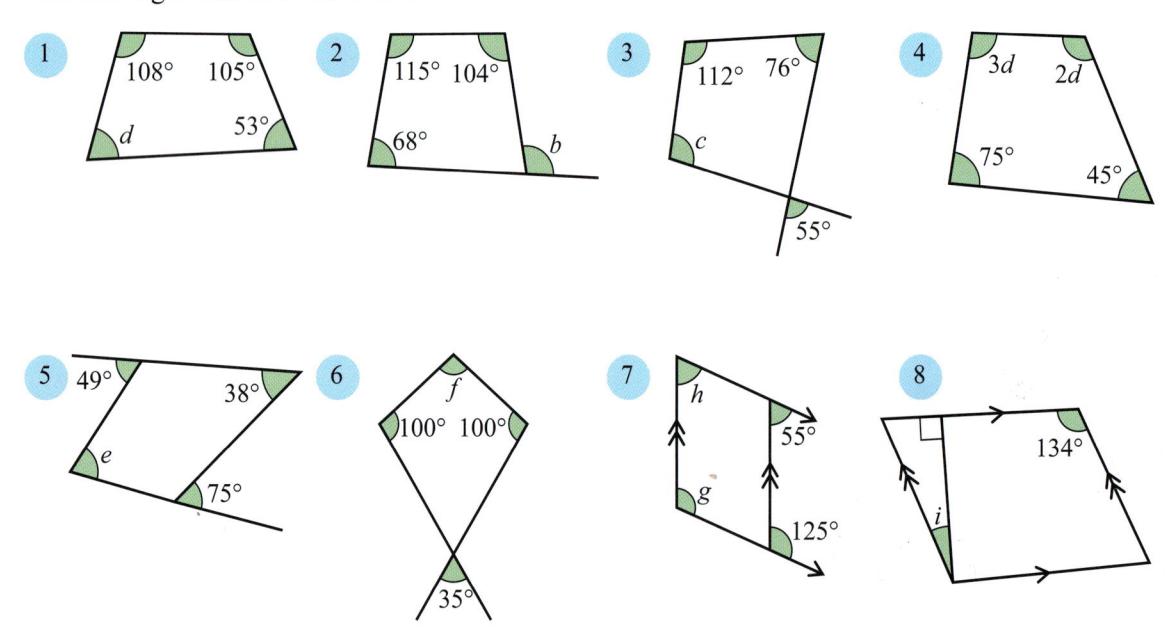

1. 108°, 105°, 53°, *d*

2. 115°, 104°, 68°, *b*

3. 112°, 76°, *c*, 55°

4. 3*d*, 2*d*, 75°, 45°

5. 49°, 38°, 75°, *e*

6. *f*, 100°, 100°, 35°

7. *h*, 55°, *g*, 125°

8. 134°, *i*

9. ABCE is a rectangle.
   Work out the value of AD̂E.
   Give reasons for your answer.

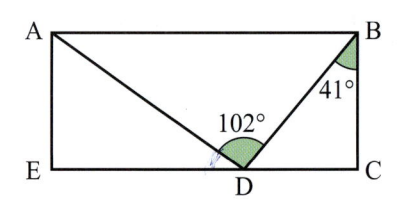

   (Diagram: rectangle ABCE with point D on EC, angle ADB = 102°, angle DBC = 41°)

10 Work out the value of TR̂S.
Give reasons for your answer.

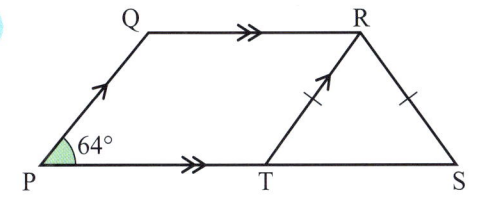

11 Work out the value of BD̂C if CB̂D is one fifth the size of AB̂C. Give reasons for your answer.

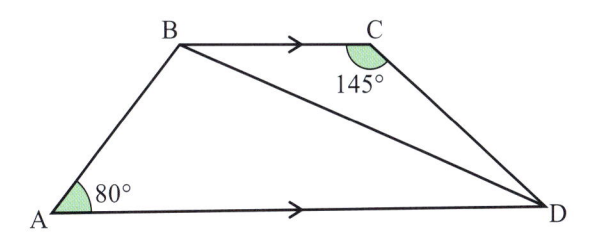

12 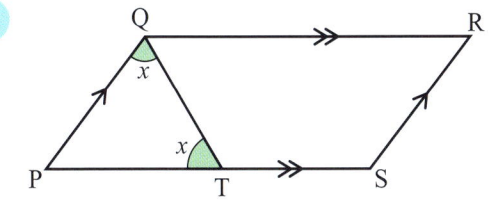 PQRS is a parallelogram.
Prove that triangle PQT is equilateral if PQ̂R = 120°.

Need more practice with angles?

Find the angles marked with letters.

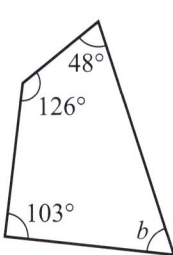

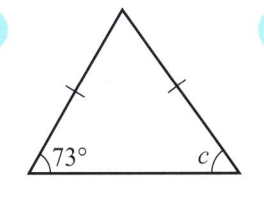

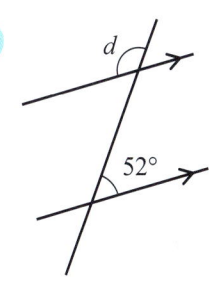

1. (quadrilateral with 108°, 86°, 75°, a)
2. (quadrilateral with 48°, 126°, 103°, b)
3. (isosceles triangle with 73°, c)
4. (parallel lines with 52°, d)
5. (angles around a point: 88°, 150°, e)
6. (parallel lines with 68°, 115°, f, g)
7. (triangle with 70°, 32°, h)
8. (triangle with 80°, i)

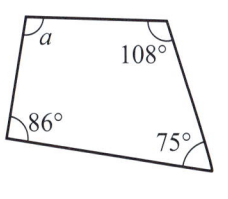

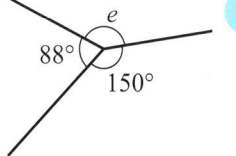

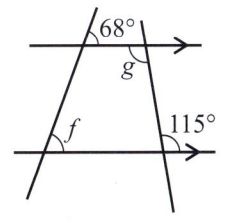

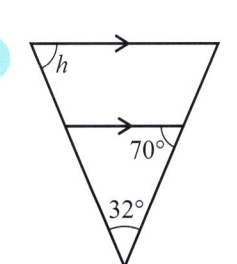

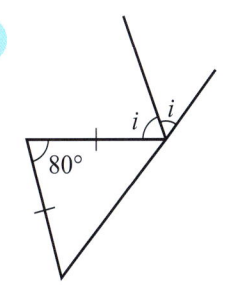

9 Angles 114°, 109°, 76°, with exterior angle j.

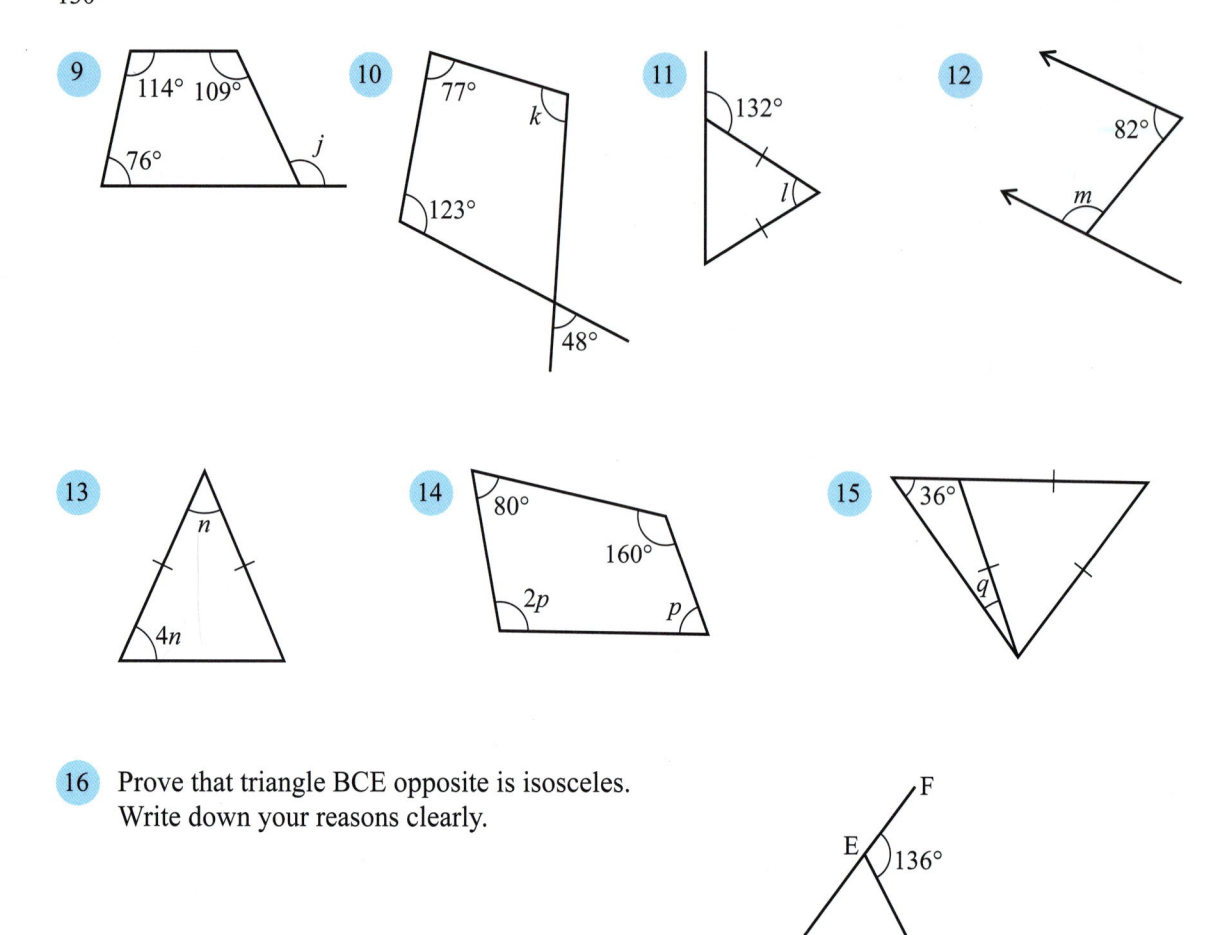

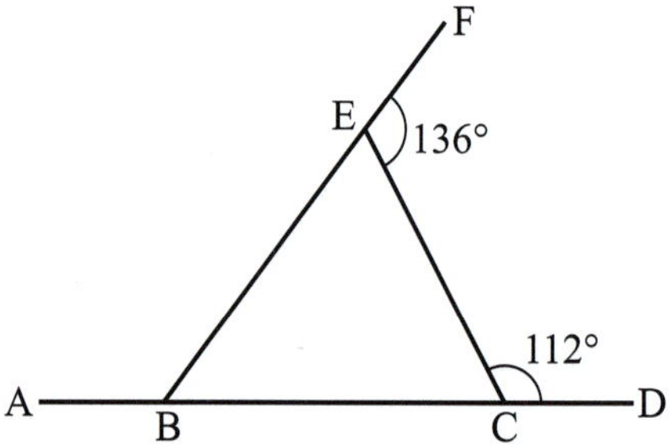

10 Quadrilateral with angles 77°, k, 123°, and exterior 48°.

11 Isosceles triangle with 132° exterior, angle l.

12 Reflex/arrow shape with 82° and m.

13 Isosceles triangle with apex n and base angle 4n.

14 Quadrilateral with angles 80°, 160°, 2p, p.

15 Triangle with 36° at top, angle q, with marked equal sides.

16 Prove that triangle BCE opposite is isosceles.
Write down your reasons clearly.

(Diagram: Triangle ABE with C on AD extended, E on BF. Angle FEC = 136°, angle BCD = 112°, with A, B, C, D collinear.)

17 Two angles in a triangle are both 30° more than the third angle.
Write down the values of all the angles in the triangle.

18 Triangle with angles 2x, 4x, 8x, x.

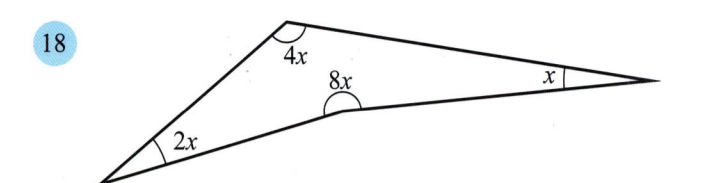

Write down the actual value of each angle in this quadrilateral.

131

Extension questions with angles

Find the angles marked with letters.

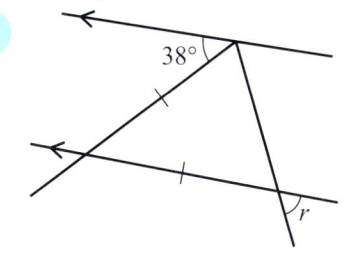

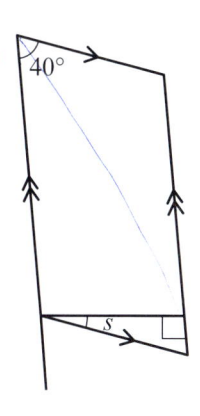

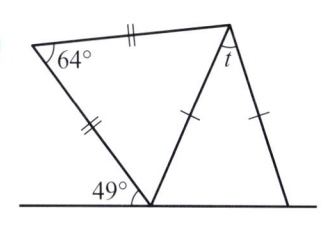

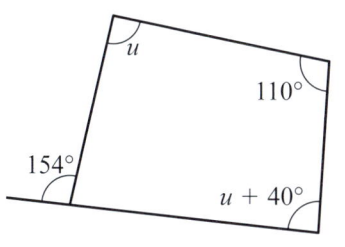

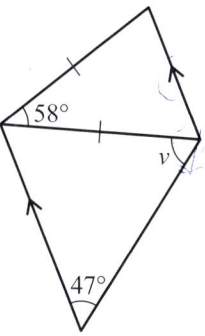

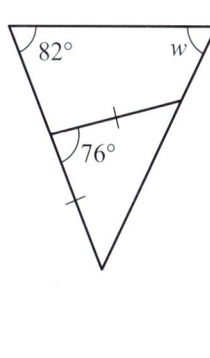

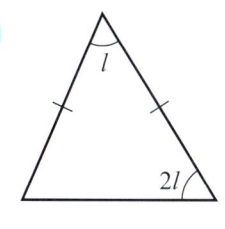

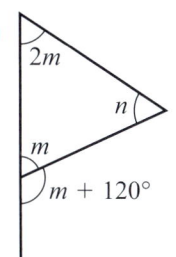

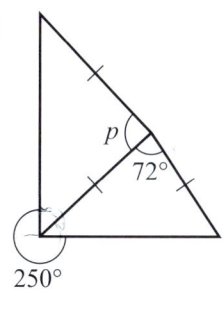

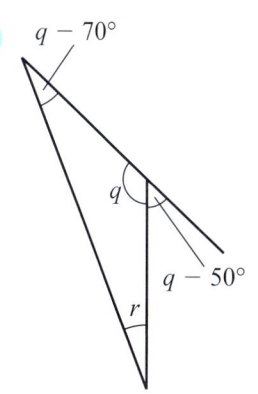

1. [diagram with 38° and angle r]

2. [diagram with 40° and angle s]

3. [diagram with 64°, 49° and angle t]

4. [quadrilateral with u, 110°, 154°, $u + 40°$]

5. [diagram with 58°, 47° and angle v]

6. [diagram with 82°, 76° and angle w]

7. [triangle with l and $2l$]

8. [triangle with $2m$, n, m, $m + 120°$]

9. [diagram with p, 72°, 250°]

10. [diagram with $q - 70°$, q, $q - 50°$, r]

11. Explain clearly why triangle BCE opposite is isosceles.

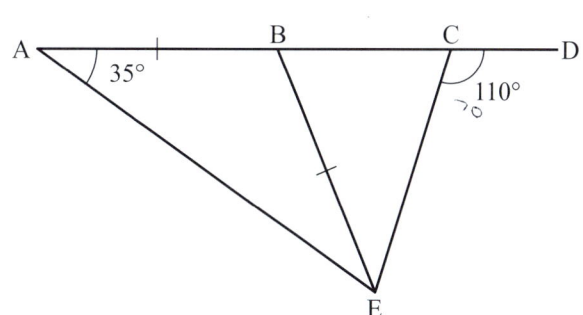

[diagram showing points A, B, C, D on a line with 35° at A, 110° at C, and point E below]

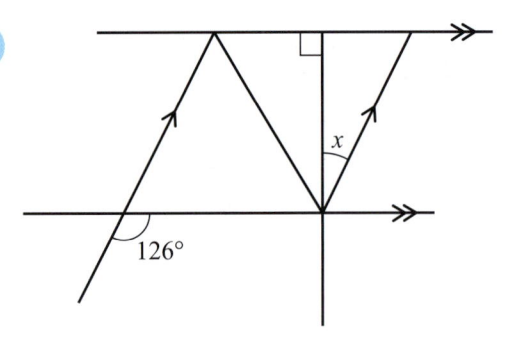

12. Work out the value of angle x.

13. A quadrilateral can be split into two triangles.
    (a) Explain why the sum of the angles in a quadrilateral is 360°.
    (b) Find the sum of the angles in a pentagon.

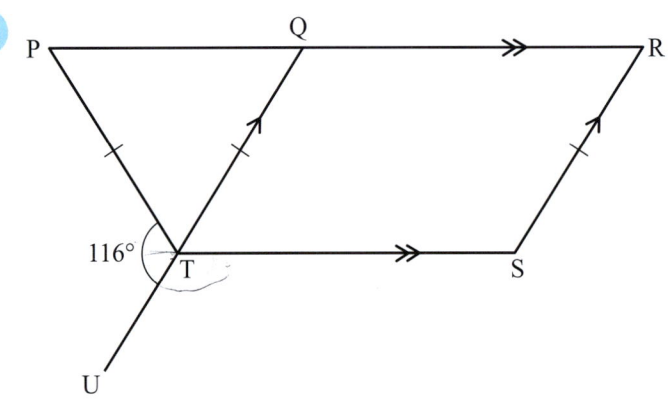

14. Work out the value of $R\hat{S}T$.
    Give full reasons for your answer.

✗ Spot the mistakes 4 ✗

Areas and angles

Work through each question below and explain clearly what mistakes have been made. Beware – some questions are correctly done.

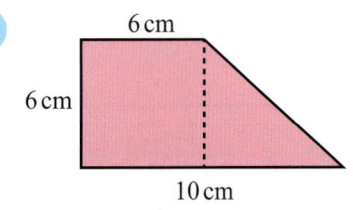

1. area of square = 6 × 6 = 36
   area of triangle = $\frac{1}{2}$ × 10 × 6 = 30
   total area = 36 + 30 = 66 cm²

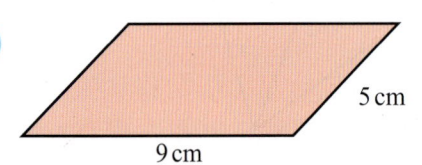

2. area of parallelogram = 9 × 5
   = 45 cm²

133

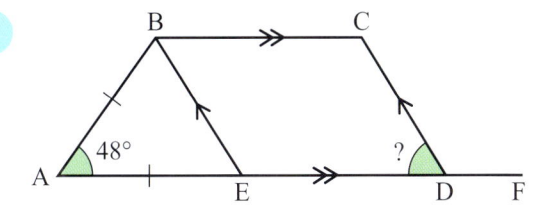

3 Calculate the value of CD̂E.
AÊB = 48° (isosceles triangle)
BÊD = 132° (angles on a straight line add up to 180°)
CD̂F = 132° (corresponding angles)
CD̂E = 48° (angles on a straight line add up to 180°)

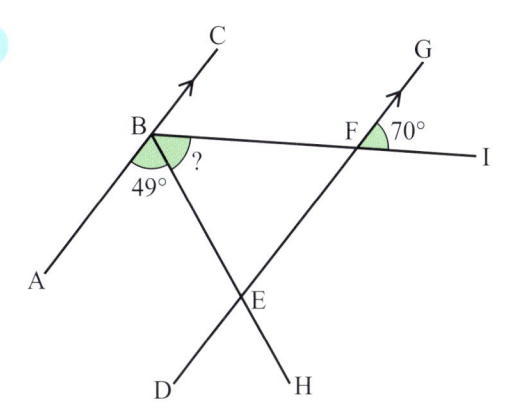

4 Calculate the value of EB̂F.
BF̂E = 70° (vertically opposite angles are equal)
CB̂F = 70° (alternate angles)
EB̂F = 180° − 70° − 49° = 61°
(angles on a straight line add up to 180°)

5 A square has an area of 36 cm² so the length of one side = 36 ÷ 4 = 9 cm.

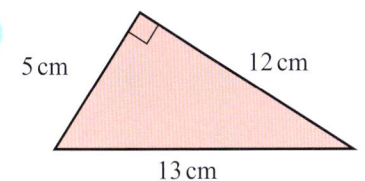

6 area of triangle = $\frac{1}{2} \times 13 \times 5$
= 32.5 cm²

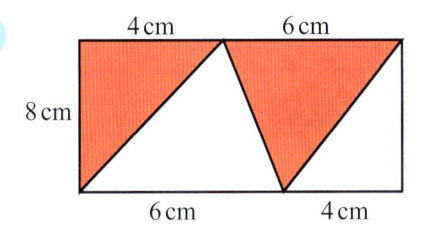

7 total red area = $\frac{1}{2} \times 4 \times 8 + \frac{1}{2} \times 6 \times 8$
= 16 + 24
= 40 cm²

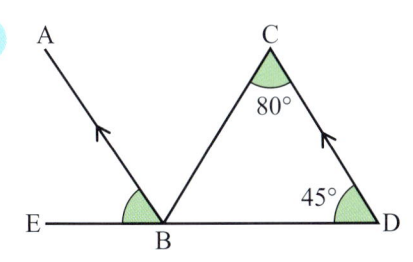

8 AB̂C = 100° (alternate angles add up to 180°)
CB̂D = 180° − 80° − 45° = 55° (angles in a triangle add up to 180°)
AB̂E = 180° − 100° − 55° = 25° (angles on a straight line add up to 180°)

9 The two parallel sides of a trapezium
are 6 cm and 12 cm.
Its area is 108 cm².
Height of trapezium = 108 ÷ (6 + 12) = 6 cm

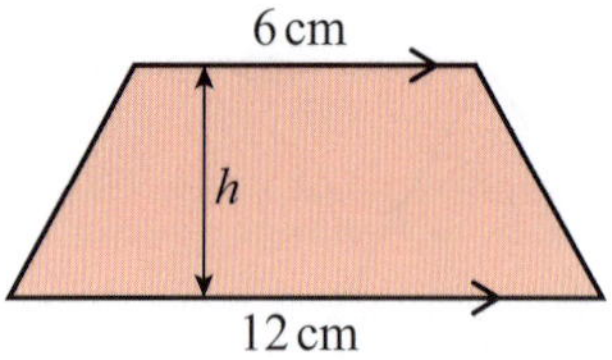

10 One box of fertiliser covers 20 m² and
costs £4.99.
How much does it cost to cover the
lawn opposite with fertiliser?
whole shape = (15 × 20) + (8 × 8) = 364
flower area = $\frac{1}{2}$ × 5 × 12 = 30
lawn area = 364 − 30 = 334 m²
number of boxes = 334 ÷ 20 = 16.7
cost = 16 × 4.99 = £79.84

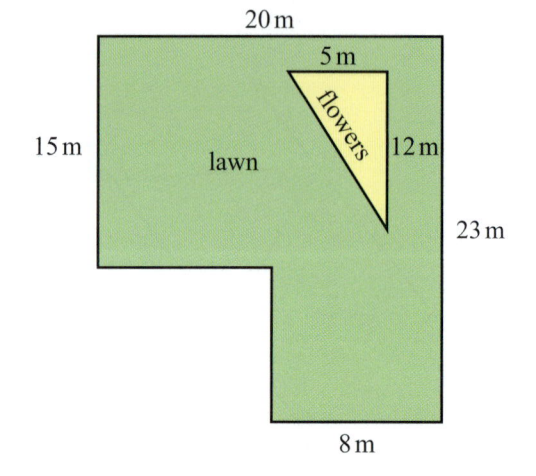

CHECK YOURSELF ON SECTIONS 2.5 and 2.6

1 Finding areas involving rectangles and triangles

(a) Find the yellow area.

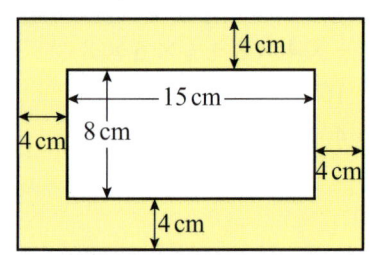

(b) Find the area of this shape.

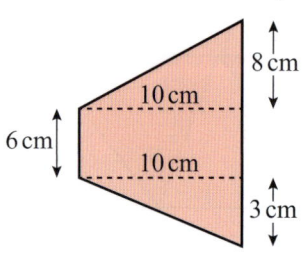

(c) The area of a tringle is 48 cm².
Find the base of the triangle if
the height is 8 cm.

(d) Find the area of this irregular shape.

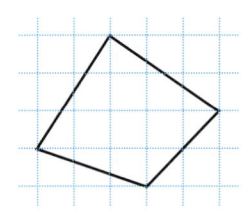

2 Finding areas of parallelograms and trapeziums

Find the area of each shape below.

(a) 14 cm, 12 cm, 13 cm, 6 cm

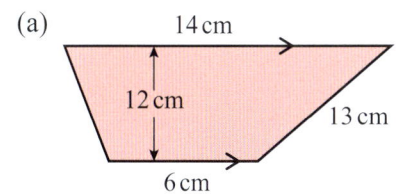

(b) 8 cm, 10 cm, 15 cm

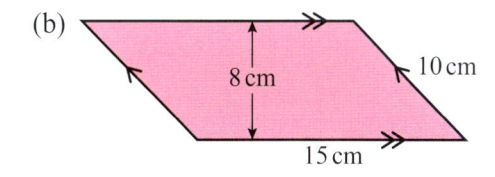

3 Reviewing basic angle calculations

(a) A, C, 39°, B

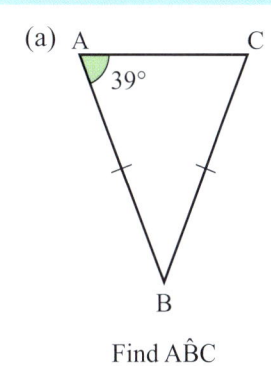

Find AB̂C

(b) Q, P 62°, R, S

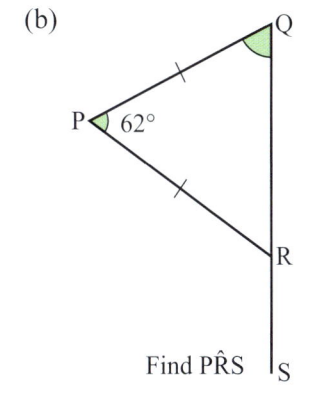

Find PR̂S

(c) C, 19°, B, A, D

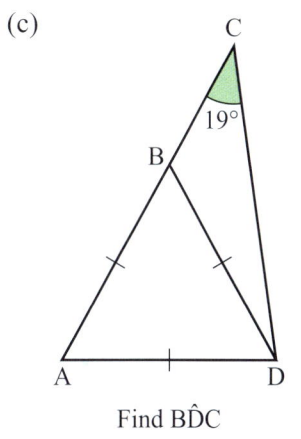

Find BD̂C

4 Calculating angles with parallel lines

(a) G, B, A, C, 78°, D, E, F, H

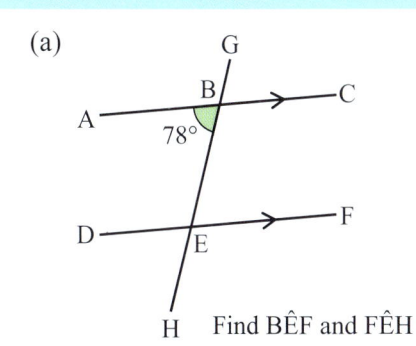

Find BÊF and FÊH

(b) P, R, 50°, 61°, T, Q, S

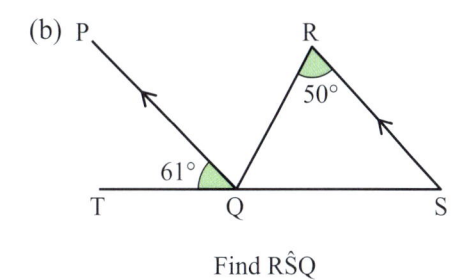

Find RŜQ

5 Calculating angles in a quadrilateral

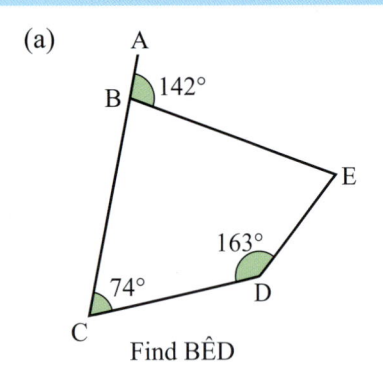

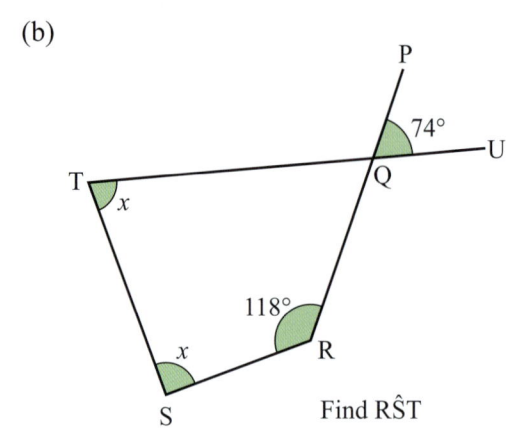

(a) Find BÊD (with angles 142° at A, 74° at C, 163° at D)

(b) Find RŜT (with 74° exterior at Q on line PU, 118° at R, x at T, x at S)

2.7 Applying mathematics 2

In section 2.7 you will apply maths in a variety of situations.

1 An Airbus 360 leaves Paris at 07.00 and arrives in New York at 10.20.
   A cargo plane leaves Paris at 07.10 and flies at half the speed of the Airbus. When should it arrive in New York?

2 The area of the 'U' shape is 175 cm².
   (a) Find the area of each small square.
   (b) Work out the length of the perimeter of the shape.

3 A school has a total of 852 pupils.
   There are 24 more girls than boys. How many girls are there?

4 A car uses 8 litres of petrol for every 50 km travelled.
   Petrol costs £1.38 per litre.
   Calculate the cost in £'s of travelling 850 km.

5 A floor measuring 5 m by 3.6 m is to be covered with square tiles of side 10 cm.
   A packet of 20 tiles costs £18.95. How much will it cost to tile the floor?

6 In a 'magic square' all rows (↔), columns (↕) and main diagonals (⊠) add up to the same 'magic number'. Copy and complete this magic square.

11			10
2	13	16	
		4	
7	12		6

7 Patrick says that SR̂U = 128°.
Is he correct?
Justify your answer fully.

8 A jar with 8 chocolates in it weighs 160 g.
The same jar with 20 chocolates in it weighs 304 g.
How much does the jar weigh on its own?

9 A book has 648 pages. Gina has read 42 pages in 3 days. At that rate how long will it take her to read the rest of the book?

10 Will cuts a right-angled triangular piece of wood as shown opposite.

He then cuts away the yellow trapezium.

Work out the blue area of wood remaining.

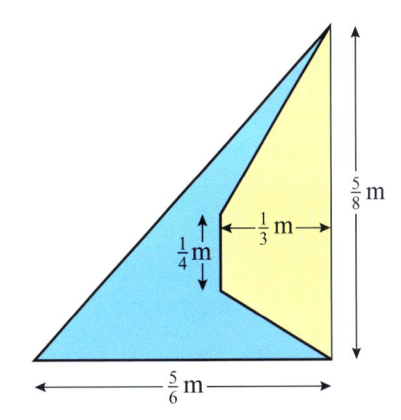

137

UNIT 2 MIXED REVIEW

Part one

1 Work out

(a) $\dfrac{3}{5} + \dfrac{1}{15}$ (b) $\dfrac{3}{8} + \dfrac{1}{4}$ (c) $\dfrac{3}{8} - \dfrac{1}{15}$

2 What is the name of the triangle with two equal angles?

3 The equation of a line is $y = x - 2$. Some points on the line are:
$(0, -2)\ (1, -1)\ (2, \Box)\ (3, \Box)\ (4, \Box)$
Fill in the missing numbers and then draw the line.

4 Copy and complete this table showing equivalent fractions, decimals and percentages.

fraction	decimal	percentage
		16%
	0.7	
$\dfrac{3}{20}$		

5 Work out $\left(\dfrac{3}{7} \times \dfrac{3}{4}\right) + \left(\dfrac{1}{2} \times \dfrac{5}{7}\right)$

6 The area of this shape is 126 cm². Find the value of x.

(9 cm top, 12 cm left side, x cm bottom)

7 A vet treats 36 sick mice with a new antibiotic.

After 6 hours $\dfrac{1}{3}$ of the mice have recovered and are running around happily.

After 12 hours $\dfrac{3}{4}$ of the remaining mice are cured but unfortunately the others have died.

(a) How many mice eventually recovered?

(b) How many mice died?

8 Four friends were eating popcorn.
Sheena ate $\frac{1}{3}$, George ate $\frac{1}{4}$ and Dan ate $\frac{1}{6}$.
Jade ate the rest. What fraction did Jade eat?

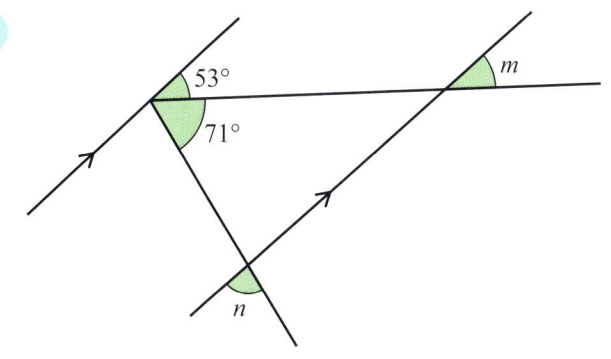

9 Find the values of *m* and *n*.

(diagram showing angles 53°, 71°, *m*, and *n* with two parallel lines)

10 A wheat field is a rectangle measuring 250 m by 800 m.
Each hectare produces 4.7 tonnes of wheat.
How much wheat is produced in this field?
[1 hectare = 10 000 m²]

11 Work out
(a) $2\frac{3}{4} \times 3\frac{1}{3}$
(b) $1\frac{1}{2} \div 3\frac{7}{8}$
(c) $3\frac{2}{5} \div 1\frac{5}{6}$

Part two

1 The letters from A to Z are shown on the grid. Decipher the following messages

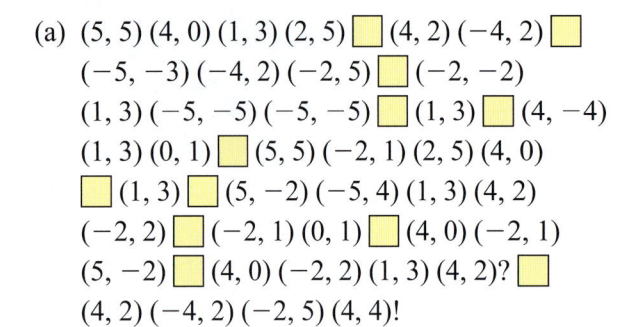

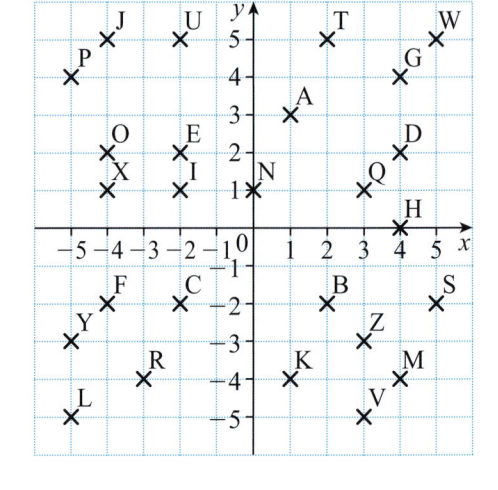

(a) (5, 5) (4, 0) (1, 3) (2, 5) ☐ (4, 2) (−4, 2) ☐
(−5, −3) (−4, 2) (−2, 5) ☐ (−2, −2)
(1, 3) (−5, −5) (−5, −5) ☐ (1, 3) ☐ (4, −4)
(1, 3) (0, 1) ☐ (5, 5) (−2, 1) (2, 5) (4, 0)
☐ (1, 3) ☐ (5, −2) (−5, 4) (1, 3) (4, 2)
(−2, 2) ☐ (−2, 1) (0, 1) ☐ (4, 0) (−2, 1)
(5, −2) ☐ (4, 0) (−2, 2) (1, 3) (4, 2)? ☐
(4, 2) (−4, 2) (−2, 5) (4, 4)!

(b) Change the seventh word to: (5, 5) (−2, 1) (2, 5) (4, 0) (−4, 2) (−2, 5) (2, 5).
Change the last word to: (4, 2) (−4, 2) (−2, 5) (4, 4) (−5, −5) (1, 3) (5, −2).

(c) (5, 5) (4, 0) (1, 3) (2, 5) ☐ (4, 2) (−4, 2) ☐ (−5, −3) (−4, 2) (−2, 5) ☐ (−2, −2)
(1, 3) (−5, −5) (−5, −5) ☐ (1, 3) ☐ (4, 2) (−2, 2) (1, 3) (4, 2) ☐ (−5, 4) (1, 3)
(−3, −4) (−3, −4) (−4, 2) (2, 5)? ☐ (−5, 4) (−4, 2) (−5, −5) (−5, −3) (4, 4) (−4, 2)
(0, 1)!

2 Look at the graph in question **1**. Write down the equation of the line through

(a) T and B   (b) P and G   (c) G and C

3 Work out $\frac{8}{25} + 0.25$

4 The area of the triangle is equal to the area of the trapezium. Calculate the height of the triangle.

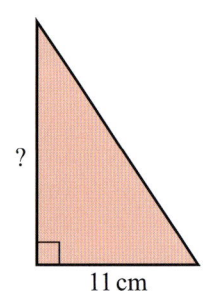

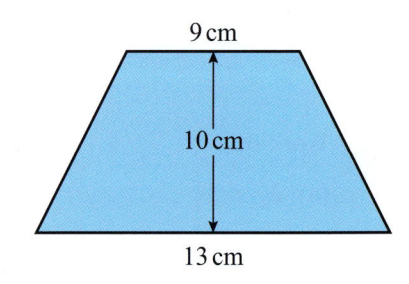

9 cm
10 cm
13 cm
?
11 cm

5 Katya says that $2\frac{3}{4} > \frac{17}{6}$. *Explain clearly* whether Katya is correct or not.

6 A rectangle has an area of 40 cm² with its longest side equal to 8 cm.
A square has an area of 49 cm².
Which shape has the longer perimeter and by how much?

7 Which line is steeper on the graph opposite: P or Q? Give the values of their gradients to support your answer.

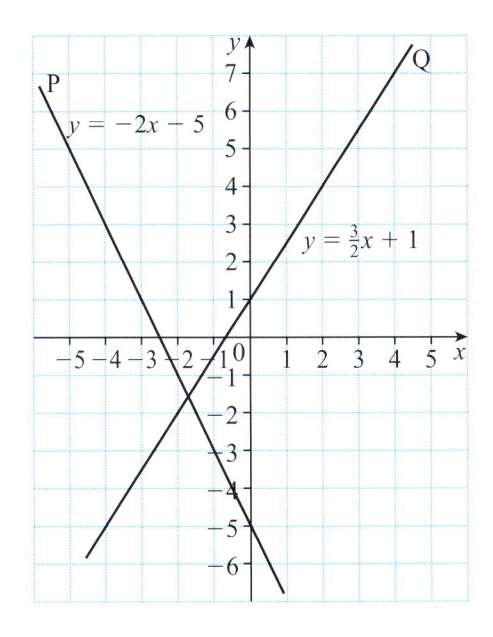

8 How many panes of glass 30 cm by 20 cm can be cut from a sheet which is 1 metre square?

9 Grass seed should be sown at the rate of $\frac{3}{4}$ of an ounce per square yard.

One packet of seed contains 3 lb of seed. How many packets of seed are needed for a rectangular garden measuring 60 feet by 36 feet? [3 feet = 1 yard, 16 ounces = 1 lb]

10 Chen invests £7800 in a business. Two years later he checks the value of his investment and finds that it has increased to $3\frac{5}{6}$ of its original value.

Chen is pleasantly surprised. How much money is his investment now worth?

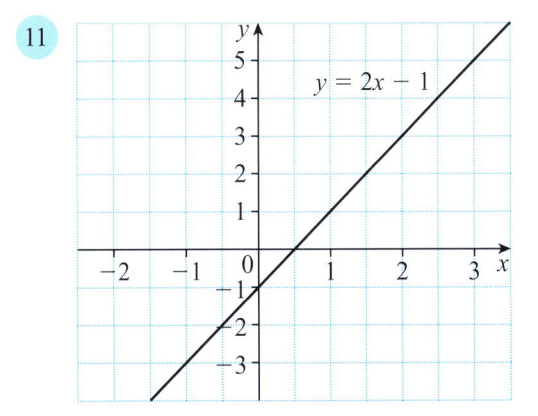

11 Grayson says the gradient of the line opposite is 1. Sophia does not agree. Who is correct and why?

Puzzles and Problems 2

Cross numbers

Make four copies of the pattern below and complete the puzzles using the clues given. To avoid confusion it is better not to write the small reference numbers 1–18 on your patterns.

Part A [No calculators]

Across

1. 499 + 43
3. 216 × 7
5. 504 ÷ 9
6. 8214 − 3643
8. Half of 192
9. 20% of 365
10. Prime number between 30 and 36
11. 213 + 62 + 9
13. 406 ÷ 7
15. 316 × 23
17. 1000 − 731
18. Next prime number after 200

Down

1. 1% of 5700
2. 600 − 365
4. 6^3
7. 4488 ÷ 6
8. $30^2 + 3 \times 6$
9. 10 000 − 2003
11. 4 × 4 × 4 × 4
12. 58.93 × (67 + 33)
14. 1136 − 315
16. $11^2 - 10^2$

In parts **B**, **C** and **D** a calculator may be used [where absolutely necessary!]. Write any decimal points on the lines between squares.

Part B

Across

1. $9 \times 10 \times 11$
3. Ninety less than ten thousand
5. $\left(7\tfrac{1}{2}\right)^2$ to the nearest whole number
6. $140.52 \div 0.03$
8. Last two digits of 99^2
9. $3^2 + 4^2 + 5^2 + 6^2$
10. Angle between the hands of a clock at 2.00 pm
11. Eight pounds and eight pence
13. Next prime number after 89
15. 11% of 213
17. 3.1 m plus 43 cm, in cm
18. Area of a square of side 15 cm.

Down

1. $\dfrac{5 \times 6 \times 7 \times 8}{2} - 11 \times 68$
2. 26% as a decimal
4. 0.1^2
7. Next in the sequence $102\tfrac{1}{2}$, 205, 410
8. $1 - 0.97$
9. 52% of £158.50
11. $0.0854 \div (7 - 6.99)$
12. $10^3 + 11^3$
14. $3 \times 5 \times 7^2$
16. Half of a third of 222

Part C

Across

1. Next square number after 144
3. 5.2 m written in mm
5. Total of the numbers on a dice
6. $0.1234 \div 0.01^2$
8. Ounces in a pound
9. Inches in a yard
10. $3^4 + 56.78 \times 0$
11. Next in the sequence 1, 2, 6, 24, 120
13. One foot four inches, in inches
15. 234 m written in km
17. $\tfrac{1}{25}$ as a decimal
18. [Number of letters in 'ridiculous']^2

Down

1. $1\tfrac{4}{5}$ as a decimal
2. $\dfrac{34^2 + 319.2}{1.4 + 0.2}$
4. 66% as a decimal
7. Days in a year minus 3
8. Number of minutes between 13.22 and 15.12
9. Seconds in an hour
11. Double 225 plus treble 101
12. A quarter to midnight on the 24 h clock
14. $2^3 \times 3 \times 5^2$
16. $\left(5\tfrac{1}{3}\right)^2$ to the nearest whole number

Part D

Across

1. 20% of 15% of £276
3. $81.23 \times 9.79 \times 11.2$, to the nearest thousand
5. Three dozen
6. 1.21 m in mm
8. Solve $2x - 96 = 72$
9. Inches in two feet
10. $6.6 \div 0.1$
11. $\frac{1}{4} - \frac{1}{5}$ as a decimal
13. Volume of a cube of side 4 units
15. $555 + 666 + 777$
17. A gross
18. $\left(19\frac{1}{4}\right)^2$ to the nearest whole number

Down

1. Next in the sequence 25, 36, 49, 64
2. $900 - \left(\frac{17 \times 12}{3}\right)$
4. 0.2×0.2
7. Solve $x^3 = 1$ million
8. $9 - 0.36$
9. $8^3 + 9^3 + 10^3$
11. 99% as a decimal
12. 20% of 2222
14. $0.2055 \div 0.0005$
16. 4 score plus ten

Mental Arithmetic Practice 2

There are two sets of mental arithmetic questions in this section. Ideally a teacher will read out each question twice, with pupils' books closed. Each test should take about 20 minutes.

Test 1

1. Share a cost of £72 between 8 people.
2. Write three fifths as a percentage.
3. How many angles has a pentagon?
4. I have five 20p, six 10p and three 2p coins. How much do I have?
5. Write the number seventeen thousand and twelve in figures.
6. Change two and a quarter metres into centimetres.
7. A train leaves at 7.40 and arrives at 9.30. How long is the journey in minutes?
8. Write three hundredths as a decimal.
9. Take away 18 from 300.
10. Work out ten per cent of £42.
11. A plane flies at 140 km/h for three hours. How far does it fly?
12. What five coins make 62p?
13. The product of two numbers is forty-five. What are the two numbers? Give two possible answers.
14. How many 5p coins do I need for 65p?
15. How many centimetres are there in a kilometre?
16. What is the cost of three DVDs at £2.99 each?
17. A shirt costs £40. How much do I pay if there is a ten per cent discount?

18. A drink costs £1.65. What is the change from £5?
19. What number is half way between 5 and 5.3?
20. What is the perimeter of a square which has an area of 36 cm^2?
21. I have three mice and two snakes. What percentage of my pets are mice?
22. Oranges cost 75 pence for five. How much does one cost?
23. Greg saves 25 pence a day. How long will it take to save four pounds?
24. How many lengths of 8 cm can be cut from 60 cm?
25. Increase eighty pounds by 25 per cent.

Test 2

1. What four coins make 42p? Give two possible answers.
2. I buy two pens at 99 pence each. What change do I get from £5?
3. What is 20 per cent of sixty kilograms?
4. What number is three times as big as eighteen?
5. I have ninety-four 2 pence coins. How much is that in pounds and pence?
6. What is the smaller angle between the hands of a clock at two o'clock?
7. One pound is the same as 1.5 euros. How many euros do I get for twenty pounds?
8. A football costs £8.95. Find the change from £20.
9. A book is six millimetres thick. How tall is a pile of fifty books? Give your answer in metres.
10. Add together £2.75 and £2.50.
11. Write one twentieth as a percentage.
12. In a room sixteen out of fifty children are boys. What percentage is that?
13. How many 5p coins are needed to make £4?
14. Two angles of an isosceles triangle are each 65°. What is the third angle?
15. A lottery prize of eight million pounds is shared equally between 100 people. How much does each person receive?
16. Add together 11, 27 and 9.
17. What is two thirds of thirty-nine?
18. Find the sum of the first four prime numbers.
19. A square has sides of length one metre. Find the area of the square in square centimetres.
20. If May 11th is a Monday, what day of the week is May 20th?
21. True or false: 'There are six inches in a foot'.
22. How many minutes are there between eleven a.m. and two p.m. on the same day?
23. What is three point nought three multiplied by one thousand?
24. Write down any square number greater than seventy.
25. A coach starts at four fifty. It takes twenty-five minutes. At what time does it arrive?

146

> A long time ago! 2

The four colour theorem

If you need to colour the areas on a map (in geography, history, etc.), it should be possible to use no more than four colours. At no boundary between two areas must the same colour be used for both areas.

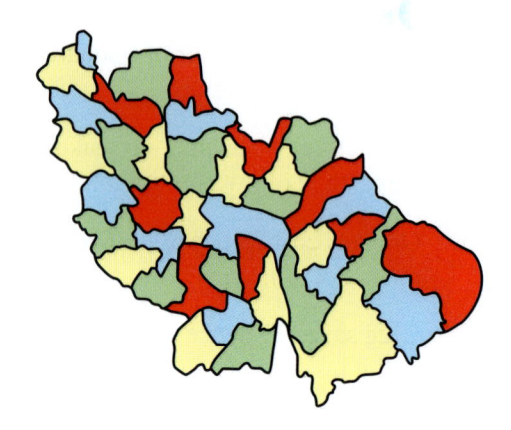

You may have two areas of the same colour meeting at a single point if necessary. A gentleman called August Ferdinand Möbius first wrote about this problem in the nineteenth century.

Exercise

Make a rough copy of each map below and try to colour each section using four colours only. The colour in one section must not be the same as that in any section next to it.

1

2

3

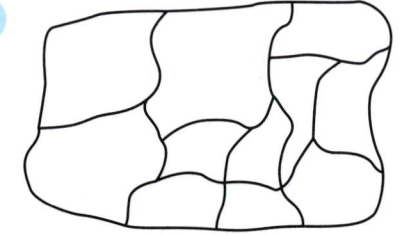

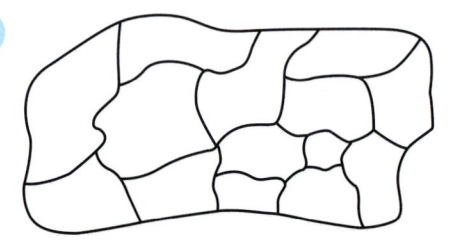

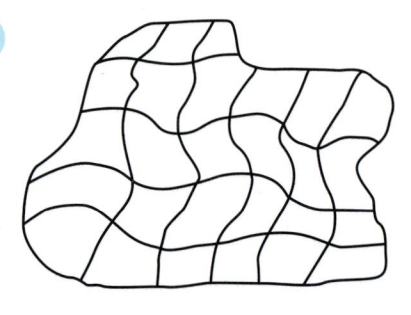

4 Have you managed with four colours only so far? Now draw your own map and see if no more than four colours are needed to fill it in.

At last! This theorem was finally proved to be correct late in the twentieth century by using a computer programme.

UNIT 3

3.1 Properties of numbers

In section 3.1 you will:
- review prime numbers
- use factors and multiples of numbers
- learn about square numbers and cube numbers

Prime numbers

A prime number has 2 factors only (ie. it is divisible by only two different numbers: by itself and by one). The first six prime numbers are 2, 3, 5, 7, 11 and 13.
Note that 1 has only one factor so is *not* a prime number.

Exercise 1M

1. The prime numbers up to 100 or 200 can be found as follows:
   - Write the numbers in 8 columns (leave space underneath to go up to 200 later).
   - Cross out 1 and draw circles around 2, 3, 5 and 7.
   - Draw 4 vertical lines to cross out the even numbers (apart from 2).
   - Draw 6 diagonal lines to cross out the multiples of 3.
   - Draw 2 diagonal lines to cross out the multiples of 7.
   - Cross out any numbers ending in 5.
   - Draw circles around all the numbers which have not been crossed out. These are the prime numbers. Check that you have 25 prime numbers up to 100.

1	2	3	4	5	6	7	8
9	10	11	12	13	14	15	16
17	18	19	20	21	22	23	24
25	26	27	28	29	30	31	32
33	34	35	36	37	38	39	40
41	42	43	44	45	46	47	48
49	50	51	52	53	54	55	56
57	58	59	60	61	62	63	64
65	66	67	68	69	70	71	72
73	74	75	76	77	78	79	80
81	82	83	84	85	86	87	88
89	90	91	92	93	94	95	96
97	98	99	100	101	102	103	104

↑ A   ↑ B

2 Selmin looked at her circled prime numbers and she thought she noticed a pattern. She thought that all the prime numbers in columns A and B could be written as the sum of two square numbers.

For example $17 = 1^2 + 4^2$
$41 = 4^2 + 5^2$

Was Selmin right? Can *all* the prime numbers in columns A and B be written like this?

3 Extend the table up to 200 and draw in more lines to cross out multiples of 2, 3 and 7.
You will also have to cross out any multiples of 11 and 13 which would otherwise be missed. (Can you see why?)
Does the pattern Selmin noticed still work?

4 Write down the two numbers in each line which are prime.
(a) 14, 17, 21, 27, 29, 39
(b) 41, 45, 49, 51, 63, 67
(c) 2, 57, 71, 81, 91, 93

5 Alicia writes down all the prime numbers that are even.
What does she write down?

6 Write down two prime numbers which add up to another prime number.
Do this in three ways.

Exercise 2M

1 How many of the prime numbers between 1 and 100 are odd?

2 Find three pairs of prime numbers with a difference of 4 between the numbers.

3 When two prime numbers are added the answer is 22.
What could the two numbers be?

4 (a) List the prime numbers ending in 1 which are smaller than 100.
(b) List the prime numbers ending in 7 which are smaller than 100.
(c) Apart from 5 why do no prime numbers end in 5?

5 Answer *true* or *false* for the statement below:

'For all whole numbers greater than one there is at least one prime number between that number and its double.'

6 A rectangle has an area of 23 cm².
Its length and width are both a whole number of centimetres.
What is the perimeter of the rectangle?

7 Find three prime numbers which add up to another prime number.

8 (a) Multiply the first two prime numbers together and then add 1. Is the answer a prime number?
(b) Work out $(2 \times 3 \times 5) + 1$. Is the answer prime?
(c) Work out $(2 \times 3 \times 5 \times 7) + 1$. Is the answer prime?
(d) Work out $(2 \times 3 \times 5 \times 7 \times 11) + 1$. Is the answer prime?
(e) Do we always get a prime number using this method?

Multiples

The *multiples* of 5 divide by 5 with no remainder.

The first four multiples of 5 are 5, 10, 15, 20.

The first four multiples of 6 are 6, 12, 18, 24.

'The multiples of 5 are the numbers in the 5 times table'

Factors

The *factors* of 8 are 1, 2, 4, 8
because $1 \times 8 = 8$ and $2 \times 4 = 8$

Exercise 3M

1 Copy and complete
(a) 25, 30, 35 and 60 are all multiples of ☐
(b) 14, 21, 35 and 70 are all multiples of ☐
(c) 8, 12, 20 and 28 are all multiples of ☐ and ☐

2 Write down the first four multiples of 37.

3 Write down all the factors of (a) 24 (b) 60 (c) 85

4 Find two 1 digit numbers that have 4 factors.

5 Find two numbers less than 20 that have 6 factors.

6 Find three numbers that are multiples of both 3 and 4.

7 What is the smallest number with exactly 3 factors.

8 Write down the numbers in the hoop which are
(a) multiples of 12
(b) factors of 12

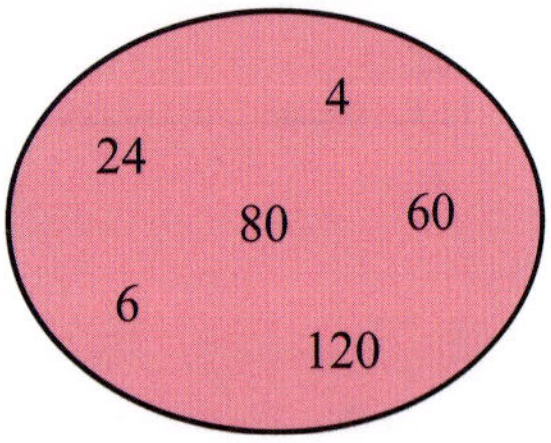

(Hoop contains: 24, 4, 80, 60, 6, 120)

9 Find three numbers that are multiples of 2, 3 and 5.

10 The number in each circle is the product of the numbers in the squares on either side. Find the missing numbers.

(a) circles: 56, 42, 48

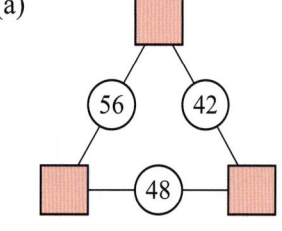

(b) circles: 36, 45, 20

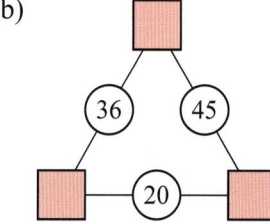

(c) circles: 84, 60, 35

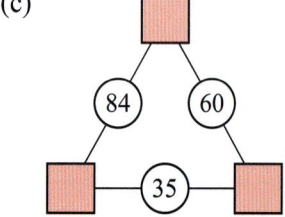

(d) circles: 18, 99, 22

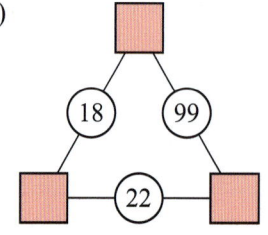

11 What is the smallest number with exactly
(a) 4 factors
(b) 5 factors?

12 Write down a 3 digit number that does not have 2, 3 or 7 as a factor.

Prime factors

Factors of a number which are also prime numbers are called *prime factors*.

24 = 2 × 2 × 2 × 3   Numbers can be written as products
60 = 2 × 2 × 3 × 5   of prime factors as shown.

These prime factors can be found by using a 'factor tree' as shown on the next page.

Factor trees

(a) Here is a factor tree for 60

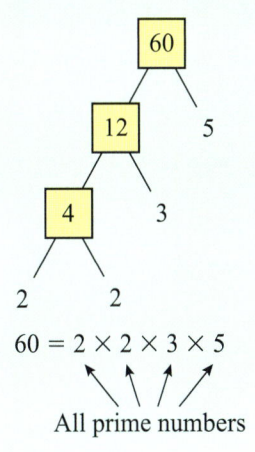

```
        60
       /  \
      12   5
     /  \
    4    3
   / \
  2   2
```

60 = 2 × 2 × 3 × 5
All prime numbers

Use pairs of factors to make each number.

(b) Here is a factor tree for 24

```
        24
       /  \
      6    4
     /\   /\
    3  2 2  2
```

24 = 3 × 2 × 2 × 2
Product means multiply

Exercise 4M

1. Complete these factor trees.
   (a) 30 / 2, 15
   (b) 70 / 5, 14
   (c) 100 / 10, 10

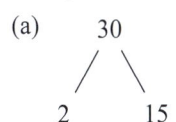

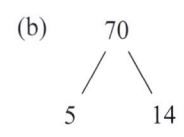

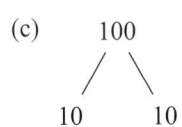

2. Write the following numbers as products of their prime factors.
   (a) 30
   (b) 70
   (c) 100

3. William draws the factor tree below for 90.

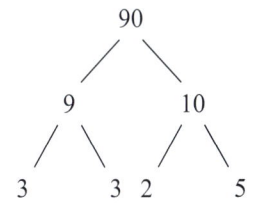

```
        90
       /  \
      9    10
     /\   /\
    3  3 2  5
```

   Ara draws the factor tree below for 90.

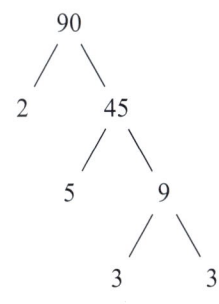

```
        90
       /  \
      2    45
          /  \
         5    9
             / \
            3   3
```

   Which factor tree is correct? Give reasons for your answer.

4. Write each number below as a product of its prime factors by first drawing a factor tree.
   (a) 40
   (b) 72
   (c) 120
   (d) 29
   (e) 150
   (f) 102
   (g) 350
   (h) 550
   (i) 1500
   (j) 2464
   (k) 4620
   (l) 98 175

5 (a) Write each of 26, 22, 312, 104 and 78 as a product of its prime factors.
   (b) Use the above answers to decide which of the above numbers will divide exactly into 312. Justify your answer.

L.C.M. and H.C.F.

The first few multiples of 4 are 4, 8, 12, 16, ⑳, 24, 28...

The first few multiples of 5 are 5, 10, 15, ⑳, 25, 30, 35 ...

The *Least Common Multiple* (L.C.M) of 4 and 5 is 20.

It is the lowest number which is in both lists.

Exercise 5M

1 Find the L.C.M. of
   (a) 6 and 9
   (b) 8 and 12
   (c) 14 and 35
   (d) 2, 4 and 6
   (e) 3, 5 and 10
   (f) 4, 7 and 9

The factors of 12 are 1, 2, 3, ④, 6, 12

The factors of 20 are 1, 2, ④, 5, 10, 20

The *Highest Common Factor* (H.C.F.) of 12 and 20 is 4.

It is the highest number which is in both lists.

2 The table shows the factors and common factors of 24 and 36

number	factors	common factors
24	1, 2, 3, 4, 6, 8, 12, 24	1, 2, 3, 4, 6, 12
36	1, 2, 3, 4, 6, 9, 12, 18, 36	

   Write down the H.C.F. of 24 and 36.

3 Find the H.C.F. of
   (a) 12 and 18
   (b) 22 and 55
   (c) 45 and 72
   (d) 12, 18 and 30
   (e) 36, 60 and 72
   (f) 20, 40 and 50

4 Don't confuse your L.C.M. s with your H.C.F. s!
   (a) Find the H.C.F. of 12 and 30.
   (b) Find the L.C.M. of 8 and 20.
   (c) Write down two numbers whose H.C.F. is 11.
   (d) Write down two numbers whose L.C.M. is 10.

5. One musician busks outside the library every 40 minutes. Another musician busks outside the library every 50 minutes. If they are both outside the library at 10:30 am, when will they both be outside the library again at the same time?

6. Josiah spends £3.51 on the stamps for some letters, Natalie spends £2.16 on stamps for her letters.
What is the cost of one stamp if Josiah and Natalie buy 21 stamps in total?

L.C.M and H.C.F. with a Venn diagram

The prime factors of two numbers can be written in a Venn diagram.

For example, $924 = 2 \times 2 \times 3 \times 7 \times 11$
and $1386 = 2 \times 3 \times 3 \times 7 \times 11$

Venn diagram

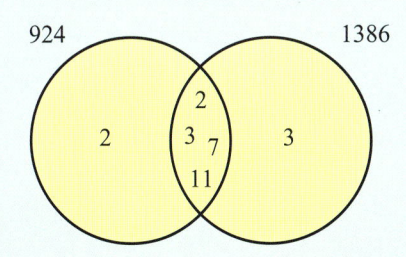

Multiply the numbers in the intersection to find the H.C.F.
H.C.F. $= 2 \times 3 \times 7 \times 11 = 462$

Multiply *all* the numbers in the Venn diagram to find the L.C.M.
L.C.M. $= 2 \times 2 \times 3 \times 3 \times 7 \times 11 = 2772$

Exercise 5E

1. The Venn diagram opposite shows the prime factors for 30 and 165.
Work out
   (a) the H.C.F. of 30 and 165
   (b) the L.C.M. of 30 and 165

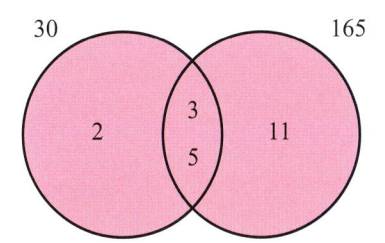

2. (a) If $315 = 3 \times 3 \times 5 \times 7$ and $273 = 3 \times 7 \times 13$, draw a Venn diagram for the prime factors of 315 and 273.
   (b) Work out the H.C.F. of 315 and 273.
   (c) Work out the L.C.M of 315 and 273.

3 (a) If $1386 = 2 \times 3 \times 3 \times 7 \times 11$ and $858 = 2 \times 3 \times 11 \times 13$, draw a Venn diagram for the prime factors of 1386 and 858.

(b) Work out the H.C.F. of 1386 and 858.

(c) Work out the L.C.M. of 1386 and 858.

4 Draw factor trees then Venn diagrams to find the H.C.F. and L.C.M. of each pair of numbers below.

(a) 650 and 1365 (b) 315 and 270 (c) 1170 and 10 725

5 A number P has the prime factors 11 and 17 only.
Another number Q has a highest common factor with number P of 17.
Write down the values of P and Q if Q is between 350 and 370.

Square numbers

A square number is obtained by multiplying a number by itself.

3×3 is written 3^2 (we say '3 squared ...')

4×4 is written 4^2

$3^2 = 9$

Exercise 6M

1 Work out

(a) $3^2 + 4^2$ (b) $1^2 + 2^2 + 3^2$ (c) $9^2 + 10^2$

2 The sum of the square numbers 9 and 81 is 90.
Find a pair of square numbers with a sum of

(a) 13   (b) 73   (c) 40   (d) 181
(e) 125 (f) 97   (g) 74   (h) 113

3 Here is a 6×6 square divided into 9 smaller squares.
Draw a 5×5 square and design a pattern which divides it into nine smaller squares.

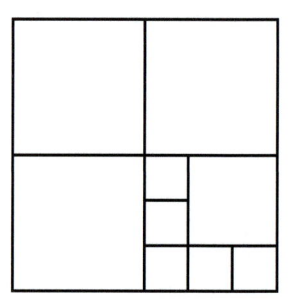

4 Which square number is between

(a) 50 and 70 (b) 70 and 100 (c) 150 and 180?

5 (a) Write down this sequence and fill in the missing numbers

   1   = 1   = 1^2
   1 + 3   = 4   = 2^2
   1 + 3 + 5   = ☐   = ☐^{2}
   1 + 3 + 5 + 7 = ☐   = ☐^{2}

   (b) Write down the next five lines of the sequence.

6 Liam says that if you multiply two square numbers together, you will always get another square number. Is Liam correct?

7 What number when multiplied by itself gives
   (a) 49   (b) 121   (c) 169

8 Look at the numbers in the pentagon.
   Write down the numbers which are
   (a) factors of 16   (b) prime numbers
   (c) multiples of 3   (d) square numbers

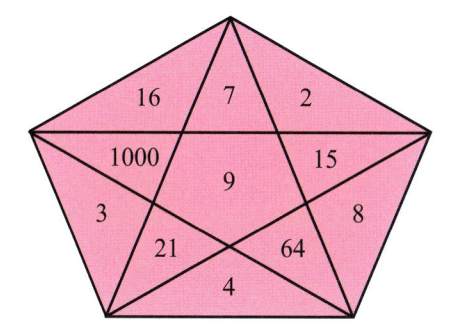

   (Numbers in pentagon: 16, 7, 2, 1000, 9, 15, 3, 8, 21, 64, 4)

9 Find a pair of square numbers with a difference of
   (a) 7   (b) 80   (c) 84   (d) 300
   (e) 45   (f) 32   (g) 39   (h) 105

10 (a) Does $(2 + 3)^2$ equal $2^2 + 3^2$?
   (b) Does $(5 + 6)^2$ equal $5^2 + 6^2$?
   (c) Explain why $(a + b)^2$ is not equal to $a^2 + b^2$ for all values of a and b.

11 Does $(a \times b)^2$ equal $a^2 \times b^2$ for all values of a and b? Justify your answer.

Cube numbers

$1 \times 1 \times 1 = 1^3 = 1$ (we say '1 cubed')
$2 \times 2 \times 2 = 2^3 = 8$ (we say '2 cubed')
$3 \times 3 \times 3 = 3^3 = 27$ (we say '3 cubed')

The numbers 1, 8, 27 are the first three *cube* numbers.

Exercise 7M

1 Work out values of the first ten cube numbers.

2 The odd numbers can be added in groups to give an interesting sequence:

$$1 = 1 = 1^3$$
$$3 + 5 = 8 = 2^3$$
$$7 + 9 + 11 = 27 = 3^3$$

Write down the next three rows of the sequence to see if the sum of each row always gives a cube number.

3 Work out the values of
(a) $(-2)^3$ (b) $(-3)^3$ (c) $(-4)^3$ (d) $(-5)^3$
(e) Comment on your answers.

4 The difference between two cube numbers is 61.
Write down the two cube numbers.

5 The *square root* of a number is the number which is multiplied by itself to give that number. The symbol for square root is $\sqrt{}$.
So $\sqrt{9} = 3$, $\sqrt{16} = 4$, $\sqrt{100} = 10$
Work out
(a) $\sqrt{25}$ (b) $\sqrt{81}$ (c) $\sqrt{49}$ (d) $\sqrt{1}$

6 Copy the following and fill in the spaces.
(a) $7^2 = 49, \sqrt{49} = \square$ (b) $14^2 = 196, \sqrt{196} = \square$
(c) $21^2 = 441, \sqrt{\square} = 21$ (d) $3.3^2 = 10.89, \sqrt{\square} = 3.3$

7 (a) What number multiplied by itself three times gives 125?
This number is called the *cube root* of 125.
The symbol for cube root is $\sqrt[3]{}$.
So $\sqrt[3]{64} = 4$ because $4 \times 4 \times 4 = 64$.
(b) Work out the value of $\sqrt[3]{216}$

8 Work out
(a) $\sqrt[3]{729}$ (b) $\sqrt[3]{343} - \sqrt[3]{8}$ (c) $\sqrt[3]{1} + \sqrt[3]{8} + \sqrt[3]{27}$

9 Work out
(a) $\sqrt[3]{512} - \sqrt{49}$ (b) $3^2 + \sqrt[3]{125} - \sqrt{64}$ (c) $\sqrt[3]{(116 + 100)} - \sqrt{25}$

10 Work out

(a) $\sqrt[3]{-8}$ (b) $\sqrt[3]{-125}$ (c) $\sqrt[3]{-1000}$

Comment on your answers.

Satisfied numbers

The number 4 is an even number *and* a square number. It *satisfies* both categories.

1 Copy the grid below and use a pencil for your answers (so that you can rub out mistakes). Write the numbers from 1 to 9, one in each box, so that all the numbers satisfy the conditions for both the row and the column.

	Number between 5 and 9	Square number	Prime number
Factor of 6	6	?	?
Even number	?	?	?
Odd number	?	?	?

2 Copy the grid and write the numbers from 1 to 9, one in each box.

	Prime number	Multiple of 3	Factor of 16
Number greater than 5			
Odd number			
Even number			

3 This one is more difficult. Write the numbers from 1 to 16, one in each box. There are several correct solutions. Ask a friend to check yours.

	Prime number	Odd number	Factor of 16	Even number
Numbers less than 7				
Factor of 36				
Numbers less than 12				
Numbers between 11 and 17				

4 Design a grid with categories of your own and ask a friend to solve it.

Happy numbers

- (a) Take any number, say 23.
  (b) Square the digits and add: $2^2 + 3^2 = 4 + 9 = 13$
  (c) Repeat (b) for the answer: $1^2 + 3^2 = 1 + 9 = 10$
  (d) Repeat (b) for the answer: $1^2 + 0^2 = 1$
      23 is a so-called 'happy' number because it ends in one.

- Take another number, say 7.
  Write 7 as 07 to maintain the pattern of squaring and adding the digits.
  Here is the sequence:

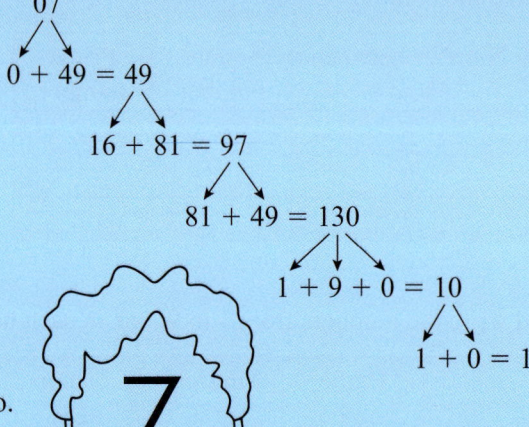

  $$07$$
  $$0 + 49 = 49$$
  $$16 + 81 = 97$$
  $$81 + 49 = 130$$
  $$1 + 9 + 0 = 10$$
  $$1 + 0 = 1$$

  So 7 is a happy number also.

  With practice you may be able to do the arithmetic in your head and write:
  $07 \rightarrow 49 \rightarrow 97 \rightarrow 130 \rightarrow 10 \rightarrow 1$.
  You may find it helpful to make a list of the square numbers $1^2, 2^2, 3^2, \ldots 9^2$.

- Your task is to find all the happy numbers from 1 to 100 and to circle them on a grid like the one shown. This may appear to be a very time-consuming and rather tedious task! But remember: Good mathematicians always look for short cuts and for ways of reducing the working.

  So think about what you are doing and good luck!

  As a final check you should find that there are 20 happy numbers from 1 to 100.

1	2	3	4	5	6	7	8	9	10
11	12	13	14	15	16	17	18	19	20
21	22	23	24	25	26	27	28	29	30
31	32	33	34	35	36	37	38	39	40
41	42	43	44	45	46	47	48	49	50
51	52	53	54	55	56	57	58	59	60
61	62	63	64	65	66	67	68	69	70
71	72	73	74	75	76	77	78	79	80
81	82	83	84	85	86	87	88	89	90
91	92	93	94	95	96	97	98	99	100

Need more practice with properties of numbers?

1 Which numbers below are not square numbers?

    1   4   8   25   49   84

2 The table shows the factors and common factors of 18 and 24

number	factors	common factors
18	1, 2, 3, 6, 9, 18	}1, 2, 3, 6
24	1, 2, 3, 4, 6, 8, 12, 24	

Write down the H.C.F. of 18 and 24.

3 Write each number below as a product of its prime factors by first drawing a factor tree.

    (a) 60   (b) 210   (c) 390   (d) 112

4 Write down two prime numbers between 30 and 40.

5 The digit sum of 16 is 7 [1 + 6]. How many factors has 16?

6 (a) Find the digit sum and the number of factors of
       (i) 24   (ii) 84

   (b) Can you find any other 2 digit numbers whose digit sum is equal to the number of its factors?

7 The number 345 has 3 and 5 as factors.
Write another 3 digit number which has 3 and 5 as factors.

8 Rory can swim a length in 40 seconds and Arlo can swim a length in 70 seconds. They both start swimming from one end of the pool at the same time.

How many more lengths will Rory have completed than Arlo when they are both back for the first time at that end of the pool at the same time?

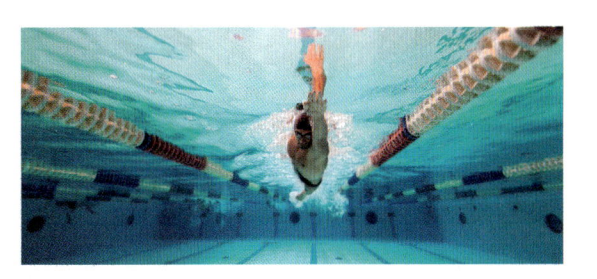

9 The factor tree for the number n is shown opposite. p is a prime number. Explain what this tells you about the number n?

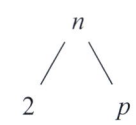

          n
        / \\
      2   p

10 *Lagrange's theorem.* A famous mathematician called Lagrange proved that every whole number could be written as the sum of four or fewer square numbers.

For example: $21 = 16 + 4 + 1$
$19 = 16 + 1 + 1 + 1$
$35 = 25 + 9 + 1$

Check that the theorem applies to the following numbers.

(a) 10   (b) 24   (c) 47   (d) 66   (e) 98
(f) 63   (g) 120   (h) 141   (i) 423

If you can find a number which needs more than four squares you will have disproved Lagrange's theorem and a new theorem will be named after you.

Extension questions with properties of numbers

1 The number 432 has 2 and 9 as factors.
Write another 3 digit number which has 2 and 9 as factors.

2 Which number less than 100 has the most prime factors?

3 Which number less than 1000 has the most *different* prime factors? (You cannot repeat a factor.)

4 What is the smallest whole number which is exactly divisible by all the numbers from 1 to 10 inclusive?

5 Use a Venn diagram to find the highest common factor and the lowest common multiple of 1911 and 2002.

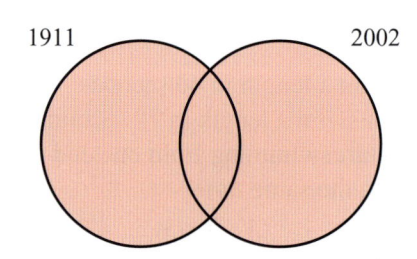

1911   2002

6 In its prime factors, $588 = 2 \times 2 \times 3 \times 7 \times 7$.
What is the smallest number by which you can multiply 588 so that the answer is a square number?

7 Write 8820 in its prime factors. What is the smallest number by which you can multiply 8820 so that the answer is a square number?

8 The ground floor of a house is 10 m by 10 m.
It is split into four rooms.
One of the rooms is a 6 m square and one room
is a 4 m by 6 m rectangle.

One of the other rooms is a square and one is
a rectangle.
What is the area of the smaller square room?

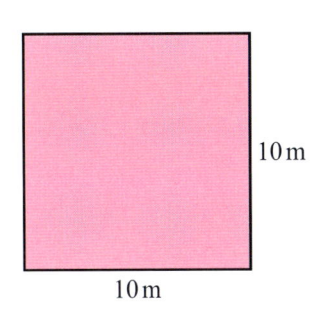

10 m

10 m

(a) Is 307 a prime number?

You might think that we need to test whether 307 is divisible by
2, 3, 4, 5, 6, 7, 8, ... 306. This would be both tedious and unnecessary.

In fact, if 307 is divisible by any number at all it will certainly be divisible by a prime number less than $\sqrt{307}$.

Since $\sqrt{307}$ is about 17.5, we only need to test whether 307 is divisible by
2, 3, 5, 7, 11, 13, 17.

Using a calculator, we find that 307 is not divisible by any of these, so we know that 307 *is* a prime number.

(b) Is 689 a prime number?

Since $\sqrt{689} \approx 26.2$, we only need to test whether 689 is divisible by
2, 3, 5, 7, 11, 13, 17, 19, 23.

Using a calculator we find that 689 is divisible by 13.
We do not need to go any further than this.

We now know that 689 is *not* a prime number.

9 Use your calculator to find which of the following are prime numbers.
 (a) 293 (b) 407 (c) 799 (d) 335
 (e) 709 (f) 1261 (g) 923 (h) 1009

10 One very large prime number is $2^{86243} - 1$. The number has 25 962 digits.
 (a) How long would it take to write out this number, assuming that you could maintain a rate of 1 digit every second? Give your answer in hours, minutes and seconds.
 (b) How many pages would you need to write out this number if you could write 50 digits on a line and 30 lines on a page?

3.2 Further arithmetic

In section 3.2 you will:

- Practise arithmetic with whole numbers and decimals

Reminder

327 × 45

```
   327
 ×  45
------
  1635   (327 × 5)
 13080   (327 × 40)
------
 14715
```

1161 ÷ 27

```
      4 3
 27)1161
   -108↓    (27 × 4)
   ----
      81
     -81    (27 × 3)
     ---
       0
```

Exercise 1M

1 Work out

(a) 36 × 29 (b) 54 × 21 (c) 312 × 24
(d) 207 × 32 (e) 27 × 27 (f) 241 × 32
(g) 480 ÷ 15 (h) 714 ÷ 21 (i) 962 ÷ 26

2 Copy and complete

(a) 32 × 17 = ☐☐☐
(b) 11 × ☐☐☐ = 3575
(c) ☐☐ × 17 = 408
(d) 22 × 55 = ☐☐☐☐

3 56 people decide to go to an Amusement Park.
A ticket for the day is £48 per person.
42 of the people travel by coach which costs £16 per person.
The rest of the people travel in 4 cars.
The petrol for each car is £28.
All the 56 people agree to pay an equal amount for the Park ticket and the travel.
How much does each person pay?

4 Eggs are packed twelve to a box. How many boxes are needed for 444 eggs?

5 In this multiplication the missing digits are 2, 3, 4, 5.
Find the missing numbers

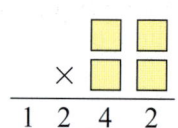

```
        ☐☐
      × ☐☐
      -----
      1 2 4 2
```

6 How many 23-seater coaches will be needed for a school trip for a party of 278?

7 Joe wants to buy as many 34p stamps as possible. He has £5 to spend. How many can he buy and how much change is left?

8 Angelina pays a £1500 deposit for a holiday to Italy followed by 12 monthly instalments of £367.
How much does she pay in total for her holiday?

9 Each class of a school has 31 pupils plus one teacher and there are 15 classes in the school.
The school hall can take 26 rows of chairs with 18 chairs in a row. Is that enough chairs for all the pupils and teachers?

10 When Philip was digging a hole in his garden he struck oil! The oil came out at a rate of £17 for every minute of the day and night.
How much does Philip receive in a 24-hour day?

Reminder

Adding and subtracting decimals – line up the decimal points.

$$2.1 \times 0.03 = 0.063 \qquad \frac{0.7}{0.02} = \frac{70}{2} = 35$$

Exercise 2M

1 Work out
(a) 0.8×0.004
(b) $6 - 1.37$
(c) $7.32 \div 3$
(d) $1.2 \div 0.04$
(e) 1.54×0.9
(f) 0.37^2
(g) $0.32 \div 0.8$
(h) $(2.41 + 0.29)^2$
(i) 0.9^3

2 Gavin spends £4.90 on two items in a shop. One item cost 40p more than the other.
How much did each item cost?

3 Eight ice-creams can be bought for £13.60.
How many ice-creams can be bought for £22.10?

4 Two books cost £18.90 in total.
One book is two-and-a-half times the price of the other.
How much does each book cost?

5 Given that 26 ÷ 8 = 3.25, write down the values of:
(a) 26 ÷ 0.8 (b) 2.6 ÷ 0.8 (c) 0.26 ÷ 0.8

6 Read the newspaper cutting from 'The Times'.
The spray costs £3.99 for 125 ml.
Work out the cost per litre of 'Expert Sensitive Refreshing Facial Spritz'.
(Remember: 1 litre = 1000 ml)

7 *Explain clearly* why 3 ÷ 0.01 = 300.

8 Which is greater and by how much:
0.48^2 or 46.16 ÷ 200?

9 Answer true or false:
$40 \times 4.5 \times 5^2 = (0.314 + 0.17 + 0.016) \times 3^2 \times 1000$

> According to the can it is a "gentle facial spritz specially formulated to refresh and hydrate. Hypoallergenic and fragrance-free it instantly cools and refreshens skin. Lanolin free. Dermatologically tested". Just one small word gives the game away that this is a triumph of marketing over common sense: the only listed ingredient is "Aqua".
> Boots confirmed yesterday that it is selling water at £3.99 for little more than a cupful. Its Expert Sensitive Refreshing Facial Spritz is exactly what it says on the can: water.

10 The perimeter of a square room is 20.8 m. Calculate the area of the room.

Hidden words

(a) Start in the top left box.
(b) Work out the answer to the calculation in the box.
(c) Find the answer in the top corner of another box.
(d) Write down the letter in that box.
(e) Repeat steps (b), (c) and (d) until you arrive back at the top left box. What is the message.

1

6.4	66	274	985	12
5 × 15	L $2^3 + 3^3$	N 20% of 50	E 15 × 100	S 756 ÷ 9
422	75	1.68	10	2.4
N 10^3	S 150 − 67	R 8 × 22	C 8.7 ÷ 10	I 37 + 385
3.85	176	0.87	1000	83
U 0.16 × 10	E 421 − 147	H 5 + 1.4	F 8.4 ÷ 5	O 385 ÷ 7
55	1500	1.6	35	84
L 1000 − 15	I $\frac{2}{3}$ of 99	N 0.4 × 6	I 25% of 48	S 5.32 − 1.47

2

612	0.8	0.77	0.2	0.62
	T	W	V	T
1.8 + 8.2	5% of 400	$2^3 \times 6$	5×69	20% of 65
32	10	13	18	250
C	B	R	E	U
$50\,000 \div 200$	$\frac{2}{5}$ of 450	0.6×2.6	80% of 80	$0.9^2 - 0.1^2$
1.56	0.6	180	0.15	64
E	R	E	S	S
$\frac{3}{8}$ of 48	$\frac{1}{2}$ of 0.3	$(0.2)^2$	0.32×10^2	$806 - 194$
0.04	0.27	20	48	345
A	O	D	N	E
10% of 2	$770 \div 1000$	$0.3 - 0.03$	3.1×0.2	$4.2 \div 7$

3

1.1	100.9	1.55	5.14	1
	Y	D	O	I
5.2 + 52	0.1% of 40 000	0.5×11	$\frac{1}{3}$ of 19.5	$0 \div 0.07$
1000	84	6.5	57.2	5100
E	E	R	C	D
$26.6 \div 7$	$\frac{1}{100}$ of 170	$999 + 998$	$77 \div 100$	2.1×40
0.2	3.5	6.4	0.08	3.8
U	H	D	S	H
half of 199	$10^5 \times 0.01$	5.1×1000	100×0.011	0.6×0.7
0.77	14.7	1997	5.5	40
A	W	D	T	O
2.1×9	$46.26 \div 9$	0.4×0.2	$4.2 - 0.7$	100×0.002
0.42	0	99.5	1.7	18.9
I	N	F	N	N
$25.1 - 18.7$	$0.15 + 1.4$	$100 \times 0.1 \times 0.1$	$6 + 8.7$	$111 - 10.1$

4

45 H $\frac{1}{2}+\frac{1}{4}$	4 C 2^4	371 A $10 \div 1000$	21 S $5 \div 8$	0.51 S $21 - 5 \times 4$
896 M $1^2 + 2^2 + 3^3$	0.06 E $51 \div 100$	0.05 L 1% of 250	0.01 E $5 \times (5-2)^2$	34 Y 5.1×100
0.625 T $\frac{2}{3} \times \frac{1}{5}$	1 O $6000 \div 20$	$\frac{3}{4}$ M $4 + 5 \times 6$	$\frac{3}{8}$ S 0.3×0.2	32 I 53×7
510 C $\frac{3}{5}$ of 35	16 A $\frac{1}{2} - \frac{1}{8}$	2.5 Y $9 \times 10^2 - 2^2$	300 N $\frac{1}{4} - 0.2$	$\frac{2}{15}$ C $20 \div (12 - 7)$

✘ Spot the mistakes 5 ✘

Number properties and arithmetic

Work through each question below and explain clearly what mistakes have been made. Beware – some questions are correctly done.

1. The lowest common multiple of 18 and 30 is 6.

2. $3^3 = 9$

3. Work out $5542 \div 17$ so $17\overline{)55^24^72}$ with 3 1 4 r 4 above, so the answer is 314 remainder 4

4. $0.072 = \frac{72}{100} = \frac{18}{25}$

5. Express 13 923 as a product of its prime factors.

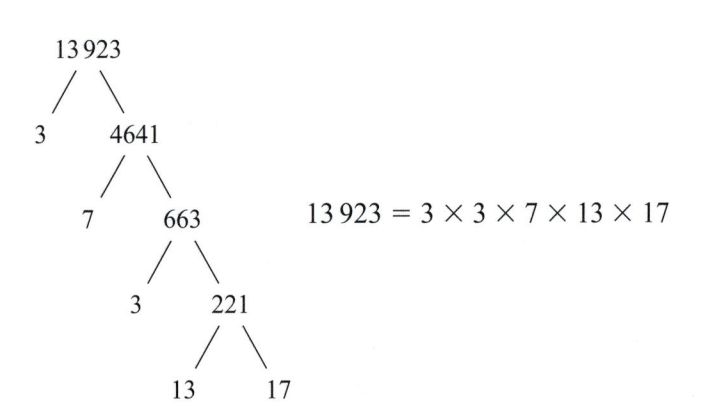

   13 923
   ╱ ╲
   3   4641
       ╱ ╲
       7   663
           ╱ ╲
           3   221
               ╱ ╲
               13 17

   $13\,923 = 3 \times 3 \times 7 \times 13 \times 17$

6    $(-4)^3 + (-3)^2 = -64 + (-9) = -73$

7    $1428 = 2 \times 2 \times 3 \times 7 \times 17$ and $306 = 2 \times 3 \times 3 \times 17$

So lowest common multiple $= 2 \times 2 \times 3 \times 7 \times 17 \times 2 \times 3 \times 3 \times 17$
$$= 436\,968$$

8    $0.32 \times 0.6 = 1.92$

9   A box contains 24 iPads. Each iPad is worth £349. Imi has 26 boxes. What is the value of these 26 boxes?

Number of iPads $= 26 \times 24$
$$= 624$$

```
   26
 × 24
 ----
  104
  520
 ----
  624
```

Value $= 624 \times 349$
$$= £49\,296$$

```
    624
  × 349
  -----
   5616
  24960
  18720
  -----
  49296
```

10    $\sqrt{22.09} = 4.7$ because $4.7 \times 4.7 = 22.09$

```
    47
  × 47
  ----
   329
  1880
  ----
  2209
```

CHECK YOURSELF ON SECTIONS 3.1 AND 3.2

1   Reviewing prime numbers

(a) Write down all the prime numbers between 50 and 60.

(b) Write 100 as the sum of two prime numbers in two different ways.

2   Using factors and multiples of numbers

(a) Find the L.C.M. of 8 and 12.

(b) Find the H.C.F. of 60 and 75.

(c) Express 735 as a product of its prime factors.

3   Square numbers and cube numbers

(a) Work out $1^1 \times 2^2 \times 3^3$

(b) Work out   (i) $\sqrt{81}$ (ii) $4^3 + 5^3$ (iii) $\sqrt{6^2 + 8^2}$

(c) x, y and z are whole numbers such that $x^2 + y^2 = z^2$.
Find the values of x, y and z.

(d) $\sqrt[3]{n} = 8$. Write down the value of n.

4   Arithmetic with whole numbers and decimals

(a) 27×35 (b) 54×327 (c) $1620 \div 36$

(d) How many 49-seater coaches are needed to take 530 people on a trip to Liverpool?

(e) Find the missing numbers

$5.1 \rightarrow \boxed{\times 2.4} \xrightarrow{?} \boxed{+ 0.76} \xrightarrow{?} \boxed{\div 5} \xrightarrow{?}$

(f) Work out $0.2 \div 0.005$

(g) The perimeter of the rectangle shown is 22.6 cm.
Work out the area of the rectangle.

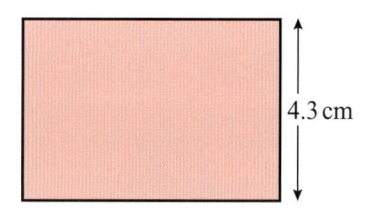

4.3 cm

3.3 Averages and range

In section 3.3 you will:

- review the mean, median, mode and range
- compare sets of data using averages and range
- find averages from frequency tables

The mean
All the data is added and the total is divided by the number of items.

The median
When the data is arranged in order of size, the median is the one in the middle.
If there are two 'middle' numbers, the median is in the middle of these two numbers.

The mode
The number which occurs most often.
A set of data may have more than one mode.

The range
The difference between the largest value and the smallest value.
The range is a measure of how *spread* out the data is. The range is *not* an average.

Exercise 1M

1. Carys and Nina play cricket. During one month they score the runs shown below.
   (a) Find the mean score for Carys.
   (b) Find the mean score for Nina.

Carys			
28	15	41	38
18	3	13	51
39	14		

Nina			
2	23	9	74
46	12	34	16

   (c) Who has the higher mean score and by how much?

2. The shoe sizes of 8 people are: 8, 4, 6, 10, 7, 6, 6, 9
   Find (a) the mean   (b) the median
         (c) the mode   (d) the range

3. (a) Copy and complete: 'For the set of numbers 7, 7, 8, 10, 11, 12, 12, 13, there are ☐ modes. The modes are ☐ and ☐.'
   (b) Find the mode or modes for this set of numbers 2, 3, 3, 3, 5, 5, 7, 8, 8, 8, 10, 10, 11, 11, 12, 12, 12, 14, 15.

4. (a) Calculate the mean of the numbers 8, 5, 3, 8, 7, 5, 6
   (b) Calculate the new mean when the lowest number is removed.

5. The range for nine numbers on a card is 56.
   One number is covered by a piece of blu-tac.
   What could that number be?

55	22	13
38	61	10
24	44	

6. Rena throws a dice ten times and wins 50p if the median score is more than 4.
   The dice shows 5, 6, 5, 2, 1, 4, 6, 3, 6, 2.
   Find the median score.
   Does she win 50p?

7  The temperatures in seven towns across the UK were recorded at 03:00.

Grantham	−1°C	Taunton	0°C
Aberdare	1°C	Burnley	−5°C
Loughborough	−2°C	Portrush	−4°C
Perth	−7°C		

What was the median temperature?

8 Colin has five cards. The mean of the five cards is 7.
The range of the five cards is 8.
What numbers are on the two other cards?

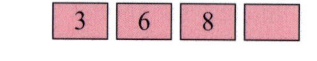

[7] [7] [7] [ ] [ ]

9 There were five people living in a house.
The *median* age of the people was 21 and the range of their ages was 3.
Write each sentence below and write next to it whether it is *True*, *Possible* or *False*.

(a) Every person was either 20 or 21 years old.

(b) The oldest person in the house was 24 years old.

(c) The mean age of the people was less than 21 years.

10 Meg has four cards. The mean of the four cards is 5.
What number is on the final card?

[3] [6] [8] [ ]

11 (a) Sid has three cards. Find the mean.

[5] [2] [11]

(b) Sid takes another card and the mean goes up by 2.
What number is on the new card?

[5] [2] [11] [ ]

12 Cath has five cards. There are two modes which are 11 and 16. The total on all five cards is 69.

(a) Write down the number on each card.

(b) Write down the median.

13 Will has four cards. The mean for three of the cards is 7.
When the fourth card is included, the mean for all four cards is 6.
Write down the number on the fourth card.

Comparing sets of data

The table below shows how many portions of fruit and vegetables are eaten by Calvin and Amy from Monday to Friday one week.

	M	T	W	Th	F
Calvin	1	2	3	4	5
Amy	3	3	3	3	3

Calvin mean $= \frac{15}{5} = 3$

Amy mean $= \frac{15}{5} = 3$

They both have the same average but clearly their pattern of eating is different. To compare the data we use a measure of how *spread out* the data is in addition to comparing an average.

Calvin range $= 5 - 1 = 4$

Amy range $= 3 - 3 = 0$

Amy's portions each day are the same because the range is 0. Calvin's portions each day can differ by up to 4 on any one day.

To compare two sets of data, always write at least two things:
1. Compare an average (i.e. mean, median or mode).
2. Compare the range of each set of data (this shows how spread out the data is).

Exercise 2M

1. 20 children were asked how many baths or showers they had each week (10 children from Year 8 and 10 children from Year 9). The results are given in the graphs below.

   (a) Work out the mean and range for Year 8.

   (b) Work out the mean and range for Year 9.

   (c) Write a sentence to compare the number of baths or showers taken by children in Year 8 and Year 9.

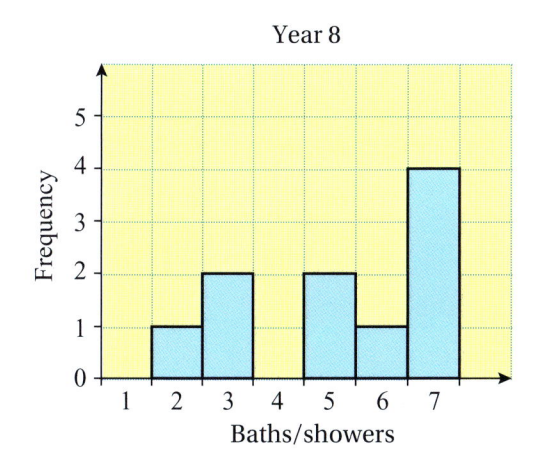

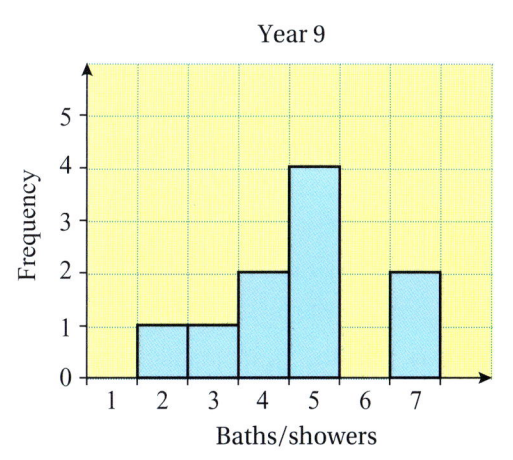

2 Helen and Nadia record their best ten times for a swimming race. The times (in seconds) are shown below:

Helen: 75, 70, 69, 70, 74, 69, 73, 69, 67, 74

Nadia: 78, 81, 80, 76, 80, 79, 69, 79, 80, 78

(a) Find the mean time for Helen.

(b) Find the range for Helen.

(c) Find the mean time for Nadia.

(d) Find the range for Nadia.

(e) Who is generally quicker? Give reasons for your answers.

3 The yearly salaries of people working in Carwells Bakery is shown below.

| £14 000 | £12 000 | £12 000 | £13 000 | £14 000 | £12 000 |
| £13 000 | £12 000 | £75 000 | £13 000 | £12 000 | £14 000 |

(a) Work out the mean, median and mode for these salaries.

(b) Some workers want a pay rise. Which average should they use to support their argument?

(c) The bakery want to attract more workers. Which average should they use to advertise the pay?

4 12 pupils in Year 7 and 12 pupils in Year 11 were asked how many hours of T.V. they watched each day. The results are recorded below:

Year 7   6 7 4 4 2 6 4 5 7 1 3 3
Year 11   2 1 1 5 3 5 6 8 4 3 1 2

(a) Work out the median and range for each of Year 7 and Year 11.

(b) Write a sentence to compare the number of hours of T.V. watched each day by pupils in Year 7 and Year 11.

5 The amount (in pounds) that three sales people have sold in each of the last five months is shown below.

Olga	7500	6300	6100	8900	8300
Austin	7200	6600	6000	6100	6500
Mia	6700	7900	7300	6900	7200

(a) Find the mean, median and range for each person.

(b) The manager is thinking of promoting Olga or Mia. Who do you think deserves to be promoted and why?

6 The heights (in metres) of the players in two football squads are shown below:

Catcott: 1.85, 1.95, 1.66, 1.98, 1.88, 1.91, 1.81, 2, 1.82, 1.93, 1.88, 1.81, 1.89, 1.95, 1.86

Tipperton: 1.87, 1.99, 1.93, 1.85, 1.94, 1.86, 1.87, 1.96, 1.92, 1.93, 1.85, 1.99, 1.97, 1.89, 1.96

(a) Find the median height for Catcott.
(b) Find the range for Catcott.
(c) Find the median height for Tipperton.
(d) Find the range for Tipperton.
(e) Which team generally has taller players? Give reasons for your answers.

7 18 children were asked how often they ate meat each week (10 children from Year 9 and 8 children from Year 11). The results are given in the graphs below.

(a) Work out the mean and range for Year 9.
(b) Work out the mean and range for Year 11.
(c) Write a sentence to compare the number of times meat is eaten each week by children in Year 9 and Year 11.

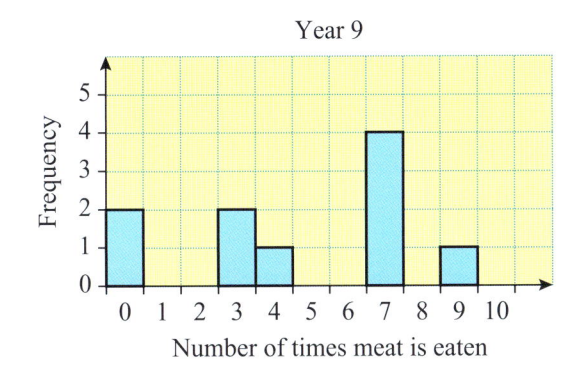

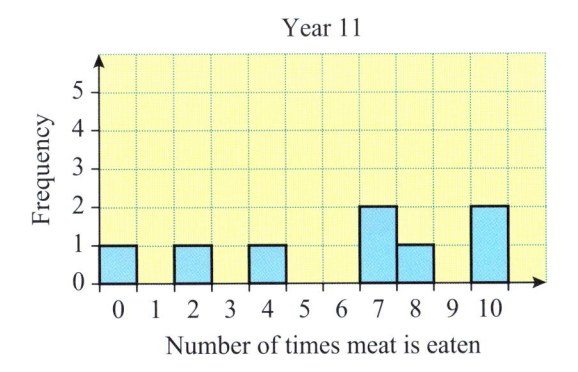

Averages from frequency tables

Twenty children were asked how many computer games they had bought during one year. The results are below.

    5   4   4   0   1   2   2   6   1   2
    3   5   2   5   1   0   3   3   5   2

This data can be recorded in a frequency table.

Number of computer games	0	1	2	3	4	5	6
Frequency (number of children)	2	3	5	3	2	4	1

Use the table to work out the mean number of computer games.

$$\text{mean} = \frac{(2 \times 0) + (3 \times 1) + (5 \times 2) + (3 \times 3) + (2 \times 4) + (4 \times 5) + (1 \times 6)}{20}$$

total number of children

$$\text{mean} = \frac{56}{20} = 2.8$$

Exercise 2E

1 The table below shows the number of children in each of 100 families.

Number of children	0	1	2	3	4	5	6	7
Frequency	4	24	22	19	15	7	7	2

Copy and complete: mean number of children $= \dfrac{(4 \times 0) + (24 \times 1) + (...)}{100} = \dfrac{\square}{100} = \square$

2 The table below shows the number of cars for each house on Carter Road in Romford.

Number of cars	0	1	2	3
Frequency	7	12	11	10

Copy and complete:

mean number of cars

$= \dfrac{(7 \times 0) + (12 \times 1) + (...) + (...)}{40}$

$= \dfrac{\square}{40} = \square$

3 Two dice are thrown several times. The scores on each dice are shown below.

Score on dice A	1	2	3	4	5	6
Number of throws	4	5	3	2	6	5

Score on dice B	1	2	3	4	5	6
Number of throws	7	6	9	5	6	7

Which dice had the greater mean score and by how much?

4 Hatton United play 25 games of football. The number of goals scored in each match is shown below:

1 3 2 4 4 2 1 0 5 0 1 1 2
0 1 1 4 2 2 1 2 0 1 3 5

(a) Record this data in a frequency table.
(b) By how much is the mean number of goals scored greater than the modal number of goals scored?

Finding the median

Consider the number of cars on Carter Road in question **2**.

Number of cars	0	1	2	3
Frequency	7	12	11	10

There are 40 cars in total.
The median is the mid-value so half way between the 20th and 21st values.

There are 19 values of 0 or 1 so 20th and 21st values are both 2 so the median is 2 cars.
Remember: if the median lies between two values (eg. 2 and 3) then it lies exactly half way between these values (ie. 2.5).

5 The table below shows the number of coats owned by 60 people.

Number of coats	0	1	2	3	4
Frequency	13	4	11	10	22

Which is greater and by how much: the median number of coats or the mean number of coats?

6 The table below shows the number of pets in each of 50 families.

Number of pets	0	1	2	3	4	5	6
Frequency	6	19	10	6	5	2	2

(a) Write down the modal number of pets (the mode).
(b) Write down the range for the number of pets.
(c) Find the mean number of pets.
(d) Find the median number of pets.

7 The number of daily portions of fruit and vegetables eaten by 24 people is shown in the table below:

Number of portions	0	1	2	3	4	5	6
Frequency	2	2	2	6	2	8	2

(a) Find the mean number of portions eaten each day.
(b) Danny joins the group of people. The mean number of portions increases to 3.6. How many portions does Danny eat each day?
(c) What, if anything, happens to the median number of portions when Danny joins the group of people?

Need more practice with averages and range?

1 In a science test the marks for the boys were 13, 16, 9, 13, 18, 15 and the marks for the girls were 12, 16, 19, 17.

Is the mean mark for the boys greater than the mean mark for the whole class?
Justify your answer fully.

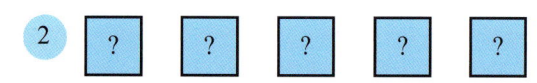

2 ? ? ? ? ?

The five numbers above have a mean average equal to 8.
The mode is 11 and the median is 9.
Write down all the numbers if the range is 8.

3 Lynne caught twelve fish.
Their masses were:

135 g, 245 g, 200 g
285 g, 276 g, 90 g, 180 g
210 g, 80 g, 300 g, 90 g, 225 g

(a) Find the modal mass (the mode).
(b) Find the median mass.
(c) Find the range.
(d) Find the mean mass.

4 Mark has thrown a dice nine times and the mean score on the dice has been 3.
He scores a 6 with his next throw. What is the mean score for all 10 throws?

5 A golfer records his scores for seven rounds of golf as below:

79   87   79   83   89   79   78

He tells his friends that his average score is 79.
Is he telling the truth? Explain your answer fully.

6 The Council is investigating the amount of rubbish placed in dustbins.
On one road there are six houses. The mean number of rubbish bags in a dustbin is 6.
The number of rubbish bags in the first five dustbins are 8, 6, 4, 5 and 4.
How many rubbish bags are there in the sixth dustbin?

7 The seven numbers opposite have a mode of 3 and 10.
Their range is 8.
Write down what the missing numbers could be.

| 10 | 10 | 10 | ? | ? | ? | ? |

8 The shoe sizes for the Freeman family and the Davidson family are shown below.

| The Freeman family: | 11 | 5 | 5 | 10 | 6 | |
| The Davidson family: | 4 | 8 | 5 | 4 | 9 | 10 |

Use an average and the range to compare the shoe sizes of the Freeman family and the Davidson family.

Extension questions with averages and range

1 The table below shows how many goals in each match that a striker has scored during one season.

Number of goals	0	1	2	3	4
Number of matches	14	8	5	2	1

Use the mean to show whether the striker has averaged more than one goal per match or not.

2 Mei and Brody both work out at the gym. The number of trips to the gym for each person during one year is shown in the table below.

Gym trips per week	0	1	2	3	4	5
Mei number of weeks	2	5	11	12	14	8
Brody number of weeks	3	9	17	11	10	2

Who makes more trips to the gym during this year and by how many?

3 The tables below show maths test marks out of 10 for class A and class B.

Class A

Mark	0	1	2	3	4	5	6	7	8	9	10
Number of pupils	0	0	1	1	1	3	2	12	7	2	1

Class B

Mark	0	1	2	3	4	5	6	7	8	9	10
Number of pupils	0	0	0	0	0	6	8	9	0	6	0

(a) Work out the mean, median, mode and range for each class (give answers to 1 decimal place if necessary).

(b) Which class as a whole do you think did better in this test? Give reasons for your answer.

4 The 09.38 train to Denby often arrives late at Holton. The data below shows how late the train is on twenty occasions. The times are given in minutes.

    2   5   11   31   0   12   11   2   33   11
   25   25   23   0   11   8   27   25   2   8

(a) Display this data in a frequency table like that shown in question **3**.

(b) A passenger survey states that on average the train is 11 minutes late. Is this correct? Explain your answer fully.

5 n | ? | ? | ? | ?

The number n is the lowest whole number on the five cards above.

The median is 4 more than this lowest number.

The range is 9.

The highest number is the mode.

The mean average is $(n + 5)$.

Write down an expression for each number on the five cards above.

6 Pavel visits 19 streets on Halloween night and records how many pumpkins he sees.
This is shown in the table below.

Number of pumpkins	6	7	8	9	10	11
Number of streets	1	2	4	4	5	3

(a) Work out the mean, median, mode and range for this data.

(b) Pavel then visits one more street where he sees 19 pumpkins. Explain how each of the mean, median, mode and range might change when this is added to the other results.
Justify each of your answers.

CHECK YOURSELF ON SECTION 3.3

1 Reviewing the mean, median, mode and range

Consider 9, 13, 8, 3, 15, 4, 8, 12
Find the (a) mean (b) median (c) mode (d) range

2 Comparing sets of data using averages and range

The Warriors and the Sabres are two basketball teams.
The ages (in years) of the players in each team are listed below:

     The Warriors: 24   22   17   28   22   19   31   27   21   27
     The Sabres: 28   24   18   20   19   30   27   19   24   18

Use the mean and range to write a sentence to compare the ages of the players for the Warriors and the Sabres.

3 Finding averages from frequency tables

The table below shows the number of computers owned by each of 80 families.

Number of computers	0	1	2	3	4	5
Frequency	8	14	13	20	16	9

Find (a) the modal number of computers
      (b) the mean
      (c) the median

3.4 Displaying and interpreting data

In section 3.4 you will:
- review charts
- draw and use stem and leaf diagrams
- display data in groups
- draw and use pie charts

Reviewing charts

Exercise 1M

1. The bar charts show the sale of different things over a year but the labels on the charts have been lost. Decide which of the charts A, B, C or D shows sales of:
   (a) Christmas trees
   (b) Crisps
   (c) Flower seeds
   (d) Greetings cards [including Christmas, Valentine's Day, etc.]

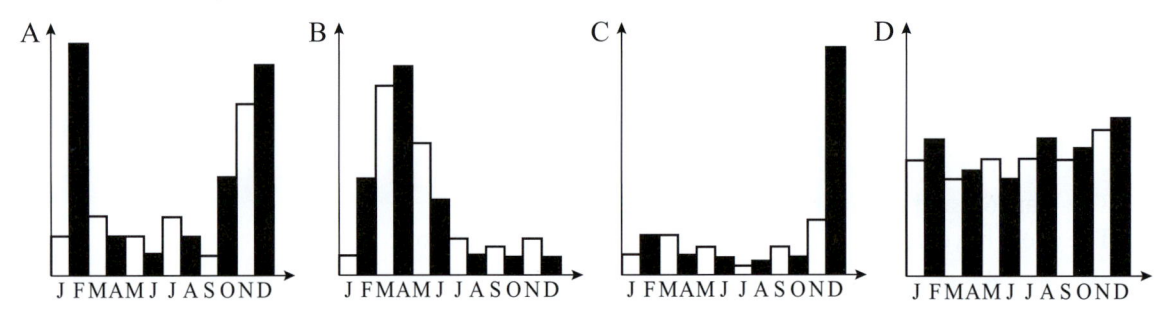

2. The number of people staying in two different hotels in each month of the year is shown below.

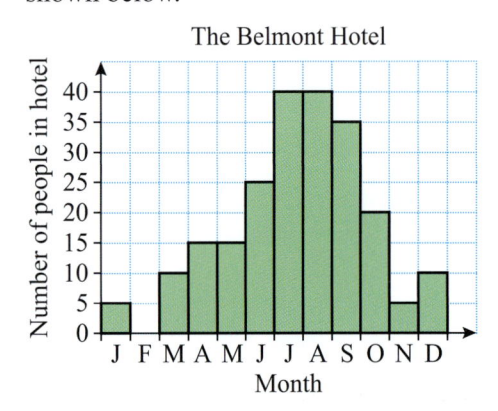

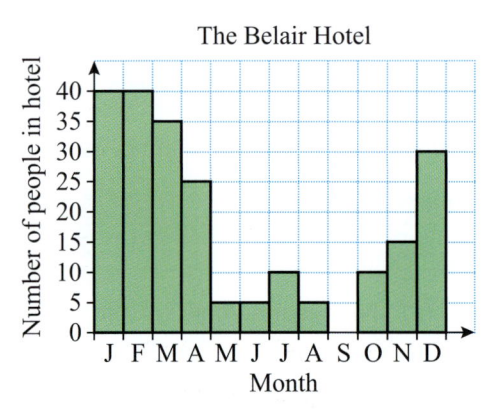

(a) How many people stayed in the 'Belmont' in July?

(b) How many people stayed in the 'Belair' in July?

(c) What was the total number of people staying in the two hotels in April?

(d) One hotel is in a ski resort and the other is by the seaside. Which is in the ski resort?

3. Some people were asked to state which was their favourite T.V. programme from the list below.

Eastenders	E
MTV	M
Football Highlights	F
Neighbours	N
The Simpsons	S

The replies were:

S N S M N E M F N M E M M E N
F S N M M E S E N S E N N E N
N M E N N E M F N S E M N F N

(a) Make a tally chart and then draw a bar chart to show the results.

		Tally	Total
Eastenders	E		
MTV	M		
Football Highlights	F		
Neighbours	N		
The Simpsons	S		

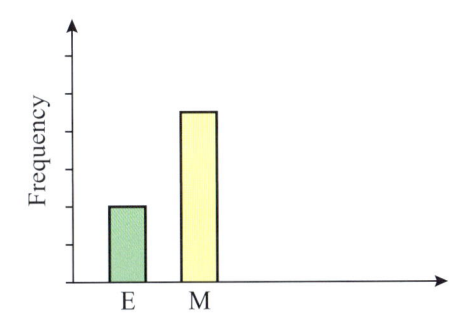

(b) Which programme was the most popular?

(c) How many more people liked Eastenders compared to the Simpsons?

4

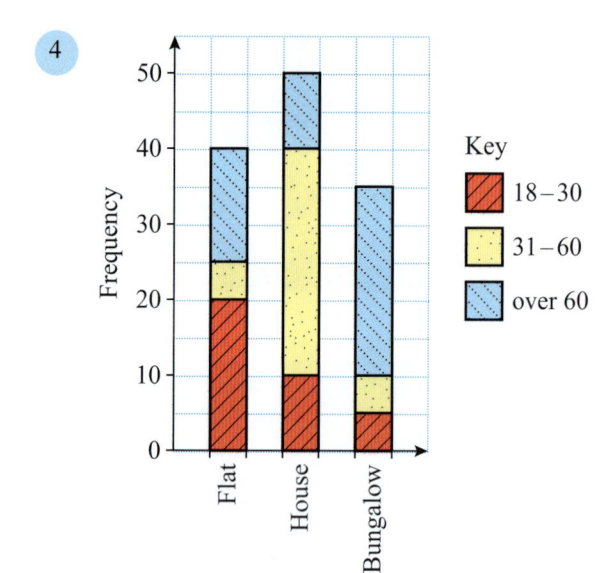

The bar chart opposite shows the type of dwelling people of different age groups live in. This is for one small area in a town.

(a) How many 31–60 year olds live in a house?

(b) A 70 year old is looking for somewhere to live. Which type of dwelling would you most expect this person to be interested in? Give a reason for your answer.

(c) Which type of dwelling is most popular with the 18–30 year olds? Why do you think this is?

Key: 18–30, 31–60, over 60

5 The chart opposite shows the agricultural production figures for four crops in Pakistan. Pakistan had low rainfall but in later years major irrigation schemes were introduced. About 50% of the population is employed in agriculture.

Describe how the production of the four crops changed over the years from 1960 to 2000.

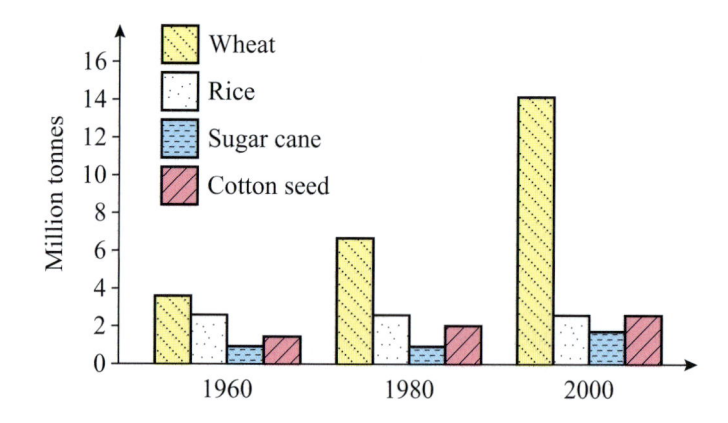

Stem and leaf diagrams

Data can be displayed in groups in a stem and leaf diagram.
Here are the marks of 20 girls in a science test.

| 47 53 71 55 28 40 45 62 57 64 |
| 33 48 59 61 73 37 75 26 68 39 |

We will put the marks into groups 20–29, 30–39 … 70–79.

We will choose the tens digit as the 'stem' and the units as the 'leaf'.

The first four marks are shown [47, 53, 71, 55]

Stem (tens)	Leaf (units)
2	
3	
4	7
5	3 5
6	
7	1

The complete diagram is below … and then with the leaves in numerical order:

Stem	Leaf
2	8 6
3	3 7 9
4	7 0 5 8
5	3 5 7 9
6	2 4 1 8
7	1 3 5

'unordered' stem and leaf

Stem	Leaf
2	6 8
3	3 7 9
4	0 5 7 8
5	3 5 7 9
6	1 2 4 8
7	1 3 5

'ordered' stem and leaf

A key is needed.

Key
4|7 means 47 in the test

The diagram shows the shape of the distribution.

Exercise 2M

1 The marks of 24 children in a test are shown

```
41  23  35  15  40  39  47  29
52  54  45  27  28  36  48  51
59  65  42  32  46  53  66  38
```

Stem	Leaf
1	
2	3
3	5
4	1
5	
6	

Key
3|5 means 35 marks

(a) Draw an ordered stem and leaf diagram. The first three entries are shown.

(b) Write down the range for these marks.

2 Here is the stem and leaf diagram showing the masses, in kg, of some people on a bus.

(a) Write down the range of the masses.
(b) How many people were on the bus?
(c) What is the median mass?
(d) Is the median mass greater or less than the mean mass?
Give reasons for your answer.

Stem (tens)	Leaf (units)
3	3 7
4	1 2 7 7 8
5	1 6 8 9
6	0 3 7
7	4 5
8	2

Key
7|4 means 74 kg

3 The ages of the people in a small company are shown opposite in the stem and leaf diagram.

The median age is 40 and the modal age is 42.

(a) Write down the values of A and B.
(b) Work out the mean age of these people.

Stem	Leaf
2	1 3 7 8
3	4 4 5 6 9 9
4	A 2 2 B 7
5	0 1 7
6	2 5

Key: 3|6 means 36 years old

4 The ages of people in a swimming pool are recorded at two different times of the day.
The information is shown below:

8:30 am: 24 52 31 55 40 37 58 61 25 46 45
44 67 68 75 73 28 20 59 65 39

7:45 pm: 30 41 53 22 72 54 35 47 59
44 67 46 38 59 29 47 28

Stem	Leaf
2	
3	
4	
5	
6	
7	

(a) Draw an ordered stem and leaf diagram for each set of data.
You must include a key for each.

(b) Use the medians and ranges to compare the ages of the people at the two times of the day.

5 In this question the stem shows the units digit and the leaf shows the first digit after the decimal point.

Draw the ordered stem and leaf diagram using the following data:

2.4 3.1 5.2 4.7 1.4 6.2 4.5 3.3
4.0 6.3 3.7 6.7 4.6 4.9 5.1 5.5
1.8 3.8 4.5 2.4 5.8 3.3 4.6 2.8

Key
3|7 means 3.7

Stem	Leaf
1	
2	
3	
4	
5	
6	

(a) What is the median?
(b) Write down the range.

6 The lengths of tadpoles in two ponds are measured.
The stem and leaf diagram for these lengths from pond A is shown opposite.

Stem	Leaf
3	4 5 5 6
4	1 2 3 3 6 7 7 9
5	2 4 5 8 8 8 9 9
6	0 1 1 4 5 5 8 9
7	2 2 2 3 7
8	0 1

Key: 6|8 means 6.8 cm

The lengths (in cm) from pond B are shown opposite.

(a) Draw an ordered stem and leaf diagram for the lengths from pond B.

(b) In which pond are the lengths generally greater? Give full reasons for your answer (ie. consider averages and the spread).

(c) In pond A, what fraction of the tadpoles were longer than 5.9 cm?

4.3 4.5 5.2 6.8 3.6 7.2
4.0 4.6 3.9 4.1 3.5 4.8
5.9 3.6 4.5 4.4 5.6 6.3
3.8 9.1 4.0 6.8 4.5 4.8
5.6 3.5 4.3 3.6 3.9

Displaying data in groups

- Here are the ages of the people at a wedding.

  33 11 45 22 50 38 23 54 18 72   5 58
  37   3 61 51   7 62 24 57 31 27 66 29
  25 39 48 15 52 25 35 18 49 63 13 74

  With so many different numbers over a wide range it is helpful to put the ages into *groups*.

  Inequalities can be used to identify a *group*.

  For example, let Age = A

  The group $10 \leq A < 20$ means all ages from 10 to 20, including 10 but not including 20.

> Ages are *continuous* data because any age value can be taken.
>
> *Discrete* data is when there can be no values between the data values. For example a family can have 2 or 3 children but not 2.4 children!

- A tally chart can be drawn up.

Ages (A)	Tally	Total (Frequency)
$0 \leq A < 10$	|||	3
$10 \leq A < 20$	ⅢⅠ	5
$20 \leq A < 30$	ⅢⅠ ||	7
$30 \leq A < 40$	ⅢⅠ |	6
$40 \leq A < 50$	|||	3
$50 \leq A < 60$	ⅢⅠ |	6
$60 \leq A < 70$	||||	4
$70 \leq A < 80$	||	2

- Draw a frequency diagram.

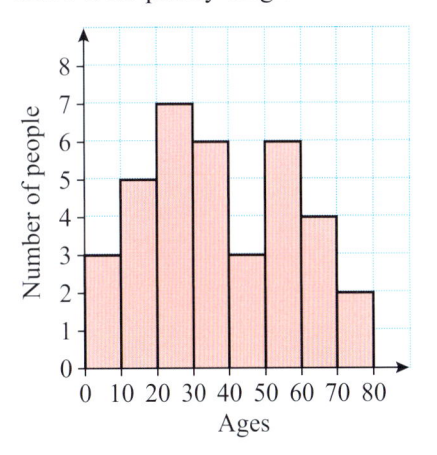

Exercise 3M

1. A drug company claims that its new nutrient pill helps people to improve their memory. As an experiment two randomly selected groups of people were given the same memory test. Group A took the new pills for a month while group B took no pills. Here are the results of the tests (a high score indicates a good memory).

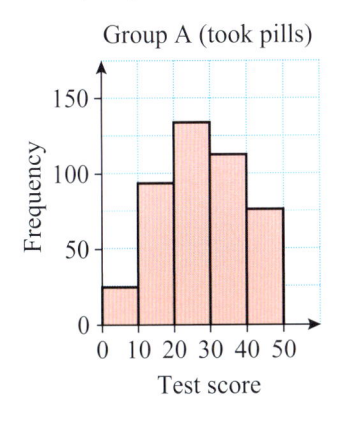

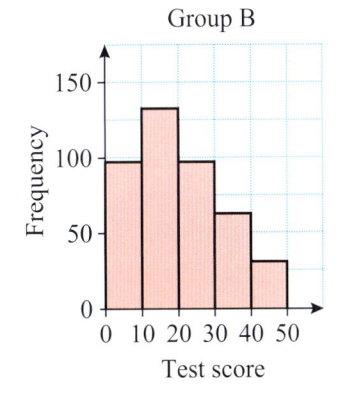

   Does it appear that the new pills did in fact help to improve memory?

2. Tom has lots of snakes and he likes to weigh them every week. The weights are shown.

(a) How many snakes weigh between 60 and 80 grams?
(b) How many snakes weigh less than 40 grams?
(c) How many snakes does he have altogether?

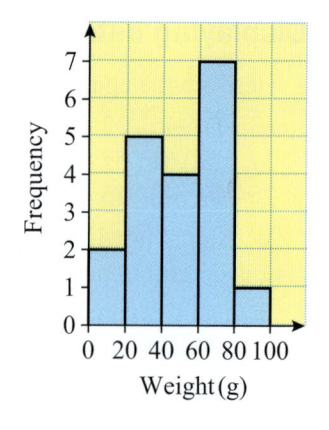

3. The heights, in cm, of 30 children are shown below.

```
134  146  141  147  151  141  137  159  142  146
151  157  143  154  146  143  149  151  141  148
136  144  147  152  147  137  133  140  139  155
```

(a) Put the heights into groups.

Class interval	Frequency
$130 \leq h < 135$	
$135 \leq h < 140$	
$140 \leq h < 145$	
$145 \leq h < 150$	

and so on.

(b) Draw a frequency diagram.

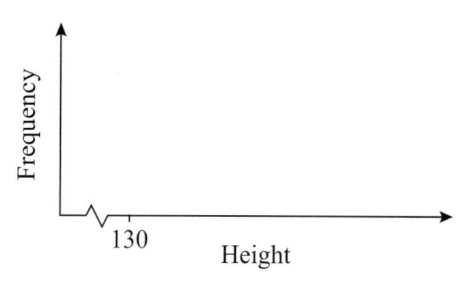

(c) How many children were *more than* 140 cm tall?

4. A group of 7 year-olds were each accompanied by one of their parents on a coach trip to a zoo. Each person on the coach was weighed in kg. Here are the weights.

```
21.1,  45.7,  22.3,  26.3,  50.1,  24.3,  44.2,
54.3,  53.2,  46.0,  51.0,  24.2,  56.4,  20.6,
25.5,  22.8,  52.0,  26.5,  41.8,  27.5,  29.7,
55.1,  30.7,  47.4,  23.5,  59.8,  49.3,  23.4,
21.7,  57.6,  22.6,  58.7,  28.6,  54.1.
```

(a) Put the weights into groups.
(b) Draw a frequency diagram.
(c) Why is the shape of the frequency diagram different to the diagram you drew in question 2?
(d) What shape of frequency diagram would you expect to obtain if you drew a diagram to show the heights of pupils in your class?

Class interval	Frequency
$20 \leq h < 25$	
$25 \leq h < 30$	
$30 \leq h < 35$	
⋮	

5 The ages (*A*) of people in a Sports Club at 4:30 p.m. one day is shown below.
The ages are in years.

15	24	29	41	34	20	13	12	38
34	11	45	63	13	22	45	32	11
24	17	20	35	13	29	17	20	54

(a) Make a tally chart with groups $10 \leq A < 20$, $20 \leq A < 30$, etc.
(b) Draw a frequency diagram.
(c) Draw a stem and leaf diagram.
(d) Write down the median age.
(e) Which diagram is most useful – the frequency diagram or the stem and leaf diagram?
Give reasons for your answer.
(f) What fraction of the people are younger than 20 years old?
(g) What percentage of the people are older than 19 years old?
(h) Describe how the ages are distributed (ie. what happens to the number of people as the ages increase?).

6 A teacher has a theory that pupils' test results are affected by the amount of T.V. watched at home.

With the willing cooperation of the children's parents, the pupils were split into two groups:
   Group X watched at least two hours of T.V. per day.
   Group Y watched a maximum of half an hour per day.

The pupils were given two tests: one at the start of the experiment and another test six months later. Here are the results:

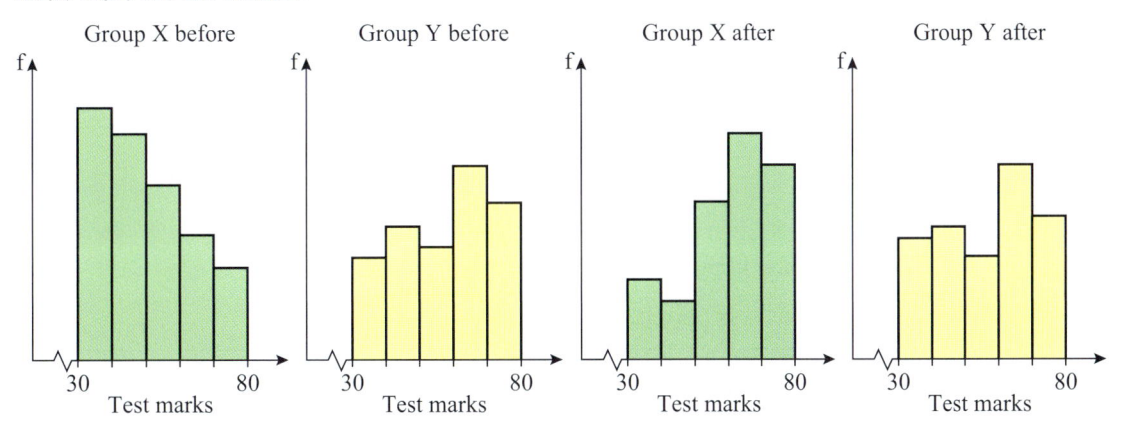

Group X before   Group Y before   Group X after   Group Y after
(Test marks 30–80 for each)

Look carefully at the frequency diagrams. What conclusions can you draw?
Was the teacher's theory correct? Give details of how the pupils in group X and in group Y performed in the two tests.

Drawing and using pie charts

Exercise 4M

1 The pie chart shows the results of a survey in which 80 people were asked how they travelled to work.
Copy this table and fill it in.

Method	Car	Walk	Train	Bus
Number of people				

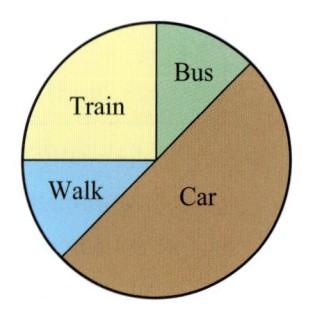

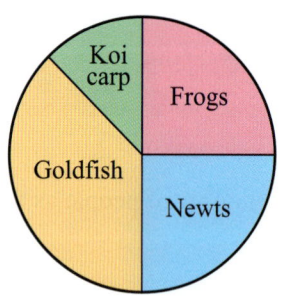

2 Jodie counted the different animals in her pond. Altogether there were 200 animals or fish.
(a) *About* how many frogs were there?
(b) *About* how many goldfish were there?

3 In 2017 and 2018 children were asked in a survey to say which country they would most like to go to for a holiday. The pie charts show the results.

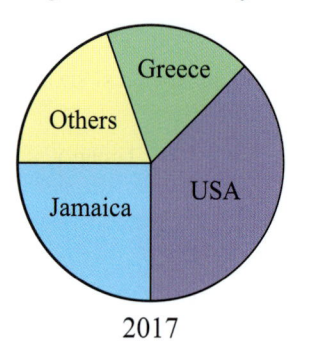

100 children answered in each year

Countries in the 'others' section had only one or two votes each.

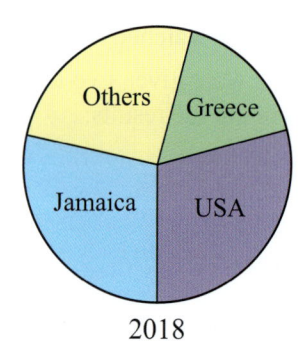

2017

2018

(a) Which was the most popular country in the 2017 survey?
(b) Which country was less popular in 2018 than in 2017?
(c) *Roughly* how many children said 'Jamaica' in the 2017 survey?

4 In a survey children were asked what *pests* they had at home.
Five twelfths of the children said, 'my sister'.
What angle would you draw for the 'my sister' sector on a pie chart?

5 The children at a school were asked to state their favourite colour. Here are the results.

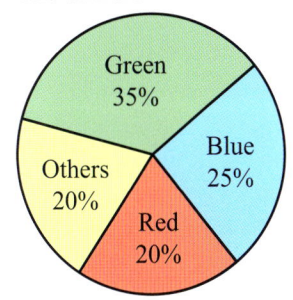

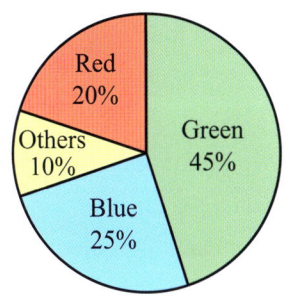

There were 80 boys   There were 60 girls

John says 'The same number of boys and girls chose red.'
Tara says 'More boys than girls chose blue.'

(a) Use both charts to explain whether or not John is right.
(b) Use both charts to explain whether or not Tara is right.

6 Lara had £24 to spend on presents.
The pie chart shows how much she spent on each person.
How much did she spend on
(a) her mum   (b) her dad
(c) her brother   (d) her grandma
(e) her friend   (f) her auntie?

[Make sure that your answers add up to £24.]

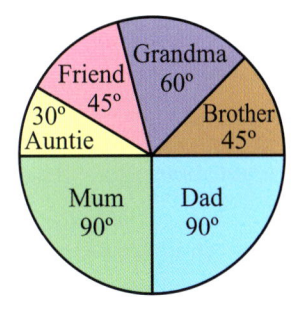

Calculating angles in pie charts

A farmer divides his land into three parts.
He uses 5 acres for corn, 3 acres for carrots and 2 acres for pigs.

(a) Add the three parts: 5 + 3 + 2 = 10 acres
(b) 10 acres = 360°
    1 acre = $\frac{360}{10}$ = 36°
(c) For corn, 5 acres = 5 × 36° = 180°
    For carrots, 3 acres = 3 × 36° = 108°
    For pigs, 2 acres = 2 × 36° = 72°

This pie chart shows the after-school
activities of 200 pupils.

(a) The number of pupils = $\frac{36}{360}$ × 200 = 20 doing drama

(b) The number of pupils = $\frac{144}{360}$ × 200 = 80 doing sport

(c) The number of pupils = $\frac{45}{360}$ × 200 = 25 doing computing

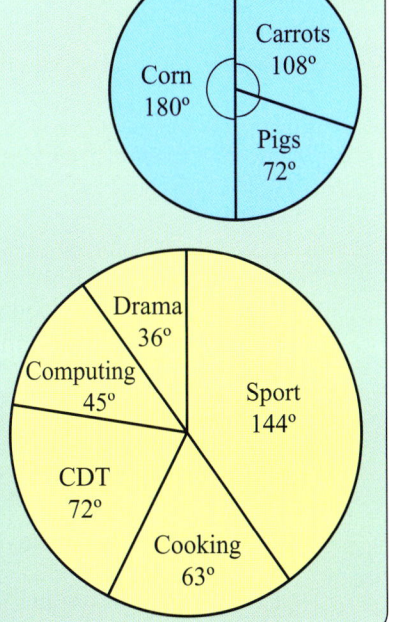

Exercise 5M

1 A 'Chewit' bar contains these four ingredients:

    Oats   6 g   Sugar   3 g
    Barley   9 g   Rye   18 g

(a) Work out the total weight of the ingredients.
(b) Work out the angle on a pie chart for 1 g of the ingredients [ie. 360° ÷ (total weight)].
(c) Work out the angle for each ingredient and draw a pie chart.

2 At the 'Crooked Corkscrew' last Friday, 120 customers ordered meals.

  40 ordered beefburger
  20 ordered ham salad
  16 ordered curry
  25 ordered cod
  19 ordered chicken.

Draw a pie chart to show this information.

In questions **3**, **4**, and **5** work out the angle for each sector and draw a pie chart.

3 Number of programmes per night.

Programme	Frequency
News	2
Soap	5
Comedy	4
Drama	5
Film	2

4 Pupils' favourite sports.

Sport	Frequency
Rugby	5
Football	7
Tennis	4
Squash	2
Athletics	3
Swimming	3

5 Periods per subject.

Subject	Frequency
Maths	5
English	5
Science	6
Humanities	4
Arts	4
Others	16

6 Six hundred families travelling home on a ferry were asked to name the country in which they had spent most of their holiday. The pie chart represents their answers.

(a) How many stayed longest   (i) in Portugal?
                              (ii) in Spain?
(b) What angle represents holidays in Switzerland?
(c) How many families stayed longest in Switzerland?

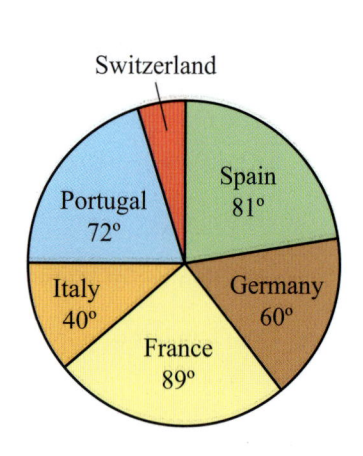

Pie chart sectors: Switzerland, Portugal 72°, Spain 81°, Italy 40°, Germany 60°, France 89°

7 The average number of presents received at Christmas by different age groups is shown in the bar chart below.

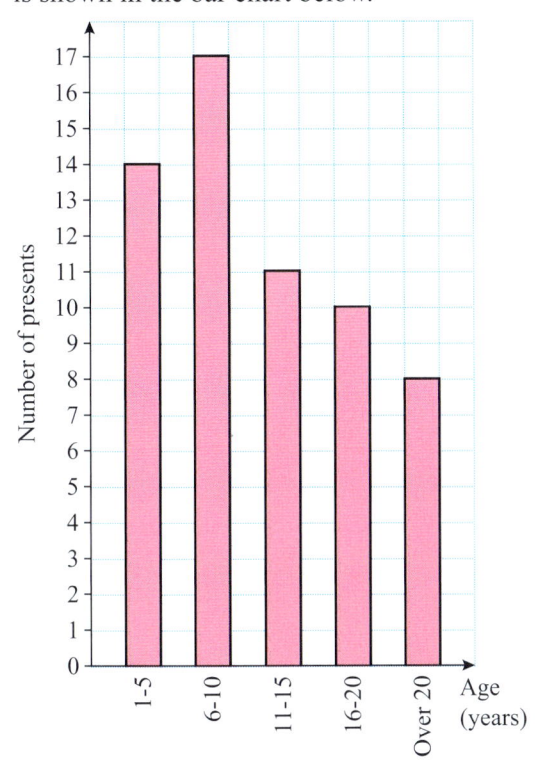

A pie chart is to be drawn to show this information.

(a) Explain clearly why an angle of 84° is used to show the number of presents for 1–5 year-olds.

(b) Draw the full pie chart for this information.

(c) Which chart do you think shows this data in the most useful way? Give reasons for your answer.

8 On one morning there are 160 recycling bins outside the houses on Parker Street.

$\frac{1}{10}$ of the boxes are for cardboard.

$\frac{3}{8}$ of the boxes are for paper.

The remaining boxes are for bottles.

A pie chart is to be drawn to show this information.

(a) What fraction of the boxes are for bottles?
(b) What angle will be drawn on the pie chart for bottle boxes?
(c) How many boxes for bottles are there?

9 In a survey the children at a school were asked to state their favourite sport in the Olympics.

(a) Estimate what fraction of the children chose gymnastics.

(b) There are 120 children in the school. Estimate the number of children who chose athletics.

(c) 15% of the children chose swimming. How many children was that?

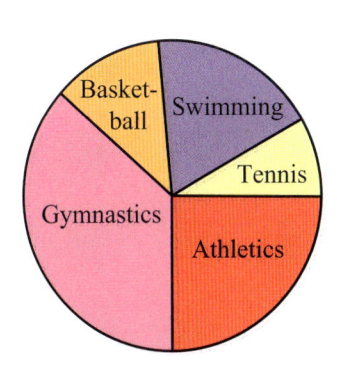

Need more practice with displaying and interpreting data?

1 This table shows the number of different sorts of snacks sold by a shop.

	Mon	Tu	Wed	Th	Fri
Mars	3	1	0	0	3
Snickers	0	4	1	2	2
Twix	2	2	1	3	4
Aero	5	0	0	1	4
Crunchie	2	3	4	1	1
Kit Kat	5	0	2	1	1

(a) How many snacks were sold on Thursday?

(b) Each Aero costs 45p. How much was spent on Aeros in the whole week?

(c) Draw a bar chart to show the number of each kind of snack sold in a week.

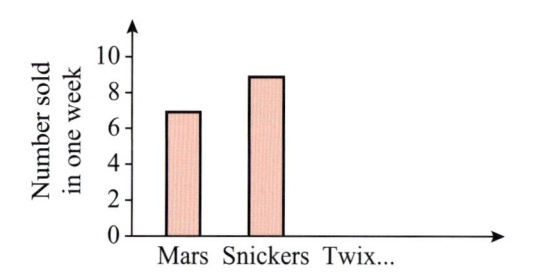

2 Shruti started with one frog but it laid eggs and now she has lots! One day she measures all her little pets. Here are the lengths in mm.

    82 63 91 78 27 93 87 48 22 15
    42 28 84 65 87 55 79 66 85 38

(a) Make a tally chart and then draw the frequency diagram.

Length (mm) (L)	Tally	Frequency
$0 < L \leq 20$		
$20 < L \leq 40$		
$40 < L \leq 60$		
$60 < L \leq 80$		
$80 < L \leq 100$		

(b) Draw a stem and leaf diagram for this data.

(c) Write down the modal interval.

(d) Write down the median length.

(e) Which diagram is most useful for finding the median? Justify your answer.

3 Farmer Gray rears pigs. As an experiment, he decided to feed half of his pigs with their normal diet and the other half on a new high fibre diet. The diagrams show the weights of the pigs in the two groups.

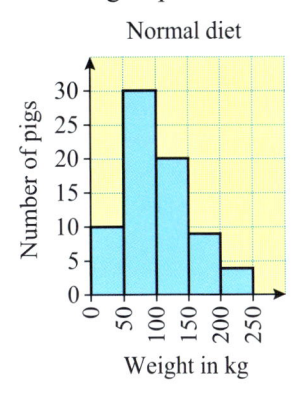

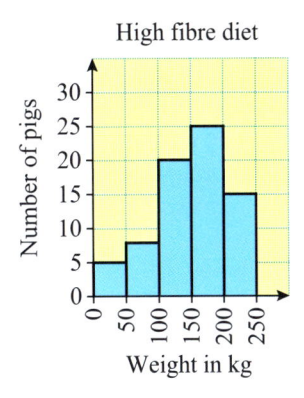

In one sentence describe what effect the new diet had.

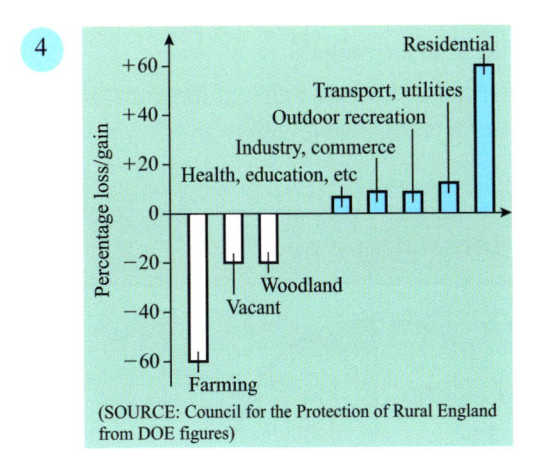

4 This chart shows changes of land use in rural areas in England between 1960 and 2000.

(a) What was the change in the area of land used for farming?

(b) Write down three activities that would go in the 'outdoor recreation' category.

(c) Describe the main features of the chart.

(SOURCE: Council for the Protection of Rural England from DOE figures)

5 This diagram shows the temperature and rainfall readings in one week.
The rainfall is shown as the bar chart.
The temperature is shown as the line graph.

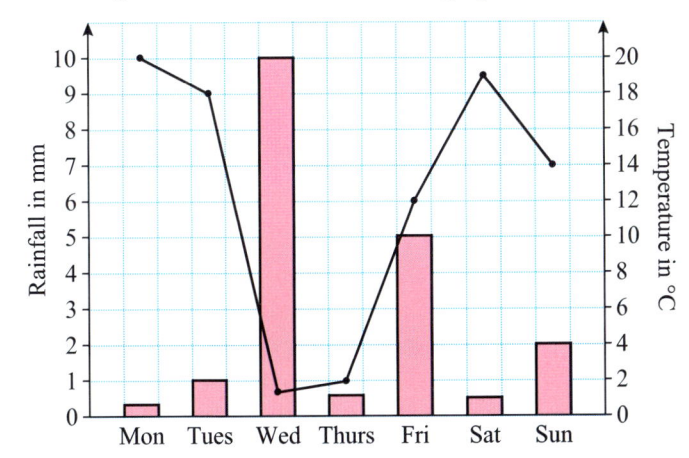

(a) Use both graphs to describe the weather on Monday.

(b) On which day was the weather cold and wet?

(c) Compare the weather on Thursday and Saturday.

6 A hidden observer watched Anna in a 60 minute maths lesson.
This is how she spent her time:

Looking for a calculator	8 minutes
Sharpening a pencil	7 minutes
Talking	32 minutes
Checking the clock	2 minutes
Working	4 minutes
Packing up	7 minutes

Draw an accurate pie chart to illustrate Anna's lesson.

7 The stem and leaf diagram below shows the test marks (out of 50) for a class.

Stem	Leaf
0	8 9
1	3 3 6 9
2	4 5 5 5 7 7 8
3	1 1 2 2 3 5 6 6 8 9 9
4	2 3 3 6 7

(a) Mitchell says that the median mark is 31. Is he correct? Explain your answer fully.
(b) The pass mark is 20. What percentage of the students failed?
(c) Criticise the stem and leaf diagram (ie. what is wrong with it?).

Extension questions with displaying and interpreting data

1 The pie chart illustrates the sales of four brands of petrol.
(a) What percentage of total sales does BP have?
(b) If Shell accounts for 35% of total sales, calculate the angles x and y.

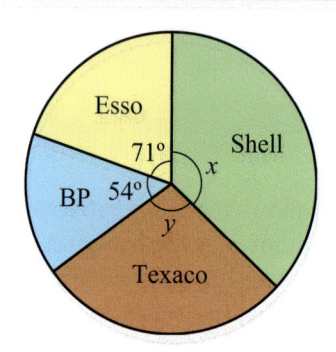

2 The heights of children in two classes is shown below in a back to back stem and leaf diagram.

```
        class P         |      class Q
                      7 | 13 | 2 6 6
                  4 1 0 | 14 | 1 3 6 7 7 9
          8 7 7 7 6 6 3 2 | 15 | 4 5 5 5 7 8 9 9 9
        8 6 6 6 6 3 2 1 0 | 16 | 0 0 1 1 2 4 8 8 8
                9 8 8 7 5 4 | 17 | 2 3 5
```

Key: 8|16 means 168 cm   Key: 15|7 means 157 cm

Make sure you always read the stem first (ie. read backwards for class P)

(a) For each of class P and class Q, draw up a frequency table with the intervals
    130 ≤ height < 140, 140 ≤ height < 150, etc.
(b) For each of class P and class Q, draw a frequency diagram.
(c) Work out the mean, median and range for each of class P and class Q.
(d) Compare the heights of the children in class P and class Q using the evidence from earlier in the question.

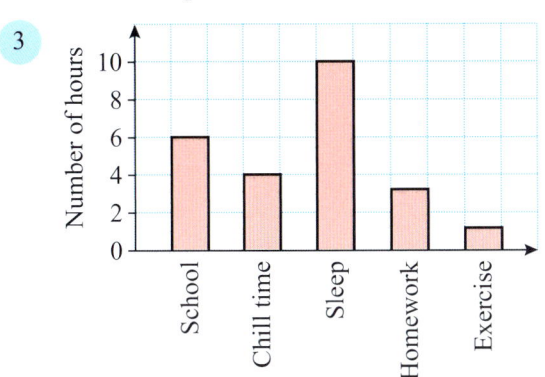

3 The bar chart shows an average day for Lamara. She draws the pie chart below to show this information but makes a mistake. Describe fully what she has done wrong.

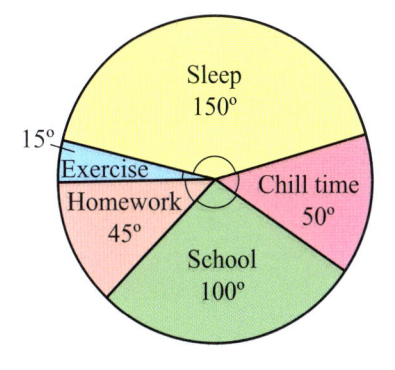

4 The stem and leaf diagram below shows the pulse rates of some people in beats per minute.

Stem	Leaf
5	4 6
6	3 3 5 9
7	1 4 6 6 8 8 9 9
8	2 3 6 7 7
9	1

Key: 6|3 means 63 beats per minute

(a) Work out the median pulse rate.
(b) Toby joins the group of people which makes the mean pulse rate become 75.
    Does the median increase, decrease or stay the same? You must explain your answer fully.

5 In a survey 320 people on an aircraft and 800 people on a ferry were asked to state their nationality.
(a) Roughly what percentage of the people on the aircraft were from the U.K.?
(b) Roughly how many people from France were on the ferry?
(c) Jill looked at the charts and said
    'There were about the same number of people from Italy on the aircraft and on the ferry'.
    Explain why Jill is wrong.

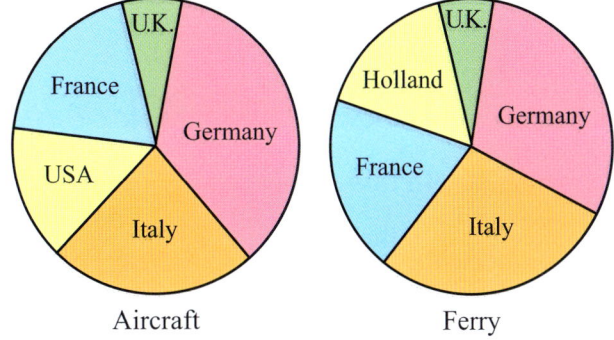

6 Here are age distribution pyramids for the U.K., Kenya and Saudi Arabia. The bars represent the percentage of the population in the age group shown.

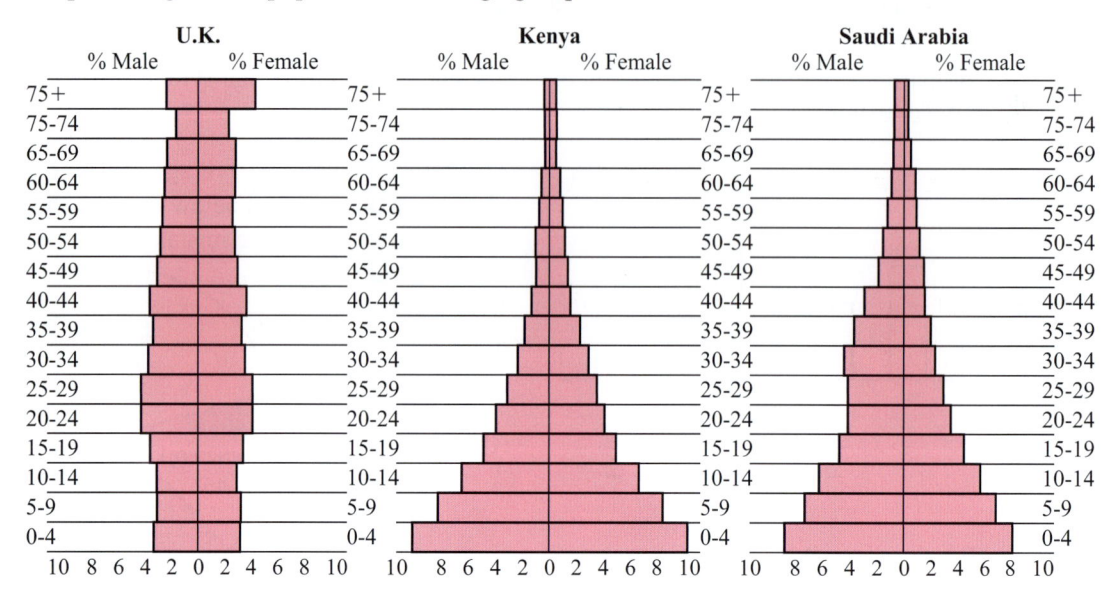

(a) For the U.K. about what percentage of the population are *male aged 20–24*?

(b) For Kenya about what percentage are *female aged 0–4*?

(c) What percentage of the population are *female aged 75+*
   (i) for the U.K.
   (ii) for Kenya?

(d) Look carefully at the charts for the U.K. and Kenya. Write a sentence to describe the main differences in the age distribution for the two countries. Write a possible explanation for the differences you observed.

(e) Look carefully at the charts for Kenya and Saudi Arabia. Do both countries have about half male and half female populations?
Explain your answer using information in the charts.

3.5 Probability 1

In this section you will learn about:

- the probability scale
- experimental probability
- expected probability
- probability involving two events

In probability we ask questions like …

'How likely is it?'

'What are the chances of …?'

'Will it rain tomorrow?'

'With global warming will my grandchildren go to school on a camel?'

Some events are certain. Some events are impossible.

Some events are in between certain and impossible.

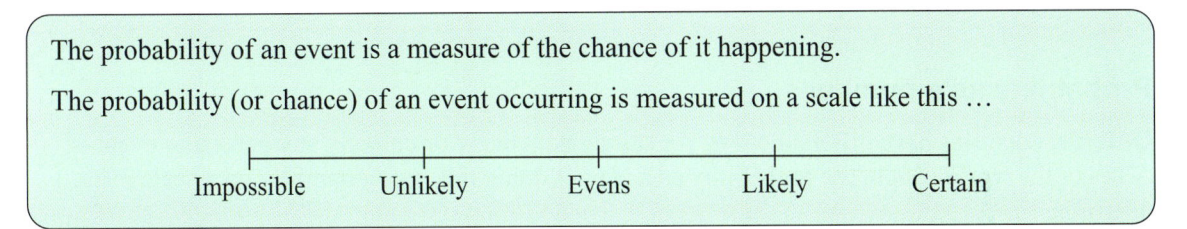

> The probability of an event is a measure of the chance of it happening.
>
> The probability (or chance) of an event occurring is measured on a scale like this …
>
> Impossible   Unlikely   Evens   Likely   Certain

Exercise 1M

Draw a probability scale like this …

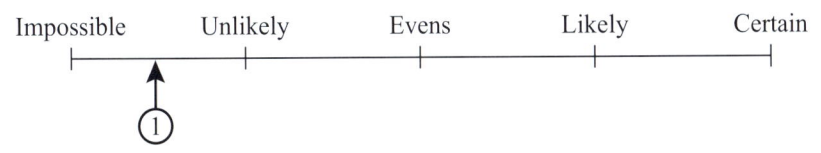

Impossible   Unlikely   Evens   Likely   Certain

Draw an arrow to show the chance of the events below happening.

[The arrow for question ① has been done for you.]

1. When a card is selected from a pack it will be an 'ace'.

2. When a coin is tossed it will show a 'head'.

3. You will discover a tarantula in your bed tonight.

4. When a drawing pin is dropped it will land 'point up'.

5. It will rain in Manchester on at least one day in April next year.

6. You get a total of one when two dice are thrown together.

7. The day after Monday will be Tuesday.

8. There will be a burst pipe in the school heating system next week and the school will have to close for three days.

⑨ You will blink your eyes in the next minute.

⑩ You will be asked to tidy your room this week.

⑪ It is 24th December. Rob says that he is very likely to be given a present the following day. Comment on what he has said.

⑫ Octavia is on holiday in Spain in the Summer. On the Tuesday it is very sunny. Octavia says 'it will probably rain tomorrow because it was so sunny today.' Comment on what she has said.

Probability as a number

Different countries have different words for saying how likely or unlikely any particular event is. All over the world people use probability as a way of doing this, using numbers on a scale instead of words.

The scale looks like this

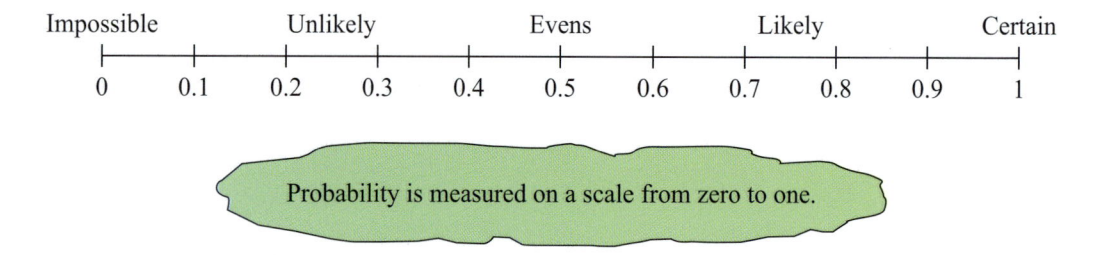

```
Impossible      Unlikely         Evens          Likely        Certain
├────┼────┼────┼────┼────┼────┼────┼────┼────┼────┤
0   0.1  0.2  0.3  0.4  0.5  0.6  0.7  0.8  0.9   1
```

> Probability is measured on a scale from zero to one.

Exercise 2M

Ⓐ Look at the events in questions ① to ⑩ in the last exercise and for each one estimate the probability of it occurring using a probability from 0 to 1.

As an example in question ① you might write 'about 0.1.' Copy each question and write your estimate of its probability at the end.

Ⓑ Now write each of the above answers as a percentage, eg. 0.1 can be written as 10%.

Experimental probability

The chance of certain events occurring can easily be predicted. For example the chance of tossing a head with an ordinary coin. Many events, however, cannot be so easily predicted.

Experiment: To find the experimental probability that the third word in the third line on any page in this book contains the letter 'a'. (You could use a non-mathematical book if you prefer.)

Step 1. We will do 50 *trials*. Write down at random 50 page numbers between 1 and 180 (say 3, 15, 16, 21, 27, etc.).

Step 2. For each page look at the third word in the third line. This is a *trial*. If there is not a third word on the third line it still counts as a trial. (The third line might be all numbers.)

> 37
>
> **Angles in triangles**
> Draw a triangle of any shape on a piece of card (and) cut it out accurately. Now tear off the three corners as shown.
>
> (third line, third word)

Step 3. If the word contains the letter 'a' this is a *success*.

Step 4. Make a tally chart like this …

Number of trials	Number of successes
⊮⊮ΙΙ	⊮ΙΙ

Step 5. Find the experimental probability that the third word in the third line on any page in this book contains the letter 'a' by doing the calculation shown below.

$$\text{Experimental probability} = \frac{\text{number of trials in which a success occurs}}{\text{total number of trials made}}$$

The 'experimental probability' is sometimes called the 'relative frequency'.

Exercise 3M

Carry out experiments to work out the experimental probability (relative frequency) of some of the following events.

Use a tally chart to record your results. Don't forget to record how many times you do the experiment (the number of 'trials').

1. Roll a dice. What is the chance of rolling a six? Perform 100 trials.

2. Toss two coins. What is the chance of tossing two tails? Perform 100 trials.

3. Pick a counter from a bag containing counters of different colours. What is the chance of picking a red counter? Perform 100 trials.

4. Roll a pair of dice. What is the chance of rolling a double? Perform 100 trials.

5. Butter a piece of toast and drop it on the floor. What is the chance of it landing buttered side down? Would you expect to get the same result with margarine? How about butter and jam? Suppose you don't toast the bread?

6. Alice throws a coin 100 times. Explain why Alice may not get 50 heads and 50 tails.

7. Sasha throws a dice 400 times. He scores a three 100 times. Do you think the dice is fair? Justify your answer.

Expected probability

For simple events, like throwing a dice or tossing a coin, we can work out the expected probability of an event occurring.

For a fair dice the *expected probability* of throwing a '3' is $\frac{1}{6}$

Getting a score on a dice is called an *outcome*.

> If all outcomes have an equal chance of happening then
>
> $$\text{Expected probability} = \frac{\text{the number of ways the event can happen}}{\text{the number of possible outcomes}}$$

Random choice: If a card is chosen at random from a pack it means that every card has an equal chance of being chosen.

> Nine identical discs numbered 1, 2, 3, 4, 5, 6, 7, 8, 9 are put into a bag.
> One disc is selected at random.
> In this example there are 9 possible equally likely outcomes of a trial.
>
> (a) The probability of selecting a '4' = $\frac{1}{9}$
>
>   This may be written p(selecting a '4') = $\frac{1}{9}$
>
> (b) p(selecting an odd number) = $\frac{5}{9}$
>
> (c) p(selecting a number greater than 5) = $\frac{4}{9}$

Exercise 4M

1. There are five paper clips. Their colours are pink, yellow, green, blue and red.
   One paper clip is chosen at random from these.
   Find the probability that it is
   (a) green   (b) blue   (c) silver

2. A hat contains 2 white balls and 1 black ball. One ball is chosen at random.
   Find the probability that it is
   (a) white   (b) black

3. One domino is selected from those shown.
   Find the probability that the total number of spots on the domino is
   (a) 11   (b) more than 10

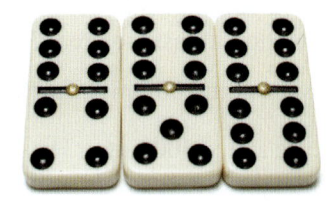

4 A pencil case contains pencils of the following colours: 6 red, 3 black, 1 green and 1 blue.
One pencil is selected without looking. Find the probability that the pencil is
   (a) red (b) black (c) green (d) not blue

5 One number is selected at random from these numbers opposite.
Find the probability that it is
   (a) an '8' (b) a '2' or '3' (c) a prime number

6 I roll an ordinary dice. Find the probability that I score
   (a) 3
   (b) 1
   (c) less than 5

7 Ten people are trying to hit the bullseye on a dartboard.
Julian says he has an equal probability to Chloe of hitting the bullseye.
Is he correct? Give a reason for your answer.

8 Eight identical discs numbered 1, 2, 3, 4, 5, 6, 7, 8 are put into a bag.
One disc is selected at random. Find the probability of selecting
   (a) a '5' (b) an odd number (c) a number less than 6

9 Nine identical discs numbered 1, 3, 4, 5, 7, 8, 10, 11, 15 are put into a bag.
One disc is selected at random. Find the probability of selecting
   (a) a '10' (b) an even number (c) a number more than 6

10 I buy a fish at random from a pond containing 3 piranhas, 2 baby sharks
and 7 goldfish. Find the probability that the fish I chose is
   (a) a goldfish (b) a baby shark
   (c) dangerous (d) glad I rescued it!
   (e) able to play the piano

11 Sienna has a bag containing 8 blue balls, 6 yellow balls and
18 red balls.
Reuben has a box containing 9 yellow balls, 27 red balls and
12 blue balls.
They each take out one ball at random.
Who is more likely to take out a red ball? Give a reason for your answer.

12 One card is selected at random from the cards shown.
Find the probability of selecting
   (a) the king of hearts (b) a joker
   (c) a 2 (d) an ace

13 A bag contains fifty balls numbered from 1 to 50.
One ball is selected at random. Find the probability that it is
(a) a multiple of 10
(b) a square number
(c) a prime number
(d) divisible by 9
(e) a cube number
(f) a factor of both 7 and 15

14 What is the probability of spinning
(a) yellow
(b) green
(c) pink or yellow
(d) blue
(e) not blue?

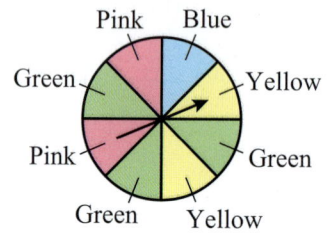

15 There are 14 discs in a bag. Grayson says that the probability of taking a blue disc when he randomly removes a disc from the bag is $\frac{1}{3}$.
Explain clearly why Grayson cannot be correct.

16 50 Christmas presents are given out randomly to some elderly people in a care home. Five of the presents are radios, 20 are books and the rest are boxes of chocolates.
(a) Mr Jackson is the first person to open a present.
What is the probability that he gets a radio?
(b) What is the probability that Mr. Jackson does not get a book?
(c) Mr Jackson in fact gets a box of chocolates. Mrs Perkins opens her present next.
What is the probability that she gets a radio?

Two events: listing possible outcomes

When an experiment involves two events, it is usually helpful to make a list of all the possible outcomes. When there is a large number of outcomes, it is important to be systematic in making the list.

- Coins
  (a) Using H for 'head' and T for 'tail', two coins can land as:

  H H
  H T
  T H
  T T

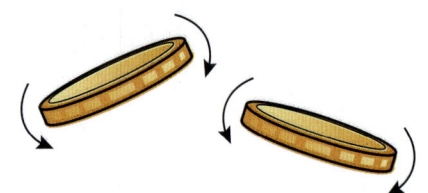

  (b) Three coins can land as:

  Notice that the outcomes in the boxes are the outcomes for two coins, as above.

  H ⌈H H⌉   T ⌈H H⌉
  H |H T| T |H T|
  H |T H| T |T H|
  H ⌊T T⌋   T ⌊T T⌋

- Two dice

  When a red dice is thrown with a white dice, the outcomes are (red dice first):
  (1, 1), (1, 2), (1, 3), (1, 4), (1, 5), (1, 6), (2, 1), (2, 2), (2, 3) … (6, 6).

  The 36 equally likely outcomes can be shown on a grid. Point A shows a 4 on the red dice and a 5 on the white dice.
  Point B shows a 2 on the red dice and a 4 on the white dice.

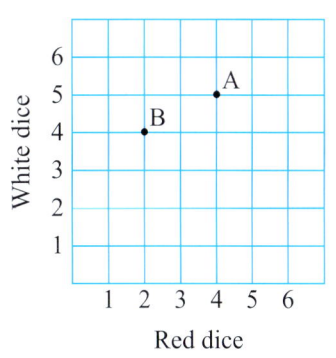

  The probability of getting a total of 10 on two dice can be found:

  $$p(\text{total is } 10) = \frac{(\text{number of ways of getting a total of 10})}{(\text{number of possible outcomes})}$$

  $$= \frac{3}{36}$$

Exercise 5M

1. A bag contains a 1p coin, a 10p coin and a 20p coin. Two coins are selected at random.
   (a) List all the possible combinations of two coins which can be selected from the bag.
   (b) Find the probability that the total value of the two coins selected is
      (i) 11p
      (ii) 30p

2. Two dice are rolled together and the *difference* is found. In the grid the point X has a difference of 3 obtained by rolling a 2 and a 5.

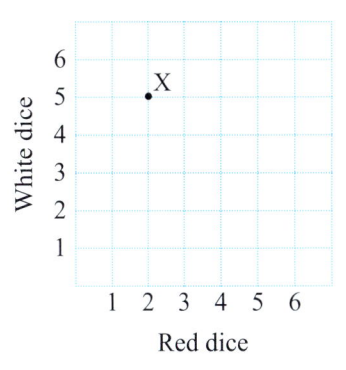

   Find the expected probability of obtaining a difference of
   (a) 3
   (b) 0

3. The four cards shown are shuffled and placed face down on a table.

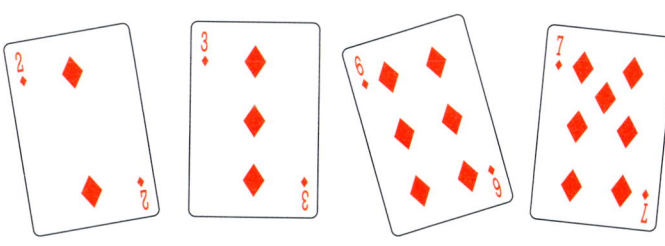

   Two cards are selected at random.
   (a) List all the possible pairs of cards which could be selected.
   (b) Find the probability that the total of the two cards is
      (i) 5   (ii) 9

4 (a) List all the outcomes when three coins are tossed together.

   (b) Find the probability of getting
       (i) exactly one head
       (ii) three tails

5 The spinner shown has six equal sections on the outside and three equal sections in the middle. The spinner shows a '5' and an 'A'.

   Find the probability of spinning
   (a) a 'C'
   (b) a '7'
   (c) a '6' and an 'F' at the same time

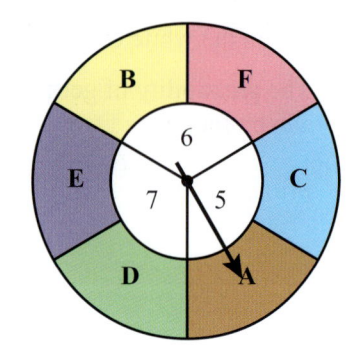

6 Dylan and Olga take turns to throw a coin and a dice. They play a game where Dylan gets a point if he gets a head on the coin and a square number on the dice. Olga gets a point if she gets a tail on the coin and an even number on the dice.

   (a) If they each throw 100 times, who is more likely to win?
       Give a full reason for your answer.

   (b) Get a partner, a coin and a dice. Play the game above.
       Do you get the results you expected in part (a)?

Need more practice with probability?

1 A bag contains 2 red balls, 4 white balls and 5 blue balls. One ball is selected at random.
   Find the probability of selecting

   (a) a red ball   (b) a white ball   (c) not a white ball

2 Evelyn throws a fair dice five times and gets scores of 2, 5, 6, 1 and 3.
   She throws the dice one more time. What is the probability that she will get a 4?

3 A box of crayons contains the following colours.

2 red	6 yellow
8 blue	3 orange
1 green	4 brown

   A crayon is chosen at random.
   Which colour has a probability $\frac{1}{3}$ of being chosen?
   Justify your answer.

4 The horse 'Optimist' wins seven races out of seven. Owen says that 'Optimist' is dead certain to win the next race.
Is Owen correct?
Explain your answer fully.

5 Maya throws a coin 600 times and it lands on tails 311 times.
Do you think the coin is fair?
Give a reason for your answer.

6 The alphabet bricks are put in a bag and one brick is selected at random.
Find the probability that the letter chosen is
(a) a vowel
(b) the letter 'z'
(c) a letter in the word 'HAT'
(d) a letter in the word 'MUSIC'

7 Two bags contain numbered discs as shown.
One disc is selected at random from each bag.
(a) Draw a grid to show all the possible outcomes.
(b) Find the probability that
  (i) the total of the two numbers is 6
  (ii) the total of the two numbers is less than 5

8 For this question you need a dice.
(a) Copy the table below and fill in the second row.

Number of rolls of dice	12	24	36	48	60
Number of 4s expected					
Actual number of 4s					

(b) Now roll the dice 60 times, filling in the third row every 12 rolls.
(c) Comment on your results.

Extension questions with probability

1 A red dice is thrown first and then a blue dice is thrown.
(a) Find the probability that the score on the blue dice is the same as the score on the red dice.
(b) Find the probability that the score on the blue dice is one more than the score on the red dice.

2 Caleb has a box containing red, blue, green and yellow balls. Caleb is going to randomly remove one ball.
The probability of taking a red ball is 0.1. There are an equal number of blue, green and yellow balls. What is the probability of Caleb removing a green ball?

3 Two spinners, with equal sectors, are numbered 0, 1, 2, … 9.
The two spinners are spun together and the difference between the scores is recorded. So a '5' and a '9' gives a difference of 4.

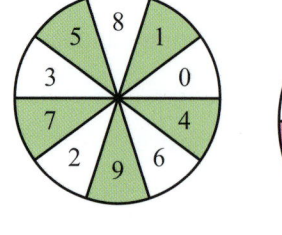

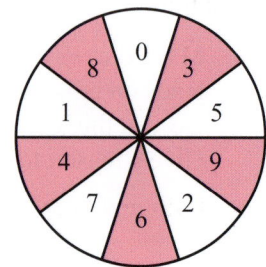

(a) Draw a grid to show all the possible outcomes and write the difference for each outcome.
(b) Find the probability of obtaining
  (i) a difference of 4   (ii) a difference of 9
(c) What is the most likely number for the difference?

4 Two sixes need to be thrown to start a board game. Sabina says that the probability of this happening would be close to zero on a probability scale.

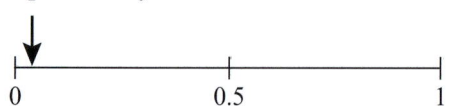

Is she correct? Explain your answer fully.

5 A bag contains some red, blue and green balls. One ball is to be randomly removed.
The probability of a blue ball being taken is $\frac{1}{8}$ and the probability of a green ball being taken is $\frac{2}{5}$.
(a) What is the least number of balls that could be in the bag?
(b) The number of balls in the bag is twice the answer found in part (a). How many of them are red?

6 (a) List all outcomes when four coins are tossed together.
(b) Find the probability of getting
  (i) exactly two heads
  (ii) exactly one tail
  (iii) four heads

7 (a) How many outcomes are possible when one coin is tossed five times?
(b) In a soccer knock-out competition, Barcelona won the toss five times in a row. What is the probability of this happening?

✗ Spot the mistakes 6 ✗

Data and probability

Work through each question below and explain clearly what mistakes have been made. Beware – some questions are correctly done.

1. Callum examines the numbers

       7   12   9   1   14   7   2   11

   Callum works out that the mode is equal to the median.

2. The pie charts below show the proportion of students who study foreign languages at two schools.

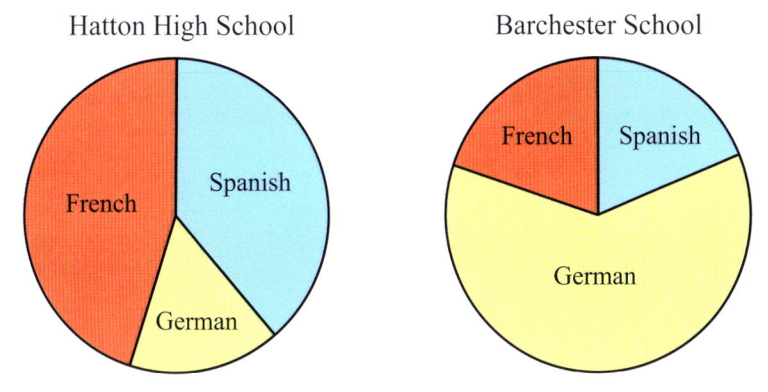

   Hatton High School   Barchester School

   (French, Spanish, German)   (French, Spanish, German)

   Alyssa says that more students study spanish in Hatton High School than in Barchester School.

3. Tyler has a bag containing green beads and yellow beads. The probability of randomly removing a yellow bead is $\frac{3}{5}$. There are more than six beads in the bag.

   Tyler says that the smallest possible number of beads in the bag must be 15 because $\frac{3}{5}$ of 15 equals 9 yellow beads, which is a whole number.

4.
Number of pets	Frequency
0	8
1	7
2	14
3	11
4	5
5	2

   The table opposite shows how many pets are owned by each family in a small village.

   Kiara says that the mode for this data is 14.

5 Two spinners each have the numbers 1 to 4 written on them. When both spinners are used, what is the probability that the total score will be 6?

Solution:

+	1	2	3	4
1	2	3	4	5
2	3	4	5	6
3	4	5	6	7
4	5	6	7	8

Probability of a score of 6 is

$$\frac{3}{24} = \frac{1}{8}$$

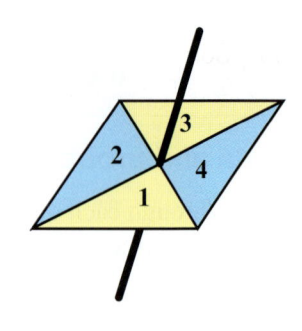

6 A cricketer has a mean average score of 34 after 9 innings. What does the cricketer score in the next innings if the mean average increases to 35.5?

Solution: total score after 9 innings = 9 × 34 = 306
total score after 10 innings = 10 × 35.5 = 355
Cricketer scored 355 − 306 = 49 in the next innings.

7 The ages (in years) of some people are given below. Draw a frequency diagram.

11	32	17	29	24	34	12
29	43	26	29	14	30	45
38	23	25	18	36	17	22

Frequency table is:

Age (A)	Frequency
$10 \leq A < 20$	6
$20 \leq A < 30$	9
$30 \leq A < 40$	4
$40 \leq A < 50$	2

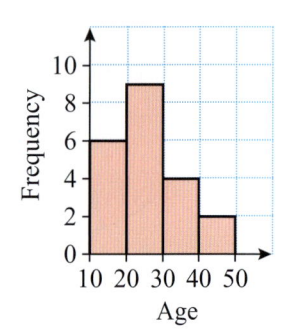

8 There are 20 people in a football squad. Four of them are left-footed and six of them wear orange football boots.

Julia says that if one person is randomly chosen then the probability of that person being left-footed or wearing orange football boots is $\frac{10}{20}$ so $\frac{1}{2}$

9 The weights of some dogs are shown in the stem and leaf diagram below.

Stem	Leaf
21	6 7 7
22	2 3 3 3 5 8
23	4 5 7 7 7
24	8 9
25	3 3 6 7

Key: 23|7 means 23.7 kg

Harvey calculates that the mean average weight is equal to the median weight.

10 Some people are asked where they would most like to go on holiday. Their responses are shown in the pie chart below.

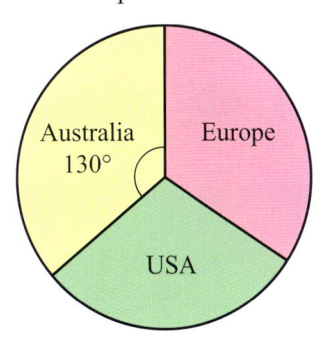

$\frac{5}{12}$ of the people chose Europe.

What fraction of the people chose USA?

Solution: Australia fraction $= \frac{130}{360} = \frac{13}{36}$

Australia + Europe fraction $= \frac{13}{36} + \frac{5}{12} = \frac{13}{36} + \frac{15}{36}$

$= \frac{28}{36} = \frac{7}{9}$

USA fraction $= 1 - \frac{7}{9} = \frac{2}{9}$

CHECK YOURSELF ON SECTIONS 3.4 AND 3.5

1 Stem and leaf diagrams

Draw an ordered stem and leaf diagram for the ages given below.

| 33 | 45 | 76 | 59 | 57 | 64 | 48 | 63 | 55 | 65 |
| 64 | 45 | 31 | 52 | 73 | 57 | 68 | 57 | 44 | 52 |

2 Displaying data in groups

At a medical inspection the 11/12 year-olds in a school have their heights measured. The results are shown.

136.8, 146.2, 141.2, 147.2, 151.3, 145.0, 155.0,
149.9, 138.0, 146.8, 157.4, 143.1, 143.5, 147.2,
147.5, 158.6, 154.7, 144.6, 152.4, 144.0, 151.0.

(a) Put the heights into groups

Class interval	Frequency
$135 \leq h < 140$	
$140 \leq h < 145$	
$145 \leq h < 150$	
$150 \leq h < 155$	
$155 \leq h < 160$	

(b) Draw a frequency diagram

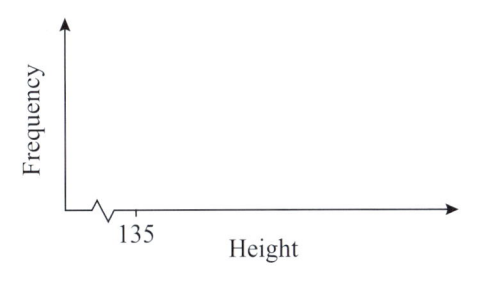

3 Pie charts

In a survey 900 children at a school were asked to state their favourite sport in the Olympics.

(a) How many chose swimming?
(b) How many chose gymnastics?
(c) How many chose either tennis or basket ball?

4 Expected probability

A bag contains 1 blue ball, 3 red balls and 7 white balls.

(a) If I select a ball at random from the bag without looking, what colour ball am I most likely to select?
(b) What is the probability I select:
   (i) a white ball
   (ii) a red ball
   (iii) a green ball
   (iv) a blue ball?

5 Probability involving two events

A spinner and a dice are spun and rolled at the same time.

(a) List all the possible outcomes.
(b) What is the probability of getting a total score which is
   (i) equal to 22
   (ii) greater than 22?

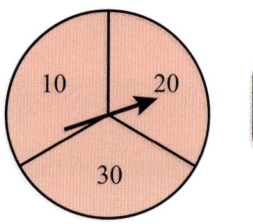

3.6 Applying mathematics 3

In section 3.6 you will apply maths in a variety of situations.

1. Jesse is paid a basic weekly wage of £65 and then a further 30p for each item completed. How many items must be completed in a week when she earns a total of £171.50?

2. Copy each calculation and find the missing numbers.

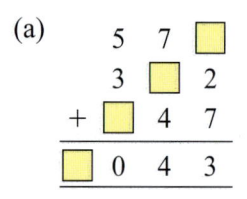

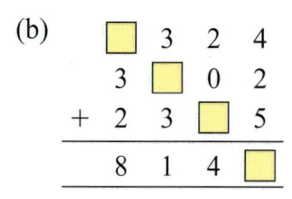

(a)
```
    5 7 □
    3 □ 2
  + □ 4 7
  ─────────
  □ 0 4 3
```

(b)
```
    □ 3 2 4
    3 □ 0 2
  + 2 3 □ 5
  ─────────
    8 1 4 □
```

3 This is a number triangle.
The numbers along each edge add up to 9.

Copy and complete the triangle.

The six numbers are 1, 2, 3, 4, 5, 6.

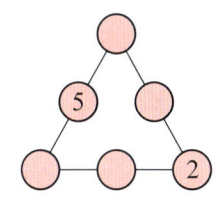

4 Mel needs to substitute the values $a = -3$ and $b = -4$ into the expression $a^2 - b$.
She gets the answer -5.
Is she correct? Explain your answer fully.

5 In the diagram opposite,
$BD = ED$ and $C\hat{B}D = 130°$.
Work out the size of $B\hat{E}F$.
Give full reasons for your answer.

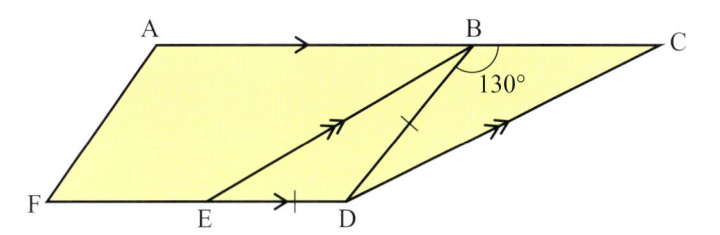

6

(a) Copy the graph opposite which shows the line $y = 3x - 4$.

(b) Copy and complete the coordinates (0, 2) (2, ?) (4, ?) which lie on the line $y = 3x + 2$. Mark these points on the graph and join them up to show the line $y = 3x + 2$.

(c) How are the two lines on your graph related?
Where do they each cross the y axis?
How does all this connect to their equations?

(d) Draw the line $y = 3x - 2$ directly onto your graph (do not work out several coordinates first!)

7 The base of a triangle is equal to its height.
Its area is equal to the area of the trapezium shown opposite.

Calculate the height of the triangle.

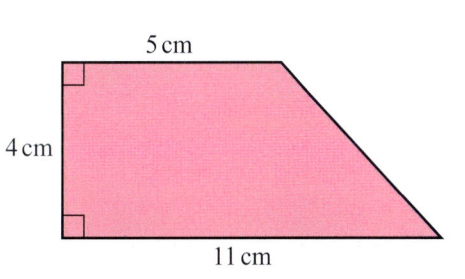

8 Work out (a) $1^1 + 2^2 + 3^3 + 4^4$

(b) $\frac{1}{3} \times \frac{2}{4} \times \frac{3}{5} \times \ldots \times \frac{9}{11} \times \frac{10}{12}$

9 The five numbers opposite have mode 2 and median 3.

One more number is added to these which makes the mean equal 5.

Write down the value of this extra number which is added to the list.

| 2 | ? | ? | 5 | 8 |

+ | ? |

10 The test results of 50 students are shown below.

Mark	5	6	7	8	9	10
Frequency	0	2	12	17	10	9

What percentage of the students scored 8 marks or more?

UNIT 3   MIXED REVIEW

Part one

1 Copy and complete
  (a) $0.71 \times 10 = \square$
  (b) $1.52 \times \square = 152$
  (c) $86.2 \div \square = 8.62$
  (d) $406 \div \square = 0.406$
  (e) $0.014 \times \square = 1.4$
  (f) $0.1 \times 1000 = \square$

2 (a) Write down the first five multiples of 4.
  (b) Write down the factors of 12.
  (c) Which of the factors of 12 are prime numbers?

3 (a) What is the probability of rolling a dice and getting a six?
  (b) What is the probability of not getting a six?

4 Different batteries were tested to see how long a set of 'chattering teeth' keep working. The winning battery worked for 8 minutes. Each battery costs 90p. How much would it cost to keep the teeth chattering for four hours?

5 Draw a factor tree then express 112 as a product of its prime factors.

6 Find the number.
  (a) a multiple of 11
      a multiple of 7
      the product of its digits is 6
  (b) a square number
      a 3 digit number
      the product of its digits is 20

7 A bag contains four balls. The probability of selecting a white ball from the bag is 0.5.
A white ball is taken from the bag and left on one side.
What is the probability of selecting a white ball from the bag now?

8 Each card opposite has a whole number on it.
The mode is 9 and the median equals the
range which equals 7.

Write down the five numbers if the mean average is as large as possible.

9 Answer true or false
(a) $4^2 = 2^4$
(b) $1 \div 100 = (0.1)^2$
(c) 3^3 is greater than 4^2

10 The test results of 100 students are shown below.

Mark	5	6	7	8	9	10
Frequency	10	22	12	17	10	29

Work out the mean test result for these 100 students.

11 The frequency diagram shows the weights of some children.
(a) How many children weighed between 50 and 55 kg?
(b) How many children weighed over 55 kg?
(c) How many children were there in total?

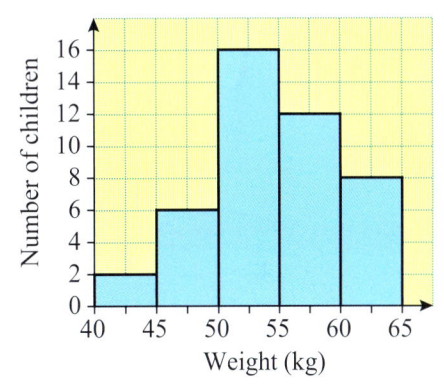

12 The cost of ham in Dan's Deli is £2.18 for 100 g.
The cost of cheese is £1.94 for 100 g.
Mr Spencer wants to buy 350 g of cheese and 150 g of ham.
He has one £10 note. Has he got enough money?
Explain your answer fully.

Part two

1 Copy and complete each chain.

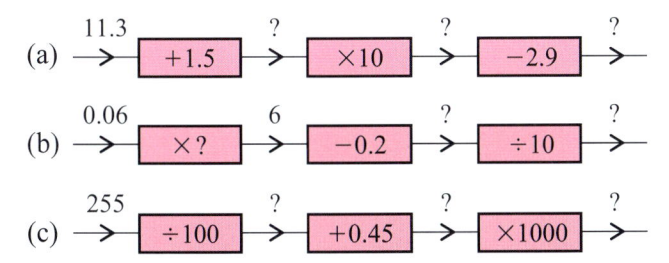

(a) 11.3 → [+1.5] → ? → [×10] → ? → [−2.9] → ?

(b) 0.06 → [×?] → 6 → [−0.2] → ? → [÷10] → ?

(c) 255 → [÷100] → ? → [+0.45] → ? → [×1000] → ?

2 Here is an age distribution pyramid for the children at a Center Parcs resort.

(a) How many girls were there aged 5–9?

(b) How many children were there altogether in the 0–4 age range?

(c) How many girls were at the resort?

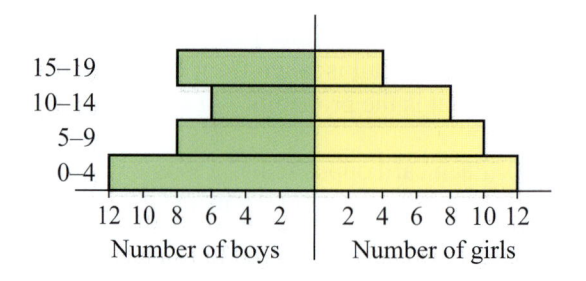

3 There were ten children on a coach journey. The mean age of the children was 11 and the range of their ages was 4. Write each statement below and then write next to it whether it is *True, Possible* or *False*.

(a) The youngest child was 9 years old.

(b) Every child was 11 years old.

(c) All the children were at least 10 years old.

4 It is not easy to burn a match completely.
In fact it takes thirteen seconds.
A box contains 47 matches.
How long would it take to completely burn the matches, one after another, in 10 boxes?

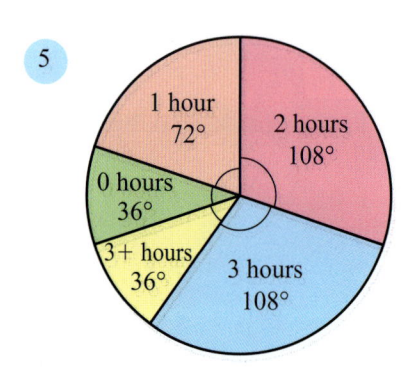

5 This pie chart shows the number of hours in one evening spent watching television by 40 children. Copy and complete the table.

Hours	Children
0	
1	
2	
3	
3+	

6 How many spots are there on twenty-four ordinary dice?

7 In a 'magic' square the sum of the numbers in any row, column or main diagonal is the same. Find x in each square.

(a)
3		
8		4
7	x	

(b)
14		7	2
x		12	
	5	9	16
15			3

8 The line graph below shows the fuel gauge reading of a car at different times throughout a day.

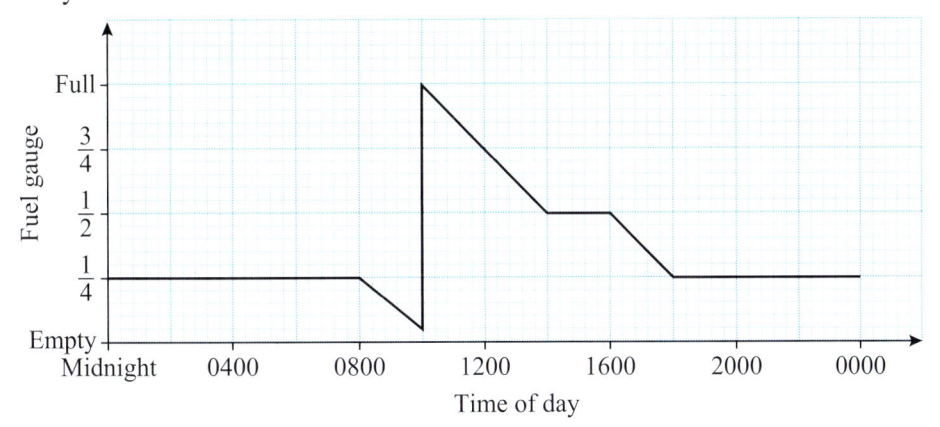

(a) Was the car moving or stationary between midnight and 8.00 am?
(b) What happened to the car at 10.00 am?
(c) How much petrol was used between 10.00 am and 2.00 pm?
(d) At what time in the evening was the car put in the garage?

9 Kelly has five cards.
The mean of the five cards is 8.
The range of the five cards is 6.

| 8 | 8 | 8 | | |

What numbers are on the other two cards?

10 The stem and leaf diagram shows the heights of some people. Calculate the difference between the median and the mean height.

Stem	Leaf
16	4 6 6
17	3 4 5 5 5 8
18	2 2 4 5 6 6 9
19	0 2 5 6

Key: 17|5 means 1.75 m

11 Write the numbers in order of size, smallest first.
(a) 0.71, 0.605, 0.65, 0.7, 0.702
(b) 0.99, 0.08, 0.079, 0.1
(c) 2^3, 3^2, 1^3, (2×3), 0.007×10^2

12 A spinner has the numbers 1 to 4 on it. The spinner is spun and one dice is thrown. The numbers on the spinner and dice are multiplied together.
What is the probability of getting a product of more than 16?

Puzzles and Problems 3

1. In these triangle puzzles the numbers a, b, c, d are connected as follows:

   $a \times b = c$

   $c \times b = d$

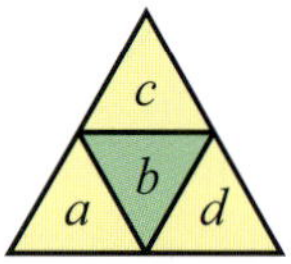

   For example: (triangle with $a=2$, $b=5$, $c=10$, $d=50$)

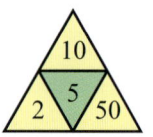

   Copy and complete the following triangles.

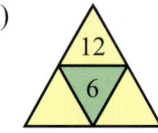

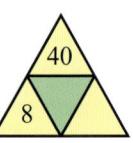

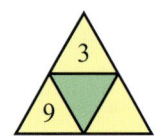

   (a) $a=4$, $b=7$
   (b) $b=6$, $c=12$
   (c) $b=3$, $d=63$
   (d) $a=8$, $c=40$
   (e) $b=9$, $c=3$
   (f) $b=3$, $d=12$

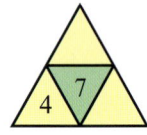

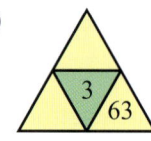

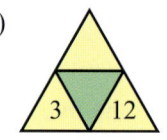

2. Write the digits 1 to 9 so that all the answers are correct.

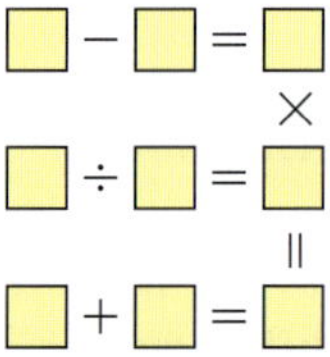

   $\square - \square = \square$
   $\square \div \square = \square$
   $\square + \square = \square$

   (with $\times$ and $=$ connecting columns)

3. Each of these calculations has the same number missing from all three boxes. Find the missing number in each calculation.

   (a) $\square \times \square - \square = 12$
   (b) $\square \div \square + \square = 9$
   (c) $\square \times \square + \square = 72$

4. In the circle write $+$, $-$, $\times$ or $\div$ to make the calculation correct.

   (a) $9 \times 5 \bigcirc 3 = 48$
   (b) $8 \times 5 \bigcirc 2 = 20$
   (c) $8 \bigcirc 9 - 5 = 67$
   (d) $12 \bigcirc 2 + 4 = 10$
   (e) $60 \div 3 \bigcirc 5 = 15$

5 Write the following with the correct signs.

(a) $5 \times 4 \times 3 3 = 63$

(b) $5 + 4 3 2 = 4$

(c) $5 \times 2 \times 3 1 = 31$

6 Draw four straight lines which pass through all 9 points, without taking your pen from the paper and without going over any line twice. [Hint: Lines can extend beyond the square.]

7 Draw six straight lines to pass through all 16 points, subject to the same conditions as in question **6**.

In questions **8** and **9** each letter stands for a different single digit from 0 to 9. The first digit of a number is never zero. Find the value of each letter.

8 (a) M E
         M E +
         ─────
         A M
   [Find two solutions]

(b) K L M
       L M
     M L M +
     ───────
     L M M

(c) N A V E
     W A V E
     R A V E +
     ─────────
     S E V E

Work out E, V, A and S, You will find that N, W and R can each have three different values.

Some of these questions have more than one solution.

9 (a) O N E
         O N E +
         ───────
         T W O

(b) C U T
     C O T
       I F +
     ───────
     O A T

(c) S O N
     S U N
       I S +
     ───────
     O W N

(d) T O U R
     S O U R
     R O A R +
     ─────────
     P E R R

(e) F O U R
     F I V E +
     ─────────
     N I N E

Mental Arithmetic Practice 3

There are two sets of mental arithmetic questions in this section. Ideally a teacher will read out each question twice, with pupils' books closed. Each test of 25 questions should take about 15–20 minutes.

Test 1

1. How many 20p coins do I need to make £300?
2. How much more than £128 is £400?
3. Work out 10% of £6000.
4. Two angles in a triangle are thirty-five and seventy-five degrees. What is the third angle?
5. A 50p coin is 2 mm thick. What is the value of a pile of 50p coins 2 cm high?
6. How many minutes are there in three and a half hours?
7. What is the perimeter of a square whose area is four centimetres squared?
8. A man died in 2003 aged 58. In what year was he born?
9. By how much is half a metre longer than 5 millimetres? (answer in mm)
10. A string of length 590 cm is cut in half. How long is each piece?
11. My watch reads twenty past seven. It is 25 minutes fast. What is the correct time?
12. By how much is four kilograms more than 700 grams?
13. What is a quarter of four hundred and ten?
14. A train travels at an average speed of 45 mph. How far does it travel in 3 hours?
15. A half is a third of a certain number. What is the number?
16. From eight times seven take away nine.
17. Find two ways of making 66p using five coins.
18. *Roughly* how many litres are there in 10 gallons?
19. A plane was due to arrive at noon on Tuesday but arrived at 7 a.m. on Wednesday. How many hours late was the plane?
20. How many square centimetres are there in one square metre?
21. Add together 18, 20 and 42.
22. Next in the sequence 10, 7, 4, 1.
23. One per cent of a billion pounds.
24. Eleven squared plus ten squared.
25. What is one twentieth as a percentage?

Test 2

1. I want to buy 4 DVDs, each costing £6.49. To the nearest pound, how much will the 4 DVDs cost in total?
2. What is the total of 67 and 953?
3. A triangle has a base of 6 cm and a height of 8 cm. What is its area?
4. Work out three squared plus four squared.
5. What number is exactly mid-way between 2.8 and 2.9?
6. How many magazines costing 85p can I buy with £10?

7. Sam is 28 cm taller than Holly who is 1.37 m metres tall. How tall is Sam?

8. Write 9 divided by 100 as a decimal.

9. What number is next in the pattern 8, 4, 2, 1, 0.5, …?

10. What is a tenth of 3.6?

11. How many lines of symmetry do all rectangles have?

12. I think of a number and subtract 7. The result is equal to 8 times 6. What is the number?

13. What number is 10 less than eight thousand?

14. The pupils in Shane's class are given lockers numbered from 42 to 64. How many pupils are there in Shane's class?

15. What is a quarter of a half?

16. A toy train travels 5 metres in two seconds. How far will it go in one minute?

17. Write the number '$3\frac{1}{2}$ million' in figures.

18. Work out 400 times 300.

19. How much longer is 8.5 metres than 835 centimetres?

20. Write down the next prime number after 32.

21. Ten cubed plus nine squared.

22. What is the perimeter of a rectangle with sides 7 cm and 35 cm?

23. How many 2p coins do you need to make £5?

24. Increase a price of £500 by 5 per cent.

25. A quadrilateral has three angles of 80°. What is the fourth angle?

A long time ago! 3

Pounds, shillings and pence

In horse racing, the length of a race is often measured in furlongs.
Do you know how many furlongs make one mile?

A person throwing a party might buy a firkin of beer.
How many gallons would this be?
These are imperial units, which are covered later in this book.
Actually 8 furlongs make one mile and 9 gallons make one firkin.

Your grandparents (and maybe parents!) used to buy things with shillings, tanners and two bob coins.
One penny was written as 1d. 12 pennies made 1 shilling (written as 1s.)
20 shillings made 1 pound.
21 shillings made 1 guinea.
(A 'tanner' was a 6d. coin and 2s. was sometimes called a 'two bob' coin)

1s. = 12d.
£1 = 20s.

Mary wants to buy a car for £27 16s. 4d.
and a bike for 5s. 10d.
How much does she spend in total?

```
  £   s.  d.
 27  16   4
      5  10
 ─────────
 28   2   2
  1   1
```

Add the pennies first. Every 12 pennies are carried over as 1 shilling.
Next add the shillings. Every 20 shillings are carried over as 1 pound.

Mary spends a total of £28 2s. 2d.

Exercise

Try these questions from a 1927 arithmetic test.

1.
```
   £  s. d.
   5  3  7
 + 2  5  9
```

2.
```
   £  s.  d.
   3  14  8
 + 6  12  3
```

3.
```
   £  s.  d.
   8  13   4
 + 4  17  10
```

4.
```
         £  s.  d.
 from    8  19   3
 take    4  13   9
```

5.
```
         £  s.  d.
 from   16   4   8
 take    7  10   4
```

6.
```
         £  s.  d.
 from   17   3   2
 take   10  14   8
```

7. How many $\frac{1}{2}$d. stamps could I buy with a 'two bob' coin?

8. How many oranges can I get for 3s. at the cost of seven oranges for 6d.?

9. How much must be added to 15s. 6d. to make a guinea?

10. I have bought a cake for 1s. 3d. and some jam for 5d. How much change should I have out of 2 shillings?

11. I have been for a week's holiday and spent 6d. a day while I was away. How much should I have left out of 4s.?

12. **RESEARCH:** There were many units used in the nineteenth century for length, weight and capacity. Examples are 'barleycorns' and 'kilderkins'.
    (a) How many different units can you find?
    (b) Can you discover where any of the names come from?

UNIT 4

4.1 Percentages

In section 4.1 you will:
- review the conversion of fractions, decimals and percentages
- express one number as a percentage of another number
- work out percentage increases and decreases

Fractions, decimals and percentages review

Reminder

$$0.35 = \frac{35}{100} = \frac{7}{20}$$

$$28\% = \frac{28}{100} = \frac{7}{25}$$

Cancel down fractions

'Per cent' means 'out of 100'

$$\frac{19}{50} = \frac{38}{100} = 38\%$$

$$64\% = \frac{64}{100} = 0.64$$

Exercise 1M

1. Change these percentages into decimals.
   (a) 37% (b) 60% (c) 6% (d) 19% (e) 45%

2. Write True or False for each of the following statements.
   (a) $0.09 = \frac{1}{9}$
   (b) $0.25 > \frac{1}{4}$
   (c) $0.2 = \frac{1}{5}$
   (d) $0.4 > 4\%$
   (e) $65\% = 0.65$
   (f) $\frac{3}{5} = 35\%$

3. 5% of people who go to the beach get sunburnt. What fraction of people who go to the beach do not get sunburnt?

4 Mary uses 39 out of 52 cards to build a tower of cards.
   (a) What fraction of all the cards did she use?
   (b) What percentage of all the cards did she use?

5 Convert these percentages into fractions.
   (a) 49%   (b) 8%   (c) 15%

6 Which test mark below is the greater percentage?

   11 out of 25 or 9 out of 20

7 Write down which fractions are equivalent to the given percentage.

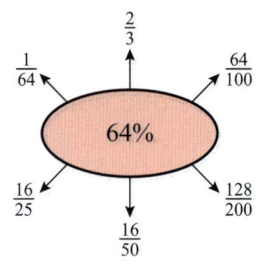

   Centre: 64%
   Surrounding: $\frac{1}{64}$, $\frac{2}{3}$, $\frac{64}{100}$, $\frac{16}{25}$, $\frac{16}{50}$, $\frac{128}{200}$

8 Write each set of numbers below in order of size, smallest first.
   (a) $\frac{3}{4}$, 0.8, $\frac{7}{10}$
   (b) 0.57, $\frac{11}{20}$, 60%
   (c) 24%, $\frac{1}{4}$, $\frac{1}{5}$
   (d) $\frac{21}{25}$, 0.8, 82%

9 There are five groups of *equivalent* fractions, decimals and percentages below. Write down each group. (Beware: there are two odd ones out.)

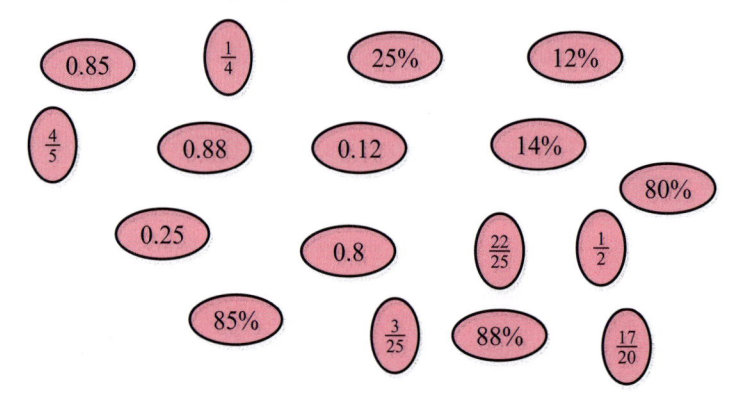

   0.85, $\frac{1}{4}$, 25%, 12%, $\frac{4}{5}$, 0.88, 0.12, 14%, 80%, 0.25, 0.8, $\frac{22}{25}$, $\frac{1}{2}$, 85%, $\frac{3}{25}$, 88%, $\frac{17}{20}$

Expressing one number as a percentage of another number

25 children are playing rounders. 8 are boys.
What percentage of the children playing rounders are boys?

8 out of 25 = $\frac{8}{25} = \frac{32}{100} = 32\%$

Exercise 2M

1. Danny plays 25 games of pool and wins 16 of them.
   What percentage of the games did he *not* win?

2. Three tenths of Lorna's books were Science Fiction.
   What percentage of her books were *not* Science Fiction?

3. Tania scored 60 out of 150 in a test.
   What percentage did she score?

4. 500 people were asked what their favourite film was.
   85 of them said 'Lord of the Rings'.
   What percentage of the people chose 'Lord of the Rings'?

5. Change each of the following into a percentage then put them in order of size, starting with the smallest.

   A. 7 out of 25   B. 13 out of 20   C. 18 out of 60   D. 50 out of 200

6. Mark spent $\frac{3}{5}$ of his money on a computer game and $\frac{3}{20}$ of his money on food.
   What percentage of his money has he got left?

7.
	Drive	Do not drive	Total
Male	160	40	200
Female	165	85	250
Total	325	125	450

   450 people are asked if they drive or not. The information is shown in the table opposite.

   (a) What percentage of the males do not drive?
   (b) What percentage of the people who do not drive are female?
   (c) What percentage of the females drive?
   (d) How many more males would need to learn to drive if the percentage of males who do not drive is to decrease to 15%?

Reminder: $\frac{1}{3} = 33\frac{1}{3}\%$ $\frac{2}{3} = 66\frac{2}{3}\%$

To change more 'tricky' numbers into a percentage, write the two numbers as a fraction then multiply by 100.

---

19 people are asked if they can drive a car. 13 of them replied with a 'yes'.
What percentage of the people can drive?

13 out of 19 = $\frac{13}{19} \times 100$ = 68.42 (using a calculator)
                                    = 68% (to the nearest %)

Exercise 3M

You may use a calculator. Give all answers to the nearest percentage.

1. There are 31 children in a class. 17 of them are girls. What percentage of the class are girls?

2. A football team scores 91 goals during one season. Crespo scores 28 of the goals. What percentage of his team's goals did he score?

3. Boris drank one third of his drink. What percentage of his drink did he have left?

4.

D	O	W	E	N
E	E	D	S	O
M	A	N	Y	T
E	S	T	S	?

What percentage of the letters in this grid are
 (a) the letter N
 (b) the letter E

5. Some bronze is made with 163 g copper, 23 g tin and 4 g aluminium. What percentage of the bronze is
 (a) copper (b) tin?

6.
```
          1
        1   1
      1   2   1
    1   3   3   1
  1   4   6   4   1
1   5  10  10   5   1
```
This triangle is known as Pascal's triangle.
What percentage of the numbers are prime numbers?
(Remember: 1 is *not* prime.)

7. Some children were asked what their favourite pet was.
The results are shown in this table.
What percentage of all the children chose
 (a) dog
 (b) gerbil
 (c) rabbit

Type of pet	Number of children
cat	87
dog	136
hamster	49
rabbit	63
gerbil	24

8. The table below shows how many fish have been caught by five people on a fishing trip.

Name	Aaron	Lillian	Emma	Deven	Nadya
Number of fish	11	9	12	8	10

Who caught 16% of all the fish?

9. A company makes money from hotels, restaurants and leisure clubs. The pie chart opposite shows what proportion of the company's profit comes from each of these. One of these produces a profit of £499 502 out of the company's total profit of £1 218 296. Which part of the business produced this profit?

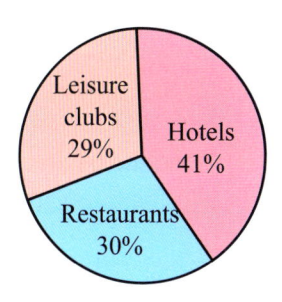

Leisure clubs 29%
Hotels 41%
Restaurants 30%

Percentage increases and decreases

Change common percentages into fractions:

$66\frac{2}{3}\%$ of $30 = \frac{2}{3}$ of $30 = (30 \div 3) \times 2 = 20$

Also use multiples of 10%: $10\% = \frac{1}{10}$

To work out 20%, find 10% then multiply by 2
To work out 30%, find 10% then multiply by 3 and so on.

In a sale the price of a shirt is reduced by 20%. Find the sale price if the normal price is £30.

10% of £30 = $\frac{1}{10}$ of 30 = £3

20% of £30 = 2 × £3 = £6

Sale price = 30 − 6 = £24

Exercise 4M

1. Work out
   (a) 80% of £200
   (b) $66\frac{2}{3}\%$ of £33
   (c) 70% of £400
   (d) 20% of £60
   (e) 5% of £80
   (f) 15% of £80

2. Which is larger?   30% of £40   or   25% of £60

3. Which is larger?   50% of £70   or   5% of £700

4. There are 48 dolphins in a pod. Seventy-five per cent of the dolphins are adults.
   How many adult dolphins are there?

5. There are 220 children in a school. 60% of the children have school meals. How many children have school meals?

6. Find the odd one out
   (a) 75% of £200
   (b) 70% of £210
   (c) 30% of £500

7. A train company increases its prices by 15%. If a ticket costs £40 now, how much will it cost after the price increase?

8. On 6th July 350 people go to the cinema. 40% more people go to the cinema on 13th July. 20% more people go to the cinema on 20th July compared to 13th July. How many people go to the cinema on 20th July?

9. A marathon runner weighs 60 kg at the start of a race. During the race his weight is reduced by 5%. How much does he weigh at the end of the race?

10. Find the sale price of each item below. The normal prices are shown in boxes.
    (a) £60, 30% off marked price
    (b) £20, 25% off!
    (c) £700, 20% off normal price
    (d) £16, 75% off
    (e) £36, $33\frac{1}{3}\%$ discount off the shown price
    (f) £62 000, 5% off normal price

11. Mr. Jenkins invests £2000 in a bank. Each year he receives 5% interest (extra money) on the money in the bank at the start of the year.
    How much money does he have in the bank after
    (a) 1 year
    (b) 2 years
    (c) 3 years?

12. People often have to pay Value Added Tax (VAT) when they buy things.
    The usual rate of VAT is 20%.
    A computer costing £800 + VAT will cost £800 + £160 (20% of 800) = £960.
    How much will each item below cost if VAT is added?
    (a) T.V. £520
    (b) fridge £240
    (c) sofa £1400
    (d) bed £650

13. Jack and Maddy take delivery of 2200 poppies to sell for charity.
    Jack takes 65% of the poppies.
    He then sells 80% of these poppies.
    How many poppies does Jack end up with unsold?

> **Harder percentages of a number**
>
> $1\% = \frac{1}{100}$. To find 1% of a number, divide the number by 100.
>
> Find 16% of a number.
>
> Divide the number by 100 to find 1% then multiply by 16 to find 16% of the number.

Increase £18 by 29%
1% of 18 = 18 ÷ 100
29% of 18 = (18 ÷ 100) × 29 = 5.22 = £5.22
'increase' so answer = 18 + 5.22 = £23.22
Note: When using a calculator, use the % button.

Exercise 5M

Use a calculator when needed.

1. Which is larger? 8% of £23 or 9% of £21

2. Work out the following, giving the correct units in your answers.
   (a) 73% of 3000 kg
   (b) 14% of 530 km
   (c) 3% of $235
   (d) 86% of 17 km
   (e) 47% of 600 m
   (f) 98% of 7100 g

3. Find 3.2% of £7000.

4. A ticket to New York City costs £230. The price of the ticket is increased by 4%. What is the new price of the ticket?

5. John weighs 80 kg. Over the next year his weight increases by 6%. What is his new weight?

6. (a) Increase £70 by 16%.
   (b) Decrease £190 by 2%.
   (c) Decrease £280 by 28%.
   (d) Increase £4100 by 9%.

7. During the day a person might shrink in height by between 0.5% and 1%. Donald is 1.8 m when he wakes up. If he shrinks by 0.7% during the day, how tall is he at the end of the day?

8. Murphy works at a market. He buys fleeces at £16 each and tries to sell them at £20 each.
   He finds that he is not selling many so reduces the selling price by 12%.
   Will he still make money if he sells the fleeces at this new price? Explain your answer fully.

9. At the Chapel School there are 150 boys and 125 girls in Year 7. During the summer the number of boys decreases by 4% and the number of girls increases by 4%.
   Tami says that the total number of children in Year 7 remains the same.
   Is she correct? Explain your answer fully.

10. In 2018 the entrance fee to an exhibition of famous jewellery was £5 and 37 840 visitors came.
    In 2019 the entrance fee was reduced by 5% and the number of visitors increased by 12.5%.
    How much was paid in entrance fees in 2019?

11. The population of a city is 420 000 people at the end of 2017.
    By the end of 2018 it has increased by 6% of this value.
    The population then starts to go down.
    By the end of 2019 it has decreased by 6% of its value at the end of 2018.

    (a) What is the difference between the population at the end of 2017 and the end of 2019?
    (b) Does this answer surprise you, given that the population went up by 6% then down by 6%? Give a reason for your answer.

12. Harry works too hard. At the end of week 1, he has worked for 50 hours during that week. In each following week, the number of hours he works increases by 14% of the hours worked in the previous week.
    In which week does he first work for more than half the hours in a week?
    Show all your working out.

Need more practice with percentages?

1. Tom has 20 pieces of fruit. 7 pieces of fruit are apples.
   What percentage of the fruit are the apples?

2 Copy and complete this table.

	Fraction	Decimal	Percentage
(a)	$\frac{7}{10}$		
(b)			24%
(c)		0.46	
(d)			95%
(e)	$\frac{3}{20}$		

3 A 925 g cake contains 200 g of self-raising flour. What percentage of the cake is self-raising flour? Give the answer to the nearest %.

4 16 children were playing in the park. 9 of them were wearing sandals. What percentage of the children were *not* wearing sandals? Give the answer to the nearest %.

5 There are 860 children in a school. 15% cycle to school, 65% walk to school and the rest go by bus.
 (a) How many walk to school?
 (b) How many go by bus?

6 A lizard weighs 500 g. While escaping from a predator it loses its tail and its weight is reduced by 5%. How much does it weigh now?

7 The number of males and females in various groups on Duke of Edinburgh expeditions are shown in the table below.

Group	A	B	C	D	E	F
Male	7	11	23	4	12	12
Female	13	14	27	6	28	24

70% of one group is female. Which group is this?

8 At an international rugby match 37% of the crowd were from the U.K., 51% were from France and the remaining spectators came from the rest of the world. There were 31 080 people from the U.K.
How many spectators came from the rest of the world?

9 Marie earns £340 each week. She is given a 6.5% pay rise. How much does she earn each week after the pay rise?

10 A hen weighs 3 kg. After laying an egg, her weight is reduced by 2%. How much does she weigh now?

Extension questions with percentages

1 Using a calculator we find that 13.2% of £12.65 = £1.6698.
This answer has to be rounded off to the nearest penny, since the penny is the smallest unit of currency. So 13.2% of £12.65 = £1.67, to the nearest penny.

Work out, to the nearest penny
(a) 7% of £16.34
(b) 38% of £7.83
(c) 16% of £39.18
(d) 4.5% of £12.60
(e) 135% of £310.19
(f) $6\frac{1}{2}$% of £14.37

2 A computer costs £585 plus VAT at 20%.
How much does the computer cost in total?

3 The bill for a meal is £63.45. The restaurant adds on a service charge of 15% of the meal price. How much will the meal cost including the service charge?

4 A shop does the deal shown opposite.
A vacuum cleaner costs £282.
How much is one of the monthly instalments?

(35% deposit + 10 equal monthly instalments)

5 A car costs £18 500 new. Each year it loses 12% of its value at the start of the year.
How much is the car worth after (a) 1 year (b) 4 years?

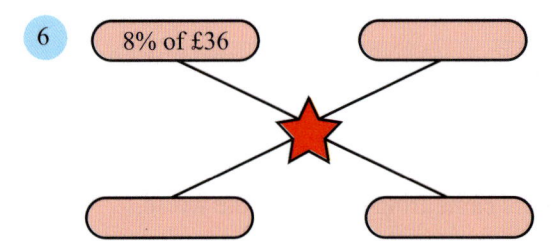

6 8% of £36

Write down three more percentage questions which give the same answer as the one shown above.

7   The value of investments can rise and fall. Phil invests £12 000 in a business.
    At the end of year 1 its value increases by 14%, at the end of year 2 it increases by 9% but at the end of year 3 it decreases by 20%.

    (a) What is the value of Phil's investment at the end of year 3.

    (b) Would Phil have been better off putting his money in a bank which guaranteed to add 2% to his money each year? Give a reason for your answer.

8   The base and the height of a triangle are increased by 50%. Work out the area of the larger triangle as a percentage of the area of the smaller triangle.
    Does this answer surprise you given that the base and height were only increased by 50%?

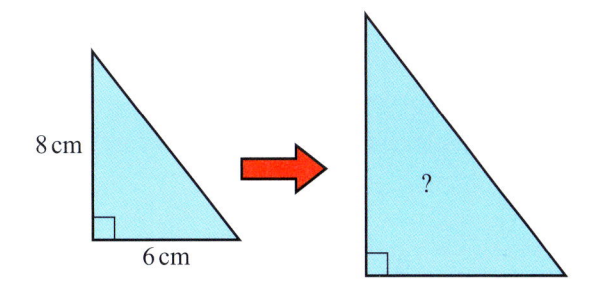

9   The cash price of a cooker is £672.
    Two stores offer the following deals.

Home Buys	Kitchen Sense
£90 deposit plus 12 monthly instalments of £48.50	20% of cash price as a deposit plus 24 monthly instalments of £23

    Which of the above payment plans is more expensive and by how much?

10 Brianna buys 20 shirts at £8 each, 12 cardigans at £12 each and 10 jackets at £15 each.
    She increases the prices by the percentages shown opposite before selling the items at a market.

    She manages to sell 16 shirts, 10 cardigans and 7 jackets.

shirt	75%
cardigan	$66\frac{2}{3}$%
jacket	80%

    (a) How much profit did she make?

    (b) What was the percentage profit? (This means 'express the profit as a percentage of the money Brianna had to pay out at the start'.) Give the answer to the nearest %.

4.2 Proportion and ratio

In section 4.2 you will learn how to:

- tackle problems involving proportion
- use ratios

Proportion is used to compare part of something to the whole.
A proportion is expressed as a fraction, decimal or percentage.

(a) There are 8 boys and 11 girls in a class of 19 children.
   The proportion of girls in the class is $\frac{11}{19}$.

(b) If 4 bottles of lemonade contain 10 litres, how much lemonade is there in 7 bottles?
   Find the amount in 1 bottle first.
   4 bottles contain 10 litres
   1 bottle contains $10 \div 4 = 2.5$ litres
   7 bottles contain $2.5 \times 7 = 17.5$ litres

Exercise 1M

1. Count the children in your class.
   What proportion of the class went to the same junior school as you?

2. The diagram shows how the government spends money on transport. Estimate, as a percentage, what proportion is spent on roads.

3. 5 tea pots cost £7.50. Find the cost of 50 tea pots.

4. A machine fills 1000 bottles in 5 minutes.
   How many bottles will it fill in 2 minutes?

5. Fishing line costs £1.80 for 50 m. Find the cost of 3000 m.

6. A train travels 30 km in 90 minutes.
   How long will it take to travel 55 km at the same speed?

7. Find the cost of 7 skateboards if 4 skateboards cost £174.

8. If 6 cauliflowers can be bought for £5.22, how many can be bought for £13.92?

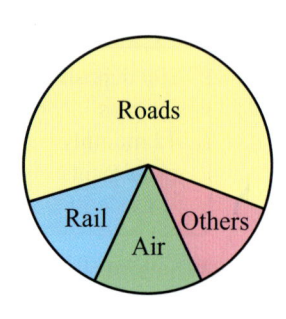

9 10 bags of corn will feed 60 hens for 3 days. Copy and complete the following.

   (a) 30 bags of corn will feed ☐ hens for 3 days.

   (b) 10 bags of corn will feed 20 hens for ☐ days.

   (c) 10 bags of corn will feed ☐ hens for 18 days.

   (d) 30 bags of corn will feed 90 hens for ☐ days.

10 Gideon makes puppets. He takes 5 hours to paint 8 bodies, 2 hours to paint 5 heads and $1\frac{1}{2}$ hours to paint 4 pairs of feet.

   (a) How long will it take Gideon to paint the bodies, heads and feet on 15 puppets?

   (b) What assumptions do you have to make to answer part (a)?

Which carton of cereal below is the better value?

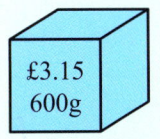

£3.15 600g

£4.75 950g

600 g costs 315p

1 g costs $\frac{315}{600}$

1 g costs 0.525p

950 g costs £4.75

1 g costs $\frac{475}{950}$

1 g costs 0.5p

1 g costs less for the larger box so the 950 g box is better value.

Exercise 1E

1 Which bottle of wine opposite is the better value?
   Show working out to justify your answer.

   750 ml   £12

   1200 ml £18

2 Harrison buys 400 yards of ribbon for £10.30 and Alexa buys 580 yards of ribbon for £14.50. Who gets the better deal? You must justify your answer.

3 Jack uses 32 litres of petrol to travel 270 km.
How much petrol does Jack use to travel 351 km?

4 Usually it takes 12 hours for 5 men to build a wall.
How many men are needed to build a wall twice as big in 6 hours?

5 A shop has a special deal on the smaller box of cookies opposite. The customers can buy two boxes and get a third box free.

Cookies 450g — £4.32

Cookies 200g — £2.76

(a) Which is the better value – the large box or the smaller boxes with the deal?

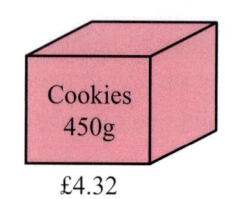

(b) Why might a customer not want to go for the deal?

6 4 machines produce 5000 batteries in 10 hours.
How many batteries would 6 machines produce in 8 hours?

7 In the army all holes are dug 4 feet deep.
It takes 8 soldiers 36 minutes to dig a hole 18 feet long by 10 feet wide.
How long will it take 5 soldiers to dig a hole 20 feet by 15 feet?

8 A biscuits recipe is shown opposite.

(a) How much of each ingredient is needed to make 18 biscuits?

(b) A chef has 105 g of black treacle. Is this enough to make 54 biscuits?

(c) Another chef has 325 g butter. What is the greatest amount of biscuits the chef could make?

> Makes 12 biscuits
> 100 g butter
> 50 g caster sugar
> 100 g soft brown sugar
> 25 g black treacle
> 175 g flour
> 1 tablespoon ground ginger

9 It takes b beavers n hours to build a dam.
How long will it take $b + 5$ beavers to build the same size dam?

Ratio

Ratio is used to compare parts of a whole.

> The ratio of shaded squares to unshaded squares is 4:10.
>
> Each part of the ratio can be multiplied or divided by the same number.
> This does not change the ratio.
> 4:10 is the same ratio as 2:5 (divide each part of ratio by 2)
>
> 2:5 is the simplest form for this ratio.

Exercise 2M

1. One evening a vet sees 10 dogs and 6 cats.
   Write down the ratio of dogs to cats in simplified form.

2. Copy this diagram. Colour in so that the ratio of coloured squares to uncoloured squares is 2:3.

3. There are 33 people on a bus. Nineteen are men.
   Write down the ratio of men to women.

4. Write these ratios in simplified form.
   (a) 5:20   (b) 8:10   (c) 4:44
   (d) 16:12   (e) 10:8:6 (f) 21:35
   (g) 65:25   (h) 16:24:80 (i) 42:21:28

5. Look at the pyramids in this photo.
   There are 12 yellow pyramids.
   There are 5 less green pyramids than yellow. There are as many blue pyramids as green.
   Find the ratio of blue pyramids to yellow pyramids.

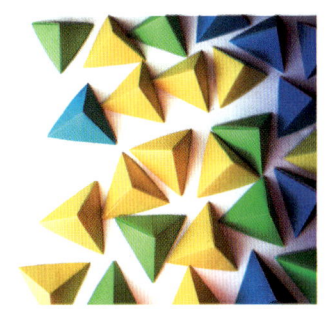

6. John is 1.8 m tall and Alice is 135 cm tall.
   Write down the ratio of John's height to Alice's height.
   Give the ratio in simplified form.

7 For each pair of ratios below, write down the value of *n* that makes the ratios *equivalent* to each other.

(a) 8:2 = *n*:1   (b) 4:12 = 1:*n*   (c) 70:40 = *n*:4
(d) 24:30 = 12:*n* (e) 22:33 = 2:*n*   (f) 48:32 = 6:*n*

8 Pablo needs to mix blue, red and green paint in the ratio 3:4:6. He uses 12 tubes of blue, 16 tubes of red and 28 tubes of green. Does he create the correct ratio of paint? Give clear reasons for your answer.

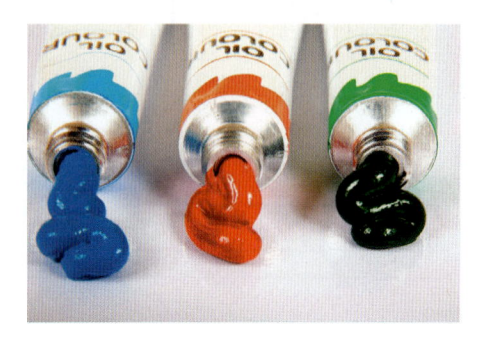

9 Brooke has £60 and Wyatt has £80. They both earn £10 an hour for their jobs. What is the least number of hours more that they must each work for so that the ratio of Brooke's money to Wyatt's money is 6:5?

10 Carl says that the ratio of his mother's age to his sister's age can never be 1:1. Is he correct? Justify your answer.

11 The lengths of the sides of the small triangle compared to the lengths of the sides of the larger triangle are in the ratio 1:4. Work out the ratios of the areas of the two triangles.

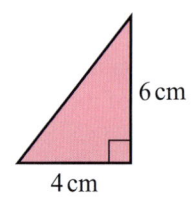

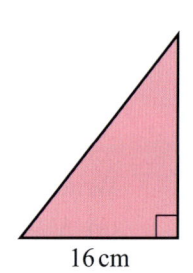

Share £35 in the ratio 5:2

The ratio 5:2 means we are dividing into '5 + 2' = 7 parts

£35 is split into 7 parts so 1 part = £5

5 parts = 5 × £5 = £25 and 2 parts = 2 × £5 = £10

Exercise 3M

1 Share £36 in the ratio   (a) 3:1   (b) 1:5   (c) 2:1

2 Share £75 in the ratio   (a) 2:3   (b) 11:14 (c) 8:7

3 There are 28 children in a class. The ratio of boys to girls is 4:3.

    (a) How many boys are in the class?

    (b) How many girls are in the class?

4 The ratio of dark chocolates to milk chocolates in a box is 2:3. If there are 18 dark chocolates, how many milk chocolates are in the box?

5 Natasha and Ning are given some money in the ratio 5:3. If Ning receives £24, how much does Natasha get?

6 In a hall, the ratio of chairs to tables is 9:2. If there is a total of 99 chairs and tables, how many chairs are there?

7 Mark and Amy share some sweets in the ratio 4:5. If Mark gets 28 sweets, how many sweets do they share out in total?

8 Neil, Pippa and Mel have newspaper rounds. Each week they earn a total of £28 in the ratio 3:5:6. How much money does Pippa earn?

9 In a kitchen drawer, there is a total of 36 knives, forks and spoons in the ratio 4:3:5. How many knives are there?

10 Chun Kit mixes some blue paint and some yellow paint in the ratio 7:4 to make up 33 litres of paint.

    (a) How much yellow paint did she use?

    (b) What is the ratio of blue paint to yellow paint if 3 more litres of yellow paint are added to the total mixture?

11 Baldeep, Millie and Mike work for a number of hours in the ratio 7:3:2. Baldeep worked for 42 hours, which was the most. How many hours did Millie and Mike work for in total?

12 On a bus, the ratio of children to adults is 4:1. What proportion of the people are adults?

13 Rob, Louise, Steve and Gemma win £40 000 and divide it in the ratio 23:34:13:10. How much does each person get?

14 Three people are standing in a lift. Their combined weight is 232 kg split in the ratio 8:11:10. The lightest person gets out of the lift and a heavier person gets in so that the ratio of the weights of the people now in the lift is 11:10:12. What is the combined weight of the three people in the lift now?

Need more practice with proportion and ratio?

1. A soup contains 150 g of water and 50 g of vegetables.
   What proportion of the soup is vegetables?

2. The total cost of 8 magazines is £12. What is the total cost of 12 magazines?

3. The chart shows how children travel to Maxwell High School.
   (a) What proportion travel by bus?
   (b) What proportion walk?

4. Manu says that the ratio 25 kg : 500 g can be simplified to 500:1. Cerys does not agree.
   Who is correct? Give full reasons for your answer.

5. Ayden and Stella each do a newspaper round.
   In total they deliver 275 newspapers split between Ayden and Stella in the ratio 4:7.
   How many newspapers does Stella deliver?

6. Which of the four ratios below is the odd one out?
   28:24   7:6   21:16   35:30

7. The ratio of red crayons to blue crayons in pencil case A is 5:3 and in pencil case B is 2:1.
   Which pencil case has the higher proportion of red crayons? Justify your answer.

8. Ishaan and Faith spend 75 minutes and 60 minutes respectively roller skating one morning.
   In the afternoon their ratio of times spent roller skating remains the same.
   How long does Faith roller skate for if Ishaan skates for 90 minutes?

9. The prices of two boxes of chocolates are shown opposite. Which size is the better value? Explain your answer fully.

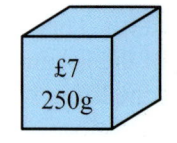

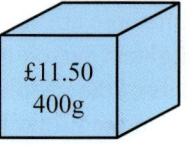

   £7 250g   £11.50 400g

10. The ratio of Tabi's height and Colin's height is 4:5 and the sum of their heights is 3.15 m. Two years later the ratio of their heights has changed to 5:6 and the sum of their heights is 3.3 m. By how much has Tabi grown during these two years?

Extension questions with proportion and ratio

1. Max, Ava and Anna are given some money in the ratio 8:3:10. Anna gets £50 more than Max. How much money does Ava get?

2. Write these ratios in simplified form.
   (a) 6 m : 50 cm
   (b) 2.5 kg : 100 g
   (c) 1.2 km : 300 m
   (d) 8 cm : 5 mm
   (e) 2 km : 2 cm
   (f) 4.5 m : 30 cm : 600 mm

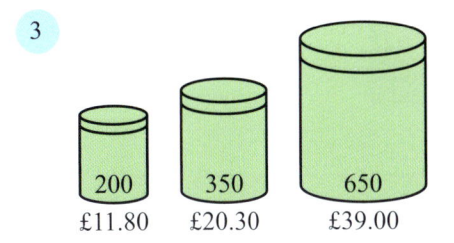

3. The pots opposite show the number of health supplement tablets and their prices given below. Which pot is the best value? Explain your answer fully.

   200 — £11.80
   350 — £20.30
   650 — £39.00

4. A machine has two cogs connected by a belt. One cog has 70 teeth and the other cog has 30 teeth.
   (a) When the larger cog rotates once, how many times does the smaller cog rotate?
   (b) How many times will the larger cog rotate when the smaller cog rotates 42 times?

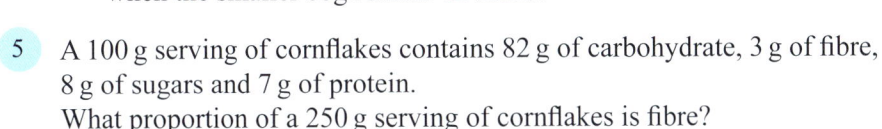

5. A 100 g serving of cornflakes contains 82 g of carbohydrate, 3 g of fibre, 8 g of sugars and 7 g of protein.
   What proportion of a 250 g serving of cornflakes is fibre?

6. The ratio of dogs to cats in Henton is 3:2 and in Banwell is 5:3. The ratio of the total number of dogs and cats in Henton compared to Banwell is 3:2. The total number of dogs and cats in Henton and Banwell is 30 000.
   Work out the ratio of the number of cats in Henton compared to the number of cats in Banwell.

7. The ratio of apples to oranges in a grocers is 3:2. The ratio of apples to pears in the same grocers is 3:4. Tilly says that there are twice as many pears as oranges. Is she correct? Justify your answer.

8.
Recipe for 20 muffins
2 eggs
250 g sugar
400 g flour
250 g milk
75 g chocolate chips

Mason has 6 eggs, 900 g of sugar, 900 g of flour, 750 g of milk and 300 g of chocolate chips.
Explain clearly whether Mason has got enough ingredients to make 50 muffins.

9. Lily earns £1600 each month. She pays her rent with $\frac{3}{8}$ of the money then uses 30% of the remaining money for her food. She splits the remaining money in the ratio 9:5 on entertainment and savings. Work out the difference between her rent and her savings each month.

10. The area of the triangle opposite is 24 cm².
The ratio $b:x = 4:5$
Work out the actual perimeter of the triangle.

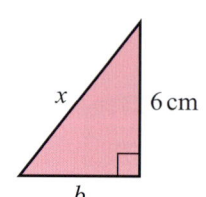

6 cm

✗ Spot the mistakes 7 ✗

Percentages, proportion, ratio

Work through each question below and explain clearly what mistakes have been made.
Beware – some questions are correctly done.

1. Increase £40 by 5%.
   Solution: 5% of 40 = 40 ÷ 5 = 8
   Answer = 40 + 8 = £48

2. Some green paint is made by mixing blue and yellow in the ratio 3:5.
   Danielle says that $\frac{3}{5}$ of the paint mixture is blue.

3. It costs Ron a total of £90 to sell ice-creams for a day. One day he sells 90 ice creams at £1.70 each. What is his profit as a percentage of the total costs?

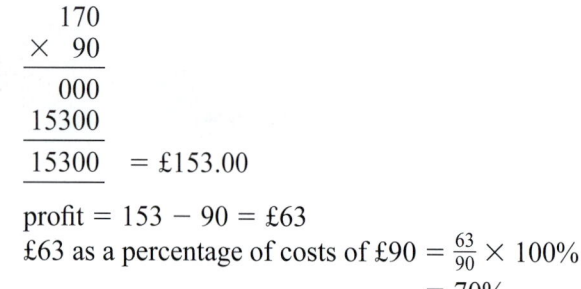

   ```
       170
    ×   90
    ------
       000
     15300
    ------
     15300   = £153.00
   ```

   profit = 153 − 90 = £63
   £63 as a percentage of costs of £90 = $\frac{63}{90} \times 100\%$
   = 70%

4 Some sweets are shared between Ian, Anya and Vitali in the ratio 2:5:3.
If Anya gets 40 sweets, how many sweets does Vitali get?
Solution: number of shares = 2 + 5 + 3 = 10 shares
one share = 40 ÷ 10 = 4 sweets
Vitali gets 3 shares = 3 × 4 = 12 sweets

5 Simplify the ratio 5 km : 200 m.
Solution: 5:200 = 1:40

6 Work out 2% of £12.
Solution: 2% of 12 = 0.2 × 12
= 2.4
= £2.40

7 All the sides of this rectangle are increased by 20%.
Work out the new area of the rectangle.

6 cm
9 cm

Solution: area = 6 × 9 = 54
10% of 54 = 5.4
so 20% of 54 = 10.8
new area = 54 + 10.8 = 64.8 cm²

8
Chocolate
300 g
£4.08

Buy one, get one free

Chocolate
450 g
£5.49

Jess needs to buy 900 g of chocolate as cheaply as possible.

Solution:
3 × 300 g = 3 × 4.08 = £12.24
2 × 450 g = 2 × 5.49 = £10.98
So Jess buys two 450 g amounts of chocolate.

9 Simplify the ratio $\frac{3}{5} : \frac{2}{3}$

Solution: $\frac{3}{5} \times 15 : \frac{2}{3} \times 15 = 9:10$

10 A father is 28 years old and his daughter is 4 years old.
Work out the ratio of their ages in two years time.

Solution: ratio of ages = 28:4
= 7:1
in 2 years time, ratio = 9:3
= 3:1

241

CHECK YOURSELF ON SECTIONS 4.1 AND 4.2

1 Conversion of fractions, decimals and percentages

Copy and complete this table.

	Fraction	Decimal	Percentage
(a)		0.08	
(b)	$\frac{4}{5}$		
(c)		0.9	
(d)			32%
(e)	$\frac{18}{25}$		

2 Expressing one number as a percentage of another number

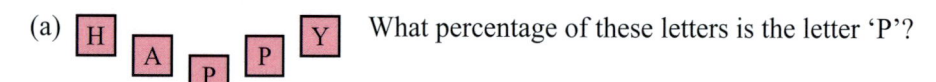

(a) H A P P Y What percentage of these letters is the letter 'P'?

(b) Andrew scored 12 out of 17 in a maths test, 33 out of 48 in an English test and 20 out of 32 in a science test. In which test did Andrew score his highest percentage?

3 Percentage increases and decreases

(a) A camera costs £300. It is reduced in price by 5%. What is the new price?

(b) Increase £720 by 12%.

4 Tackling problems involving proportion

(a) 22 children are playing football. Nine of the children are in Year 7, the rest are in Year 8. What proportion of the children are in Year 8?

(b) Find the cost of 7 toys if 9 toys cost £78.84.

(c) Which box of chocolates is the better value? Explain your answer fully.

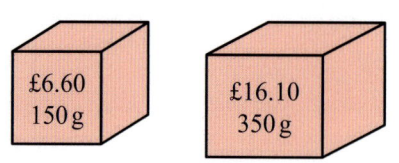

£6.60 150 g

£16.10 350 g

5 Using ratios

(a) Write the ratio 12:32 in simplified form.

(b) During one week Urma and Terry eat 15 ice-creams in the ratio 3:2. How many ice-creams does Urma eat?

(c) Janet buys gifts for her husband and son. She spends money in the ratio 3:7. If she spends £56 on her son, how much does she spend in total on the gifts?

4.3 Constructing triangles

In section 4.3 you will learn how to:

- construct triangles with a protractor and ruler
- construct triangles with three sides given

A triangle is an extremely rigid structure. It is used extensively in the real world to support many objects such as the roof on your house or the brackets holding up your bookshelf.

Draw the triangle ABC full size and measure the length x.

(a) Draw a base line *longer than* 8.5 cm
(b) Put the centre of the protractor on A and measure an angle 64°. Draw line AP.
(c) Similarly draw line BQ at an angle 40° to AB.
(d) The triangle is formed. Measure $x = 5.6$ cm.

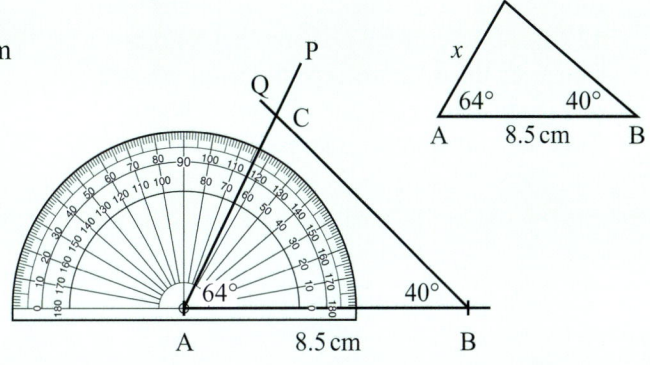

Exercise 1M

1 Construct each triangle below. Measure the third angle in each triangle. Is it what you would expect?

(a) 70°, 70°, 6 cm

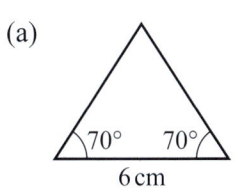

(b) 35°, 35°, 7 cm

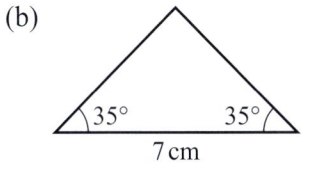

(c) 85°, 40°, 7 cm

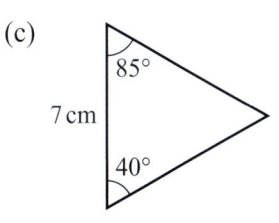

2 Construct each triangle below. Measure the lengths of the sides marked x.

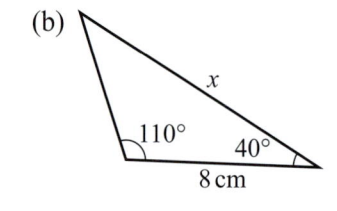

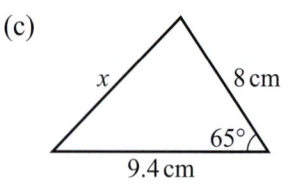

(a) Triangle with base 8 cm, angles 40° and 60°, side x opposite the 60° angle.

(b) Triangle with base 8 cm, angles 110° and 40°, side x.

(c) Triangle with sides 8 cm and 9.4 cm, angle 65°, side x.

3 Construct triangle PQR where PR = 6.8 cm, $R\hat{P}Q = 72°$ and $P\hat{R}Q = 60°$. Measure the length of QR.

4 Construct the parallelogram shown below.

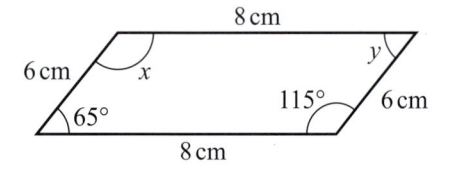

Parallelogram with sides 8 cm and 6 cm, angles 65° and 115°, with x and y marked.

Measure the size of x and y.

5 Emma walks 5 km due South from home then 12 km due East to her grandmother's house. Construct the diagram opposite using a scale of 1 cm to 1 km. How far is Emma's home from her grandmother's house?

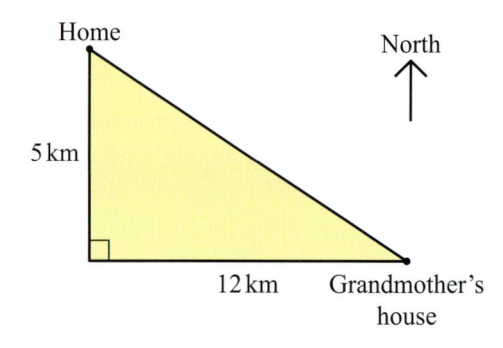

6 Construct the shape opposite and measure the side marked x.

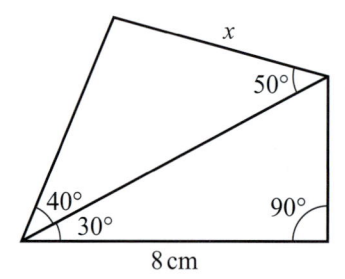

Triangles with three sides given

Draw triangle XYZ and measure XẐY.

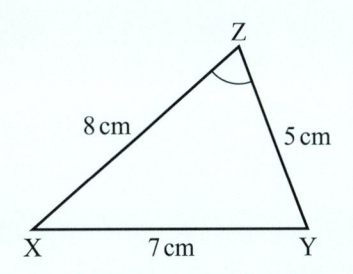

(a) Draw a base line longer than 7 cm and mark X and Y exactly 7 cm apart.

(b) Put the point of a pair of compasses on X and draw an arc of radius 8 cm.

(c) Put the point of the pair of compasses on Y and draw an arc of radius 5 cm.

(d) The arcs cross at the point Z so the triangle is formed.

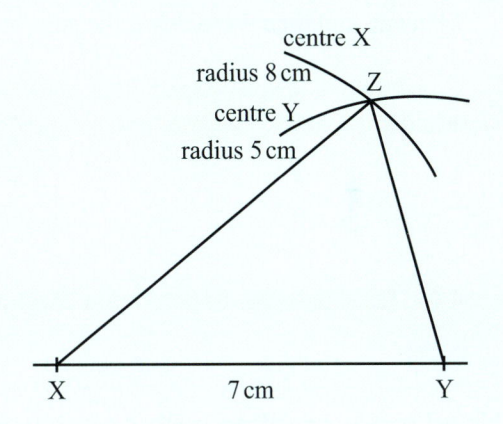

Measure XẐY = 60°

Exercise 2M

Use a ruler and a pair of compasses to construct the triangles in questions 1 to 4. For each triangle, measure the angle x.

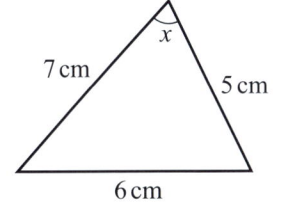

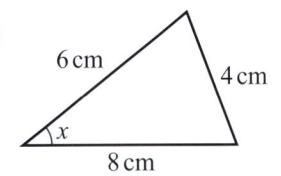

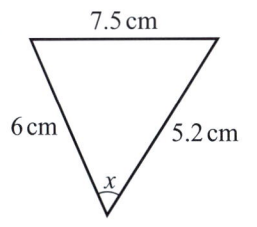

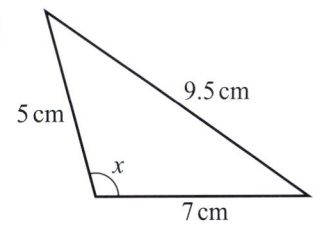

1. [Triangle: 7 cm, 5 cm, 6 cm, angle x at top]

2. [Triangle: 6 cm, 4 cm, 8 cm, angle x]

3. [Triangle: 7.5 cm, 6 cm, 5.2 cm, angle x at bottom]

4. [Triangle: 9.5 cm, 5 cm, 7 cm, angle x]

5. Construct triangle XYZ where XY = 6.7 cm, YZ = 8.2 cm and ZX = 7.9 cm. Measure XẐY.

6. Construct the shape opposite then measure angle x.

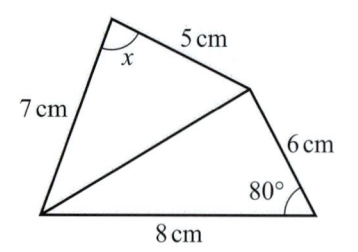

7. Construct a quadrilateral ABCD where AB = 6.1 cm, BC = 5.3 cm, CD = 6.2 cm, AD = 6.8 cm and AC = 8 cm (you may find it useful to sketch the shape first). Measure and then write down the sum of angles $A\hat{B}C$ and $A\hat{D}C$.

8. Construct the shape opposite then measure angle x.

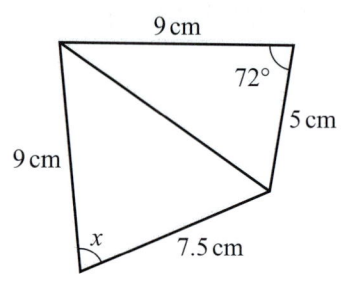

Need more practice with constructing triangles?

1. Construct triangle ABC where AC = 7.2 cm, $B\hat{A}C = 34°$ and $A\hat{C}B = 103°$. Measure the length of AB.

2. Construct each triangle below. Measure the lengths of the sides marked x.
   (a)
   (b)
   (c)

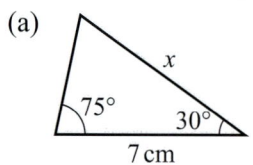

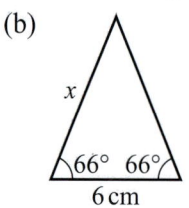

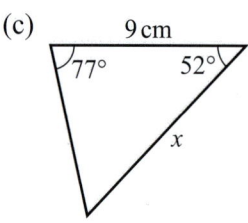

3. Construct each triangle below. For each triangle, measure the angle x.
   (a)
   (b)

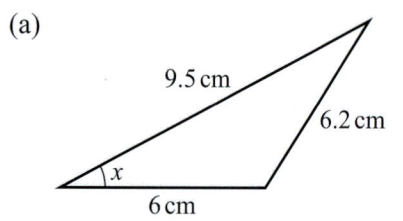

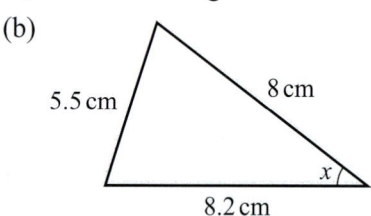

4. Marie and Leo both construct triangle ABC with sides 6 cm, 8 cm and 10 cm. Marie measures $A\hat{B}C$ and says the answer is 37°. Leo measures $A\hat{B}C$ and says the answer is 53°. Explain why this might have happened?

Extension questions with constructing triangles

1. Construct the rhombus shown opposite. Measure the size of *m* and *n*.

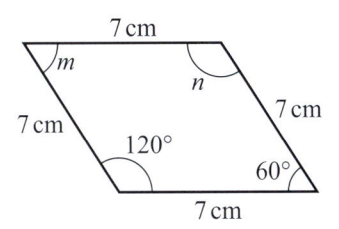

2. Construct the shape shown opposite. Measure the angle *x*.

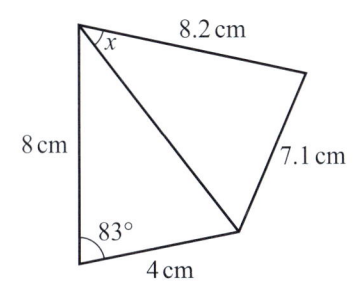

3. Construct each shape below and measure the lengths of the sides marked *x*.

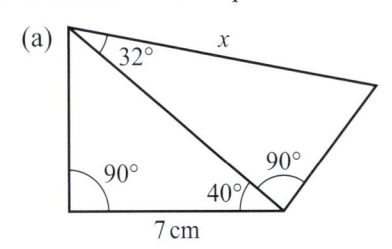

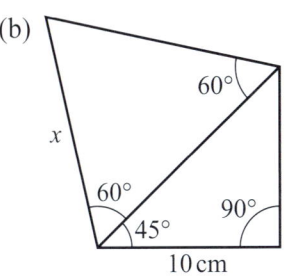

   (a)

   (b)

4. A rhombus has four equal sides as shown in question 1.

   Construct a rhombus WXYZ where WZ = 8 cm, $X\hat{W}Z = 50°$ and $Y\hat{Z}W = 130°$. Measure $X\hat{Y}Z$.

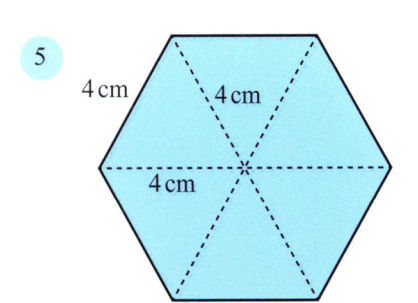

5. A regular hexagon is made from six equilateral triangles. Construct the hexagon shown opposite.

6. A disused airfield is to be sold at a price of £5500 per hectare. (1 hectare = 10 000 m²) The outline of the airfield is a quadrilateral but it is not a rectangle. The area can be found by splitting it into two triangles and then finding the area of each part.
Find the selling price of the airfield.

[Use a scale of 1 cm to 100 m]

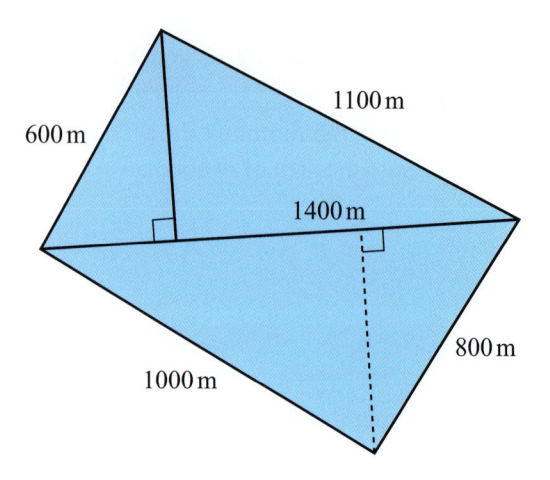

4.4 Two dimensional shapes

In section 4.4 you will review:

- recognising different polygons, particularly types of quadrilaterals
- identifying symmetry properties of quadrilaterals

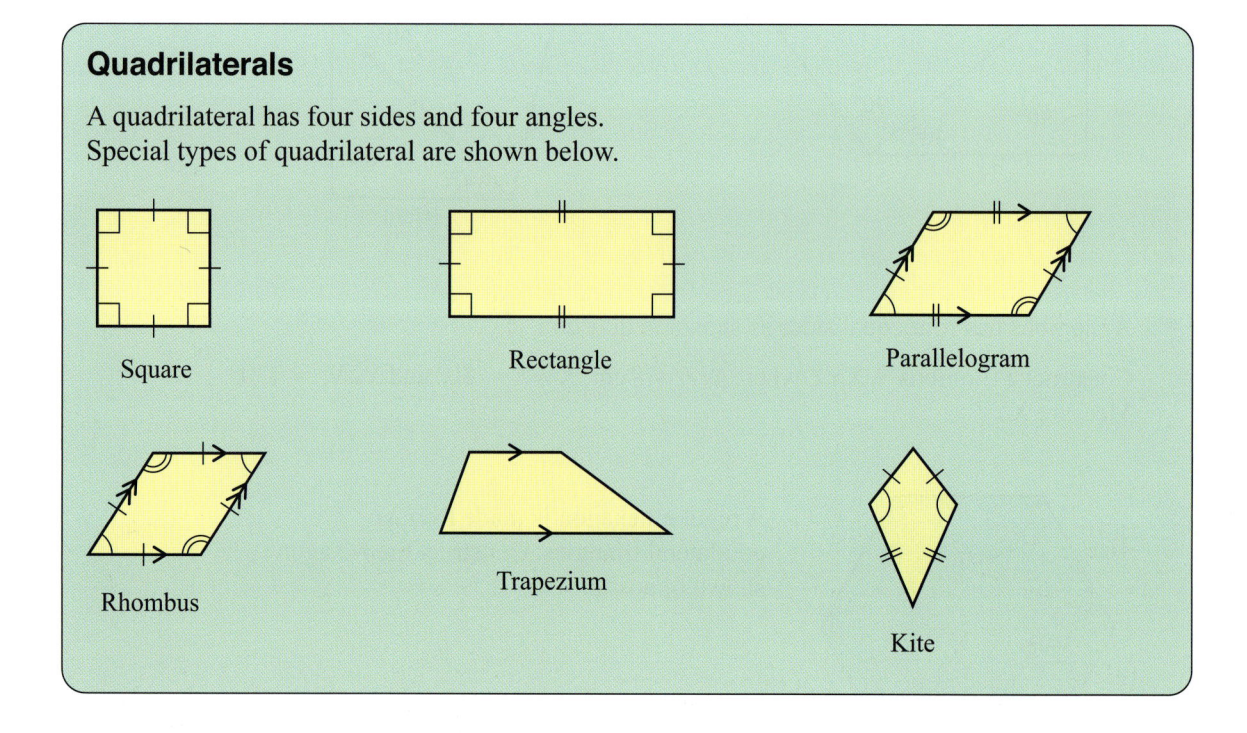

Quadrilaterals

A quadrilateral has four sides and four angles.
Special types of quadrilateral are shown below.

Square

Rectangle

Parallelogram

Rhombus

Trapezium

Kite

Polygons

A polygon is a shape with straight sides.

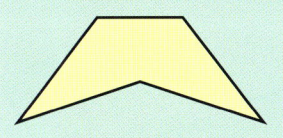

This is a five-sided polygon or pentagon.

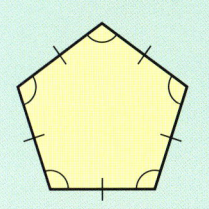

A *regular* polygon has all its sides and angles equal.
This is a *regular* pentagon.

Names of common polygons:

hexagon (6 sides), heptagon (7 sides), octagon (8 sides), nonagon (9 sides), decagon (10 sides).

Exercise 1M

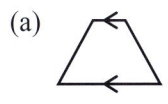

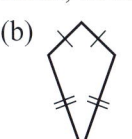

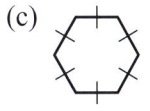

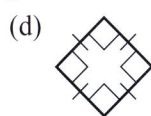

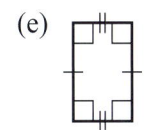

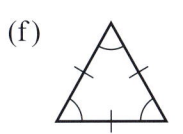

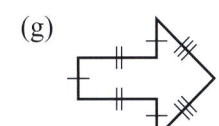

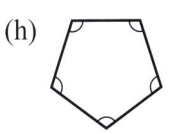

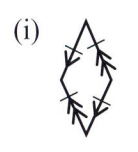

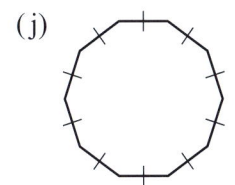

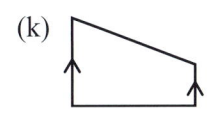

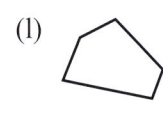

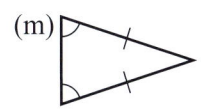

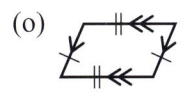

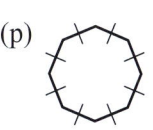

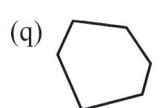

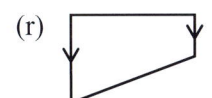

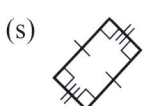

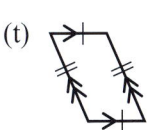

1 Write down the name for each shape below. If the shape has a special name like 'parallelogram' or 'kite' write that name. If not, write 'quadrilateral', 'hexagon', 'regular pentagon' and so on.

(a) (b) (c) (d)

(e) (f) (g) (h)

(i) (j) (k) (l)

(m) (n) (o) (p)

(q) (r) (s) (t)

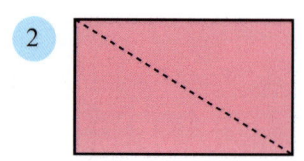

2. A diagonal joins one corner (vertex) of a polygon to another corner.

   Draw any rhombus. Write as many facts as possible about the diagonals of a rhombus.

3. Explain clearly why both of these shapes are trapeziums.

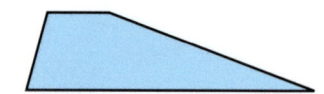

4. A quadrilateral has one pair of equal angles and no parallel sides. Which quadrilateral is it?

5. Which shape below is not a regular polygon?

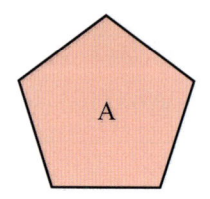

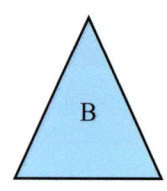

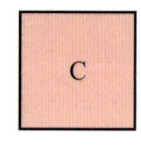

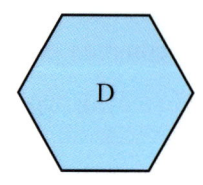

6. What changes must be made to a rhombus for it to become a square?

7. Name any quadrilaterals which have one but not two pairs of equal angles.

8. If one line is drawn inside the parallelogram opposite to create a trapezium, what other shapes might be created at the same time?

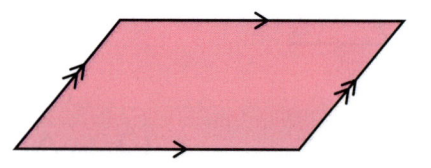

Symmetry – a reminder

A shape has *line symmetry* if half of its shape matches the other half exactly.

A shape has *rotational symmetry* if it fits onto itself when rotated (turned) before it gets back to its starting position.

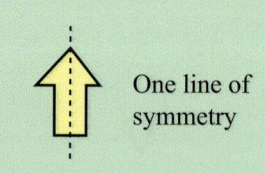

One line of symmetry

Shape A fits onto itself three times when rotated through a complete turn. We say it has rotational symmetry of *order 3*.

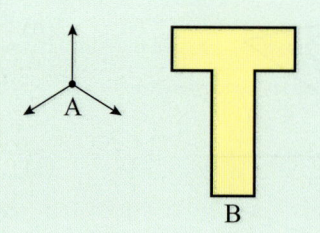

Shape B can only fit onto itself in its starting position. We say it has rotational symmetry of *order 1*.

Exercise 2M

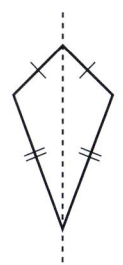

1. The diagram shows one line of symmetry for a kite. How many more lines of symmetry does a kite have?

2. Draw a rectangle and show all its lines of symmetry.

3. Which common quadrilaterals have two lines of symmetry only?

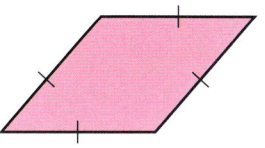

4. What is the order of rotational symmetry of this rhombus?

5. Which quadrilateral has rotational symmetry of order 4.

6. Draw a quadrilateral which has one line of symmetry only and one pair of parallel sides only.

7. What is the order of rotational symmetry of an equilateral triangle?

8. What is the order of rotational symmetry of this hexagon?

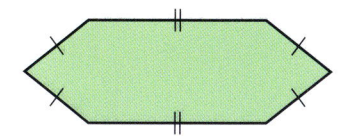

9. How many of the quadrilaterals below have rotational symmetry of order 2?

    kite   square   parallelogram   rectangle   trapezium   rhombus

10. Which of the quadrilaterals in question 9 have rotational symmetry of order 1 (ie. no rotational symmetry).

Need more practice with two dimensional shapes?

1. Is a parallelogram a type of rectangle?

2. Is a rectangle a type of parallelogram?

3 Callum says that all trapeziums have one line of symmetry only.
Is he correct? Justify your answer.

4 Which quadrilaterals can be drawn by starting with the diagram opposite?

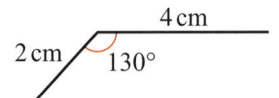

5 Write down the letter for which bucket each of the 6 quadrilaterals will drop into when they pass through the sorting machine.

parallelogram   square   rectangle   trapezium   kite   rhombus

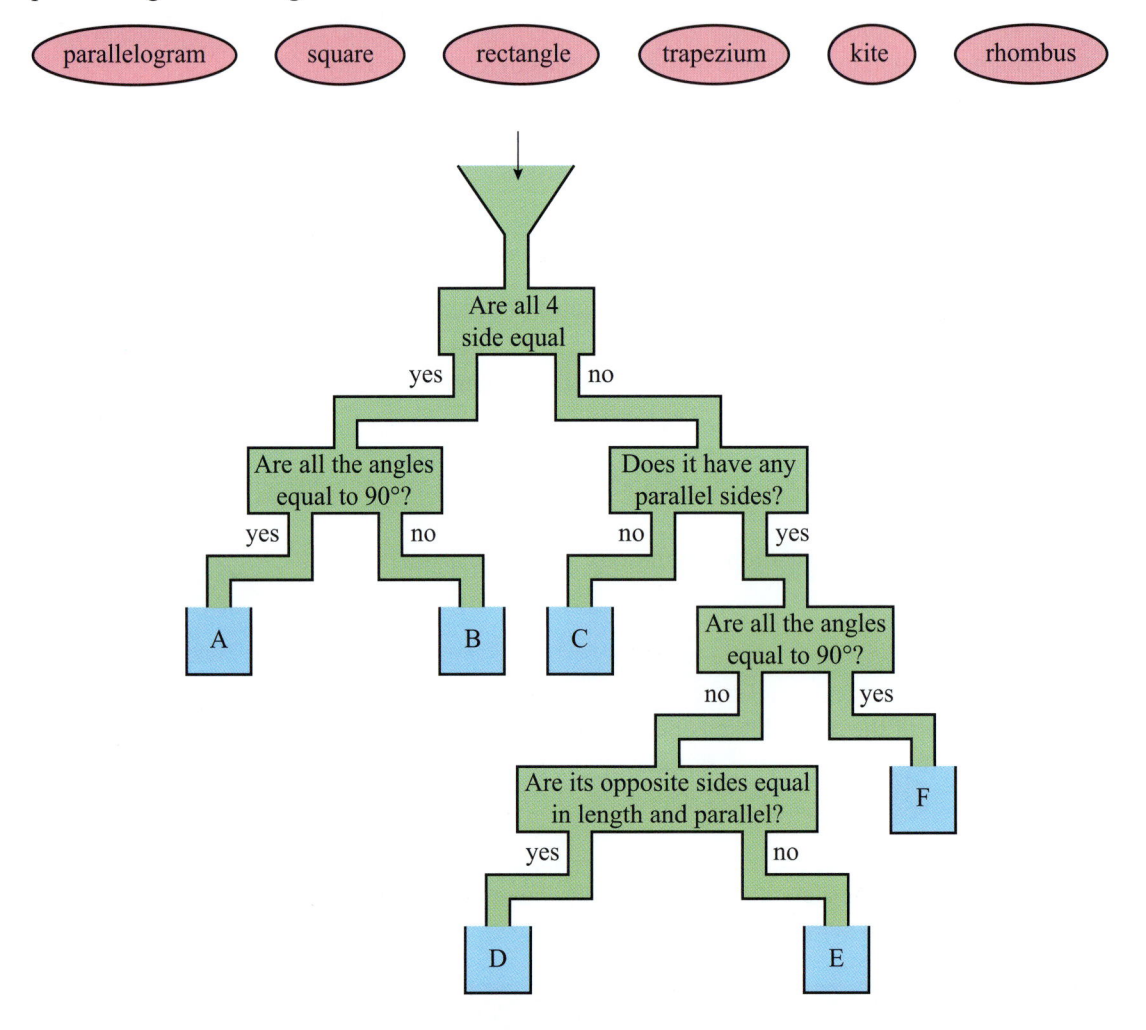

6 Draw a square, rectangle, parallelogram, rhombus, trapezium and kite.

For each of these quadrilaterals, write its name and describe the rules that make it that particular shape.

Discuss these rules with a partner and then as a class.

Extension questions with two dimensional shapes

Investigation – triangles and quadrilaterals

On a square grid of 9 dots it is possible to draw several different triangles with vertices on dots. A vertex (plural vertices) is where two lines meet. Look at the three examples below:

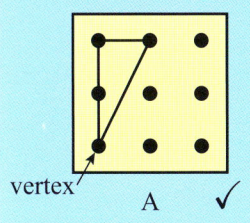

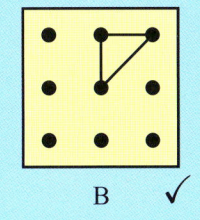

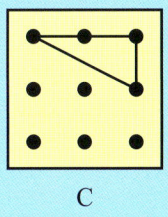

vertex   A ✓   B ✓   C

A and B are different triangles but C is the same as A. If a triangle could be cut out and placed exactly over another triangle then the two triangles are the same. The two triangles are called *congruent*.

Part A
Copy A and B above and then draw as many different triangles as you can.
Check carefully that you have not repeated the same triangle.

Part B
On a grid of 9 dots it is also possible to draw several different *quadrilaterals*.

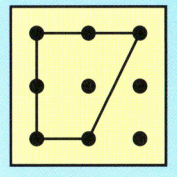

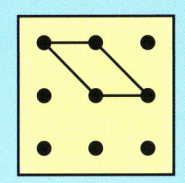

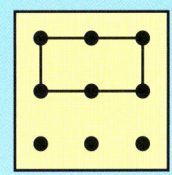

Copy the three shapes above and then draw as many other different quadrilaterals as possible. You are doing well if you can find 12 shapes but there are a few more!

Check carefully that you have not repeated the same quadrilateral. (Congruent shapes are not allowed.)

CHECK YOURSELF ON SECTIONS 4.3 AND 4.4

1   Constructing triangles with a protractor and ruler

Construct the triangle opposite.
Measure QR.

2 Constructing triangles with three sides given

(a) Construct the triangle below.

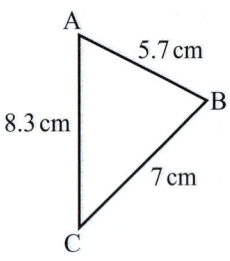

A, 5.7 cm, B, 8.3 cm, 7 cm, C

Measure AĈB.

(b) Construct triangle PQR where PQ = 4.9 cm, QR = 6.4 cm and PR = 5 cm. Measure PR̂Q.

3 Recognising different polygons, particularly types of quadrilaterals

Match each quadrilateral to the correct name below:

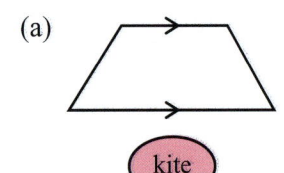

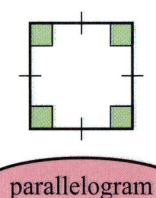

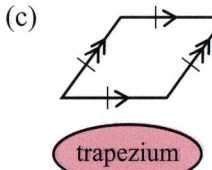

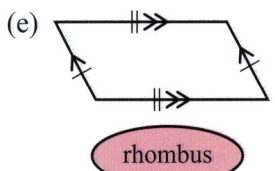

(a) kite

(b) parallelogram

(c) trapezium

(d) square

(e) rhombus

(f) Write down the rules that make a rhombus.

(g) Write down which shapes below are polygons.

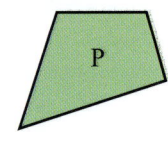

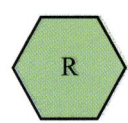

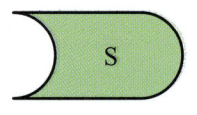

P   Q   R   S

(h) How many sides has a decagon?

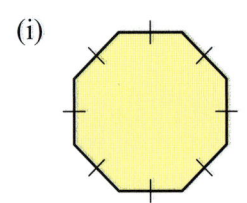

(i) Copy and complete the sentence below:

'This shape is a r————— o———————.'

4 Identifying symmetry properties of quadrilaterals

(a) What is the order of rotational symmetry of a parallelogram?

(b) What is the order of rotational symmetry of the trapezium below?

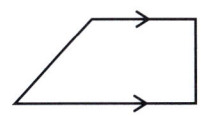

(c) *Explain* why the lines of symmetry for the rectangle below are *not* correct.

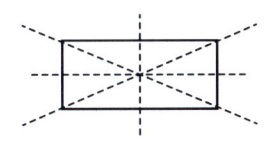

4.5 Translation

In section 4.5 you will learn about:

- translating shapes

A **translation** is a transformation in which every point of the object moves the same distance in a parallel direction.

A translation can be described by two instructions, the move parallel to the *x* axis and the move parallel to the *y* axis.

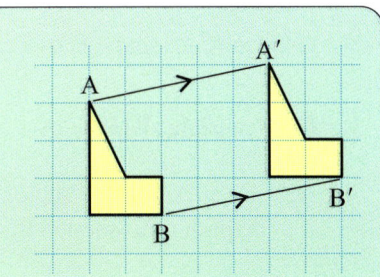

We use a **translation vector**, not words.

A translation vector is a vertical bracket as shown below:

$\begin{pmatrix} 5 \\ 1 \end{pmatrix}$ The number at the *top* shows 5 units to the *right*.
The number at the *bottom* shows 1 unit *up*.

If the number at the top was −5 it would be 5 units to the *left*.
If the number at the bottom was −1 it would be 1 unit *down*.

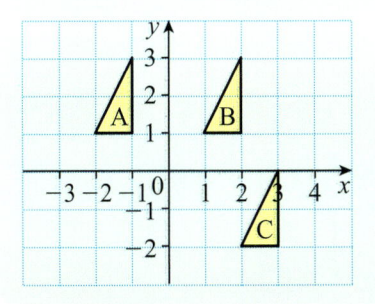

The translation of B to C is $\begin{pmatrix} 1 \\ -3 \end{pmatrix}$

The translation of C to A is $\begin{pmatrix} -4 \\ 3 \end{pmatrix}$

The translation of A to B is $\begin{pmatrix} 3 \\ 0 \end{pmatrix}$

Exercise 1M

1. Use translation vectors to describe the following translations.

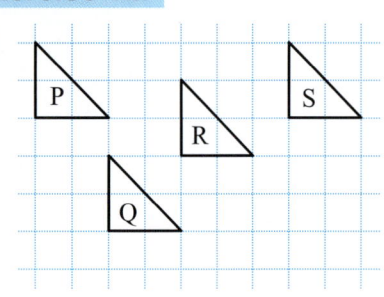

(a) P → Q
(b) Q → S
(c) R → P
(d) S → P

2. (a) Draw shape A as shown.

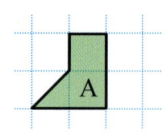

(b) Translate shape A by $\begin{pmatrix} 5 \\ 0 \end{pmatrix}$. Label the new shape B.

(c) Translate shape B by $\begin{pmatrix} 0 \\ -3 \end{pmatrix}$. Label the new shape C.

(d) Translate shape C by $\begin{pmatrix} -3 \\ -1 \end{pmatrix}$. Label the new shape D.

(e) Use a translation vector to describe the single translation which would move shape A onto shape D.

3. Use translation vectors to describe the following translations.

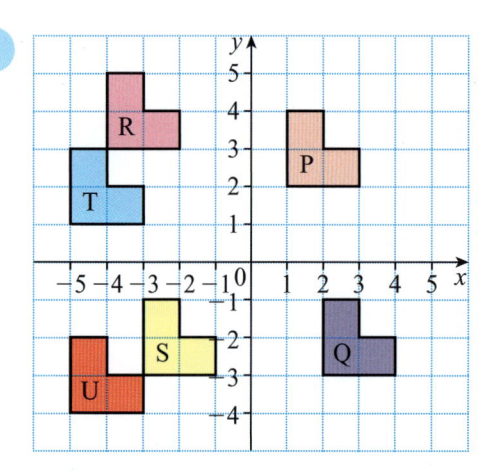

(a) P to R
(b) P to S
(c) S to Q
(d) T to Q
(e) Q to T
(f) R to U
(g) U to S

4. A computer controls a pen which starts at A opposite. Use translation vectors to describe the 8 translations required to draw the shape given.

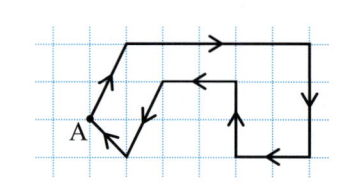

5. What shape do you move to when you

   (a) translate shape A by $\begin{pmatrix} -2 \\ -1 \end{pmatrix}$

   (b) translate shape E by $\begin{pmatrix} 5 \\ 3 \end{pmatrix}$

   (c) translate shape D by $\begin{pmatrix} 3 \\ -2 \end{pmatrix}$

   (d) translate shape B by $\begin{pmatrix} -5 \\ 0 \end{pmatrix}$?

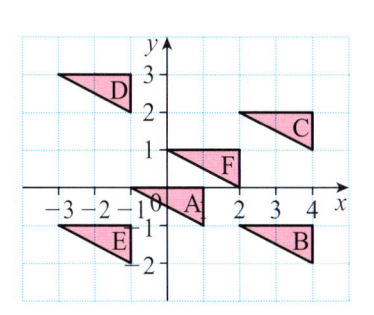

6. Shape P is translated to shape Q by $\begin{pmatrix} 3 \\ 2 \end{pmatrix}$ then shape Q is translated to shape R by $\begin{pmatrix} 2 \\ 6 \end{pmatrix}$.

   Write down the translation vector which moves shape R to shape P.

7. In the computer game shown opposite, a rocket R has to rescue people from 7 escape pods (▽).

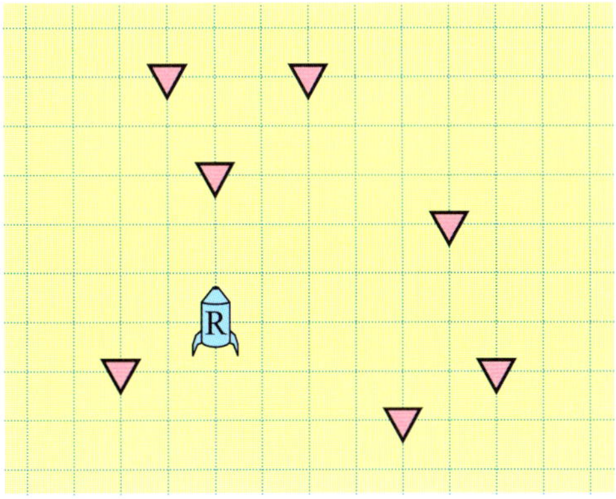

   (a) Give instructions using translation vectors so that the rocket gets to every escape pod.

   (b) It takes 1 minute for the rocket to move one square left, right, up or down. The people in the escape pods will run out of air after 30 minutes. Will your instructions in part (a) enable everyone to be rescued in time? If not, find a new set of instructions for the rocket so that everyone will be saved!

8. Shape A is translated to shape B with the translation vector $\begin{pmatrix} -m \\ n \end{pmatrix}$.

   Write down the translation vector which moves shape B to shape A.

4.6 Reflection

In section 4.6 you will:
- review symmetry
- reflect shapes

Rotational symmetry

The shape B fits onto itself three times when rotated through a complete turn. It has *rotational symmetry of order 3*.

The shape C fits onto itself six times when rotated through a complete turn. It has rotational symmetry of order 6.

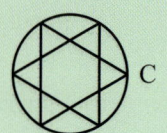

Exercise 1M

For each diagram decide whether or not the shape has rotational symmetry. For those diagrams that do have rotational symmetry state the order.

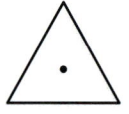

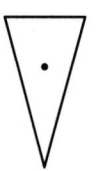

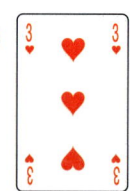

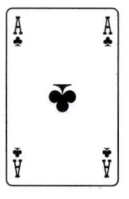

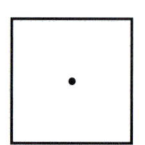

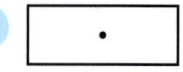

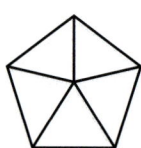

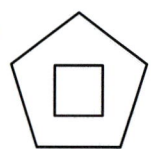

In questions 17 to 22 copy each diagram and complete it so that the final design has rotational symmetry of the order stated.

17 Order 4

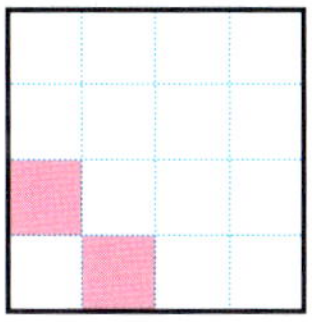

18 Order 4

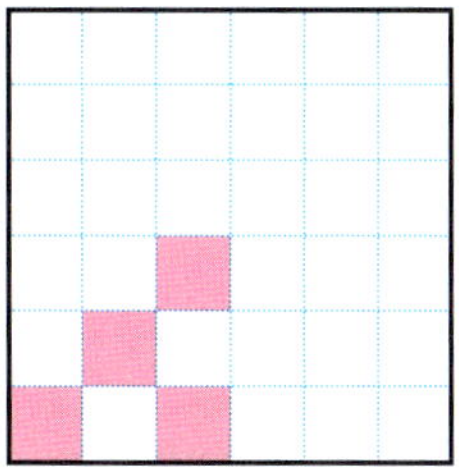

19 Order 4

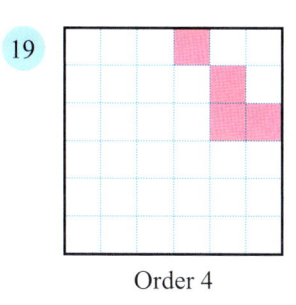

20 Order 2

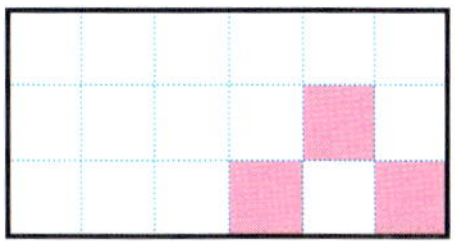

21 Order 4

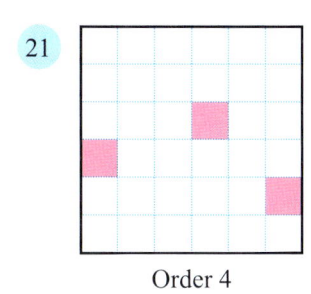

22 Order 2

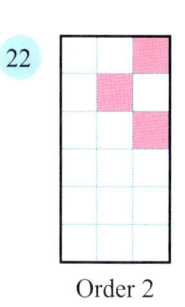

Symmetry review

Exercise 2M

1. (a) Does this shape have rotational symmetry?
   (b) Does this shape have line symmetry?

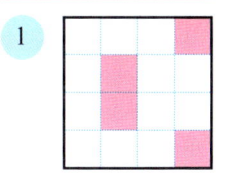

2. Draw a 4 × 4 grid like the one above. Shade four squares to make a pattern with rotational symmetry but no line symmetry.

3. Draw a 3 × 3 grid. Shade three squares to make a pattern with line symmetry but not rotational symmetry.

4. Draw a 4 × 4 grid and shade four squares to make a pattern with no line symmetry and no rotational symmetry.

5. In the diagram three vertices of a rectangle are given. Find the coordinates of the fourth vertex and write down the equations of any lines of symmetry. The answers are shown on the next page.

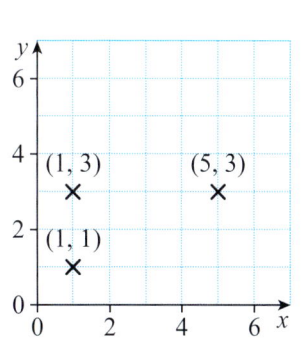

Shape	Vertices given	Other vertex	Lines of symmetry
Rectangle	(1, 1), (1, 3), (5, 3)	(5, 1)	$x = 3, y = 2$

Draw axes with values of x and y from -10 to $+10$.

Draw the shapes given below then copy and complete the given table.

	Shape	Vertices given	Other vertex	Lines of symmetry
(a)	Rectangle	(1, 6), (1, 10), (3, 6)	?	? , ?
(b)	Rectangle	(4, 3), (4, −1), (10, 3)	?	? , ?
(c)	Rectangle	(5, −2), (10, −2), (5, −3)	?	? , ?
(d)	Isosceles triangle	(5, −10), (10, −8)	?	$y = -8$ only
(e)	Isosceles triangle	(2, −4), (0, −8)	?	$x = 2$ only
(f)	Rhombus	(−6, 4), (−8, 7), (−6, 10)	?	? , ?
(g)	Square	(3, 3), (3, −3), (−3, −3)	?	Give four lines.
(h)	Trapezium	(−8, −2), (−7, 1), (−5, 1)	?	$x = -6$ only
(i)	Parallelogram	(−8, −5), (−4, −5), (−5, −8)	Give three possibilities	none
(j)	Parallelogram	(−3, 4), (−2, 6), (−1, 6)	Give three possibilities	none
(k)	Square	(6, 6), (6, 9)	Give two points	$y = x$ is one line. Find three more.

Reflection

A reflection is a transformation in which points are mapped to images by folding along a mirror line.

Exercise 3M

Copy each diagram and, using a different colour, shade in as many squares as necessary so that the final pattern has mirror lines shown by the broken lines. For each question write down how many new squares were shaded in.

Be careful when the mirror line is a diagonal line. You can check your diagram by folding along the mirror line.

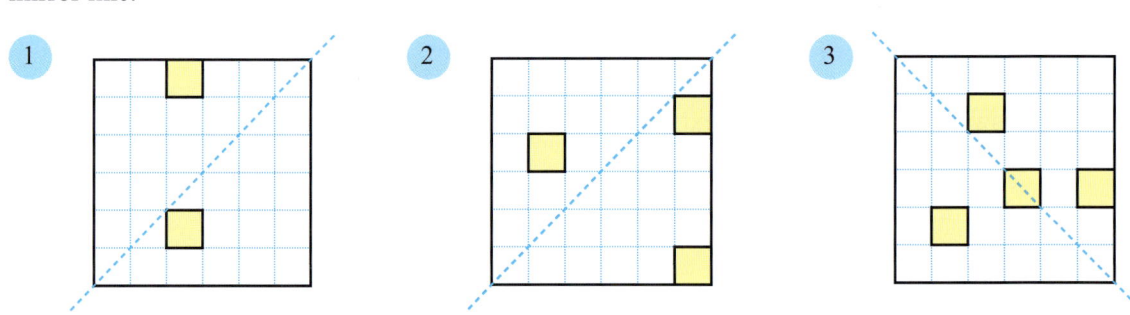

4

5

6

7

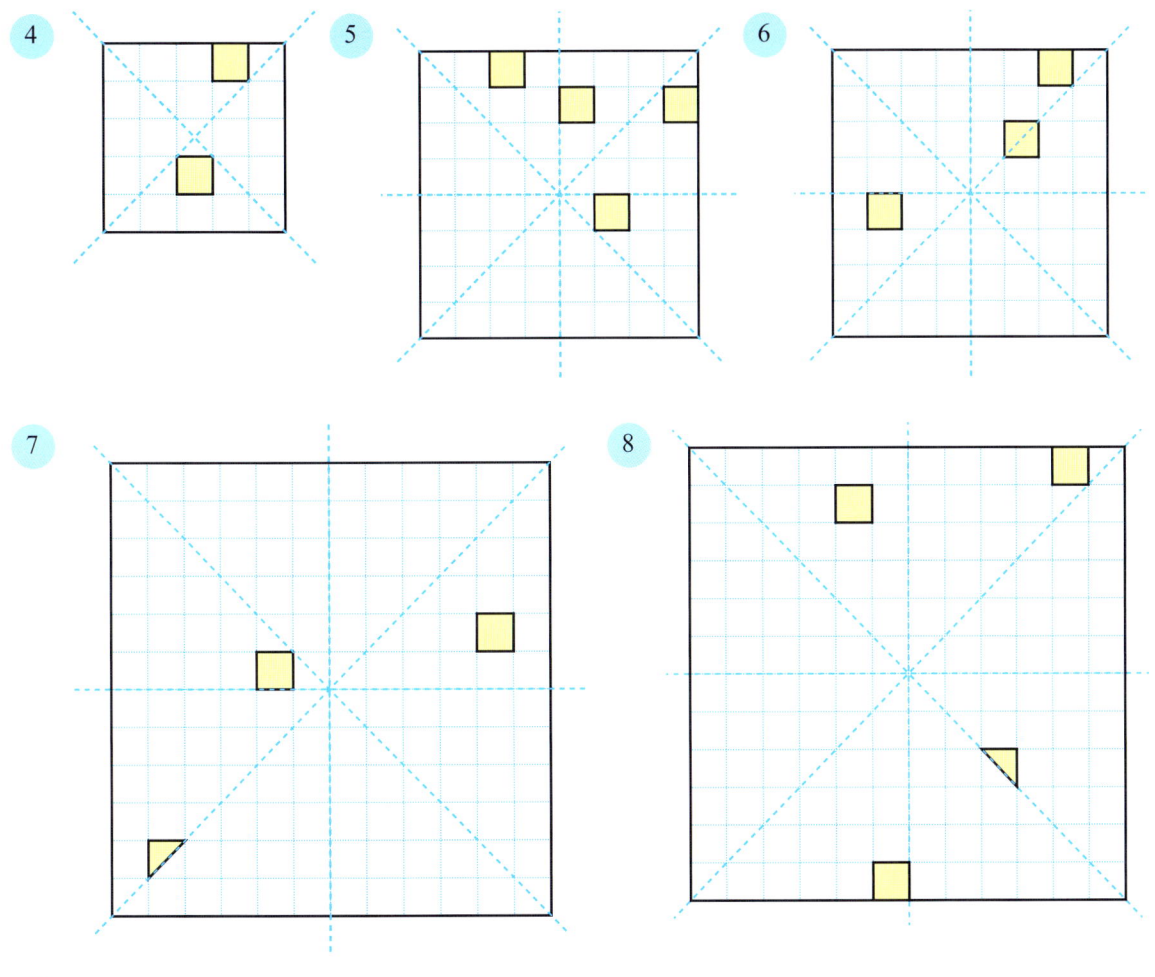

8

9 You have 3 square pink tiles and 2 square white tiles, which can be joined together along whole sides.

So this ▨▢ is allowed but this ▢▨ is *not* allowed.

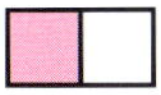

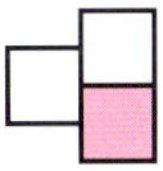

Draw as many diagrams as possible with the 5 tiles joined together so that the diagram has line symmetry.

For example Fig. 1 and Fig. 2 have line symmetry but Fig. 3 does not have line symmetry so Fig. 3 is not acceptable.

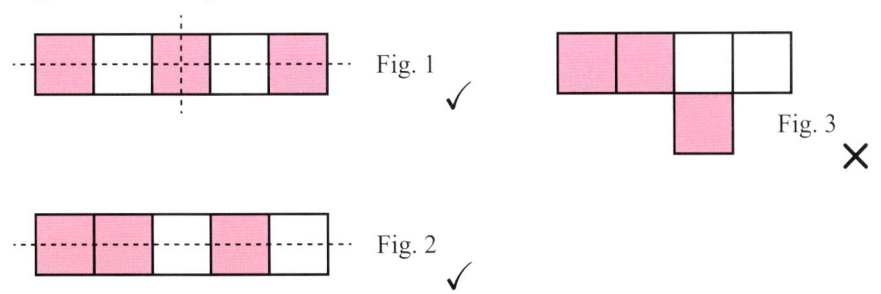

Fig. 1 ✓

Fig. 2 ✓

Fig. 3 ✗

10 Now you have 2 pink tiles and 2 white tiles. Draw as many diagrams as possible with these tiles joined together so that the diagram has line symmetry.

11 Finally with 3 pink tiles and 3 white tiles draw as many diagrams as possible which have line symmetry.

Here is one diagram which has line symmetry.

12 Shape A is a single square. Shape B consists of four squares.

Draw three diagrams in which shapes A and B are joined together along a whole edge so that the final shape has line symmetry.

13 Shape C is a single square. Shape D consists of five squares.

Draw four diagrams in which shapes C and D are joined together along a whole edge so that the final shape has line symmetry.

Using coordinates

(a) Triangle 2 is the image of triangle 1 under reflection in the line $x = -1$. We will use the shorthand '△' for 'triangle'.

(b) △3 is the image of △1 under reflection in the line $y = x$.

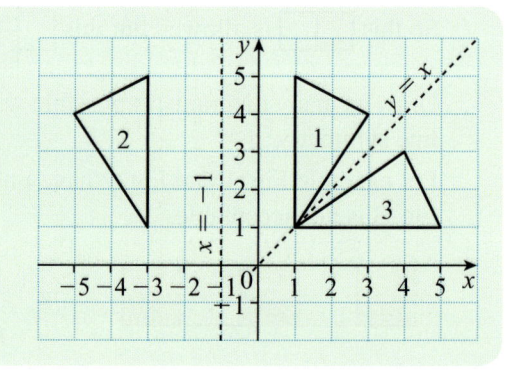

Exercise 4M

1. Copy the diagram.
  (a) Reflect the shape in the y axis. Label the image A.
  (b) Reflect the shape in the x axis. Label the image B.

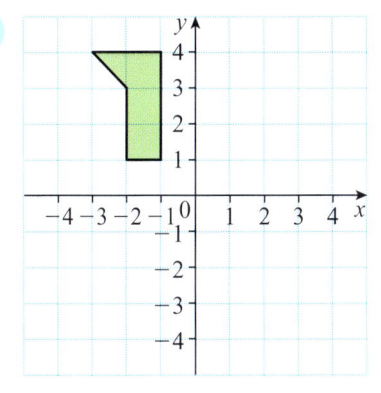

2. Copy the diagram onto squared paper.
  (a) Reflect shape A in the line $x = 3$. Label the image B.
  (b) Reflect shape A in the line $y = 1$. Label the image C.
  (c) Reflect shape A in the y axis. Label the image D.

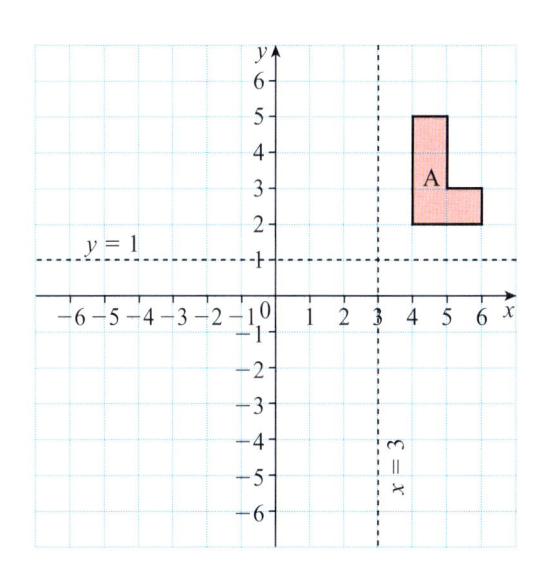

3. 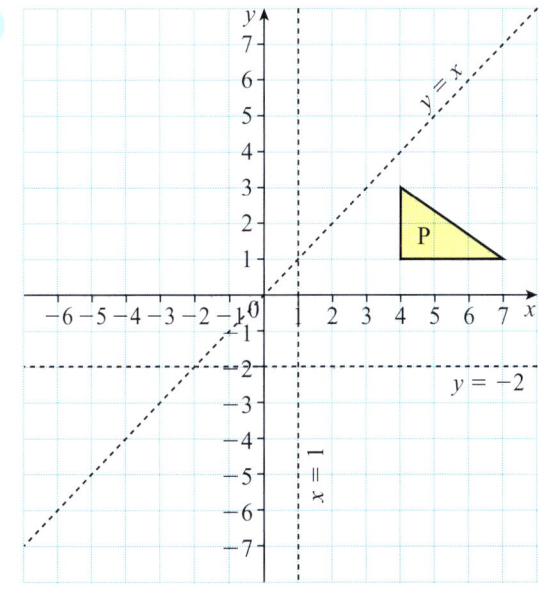 Copy the diagram onto squared paper.
  (a) Reflect shape P in the line $y = -2$. Label the image Q.
  (b) Reflect shape P in the line $x = 1$. Label the image R.
  (c) Reflect shape P in the line $y = x$. Label the image S.

4 (a) Draw an x axis from -8 to 7 and a y axis from -5 to 6.

   (b) Draw a triangle with vertices (corners) at $(2, 2)$, $(2, 5)$ and $(4, 5)$. Label this triangle A.

   (c) Reflect triangle A in the line $x = 4$. Label the image B.

   (d) Reflect triangle B in the line $y = 1$. Label the image C.

   (e) Reflect triangle C in the line $x = -1$. Label the image D.

5 Write down the equation of the mirror line for the following reflections.

   (a) A to B

   (b) B to C

   (c) B to D

   (d) D to E

   (e) G to F

   (f) F to C

   Note: The x axis has equation $y = 0$.
   The y axis has equation $x = 0$.

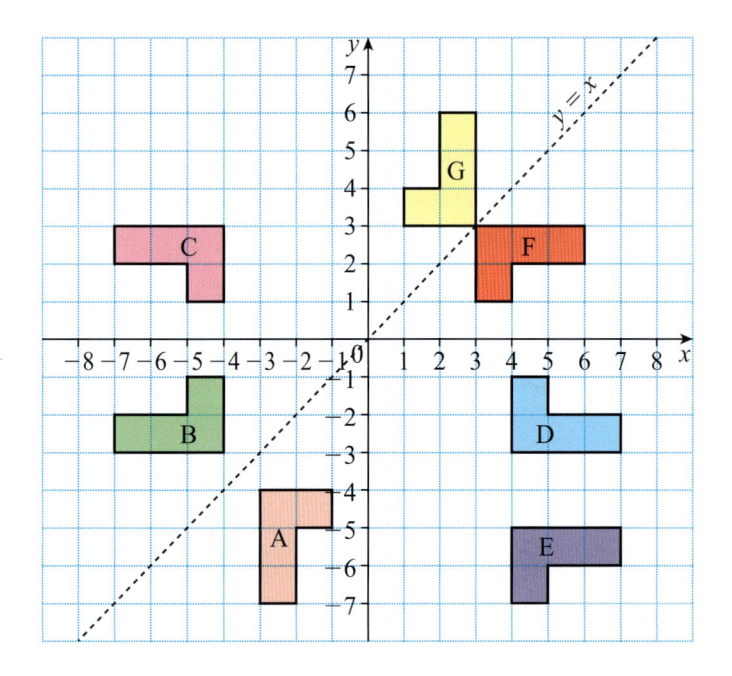

6 (a) Draw x and y axes from -4 to 4.

   (b) Draw a rectangle with vertices at $(-2, 1)$, $(-2, 4)$, $(-3, 4)$ and $(-3, 1)$. Label this rectangle P.

   (c) Reflect rectangle P in the line $x = -1$. Label the image Q.

   (d) Reflect rectangle Q in the line $x = -1$. What do you notice? Explain clearly why this has happened.

7 (a) Draw an x axis from 0 to 12 and a y axis from 0 to 4.

   (b) Draw a triangle with vertices at $(1, 1)$, $(2, 1)$ and $(2, 3)$. Label this triangle A.

   (c) Reflect △A in the line $x = 3$ then reflect the new △ in the line $x = 6$ then reflect this new shape in the line $x = 9$. Label the final triangle B.

   (d) If △A is reflected directly to △B, write down the equation of the mirror line.

4.7 Rotation

In section 4.7 you will learn how to:
- rotate shapes

In these diagrams the shaded shape has been rotated onto the unshaded shape.

In the first diagram the shaded shape is rotated 90° (1 right angle) anticlockwise around point A.

In the second diagram the shaded shape is rotated 180° (2 right angles) around point B.
Notice that for a 180° rotation it makes no difference whether you turn clockwise or anticlockwise.

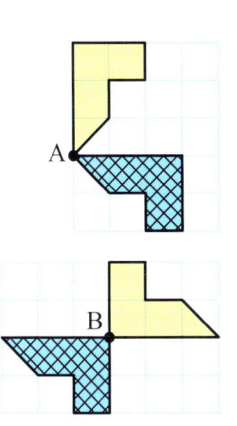

Exercise 1M

In questions 1 to 9 copy each diagram and then draw its new position after it has been turned. You can use tracing paper if you wish.

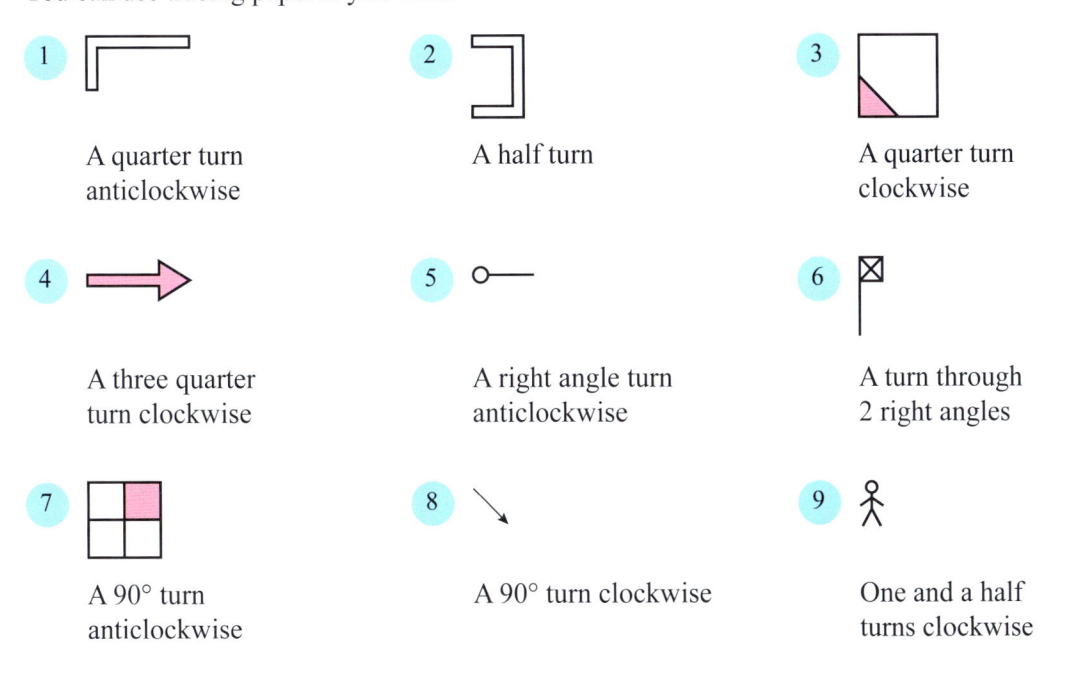

1. A quarter turn anticlockwise

2. A half turn

3. A quarter turn clockwise

4. A three quarter turn clockwise

5. A right angle turn anticlockwise

6. A turn through 2 right angles

7. A 90° turn anticlockwise

8. A 90° turn clockwise

9. One and a half turns clockwise

In questions 10 to 15 describe the rotation. Give the angle and the direction.

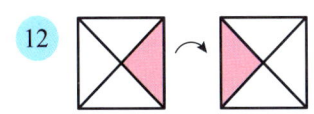

10.

11.

12.

13 V ⤳ ⟩   14 ◓ ⤳ ◒   15 ⌒ ⤳ ⊃

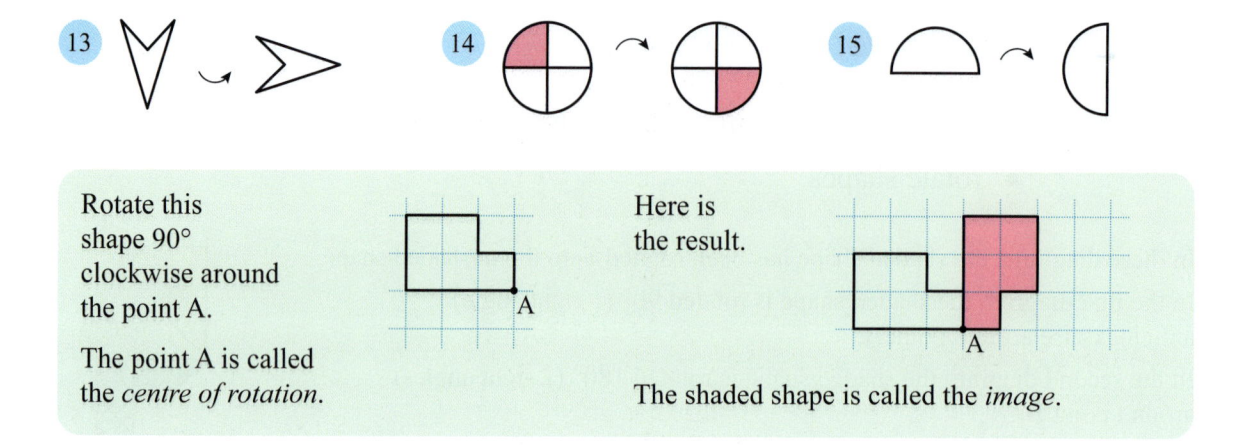

> Rotate this shape 90° clockwise around the point A.
>
> The point A is called the *centre of rotation*.
>
> Here is the result.
>
> The shaded shape is called the *image*.

Exercise 2M

Use tracing paper if you wish.

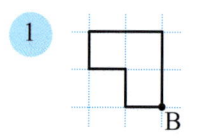

1. (a) Copy this shape on squared paper.
   (b) Draw the image of the shape after a quarter turn clockwise around the point B.

In questions 2 to 4 copy the shape on squared paper and then draw and shade its new position.

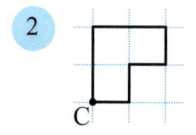

2. Half turn around the point C

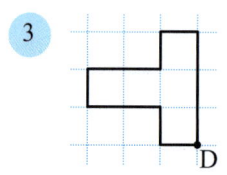

3. Quarter turn clockwise around the point D

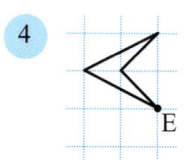

4. Turn 90° anticlockwise around the point E

5. The diagram shows shapes which have been rotated about the points A, B, C, D and E.

   Which shape do you get when you
   (a) rotate shape R 90° clockwise about A
   (b) rotate shape R 90° clockwise about B
   (c) rotate shape Q 180° about C
   (d) rotate shape S 90° anticlockwise about D
   (e) rotate shape P 180° about E

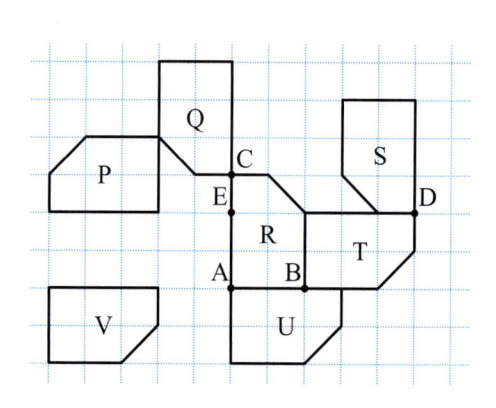

6. Draw this shape on squared paper.
   Draw the image of the shape
   (a) after a 90° rotation clockwise about A
   (b) after a 180° rotation about B
   (c) after a 90° rotation anticlockwise about C
   (d) after a 45° rotation clockwise about A

Using coordinates

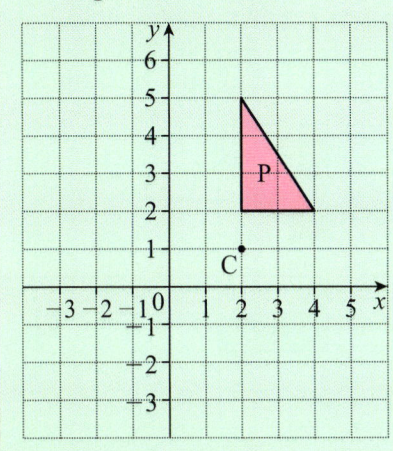

Triangle P is to be rotated 90° anticlockwise about the point C (2, 1).

Maybe use tracing paper. Hold pencil on point C then turn the tracing paper 90° anticlockwise.

Triangle Q is the image of P.

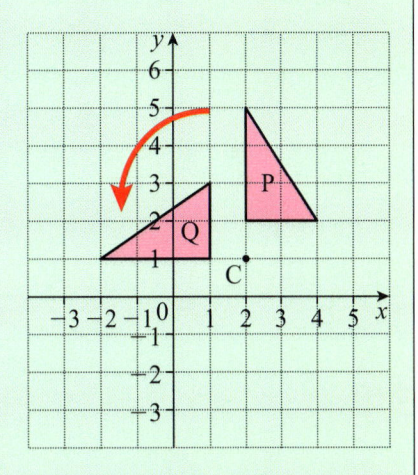

Note: we need three things to describe fully a rotation.
(1) the angle
(2) the direction (clockwise or anticlockwise)
(3) the centre of rotation

Exercise 3M

1. Copy the diagram opposite.
   (a) Rotate shape A 90° clockwise about (0, 0). Label the image C.
   (b) Rotate shape B 90° anticlockwise about (0, 0). Label the image D.

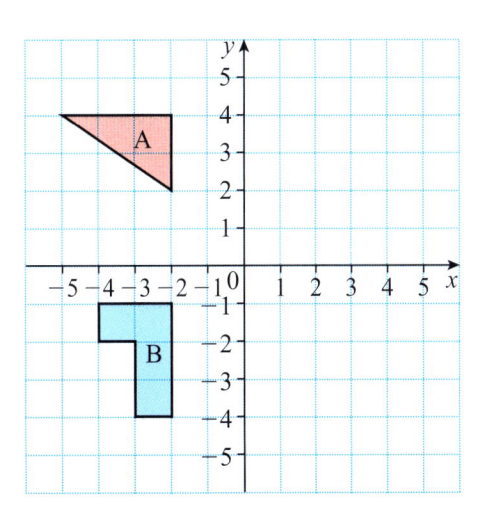

2 (a) Draw x and y axes from -5 to 5.
  (b) Draw a rectangle with vertices at $(1, -2)$, $(1, -4)$, $(5, -4)$ and $(5, -2)$. Label this rectangle P.
  (c) Rotate P 90° anticlockwise about $(1, -1)$. Label the image Q.
  (d) Rotate Q 180° about $(0, -1)$. Label the image R.

3 A shape is rotated 90° clockwise about the origin $(0, 0)$ then the new shape is rotated 180° about the origin. This new shape is then rotated 90° anticlockwise about the origin. Describe what has happened to the original shape to give the final image.

4 For each rotation below, give the angle of rotation, direction and centre of rotation.
Use tracing paper to help you.
  (a) A to B
  (b) B to C
  (c) D to C

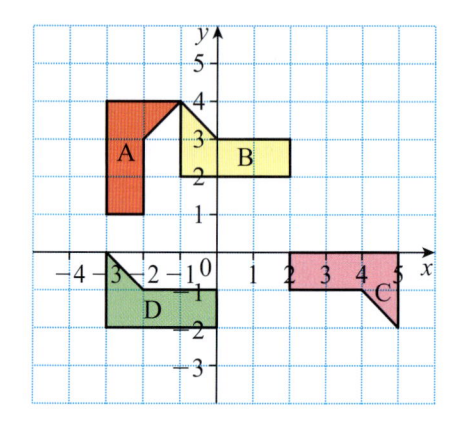

5 Copy the diagram opposite.
  (a) Rotate H 90° anticlockwise about $(6, -1)$.
  (b) Rotate T 90° anticlockwise about $(11, 1)$.
  (c) Rotate A 180° about $(8, 1)$.

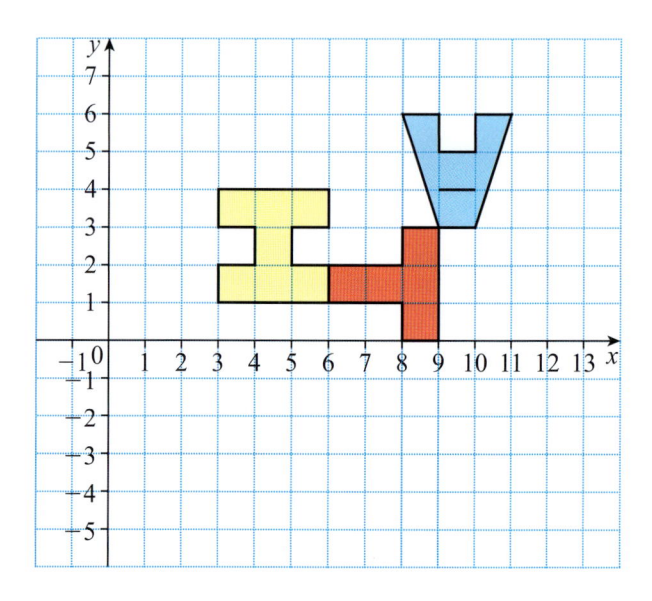

6 A triangle A is rotated 90° anticlockwise about $(1, 2)$.
The new triangle is labelled B.
Triangle B is now rotated 180° about $(1, 2)$ and the new triangle is labelled C.
Describe fully the angle of rotation, direction and centre of rotation which moves A to C in one single rotation.

7 (a) Draw x and y axes from -6 to 6.
   (b) Draw a triangle with vertices at $(-2, -2)$, $(-2, -3)$ and $(-5, -2)$. Label this triangle P.
   (c) Rotate P 90° clockwise about $(-1, -1)$. Label the image Q.
   (d) Rotate Q 180° about the origin $(0, 0)$. Label the image R.
   (e) Rotate R 90° clockwise about $(4, 1)$. Label the image S.
   (f) Rotate S 180° about $(3, -1)$. Label the image T.
   (g) T can be rotated to Q in one single rotation.
       Give the angle of rotation, direction and centre of rotation.

Need more practice with translation, reflection and rotation?

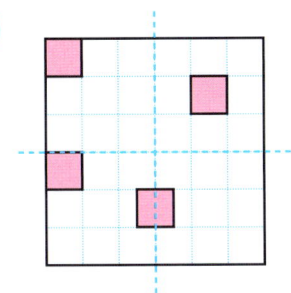

1 Copy this diagram and shade in as many squares as necessary so that the final pattern has mirror lines shown by the broken lines. Write down how many new squares were shaded in.

2 Copy the shape shown opposite on squared paper. Rotate the shape 90° clockwise about the point C.

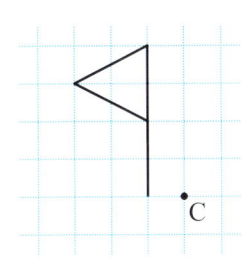

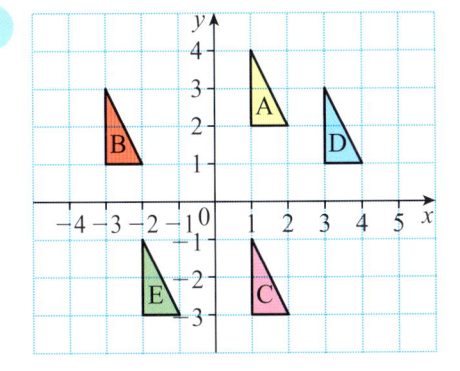

3 Use translation vectors to describe the following translations.
   (a) A to B   (b) B to C
   (c) C to E   (d) E to A
   (e) D to C   (f) D to A

4 Do any of these letters have both line symmetry and rotational symmetry?

N   Z   E   H   T

5   Copy the diagram opposite.
    (a) Reflect the triangle in the line $y = 1$.
    (b) Reflect the triangle in the line $x = -3$.
    (c) Reflect the triangle in the line $x = \frac{1}{2}$.

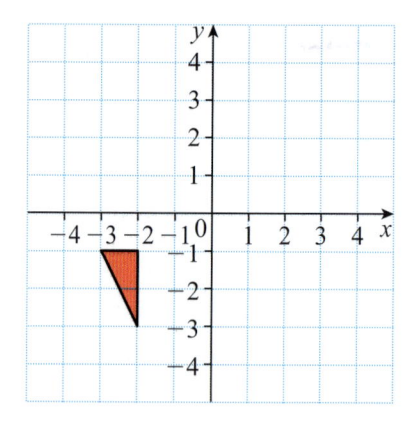

6   (a) Draw x and y axes from -5 to 5.
    (b) Draw a rectangle with vertices at (2, 1), (2, 4), (4, 4) and (4, 1). Label this rectangle A.
    (c) Translate A by $\begin{pmatrix} -5 \\ 1 \end{pmatrix}$. Label the image B.
    (d) Translate B by $\begin{pmatrix} 4 \\ -7 \end{pmatrix}$. Label the image C.
    (e) Translate C by $\begin{pmatrix} -6 \\ 1 \end{pmatrix}$. Label the image D.
    (f) Write down the translation vector which translates D to B.

7   (a) If this umbrella was viewed from above would it have rotational symmetry?
    (b) If so what is the order of rotational symmetry?

8   Copy the diagram opposite.
    (a) Rotate the shape 90° anticlockwise about (0, 0).
    (b) Rotate the shape 180° about (0, 0).

Extension questions with translation, reflection and rotation

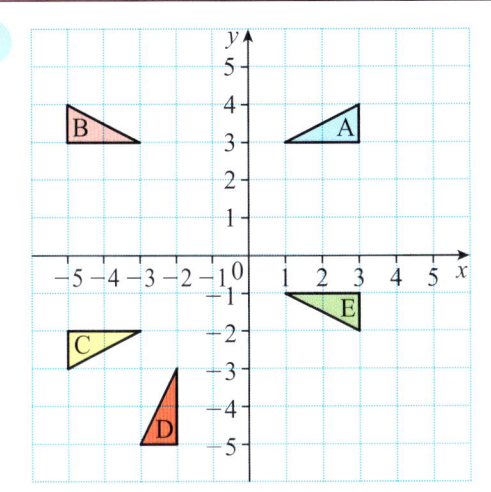

1 Write down the equation of the mirror line for the following reflections.
(a) A to B
(b) B to C
(c) C to D
(d) E to A

2 (a) Draw x and y axes from -6 to 6.
(b) Draw a triangle with vertices at $(-6, -3)$, $(-3, -3)$, and $(-3, -4)$. Label the triangle A.
(c) Reflect triangle A in the x axis. Label the image B.
(d) Reflect triangle B in the y axis. Label the image C.
(e) Triangle C can be directly rotated back to triangle A. Write down the angle of rotation and the centre of rotation.

3 For each rotation below, give the angle of rotation, direction and centre of rotation. Use tracing paper to help you.
(a) P to Q
(b) Q to R
(c) R to S
(d) S to T

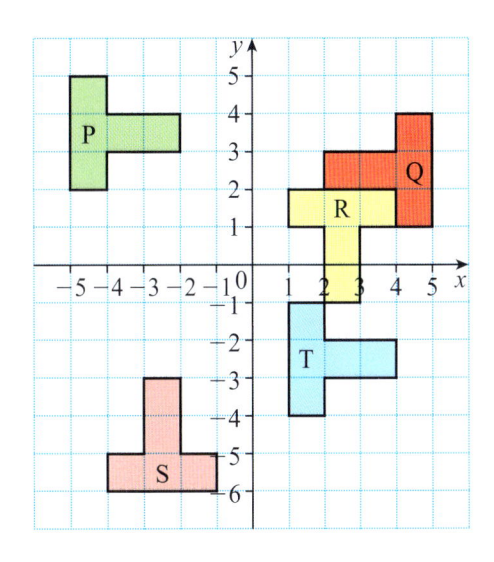

4 An L-shape is rotated $180°$ about $(0, 0)$.
Charlotte says that the image is not the same shape because it is upside down.
Is she correct?
Explain your answer fully.

5 (a) Draw x and y axes from -6 to 6.

(b) Draw a rectangle with vertices at $(1, -2)$, $(2, -2)$, $(2, -5)$ and $(1, -5)$. Label the rectangle A.

(c) Rotate A $180°$ about $(0, 0)$. Label the image B.

(d) Translate B by $\begin{pmatrix} -3 \\ -1 \end{pmatrix}$. Label the image C.

(e) Reflect C in the line $x = -1$. Label the image D.

(f) Translate D by $\begin{pmatrix} 2 \\ -6 \end{pmatrix}$. Label the image E.

(g) Rectangle E is reflected onto rectangle A. Write down the equation of the mirror line.

6 Describe fully each transformation below – either a translation, reflection or rotation.

(a) A to B
(b) B to C
(c) C to D
(d) D to E
(e) F to C
(f) G to A
(g) G to H
(h) E to H
(i) G to D
(j) H to I

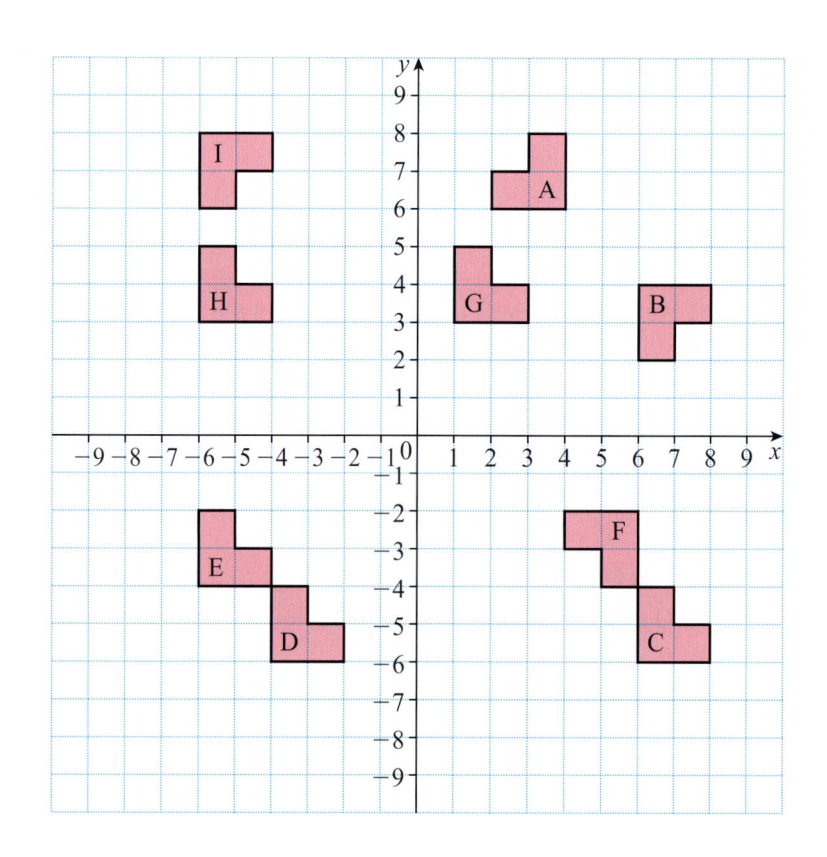

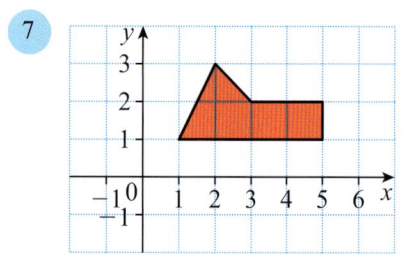

7 Describe three consecutive transformations that will move the shape opposite into two new positions then finally back to this starting position.

The tile factory: an activity

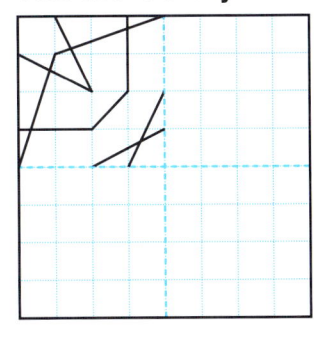

1. Copy this square and pattern onto the top left hand corner of a piece of A4 centimetre squared paper.

2. Lightly mark the reflection lines on the diagram as shown.

3. Use these lines to help you reflect the pattern across … … and then down.

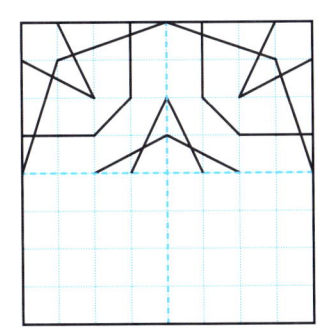

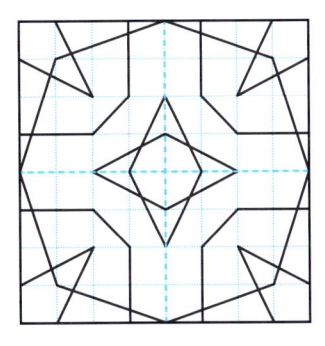

4. Repeat the process with the same tile so that your tile neatly covers the piece of paper as shown on the right.

5. Now colour or shade in your work as neatly and symmetrically as you can.

✗ Spot the mistakes 8 ✗

Two dimensional shapes, transformations and constructing triangles

Work through each question on the next 2 pages and explain clearly what mistakes have been made. Beware – some questions are correctly done.

1. How many lines of symmetry does a rectangle have?

   Answer: 4

2. AC is the diagonal of a rhombus. AC = 9 cm. Find the length MC.

   Answer: MC = 4.5 cm

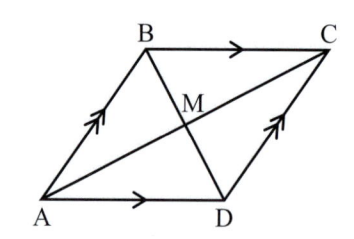

3. Triangle A is to be reflected in the line $y = -1$.

   The solution is shown opposite.

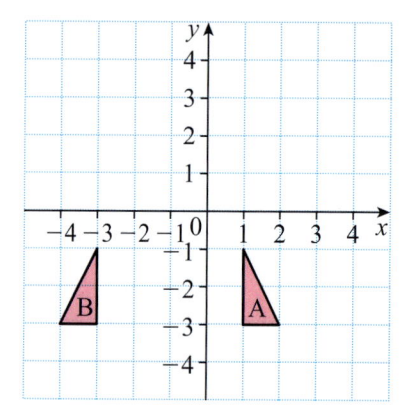

4. Shape P is translated by $\begin{pmatrix} 5 \\ -3 \end{pmatrix}$ to shape Q.

   Shape Q is translated by $\begin{pmatrix} 4 \\ 1 \end{pmatrix}$ to shape R.

   What translation vector will translate shape R to shape P?

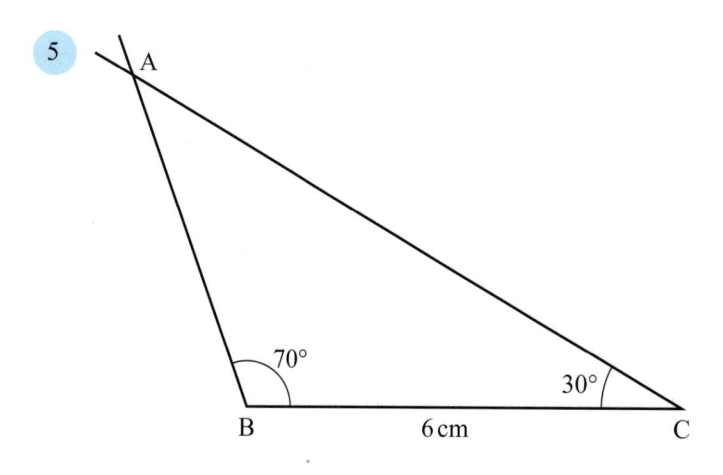

   Answer: $\begin{pmatrix} 5 \\ -3 \end{pmatrix} + \begin{pmatrix} 4 \\ 1 \end{pmatrix} = \begin{pmatrix} 9 \\ -2 \end{pmatrix}$

5. A triangle ABC is to be constructed with BC = 6 cm, $A\hat{B}C = 70°$ and $A\hat{C}B = 30°$.

   The solution is shown opposite.

6 What is the order of rotational symmetry of a kite?

Answer: 2

7 (a) Rotate shape A 90° clockwise about (0, 0). Label the image B.
(b) Reflect B in the *x* axis. Label the image C.
(c) Rotate C 90° anticlockwise about (0, 0). Label the image D.
(d) D is reflected back to A. What is the mirror line?

The solution is shown opposite and the answer to part (d) is 'the *y* axis'.

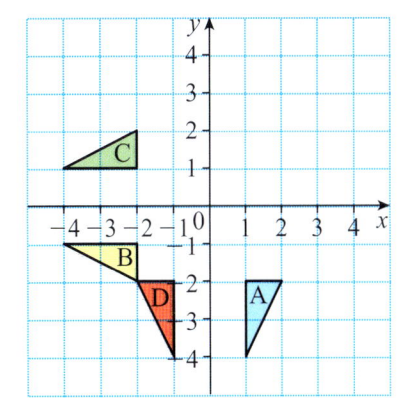

8 Shape P is to be rotated 90° clockwise about (0, 1).
The solution is shown opposite.

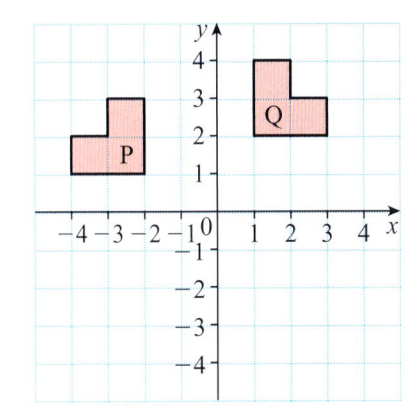

9 Describe a trapezium.

Solution: A trapezium has one pair of parallel sides and two pairs of equal angles as shown.

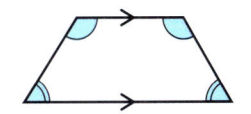

10 (a) Translate triangle P by $\begin{pmatrix} 5 \\ -5 \end{pmatrix}$.
Label the image Q.
(b) Rotate Q 90° clockwise about (0, 0). Label the image R.
The solution is shown opposite.

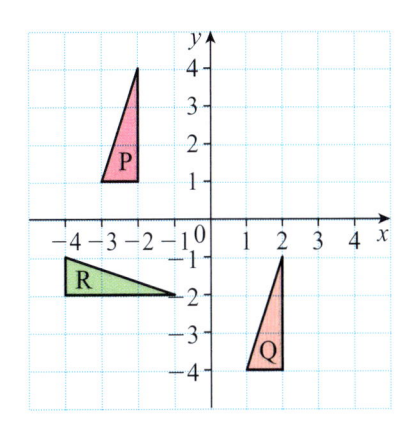

CHECK YOURSELF ON SECTIONS 4.5, 4.6 AND 4.7

1 Translating shapes

(a) Use translation vectors to describe each translation below
   (i) A to C
   (ii) C to D
   (iii) B to E

(b) Draw the triangle A on squared paper.

   Translate triangle A by $\begin{pmatrix} 4 \\ 3 \end{pmatrix}$.

   Label the image F.

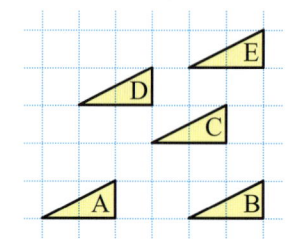

2 Reviewing symmetry

State the order of rotational symmetry of each shape

(a)   (b) 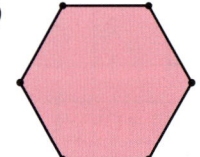   (c) 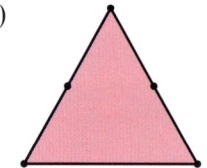   (d)

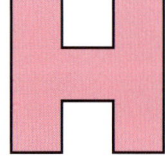

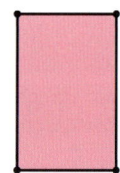

(e) 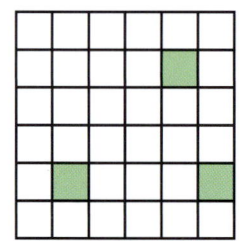 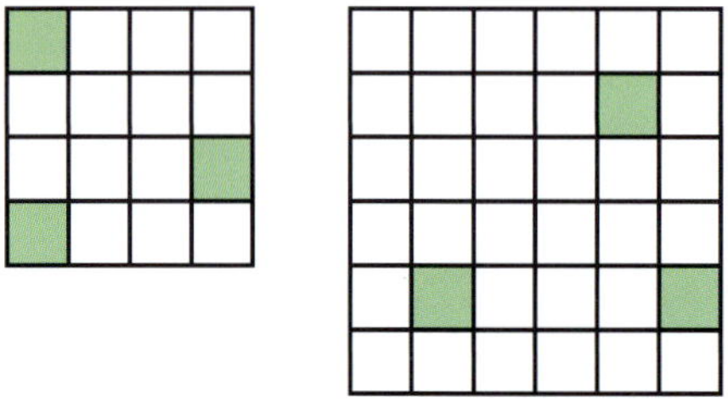 Draw the two patterns on the left and shade in the least number of squares so that the final patterns have line symmetry.

3 Reflecting shapes

Copy the diagram opposite.

(a) Reflect triangle A in the y axis.
   Label the image B.

(b) Reflect triangle A in the line $y = -1$.
   Label the image C.

(c) Write down the mirror line for the reflection of triangle P onto triangle Q.

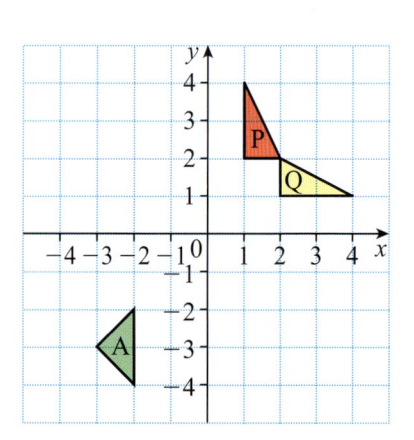

4 Rotating shapes

Copy the diagram opposite.

(a) Rotate rectangle A 180° about (−2, 0).
Label the image B.

(b) Rotate rectangle A 180° about (0, 0).
Label the image C.

(c) Triangle P is rotated to triangle Q.
Write down the angle of rotation, direction and centre of rotation.

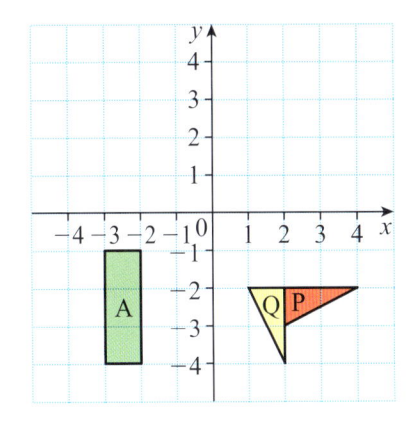

4.8 Applying mathematics 4

In section 4.8 you will apply maths in a variety of situations.

1. A school play was attended by 226 adults, each paying £1.50, and 188 children, each paying 80p. How much in £s was paid altogether by the people attending the play?

2. Write down these calculations and find the missing digits.

(a) 5 ☐ 5
   + 3 2 ☐
   ─────────
     9 0 1

(b) 3 ☐ 9
   + 5 8 ☐
   ─────────
   ☐ 5 3

(c) ☐ 1 ☐
   + 5 ☐ 4
   ─────────
     7 5 0

3. On a Saturday Dom spends 90 minutes playing a game and Morgan spends 70 minutes playing the same game. On the Sunday, Dom increases his playing time by 15% and Morgan spends 45% more time playing the game.

Who spends the longer time playing on the Sunday and what is the difference between their playing times?

4. I am a 2 digit prime number.
I am a factor of 184.
What number am I?

5) Amy plots three points on a graph. Each unit on the axes is 1 cm.
She plots A (1, 2), B (4, 2) and C (4, 6). She measures the length AC as 5 cm.
Is she correct? Explain fully how you decide on your answer.

6) Triangle PQS is equilateral and triangle QRS is isosceles.
Work out the size of QR̂S.
Give full reasons for your answer.

7) A small boat travels 350 km on 125 litres of fuel.
How much fuel is needed for a journey of 630 km?

8) A golfer has a mean average of −2 for six rounds of golf.

For his first five rounds of golf he has scores of:

−3   −1   +2   −5   −1

What did he score on his sixth round of golf?

9) Four 4s can be used to make 12: $\dfrac{44 + 4}{4}$

(a) Use three 6 s to make 2
(b) Use three 7 s to make 7
(c) Use three 9 s to make 11
(d) Use four 4 s to make 9
(e) Use four 4 s to make 3

10) Write down the ratio of area A to area B in the trapezium shown opposite.
Give the ratio in its simplest form.

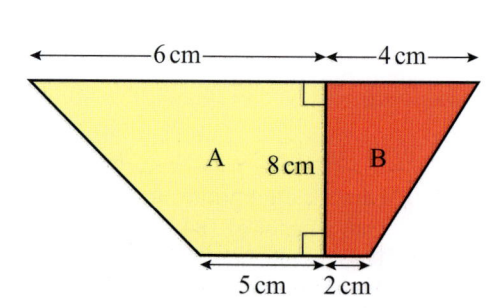

UNIT 4 MIXED REVIEW

Part one

1. The price of a computer game is £40 but it is increased by 5%. What is the new price?

2. Gwen and Tim are given £99 in the ratio 8:3. How much money does Tim get?

3. 'Any quadrilateral can be cut into two triangles'. True or false?

4. Use a protractor and ruler to construct this triangle.
   Measure the side marked x.

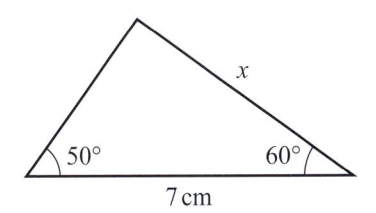

5. Copy the diagram opposite.

   (a) Translate triangle A by $\begin{pmatrix} 3 \\ 4 \end{pmatrix}$. Label the image B.

   (b) Translate triangle B by $\begin{pmatrix} 2 \\ -3 \end{pmatrix}$. Label the image C.

   (c) What translation vector will translate triangle C back to triangle A?

6. A train travels 20 km in 8 minutes.
   How long will it take to travel 25 km at the same speed?

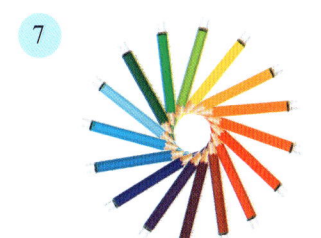

7. This shape is made using coloured pencils.
   If you ignore the different colours, what is the order of rotational symmetry of the shape?

8. Which is larger, $\frac{7}{25}$ or 27%?

9. Four and a half dozen eggs weigh 2970 g.
   How much would six dozen eggs weigh?

10 Show how the 3 by 8 rectangle can be cut into two identical pieces and joined together to make a 2 by 12 rectangle.

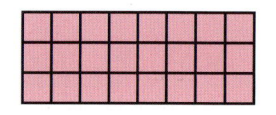

11 60 people take their driving test. 24 of these people fail the test.
What percentage of the people pass the test?

12 Colin books a holiday to Venice for £670.
The holiday firm adds an extra 12% charge when Colin pays for his holiday.
How much does Colin have to pay?

Part two

1 Without using a calculator, work out 2.5% of £220.

2 Work out $\frac{9}{20} + 0.18$.

3 Draw the two patterns on the right and shade in more squares so that the final patterns have rotational symmetry of order 2.

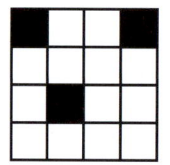

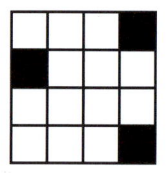

4 A rectangular window frame in a church measures 24.3 cm by 35.7 cm. 80% of the window is filled with stained glass. What is the area of stained glass in the window?

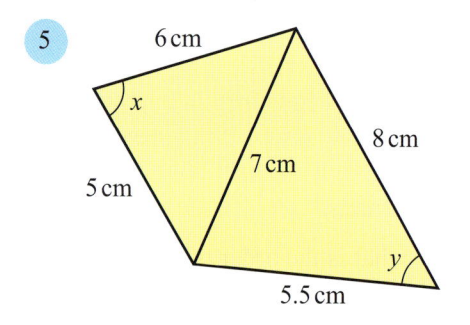

5 Use a ruler and compasses to construct this diagram.
Use a protractor to measure angles x and y.

6 A boat sails 2.4 km in 30 minutes.
How long will it take to sail one km?

7 At noon there are 324 600 starlings in a flock.
Two hours later the number has increased by 7.5%.
How many starlings are in the flock at 2.00 p.m.?

8 Work out the total cost of:
15 kg of sand at 67p per kg
3 tape measures at £4.80 each
3000 screws at 80p per hundred
Add VAT at 20%.

9 Draw a quadrilateral which has two lines of symmetry *only*.

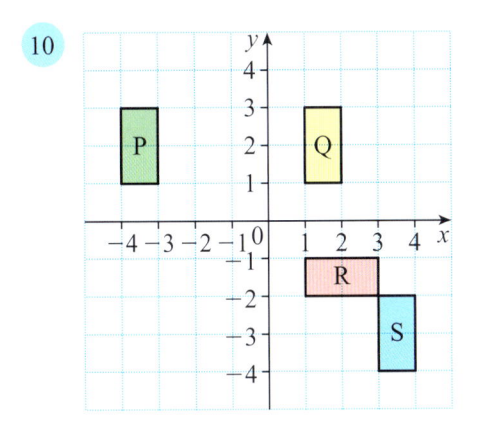

10
(a) P is reflected to Q. Write down the equation of the mirror line.
(b) Q is rotated to R. Write down the angle of rotation, direction and centre of rotation.
(c) R is rotated to S. Write down the angle of rotation, direction and centre of rotation.
(d) Write down the translation vector which will translate S to P.

11 Matt and Heather share out some pencils in the ratio 7:13.
If Matt gets 21 pencils, how many pencils does Heather get?

12 The price of a T.V. costing £650 was decreased by 20%.
Three months later the price was increased by 20%. Calculate the final price of the TV.

Puzzles and Problems 4

Cross numbers without clues

On the next two pages are cross number puzzles with a difference. There are no clues, only answers, and you have to find where the answers go.

(a) Copy out the cross number pattern.

(b) Fit all the given numbers into the correct spaces. Work logically and tick off the numbers from lists as you write them in the squares.

① Ask your teacher if you do not know how to start.

2 digits	3 digits	4 digits	5 digits	6 digits
18	375	1274	37 125	308 513
37	692	1625		
53	828	3742		
74		5181		
87				

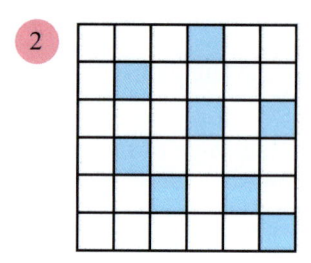

②

2 digits	3 digits	4 digits	5 digits	6 digits
13	382	2630	12 785	375 041
21	582	2725		
45	178	5104		
47		7963		
72				

③

2 digits	3 digits	4 digits	6 digits	7 digits
53	182	4483	375 615	3 745 124
63	324	4488		4 253 464
64	327	6515		8 253 364
	337			8 764 364
	436			
	573			
	683			
	875			

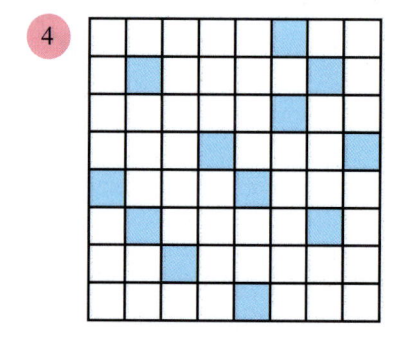

④

2 digits	3 digits	4 digits	5 digits	6 digits
27	161	1127	34 462	455 185
36	285	2024	74 562	
54	297	3473	81 072	
63	311	5304	84 762	
64	412	5360		
69	483	5370		
	535	5380		
	536			
	636			
	714			

5 *This one is more difficult.*

2 digits	3 digits	4 digits	5 digits	6 digits
16	288	2831	47 185	321 802
37	322	2846	52 314	
56	607	2856	56 324	
69	627	2873	56 337	
72	761	4359		
98	762	5647		
	768	7441		
	769			
	902			
	952			

6 *This one is more difficult.*

2 digits	3 digits	4 digits	5 digits	6 digits
21	121	1349	24 561	215 613
22	136	2457	24 681	246 391
22	146	2458	34 581	246 813
23	165	3864		
36	216	4351		
53	217	4462		
55	285	5321		
56	335	5351		
58	473	5557		
61	563	8241		
82	917	8251		
83		9512		
91				

Mental Arithmetic Practice 4

There are two sets of mental arithmetic questions in this section. Ideally a teacher will read out each question twice, with pupils' books closed. Each test should take about 20 minutes.

Test 1

1. Write down a factor of 35 greater than one.
2. How many more than 17 is 80?
3. Find the change from a £10 note if you spend £2.30.
4. The perimeter of a square is 20 cm. What is the area of the square?
5. What is two point nought one multiplied by one thousand?
6. How many fifteens are there in three hundred?
7. What is the difference between 1.7 and 8?
8. What is the remainder when 50 is divided by 7?
9. What is the cost of 3 magazines at £2.99 each?
10. Subtract the sum of 11 and 12 from 50.
11. I have one 20p, three 10p, and one 50p coin. How much money do I have?
12. What four coins make 67p?
13. A saucepan costs £17.95 new. I get a discount of £6. How much do I pay?
14. A film starts at 7.45 and ends at 9.10. How long is the film?
15. Work out 200 times 400.
16. Write the number 'one and a half billion' in figures.
17. What number is exactly mid-way between 4 and 4.1?
18. Work out two squared plus two cubed.
19. A length of 210 mm is cut from a rod of length one metre. What is the length of the remaining rod?
20. How many edges does a square based pyramid have?
21. How many lines of symmetry does a regular hexagon have?
22. An ant walks 20 cm in 5 seconds. How far will it walk in one minute?
23. Find the new price of a £50 scanner after a 10 per cent increase.
24. I think of a number and add 5. The result is equal to 6 times 7. What is the number?
25. What number is next in the sequence 4, 8, 16, 32?

Test 2

1. What is one million pence in pounds?
2. A triangle has a base of 8 cm and a height of 6 cm. What is its area?
3. True or false: 1 yard is equal to 4 feet?
4. A wire of length 590 cm is cut in half. How long is each half?

5. An aircraft begins a 45 minute flight at 10 minutes to six. When does it land?

6. What is a quarter of four hundred and twenty?

7. If the 10th of November is a Monday, what day of the week is the 20th?

8. What percentage of the numbers from 1 to 10 are prime numbers?

9. What four coins make 65 pence? Do this in two ways.

10. A lottery prize of eighteen million pounds is shared between ten winners. How much does each person receive?

11. What is the total of 55 and 66?

12. Two angles of a triangle are 45° and 30°. What is the third angle?

13. What is a half of a quarter of 100?

14. An egg box holds six eggs. How many boxes are needed for 40 eggs?

15. Add together £3.25 and £6.15.

16. Fifty people took their driving test one day and thirty-two passed. What percentage passed?

17. A regular hexagon has sides of length 15 cm. What is the perimeter of the hexagon?

18. Find the difference, in millimetres, between half a metre and one millimetre.

19. How many 20p coins do I need to make £50?

20. A clock shows five past nine but it is fifteen minutes slow. What is the correct time?

21. What is three quarters of £88?

22. What is the smaller angle between the hands of a clock at four o'clock?

23. How many centimetres are there in one kilometre?

24. How many minutes are there in $1\frac{2}{3}$ hours?

25. Add twelve to six times nine.

> A long time ago! 4

The Königsberg Problem

In the 18th century, the city of Königsberg (in Prussia) was split into parts by the River Pregel. There were seven bridges. The people of Königsberg tried to walk across all seven bridges without crossing the same bridge twice.

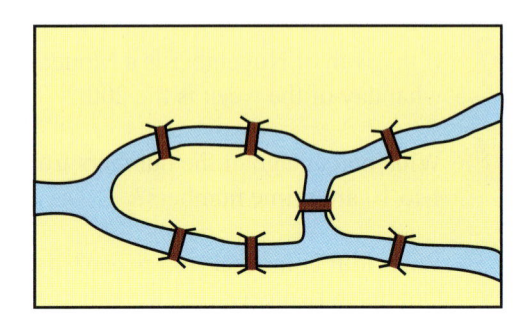

Exercise

1. Sketch the diagram above to show the river and the bridges. Use a pencil to show how you could walk across each bridge without crossing the same bridge twice.
   If you make a mistake, rub out the pencil and try again.
   If you find a way, show somebody else then show your teacher.

2. Make up a map of a city which has more than seven bridges. Get somebody else to copy your map and try to show you how to walk across each bridge without crossing the same bridge twice.

3. **RESEARCH:**

   A famous mathematician, Leonhard Euler, examined the Königsberg problem.

   (a) Find out when Euler lived.

   (b) Find out what Euler said about the Königsberg problem.

   (c) Königsberg is now called Kaliningrad and is in Russia. Find out how many of the seven bridges still exist.

   (d) Discuss as a class your main findings about the Königsberg problem.

UNIT 5

5.1 More algebra

In section 5.1 you will:
- review section 1.4, Rules of algebra
- solve equations
- form and solve equations

Review of section 1.4, Rules of algebra

Exercise 1M

1. I start with a number w, double it then subtract 18. Write down an expression for what I now have.

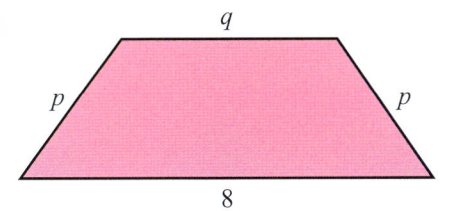

2. Write down an expression for the perimeter of this trapezium.

3. Simplify the following expressions where possible.
   (a) $5y - 2y$ (b) $8m + 2$ (c) $7x - x$ (d) $5w - 3$

4. Which pair of expressions below are equal to each other?

   $2n + 1$ $2n + n$ $n \times n \times n$ $3n$ $n + 3$

5. Simplify   (a) $\dfrac{2w}{w}$ (b) $\dfrac{w^2}{w}$

6. Expand (multiply out)
   (a) $m(n - p)$ (b) $4(3m + 2)$ (c) $n(n - 5)$

7 Which expression below is the odd one out?

| $5a \times 4b \times c$ | $2a \times 5b \times 4c$ | $2a \times 5c \times 2b$ |

8 $V = IR$ is an electrical formula. Find the value of V when $I = 0.5$ and $R = 68$.

9 (a) Write down an expression for the total area of the three rectangles shown opposite. Simplify the answer.
(b) What is the actual area when $x = 6$ cm?

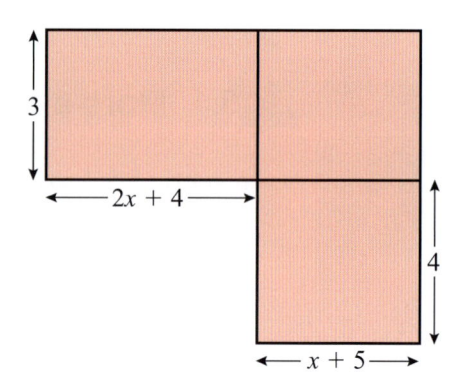

(Diagram: top-left rectangle of height 3 and width $2x + 4$; top-right square; right side height 4 and width $x + 5$.)

10 Jack says that $2x - x$ is equal to 2. Is he correct? Explain your answer fully.

11 $w = 25 - 4n$
Find w, when $n = 5$.

12 $a = 2(b - 6)$
Find a, when $b = 10$.

13 $p = 2q + 5r$
Find p, when $q = 6$ and $r = 7$.

14 $a = b(c - 7)$
Find a, when $b = 10$ and $c = 15$.

15 $y = \dfrac{x}{6} - 9$
Find y, when $x = 72$.

16 $m = n^2 + p^2$
Find m, when $n = 8$ and $p = 11$.

17 Rachel adds an expression to $3n + 4$ and gets the expression $2m + 2n + 7$. Write down the expression that Rachel added.

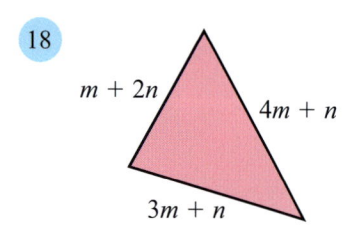

18 (Triangle with sides $m + 2n$, $4m + n$, $3m + n$.) The square has the same perimeter as the triangle. Write down an expression for the length of one side of the square.

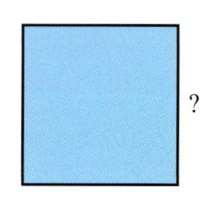

Negative numbers can be substituted into formulas

$m = 6 - n$
Find m, when $n = -2$

$m = 6 - (-2)$
$m = 6 + 2$
$m = 8$

$y = 3x + w$
Find y, when $x = 4$ and $w = -8$

$y = (3 \times 4) + (-8)$
$y = 12 - 8$
$y = 4$

Exercise 1E

1. I start with x, divide it by 9 and then subtract 14.
Write down an expression for what I now have.

2. Marie has n sweets. She eats half the sweets then gives y sweets to her brother.
They each then eat 2 more sweets.
Write down an expression for how many sweets she now has.

3. Simplify the following expression by collecting like terms.
$$8a + 4 - a - 6 - a + 1$$

4. Simplify $4n \times 7n \times 2n$

5. Use algebra to find the area of this shape.
Simplify your answer as far as possible.

(Dimensions: $2n$, $9m$, $4m$, $6n$)

6. Simplify the following expressions by collecting like terms.
   (a) $mn + mn + mn$
   (b) $3xy + 6x - 2xy + x$
   (c) $p + pq + 6pq - p$
   (d) $4a + 9 - 3a + ab + 6ba$

7. $w = 16 - p$
Find w, when $p = -3$.

8. $h = 3g - 6$
Find h, when $g = -6$.

9. $n = 5x - y$
Find n, when $x = -10$ and $y = -40$.

10. $p = m^2$
Find p, when $m = -6$.

11. $y = 3(8 - x)$
Find y, when $x = -2$.

12. $p = -2(8 + q)$
Find p, when $q = -3$.

13. $a = 2b + 2c$
Find a, when $b = -4$ and $c = -5$.

14. $y = mx + c$
Find y, when $m = 4$, $x = -6$ and $c = 3$.

15. $p = q^2 + r^2$
Find p, when $q = -5$ and $r = -3$.

16. $m = n^2 + p$
Find m, when $n = -9$ and $p = -20$.

Solving equations

- Tom is thinking of a mystery number. He knows that if he doubles the number and then adds nine, the answer is twenty-three.

  He could write $\boxed{?}$ for the mystery number.

  So $2 \times \boxed{?} + 9 = 23$

  This is an *equation*. It contains an '=' sign.

  There is one unknown number shown by the question mark.

- People prefer to use *letters* to stand for unknowns when they write equations. Tom's equation would be

  $2 \times n + 9 = 23$ where *n* is the mystery number
  or $2n + 9 = 23$ (any letter could be used)

  What is Tom's mystery number?

- Equations are like weighing scales which are balanced. The scales remain balanced if the same weight is added or taken away from both sides.

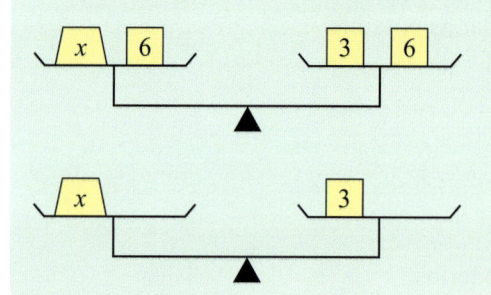

  On the left pan is an unknown weight *x* plus a 6 kg weight. On the right pan there is a 6 kg weight and a 3 kg weight.

  If the two 6 kg weights are taken from each pan, the scales are still balanced so the weight *x* is 3 kg.

Exercise 2M

Find the weight *x* by removing weights from both pans. Weights are in kg.

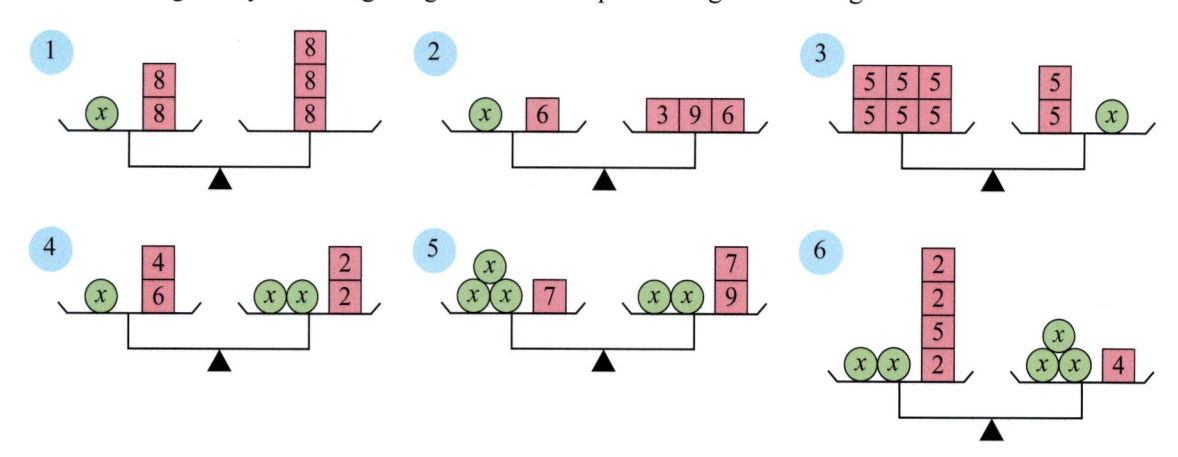

7

8

9

10

11

12

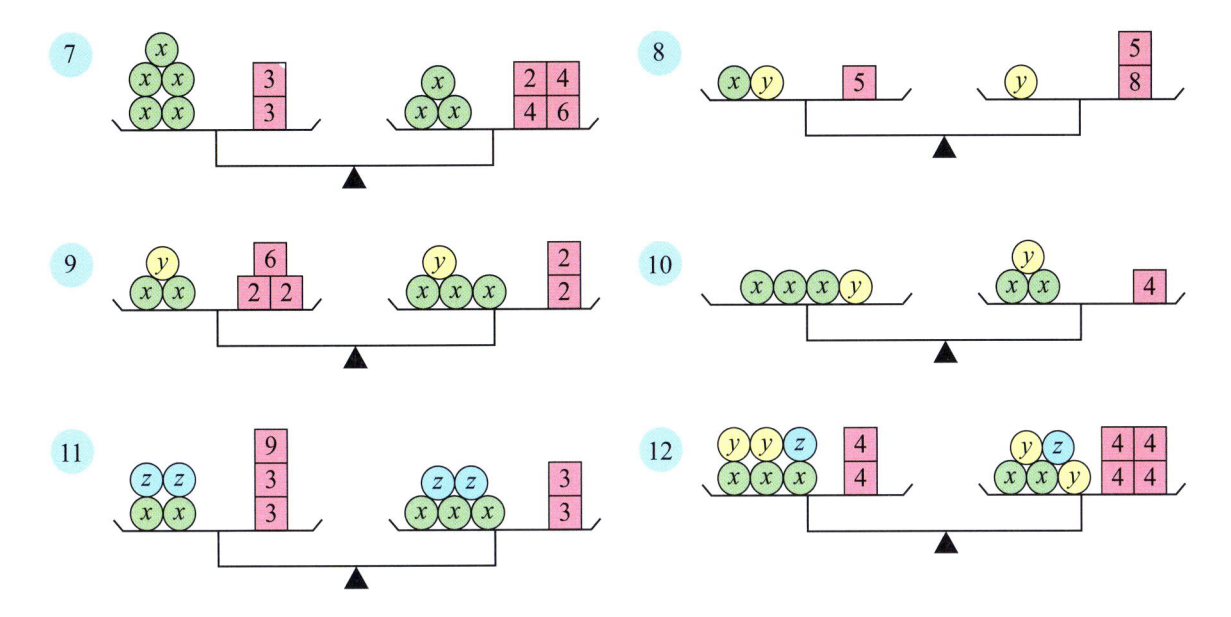

Rules for solving equations

Equations can be solved in the same way as the weighing scale problems were solved.

The main rule is

> Do the same thing to both sides

If you need to, you may:

- *add* the same thing to both sides
- *subtract* the same thing from both sides
- *multiply* both sides by the same thing
- *divide* both sides by the same thing

Solve the equations. The circles show what is done to both sides of the equation.

(a) $x + 4 = 16$
 (-4) (-4)
$x = 12$

(b) $x - 5 = 14$
 $(+5)$ $(+5)$
$x = 19$

(c) $3x = 18$
 $(\div 3)$ $(\div 3)$
$x = 6$

(d) $\dfrac{x}{2} = 6$
 $(\times 2)$ $(\times 2)$
$x = 12$

Exercise 3M

Solve the equations below.

1. $x + 6 = 19$
2. $x - 9 = 8$
3. $6 = x - 2$
4. $3 + x = 3$
5. $x - 14 = 10$
6. $17 = 5 + x$

Questions 7 to 21 involve multiplication and division.

7. $7x = 21$
8. $4x = 12$
9. $5x = 45$
10. $10 = 2x$
11. $8 = 8x$
12. $2x = 1$
13. $4x = 100$
14. $6x = 0$
15. $\dfrac{x}{3} = 2$
16. $\dfrac{x}{5} = 4$
17. $70 = 7x$
18. $3x = 2$
19. $\dfrac{x}{8} = 3$
20. $\dfrac{x}{4} = 1$
21. $10 = \dfrac{x}{12}$

Exercise 3E

Solve the equations below to find n.

1. $n - 17 = 21$
2. $5 = n + 5$
3. $15n = 45$
4. $\dfrac{n}{5} = 20$
5. $2 = \dfrac{n}{8}$
6. $3n = 1$
7. $n - \dfrac{1}{3} = \dfrac{2}{3}$
8. $120 = n + 36$
9. $3n = \dfrac{1}{3}$
10. $\dfrac{1}{2} = \dfrac{n}{10}$
11. $4n = 412$
12. $140 = n - 20$

Solve the equations below to find x.

13. $109 = x - 206$
14. $\dfrac{x}{3} = 9$
15. $0 = 15x$
16. $\dfrac{1}{5}x = 100$
17. $16\tfrac{1}{2} = x - 2\tfrac{1}{2}$
18. $\dfrac{x}{10} = 6$
19. $\dfrac{1}{2}x = 35$
20. $x + 14 = 14$
21. $x + \dfrac{1}{8} = \dfrac{1}{4}$
22. $11 = x + 1.4$
23. $0.02 = \dfrac{x}{10}$
24. $150 = 210 + x$
25. $\dfrac{1}{3} + x = \dfrac{1}{2}$
26. $x + 123 = 1000$
27. $x - 0.24 = 0.03$
28. $\dfrac{x}{11} = 145$
29. $\dfrac{x}{4} = \dfrac{1}{12}$
30. $0.2 = x + \dfrac{1}{8}$

Equations with two operations

(a) $6n - 5 = 19$
$\quad\quad +5 \quad +5$
$\quad\quad 6n = 24$
$\quad\quad \div 6 \quad \div 6$
$\quad\quad n = 4$

(b) $8x + 4 = 9$
$\quad\quad -4 \quad -4$
$\quad\quad 8x = 5$
$\quad\quad \div 8 \quad \div 8$
$\quad\quad x = \dfrac{5}{8}$

Exercise 4M

Solve the equations below to find x.

1. $4x - 1 = 11$
2. $2x + 3 = 17$
3. $6x - 9 = 15$
4. $9x + 4 = 13$
5. $7x - 6 = 15$
6. $2x - 10 = 8$
7. $7x - 10 = 25$
8. $9x = 7$
9. $5x = 2$
10. $5 + 2x = 6$
11. $8 + 3x = 26$
12. $4x - 7 = 73$

In questions 13 to 24 solve the equations to find n.

13. $5n - 9 = 31$
14. $7n + 3 = 5$
15. $8n + 3 = 59$
16. $2 + 3n = 3$
17. $2n - 38 = 62$
18. $9n + 4 = 8$
19. $7n - 40 = 100$
20. $3n - 10 = 3$
21. $6 + 10n = 6$
22. $5n - 3 = 1$
23. $7 + 2n = 19$
24. $8 + 3n = 10$

Solve the equations where the 'x' terms are on the right hand side.

(a) $7 = 5x - 8$
$\quad\quad +8 \quad +8$
$\quad\quad 15 = 5x$
$\quad\quad \div 5 \quad \div 5$
$\quad\quad 3 = x$

(b) $9 = 6 + 5x$
$\quad\quad -6 \quad -6$
$\quad\quad 3 = 5x$
$\quad\quad \div 5 \quad \div 5$
$\quad\quad \dfrac{3}{5} = x$

Exercise 5M

Solve the equations below to find x.

1. $37 = 4x + 1$
2. $7 = 2x - 5$
3. $7 = 20x - 13$
4. $33 = 2x + 9$
5. $16 = 16 + 3x$
6. $0 = 7x - 4$
7. $59 = 4x + 3$
8. $10 = 7 + 5x$
9. $9 = 8 + 4x$
10. $13x + 15 = 16$
11. $65 = 55 + 40x$
12. $31 = 3x + 29$

In questions 13 to 24 find the value of the letter in each question.

13. $5t - 4 = 8$
14. $7 = 7 + 9y$
15. $30 = 4c + 20$
16. $6x - 9 = 45$
17. $540 = 3m - 63$
18. $0 = 9p - 7$
19. $47 = 8n - 25$
20. $106 = 16 + 2w$
21. $20 = 50a + 19$
22. $2y + \frac{1}{2} = 1$
23. $2q + \frac{1}{4} = \frac{1}{2}$
24. $3x - 1\frac{1}{2} = \frac{1}{2}$

Equations with brackets

Multiply out the brackets first.

(a) $3(2n + 1) = 27$
$6n + 3 = 27$
$\boxed{-3} \; \boxed{-3}$
$6n = 24$
$\boxed{\div 6} \; \boxed{\div 6}$
$n = 4$

(b) $2(5n - 3) = 8$
$10n - 6 = 8$
$\boxed{+6} \; \boxed{+6}$
$10n = 14$
$\boxed{\div 10} \; \boxed{\div 10}$
$n = 1.4$

Alternatively divide by 2 first:
$2(5n - 3) = 8$
$5n - 3 = 4$
$5n = 7$
$n = \frac{7}{5} = 1.4$

Exercise 6M

Solve the equations below to find x.

1. $4(2x + 3) = 52$
2. $3(3x - 2) = 30$
3. $5(4x - 2) = 110$
4. $8(x + 4) = 56$
5. $2(4x + 6) = 76$
6. $5(2x - 11) = 45$
7. $4(3x - 6) = 60$
8. $10(3x + 2) = 170$
9. $6(2x - 5) = 42$
10. $4(5x - 3) = 168$

11 Make up an equation with brackets which will give the answer $x = 4$.
Ask a friend to solve the equation to see if it works.

In questions **12** to **20** find the value of the letter in each question.

12 $3(2f + 5) = 17$ **13** $5(3m - 2) = 4$ **14** $8(5a - 7) = 84$

15 $9(5x + 3) = 42$ **16** $9 = 2(2p + 3)$ **17** $15 = 5(4n - 3)$

18 $10(5w - 7) = 155$ **19** $92 = 8(5c - 1)$ **20** $2(3y + 9) = 23$

21 Make up an equation with brackets so that it looks like $a(bx + c) = 46$ where a, b and c are numbers you must work out so the equation gives $x = 5$.
Ask a friend to solve the equation to see if it works.

22 Make up any equation which gives the same x-value as the equation $4(3x - 2) = 76$.
Ask a friend to solve the equation to see if it works.

Forming equations to solve problems

Tina is thinking of a number. She tells us that when she trebles it and adds 8, the answer is 24. What number is Tina thinking of?

Let x be the number Tina is thinking of.

She tell us that $\qquad 3x + 8 = 24$

Subtract 8 from both sides: $\qquad 3x = 16$

Divide both sides by 3: $\qquad x = \dfrac{16}{3} = 5\tfrac{1}{3}$

So Tina is thinking of the number $5\tfrac{1}{3}$

Exercise 7M

In each question I am thinking of a number. Write down an equation then solve it to find the number.

1 I double the number and then add 17.
The answer is 37.

2 I multiply the number by 5 and then subtract 11.
The answer is 24.

3 I treble the number and then subtract 13.
The answer is 2.

4 I multiply the number by 4 and then add 15.
The answer is 135.

5. I multiply the number by 3 and then add 5. The answer is 16.

6. I multiply the number by 5 and then subtract 8. The answer is 4.

7. I multiply the number by 11 and then subtract 15. The answer is 7.

8. I multiply the number by 6 and then add 23. The answer is 28.

9. I multiply the number by 5 and then subtract $\frac{1}{3}$. The answer is $11\frac{2}{3}$.

10. I multiply the number by 40 and then subtract 3. The answer is 7.

11. I add 3 to the number then double the result. The answer is 20.

12. I subtract 4 from the number then treble the result. The answer is 18.

The sum of the ages of Annie, Ben and Cath is 60 years.
Ben is five times as old as Annie and Cath is 4 years older than Annie. How old is Annie?

Let the age of Annie be x years (a *general rule is to let x be the quantity you are asked to find*).

Write down the ages of each person using x.

Annie	Ben	Cath
x	$5x$	$x + 4$

Ben is five times as old as Annie so Ben's age is $5x$ years.
Cath is 4 years older than Annie so Cath's age is $x + 4$ years.

The sum of the ages is 60 years.
$$x + 5x + x + 4 = 60$$
$$7x + 4 = 60$$
$$7x = 56$$
$$x = 8$$

Annie is 8 years old.

Exercise 7E

1. The total mass of four boxes A, B, C and D is 133 kg. Box C is three times as heavy as box B and box A is 20 kg heavier than box C. Box D is 7 kg lighter than box B.

   (a) Copy and complete the table below to show an expression for the mass of each box.

box	A	B	C	D
mass		x		

   (b) Write down an equation in terms of x.

   (c) Solve the equation to find x.

   (d) Write down the actual mass of each box.

2 The total mass of three coins A, B and C is 33 grams. Coin B is twice as heavy as coin A and coin C is 3 grams heavier than coin B.

(a) Copy and complete the table below to show an expression for the mass of each coin.

coin	A	B	C
mass	x		

(b) Write down an equation in terms of x.

(c) Find the actual mass of coin A.

3 In a quadrilateral ABCD, BC is twice as long as AB and AD is three times as long as AB. Side DC is 10 cm long.
The perimeter of ABCD is 31 cm.
Write an equation and solve it to find the length of AB.

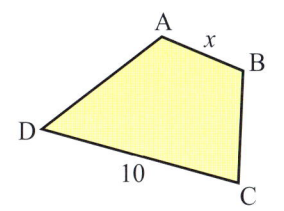

4 The length of a rectangle is twice its width.
If the perimeter is 48 cm, find its width.

5 The length of a rectangle is four times its width. If the perimeter of the rectangle is 50 cm, find its width.

6 The width of a rectangle is $(x + 4)$ and its perimeter is $(8x + 12)$.

(a) Find the length of the rectangle (in terms of x).

(b) Find x if the length of the rectangle is 20 cm.

7 Remember: the angles in a triangle add up to 180° and the angles in a quadrilateral add up to 360°.
For each shape, write down an equation then solve it to find x.

(a)

(b)

(c)

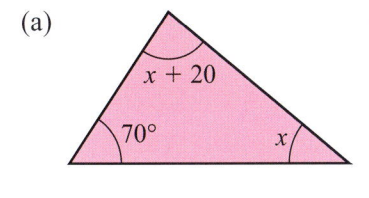

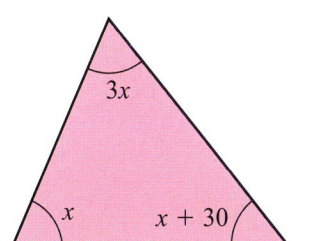

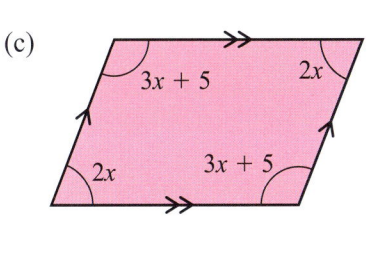

8 The angles of a triangle are A, B and C. Angle B is three times as big as angle A. Angle C is 45° bigger than angle A. Find the size of angle A.
(Hint: let the size of angle A be $x°$)

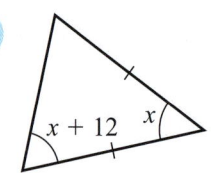

9 The diagram shows two angles in an isosceles triangle.
Find the angles in the triangle.

(triangle with angles $x + 12$ and x)

10 Number walls are formed by adding adjacent numbers to get the number in the brick above.
Find n in these walls.

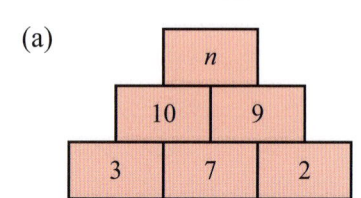

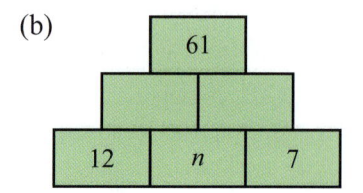

(a)
```
      n
   10   9
  3   7   2
```

(b)
```
      61
   __   __
  12   n   7
```

Need more practice with equations?

Solve the equations below.

1 $8x = 56$

2 $76 = x + 48$

3 $\dfrac{x}{6} = 10$

4 $49 = 7x$

5 $8 = \dfrac{x}{9}$

6 $5x - 7 = 23$

7 $9x + 4 = 58$

8 $6x - 15 = 57$

9 $10x + 3 = 43$

10 $8x + 47 = 79$

11 $27 = 3x - 6$

12 $74 = 20 + 6x$

13 Ayden and Emily are trying to solve the equation $\dfrac{n}{2} = 6$.

Ayden says the answer is $n = 12$ and Emily says the answer is $n = 3$.
Who is correct? Explain what mistake the other person has made.

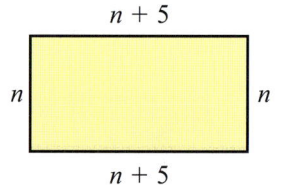

14 (rectangle with length $n + 5$ and width n)

The length of a rectangle is 5 cm more than its width.
The perimeter of the rectangle is 38 cm.
Form an equation in terms of n then work out the width of the rectangle.

15 Write down an equation involving x for the triangle opposite then find the value of x.

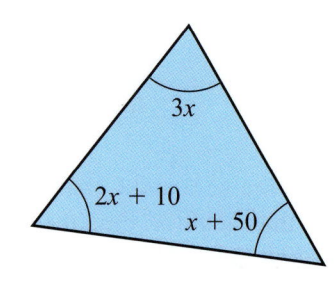

(triangle with angles $3x$, $2x + 10$, and $x + 50$)

16 Trinity's mother is 3 times older than Trinity. Trinity's brother is 7 years older than Trinity. The sum of all three ages is 67.

(a) Copy and complete the table below to show an expression for the age of each person.

Person	Trinity	Mother	Brother
Age	x		

(b) Write down an equation in terms of x.

(c) Work out the actual age of each person.

Solve the equations below.

17 $5x = 4$

18 $3x = 1$

19 $6x = 5$

20 $3x + 2 = 4$

21 $5x - 13 = 3$

22 $7x - 1 = 4$

23 $4(2x + 5) = 60$

24 $6(x - 3) = 66$

25 $5(4x - 7) = 85$

26 $2(4x + 9) = 42$

27 $3(3x + 5) = 69$

28 $7(10x + 4) = 168$

Extension questions with equations

Solve the equations below.

1 $\dfrac{x}{6} = \dfrac{1}{3}$

2 $5x = \dfrac{1}{4}$

3 $x + \dfrac{1}{6} = \dfrac{1}{2}$

4 $\dfrac{1}{4}x = 6$

5 $\dfrac{1}{5}x = 0.25$

6 $7 = 5x + 4$

7 $6x - 7 = 12$

8 $8x - 19 = 18$

9 $14 = 3x + 7$

10 The triangle opposite is equilateral. Set up an equation in terms of x then find the value of x.

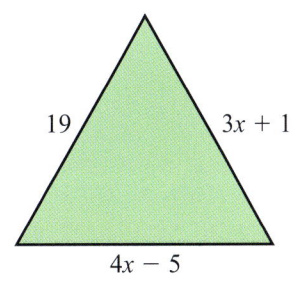

Sides: 19, $3x + 1$, $4x - 5$

11 Find the value of x in the rectangle opposite.

$6x - 3$, $3x + 12$

12 (a) Find the value of x in the rectangle opposite.
(b) Work out the actual perimeter of the rectangle.

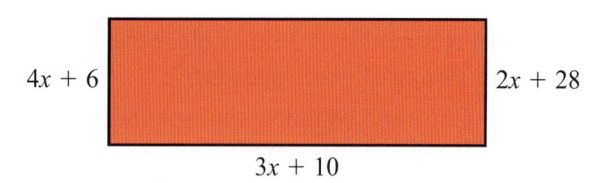

$4x + 6$ $2x + 28$
$3x + 10$

13 The sum of four consecutive whole numbers is 70. Let the first number be x. Write an equation and solve it to find the four numbers.

14 The total distance from P to T is 181 km. The distance from Q to R is twice the distance from S to T. R is midway between Q and S. The distance from P to Q is 5 km less than the distance from S to T. Find the distance from S to T.

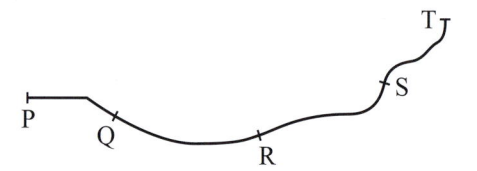

15 A parallelogram has angles of $n°$ and $(n + 6)°$. Find the angles of the parallelogram.

16 Find x and work out the actual area of this square.

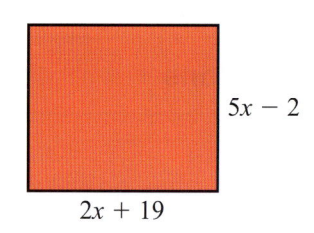

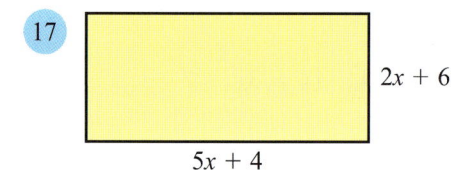

$5x - 2$
$2x + 19$

17 The actual perimeter of the rectangle opposite is 146 cm. Work out the actual area of this rectangle.

$2x + 6$
$5x + 4$

Solve the equations below.

18 $5(2x - 3) = 25$

19 $4(3x + 1) = 15$

20 $3(2x - 7) = 8$

21 $6x + 2 = 3x + 20$

22 $5x - 4 = x + 28$

23 $9x - 3 = 3x + 39$

24 $4(2x - 3) = 3(2x + 6)$

25 $6(5x + 4) = 4(5x + 16)$

26 $2(3x - 8) = 2(2x + 7)$

5.2 Interpreting graphs

In section 5.2 you will:

- read and draw line graphs in real life situations
- interpret and draw travel graphs

Exercise 1M

1. This graph converts rupees into pounds. The rupee is the currency in India

   (a) Convert into pounds
   - (i) 280 rupees
   - (ii) 110 rupees
   - (iii) 250 rupees
   - (iv) 360 rupees

   (b) Convert into rupees
   - (i) £5.00
   - (ii) £2.40
   - (iii) £4.20
   - (iv) £0.80

   (c) On holiday in India, Jason bought fish and chips for 300 rupees. How much did the meal cost in pounds?

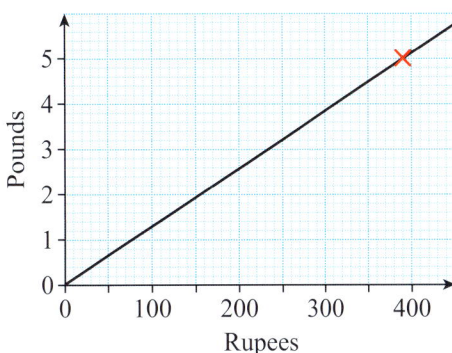

2. The graph shows the cost of making calls to two directory enquiry numbers.

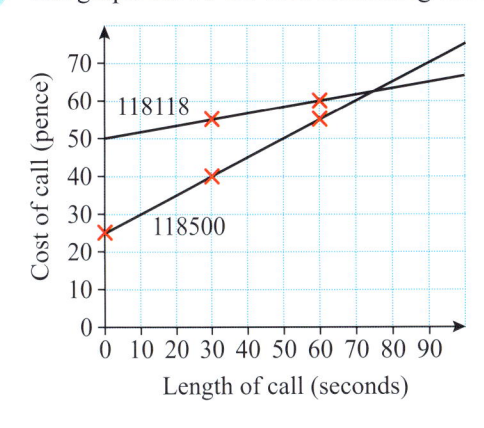

   (a) How much does it cost for a 50 second call to 118500?

   (b) Using 118118, for how long can you call for 55p?

   (c) At what length of call do both numbers cost the same?

   (d) What would be the cost of a two minute call to 118500?

3. Draw a graph to convert kilograms into pounds. Draw a line through the point where 3 kg is equivalent to 6.6 pounds. Use a scale of 1 cm to 1 pound across the page and 2 cm to 1 kg up the page.
   Use your graph to convert
   (a) 1.2 kg into pounds
   (b) 2 pounds into kg

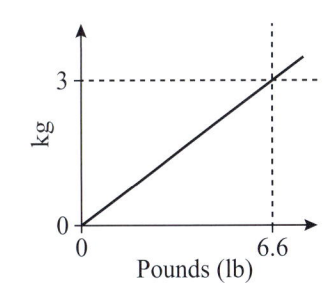

4 The graph shows the minimum distance between cars at different speeds in good or bad weather.

(a) Think carefully and decide which line is for good weather and which line is for bad weather.

(b) A car is travelling at 50 m.p.h. in good weather. What is the minimum distance between cars?

(c) In bad weather John is driving 60 metres behind another car. What is the maximum speed at which John should drive?

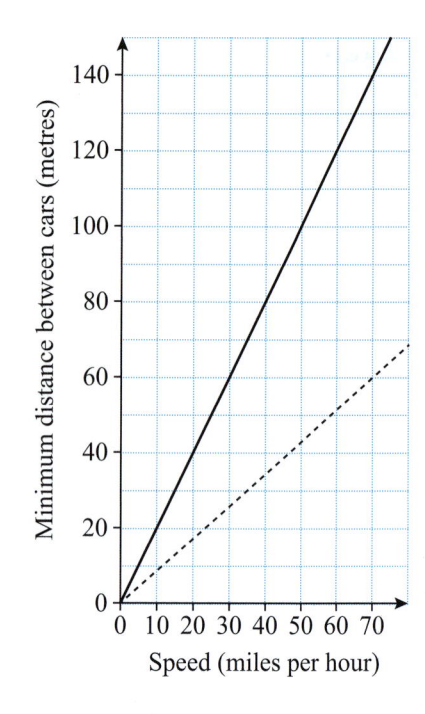

5 A mobile phone company charges £10 a month rental plus 20p per minute for calls.

Minutes of calls	0	20	40	60	80
Cost in £	10	14	18	22	26

(a) Draw a graph to show this information.
(b) Use your graph to find the total cost of making 65 minutes of calls.

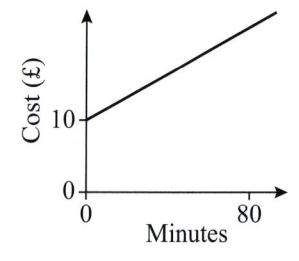

Travel graphs

- This graph shows the details of a cycle ride that Jim took starting from his home.

  (a) In the first hour Jim went 30 km so his speed was 30 km/h.
  (b) He stopped for $\frac{1}{2}$ hour at a place 30 km from his home.
  (c) From 09.30 until 11.00 he cycled back home. We know that he cycled back home because the distance from his home at 11.00 is 0 km.
  (d) The speed at which he cycled home was 20 km/h.

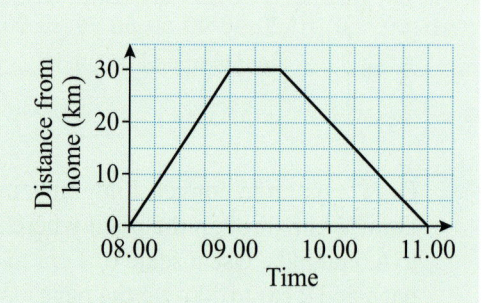

Exercise 2M

1. The graph shows a car journey from A to C via B.
   (a) How far is it from A to C?
   (b) For how long does the car stop at B?
   (c) When is the car half way between B and C?
   (d) What is the speed of the car
       (i) between A and B?
       (ii) between B and C?

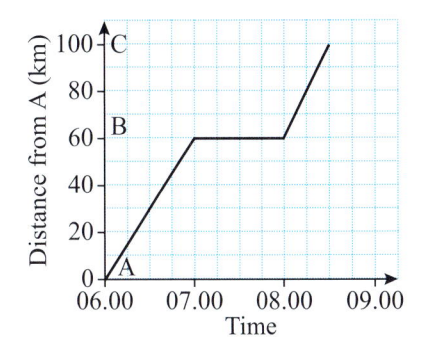

2. The graph shows a car journey from Lemsford.
   (a) For how long did the car stop at Mabley?
   (b) When did the car arrive back at Lemsford?
   (c) When did the car leave Mabley after stopping?
   (d) Find the speed of the car
       (i) from Mabley to Nixon
       (ii) from Nixon back to Lemsford.

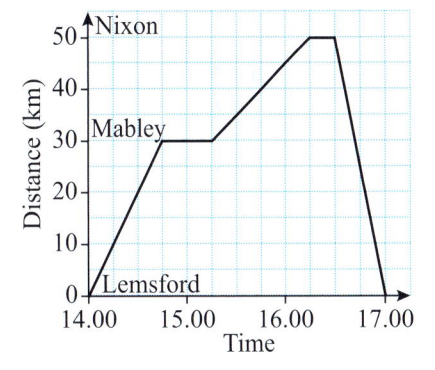

3. The graph shows the journey of a coach and a lorry along the same road between Newcastle and Carlisle.

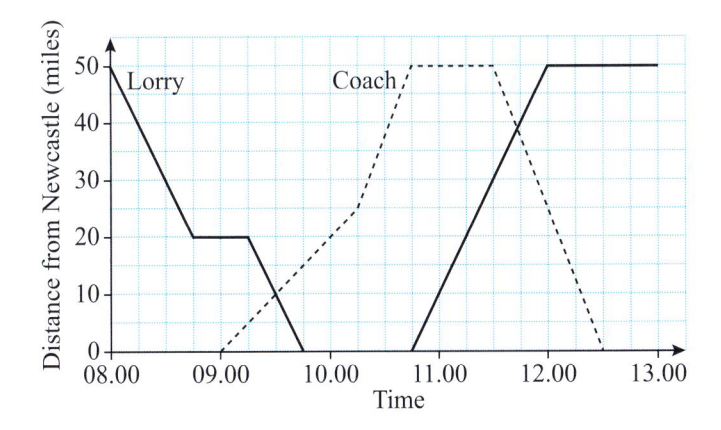

   (a) How far apart were the two vehicles at 09.15?
   (b) At what time did the vehicles meet for the first time?
   (c) At what speed did the coach return to Newcastle?
   (d) What was the highest speed of the lorry during its journey?

4 The diagram shows the travel graphs of five objects.
Which graph shows:

(a) a car ferry from Dover to Calais

(b) a hovercraft from Dover to Calais

(c) a car ferry from Calais to Dover

(d) a buoy outside Dover harbour

(e) a cross channel swimmer from Dover?

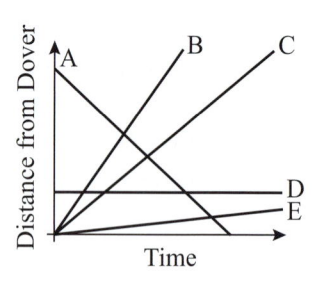

In questions **5** to **8** use the same scales as in question **3** of this exercise.

5 At 17.00 Lisa leaves her home and cycles at 20 km/h for 1 hour. She stops for $\frac{1}{4}$ hour and then continues her journey at a speed of 40 km/h for the next $\frac{1}{2}$ hour. She then stops for $\frac{3}{4}$ hour. Finally she returns home at a speed of 40 km/h.

Draw a travel graph to show Lisa's journey.
When did she arrive home?

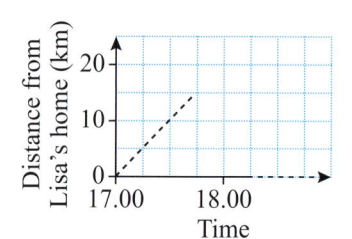

6 As Mrs Sadler leaves home in her car at 13.00 she encounters heavy traffic and travels at only 20 km/h for the first $\frac{1}{2}$ hour. In the second half hour she increases her speed to 30 km/h and after that she travels along the main road at 40 km/h for $\frac{3}{4}$ hour. She stops at her destination for $\frac{1}{2}$ hour and then returns home at a steady speed of 40 km/h. Draw a graph to find when she returns home.

7 Declan leaves home at 13.00 on his horse and rides at a speed of 20 km/h for one hour. Declan and his horse then rest for 45 minutes and afterwards continue their journey at a speed of 15 km/h for another one hour.
At what time do they finish the journey?

8 Kate lives 80 km from Kevin. One day at 12.00 Kate cycles towards Kevin's home at 25 km/h. At the same time Kevin cycles at 30 km/h towards Kate's home

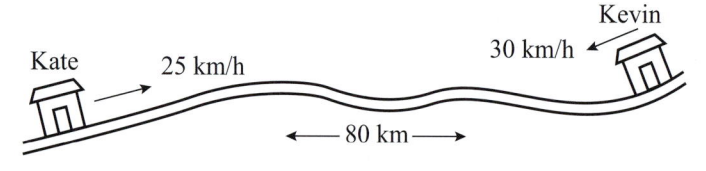

Draw a travel graph with 'Distance from Kate's home' on the vertical axis.
Approximately when and where do they meet?

Need more practice with interpreting graphs?

1. Jerome was not well one day. The graph shows his temperature between 07.00 and 13.00.
   (a) What was his temperature at 10.30?
   (b) At what time was his temperature highest?
   (c) At what two times was his temperature 38.5°C?
   (d) Between which two times did his temperature rise most quickly?

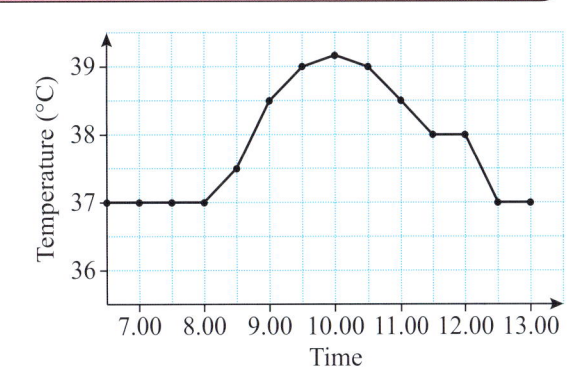

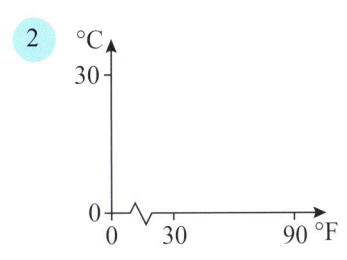

2. Draw a graph to convert temperatures from °F to °C.
   Draw a line through the points 50°F = 10°C and 86°F = 30°C.
   Use the graph to convert:
   (a) 77°F into °C
   (b) 15°C into °F

3. A man climbing a mountain measures his height above sea level after every 30 minutes; the results are shown on the graph.
   (a) At what height was he at 10.00?
   (b) At what height was he at 13.30?
   (c) Estimate his height above sea level at 09.45.
   (d) At what two times was he 2200 m above sea level?
   (e) How high was the mountain? (He got to the top!)
   (f) How long did he rest at the summit?
   (g) How long did he take to reach the summit?

4. The graph shows the motion of a train as it accelerates away from Troon.
   (a) How far from Troon is the train at 08.45?
   (b) When is the train half way between R and S?
   (c) Find the speed of the train
      (i) from R to S
      (ii) from Q to R
      (iii) (harder) from P to Q
   (d) How long does it take the train to travel 100 km?

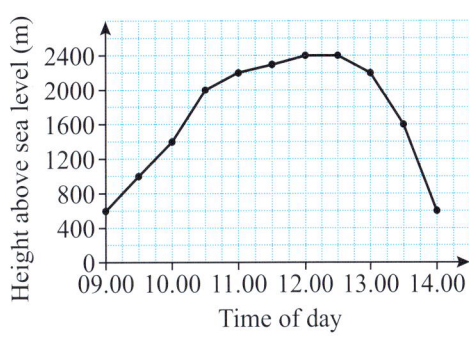

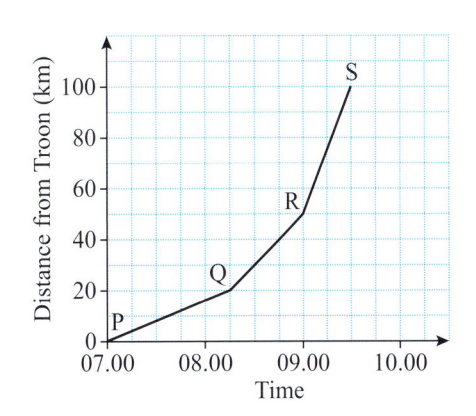

5 The cost of hiring a tank for filming depends on the duration of the hire.

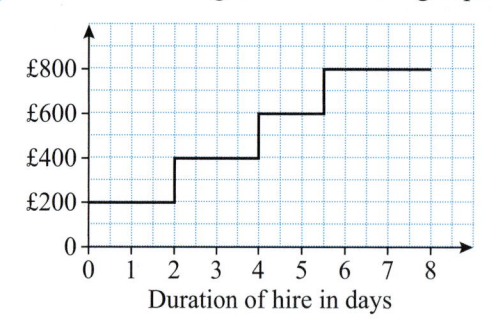

(a) How much does it cost to hire the tank for
  (i) 1 day   (ii) $4\frac{1}{2}$ days   (iii) 3 days?

(b) What is the minimum hire charge?

Extension questions with interpreting graphs

In questions **1** and **2** use a scale of 4 squares to 1 hour across the page and 2 squares to 10 km up the page.

1 At 12.00 Amar leaves home and drives at a speed of 30 km/h. At 12.30 he increases his speed to 50 km/h and continues to his destination which is 65 km from home. He stops for $\frac{1}{2}$ hour and then returns home at a speed of 65 km/h.
Draw and use a graph to find the time at which he arrives home.

2 At 08.00 Chew Ling leaves home and cycles towards a railway station which is 65 km away. She cycles at a speed of 30 km/h until 09.30 at which time she stops to rest for $\frac{1}{2}$ hour. She then completes the journey at a speed of 20 km/h.
At 09.45 Chew Ling's father leaves their home in his car and drives towards the station at 60 km/h.
(a) Draw a travel graph.
(b) At what time does Chew Ling arrive at the station?
(c) When is Chew Ling overtaken by her father?

In questions **3** and **4** use a scale of 2 squares to 15 minutes across the page and 1 square to 10 km up the page.

3 At 01.00 a bank robber leaves a bank as the alarm sounds and sets off along a motorway at 80 km/h towards his hideout which is 150 km from the bank.

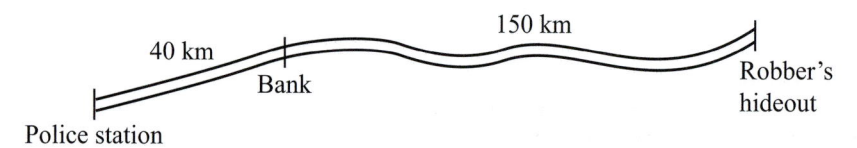

As soon as the alarm goes off a police car leaves the police station, which is 40 km from the bank, and drives at 80 km/h to the bank. After stopping at the bank for 15 minutes, the police car chases after the robber at a speed of 160 km/h.

Draw a travel graph with 'Distance from police station' on the vertical axis.

(a) Find out if the police caught the robber before the robber reached his hideout.

(b) If the robber was caught, say when. If he was not caught say how far behind him the police were when he reached his hideout.

4 The diagram shows three towns A, B and C. The distance from A to B is 50 km and the distance from B to C is 110 km. At the same moment 3 cars leave A, B and C at the speeds shown and in the directions shown.

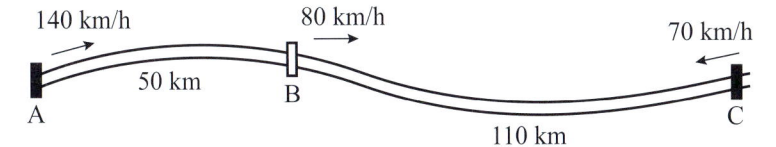

140 km/h   80 km/h   70 km/h
A   50 km   B   C
                        110 km

The cars from A and C are trying to intercept the car from B as quickly as possible.

(a) Which car intercepts the car from B first?

(b) After how many minutes does the car from A catch the car from B?

✗ Spot the mistakes 9 ✗

Algebra and interpreting graphs

Work through each question below and *explain clearly* what mistakes have been made. Beware – some questions are correctly done.

1 Solve $\quad 5x - 1 = 3$

Answer: $\quad 5x - 1 = 3$
$\qquad 5x = 2$
$\qquad x = \dfrac{2}{5}$

2
$4n + 6$
$2n + 24$

The perimeter of the equilateral triangle is equal to the perimeter of the rectangle. Find an expression for the length of one side of the triangle.

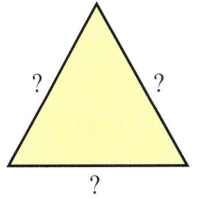

Answer: perimeter of rectangle $= 4n + 6 + 2n + 24$
$\qquad\qquad\qquad\qquad\qquad\; = 6n + 30$

The 3 sides of the equilateral triangle are equal in length.
The length of one side $= (6n + 30) \div 3 = 2n + 10$

3. Simplify $5xy + 6y - 2xy + yx - y$
Answer: $3xy + 6y + yx$

4. Solve $3(2n + 5) = 17$
Answer: $6n + 5 = 17$
$6n = 12$
$n = 2$

5. Conan uses the conversion graph opposite to work out how many dollars are equivalent to £3. His answer is $2.80

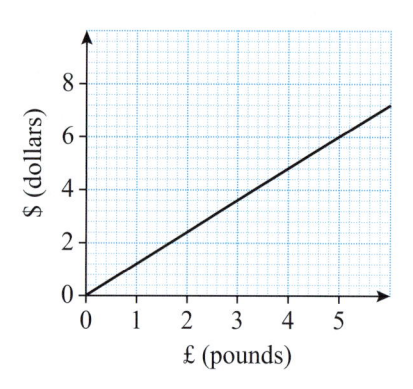

6. I think of a number, multiply it by 7 then subtract 3. The answer is 2. What number did I think of?
Solution: Let the number be n.
$7n - 3 = 2$
$7n = 5$
$n = \frac{5}{7}$
so the number is $\frac{5}{7}$

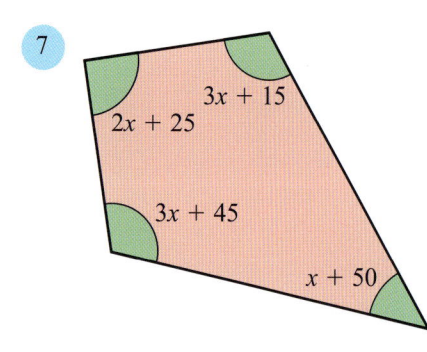

7. Work out the actual value of each angle in the quadrilateral opposite.
Answer: $3x + 15 + x + 50 + 3x + 45 + 2x + 25 = 360$
$9x + 135 = 360$
$9x = 225$
$x = 25$
Angles are 90°, 75°, 120° and 75°

8. Find the value of P when $n = 3$ if $P = 2n^2 + 3$.
Answer: $2n = 6$ so $P = 6^2 + 3 = 36 + 3 = 39$

9. At 09.00 Olivia leaves her home and drives at 30 km/h for half an hour. She then travels another 10 km during the next 30 minutes. She stops at a garage for 15 minutes then travels 10 km in the next quarter of an hour. She stops at a shop for 30 minutes then drives all the way home in one hour.
Draw a travel graph then work out the speed she travelled at during the last hour to get home.

Solution:

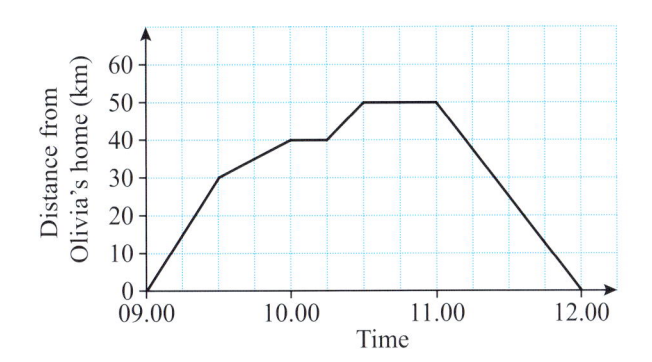

Olivia's speed when returning home = 50 km/h.

10 Austin has four times more money than Taylor. Diya has £20 more than Austin. In total they have £200. How much money does each person have?

Solution: Taylor: x, Austin: $4x$, Diya: $x + 20$
$$x + 4x + x + 20 = 200$$
$$6x + 20 = 200$$
$$6x = 180$$
$$x = 30$$

so Taylor: £30, Austin: £120, Diya: £50

CHECK YOURSELF ON SECTIONS 5.1 AND 5.2

1   Review of section 1.4 Rules of algebra

Simplify   (a) $mn + m + nm$ (b) $\dfrac{6x}{x}$ (c) $5m \times 3n$

(d) Expand $7(3n - 5)$ (e) $y = 3x + 4z$
Find y when $x = 8$ and $z = -5$.

2   Solving equations

Solve   (a) $3n - 7 = 23$ (b) $\dfrac{m}{6} = 5$

(c) $7 = 6 + 5w$ (d) $4(2n - 9) = 20$

3   Forming and solving equations

(a) I think of a number, treble it then add 9. The answer is 10.
Form an equation then find the value of my number.

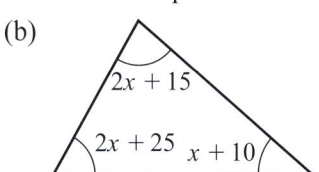

(b) Form an equation then find the value of x.
Write down the actual value of each angle in the triangle.

Triangle with angles $2x + 15$, $2x + 25$, $x + 10$.

4 Reading and drawing line graphs in real life situations

This line graph shows the average daily temperature in Sweden.

(a) What was the temperature in June?
(b) In which month was the temperature 7°C?
(c) In which two months was the temperature 3°C?
(d) Between which two months was there the largest increase in temperature?
(e) What was the range of temperature over the year?

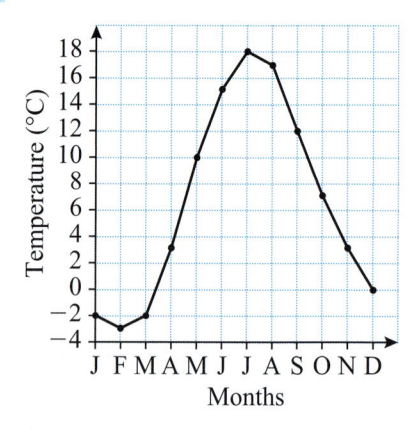

5 Interpreting and drawing travel graphs

A car leaves London at 09.00 and travels at a speed of 10 km/h for 1 hour.
It then travels at a speed of 60 km/h for half an hour.
The car then stops for one hour before returning to London at a speed of 40 km/h.
Draw a travel graph for this journey. At what time did the car return to London?

[Use a scale of 4 squares to 1 hour and 2 squares for 10 km.]

5.3 Number review

In section 5.3 you will review:
- multiples, factors, prime numbers, H.C.F. and L.C.M.
- fractions, decimals and percentages
- long multiplication and division
- adding, subtracting, multiplying and dividing decimals
- using percentages and fractions
- using ratios

Multiples, factors and prime numbers

The first six *multiples* of 5 are 5, 10, 15, 20, 25, 30
The factors of 8 are 1, 2, 4, 8
The first five prime numbers are 2, 3, 5, 7, 11

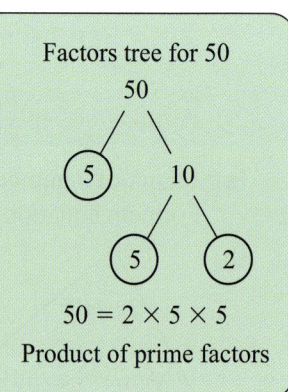

Factors tree for 50

$50 = 2 \times 5 \times 5$

Product of prime factors

Exercise 1M

1 Write down the odd one out.
   (a) Factors of 24:   2, 3, 8, 24, 48
   (b) Factors of 50:   2, 5, 10, 20, 25
   (c) Multiples of 11:   22, 66, 88, 111
   (d) Multiples of 15:   1, 15, 30, 45

2 Write down two prime numbers whose sum is a prime number.

3 Write down the 1-digit numbers that have three factors.

4 (a) Write down the first six multiples of 4.
   (b) Write down the first six multiples of 5.
   (c) Write down the lowest common multiple (L.C.M.) of 4 and 5.

Reminder: The L.C.M. is the lowest number which is in both lists.

5 The table shows the factors and common factors of 12 and 18

Number	Factors	Common factors
12	1, 2, 3, 4, 6, 12	1, 2, 3, 6
18	1, 2, 3, 6, 9, 18	

Write down the highest common factor (H.C.F.) of 12 and 18.

The H.C.F. is the highest number which is in both lists.

6 Find the H.C.F. of
   (a) 9 and 12   (b) 24 and 36   (c) 12 and 16

7 Why is this factor tree for 180 not correct?

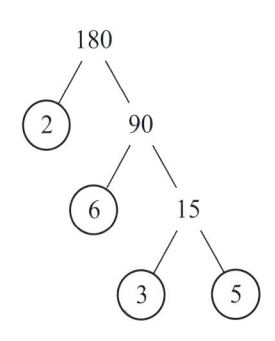

$180 = 2 \times 3 \times 5 \times 6$

8 Express 150 as a product of its prime factors.

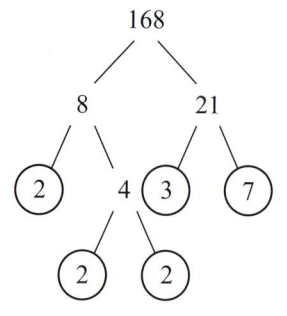

9

72 = 2 × 2 × 2 × 3 × 3   168 = 2 × 2 × 2 × 3 × 7

Factor trees for 72 (branches: 8, 9 → 2, 4, 3, 3 → 2, 2) and 168 (branches: 8, 21 → 2, 4, 3, 7 → 2, 2).

Use the results from the factor trees opposite to find:
(a) the H.C.F. of 72 and 168
(b) the L.C.M. of 72 and 168

10 Use factor trees to find the H.C.F. and L.C.M. of 105 and 385.

Fractions, decimals, percentages

Exercise 2M

1 Find the missing number to make these fractions equivalent.

(a) $\dfrac{3}{4} = \dfrac{\square}{12}$ (b) $\dfrac{4}{7} = \dfrac{\square}{35}$ (c) $\dfrac{6}{10} = \dfrac{\square}{5}$ (d) $\dfrac{3}{8} = \dfrac{\square}{32}$

(e) $\dfrac{3}{8} = \dfrac{9}{\square}$ (f) $\dfrac{4}{5} = \dfrac{12}{\square}$ (g) $\dfrac{8}{9} = \dfrac{16}{\square}$ (h) $\dfrac{1}{3} = \dfrac{5}{\square}$

2 Copy and use the two diagrams opposite to explain why $\dfrac{2}{3} + \dfrac{1}{4} = \dfrac{11}{12}$

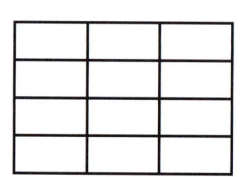

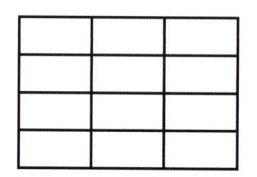

3 Which of the following calculations does not equal $\dfrac{2}{5}$?
You must fully justify your answer.

$\dfrac{3}{20} + \dfrac{1}{4}$ $\dfrac{9}{10} - \dfrac{1}{2}$ $\dfrac{24}{35} - \dfrac{2}{7}$ $\dfrac{1}{5} + \dfrac{1}{3}$

4 Convert these fractions into decimals.

(a) $\dfrac{3}{10}$ (b) $\dfrac{1}{4}$ (c) $\dfrac{32}{40}$ (d) $\dfrac{24}{200}$ (e) $\dfrac{9}{100}$

5 Copy and complete

(a) $\dfrac{1}{5} = \dfrac{20}{100} = \square\%$ (b) $\dfrac{3}{20} = \dfrac{15}{100} = \square\%$ (c) $\dfrac{1}{25} = \dfrac{4}{100} = \square\%$

(d) $\dfrac{9}{20} = \dfrac{\square}{100} = \square\%$ (e) $\dfrac{11}{50} = \dfrac{\square}{100} = \square\%$ (f) $\dfrac{11}{25} = \dfrac{\square}{100} = \square\%$

6 Lily writes the following on a whiteboard.

$$\frac{2}{5} \times \frac{1}{2} = \frac{4}{10} \times \frac{5}{10} = \frac{20}{100} = \frac{1}{5}$$

Her teacher says that this is long-winded. Explain how Lily could do this question in a quicker way.

7 Write down each fraction with its equivalent percentage.
(a) $\frac{1}{3}$ (b) $\frac{2}{5}$ (c) $\frac{3}{4}$ (d) $\frac{3}{100}$ (e) $\frac{2}{3}$ (f) $\frac{1}{1000}$

8 Work out
(a) $\frac{4}{7} \div \frac{7}{8}$ (b) $\frac{3}{7} \div \frac{4}{5}$ (c) $\frac{1}{4} \div \frac{2}{5}$ (d) $\frac{2}{9} \div \frac{3}{4}$

9 Write the following in order of size, smallest first
(a) $\frac{3}{4}$, 60%, 0.7 (b) 5%, $\frac{1}{50}$, 0.03 (c) $\frac{3}{9}$, 0.3, 23%

10 Which number is larger: $1\frac{1}{7}$ or $\frac{7}{6}$? Explain your answer fully.

Long multiplication and division

Exercise 3M

Work out

1 56 × 35 **2** 72 × 41 **3** 125 × 19 **4** 214 × 36

5 Copy and complete.
(a) ☐ ÷ 25 = 15 (b) ☐ ÷ 33 = 17 (c) ☐ ÷ 27 = 42

6 Work out
(a) 784 ÷ 14 (b) 544 ÷ 32 (c) 806 ÷ 31 (d) 1035 ÷ 23

7 There are 47 seats on a coach.
How many coaches will be needed to transport 206 people to a concert?

8 A ferris wheel rotates one whole circle every 96 seconds. How many complete circles will the wheel manage if it turns steadily for 4 hours?

9 There are twenty-two balls in a set of snooker balls.
Each ball weighs 154 grams.
Calculate the total weight of the set of snooker balls.

10 Chocolates are packed eighteen to a box.
How many boxes are needed for 648 chocolates?

Calculations involving decimals

Exercise 4M

1 Copy and complete

(a) 6.☐4
   + ☐.7☐
   ─────
     8.27

(b) 4.7☐
   + 4.☐5
   ─────
     ☐.10

(c) 6.☐72
   + ☐.2☐9
   ──────
     8.09☐

2 Copy and complete

(a) $0.72 \times \square = 7.2$
(b) $\square \times 100 = 170$
(c) $10 \times \square = 16$
(d) $100 \times \square = 85.4$
(e) $3.2 \times \square = 3.2$
(f) $\square \times 100 = 2$

3 What number when multiplied by 7 gives an answer of 16.8?

4 Copy and complete the cross number.

Clues across
1. $5.7 \div 3$
3. 0.8×3
5. $6^2 \times 0.5$
6. $44.8 \div 8$
7. $9^2 \div 10 + 0.3$
8. $(10\% \text{ of } 23) \times 3$
10. $8^2 + 5^2 + (0.1^2 \times 100)$
11. $46.4 + 47.6$

Clues down
1. $0.017 \times 1000 + 10^2$
2. $1078 \div 11$
3. 50.8×5
4. $4^3 - 4^2 - (4 \div 2)$
7. $44.5 \div 5$
8. $3 \times 2 \times 5 \times 2$
9. 11×0.4

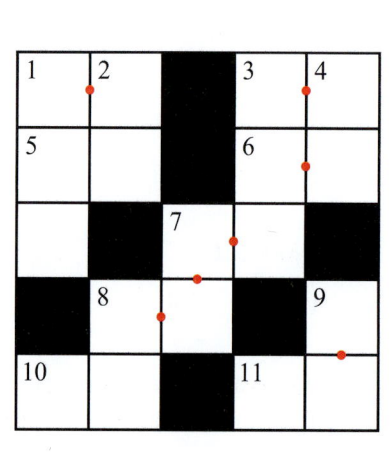

5 Five people share the cost of a meal which costs £42.
How much does each person pay?

6 Timon says that $\frac{2}{0.4}$ is the same as $\frac{20}{4}$.

Is he correct? Explain your answer fully.

7 Work out
(a) 8.23×4
(b) $3.12 \div 4$
(c) $6.2 \div 5$
(d) 0.85×4
(e) $31.8 \div 6$
(f) 7×1.23
(g) $9.94 \div 7$
(h) 6×8.02
(i) $4 \div 0.2$
(j) $8 \div 0.05$
(k) 0.2×0.12
(l) $4.2 \div 0.005$

Using percentages and fractions

Exercise 5M

1 Copy and complete

(a) $\frac{1}{\square}$ of $35 = 5$
(b) $\frac{1}{\square}$ of $121 = 11$
(c) $\frac{1}{\square}$ of $74 = 37$

(d) $\frac{2}{5}$ of $45 = \square$
(e) $\frac{2}{\square}$ of $12 = 8$
(f) $\frac{7}{\square}$ of $3000 = 210$

2 There are four hundred and fifty mushrooms in a garden and $\frac{3}{50}$ of them are poisonous. How many of the mushrooms are poisonous?

3 In one week 400 people took their driving test and three fifths of them passed. How many people passed the test that week?

4 Harvey earns £1300 each month. He is given a 5% pay rise. How much does Harvey now earn each month?

5 A piece of wood is 85.6 cm long. 25% of the wood is cut off. How long is the remaining piece of wood?

6 Copy and complete

(a) $\frac{1}{4} = \square\%$
(b) $\frac{2}{5} = \square\%$
(c) $\frac{1}{3} = \square\%$
(d) $\frac{1}{50} = \square\%$

7 220 people out of 550 catch flu one winter.
What percentage of these people do not catch flu?

8 Write in order of size, smallest first.

(a) 22%, $\frac{1}{4}$, 0.15, $\frac{1}{5}$ (b) $\frac{3}{5}$, 52%, 0.05, $\frac{1}{8}$ (c) 0.7, $\frac{2}{3}$, 66%, 0.17

9 Which is greater: 5% of 800 or 18% of 300? Explain why you chose your answer.

10 A factory produces forty-five thousand clocks every week and, when tested, two per cent of them are not accurate. How many inaccurate clocks are made each week?

11 Work out 22% of $\frac{2}{3}$ of 480.

12 Work out (5% of £30) + (4% of £200) + (11% of £1200).

Using ratios

Exercise 6M

1 Write these ratios in simplified form.

(a) 21 : 49 (b) 8 : 32 : 12 (c) 0.6 : 0.3
(d) 0.15 : 0.6 : 0.75 (e) 2 kg : 400 g (f) 6 cm : 4 mm

2 7 sweaters cost £273 and 9 jackets cost £567.
Which cost more: 11 jackets or 17 sweaters and by how much more?

3 Blue, yellow and green paint are mixed in the ratio 5 : 7 : 2.
If 20 litres of blue paint are used, how much yellow and green paint is used in total?

4 Tins of fruit cocktail are sold in 3 sizes as shown opposite. Which size is the best value?

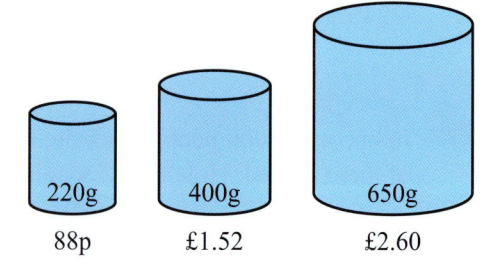

220g — 88p
400g — £1.52
650g — £2.60

5 A will of £48 000 is split between Joel and his sister in the ratio 3 : 5.
Joel then splits his money between himself and his children in the ratio 4 : 5.
How much money do his children get?

6 Express the ratio 2000 : 60 000 in the form 1 : n.

7 The ratio of the lengths of the sides of the two squares shown is 1 : 6.
Work out the area of the larger square.

Area = 9cm²
Area = ?

8 **300 g shortcrust pastry**
   210 g flour
   90 g butter

   A chef needs to make 750 g of shortcrust pastry using the recipe shown opposite.
   The chef has 400 g of flour in the kitchen.
   How much more flour is needed to make the pastry?

Need more practice with number work?

1. Work out
   (a) $11 - 3.2$
   (b) $4.2 + 7.4 + 6$
   (c) $32.7 - 19$
   (d) 1.4×0.03

2. What is the smallest number with two factors?

3. Write down the L.C.M. of 3 and 7.

4. There are 23 seats in each row at a football stadium.
   How many seats are there in 35 rows?

5. Find the remainder when 276 is divided by 11.

6. On average Lian checks her phone 37 times each day. How many times does she check her phone during the month of July?

7. Change these decimals into fractions (cancel down when possible).
   (a) 0.2
   (b) 0.9
   (c) 0.03
   (d) 0.11
   (e) 0.43
   (f) 0.03
   (g) 0.15
   (h) 0.85
   (i) 0.24
   (j) 0.05

8. Reduce £250 by 3%.

9. The number of students in a school is 1200. In a nearby college there are 1250 students.
   The number of students in the school increases by 11% in the following year and the number of students in the college increases by 6%.
   Which has more students now – the school or the college?
   Write down the difference in the number of students.

10 Copy and complete the factor tree opposite then express 140 as the product of its prime factors.

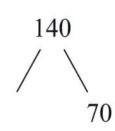

```
    140
   /  \
      70
```

11 Copy and complete

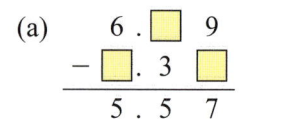

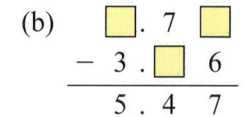

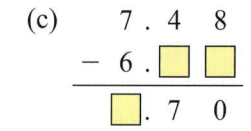

(a) 6 . ☐ 9
    − ☐ . 3 ☐
    ─────────
      5 . 5 7

(b) ☐ . 7 ☐
    − 3 . ☐ 6
    ─────────
      5 . 4 7

(c) 7 . 4 8
    − 6 . ☐ ☐
    ─────────
      ☐ . 7 0

12 Work out the perimeter of the triangle shown opposite.

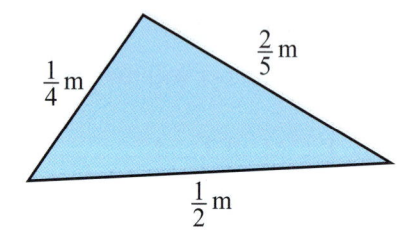

Sides: $\frac{1}{4}$ m, $\frac{2}{5}$ m, $\frac{1}{2}$ m

13 £700 is shared between Carl, Amy and Justin in the ratio 3 : 5 : 2. How much more money does Amy get than Justin?

14 Copy and complete the table

	Fraction	Decimal	Percentage
(a)			40%
(b)		0.15	
(c)	$\frac{3}{25}$		
(d)			16%
(e)		0.04	

15 Find the difference between the answers to $\frac{3}{5} \times \frac{2}{3}$ and $\frac{1}{4} \div \frac{2}{3}$.

Extension questions with number work

1 Jacob is paid a work bonus of £6500. He spends 40% of this on a holiday and saves $\frac{5}{6}$ of the remaining money. He uses the left over money to buy presents and clothes in the ratio 9 : 4. How much money does he spend on clothes.

2 Work out

(a) $1\frac{2}{3} - \frac{6}{7}$

(b) $2\frac{1}{2} \times 1\frac{2}{3}$

(c) $1\frac{5}{6} \div 3\frac{1}{3}$

(d) $5\frac{1}{2} \times \frac{3}{22}$

(e) $2\frac{3}{4} + 1\frac{1}{6}$

(f) $2\frac{1}{3} + 1\frac{5}{12} - 2\frac{1}{6}$

3. The Venn diagram shows the prime factors of 294 and 693. Work out
   (a) the H.C.F. of 294 and 693
   (b) the L.C.M. of 294 and 693

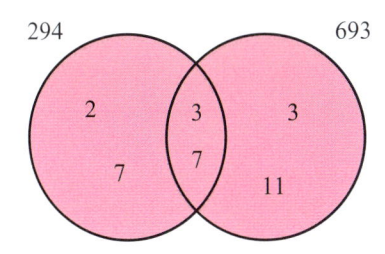

294: 2, 7 | shared: 3, 7 | 693: 3, 11

4. The colours of a flag are red, green and yellow in the ratio 5 : 3 : 4. What fraction of the flag is red?

5. The height of a plant increases by a third over a 3 month period. It is now 48 cm high. How tall was the plant at the start of the 3 month period?

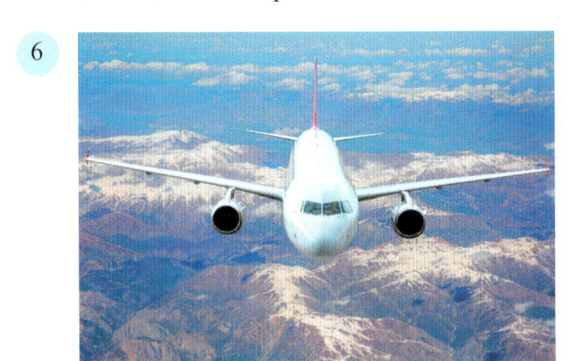

6. Sophie books a holiday priced at £2180. She pay a 15% deposit immediately.
The remaining money is to be paid in 12 equal monthly instalments. Unfortunately an extra 20% fuel charge is added to this remaining money to be paid. How much is each monthly payment?

7. Work out
   (a) $5 \div 0.2$
   (b) $6 \div 0.05$
   (c) $4.3 \div 0.02$
   (d) $0.12 \div 0.004$

8. Some test percentages for six people are shown in the table.

Zak	35%
Bella	80%
Eric	40%
Vanya	28%
Arna	85%
Julia	60%

   Their actual test marks are shown below:

   $\frac{75}{125}$ $\frac{17}{20}$ $\frac{7}{25}$

   $\frac{105}{300}$ $\frac{68}{85}$ $\frac{30}{75}$

   Match up each person to the correct test mark.

9. Draw factor trees then a Venn diagram to find the H.C.F. and L.C.M. of 5720 and 1638.

10. The ratio of dogs to cats in a town is 7 : 8.
The ratio of cats to rabbits in the same town is 4 : 1.
What is the ratio of dogs to rabbits?

5.4 Rounding numbers

In section 5.4 you will:
- round off to decimal places and significant figures
- calculate using estimates

Round to decimal places

- Using a calculator to work out 25 ÷ 9, the answer is 2.777777.

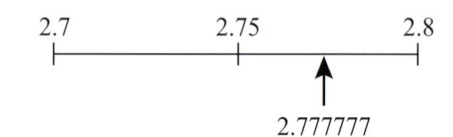

  On a number line we can see that the answer is nearer to 2.8 than to 2.7. We will **round off** the answer to 2.8 correct to 1 **decimal place**.

  Using a calculator to work out 11% of 21.23, the answer is 2.3353.

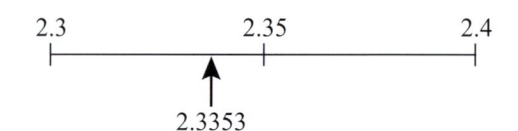

  On a number line we can see that the answer is nearer to 2.3 than to 2.4. So the answer is 2.3, correct to 1 decimal place (1 d.p. for short).

Suppose the calculator shows 1.75. This number is exactly half way between 1.7 and 1.8. Do we round up or not? The rule for rounding off to 1 decimal place is:

> If the figure in the 2nd decimal place is 5 or more, round up. Otherwise do not.

Rounding to 2 decimal places – leave 2 digits after the decimal point when rounding off. If the figure in the 3rd decimal place is 5 or more, round up. Otherwise do not.

2.6382 = 2.64 to 2 d.p.   5.7326 = 5.73 to 2 d.p.
   ↑   ↑
round up   round down

Exercise 1M

1. Round these numbers to 1 decimal place.
   (a) 2.41   (b) 8.94   (c) 4.65   (d) 12.47   (e) 16.35

2. Round these numbers to 2 decimal places.
   (a) 1.924   (b) 4.065   (c) 9.997   (d) 65.374   (e) 14.043

3 Write down any number greater than 50 which has been rounded off to 2 decimal places.

4 Work out these answers on a calculator and then round the answer to one decimal place.
(a) 65 ÷ 7
(b) 85 × 0.7
(c) 8.64 ÷ 11.014
(d) 8 × 16.22
(e) 1.4 × 0.97
(f) 82 ÷ 7
(g) 113 ÷ 5
(h) 0.6 ÷ 0.022

5 Work out the area of each shape opposite and round each answer to 1 decimal place.

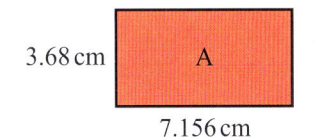

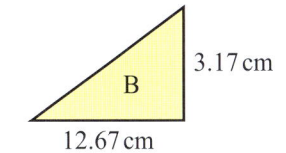

A: 3.68 cm by 7.156 cm

B: triangle, 3.17 cm and 12.67 cm

6 Work out the following on a calculator and write the answers correct to 2 decimal places.
(a) 11 ÷ 7
(b) 213 ÷ 11
(c) 1.4 ÷ 6
(d) 29 ÷ 13
(e) 1.3 × 0.95
(f) 1.23 × 3.71
(g) 97 ÷ 1.3
(h) 0.95 × 8.3

7 Measure the lines below and give the lengths in cm correct to one decimal place.
(a) _____
(b) _____
(c) _____
(d) _____
(e) _____

8 Measure the dimensions of the rectangles below.
(a) Write down the length and width in cm, correct to one decimal place.
(b) Work out the area of each rectangle and give the answer in cm², correct to one decimal place.

(i)

(ii)

9 Jermaine needs to find the product of 4.26 and 7.17. The answer is to be given to 1 decimal place. He rounds each number to 1 decimal place then multiplies the numbers.
4.3 × 7.2 = 30.96 = 31.0 to one decimal place.
This is not the correct answer. Explain clearly what he has done wrong.

10 Round the following numbers to the accuracy indicated.

(a) 6.1723 (1 d.p.) (b) 14.6958 (2 d.p.) (c) 0.010102 (2 d.p.)
(d) 712.816 (1 d.p.) (e) 3.9084 (2 d.p.) (f) 24.65298 (1 d.p.)

Round to significant figures

The most significant figure is the figure on the left of a number.

2364

2 is the 1st significant figure. The value of the number is in the 2 thousands.

We can round off numbers to significant figures. We approach from the left and start counting as soon as we come to the first figure which is not zero. Once we have started counting we count any figure, zeros included.

(a) 74.3418 = 74.3 to 3 significant figures (3 s.f.)
    ↑
   [Count 3 figures. The 'next' figure is 4 which is less than 5.]

(b) 8.1783 = 8.18 to 3 significant figures
    ↑

(c) 0.095627 = 0.096 to 2 significant figures
      ↑

(d) 5286.3 = 5300 to 2 significant figures
    ↑
   Notice that we need the two noughts after the '3' as the original number is approximately 5300.

Exercise 2M

1 Ruby says that 2, 3 and 7 are the first 3 significant figures in the number 0.023715. Is she correct?

2 Manu says that 5, 7 and 9 are the first 3 significant figures in the number 0.570937. Is he correct?

3 Write the following numbers correct to 3 significant figures.

(a) 2.1874 (b) 32.793 (c) 264.23 (d) 0.8137
(e) 0.08555 (f) 4762.4 (g) 5167 (h) 0.03372

4 Write the following numbers to the number of significant figures indicated.

(a) 42.86 (2 s.f.) (b) 6.521 (1 s.f.) (c) 0.83652 (3 s.f.)
(d) 1232.9 (3 s.f.) (e) 42777 (2 s.f.) (f) 0.06485 (2 s.f.)

5 Write down the perimeter of the pentagon opposite and give the answer to 3 significant figures. The given lengths are in metres.

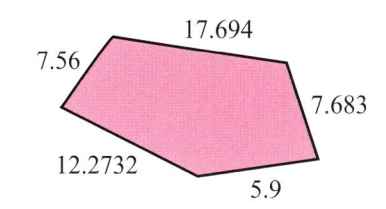

17.694
7.56
7.683
12.2732
5.9

6 How many significant figures has the number 20 000 got?

7 Work out the following on a calculator and write the answer correct to 2 significant figures.

(a) 16 ÷ 2.9 (b) 0.73 × 0.0017 (c) 16^2 ÷ 3.17

8 Write down any number that rounds to 0.0604 to 3 significant figures.

9 Which of the numbers below round off to 7.8 correct to 2 significant figures?

| 7.804 | 7.83 | 7.807 | 7.901 | 7.745 | 7.75 |

Calculating with estimates, checking results

- Hazim worked out 38.2 × 10.78 and wrote down 41.1796. He can check his answer by working with estimates.

  Instead of 38.2 use 40, instead of 10.78 use 10.
      So 40 × 10 = 400.
  Clearly Hazim's answer is wrong. He put the decimal point in the wrong place.

- Here are three more calculations with estimates.

  (a) 27.2 × 51.7 (b) 78.9 ÷ 1.923 (c) 12% of £411.55
      ≈ 30 × 50   ≈ 80 ÷ 2   ≈ 10% of £400
      ≈ 1500   ≈ 40   ≈ £40

Exercise 3M

Do not use a calculator. Decide, by estimating, which of the three answers is closest to the exact answer. Write the calculation and the approximate answer for each question (use ≈).

	Calculation	A	B	C
1.	102.6 × 9.7	90	500	1000
2.	7.14 × 11.21	30	70	300
3.	1.07 × 59.2	6	60	200
4.	2.21 × 97.8	200	90	20
5.	8.95 × 42.1	200	400	4000
6.	4.87 × 6.18	15	10	30
7.	789 × 12.3	8000	4000	800
8.	978 × 9.83	1 million	100 000	10 000
9.	1.11 × 28.7	20	30	60
10.	9.8 × 82463	8 million	1 million	800 000
11.	307.4 ÷ 1.97	50	100	150
12.	81.2 ÷ 0.99	8	0.8	80
13.	6121 ÷ 102.4	60	300	600
14.	59.71 ÷ 3.14	10	20	180
15.	1072 ÷ 987.2	0.2	1	10
16.	614 − 297.4	300	100	3000
17.	0.104 + 0.511	0.06	0.1	0.6
18.	8216.1 + 1.44	800	4000	8000
19.	51% of £8018.95	£40	£400	£4000
20.	9% of £205.49	£10	£20	£200

Exercise 4M

1. A 'Pritt Stick' costs £1.99.

    (a) Without a calculator, estimate the cost of twelve Pritt Sticks.

    (b) Find the exact cost of twelve Pritt Sticks.

2. A box of drawing pins costs £3.85.

    Estimate the cost of 20 boxes of drawing pins.

3. A painting measures 12.2 cm by 9.7 cm.

    (a) Without a calculator, estimate the area of the painting.

    (b) Use a calculator to work out the exact area of the painting.

4 A newspaper was sold at £2.95 per copy.
Estimate the total cost of 47 copies.

5 Desmond has to pay £208.50 per month for 2 years towards the cost of his car.
Estimate the total cost of his payments.

6 Two hundred and six people share the cost of hiring a train.
Roughly how much does each person pay if the total cost was £61 990?

In questions **7** and **8** there are six calculations and six answers.

Write down each calculation and insert the correct answer from the list given.
Use estimation. Do not use a calculator.

7 (a) 6.9×7.1 (b) $9.8 \div 5$ (c) 21×10.2
(d) $151.767 \div 9.9$ (e) $3114 \div 30$ (f) 4.03×1.9

Answers: 1.96   15.33   48.99   103.8   7.657   214.2

8 (a) $103.2 \div 5$ (b) 7.2×7.3 (c) 4.1×49
(d) $3.57 \div 3$ (e) $36.52 \div 4$ (f) $1.4 \div 10$

Answers: 52.56   1.19   9.13   200.9   20.64   0.14

9

Insult may leave man speechless

CAIRO A Sinai man who insulted a sheperdess was ordered by a tribal court to give her 40 camels and either have his tongue cut out or give five more camels. *(AFP)*

In this area of Egypt an average camel costs 5100 Egyptian pounds (EGP).
(a) Estimate the value in pounds of 40 camels.
(b) Estimate the value in pounds of the extra camels needed to save the man's tongue.
[£100 = 1160 EGP]

10 A footballer is paid £94 800 per week.
Estimate how much he is paid in a year.

Need more practice with rounding numbers?

1 Write the following numbers correct to 1 decimal place.
(a) 18.7864 (b) 3.55 (c) 17.0946 (d) 0.7624
(e) 5.421 (f) 11.27 (g) 10.252 (h) 7.084

2. Write the following numbers correct to 2 decimal places.
   (a) 3.75821   (b) 11.64412   (c) 0.38214   (d) 138.2972
   (e) 11.444   (f) 7.058   (g) 6.5781   (h) 5.3092

3. 731.029 = 730 (to 3 s.f.) True or false?

4. 0.061042 = 0.06 (to 3 s.f.) True or false?

5. Work out $1^2 + 2^2 + 3^2 + 4^2 + 5^2 + 6^2 + 7^2 + 8^2 + 9^2 + 10^2$, giving the answer to 2 significant figures.

6. An astronaut is 2148 km above the Earth's surface. Write this distance to 2 significant figures.

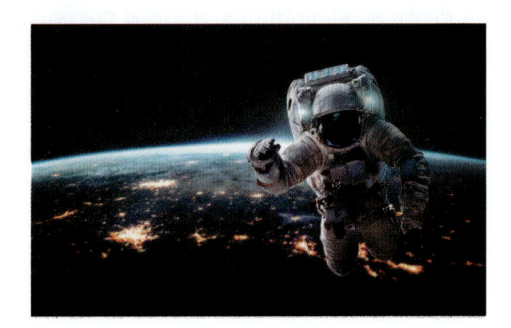

7. 17 873 people watched a cricket match. Round this figure to 3 significant figures.

8. Carter says that 21.08 × 0.997 is approximately equal to 20. Explain fully whether he is correct or not?

9. The number 0.0762 is rounded to (a) 2 decimal places and (b) 2 significant figures. What is the difference between the two answers?

10. A TV costs £297. Estimate the total cost of 62 TVs.

Extension questions with rounding numbers

1. Which number below does not round off to 0.017 when given to 2 significant figures?

   | 0.0174 | 0.0165 | 0.01751 | 0.01692 |

2. Calculate the area of the trapezium opposite. Give the answer to 1 decimal place.
   (1.9 cm, 6.32 cm, 7.149 cm)

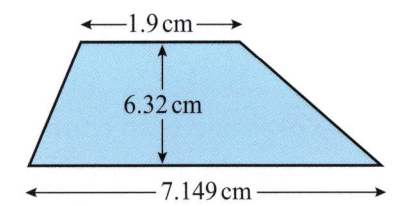

3. Write down the smallest number which would be rounded to 8.49 when given to 3 significant figures.

4 Find the sum of the first 10 cube numbers then give the answer to 1 significant figure.

5 Work out the following on a calculator and give the answer to the accuracy indicated.

(a) $\dfrac{2^3 - 0.07}{3.6^2}$ (2 d.p.)   (b) $\dfrac{(1 + 0.72)^2}{2 + 0.03}$ (3 s.f.)   (c) 69% of 21 647 (2 s.f.)

6 0.740382 = 0.7404 (to 4 s.f.) True or false?

7 Write down each calculation and insert the correct answer from the list given.
Use estimation. Do not use a calculator.

(a) 20.16 ÷ 4   (b) 39% of 60.2   (c) 4.3 × 4.1
(d) 9.02^2 (e) 160.8 ÷ 20   (f) 19.698 ÷ 0.49

Answers: 17.63   40.2   81.3604   8.04   23.478   5.04

8 Round off 2.9999999 to 4 decimal places.

9 Estimate the value of $\dfrac{15.99 + 2.03^2}{7.02 - 1.99}$

10 15.03 m   Lawn   29.8 m

Claudia's lawn is shown opposite.
A bag of fertiliser covers 48.5 m² of lawn and costs £5.85. Estimate the total cost for Claudia to cover her entire lawn with fertiliser.

CHECK YOURSELF ON SECTIONS 5.3 AND 5.4

1 Number review

(a) Draw a factor tree then express 364 as a product of its prime factors.
(b) Which calculation gives the larger answer: $\frac{3}{4} - \frac{1}{3}$ or $\frac{1}{6} + \frac{1}{4}$?
(c) Work out $2\frac{1}{2} \div 3\frac{1}{3}$
(d) A box contains 12 eggs. How many boxes are needed for 400 eggs?
(e) Some wire costs £2.30 per metre. How much does 0.7 m of wire cost?
(f) Work out 6 ÷ 0.4 + 0.6 ÷ 4
(g) Harry is awake for 16 hours each day. He goes to school for $\frac{3}{8}$ of this time. He plays sport for 15% of the remaining time. How much time does he spend playing sport each day?
(h) Some sweets are shared between Jason, Ariana, and Mariah in the ratio 7 : 4 : 8.
How many sweets does Jason get if Ariana gets 32 sweets?

2 Rounding off to decimal places and significant figures

Write the following numbers to the accuracy indicated.

(a) 0.1793 (2 d.p.) (b) 0.08437 (2 s.f.) (c) 31826 (2 s.f.)

(d) 684.67 (2 s.f.) (e) 43.1532 (1 d.p.) (f) 0.0701042 (3 s.f.)

3 Calculating using estimates

Decide, by estimating, which of the three answers is closest to the exact answer.

(a) 81.5×2.24 [1500 150 40]

(b) 0.97×38.4 [40 4 0.4]

(c) $98.1 \div 11.7$ [1 1000 10]

(d) A tin of blackcurrants cost 95p. Estimate the cost of 63 tins.

5.5 Probability 2

In section 5.5 you will learn to:
- find the probability of an event and two events

Equally likely outcomes

On this spinner there are five equal sections and two of these are blue.
The probability of spinning blue is $\frac{2}{5}$

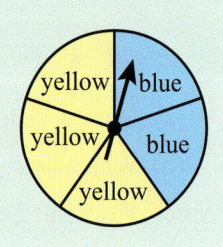

Exercise 1M

1. Cards with the letters of the word O C T O P U S are placed in a bag. One letter is selected at random.

   Find the probability of selecting

   (a) a T (b) an O

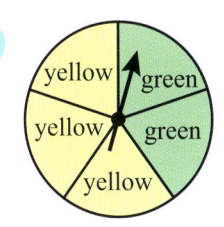

2 This spinner has five equal sections with 3 yellow and 2 green. What is the probability of spinning

(a) yellow

(b) green?

3 Bags A and B contain red and yellow balls as shown. Gary wants to get a yellow ball.

From which bag does he have the better chance of selecting a yellow ball? Explain your answer fully.

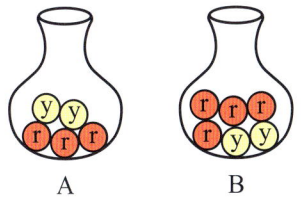

4 A fair dice is rolled. What is the probability of rolling

(a) a 5

(b) an even number

(c) a number greater than 7?

5 Four cards numbered 1, 2, 3, 4 are placed face down. One card is chosen at random.

(a) What is the probability of selecting an even number?

(b) A card numbered 5 is added to the cards above. What is now the probability of selecting an even number?

6 These balls are placed in a bag and then one ball is selected at random. There are two green balls, two red balls, and some other balls. What is the probability of selecting

(a) a green ball

(b) a green ball or a red ball?

7 These cards are shuffled and turned over. One card is picked at random. What is the probability of picking

(a) the number 6

(b) the number 4

(c) the number 8?

8 A bag contains green and yellow beads only. The total number of beads is 29.
Kelly says that the probability of removing a green bead is $\frac{1}{6}$. Ed says that the probability of removing a green bead is $\frac{1}{5}$. Explain clearly why both Kelly and Ed must be wrong.

9 There are 16 pens in a box. All of them are black. Steve chooses one of the pens at random. What is the probability that the pen is

(a) black   (b) red?

A pack of playing cards, without jokers, contains 52 cards.
There is ace, king, queen, jack, 10, 9, 8, 7, 6, 5, 4, 3, 2 of four suits.
The suits are ...

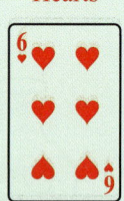

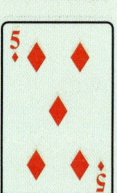

Spades   Hearts   Diamonds   Clubs

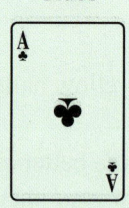

A pack of cards is shuffled and then one card is chosen at random.

(a) The probability that it is a king of hearts is $\frac{1}{52}$

(b) The probability that it is an ace is $\frac{4}{52}\left(=\frac{1}{13}\right)$

(c) The probability that it is a spade is $\frac{13}{52}\left(=\frac{1}{4}\right)$

Exercise 2M

1. One card is selected at random from a full pack of 52 playing cards.
   Find the probability of selecting

   (a) a heart
   (b) a red card
   (c) a '2'
   (d) any king, queen or jack
   (e) the ace of spades

2. A small pack of twenty cards consists of the ace, king, queen, jack and 10 of spades, hearts, diamonds and clubs.
   One card is selected at random. Find the probability of selecting

   (a) the ace of hearts
   (b) a king
   (c) a '10'
   (d) a black card
   (e) a heart

3. One card is selected at random from the cards shown.
   What is the probability of selecting

   (a) a red card (heart or diamond)
   (b) a 5
   (c) a card of the 'club' suit?

4. If Jake throws a 1 or a 4 on his next throw of a dice when playing 'Snakes and Ladders' he will climb up a ladder on the board.
   What is the probability that he will *miss* a ladder on his next throw?

5 A box contains 11 balls: 3 green, 2 white, 4 red and 2 blue.

  (a) Find the probability of selecting
   (i) a blue ball   (ii) a green ball

  (b) The 3 green balls are replaced by 3 blue balls.
   Find the probability of selecting
   (i) a blue ball   (ii) a white ball

6 Cards with numbers 1, 2, 3, 4, 5, 6, 7, 8, 9, 10 are shuffled and then placed face down in a line. The cards are then turned over one at a time from the left. In this example the first card is a '4'.

Find the probability that the next card turned over will be
  (a) 7   (b) a number higher than 4

7 Suppose the second card is a 1.

Find the probability that the next card will be
  (a) the 6   (b) an even number   (c) higher than 1

8 Suppose the first three cards are 4 1 8 ...

Find the probability that the next card will be
  (a) less than 8   (b) the 4   (c) an odd number

9 Each letter in the words of the sentence below is written on a separate card.
'I have told you a million times, don't exaggerate!'
The cards are placed in a bag and one card is selected at random.
Find the probability of selecting
  (a) an 'a'   (b) a 't'   (c) a 'b'

10 Here are two spinners. Say whether the following statements are true or false. Explain why in each case.
  (a) 'Sarah is more likely to spin a 6 than Ben.'
  (b) 'Sarah and Ben are equally likely to spin an even number.'
  (c) 'If Sarah spins her spinner six times, she is bound to get at least one 6.'

Two spinners are used. Each spinner has the numbers 1 to 4.
The outcomes are: (1, 1), (1, 2), (1, 3), (1, 4), (2, 1), (2, 2), (2, 3) …… (4, 4).
Find the probability of getting a product of 8 with the scores on the two spinners.

Draw a grid showing the possible products.

×	1	2	3	4
1	1	2	3	4
2	2	4	6	8
3	3	6	9	12
4	4	8	12	16

p (product is 8) $= \frac{2}{16} = \frac{1}{8}$

because there are 16 possible outcomes and 2 ways of getting a product of 8.

Exercise 3M

1. Three coins are tossed together.
   Find the probability of getting exactly two heads.

2. Two spinners are used. Each spinner has the numbers 1 to 5.
   Find the probability of getting a total score of 7 with the scores on the two spinners.

3. Three friends Alf, Ben and Curtis sit next to each other on a bench.
   (a) Make a list of all the different ways in which they can sit. (Use A = Alf, B = Ben and C = Curtis).
   Find the probability that
   (b) Alf sits in the middle
   (c) Alf sits next to Curtis
   (d) Ben sits at one end of the bench

4. ④ ⑥ ⑦ ⑨ Four balls as shown opposite are placed in a bag.
   One ball is randomly chosen then replaced in the bag.
   A second ball is then randomly chosen.
   (a) List all the possible pairs of numbers which could be selected.
   (b) Find the probability that the difference between the two numbers chosen is 2.

5. One ball is selected at random from a bag containing x red balls and y white balls.
   What is the probability of selecting a red ball?

6. One ball is selected at random from a bag containing w white balls, g green balls and p pink balls. Find the probability of selecting
   (a) a white ball
   (b) a pink ball
   (c) a ball which is not white

7 Sana, Liz and Carmel were asked to toss a fair coin 16 times.
Here are the results they wrote down.

Sana   H T H T H T H T H T H T H T H T
Liz   H H T H T T H T T T H H T H H T
Carmel   H H H H H H H H T T T T T T T T

One of the three did the experiment properly while the other two just made up results.
Explain what you think each person did.

Need more practice with probability?

1 A hat contains 1 red ball, 1 blue ball and 1 orange ball. One ball is selected at random.
What is the probability of selecting
 (a) a blue ball   (b) an orange ball?

2 The cards below are placed in a bag and then one card is selected at random.

[1] [2] [3] [4] [5] [6] [7] [8] [9]

Find the probability of selecting
 (a) the number 4   (b) an even number   (c) a number less than 5

3 Children in France count up to five using their fingers and thumb as shown.
Michele displays one number at random.
Find the probability that she shows
 (a) the number three
 (b) an even number
 (c) How do *you* count from 1 to 5 using your fingers?

4 A raffle has tickets numbered from 1 to 150. Maggie has ticket number 37.
What is the probability that Maggie wins the raffle?

5 A bag contains only red and blue counters. The probability of choosing a blue counter is $\frac{3}{5}$
when one counter is randomly selected. There are at least 11 blue counters in the bag.
What is the least possible number of red counters in the bag?

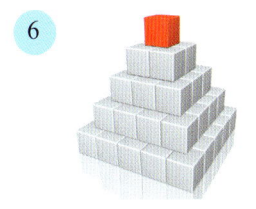

6 There are 54 white cubes and 1 red cube in the pile shown.
The cubes are jumbled up in a box and then one cube is selected
at random.
What is the probability of selecting the red cube?

7 One card is picked at random from a pack of 52.
Find the probability that it is
(a) a queen (b) the king of diamonds (c) a spade

8 A bag contains 3 black balls, 2 green balls, 1 white ball and 5 orange balls.
Find the probability of selecting
(a) a black ball (b) an orange ball (c) a white ball

9 A bag contains the balls shown. One ball is taken out at random.
Find the probability that it is
(a) yellow (b) blue (c) red

One more blue ball and one more red ball are added to the bag.
(d) Find the new probability of selecting a yellow ball from the bag.

10 Helen played a game of cards with Michelle.
The cards were dealt so that both players received two cards.
Helen's cards were a 7 and a 4. Michelle's first card was a 10.

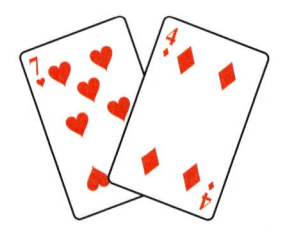

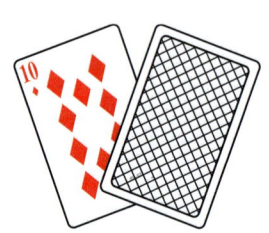

Find the probability that Michelle's second card was
(a) a picture card (a king, queen or jack)
(b) a seven

Extension questions with probability

In questions **1** to **4** a bag contains a certain number of red balls and a certain number of white balls. The tally charts show the number of times a ball was selected from the bag and then replaced. Look at the results and say what you think was in the bag each time.

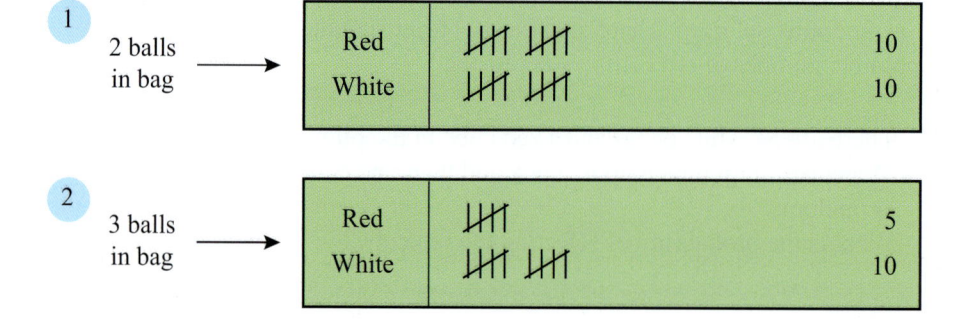

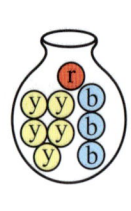

1 2 balls in bag →

| Red | |||| |||| | 10 |
| White | |||| |||| | 10 |

2 3 balls in bag →

| Red | |||| | 5 |
| White | |||| |||| | 10 |

3 3 balls in bag →

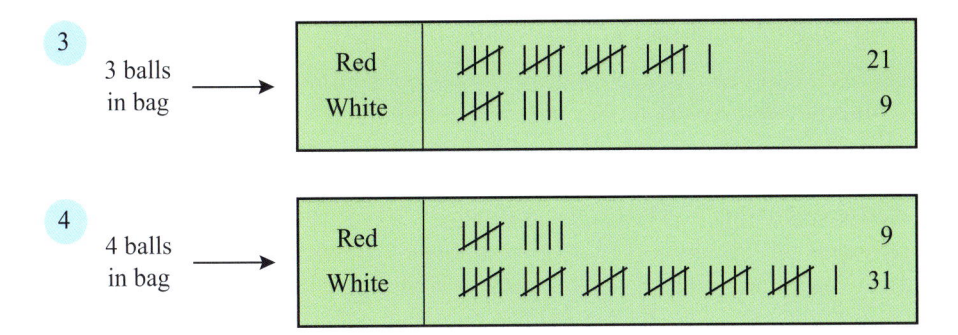

Red	⋕⋕ ⋕⋕ ⋕⋕ ⋕⋕ I	21
White	⋕⋕ IIII	9

4 4 balls in bag →

Red	⋕⋕ IIII	9
White	⋕⋕ ⋕⋕ ⋕⋕ ⋕⋕ ⋕⋕ ⋕⋕ I	31

5 It is assumed that when a baby is born, the probability of the child being female is 0.5. If triplets are born, what is the probability of two of the babies being girls and one being a boy?

6 Melissa, who is 8 years old, plays two games with her mother, 'Snakes and Ladders' and then 'Monopoly'.
Comment on the following statements:
(a) Melissa has an evens chance of winning at 'Snakes and Ladders'.
(b) Melissa has an evens chance of winning at 'Monopoly'.

7 A pack of cards is split into two piles. Pile P contains all the picture cards and aces and pile O contains all the other cards.
(a) Find the probability of selecting
   (i) the jack of hearts from pile P
   (ii) a seven from pile O
(b) All the diamonds are now removed from both piles.
Find the probability of selecting
   (i) the king of clubs from pile P
   (ii) a red card from pile O

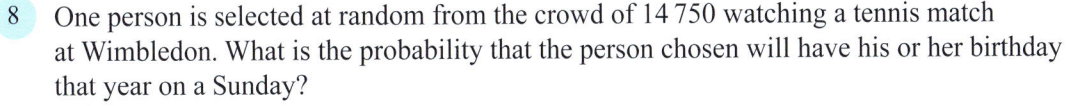

8 One person is selected at random from the crowd of 14 750 watching a tennis match at Wimbledon. What is the probability that the person chosen will have his or her birthday that year on a Sunday?

9 A bag contains 9 balls, all of which are black or white. Jane selects a ball and then replaces it. She repeats this several times. Here are her results (B = black, W = white):

B W B W B B B W B B W B B W B
B B W W B B B B W B W B B W B

How many balls of each colour do you think there were in the bag?

10 If two dice are thrown, is the probability of the total score being 4 less than, equal to or greater than the total score being 10? You must justify your answer fully.

Dice Pontoon

This is a game for two players using a dice.

Version 1

- Player A throws a dice as many times as he likes and keeps a running total for his 'score'.
  So if he throws 2, 3, 5, 1 his score is 11.
- If he throws the same number twice consecutively his score returns to zero and his turn is finished.
  So if he throws 2, 3, 5, 1, 1 his score is 0.
- He can decide to stop throwing the dice at any time to avoid the risk of losing his score.
- Player B then has his turn and throws the dice following the rules above.
- The winner is the player with the higher score.

Version 2

- The players take turns to throw the dice.
- If a player throws the same number that his opponent has just thrown then his score goes to zero.
  For example a game could go like this:

  A3   A5   A3
       B4   B1   B3

  Now B automatically loses because his score is zero.

- A player can decide to stop throwing at any time. If he does stop, his opponent may continue throwing on his own until someone wins.
  Here is another example of a game:

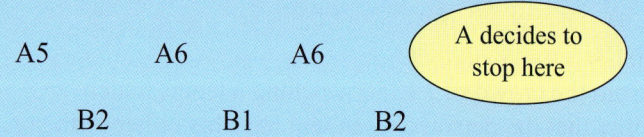

  A5   A6   A6   *A decides to stop here*

       B2   B1   B2   B3   B4   B5   B5

So A is the winner because B's score is zero after throwing two consecutive fives.

Notice that B would have won if he had thrown any number apart from 5 on his last throw.

Think about the rules of the two versions of the game and decide which version you *think* will give both players the most even chance of winning.

Which version do you think involves more skill?

It is not easy to decide which version will give both players the most even chance of winning.

One way to find out is to do an experiment.

Play each version of the game several times and make a tally chart, recording which player (first or second) won. Work out the experimental probability of each player winning for each version.

For example, if you played the game 14 times and the first player won 9 times, the experimental probability of the first player winning would be $\frac{9}{14}$.

Winner	
First player	Second player
⫼⫼ IIII	⫼⫼

Write a couple of sentences to say what the results of the experiments showed.

Try to think of any further changes to the rules which would make the game more fair or perhaps more interesting. Play the game using your changes and decide if it really does give a better game.

✘ Spot the mistakes 10 ✘

Number, work and probability

Work through each question below and explain clearly what mistakes have been made.
Beware – some questions are correctly done.

1. Some money is shared between Russell, Anton and Tara in the ratio 7 : 2 : 5. Tara gets £420. How much does Russell get?

   Solution: Total number of shares = 7 + 2 + 5 = 14
   1 share = 420 ÷ 14 = 30
   Russell gets 7 shares = 7 × 30 = £210

2. Work out 0.1087902 ÷ 1.8, giving the answer to 3 significant figures.
   Answer: 0.1087902 ÷ 1.8 = 0.060439 = 0.06044 (3 s.f.)

3. Work out $1\frac{1}{7} \times 1\frac{3}{4}$
   Answer: $1\frac{1}{7} \times 1\frac{3}{4} = \frac{8}{7} \times \frac{7}{4} = \frac{56}{28} = \frac{2}{1} = 2$

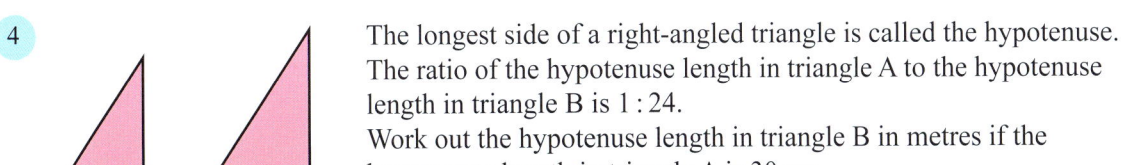

4. The longest side of a right-angled triangle is called the hypotenuse. The ratio of the hypotenuse length in triangle A to the hypotenuse length in triangle B is 1 : 24.
   Work out the hypotenuse length in triangle B in metres if the hypotenuse length in triangle A is 30 cm.
   Answer: length = 24 × 30 = 720 cm.

5. What is the probability of Tessa beating Chun at a game of badminton?
   Answer: 0.5 because Tessa is one of two players involved in the game.

6. Use factor trees to find the H.C.F. of 476 and 1050.

Solution:

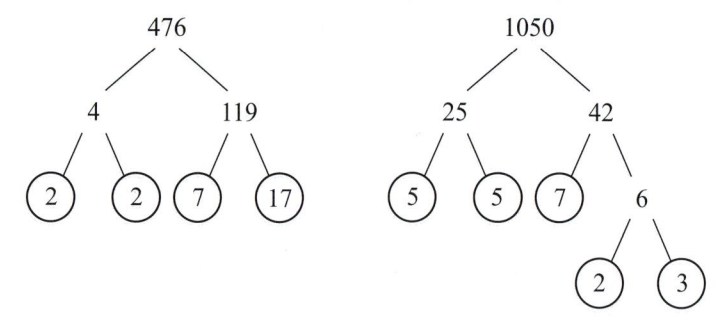

so $476 = 2 \times 2 \times 7 \times 17$ and $1050 = 2 \times 3 \times 5 \times 5 \times 7$

The factors in both numbers are 2 and 2 with 7 and 7

so H.C.F. $= 2 \times 2 \times 7 \times 7 = 196$

7. A model ship costs £25.
Its price is reduced by 20% for a sale.
After the sale it has not sold and its price is increased by 20%.
What does the model ship now cost?

Answer: It costs the original price of £25 because the price was decreased by 20% then increased by 20%.

8. A bag contains red, green and yellow balls. If one ball is randomly selected, the probability of a red ball is $\frac{1}{3}$ and the probability of a green ball is $\frac{1}{5}$. If there are 21 yellow balls in the bag, how many green balls are in the bag?

Solution: $p(\text{red or green}) = \frac{1}{3} + \frac{1}{5} = \frac{5+3}{15} = \frac{8}{15}$

so $p(\text{yellow}) = \frac{7}{15} = \frac{21}{45}$

so 45 balls in bag if 21 yellow balls in bag.

$p(\text{green}) = \frac{1}{5}$ so number of green balls $= \frac{1}{5}$ of $45 = 9$

9. Work out the perimeter of the rectangle opposite, giving the answer to 2 decimal places.

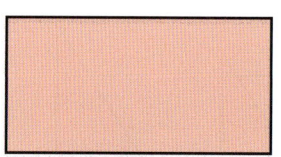

Answer: $1.324 = 1.32$ (2 d.p.)
$3.232 = 3.23$ (2 d.p.)
Perimeter $= 1.32 + 3.23 + 1.32 + 3.23 = 9.10$ cm (2 d.p.)

1.324 cm

3.232 cm

10. Work out the probability of getting a 1 and a 1 when two dice are thrown.

Answer: $p(1) = \frac{1}{6}$ so $p(1)$ and $p(1) = \frac{1}{6} + \frac{1}{6} = \frac{2}{6} = \frac{1}{3}$

CHECK YOURSELF ON SECTION 5.5

1 Finding the probability of an event and two events

(a) Write down the probability of choosing a diamond when selecting one card randomly from a standard pack of cards?

(b) There are eight balls in a bag. The probability of taking a white ball from the bag is 0.5. A white ball is taken from the bag and put on one side.
What is the probability of taking a white ball from the bag now?

(c) One coin and one dice are thrown. What is the probability of getting a square number with heads?

5.6 Applying mathematics 5

In section 5.6 you will apply maths in a variety of situations.

1 It costs 18p per minute to hire a tool.
How much will it cost to hire the tool from 08.50 to 11.15?

2 Work out the missing numbers.

(a) $204 + 360 = \Box$ (b) $273 + \Box = 800$ (c) $25 \times \Box = 1700$
(d) $\Box + 305 = 5000$ (e) $\Box - 4.1 = 27.95$ (f) $\Box \div 12 = 536$

3 Work out the value of n from the rectangle opposite then calculate the actual area of the square shown.
All lengths are in cm.

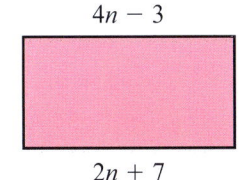

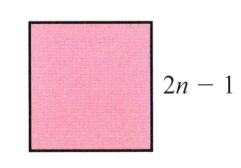

Rectangle: $4n - 3$ by $2n + 7$
Square: $2n - 1$

4 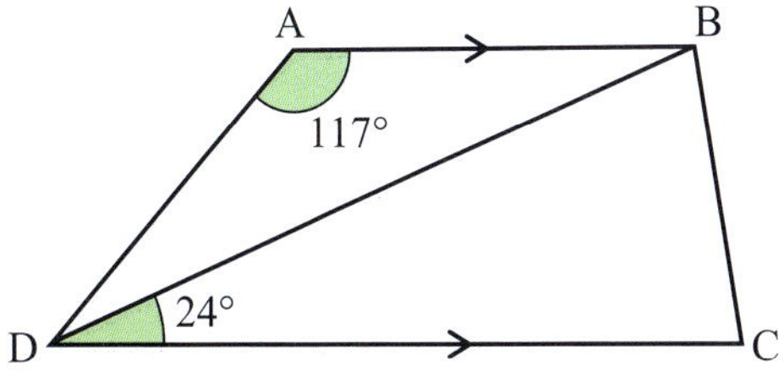 Work out the value of $A\hat{D}B$, giving reasons for your answer.

(Diagram: quadrilateral with A, B on top, D, C on bottom; angle at A = 117°, angle at D = 24°, AB parallel to DC)

5 If 1 billion is a thousand million, write 30 billion pence in pounds and pence.

6. Square ABCD can be moved onto square BCEF by either a translation, a rotation or a reflection.

   (a) Describe the translation using a vector.

   (b) What is the mirror line for the reflection?

   (c) Describe *two* possible rotations which achieve the result given. You must write down the angle of rotation, direction and centre of rotation.

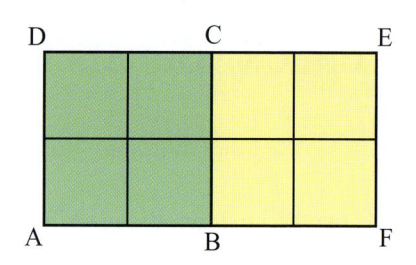

7. The diagram shows a corner torn from a sheet of graph paper measuring 18 cm by 28 cm.

   Calculate the total length of all the lines drawn on the whole sheet of graph paper.

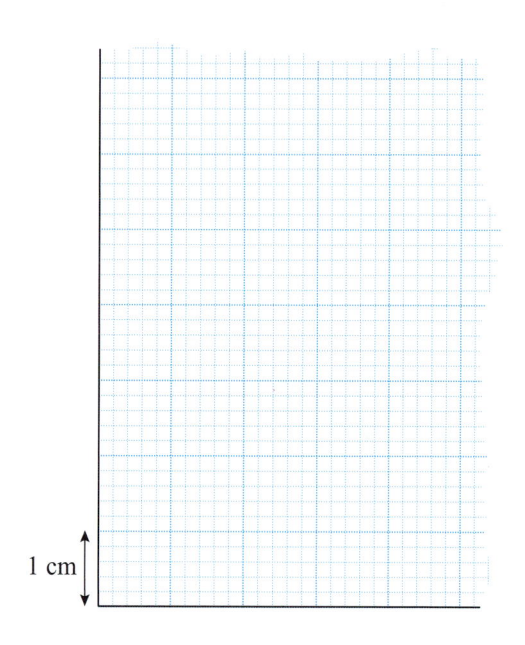

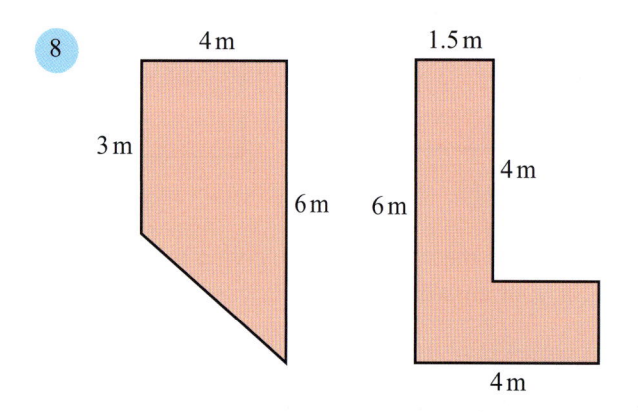

8. Laura needs to put wooden flooring in the two rooms shown opposite. The cost of the wooden flooring is £29.25 per m². 5% extra wood is bought to allow for mistakes. How much will Laura need to pay in total?

9. In this calculation use each of the digits 1, 2, 3, 4, 5, 6. Put one digit in each box to make the statement true.

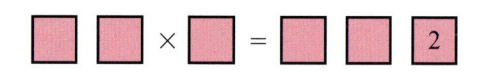

10 Faris has completed five maths tests and has a mean average score of 64%. After her sixth test her mean average score has increased to 67%. What percentage test mark did she score in her sixth test?

UNIT 5 MIXED REVIEW

Part one

Use a calculator when necessary.

1 A cake recipe calls for 500 g of flour to mix with 200 g of sugar.
   How much sugar should be used if you have only 300 g of flour?

2 Highly trained mosquitoes can be used to find oil.
   The annual profit in pounds, P, made by the mosquitoes is given by the formula.

   $P = 500m - 2$, where m is the number of mosquitoes.

   Find the profit when 10 000 mosquitoes are employed.

3 Simplify $5(3x + 6) + 4(x - 3)$

4 Joe got 27 out of 40 in a geography test. What was his mark as a percentage?

5 Copy and complete by filling in the boxes. You can use any of the numbers 1, 2, 3, 4, 5 but you cannot use a number more than once.
   (a) $\square + \square - \square = 7$
   (b) $(\square + \square) \div \square = 3$
   (c) $(\square + \square) \div (\square - \square) = 1\frac{1}{2}$
   (d) $(\square + \square + \square) \times \square = 33$

6 I think of a number. If I add 5 and then multiply the result by 10 the answer is 82.
   What number was I thinking of?

7 If $y = 3x - c$, find the value of y when $x = 3$ and $c = -8$.

8 The temperature in a centrally heated house is recorded every hour from 12.00 till 24.00; the results are shown below.

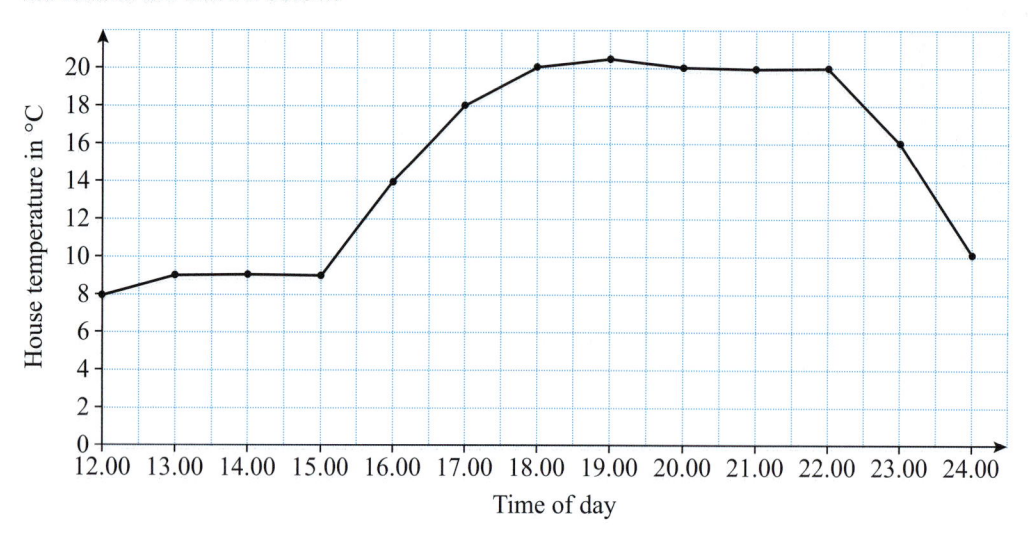

(a) What was the temperature at 20.00?
(b) Estimate the temperature at 16.30.
(c) Estimate the two times when the temperature was 18°C.
(d) When do you think the central heating was switched on?
(e) When do you think the central heating was switched off?

9 Look at this group of numbers …

   10, 19, 25, 30, 21

(a) Which of the numbers is a multiple of both 3 and 5?
(b) Which of the numbers is a prime number?
(c) Which of the numbers is a square number?
(d) Which number is a factor of another number in the group?

10 An advert for toothpaste used a photo of a model's teeth. Sales of the toothpaste rose from 25 800 per week by 4%. How many extra tubes were sold?

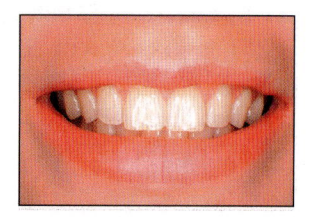

11 A worker takes 8 minutes to make 12 items. How long would it take to make 15 items?

12 During one season the probability of Hatton United winning a game is $\frac{13}{20}$ and the probability of a draw is $\frac{1}{4}$. What is the probability that Hatton United will lose a game?

13 Use a calculator to work out the following and give your answers correct to 1 decimal place.

(a) $8.62 - \dfrac{1.71}{0.55}$ (b) $\dfrac{8.02 - 6.3}{1.3 + 4.6}$ (c) $\dfrac{5.6}{1.71} - 1.08$

14 Two fifths of the children in a swimming pool are boys.
There are 72 girls in the pool. How many boys are there?

15 Solve (a) $4x - 9 = 11$ (b) $7 = \dfrac{x}{8}$ (c) $8 = 5 + 4x$

Part two

1 Write down an expression for the area of this rectangle.
Expand your answer.

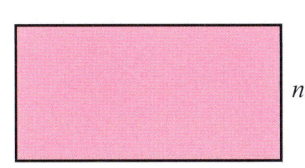

n

$n + 4$

2 The diagram shows a rectangle.
The perimeter of the rectangle is 42 cm.
Work out x.

6 cm

$8x - 5$

3 Two books cost £13.50 in total. One book is one-and-a-half times the price of the other.
How much does each book cost?

4 Charlotte says that the probability of getting 3 tails when tossing 3 coins is $\frac{1}{8}$.
Is she correct? You must justify your answer fully.

5 Solve (a) $12 = 5 + 8x$ (b) $3x - 4 = 50$ (c) $2x + \frac{1}{3} = 3\frac{1}{3}$

6 (a) Suppose the '5' button on your calculator does not work.
Show how you can make your calculator show the number 345.

(b) Suppose none of the numbers 1, 3, 5, 7, 9 work.
Show how you can make your calculator show the number 115.

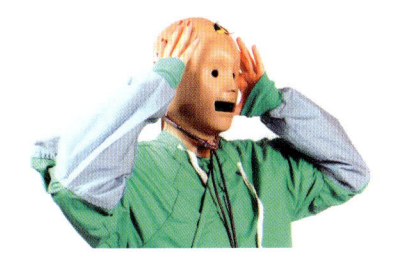

7 Crash dummies do have feelings!
Just before being 'tested' a dummy's heart rate increased from 60 beats per minute by 75%.
What is the raised heart rate?

8 Write down these calculations and find the missing digits.

(a)   5 . ☐ 5
    + 3 . 7 ☐
    ─────────
      9 . 0 9

(b)   7 . ☐ 8
    − 3 . 8 ☐
    ─────────
      ☐ . 1 5

(c)   ☐ 3 . ☐
    + 2 ☐ . 3
    ─────────
      7 0 . 0

9 The number 7.06483 is first rounded off to 4 significant figures.
   This answer is then rounded off to 2 decimal places. Write down the final answer.

10 Multiply out   (a) $5(x - 3)$ (b) $3(2x + 4)$

11 The travel graph below shows how far a crab is from the sea at certain times during one day.

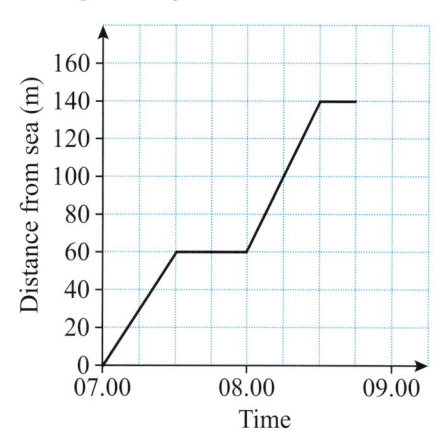

(a) What has happened to the crab between 08.30 and 08.45?

(b) The crab now returns to the sea at a speed of 70 m/h. What time does the crab reach the sea?

12 Which fraction is closer to one: $\frac{9}{10}$ or $\frac{10}{11}$? Show your working.

13 A bag contains 6 coloured balls. One ball is selected at random and then replaced in the bag. This procedure is repeated until 50 selections have been made.
Here are the results:
[B = Blue, G = Green, Y = Yellow]

B Y B Y B Y B Y B G B Y B
G B B B B Y G B Y B G B Y
Y B Y Y B B B G B B Y B
B Y B Y G B Y B Y B G B

What do you think were the colours of the balls in the bag?

14 Simplify the ratio $\frac{3}{4} : 1\frac{1}{5} : 2\frac{2}{3}$

Puzzles and Problems 5

Break the codes

1 The symbols γ, ↑, !, ⊖, ⊥ each stand for one of the digits 1, 2, 3, 5 or 9 but not in that order. Use the clues below to work out what number each symbol stands for.

(a) ↑ × ↑ = ⊥

(b) ⊖ × ↑ = ↑

(c) ⊖ + ⊖ = γ

(d) γ + ↑ = !

2 The ten symbols below each stand for one of the digits 0, 1, 2, 3, 4, 5, 6, 7, 8 or 9 but not that order.

♂ ⩔ ☐ ⊙ ↑ ✻ ⬚ △ Φ ⊠

Use the clues below to work out what number each symbol stands for.

(a) ♂ + ♂ + ♂ + ♂ + ♂ = ⩔

(b) ⩔ + ⊠ = ⩔

(c) ⩔ + ♂ = ⊙

(d) Φ + Φ + Φ + Φ = ↑

(e) ✻ × ✻ = ⬚

(f) ⊙ − Φ = △

(g) ✻ + △ = ☐

3 The ten symbols used in part 2 are used again but with different values.

(a) ⊠ × ⊙ = ⊙

(b) ⊠ + ⊠ + ⊠ = ✻

(c) ✻ − ⊠ = △

(d) △ × △ × △ = ⊙

(e) ⊙ − ⊠ = ↑

(f) ✻ + ⩔ = ✻

(g) ⊙ ÷ △ = Φ

(h) ✻ + △ = ☐

(i) ↑ − ⊠ = ⬚

(j) ♂ − △ = ↑

4 These clues are more difficult to work out.

(a) ☐ + ↑ = ☐

(b) ♂ × ☐ = ♂

(c) ⬚ × ⬚ × ⬚ = ♂

(d) ♂ − ⬚ = Φ

(e) Φ − ⬚ = △

(f) Φ − ☐ = ⊠

(g) ⊠ + ⬚ = ⊙

(h) ⩔ × ⩔ = ✻

Curves from straight lines

- On a sheet of unlined paper draw a circle of radius 8.5 cm and mark 36 equally spaced points on the circle. Use a protractor inside the circle and move around 10° for each point.

- Mark an extra 36 points in between the orininal 36 so that finally you have 72 points equally spaced around the circle.

- Number the points 0, 1, 2, 3, …… 71 and after one circuit continue from 72 to 143.

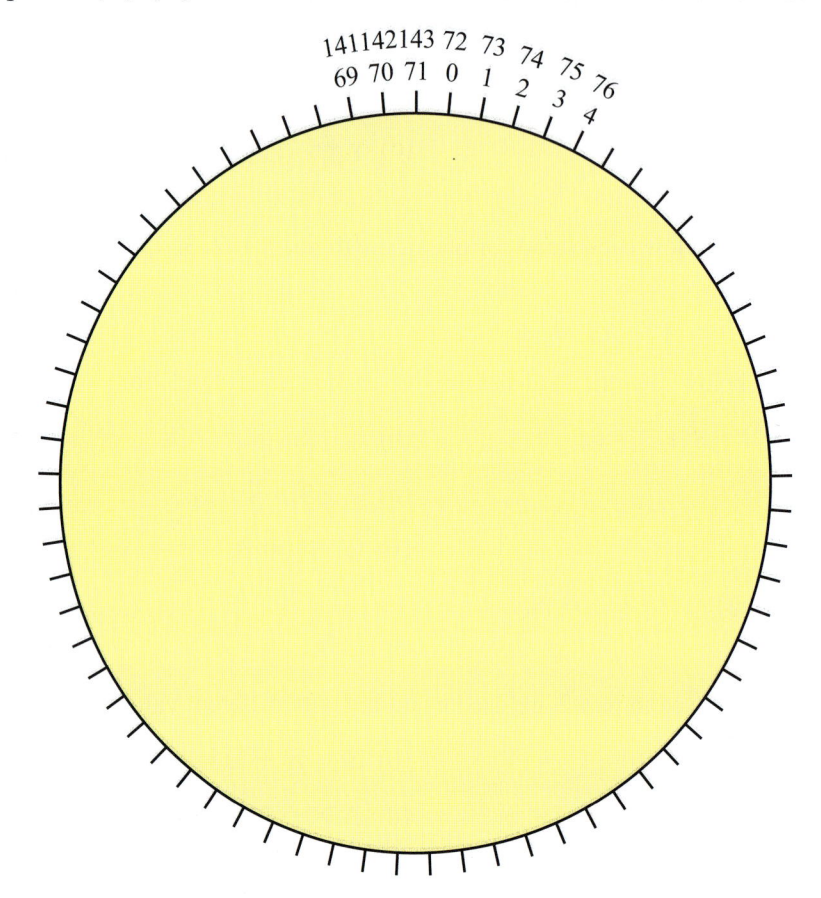

- You can obtain three different patterns as follows:

A (i) Join 0 → 10, 1 → 11, 2 → 12 etc
   (ii) Join 0 → 20, 1 → 21, 2 → 22 etc
   (iii) Join 0 → 30, 1 → 31, 2 → 32 etc

B Join each number to double that number.
   ie. 1 → 2, 2 → 4, 3 → 6, ……

C Join each number to treble that number.
   ie. 1 → 3, 2 → 6, 3 → 9, ……
   For **C** you need to continue numbering points around the circle from 144 to 215.

Mental Arithmetic Practice 5

There are two sets of mental arithmetic questions in this section. Ideally a teacher will read out each question twice, with pupils' books closed. Each test should take about 20 minutes.

Test 1

1. Write 0.07 as a fraction.
2. Jack has £336 and spends £279. How much money does he have left?
3. A triangle has three equal sides. What is its special name?
4. Subtract 0.3 from 5.
5. Write down three factors of 6.
6. What is three-fifths of 40?
7. What is the mean average of 9, 6 and 15?
8. A rectangle of length 6 cm has an area of 21 cm². What is the width of the rectangle?
9. Is the difference between 264° and 173° an acute angle or an obtuse angle?
10. Write down a prime number between 24 and 30.
11. How many sixths make up $3\frac{1}{3}$?
12. Sarah is given a bonus of 5% of £440. How much is the bonus?
13. What is the probability of getting a square number if you throw one dice?
14. Donna scores 15 out of 25 in a test. What percentage score is this?
15. What do the angles in a quadrilateral add up to?
16. What is the perimeter of a square whose area is 49 cm²?
17. Cakes cost 30p each. How many cakes can be bought with £5?
18. If $n = 3$, which is larger: $3n$ or n^2?
19. How many twenty-fours are there in seven hundred and twenty?
20. What is $6 + 4 \times \frac{1}{2}$?
21. What is five per cent of £200 000?
22. A hose of length 170 m is cut in half. How long is each piece?
23. A car travels 50 m in 10 seconds. How far will it go in 10 minutes?
24. Three angles of a quadrilateral are 80°, 90° and 100°. What is the fourth angle?
25. Add together two cubed and three cubed.

Test 2

1. Find 25% of 880.
2. Work out $301 - 102$.
3. What number is eleven less than two thousand?
4. Write 20% as a fraction.
5. 4 apples cost 96p. What is the cost of 6 apples?
6. What is the difference between six squared and two squared?
7. A triangle has two angles of 38° and 67°. What is the size of the third angle?
8. What is $-3 - (-4)$?
9. How many lines of symmetry does a parallelogram have?
10. What is the median of 1, 2, 3 and 4?

11 There are 12 beads in a bag. Seven of the beads are red. I take out one bead from the bag. What is the probability that the bead is *not* red?

12 Don buys a book for £5.35 and a drink costing 57p. How much change does he get from a £10 note?

13 What is 600 divided by 25?

14 How many fifty pence coins make £103.50?

15 What is the product of 3, 4 and 5?

16 A car travels 4 miles in 5 minutes. How far will it travel in one hour?

17 Find five-sevenths of 42.

18 What number is next in the pattern 1, 3, 6, 10, ... ?

19 How many seconds are there in one hour?

20 I treble a number and add 6. The answer is equal to half of 84. What was the number?

21 True or false '8 miles is about 5 km'.

22 Write down the sum of the numbers from one to five.

23 If apples cost 55p for 200 g, how much will 2 kg cost?

24 What is a quarter of six hundred and forty?

25 What is ten cubed take away one cubed?

A long time ago! 5

Roman numerals

Many clock faces still use roman numerals like IV and XI. At the end of a film, the year in which the film was made is often given using roman numerals. MCMLXXX means 1980.

I	one	XI	eleven
II	two	XII	twelve
III	three	XX	twenty
IV	four (one before five)	XXX	thirty
V	five	XL	forty (ten before fifty)
VI	six	L	fifty
VII	seven	LX	sixty
VIII	eight	C	hundred
IX	nine (one before ten)	CM	nine hundred
X	ten	M	thousand

Note
When we reach 10 before 50, we write XL not XXXX. Your teacher may explain this more fully.

Exercise

1 Write down the value of each of the numbers written below in roman numerals.

(a) VII (b) XIII (c) XVI (d) XXVII
(e) XVIII (f) XIX (g) XLV (h) LXXII
(i) CCCXXVII (j) XCIV (k) MMVI (l) CMXLIX

2 Write these numbers in roman numerals.

(a) 8 (b) 17 (c) 22
(d) 58 (e) 39 (f) 84
(g) 78 (h) 123 (i) 339
(j) 1265 (k) 1066 (l) 3194

3 Write this year in roman numerals.

4 Work out the questions below, giving your answers in roman numerals.

(a) VI + III (b) IX + VIII (c) XIII + XVII
(d) XL − VI (e) LIII − XVIII (f) C − XLVII
(g) LXXV + CCXXXVI (h) V × II (i) IV × IX
(j) CCCXII − CLXXIX (k) VII × VI (l) VII × XII
(m) XXIV ÷ III (n) L ÷ X (o) CXX ÷ XX
(p) XXXVI ÷ IX (q) MCC ÷ XXX (r) MCCV + CCXXVIII − XCIV

5 RESEARCH:

(a) In the ancient Greek number system, Δ was the symbol for 10. Find out the ancient Greek symbol for (i) 100 (ii) 50

(b) Find the ancient Egyptian symbols for (i) 10 (ii) 100 (iii) 1000

(c) Find out three more ancient Egyptian symbols and sketch them as carefully as you can.

(d) Can you find out why particular letters are used for certain roman numerals? For example, why is C used for 100?

UNIT 6

6.1 Metric and imperial units

In section 6.1 you will:
- convert metric units
- convert imperial units
- convert between metric and imperial units
- change units for some problems

Metric units

Length
1 cm = 10 mm
1 m = 100 cm
1 km = 1000 m

Mass
1 g = 1000 mg
1 kg = 1000 g
1 tonne = 1000 kg

Volume
1 millilitre (ml) = 1 cm^3
1 litre = 1000 ml

Exercise 1M

Copy and complete

1. 5.9 m = ☐ cm
2. 9.13 kg = ☐ g
3. 700 g = ☐ kg
4. 3.5 km = ☐ m
5. 43 mm = ☐ cm
6. 70 cm = ☐ m
7. 4 litres = ☐ ml
8. 2500 kg = ☐ t
9. 2.4 kg = ☐ g
10. 300 mm = ☐ m
11. 509 g = ☐ kg
12. 0.2 m = ☐ cm

13. Alec suggests that an adult lion weighs around 190 g.
Comment on his suggestion.

14 A chef uses 240 g and 135 g of flour when making two cakes.
He now has 0.6 kg of flour remaining.
How much flour did he have before he made the cakes?

15 Write down the difference between each pair of measurements below.
(a) 7.4 litres and 7275 ml
(b) 60 g and 0.083 kg
(c) 62 litres and 6180 ml
(d) 3.7 m and 4200 mm
(e) 5.02 kg and 4970 g
(f) 2.6 litres and 1900 cm^3

16 A long stick of rock measures 2.5 m. It is cut into sticks which measure 18 cm.
How many 18 cm sticks will there be?

17 A bag of cotswold stone weighs 25 kg. A lorry transports 85 bags.
What is the total weight of the bags? Give the answer in tonnes.

18 Write down the measurements below in order of size, starting with the smallest.

| 0.87 ℓ | 1250 mℓ | 1.1 ℓ | 489 cm^3 | 1.542 ℓ | 410 mℓ |

Imperial units

We still use imperial units. Imperial measurements were made by using appropriately sized bits of human being. The inch was measured using the thumb (we still sometimes say 'rule of thumb' when we mean rough measurement), the foot by using the foot.

Imperial units

Length
1 foot = 12 inches
1 yard = 3 feet
1 mile = 1760 yards

Mass
1 pound = 16 ounces
1 stone = 14 pounds
1 ton = 2240 pounds

Volume
1 gallon = 8 pints

Exercise 2M

1 Which is larger: 12 stones or 164 pounds?
Give a full reason for your answer.

2 Work out the difference between 58 inches and 6 feet.

3 Copy and complete

(a) 60 inches = ☐ feet
(b) $\frac{1}{4}$ pound = ☐ ounces
(c) 3 feet 2 inches = ☐ inches
(d) 7 stones 9 pounds = ☐ pounds
(e) 4 tons = ☐ pounds
(f) 6 feet 5 inches = ☐ inches
(g) 5 miles = ☐ yards
(h) 8 yards 2 feet = ☐ feet
(i) 4 stones 6 pounds = ☐ pounds
(j) $1\frac{1}{2}$ gallons = ☐ pints

4 Vitali travels $2\frac{1}{2}$ miles on his bike. How many inches is this?

5 During her lifetime, Ann donates 46 pints of blood which is badly needed by the hospitals. How many gallons of blood is this?

6 Natasha is 62 inches tall and Ian is 5 feet 11 inches tall. How much taller is Ian than Natasha?

7 Convert 1 ton 78 stones 11 pounds into ounces.

8 Which is larger and by how much: $\frac{3}{5}$ mile or 3160 feet?

Converting between metric and imperial units

1 inch ≈ 2.5 cm   1 kg ≈ 2.2 pounds
1 foot ≈ 30 cm   30 g ≈ 1 ounce
8 km ≈ 5 miles   1 gallon ≈ 4.5 litres

'≈' means 'is approximately equal to'

Divide or multiply by the appropriate number shown above.

(a) 3 feet ≈ 90 cm   (b) 11 pounds ≈ 5 kg   (c) 3 gallons ≈ 13.5 litres
    × 30   ÷ 2.2   × 4.5

Exercise 2E

1 Danny puts 8 gallons of petrol into his car. *Roughly* how many litres of petrol did Danny put into his car?

Copy and complete questions **2** to **10**

2 4 kg ≈ ☐ pounds

3 10 gallons ≈ ☐ litres

4 16 km ≈ ☐ miles

5 8 inches ≈ ☐ cm

6 44 pounds ≈ ☐ kg

7 3 m ≈ ☐ feet

8 30 miles ≈ ☐ km

9 90 g ≈ ☐ ounces

10 5 feet 4 inches ≈ ☐ cm

11 Copy each sentence and choose the number which is the best estimate.
   (a) The Prime Minister is about [1 m, 6 feet, 8 feet] tall.
   (b) A can of coke contains about [350 ml, 2 litres, 10 ml].
   (c) The perimeter of a classroom is about [30 m, 6 m, $\frac{1}{10}$ mile].
   (d) The width of one of my fingers is about [1 mm, 5 mm, 10 mm].
   (e) A bag of crisps weighs about [25 g, 500 g, 1 pound].

12 Suppose you have just won a prize which is one million grams of gold! Which of the following would you need to take away your prize?
   (a) A large suitcase
   (b) A van
   (c) A very large delivery lorry

13 The maximum height limit for children on a bouncy castle is 4 feet 6 inches. Julie is 132 cm tall. Is Julie inside the limit? Justify your answer.

14 Phil has cycled 24 km from his house. His total journey will be 19 miles. How many *more* miles does he have to cycle?

15 Rosa needs 2 gallons of petrol. Roughly how much will it cost if petrol costs £1.38 per litre?

16 A restaurant needs 9 kg of potatoes for one evening. It has 20 pounds of potatoes. Will the restaurant have enough potatoes? Justify your answer.

17 Keita's mother buys him a pair of trousers with waist size 86 cm.
Keita's waist measures 34 inches. Do the trousers fit Keita? Justify your answer.

18 Which shape opposite has the longer perimeter and by how much?

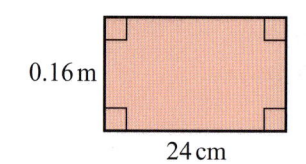

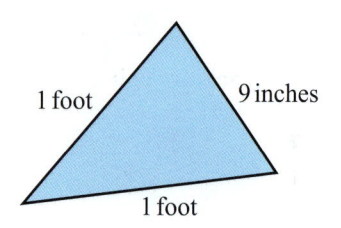

0.16 m
24 cm
1 foot
9 inches
1 foot

19 Which is longer: 1 yard or 1 metre? Explain your answer fully.

20 Amelia uses £44.73 of petrol on a journey.
If petrol costs £1.42 per litre, how many gallons of petrol did Amelia use?

Changing units

When a problem has quantities measured in different units the first thing you must do is change some of the units so that all quantities are in the same units.

1.5 m   80 cm

(a) Find the area of the rectangular table top shown.
Write 80 cm as 0.8 m.
Area of table = 1.5 × 0.8
            = 1.2 m²

(b) A piece of metal weighing 3 kg is melted down and cast into small cubes each weighing 40 g.
How many cubes can be made?
Write 3 kg as 3000 g.
Number of cubes = 3000 ÷ 40
               = 75

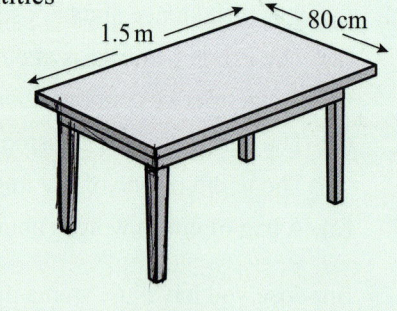

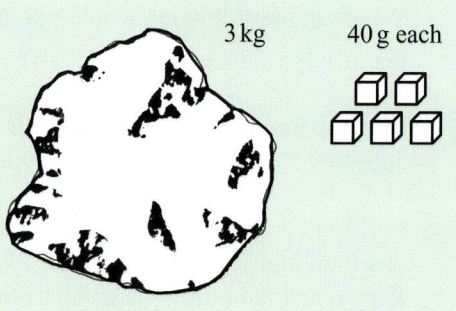

3 kg   40 g each

A *very* common error occurs where the units of an area are changed.

Here is a square of side 1 m.   Area = 1 m²

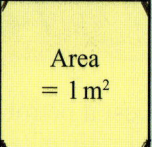

The same square has sides of 100 cm.   Area = 10 000 m²

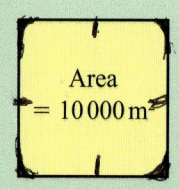

We see that 1 m² = 10 000 cm² [NOT 100 cm²!]

Exercise 3M

You may use a calculator in this exercise.

1. A piece of gold weighing 0.9 kg is melted down and cast into tiny coins each weighing 180 mg. How many coins can be made?

2. An urn containing 45 litres of water is used to fill cups of capacity 150 ml. How many cups can be filled?

3. A large lump of 'playdoh' weighing 2.1 kg is cut up into 300 identical pieces. Find the weight of each piece in grams.

4. Polly buys 3 bags of sugar weighing 0.6 kg each, a tube of toothpaste weighing 225 g and 12 packets of crisps each weighing 25 g. Find the total weight of these items in kg.

5. Find the area of each shape in m^2.
   (a) 3.4 m, 10 cm
   (b) 0.8 m, 20 cm
   (c) 90 cm, 4 m, 70 cm, 5 m

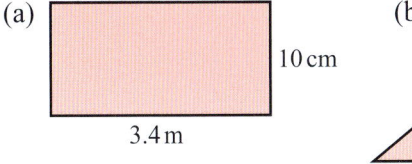

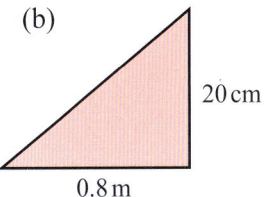

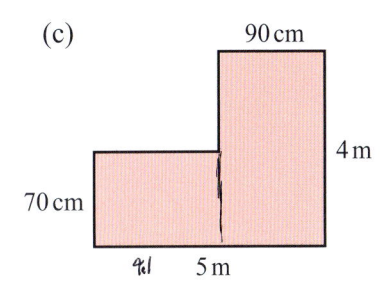

6. Water is leaking from a tap at a rate of 1.3 cm^3 per second. How many litres of water will leak from the tap in one day?

7. Every face of the rectangular block shown is painted. The tin of paint used contains enough paint to cover an area of 10 m^2. How many blocks can be painted completely?

30 cm, 50 cm, 25 cm

8. Matt has 4 pounds of butter. He buys another 750 g of butter. He needs 3 kg of butter. How much more butter does he need?

9. The diagram shows the outline of a strip of farmland.
   (a) Calculate the area of the field in hectares
       [1 hectare = 10 000 m²]
   (b) The field is sprayed with a pesticide and it takes 3 seconds to spray 100 m². How many hours will it take to spray the entire field?

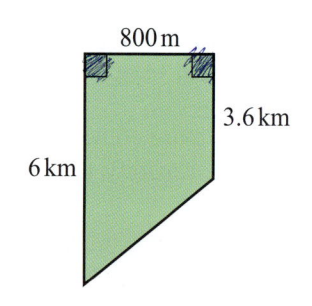

10. Steve runs 800 m in $2\frac{1}{2}$ minutes. Seb runs 1500 m in 4 minutes 30 seconds. Who is the quicker runner? Explain your answer fully.

Need more practice with metric and imperial units?

1. Elena has 375 m of a 3 km race still to run. Bella has run 2.12 km of the race. How far ahead of Bella is Elena?

2. A company uses 1.36 tonnes of gravel during a job. How many kilograms of gravel remain if the company started with 3 tonnes?

3. Which are larger?
   (a) 4 feet or 50 inches
   (b) 6 yards or 16 feet
   (c) 8 stones or 115 pounds
   (d) 5 pounds or 84 ounces
   (e) 28 pints or 3.5 gallons
   (f) 5 stones 7 pounds or 75 pounds

4. Carson is 5 feet 9 inches tall. Molly is slightly shorter at 170 cm. How much taller is Carson?

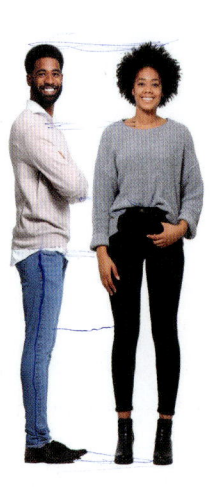

5. A rectangle measures 35 cm by 2 m. Penny says the area is 70 cm². Explain what mistake she has made.

6 A cake requires 175 g of mixed fruit. How many kilograms of mixed fruit are needed to make 12 cakes?

7 Hugo weighs 14 stones 13 pounds. During one month he loses 4 kg on a diet. How much does he now weigh?

8 When full, the large jar opposite contains 0.6 litres of liquid and the smaller jar contains 450 ml. 45 full large jars are emptied into the smaller jars.
How many smaller jars are filled up?

9 Some friends share the cost of petrol on a journey.
A litre of petrol cost £1.47 and they use 12 gallons.
Julia pays $\frac{5}{6}$ of the total cost. How much does she pay?

10 A mother gives birth to twins each weighing $5\frac{1}{2}$ pounds.
What is their total weight in kg?

Extension questions with metric and imperial units

1 A boxer must weigh no more than 10 stones just before his fight.
With two days to go he weighs 65 kg.
Roughly how much weight in pounds does he have to lose to get down to the 10 stone limit?

2 Work out the volume of this cuboid.

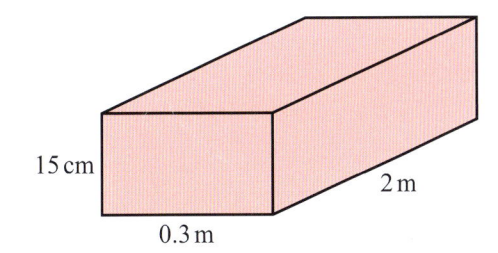

15 cm
2 m
0.3 m

3 Put these amounts in order starting with the largest.
(a) 0.55 m, 7 inches, 16 cm, 2 feet, 50 cm
(b) 0.4 kg, 1.1 pound, 0.48 kg, 9 ounces, 450 g

4 Grass seed should be sown at the rate of $\frac{2}{3}$ of an ounce per square yard. One packet of seed contains 3 pounds (lb) of seed. How many packets of seed are needed for a rectangular garden measuring 54 feet by 30 feet? [3 feet = 1 yard, 16 ounces = 1 pound (lb)]

5 Which is larger and by how much: 4 miles or 63 000 inches?

6 A barrel contains 49.5 litres of beer. Pints of beer are drawn from the barrel. How many pints of beer does the barrel provide?

7 The waterfall with the greatest flow of water in the world is the 'Guaira' between Brazil and Paraguay. Its estimated average flow is 13 000 m³ per second. The dome of St Paul's Cathedral has a capacity of 7800 m³. How long would it take the waterfall to fill the dome?

8 A square has area 4 m². It is divided into little squares each of area 16 mm². How many little squares are there in total?

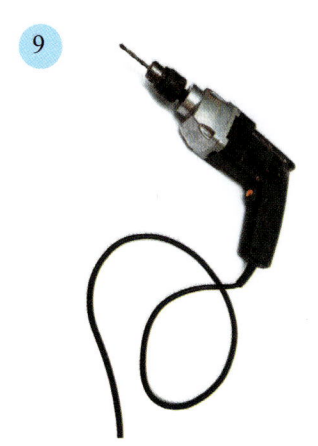

2 m

9 A carpenter requires a 12 mm drill for a certain job but he has only the imperial sizes $\frac{1}{4}$, $\frac{1}{2}$ and $\frac{3}{4}$ inch. Which of these drills is the closest in size to 12 mm?

10 Calculate the area of each shape in cm².

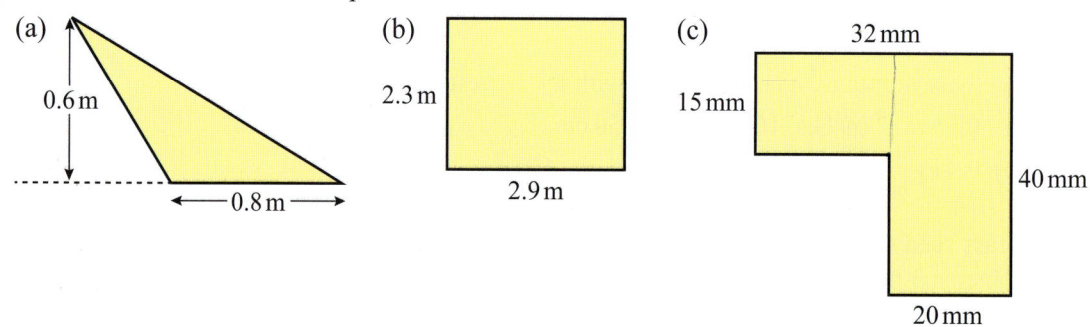

(a) 0.6 m, 0.8 m

(b) 2.3 m, 2.9 m

(c) 32 mm, 15 mm, 40 mm, 20 mm

6.2 Angles and constructions

In section 6.2 you will:
- review angle work from unit 2
- construct bisectors of lines and angles

Review of angle work

Exercise 1M

1. Write down the value of each angle listed below.
   (a) PR̂Q
   (b) TŜU
   (c) RP̂T
   (d) RT̂S
   (e) RŜT

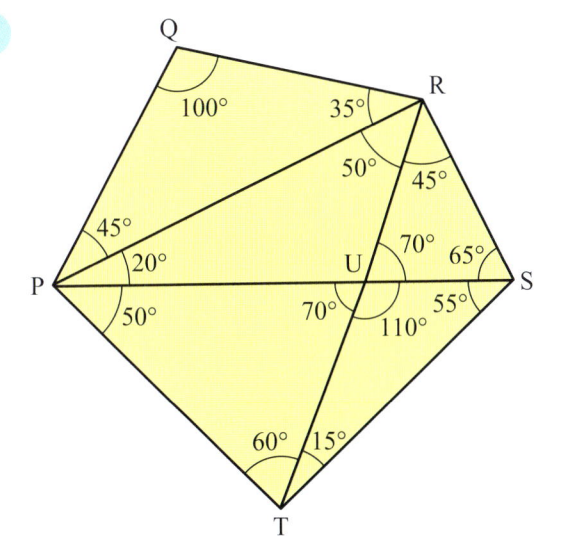

2. Use a protractor to draw the following angles accurately.
   (a) 65°   (b) 110°   (c) 170°   (d) 300°   (e) 73°   (f) 285°

3. Which angles in question 2 are *reflex*?

4. Find the angles marked with letters.

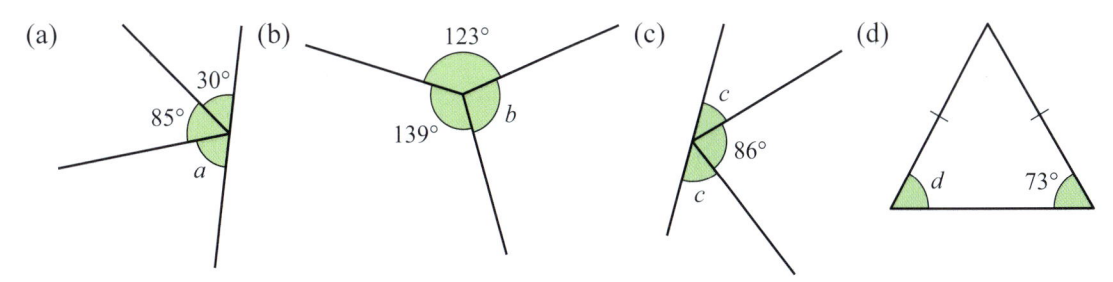

5 Find the angles marked with letters.

(a) 100°, a, b, c

(b) 75°, d, e

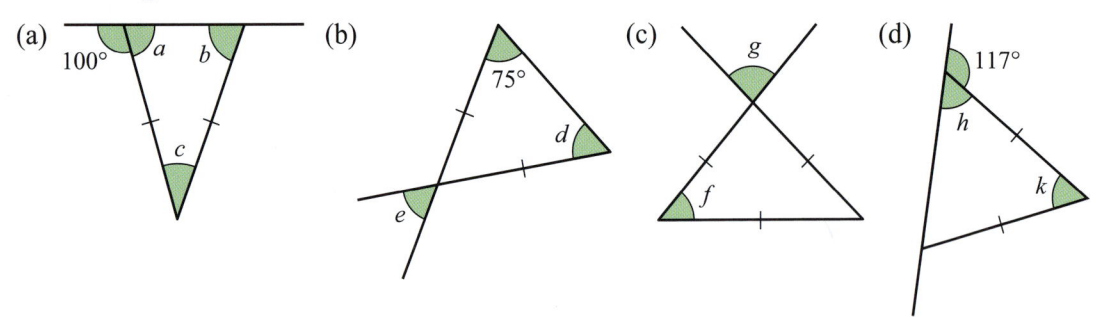

(c) g, f

(d) 117°, h, k

6 If you add together two acute angles, will the answer always be an obtuse angle? Give a reason for your answer.

7 If you add together two obtuse angles, will the answer always be a reflex angle. Explain your answer.

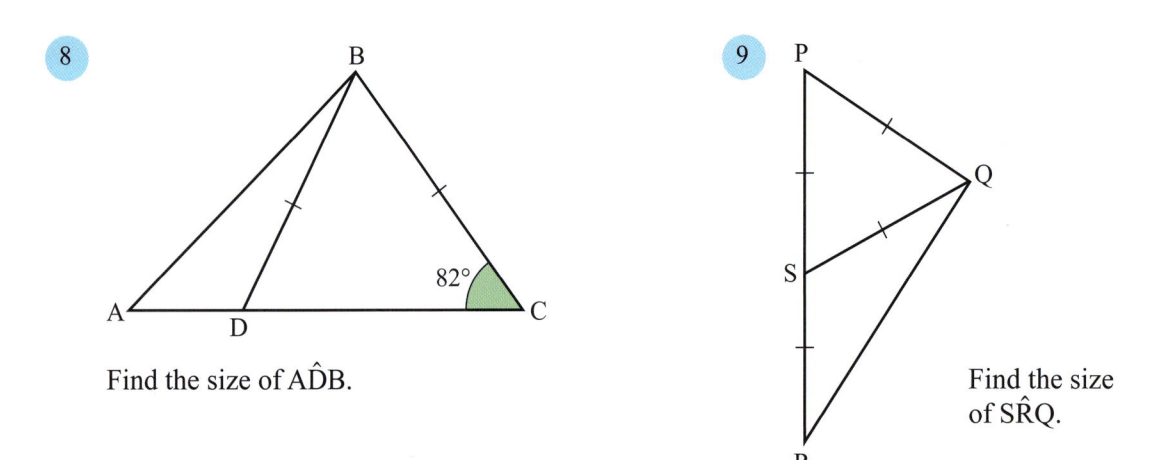

8
Find the size of AD̂B.
(Triangle with B at top, A and C at base, D on AC; angle at C = 82°)

9
Find the size of SR̂Q.
(Figure with points P, Q, S, R)

Exercise 2M

Find the angles marked with letters.

1 b, 85°, a

2 c, d, 48°, 36°, e

3 f, 153°, 106°, 74°

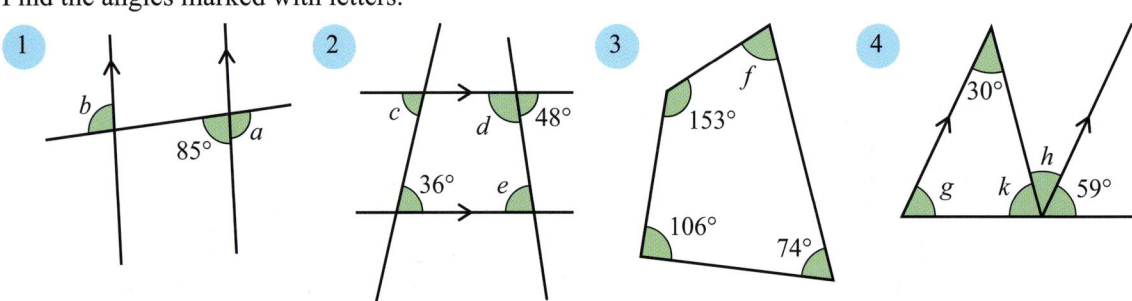

4 30°, g, k, h, 59°

5

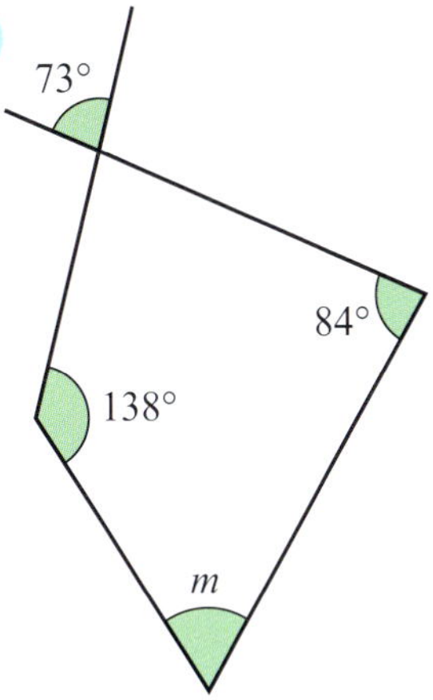

6

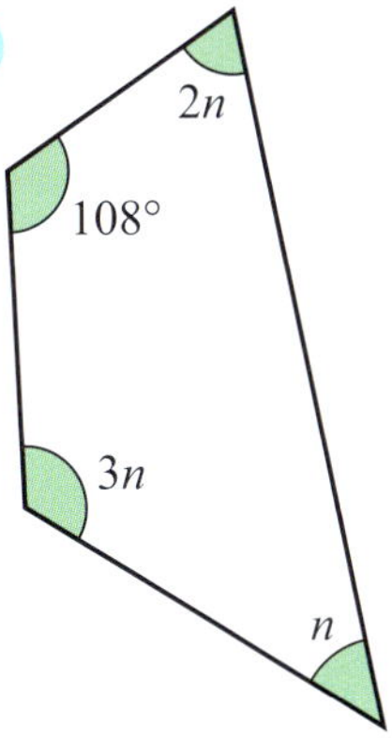

7

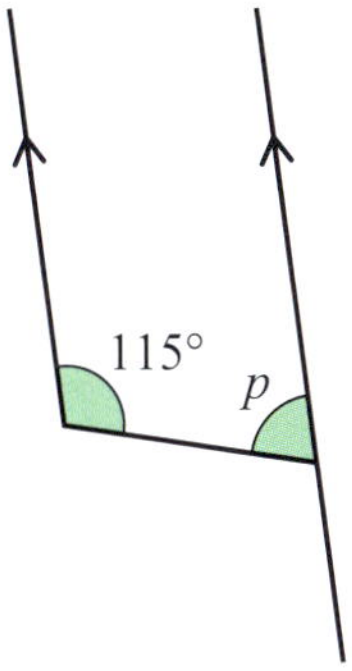

8

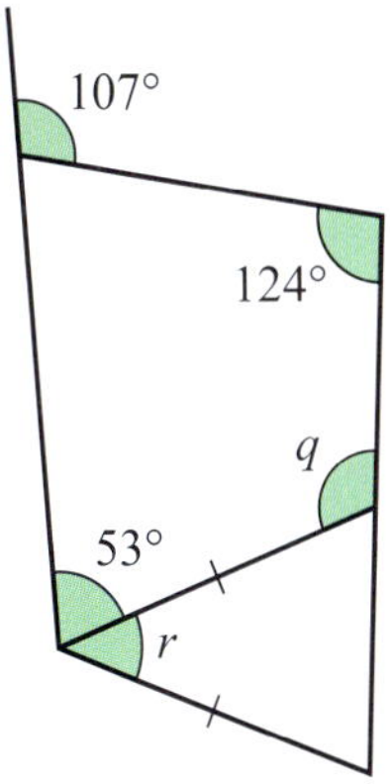

9

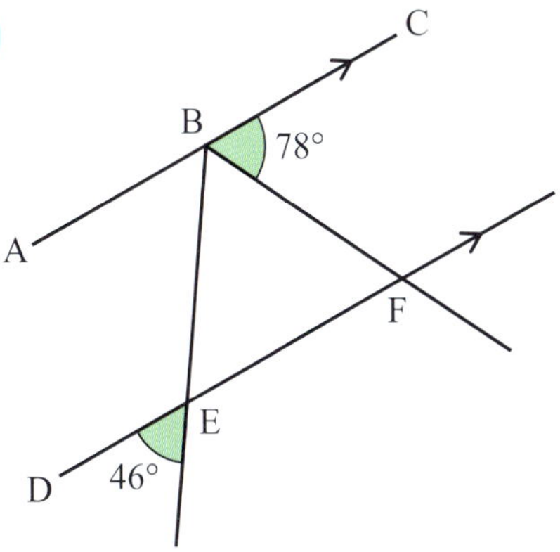

Find the size of EB̂F.

10

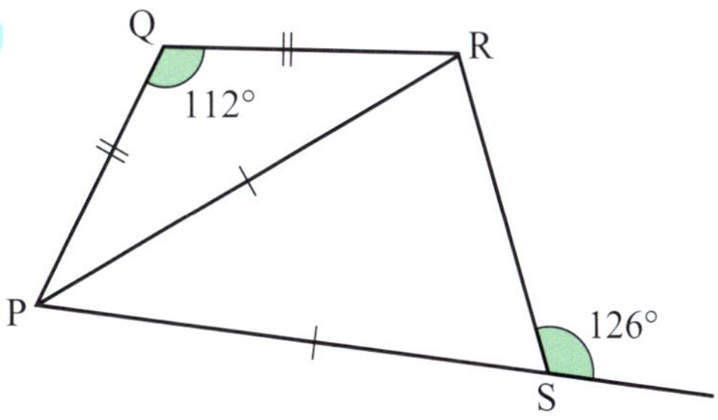

Find the size of QP̂S.

11 In the diagram KL is parallel to NM and LJ = LM.
Calculate the size of angle JLM.

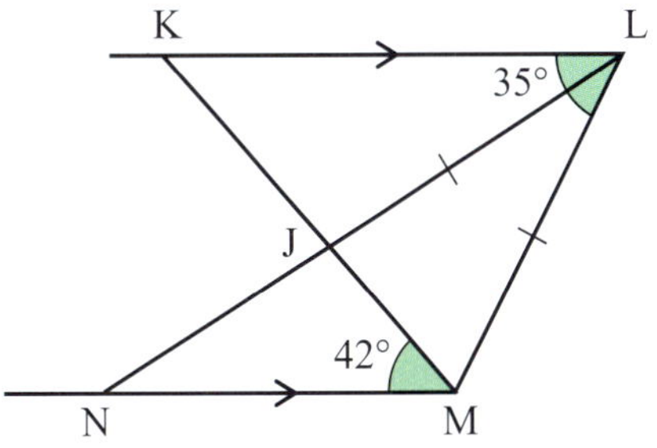

12 The diagram shows a series of isosceles triangles drawn between two lines.
Find the value of x.

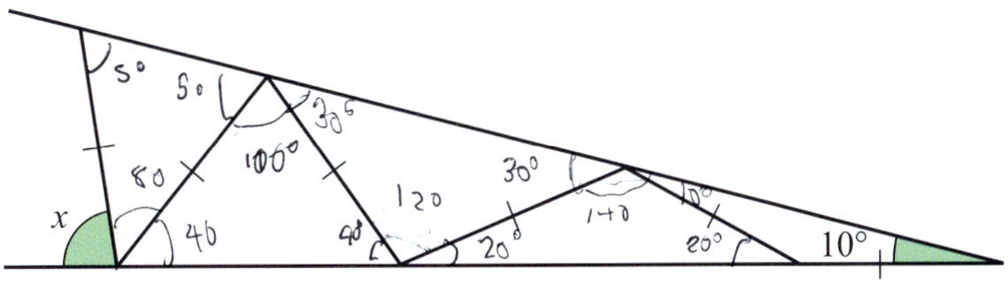

Constructing bisectors

Perpendicular bisector
Draw a line AB 8 cm long.

Set the pair of compasses to more than 4 cm (half the line AB). Put the compass point on A and draw an arc as shown.

Put the compass point on B (DO NOT LET THE COMPASSES SLIP). Draw another arc as shown.

Draw a broken line as shown.

This broken line cuts line AB in half (bisects) and is at right angles to line AB (perpendicular).

The broken line is called the perpendicular bisector of line AB.

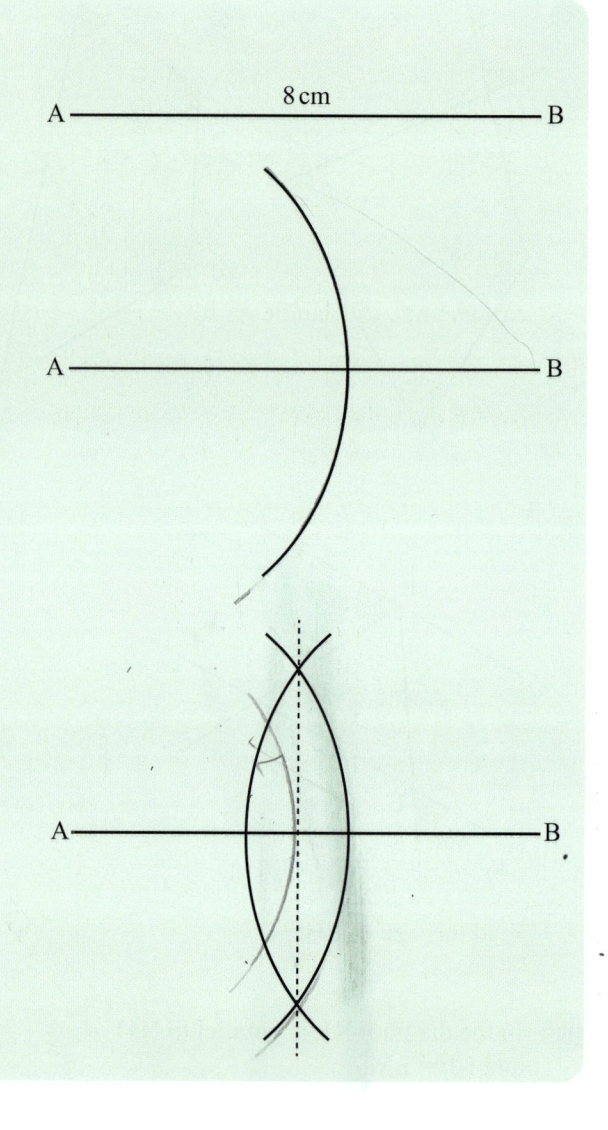

Exercise 3M

1. Draw a horizontal line AB of length 8 cm. Construct the perpendicular bisector of AB.

2. Draw a vertical line CD of length 6 cm. Construct the perpendicular bisector of CD.

3. Draw a vertical line EF of length 5 cm. Construct the perpendicular bisector of EF.

4. (a) Use a pencil, ruler and a pair of compasses only to construct the triangle ABC shown opposite.
   (b) Construct the perpendicular bisector of line AB.
   (c) Construct the perpendicular bisector of line AC.

   If done accurately, your two lines from (b) and (c) should cross exactly on the line BC.

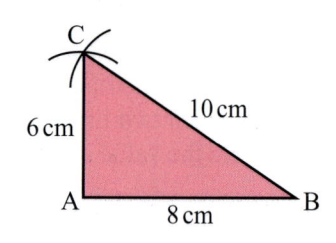

5. Draw any triangle KLM and construct

   (a) the perpendicular bisector of KM
   (b) the perpendicular bisector of KL.
       Mark the point of intersection X.

   Take a pair of compasses and, with centre at X and radius KX, draw a circle through the points K, L and M. This is the circumcircle of triangle KLM.

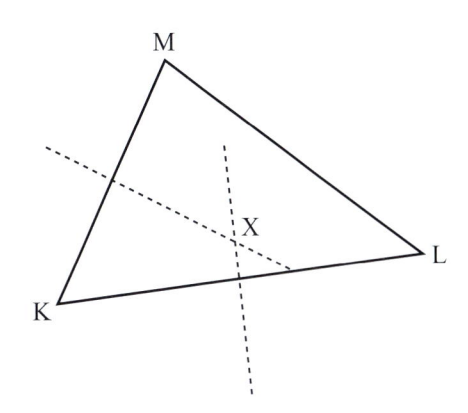

   Repeat the construction for another triangle of different shape.

Bisector of an angle

Draw any angle as shown.

Put the compass point on A and draw an arc as shown.

Put the compass point on P and draw an arc as shown.
Put the compass point on Q and draw an arc as shown.

Draw a broken line as shown.

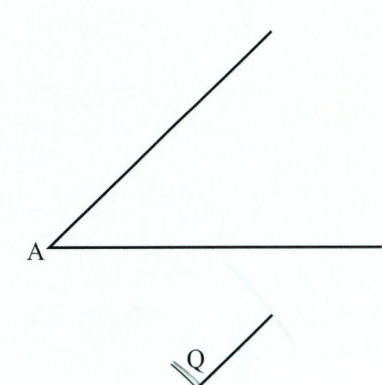

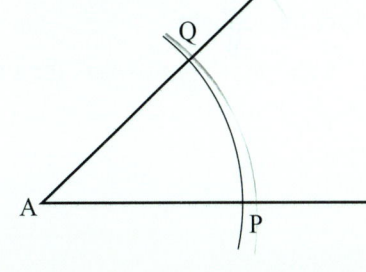

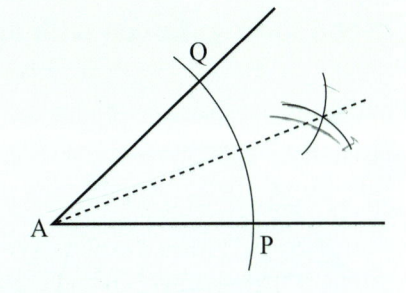

This broken line cuts the angle in half (bisects).

This broken line is called the angle bisector.

Exercise 4M

1. Draw an angle of 60°. Construct the bisector of the angle (use a protractor to measure the angles to check that you have drawn the angle bisector accurately).

2. Draw an angle of 40°. Construct the bisector of the angle.

3. Draw an angle of 130°. Construct the bisector of the angle.

4. Draw an angle of 50°. Construct the bisector of the angle.

5. Draw any triangle ABC and then construct the bisectors of angles A, B and C. If done accurately the three bisectors should all pass through one point.

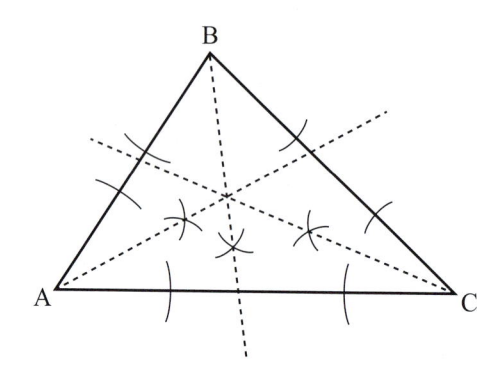

6. Draw any triangle ABC and construct the bisectors of angles B and C to meet at point Y. With centre at Y draw a circle which just touches the sides of the triangle. This is the inscribed circle of the triangle.

   Repeat the construction for a different triangle.

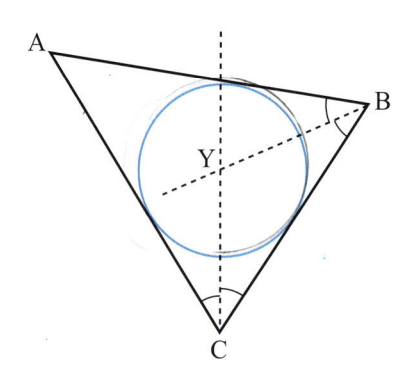

Need more practice with angles and constructions?

Find the angles marked with letters.

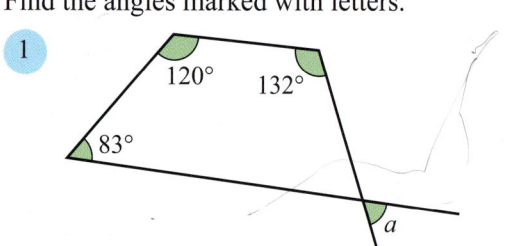

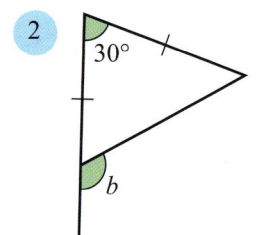

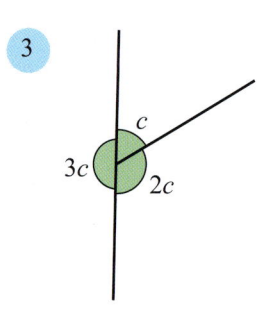

1. [diagram with angles 120°, 132°, 83°, and a]

2. [diagram with angle 30° and b]

3. [diagram with angles c, $3c$, $2c$]

4 An obtuse angle is subtracted from a reflex angle to give an acute angle. Suggest a value for each of these angles.

5 Draw any line and construct its perpendicular bisector.

6 Use a ruler and compasses only to construct the triangle shown opposite.

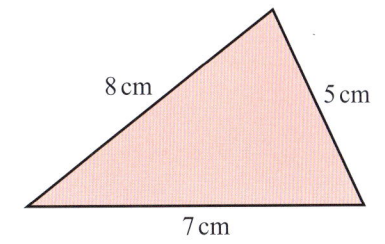

7 (a) Construct a triangle with sides 6 cm, 5.5 cm and 6.5 cm.
(b) Construct the perpendicular bisector of each side.
(c) Comment on the point where the three perpendicular bisectors intersect each other.

8 Work out the value of $A\hat{B}C$ opposite. Give full reasons for your answer.

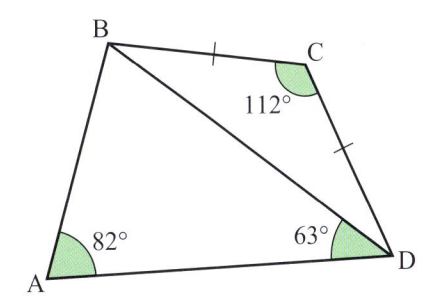

9 Use a protractor to draw an angle of 70° then construct the angle bisector. Check each angle is 35°.

10 An isosceles triangle has an angle of 40° in it. What are the possible values of the other two angles? Could there be a different set of answers? If so, give their values.

Extension questions with angles and constructions

Find the angles marked with letters.

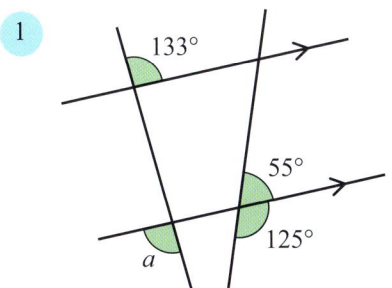

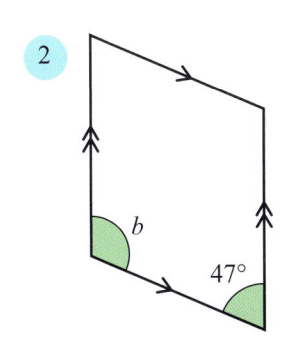

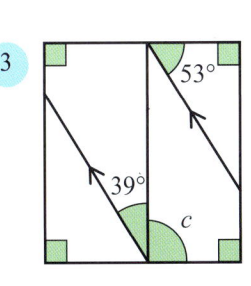

4 A rhombus has two angles, each equal to 116°. Write down the values of the other two angles.

5 (a) Construct triangle PQR shown opposite.
(b) Construct the angle bisector of QP̂R.
(c) Use a protractor to measure one of the smaller angles made in part (b).

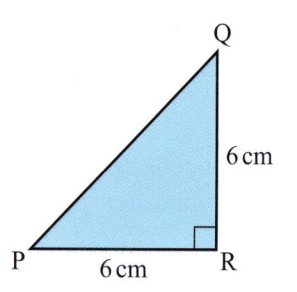

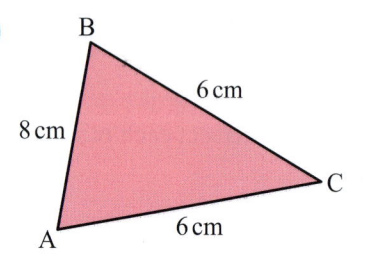

6 (a) Construct triangle ABC shown opposite.
(b) Construct the perpendicular bisector of side AB.
(c) What do you notice if you make the perpendicular bisector longer?

7 SQ = SR in the diagram opposite. Work out the value of PQ̂R.

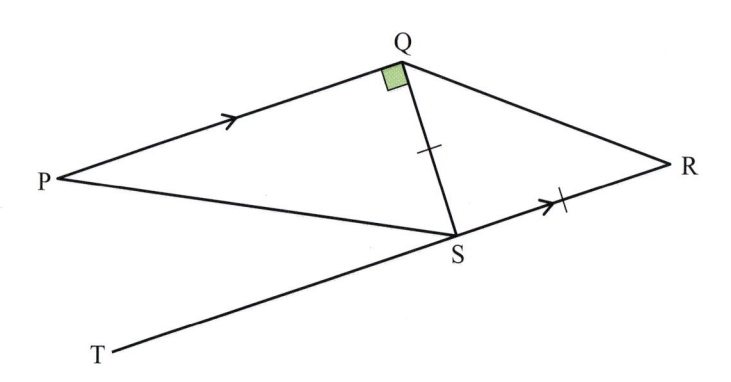

8 Use the diagram opposite to explain why the angles in a quadrilateral add up to 360°.

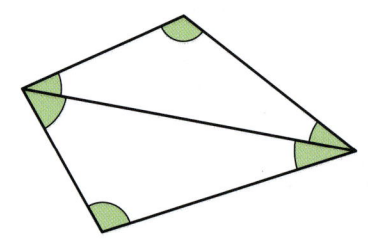

9 Use a ruler and compasses only to construct an angle of 30° (hint: construct an equilateral triangle first).

10 (a) Copy the line and dot opposite.

(b) Can you find a way of using a ruler and compasses only to construct a 90° angle with the line at the dot (hint: make use of a perpendicular bisector)?

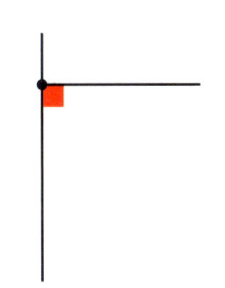

CHECK YOURSELF ON SECTIONS 6.1 AND 6.2

1 Converting metric units

Copy and complete

(a) 7.65 km = ☐ m

(b) 0.4 m = ☐ cm

(c) 7500 ml = ☐ litres

2 Converting imperial units

Copy and complete

(a) $\frac{1}{2}$ pound = ☐ ounces

(b) $2\frac{3}{4}$ gallons = ☐ pints

(c) 72 inches = ☐ feet

3 Converting between metric and imperial units

(a) Ed is 6 feet tall. Mo is 1.75 m tall. Roughly how many cm is Ed taller than Mo?

(b) Jade fills her car with 12 gallons of petrol, costing her £57.24. How much per litre did the petrol cost?

4 Changing units for some problems

(a) Which rectangle has the larger area and by how much?

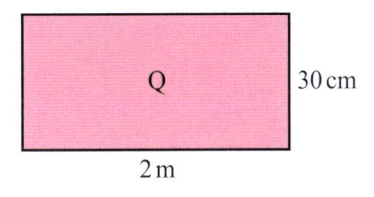

P: 70 cm by 0.9 m

Q: 30 cm by 2 m

(b) In a forest a young tree grows at a constant rate of 18 cm per day. How much in mm does it grow in one minute?

(c) Some lemonade bottles contain $2\frac{1}{2}$ litres each. A glass contains 225 ml when full. How many glasses can be filled completely from 81 bottles?

5 Review of angle work from unit 2

Find the angles marked with letters.

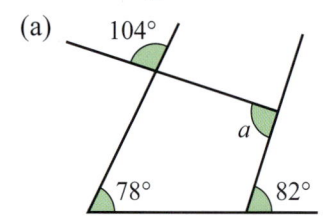

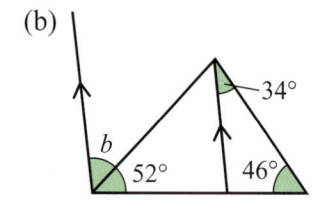

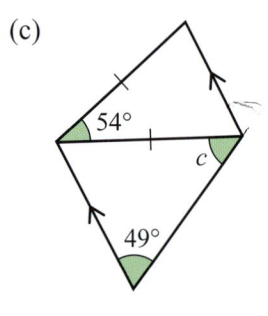

(a) 104°, 78°, 82°, angle a

(b) 34°, 52°, 46°, angle b

(c) 54°, 49°, angle c

6 Constructing bisectors

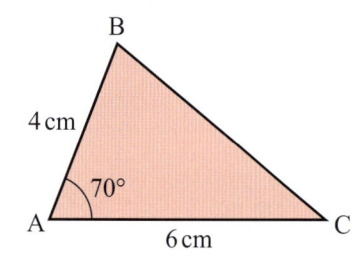

Triangle with AB = 4 cm, angle A = 70°, AC = 6 cm.

Use a ruler and protractor to draw this triangle accurately. Construct the perpendicular bisector of AC and the angle bisector of angle A. Mark with a P the point where the two bisectors meet. Measure and write down the length of AP.

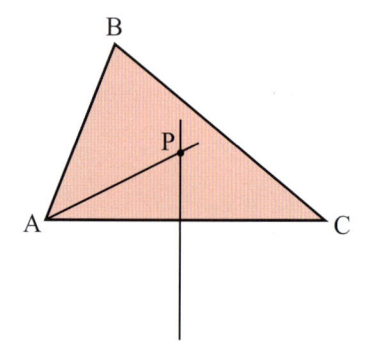

6.3 Circles

In section 6.3 you will learn how to:

- find the circumference of a circle
- find the area of a circle

Activity

Find 8 circular objects (tins, plates, buckets, wheels etc.) For each object, measure the diameter and the circumference and write the results in a table. Use a flexible tape measure for the circumference or wrap a piece of string around the object and then measure the string with a ruler. For each pair of readings, work out the ratio (*circumference ÷ diameter*).

You should find that the number in the $\frac{c}{d}$ column is about the same each time. Work out the mean value of the 8 numbers in the $\frac{c}{d}$ column.

Object	Circumference c	diameter d	$\frac{c}{d}$
Tin of tuna	28.6 cm	8.8 cm	3.25
...			
...			

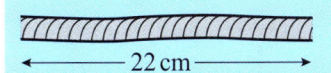

←—— 22 cm ——→

A piece of string 22 cm long will make:

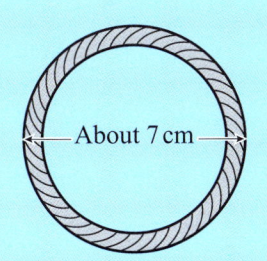

About 7 cm

A circle whose diameter is just over 7 cm.

If you divide the circumference of a circle by its diameter the number you obtain is always just over three.

Which means $\qquad \dfrac{\text{circumference}}{\text{diameter}} \approx 3$

Circumference $\approx 3 \times$ diameter

This provides a fairly good *estimate* for the circumference of any circle.

Pi

For any circle, the exact value of the ratio $\left(\dfrac{\text{circumference}}{\text{diameter}}\right)$ is a number denoted by the Greek letter π.

Since $\dfrac{\text{circumference}}{\text{diameter}} = \pi$ we can write

Circumference $= \pi \times$ diameter   Learn this formula.

Most calculators have a $\boxed{\pi}$ button, which will give the value of π correct to at least 7 significant figures: 3.141593.

Find the circumference of the circle.

Radius = 4 cm, so diameter = 8 cm

Circumference = $\pi \times 8$

$= 25.13274123 \ldots$ cm

$= 25.1$ cm correct to one decimal place

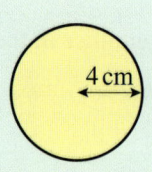

Exercise 1M

1. Calculate the circumference of each circle.
   Give each answer correct to one decimal place.

   (a) 50 cm
   (b) 37 m
   (c) 68 km
   (d) 10 cm

2. A circular mirror has diameter 60 cm. Work out its circumference, correct to one decimal place.

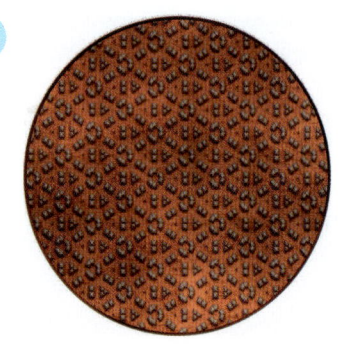

3. The radius of the manhole cover is 36 cm. Calculate its circumference and give your answer correct to the nearest cm.

4. On an army range a circle of diameter 6 km is 'out of bounds' to all personnel. Calculate the circumference of this circle.

5. Terri is decorating a box in the shape of a cylinder. She wants to put ribbon around the edges of the two circles at each end. The radius of each circle is 12 cm.
   Terri has 1.4 m of ribbon.
   Will she have enough ribbon?
   Explain your answer fully.

6 Tim walks his dog three times around a circular lake of radius 160 m. How far does he walk? Give the answer in kilometres.

7 Which shape below has the greater perimeter and by how much?

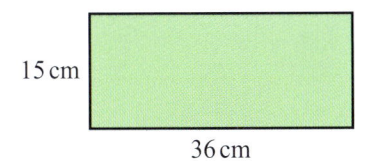

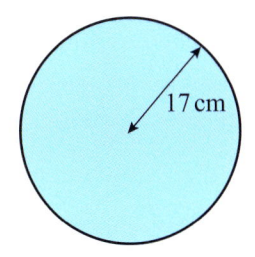

15 cm
36 cm

17 cm

8 The minute hand on a clock is 9 cm long. How far does the end of the minute hand travel in 15 minutes?

9 Calculate the perimeter of the semi-circle opposite.

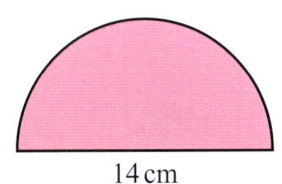

14 cm

10

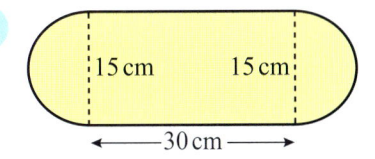

15 cm   15 cm
30 cm

The shape opposite is made from two semi-circles and a rectangle. Calculate the perimeter of the shape.

Area of a circle

(a) The circle below is divided into 12 equal sectors.

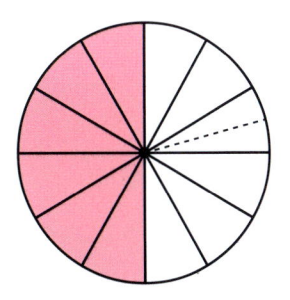

(b) The sectors are cut and arranged to make a shape which is nearly a rectangle (one sector is cut in half).

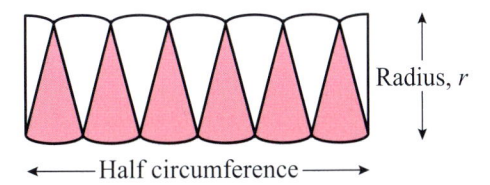

Radius, r

Half circumference

(c) The approximate area can be found as follows:
length of rectangle ≈ half circumference of circle

$$\approx \frac{\pi \times 2r}{2}$$

$$\approx \pi r$$

width of rectangle ≈ r

∴ area of rectangle ≈ $\pi r \times r$

$$\approx \pi r^2$$

If larger and larger numbers of sectors were used, this approximation would become more and more accurate.

This is a demonstration of an important result.

Area of a circle = πr^2 *Learn* this formula.

Note: πr^2 means $\pi(r^2)$ i.e. π multiplied by r^2

Find the area of each shape.

(a) 26 cm

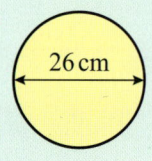

radius = 13 cm

area = πr^2

= 530.9 cm² (1 d.p.)

(b) ←3.2 cm→

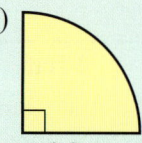

The shape is a quarter circle

area = $\dfrac{\pi (3.2)^2}{4}$

= 8.0 cm² (1 d.p.)

Exercise 2M

1. Calculate the area of each circle and give your answer correct to one decimal place.

(a) 11 mm   (b) 12 cm   (c) 20 m   (d) 13 cm

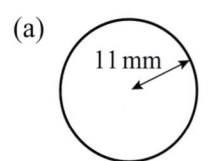

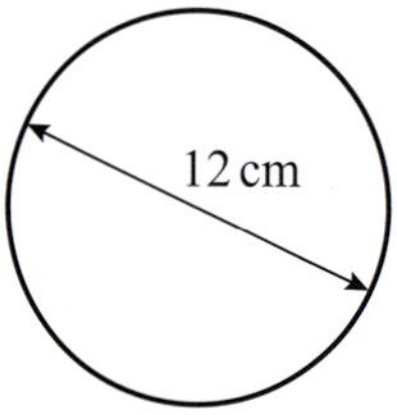

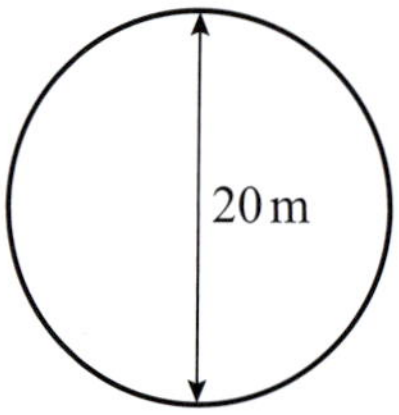

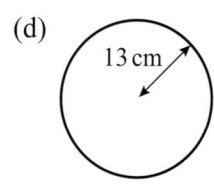

2. The dart board shown has a diameter of 53 cm. Calculate the area of the dart board.

3. Work out the area of a circular lawn which has a radius of 4.2 m.

4. The top of a mixing bowl is a circle with diameter 33 cm. Find the area of this circle.

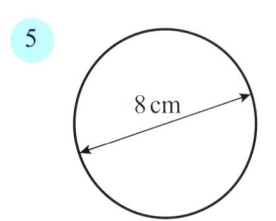

5. Nisha calculates the area of the circle opposite and gets the answer 201.1 cm². Explain clearly what mistake Nisha has made.

8 cm

6. Write the shapes below in order of area size, starting with the largest.

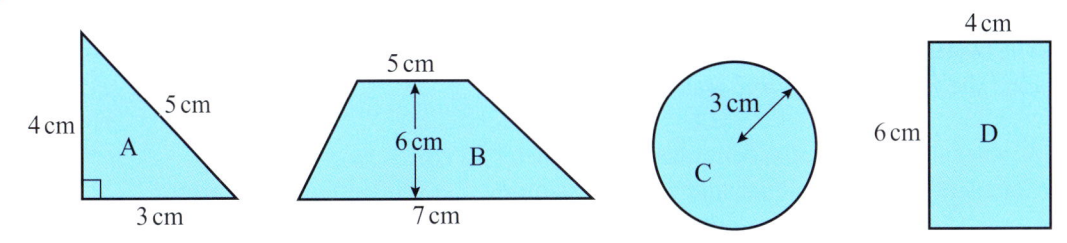

A: triangle with sides 4 cm, 5 cm, 3 cm
B: trapezium with parallel sides 5 cm and 7 cm, height 6 cm
C: circle with radius 3 cm
D: rectangle 4 cm by 6 cm

7. Calculate the area of each shape, giving each answer to one decimal place.

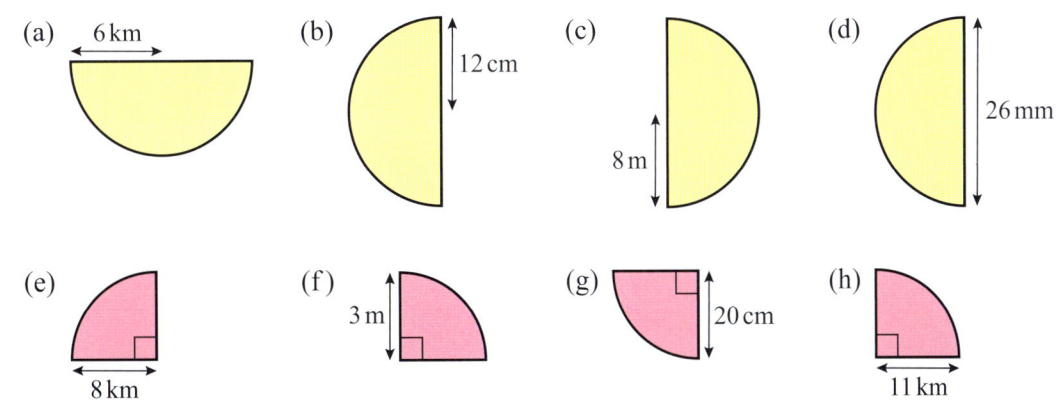

(a) semicircle, 6 km
(b) semicircle, 12 cm
(c) semicircle, 8 m
(d) semicircle, 26 mm
(e) quarter circle, 8 km
(f) quarter circle, 3 m
(g) quarter circle, 20 cm
(h) quarter circle, 11 km

Need more practice with circles?

1 Calculate (i) the circumference and (ii) the area of each circle.
Give each answer correct to one decimal place.

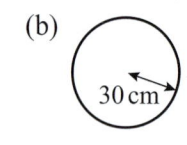

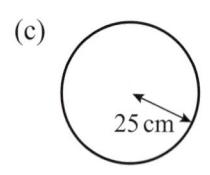

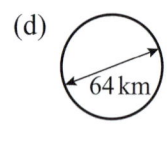

(a) 30 m   (b) 30 cm   (c) 25 cm   (d) 64 km

2 The head of a drawing pin is circular with radius 3.5 mm.
Find its circumference.

3 In the North Sea a circle of diameter 3 km is prohibited to all shipping because of sandbanks.
Calculate the circumference of this circle.

4 A top of a can has a diameter of 6.8 cm.
Calculate the circumference and area of the can top.

5 The centre island of a roundabout has radius 32 m.
Find the circumference and area of the island.

6 A water-lily leaf is almost circular with diameter 12 cm.
Calculate its circumference and area by assuming that it is perfectly circular.

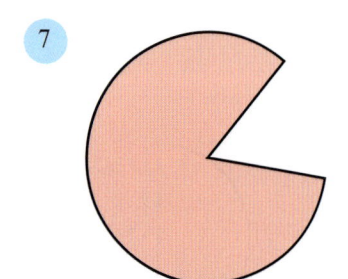

7 A circular pie has radius 14 cm.
Toni eats one sixth of the pie.
What is the area of the left over pie?

8 An artist paints a circular picture. If its radius is 20 cm,
what is its circumference and area?

9 The tyre of a bicycle has a piece of gum stuck to it.
The diameter of the tyre is 75 cm.
How far does the piece of gum move when the tyre makes one complete revolution?

10. A quarter of a 24 cm diameter pizza is cut and placed on a plate of radius 11 cm. Calculate the area of the plate that is not covered by the pizza.

Extension questions with circles

1. Calculate (i) the perimeter and (ii) the area of each shape. Give each answer correct to one decimal place.

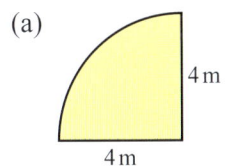

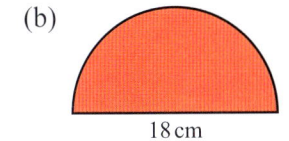

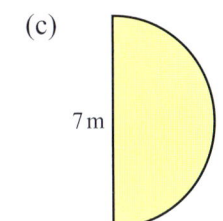

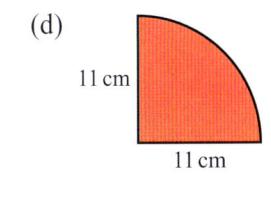

   (a) 4 m, 4 m

   (b) 18 cm

   (c) 7 m

   (d) 11 cm, 11 cm

2. A bike wheel has diameter 67 cm.
   (a) If the wheel turns one complete circle (a revolution), how far does the bike travel along the ground?
   (b) How many complete revolutions does the wheel make when the bike travels 1 km?

3. Calculate the shaded area shown opposite.

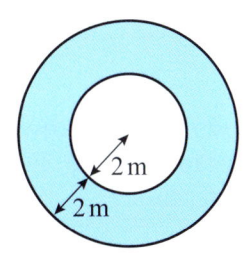

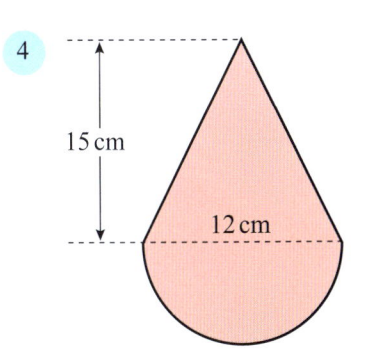

   2 m
   2 m

4. Work out the area of the shape shown opposite.

   15 cm
   12 cm

5 Lucy's bike wheels have diameter 68 cm and her sister's bike wheels have diameter 62 cm. They both cycle 500 m. How many more complete revolutions does her sister's bike do compared to Lucy's bike?

6 Circle A has radius 7 cm and circle B has diameter 28 cm. Write down the ratio of the area of circle A to the area of circle B.

7 Three holes of diameter 3 mm are cut from a circle of radius 3 cm. Calculate the remaining area inside the circle.

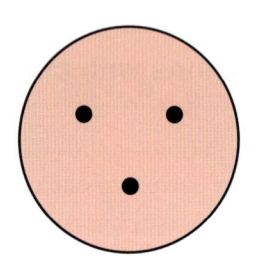

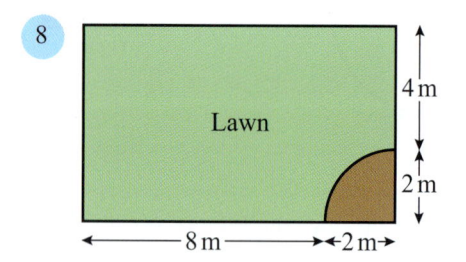

8 (a) Calculate the area of the lawn opposite.
(b) What percentage of the rectangular garden is lawn?

9 A circle has a circumference of 12.566 cm. Work out the diameter of the circle to one decimal place.

10 A bag of fertiliser costs £7.99 and covers 33 m². How much will it cost to cover the entire lawn shown opposite with fertiliser?

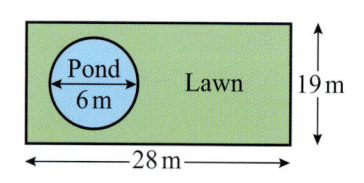

6.4 Three dimensional objects

In section 6.4 you will review how to:

- count faces, edges and vertices
- make shapes with nets

Faces, edges and vertices

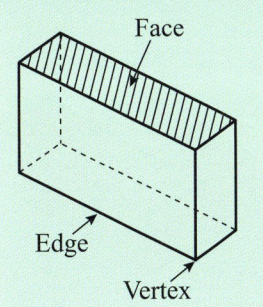

Many three-dimensional shapes have faces, edges and vertices.

'Vertices' is the plural of 'vertex'.

The *faces* of the cuboid are the flat surfaces on the shape.
A cuboid has 6 faces.

The *edges* of the cuboid are the lines where the faces meet.
A cuboid has 12 edges.

The *vertices* are where the edges meet at a point.
A cuboid has 8 vertices (corners).

Exercise 1M

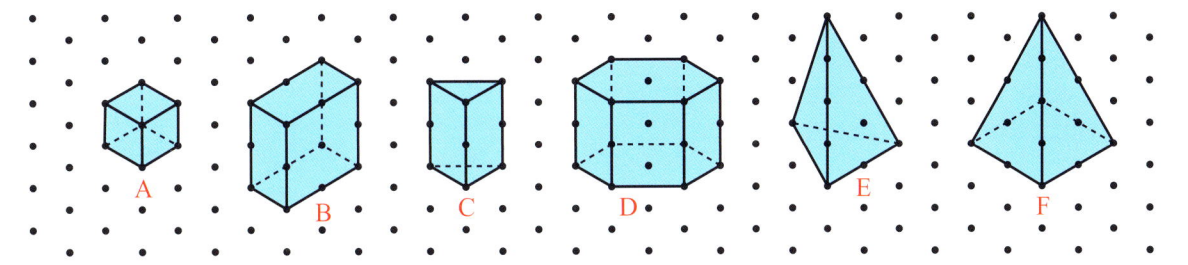

1. (a) For objects A to F, state the number of faces, edges and vertices. Write your answers in a table with columns for 'shape', 'faces', 'edges' and 'vertices'.

   (b) Try to find a connection between the number of faces, edges and vertices which applies to all the objects A to F.

2. Imagine a large cube which is cut in half along the dotted lines.
   Describe the two new solids formed.
   How many faces, edges and vertices does each solid have?

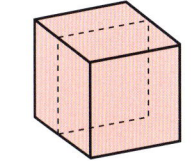

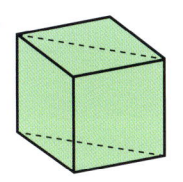

3. Suppose the same large cube is now cut in half along a different dotted line.
   Describe the two new solids formed.
   How many faces, edges and vertices does each solid have?

4. These diagrams show different solids when viewed from directly above. Describe what each solid could be. [There may be more than one correct response but you only have to give one.]

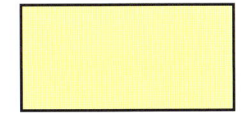

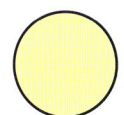

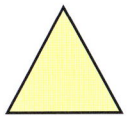

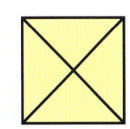

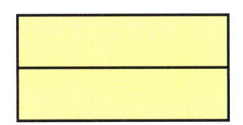

5 Describe two different ways in which you could cut a cylinder into two identical pieces. Describe and/or sketch the solids you would obtain in each case.

6 Here is an object made from four cubes.
   (a) Copy the drawing on isometric paper. (Make sure you have the paper the right way round.)
   (b) Make as many *different* objects as you can using four cubes. Draw each object on isometric paper.

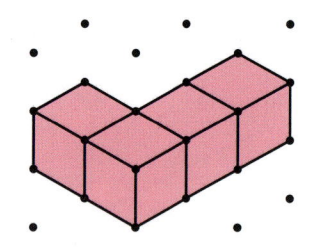

Nets for making shapes

- If the cube shown was made of cardboard, and you cut along some of the edges and laid it out flat, you would have a net of the cube. There is more than one net of a cube as you will see in the exercise below.

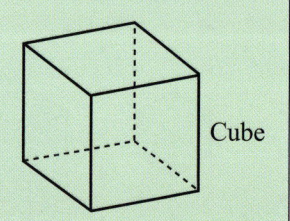

- To make a cube from card you need to produce the net shown below complete with the added 'tabs' for glueing purposes.

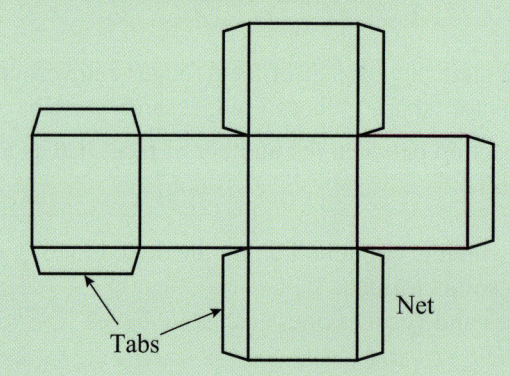

- In this section you will make several interesting 3D objects. You will need a pencil, ruler, scissors and either glue (Pritt Stick) or Sellotape.

Exercise 2M

1 Here are several nets which may or may not make cubes. Draw the nets on squared paper, cut them out and fold them to see which ones do make cubes.

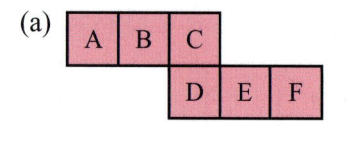

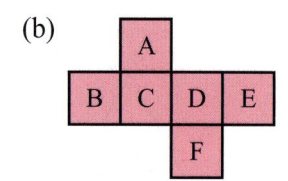

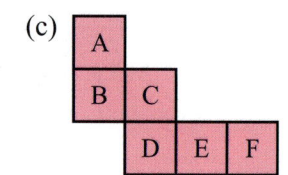

(a) A B C
         D E F

(b)   A
       B C D E
           F

(c) A
     B C
         D E F

(d)
A	B
	C	D
		E	F

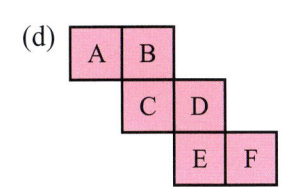

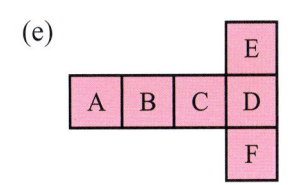

(e)
			E	
A	B	C	D
			F	

2 For the nets that *did* make cubes in question **1**, state which of the faces B, C, D, E or F was opposite face A on the cube.

3 Ask your teacher for cardboard. Use a ruler and compasses to construct this triangle in the middle of the cardboard. All lengths are in cm.

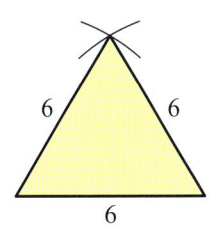

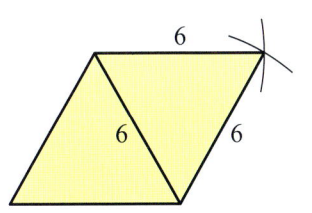

4 Use a ruler and compasses to construct this triangle joined to the first triangle.

5 Use a ruler and compasses to draw 2 more triangles joined to your first triangle.

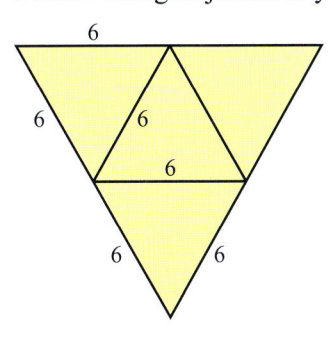

6 Draw on some flaps like this:

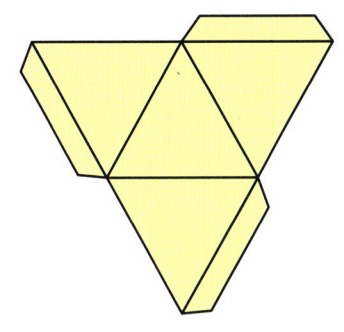

7 *Score* all the lines then cut out the net. Fold and glue to make a triangular pyramid (called a *tetrahedron*).

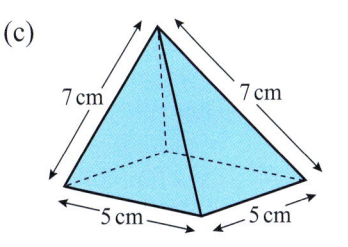

8 Draw accurately the nets for these three dimensional objects.

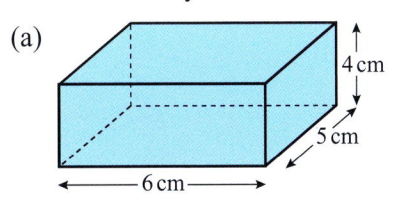

(a) 4 cm, 5 cm, 6 cm

(b) 5 cm, 3 cm, 4 cm, 7 cm

(c) 7 cm, 7 cm, 5 cm, 5 cm

Need more practice with three dimensional objects?

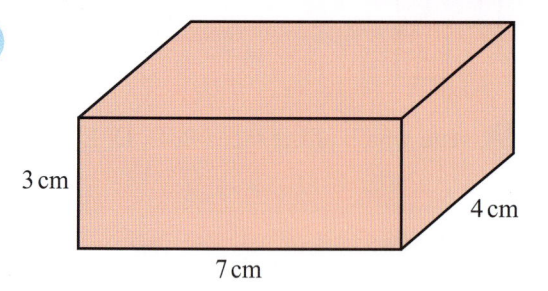

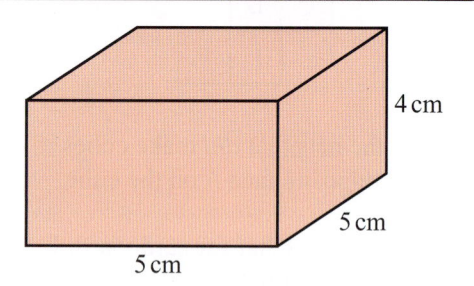

1

Draw a net for each cuboid then work out the difference between the areas of each net.

2 Suppose you cut off one corner from a cube. How many faces, edges and vertices has the remaining shape? How about the piece cut off?

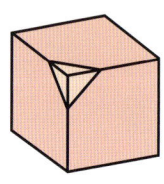

3 Draw a solid with 12 vertices, 8 faces and 18 edges.

4 Use triangle dotty paper. Draw each net then make the solid shown.
  (a) Octahedron (octa: eight; hedron: faces)
  (b) Icosahedron (an object with 20 faces)

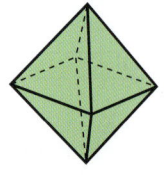

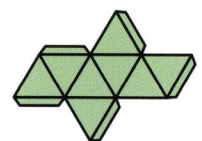

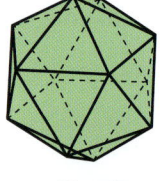

Extension questions with three dimensional objects

1 (More difficult) Here you are going to construct the net for a dodecahedron (12 faces). Take extra care with this one!

  (a) Draw a circle of radius 10 cm and construct a large pentagon using the 72° angles as shown. Draw the lines OA, OB, OC, OD, OE very faintly because it is best to rub them out as soon as we have found the positions for A, B, C, D, E.

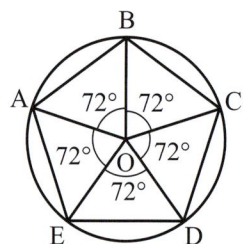

(b) Join A to C and A to D. Join B to E and B to D.
Join C to E. Mark the points V, W, X, Y, Z.

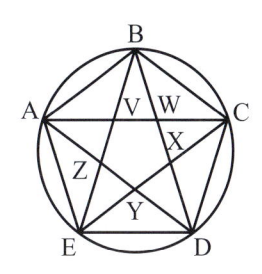

(c) Draw a line through Z and W.
Draw a line through V and X.
Draw a line through W and Y.
Draw a line through Z and X.
Draw a line through V and Y.

This pattern forms a series of regular pentagons.

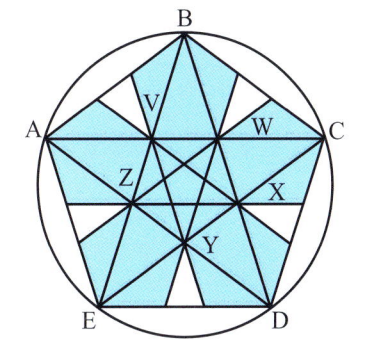

Draw the pattern of regular pentagons twice. *Remember to draw tabs before cutting out the net.* Join the two patterns of pentagons along the line PQ as shown.

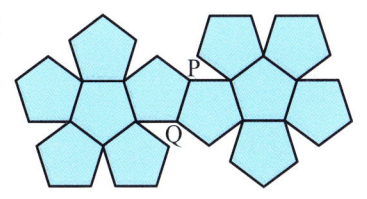

net: dodecahedron:

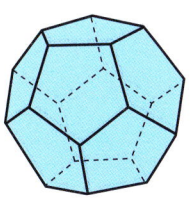

Try drawing accurately the nets shown in questions ② and ③ if you feel up to the challenge! Draw on tabs and make the solids.

② Cuboctahedron

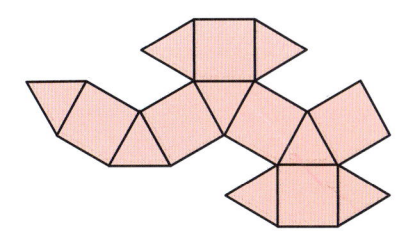

③ Truncated octahedron

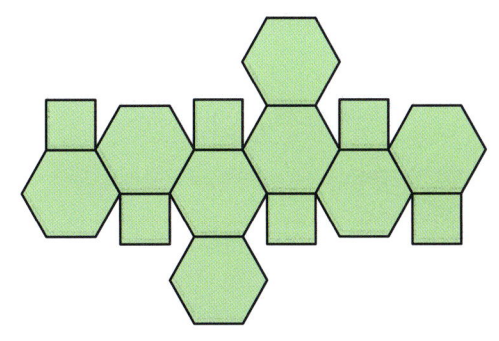

❌ Spot the mistakes 11 ❌

Units, angles, constructions, circles and three dimensional objects

Work through each question below and explain clearly what mistakes have been made. Beware – some questions are correctly done.

1 Find the area of the trapezium.

Solution: area $= \frac{1}{2}h(a + b)$

$= \frac{1}{2} \times 2 \times (30 + 60)$

$= 90 \text{ cm}^2$

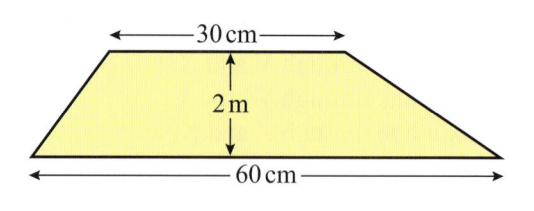

(Diagram: trapezium with top 30 cm, bottom 60 cm, height 2 m)

2 Calculate $B\hat{C}D$, giving full reasons for your answer.

(Diagram: triangle with A at top, D at bottom-left, B on segment DC, C at right. Angle at D (ADB) marked 116°, angle ABC marked 172°. Sides AD = AB marked with ×; BC = DC marked with #.)

Solution: $A\hat{B}D = \frac{1}{2}(180° - 116°)$ (isosceles triangle and angles in a triangle add up to 180°)

$= 32°$

$C\hat{B}D = 360° - (172° + 32°)$ (angles at a point add up to 360°)

$= 156°$

$B\hat{C}D = \frac{1}{2}(180° - 156°)$ (isosceles triangle and angles in a triangle add up to 180°)

$= 12°$

3 A nurse needs to convert a patient's weight from stones to kilograms. What is the weight in kilograms if the patient weighs 13 stones 5 pounds?

Answer: 13 stones 5 pounds $= 13 \times 16 + 5$

$= 213$ pounds

$= 213 \div 2.2$

$= 96.8$ kg (to 1 decimal place)

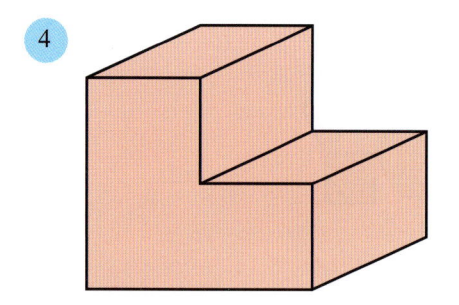

4 How many edges does this prism have?

Answer: 15

5 Calculate the area of the circle to 1 decimal place.

Answer: area $= \pi \times 12^2$
$= \pi \times 144$
$= 452.4$ cm² (to 1 decimal place)

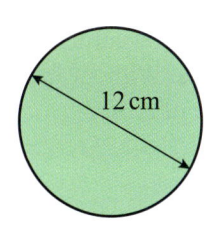

6 Draw a net for the triangular prism opposite.

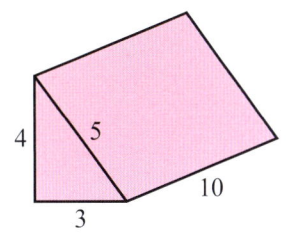

Answer:

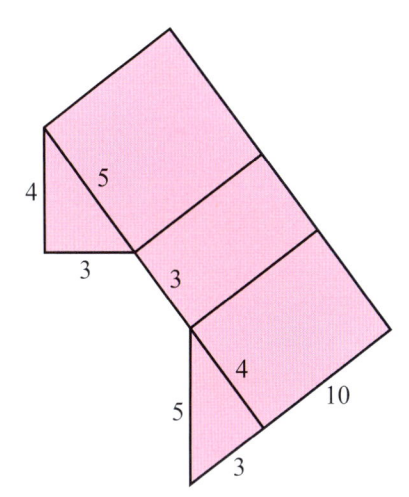

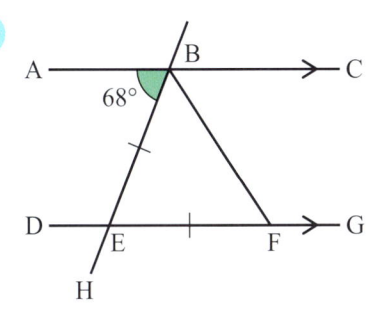

7 Find the value of BF̂E, giving full reasons for your answer.

Solution: BÊF = 68° (alternate angles)
BF̂E = 68° (isosceles triangle)

8 Find the area of a circle with radius 9 cm.
Give the answer to 1 decimal place.

Answer: area $= \pi \times 9^2$
$= 28.274^2$
$= 799.4$ cm² (to 1 decimal place)

9 Gemma does some constructions as shown opposite. Without measuring, what is the value of $A\hat{B}C$?

Answer: 45°

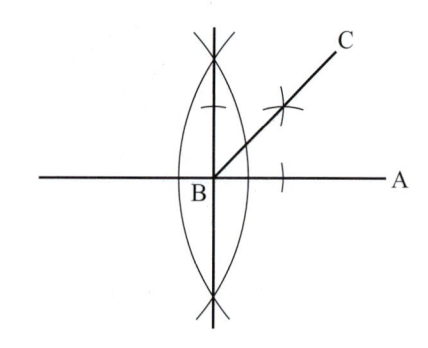

10

Work out the perimeter of this sector of a circle. Give the answer to 1 decimal place.

Solution: 60° is $\frac{1}{6}$ of 360°

so sector is $\frac{1}{6}$ of a circle

so curved length = $\frac{1}{6}$ of circumference

$= \frac{1}{6} \times \pi \times 8 = 4.2$ cm

Perimeter = 4.2 + 4 + 4 = 12.2 cm (to 1 decimal place)

CHECK YOURSELF ON SECTIONS 6.3 AND 6.4

1 Finding the circumference and area of a circle

(a) Find the circumference of each circle, correct to 1 decimal place.

(b) Find the area of each circle, correct to 1 decimal place.

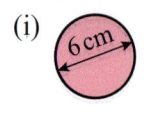

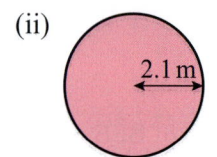

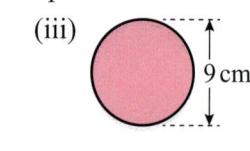

(i) 6 cm   (ii) 2.1 m   (iii) 9 cm

(c) Calculate the area of this semi-circle, correct to 1 decimal place.

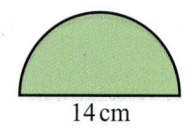

14 cm

2 Counting faces, edges and vertices

For each solid below, write down how many faces, edges and vertices there are.

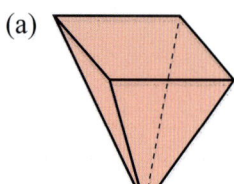

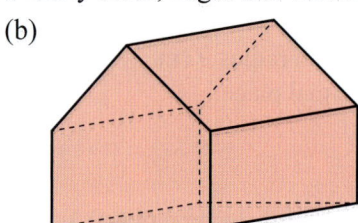

(a)   (b)

3 Making shapes with nets

(a) Draw a net for a triangular prism.

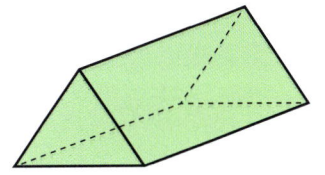

This is a tetrahedron (a triangular pyramid).

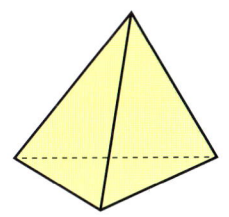

Which of these nets will make a tetrahedron?

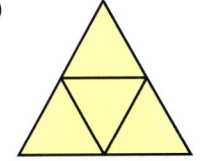

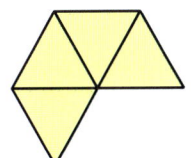

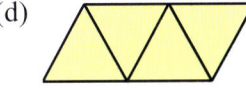

(b)   (c)   (d)

6.5 More equations

In section 6.5 you will:

- review equations covered in section 5.1
- solve equations with the unknown on both sides

Remember with equations:

You may do the same thing to both sides

Solve $15 = 9 + 7n$

$-9 \quad -9$

$6 = 7n$

$\div 7 \quad \div 7$

$\frac{6}{7} = n$ so $n = \frac{6}{7}$

Exercise 1M

1 Solve the equations below.
(a) $n - 7 = 9$
(b) $4x = 28$
(c) $8y = 40$
(d) $\frac{w}{3} = 12$
(e) $\frac{m}{9} = 9$
(f) $3n = 1$

2 Now solve these equations.
(a) $2w + 8 = 24$
(b) $7y - 5 = 9$
(c) $6x - 8 = 16$
(d) $5m + 12 = 62$
(e) $5n - 3 = 1$
(f) $7p + 4 = 6$

3 I think of a number, multiply it by 9 and add 14. The answer is 68. Write down an equation then solve it to find the number.

4 Solve these equations.
(a) $7y - 2 = 2$
(b) $13n + 10 = 12$
(c) $6m - 15 = 33$
(d) $5w - 2 = 1$
(e) $9n + 8 = 71$
(f) $7x + 5 = 8$

5 Solve
(a) $5 = 6x + 4$
(b) $10 = 7 + 8m$
(c) $6 = 5 + 2w$
(d) $13 = 10n + 6$
(e) $6 = 12m - 1$
(f) $2 = 8x - 5$

6 Lois thinks of a number. She multiplies it by 7 and subtracts 3. The answer is 5.

Write down an equation then solve it to find the number.

7 Solve
(a) $3w + 20 = 95$
(b) $\frac{1}{4}x = 9$
(c) $2p + \frac{1}{2} = 1$
(d) $5m + 8 = 8$
(e) $5y - 75 = 425$
(f) $10n = \frac{1}{2}$

8 [rectangle with width n and length $2n + 7$]

The perimeter of this rectangle is 44 cm.
Write down an equation involving n then solve it to find the actual length and width of this rectangle.

9 Repeat question **8** if the perimeter is now 68 cm.

(a) Any answers with fractions must be cancelled if possible.

Solve $6x + 7 = 11$

 ⊖7 ⊖7
$6x = 4$
 ÷6 ÷6
$x = \frac{4}{6}$

(cancel down)

$x = \frac{2}{3}$

(b) Multiply out any brackets first.

Solve $3(2x - 4) = 18$
$6x - 12 = 18$
 +12 +12
$6x = 30$
 ÷6 ÷6
$x = 5$

Exercise 2M

1 Solve these equations.
(a) $8n + 3 = 9$
(b) $10w - 5 = 3$
(c) $4y - 7 = 7$
(d) $20x - 13 = 57$
(e) $11 = 9 + 6m$
(f) $3 = 8p - 9$

2 Solve
(a) $5(x + 2) = 25$
(b) $7(2x - 1) = 21$
(c) $4(3x - 2) = 28$
(d) $2(4x + 5) = 50$
(e) $10(x - 4) = 50$
(f) $6(2x + 7) = 78$

3 [rectangle with sides 23, $3n + 2$, $4n + 5$]

(a) Write down an equation involving n.
(b) Work out the actual value of the perimeter of the rectangle.

4 Solve these equations.
(a) $15 = 7 + 10m$
(b) $4(2x + 3) = 16$
(c) $5(4x - 3) = 15$
(d) $40 = 8(n - 2)$
(e) $4y - 7 = 15$
(f) $3(6p + 5) = 21$

5 Abbie is 8 years older than her sister. Her sister is 3 years older than her brother. The sum of their ages is 50. Let Abbie's age be x. Write down an equation involving x then solve it to find Abbie's age.

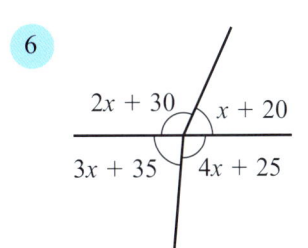

6 [diagram with angles $2x + 30$, $x + 20$, $3x + 35$, $4x + 25$]

Write down an equation involving x then solve it to find the value of each angle.

7 Solve

(a) $52 = 3 + 7p$
(b) $4 = 9w - 3$
(c) $2n + 6 = 11$
(d) $6d - 3 = 8$
(e) $0 = 3(2x - 8)$
(f) $5(4m + 1) = 20$
(g) $1 = 8n - 9$
(h) $2(6y - 5) = 20$
(i) $7 = 3 + 16q$

Equations with the unknown on both sides

(a) Solve $3n + 4 = n + 12$

$$\begin{aligned} &\text{(−n)} \quad \text{(−n)} \\ &2n + 4 = 12 \\ &\text{(−4)} \quad \text{(−4)} \\ &2n = 8 \\ &\text{(÷2)} \quad \text{(÷2)} \\ &n = 4 \end{aligned}$$

(b) Solve $7n - 5 = 3n + 23$

$$\begin{aligned} &\text{(−3n)} \quad \text{(−3n)} \\ &4n - 5 = 23 \\ &\text{(+5)} \quad \text{(+5)} \\ &4n = 28 \\ &\text{(÷4)} \quad \text{(÷4)} \\ &n = 7 \end{aligned}$$

Exercise 3M

1 Solve these equations.

(a) $6n = 4n + 18$
(b) $8n = n + 21$
(c) $15n = 5n + 70$
(d) $4n = 12 + n$
(e) $6n + 4 = 3n + 22$
(f) $8n + 9 = 6n + 23$
(g) $5n - 3 = 3n + 15$
(h) $7n - 6 = 4n + 15$
(i) $5 + 6n = 4n + 33$

2 Solve

(a) $5n + 2 = 3n + 3$
(b) $7n - 9 = 2n + 5$
(c) $8n - 4 = 4n + 11$
(d) $9n + 3 = 6n + 5$
(e) $10n - 7 = 4n + 6$

3 Solve these equations for x.

(a) $4(x + 6) = 3(x + 9)$
(b) $5(2x - 1) = 3(2x + 5)$
(c) $7(2x + 3) = 11(x + 3)$
(d) $4(4x - 1) = 9(x + 5)$
(e) $3(7x - 3) = 3(2x + 17)$
(f) $2(8x + 5) = 13(x + 1)$

4 When a girl's current weight increases by 3 stones, she will weigh three times her current weight less 1 stone. Let n be her current weight. Form an equation in terms of n then write down her current weight.

5 Max solves the equation opposite.
Identify clearly his mistake.

$$5(2x - 1) = 3x + 3$$
$$10x - 5 = 3x + 3$$
$$7x - 5 = 3$$
$$7x = 8$$
$$x = \frac{7}{8}$$

6 Ella has some money. Four times her money less £7 is equal to double her money plus £33. Form an equation then find out how much money Ella has.

Need more practice with equations?

1 Solve the equations below.

(a) $4n = 36$ (b) $4x = 3$ (c) $\frac{m}{4} = 8$

(d) $\frac{w}{7} = 4$ (e) $4p + 2 = 30$ (f) $6x - 5 = 13$

(g) $5y - 11 = 34$ (h) $3w + 12 = 36$ (i) $9m - 7 = 47$

2 Solve these equations.

(a) $8 + 2m = 18$
(b) $38 = 6n - 4$
(c) $51 = 8w + 3$
(d) $55 = 11 + 4p$
(e) $35 = 17 + 3x$

3 Solve

(a) $4(2x + 3) = 60$ (b) $3(5w - 2) = 54$ (c) $5(3x - 1) = 100$

(d) $6(2x + 5) = 66$ (e) $9(3m - 2) = 63$ (f) $7(2n + 7) = 77$

4 The perimeter of this triangle is 67 cm.
Form an equation and find the value of n.

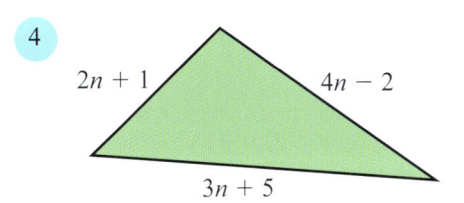

Triangle sides: $2n + 1$, $4n - 2$, $3n + 5$

5 Look at the isosceles triangle opposite and form an equation in terms of x.
Write down the value of x.

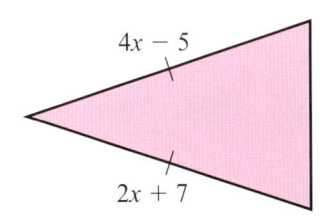

Triangle sides: $4x - 5$, $2x + 7$

6

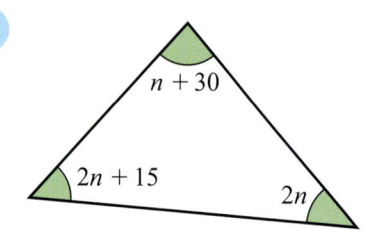

Triangle with angles $n + 30$, $2n + 15$, and $2n$.

(a) Look at the triangle opposite and form an equation in terms of n.
(b) Write down the actual value of each angle in the triangle.

7 Alice, Ben and Charlotte have a total of £137. Ben has twice as much money as Alice. Charlotte has £12 more than Ben.

(a) Copy and complete the table below to show an expression for how much money each person has.

Person	Alice	Ben	Charlotte
Amount	x		

(b) Write down an equation in terms of x.
(c) How much money does Alice have?

Extension questions with equations

1 Solve the equations below.
(a) $8n + 5 = 4n + 37$
(b) $7n - 3 = 5n + 13$
(c) $6n - 20 = 2n + 24$
(d) $10n - 4 = 5n + 16$
(e) $9n + 21 = 7n + 31$
(f) $4n + 9 = 6n - 5$
(g) $5n + 2 = 3n + 3$
(h) $12n - 8 = 8n + 3$
(i) $11n - 4 = 8n + 6$

2 Solve these equations.
(a) $5(2x + 3) = 24$
(b) $3(3x - 2) = 2$
(c) $5(3x - 2) = 11$
(d) $6(2x - 5) = 15$
(e) $5(4x + 3) = 38$
(f) $2(5x - 4) = 23$

3 Rectangle with sides 9, $2n - 3$, and $3n + 1$.

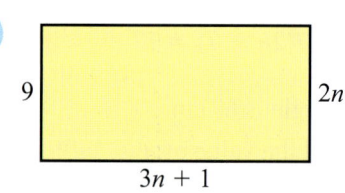

Form an equation then work out the actual area of this rectangle.

4 (a) Write down algebraic expressions for three consecutive numbers if the first number is n.
(b) Form an equation then find the value of n if the sum of the three consecutive numbers is 132.

5 Solve these equations.
(a) $\dfrac{x - 2}{4} = 2$
(b) $\dfrac{x}{4} - 2 = 2$
(c) $\dfrac{3x + 1}{5} = 5$
(d) $\dfrac{3x}{5} + 1 = 5$
(e) $\dfrac{5x - 4}{2} = 13$
(f) $\dfrac{5x}{2} - 4 = 13$

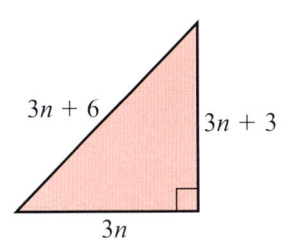

6 Work out the area of this triangle if the perimeter is 36 cm.

Sides: $3n + 6$, $3n + 3$, $3n$

7 The triangle shown opposite is isosceles. Work out the actual area of this triangle.

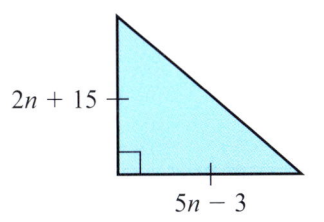

Sides: $2n + 15$, $5n - 3$

8 Solve these equations.
(a) $5(2x + 3) = 2(4x + 9)$
(b) $6(3x - 5) = 5(2x + 3)$
(c) $8(2x - 3) = 3(3x + 2)$

9 Create your own question involving a triangle which will give the equation $7n + 6 = 41$.

6.6 Sequences

In section 6.6 you will learn how to:
- find and use a rule for a sequence

- A number sequence is a set of numbers in a given order.
- Each number in a sequence is called a *term*.

Exercise 1M

1 Write down each sequence and find the next term.
(a) 2, 5, 8, 11
(b) 2, 8, 14, 20
(c) −2, 0, 2, 4
(d) 0.9, 1, 1.1, 1.2
(e) 22, 17, 12, 7
(f) 0.2, 0.5, 0.8

In questions **2** to **7** you may have to add, subtract, multiply or divide to find the next term.

2 21, 15, 9

3 0.2, 2, 20, 200

4 0.8, 1, 1.2

5 80, 40, 20, 10

6 11, 8, 5, 2

7 10 000, 1000, 100

8 Write down the sequence and find the missing numbers.

(a) ☐, 6, 12, 24, ☐

(b) 4, ☐, 10, 13, ☐

(c) ☐, 16, 8, 4, ☐

(d) ☐, 6, 3, 0, −3, ☐

The next three questions are more difficult. Find the next term.

9 1, 2, 6, 24, 120

10 $\frac{1}{3}, \frac{2}{5}, \frac{3}{7}, \frac{4}{9}$

11 2, 2, 4, 12, 48, 240

12 Golf balls can be stacked in a 'solid' pyramid.

The picture shows the view from above a pyramid with **1** ball at the top, **4** balls on the next layer and **9** balls on the next layer after that.

(a) How many balls will be on the next layer?

(b) How many balls will there be altogether in the first five layers?

Sequence rules

- For the sequence 10, 13, 16, 19, 22, … the first term is 10 and the term-to-term rule is 'add 3'.
- For the sequence 3, 6, 12, 24, 48, … the term-to-term rule is 'double' or 'multiply by 2'.

Exercise 2M

1 You are given the first term and the rule of several sequences. Write down the first five terms of each sequence.

	First term	Rule
(a)	8	add 2
(b)	100	subtract 4
(c)	10	double
(d)	64	divide by 2

2 Write down the rule for each of these sequences.

(a) 3, 10, 17, 24   (b) 100, 89, 78, 67   (c) 0.7, 0.9, 1.1, 1.3   (d) 1, 2, 4, 8, 16

3 The rule for the number sequences below is

'double and add 1'

Find the missing numbers.

(a) 2 → 5 → 11 → 23 → ☐

(b) ☐ → 7 → 15 → 31

(c) ☐ → 51 → ☐ → ☐

4 The rule for the number sequences below is

'multiply by 3 and take away 2'

Find the missing numbers.

(a) 2 → 4 → 10 → ☐

(b) ☐ → 7 → 19 → 55

(c) 1 → ☐ → ☐ → ☐

5 A sequence begins 2, 4, …

(a) What is the next term? Give a reason for your answer.

(b) Could the next term be different to your part (a) answer? Give a reason for your answer.

6 The first number in a sequence is 5. Write down a possible rule so that all the terms in the sequence are odd numbers.

7 Write down the rule for each of these sequences.

(a) 2, $2\frac{1}{2}$, 3, $3\frac{1}{2}$, 4, … (b) 5, 10, 20, 40, 80, …

(c) 1.5, 1.6, 1.7, 1.8, … (d) 81, 27, 9, 3, 1, …

(e) 1.5, 1.35, 1.2, 1.05 (f) 76, 38, 19, 9.5

(g) 1, 4, 10, 22, 46 (h) 3, 10, 31, 94

8 Write down the first six terms of these sequences.

(a) the first term is 3
the rule is 'subtract 0.3'

(b) the first term is 864
the rule is 'divide by 6'

(c) the fourth term is 60
the rule is 'add 11'

(d) the third term is 6
the rule is 'divide by 10'

(e) the first two terms are 1, 4
the rule is 'add the two previous terms'

(f) the first two terms are 0, 2
the rule is 'add the two previous terms'

(g) the first term is 3
the rule is 'multiply by 2 and then add 3'

(h) the first term is 5
the rule is 'write down the next prime number'

9 Find the first five terms of each sequence.

(a) The 2nd term is 9
The rule is 'add 5'

(b) The 4th term is 11
The rule is 'take away 3'

(c) The 3rd term is 12
The rule is 'multiply by 2'

(d) The 2nd term is 10
The rule is 'multiply by 10'

10 The rule for a sequence is 'add 3'. The first three terms of the sequence are negative numbers. Find what numbers the first term of the sequence could be.

11 The tenth number in the sequence 1, 3, 9, 27 … is 19 683.
What is (a) the ninth number
(b) the twelfth number?

Exercise 3M

1 Here is a sequence of triangles made from sticks.

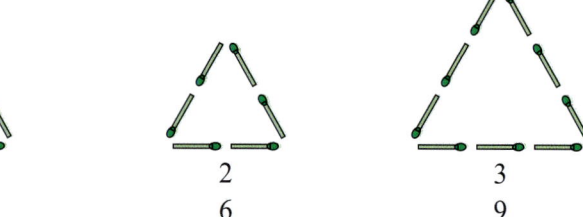

Shape number: 1   2   3
Number of sticks: 3   6   9

(a) Draw shape number 4 and count the number of sticks.

(b) Write down and complete the rule for the number of sticks in a shape:
'The number of sticks is ____ times the shape number'.

2 Louise makes a pattern of triangles from sticks.

Shape number: 1   2   3
Number of sticks: 3   5   7

(a) Draw shape number 4 and shape number 5.

(b) Make a table:

shape number	1	2	3	4	5
number of sticks	3	5	7		

(c) Write down the rule for the number of sticks in a shape.
'The number of sticks is ____ times the shape number and then add ____.'

An *arithmetic* (or linear) sequence is one where the gap between each pair of terms is always the same. This gap is known as the *difference*.

- Consider an arithmetic sequence of shapes made from sticks:

Shape number:	1	2	3
Number of sticks:	4	7	10

- There is a *rule* or *formula* which we can use to calculate the number of sticks for any shape number.
  'The number of sticks is three times the shape number add one'.
  Check that this rule works for all the shapes above and also for shape number 4 which you can draw.
- We could also write the rule using symbols. Let n stand for the diagram number and let s stand for the number of sticks.
  The rule (or formula) is '$s = 3n + 1$'.

3 In these diagrams black squares are surrounded on three sides by yellow squares. Let the number of black squares be b and let the number of yellow squares be y.

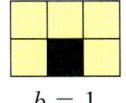

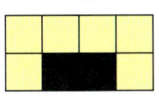

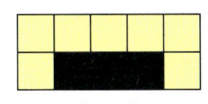

$b = 1$ $b = 2$ $b = 3$
$y = 5$ $y = 6$ $y = 7$

(a) Draw the next diagram, which has 4 black squares.

(b) Write down the rule.
   'The number of yellow squares is ……'

4 Crosses are drawn on 'dotty' paper to make a sequence.

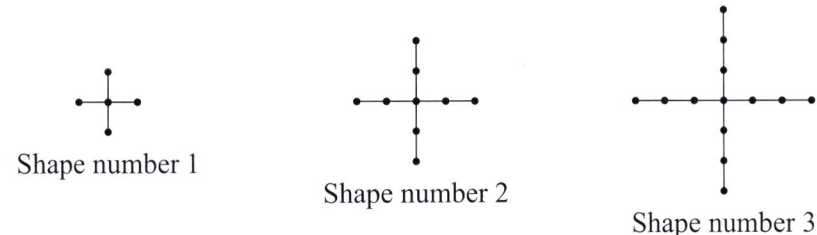

Shape number 1   Shape number 2   Shape number 3

(a) Draw shape number 4.

(b) Make a table:

shape number	1	2	3	4
number of dots	5	9	13	

(c) Write down the rule.
   'The number of dots is ____ times the shape number and then add ____.'

5 Look again at questions ①, ②, and ④. Use n for the shape number and s for the number of sticks or dots. For each question write the rule connecting n and s without using words. In each question write '$s =$.'

- Here is a sequence 4, 8, 12, 16, …

  The first term is 4×1
  The second term is 4×2
  The third term is 4×3
      ⋮   ⋮
  The 30th term is 4×30

  Consider a term n. We call this the nth term.
  The nth term is $4 \times n$ in this sequence.

  > n^{th} term = $4n$

  This formula can be used to find any term in the sequence
  eg.   15th term = $4n = 4 \times 15 = 60$
         100th term = $4n = 4 \times 100 = 400$

- In another sequence the nth term is $3n + 2$

  1st term   = $3 \times 1 + 2$ 2nd term   = $3 \times 2 + 2$ 3rd term   = $3 \times 3 + 2$
  ($n = 1$)   = 5   ($n = 2$)   = 8   ($n = 3$)   = 11

Exercise 4M

1 The nth term of a sequence is $6n$. What is the value of

    (a) the first term   (use $n = 1$)

    (b) the second term   (use $n = 2$)

    (c) the tenth term   (use $n = 10$)

2 The nth term of a sequence is $2n + 5$. What is the value of

    (a) the first term   (use $n = 1$)

    (b) the fifth term   (use $n = 5$)

    (c) the one hundredth term   (use $n = 100$)

3 Write down the first four terms of each sequence using the nth term given.

    (a) $7n$ (b) $n + 3$ (c) $3n + 1$ (d) $25 - n$ (e) $4n + 7$

4 Match up each sequence and the correct formula for the nth term from the list given.
(a) 10, 20, 30, 40, ...
(b) 3, 6, 9, 12, ...
(c) 5, 9, 13, 17, ...
(d) 50, 100, 150, 200, ...
(e) $1^2, 2^2, 3^2, 4^2, ...$
(f) 8, 10, 12, 14, ...
(g) 11, 14, 17, 20, ...
(h) 12, 24, 36, 48, ...

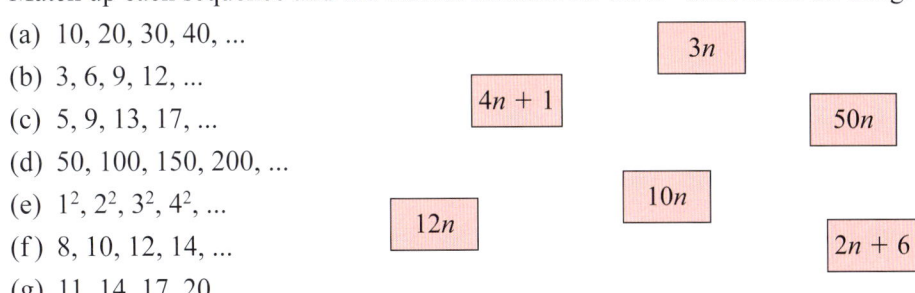

$3n$ $4n + 1$ $50n$ $10n$ $12n$ $2n + 6$ n^2 $3n + 8$

5

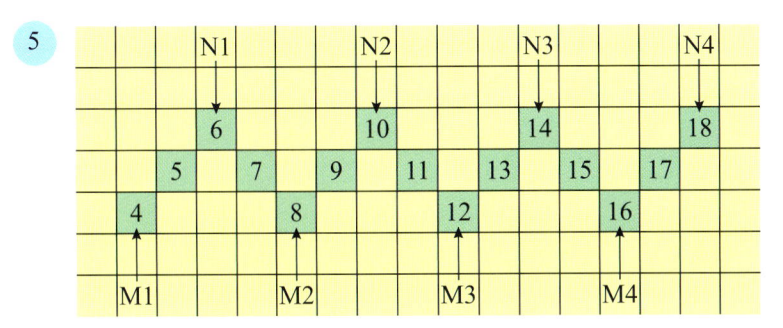

The numbers N1, N2, N3, N4 and M1, M2, M3, M4 form two sequences.
(a) Find M5, M6, N5, N6.
(b) Think of rules and use them to find M15 and N20.

6 The following are arithmetic sequences.

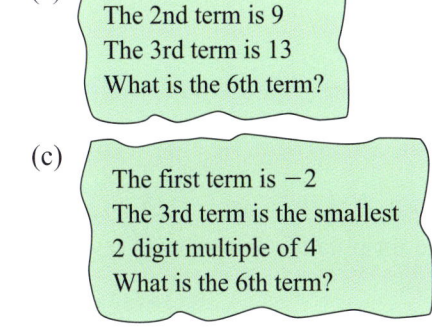

(a) The 2nd term is 9
The 3rd term is 13
What is the 6th term?

(b) The 4th term is 11
The 12th term is 27
What is the 9th term?

(c) The first term is −2
The 3rd term is the smallest
2 digit multiple of 4
What is the 6th term?

(d) The 2nd term is 9
The 5th term is six times
as large as the 1st term.
What is the 6th term?

7 Here is a sequence of touching triangles.
Find the coordinates of
(a) the top of triangle 5
(b) the top of triangle 50
(c) the bottom right corner of triangle 50
(d) the bottom right corner of triangle 100

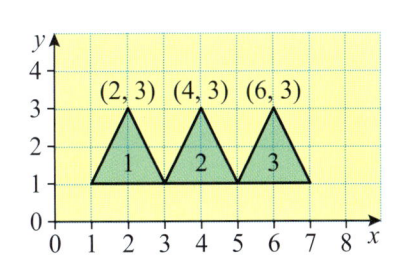

8 Sequence A: n^{th} term = $5n - 3$
Sequence B: n^{th} term = $2n + 5$
Sequence C: n^{th} term = $4n - 1$
Which of the above sequences do the following numbers belong to?
(a) 12 (b) 11 (c) 13 (d) 7 (e) 47 (f) 35

9 Write down the coordinates of the centres of squares 1, 2 and 3.
Find the coordinates of
(a) the centre of square 4
(b) the centre of square 10
(c) the top vertex of square 70

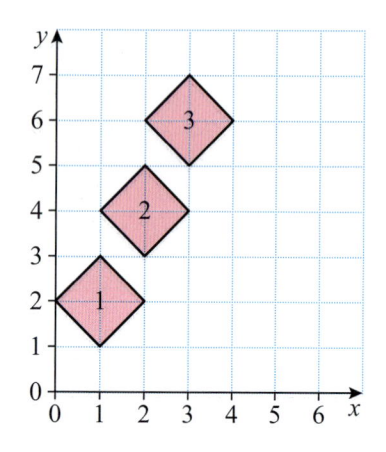

10 Here is a sequence of hexagons made from sticks.

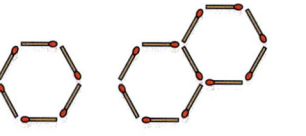

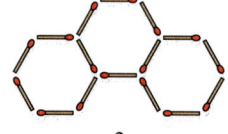

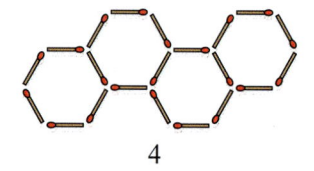

Shape number: 1   2   3   4
Number of sticks: 6   11   16   21

Let n be the shape number and s be the number of sticks.
(a) Write down a rule (or formula) for s in terms of n.
(b) How many sticks are in shape number 15?

11 Design your own sequence using sticks. Write down the formula for s in terms of n where n is the shape number and s is the number of sticks.

12 Design a sequence of squares using sticks so that $s = 6n + 2$ (n is the shape number and s is the number of sticks).

Need more practice with sequences?

1 In the sequences of squares the number of matches is shown.

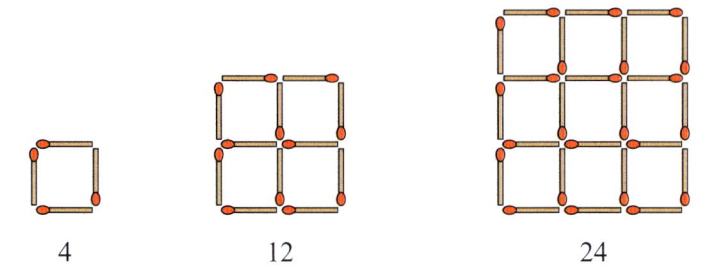

    4   12   24

(a) Draw the next square in the sequence and write down the number of matches in the square.

(b) Copy and complete the number pattern below.

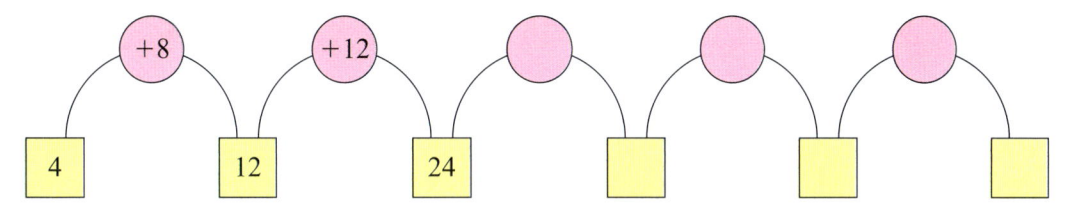

   +8   +12

4   12   24

2 The first term of an arithmetic sequence is 3.7 and the term-to-term rule is 'add 0.25'. Write down the first five terms of the sequence.

3 In this question the rule for several *different* sequences is 'add 5'.
(a) Find a sequence for which all the terms are divisible by 5.
(b) Find a sequence for which none of the terms is a whole number.
(c) Can you find a sequence with the 'add 5' rule in which all the terms are odd numbers?

4 Here is a sequence of 'steps' made from sticks.

Shape number:	1	2	3
Number of sticks:	4	8	12

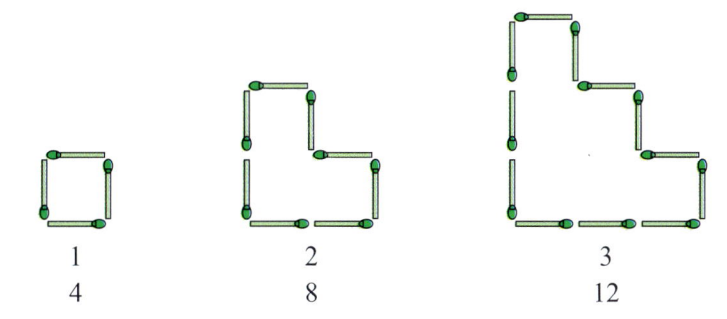

(a) Draw shape number 4 and count the number of sticks.
(b) Write down the rule for the number of sticks in a shape. 'The number of sticks is _____ times the shape number.'
(c) Write down a formula for s in terms of n where n is the shape number and s is the number of sticks.
(d) How many sticks are in shape number 50?

5 Here is a sequence of touching squares.
Copy and complete the table.

Square number	Coordinates of centre
1	(2, 2)
2	(4, 4)
3	
5	
40	
45	

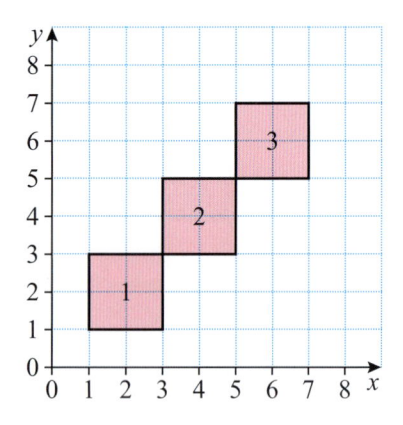

6 A sequence made from a pattern of sticks has the formula $s = 5n + 3$ where n is the shape number and s is the number of sticks.
Anton says that one of the shapes contains 39 sticks.
Marie does not agree. Who is correct? Justify your answer fully.

7 Write down the next three terms in the sequence

2, 2, 4, 6, 10, …

8 Sequence A has n^{th} term $= 6n - 2$ and sequence B has n^{th} term $= n^2 - 3$.
What is the lowest number that is in both sequence A and sequence B?

9 In an arithmetic sequence the terms go up or go down in equal steps.
For example 7, 10, 13, 16, … or 20, 18, 16, 14, …
Fill in the missing numbers in these arithmetic sequences.

(a) 2, ☐, 8, ☐, ☐, 17   (b) 10, ☐, 18, ☐, 26, 30, ☐
(c) ☐, 37, ☐, ☐, 28, 25

10 Write down 4 terms of an arithmetic sequence by using four of the numbers from the list below.

35, 33, 41, 27, 32, 29, 39, 40, 31, 38

Extension questions with sequences

1 (a) Copy this pattern and write down the next three lines. Do not use a calculator!

1 × 999 = 999
2 × 999 = 1998
3 × 999 = 2997
4 × 999 = 3996

(b) Copy this pattern and write down the next two lines.

$3 \times 5 = 15$
$33 \times 5 = 165$
$333 \times 5 = 1665$
$3333 \times 5 = 16665$

(c) Copy and complete $333\,333\,333 \times 5 =$

2 (a) Look at the pattern below and then continue it for a further three rows.

$2^2 + 2 + 3 = 9$
$3^2 + 3 + 4 = 16$
$4^2 + 4 + 5 = 25$
. . . .
. . . .
. . . .

(b) Write down the line which starts
$12^2 + \ldots$

3 (a) Copy this pattern and write down the next line.

$1 \times 9 = 9$
$21 \times 9 = 189$
$321 \times 9 = 2889$
$4321 \times 9 = 38\,889$
$54\,321 \times 9 = 488\,889$

(b) Complete this line $87\,654\,321 \times 9 =$

4 (a) Copy this pattern and write down the next line.

$1 + 9 \times 0 = 1$
$2 + 9 \times 1 = 11$
$3 + 9 \times 12 = 111$
$4 + 9 \times 123 = 1111$

(b) Find the missing numbers

$\boxed{} + 9 \times \boxed{} = 1\,111\,111$

5 (a) Copy this pattern and write down the next line.

$3 \times 4 = 3 + 3 \times 3$
$4 \times 5 = 4 + 4 \times 4$
$5 \times 6 = 5 + 5 \times 5$

(b) Copy and complete
$10 \times 11 =$
$11 \times 12 =$
$100 \times 101 =$

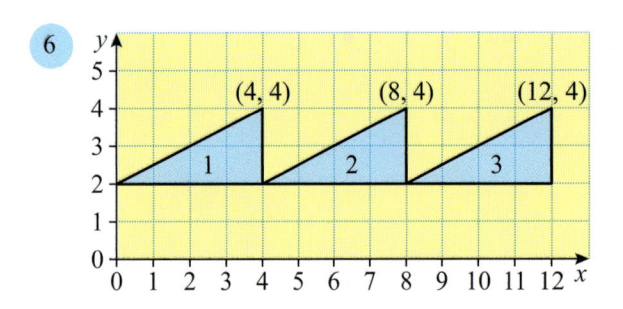

6 Find the coordinates of the top vertex of
  (a) triangle 4
  (b) triangle 20
  (c) triangle 2000

7 A famous sequence in mathematics is Pascal's triangle.
  (a) Look carefully at how the triangle is made. Write down the next row. It starts: 1 7 ...
  (b) Look at the diagonal marked A. Predict the next three numbers in the sequence 1, 3, 6, 10, 15, ...
  (c) Work out the *sum* of the numbers in each row of Pascal's triangle. What do you notice?
  (d) Without writing down all the numbers, work out the sum of the numbers in the 10th row of the triangle.

Note: 1, 3, 6, 10, 15, ... are known as triangular numbers. Research these or ask your teacher about them.

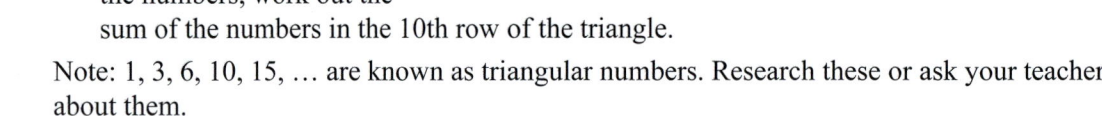

8 (a) What is the sum of all the numbers in Pascal's triangle down to and including
    (i) the 3rd row
    (ii) the 6th row?
  (b) Predict the sum of all the numbers in Pascal's triangle down to and including the 10th row.

9 Write down the coordinates of the centres of the first six squares shown on the diagram below. Find the coordinates of
  (a) the centre of square 60
  (b) the centre of square 73
  (c) the top left corner of square 90
  (d) the top left corner of square 101

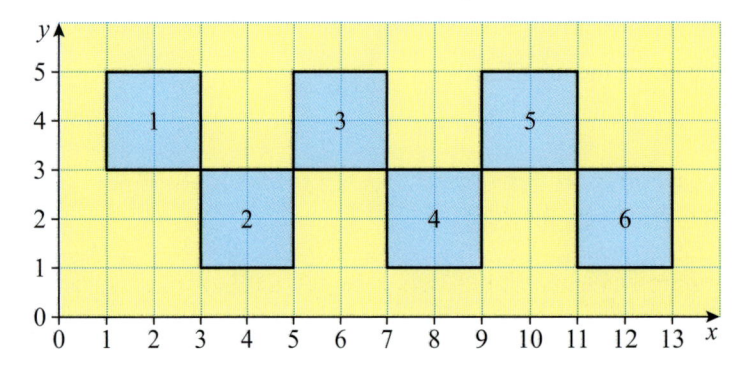

10 The odd numbers can be added in groups to give an interesting sequence.

$$1 = 1 = 1^3 \quad (1 \times 1 \times 1)$$
$$3 + 5 = 8 = 2^3 \quad (2 \times 2 \times 2)$$
$$7 + 9 + 11 = 27 = 3^3 \quad (3 \times 3 \times 3)$$

The numbers 1, 8, 27 are called *cube* numbers. Another cube number is 5^3 (we say '5 cubed').

$$5^3 = 5 \times 5 \times 5 = 125$$

Write down the next three rows of the sequence to see if the sum of each row always gives a cube number.

Investigation – count the crossovers

Two straight lines have a maximum of one crossover.

Three straight lines have a maximum of three crossovers.

Notice that you can have less than three crossovers if the lines all go through one point. Or the lines could be parallel.
In this work we are interested only in the *maximum* number of crossovers.

Four lines have a maximum of six crossovers.

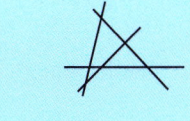

Part A Draw five lines and find the maximum number of crossovers.
Does there appear to be any sort of sequence in your results? If you can find a sequence, use it to *predict* the maximum number of crossovers with six lines.

Part B Now draw six lines and count the crossovers to see if your prediction was correct (remember not to draw three lines through one point).

Part C Predict the number of crossovers for seven lines and then check if your prediction is correct by drawing a diagram.

Part D Write your results in a table:

Number of lines	Number of crossovers
2	1
3	3
4	6
5	
6	

Predict the number of crossovers for 20 lines.

Part E Predict the number of crossovers for 2000 lines (you will need to work out a formula).

✗ Spot the mistakes 12 ✗

Equations and sequences

Work through each question below and explain clearly what mistakes have been made. Beware – some questions are correctly done.

1 Solve $5x - 3 = 2x + 15$

Solution: $5x - 3 = 2x + 15$
$3x - 3 = 15$
$3x = 12$
$x = 4$

2 Find the first 4 terms of the sequence with n^{th} term $= 2n^2 + 1$

Solution: 1st term $= 2 \times 1^2 + 1 = 4 + 1 = 5$
2nd term $= 2 \times 2^2 + 1 = 16 + 1 = 17$
3rd term $= 2 \times 3^2 + 1 = 36 + 1 = 37$
4th term $= 2 \times 4^2 + 1 = 64 + 1 = 65$

3 Solve $\dfrac{x-4}{6} = 5$

Solution: $\dfrac{x-4}{6} = 5$

$\dfrac{x}{6} = 9$

$x = 54$

4 Here is a sequence made from sticks.

Shape number:	1	2	3	4
Number of sticks:	5	9	13	17

Let n be the shape number and s be the number of sticks.
Write down a formula for s in terms of n.

Answer: The number of sticks increases by 4 each time so $s = n + 4$

5 Form an equation and work out the actual area of the square opposite. All lengths are in cm.

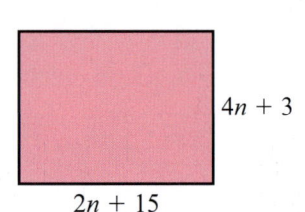

$4n + 3$

$2n + 15$

Solution: $4n + 3 = 2n + 15$
$2n + 3 = 15$
$2n = 12$
$n = 6$

length of side of square $= 2 \times 6 + 15 = 27$ cm
area of square $= 27 \times 27 = 729$ cm²

6 Find the next 3 terms of the sequence 0, 1, 1, 2, 4, 7, 13, …

Answer: 24, 44, 81 because each term is the sum of the previous 3 terms.

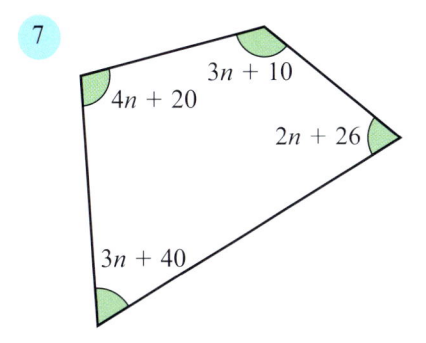

7 Form an equation to find the value of n.

Solution: $4n + 20 + 3n + 10 + 2n + 26 + 3n + 40 = 180$
$12n + 96 = 180$
$12n = 84$
$n = 7°$

Sides labelled: $3n + 10$, $4n + 20$, $2n + 26$, $3n + 40$.

8 Is 49 a number in the sequence with n^{th} term $= 3n + 7$?

Answer: Try $3n + 7 = 49$
$3n = 42$
$n = 14$

so 49 is the 14th term of this sequence.

9 Asha is 3 years older than Ryan. Ryan is twice as old as Ariana. The sum of their ages is 83. How old is Ariana?

Solution: Let Ariana's age $= x$
Asha's age $= x + 3$
Ryan's age $= 2x$
$x + x + 3 + 2x = 83$
$4x + 3 = 83$
$4x = 80$
$x = 20$

so Ariana is 20 years old.

10 Solve $4(2x - 3) = 5x + 21$

Solution: $8x - 3 = 5x + 21$
$3x = 24$
$x = 8$

CHECK YOURSELF ON SECTIONS 6.5 AND 6.6

1 Review of equations covered in section 5.1

Solve the equations below.

(a) $5n - 17 = 28$ (b) $\dfrac{m}{7} = 8$ (c) $15 = 7y + 10$

(d) $4 = 6w - 1$ (e) $3(2x - 5) = 39$ (f) $54 = 2(4p + 3)$

2 Solving equations with the unknown on both sides

Solve these equations.

(a) $5x + 3 = 2x + 24$ (b) $8m - 7 = 6m + 11$ (c) $2(3x - 4) = 4x + 7$

3 Finding and using a rule for a sequence

In these diagrams blue squares are surrounded by green squares.

(a) Draw the next diagram, which has 4 blue squares.

(b) Make a table. Fill in the missing values.

number of blue squares	1	2	3	4
number of green squares	8	10		

(c) Complete the rule:

'The number of green squares is ____ times the number of blue squares and then add ____.'

(d) Using g for the number of green squares and b for the number of blue squares, write down a formula for g in terms of b.

(e) The nth term of a different sequence is $4n + 3$. What is the value of the tenth term of this sequence?

6.7 Applying mathematics 6

In section 6.7 you will apply maths in a variety of situations.

1 Sima has the same number of 10p and 50p coins. The total value is £9. How many of each coin does she have?

2 A box has a mass of 230 g when empty. When it is full of sugar the total mass is 650 g. What is its mass when it is half full?

3 Martin has fitted together 3 patio slabs as shown opposite. Two of the slabs are rectangular and one is triangular.

He has one more triangular slab as shown here. Will it fit perfectly in the space between the two rectangular slabs? Justify your answer fully.

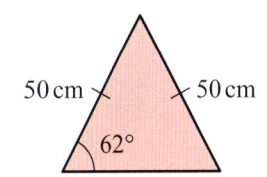

4 Look at the photo of the pile of matches.

(a) Each match is 3 mm thick. How many matches are there in a tower of height 3 cm?

(b) How high a tower can you build with 14 boxes of matches if each box contains 48 matches?

5 The two sides PQ and PT are equal in the pentagon opposite. Form an equation in terms of n then find the actual perimeter of the pentagon. All lengths are in cm.

6 A book has pages numbered 1 to 300 and the thickness of the book, without the covers, is 12 mm. How thick is each page?

7 Lily invests £5000 in a bank. After 1 year she gets 1% interest, the following year 2% interest and in the year after that 3% interest. Each year the amount of interest is worked out on how much money she has in the bank at that moment.

She hoped that the total interest after 3 years would be enough to buy an iPad for £300. Was there enough money for Lily to do this? You must justify your answer fully.

8 The Colosseum had 2680 windows when it was built. The local window cleaner charged a quarter of a denarius per window and cleaned all the windows once a week. A 'denarius' was a Roman coin.

(a) What was his total income in 3 weeks?

(b) Where is the Colosseum?

9. The rule for the number sequences is '*treble* and *subtract 1*'.
   Write down each sequence and fill in the missing numbers.

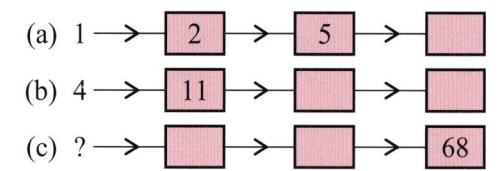

   (a) 1 → 2 → 5 → ☐

   (b) 4 → 11 → ☐ → ☐

   (c) ? → ☐ → ☐ → 68

10. A yellow circle fits perfectly inside an 8 cm square as shown.
    What percentage of the square is outside the circle?
    Give the answer to 1 decimal place.

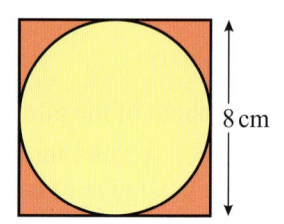

UNIT 6   MIXED REVIEW

Part one

1. What is the next number in the sequence 6, 13, 27, 55?

2. Here is the net for a cube.
   (a) When the net is folded up, which edge will be stuck to the edge JI?
   (b) Which edge will be stuck to the edge AB?
   (c) Which corner will meet corner D?

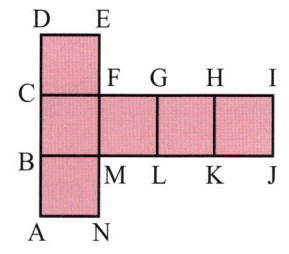

3. What is the mathematical name for a snooker ball that has been cut in half.

4. The tenth number in the sequence 1, 3, 9, 27, … is 19 683. What is the ninth number?

5. How many metres are 999 mm?

6. A jar with 8 chocolates in it weighs 160 g. The same jar with 20 chocolates in it weighs 304 g. How much does the jar weigh on its own?

7. P ——— 7 cm ——— Q   Draw a line PQ of length 7 cm.
   Construct the perpendicular bisector of PQ.

8. Solve the equations.

(a) $\frac{n}{7} = 6$ (b) $6y - 3 = 45$ (c) $8x + 7 = 12$

(d) $3 = 5w - 1$ (e) $4p = \frac{1}{2}$ (f) $75 = 4a - 17$

9. Here is a sequence of diagrams showing an arrangement of counters

Diagram 1   Diagram 2   Diagram 3

(a) Draw diagram number 4.
(b) Copy and complete this table for the diagrams so far.

Diagram Number	Counters used
1	7
2	
3	
4	

(c) Without drawing, how many counters will be needed for diagram number 5?
(d) Let n be the diagram number and c be the counters used.
Write down a formula for c in terms of n.

10. How many wine glasses of capacity 30 ml can be filled from a barrel containing 210 litres?

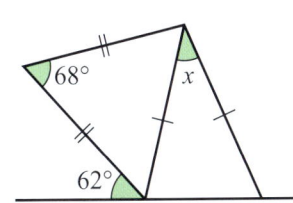

11. Find the size of angle x.

12. Unifix cubes can be joined together to make different sized cuboids.

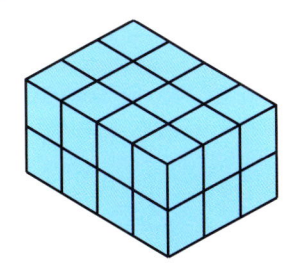

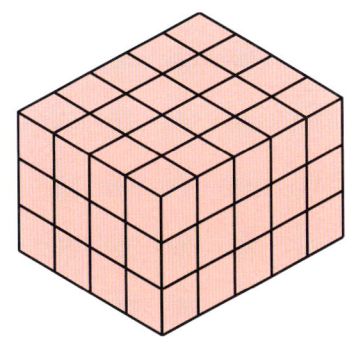

If the smaller cuboid weighs 96 g, how much does the large cuboid weigh?

13 (a) Calculate the circumference of circle A.
   (b) Calculate the area of semi-circle B.

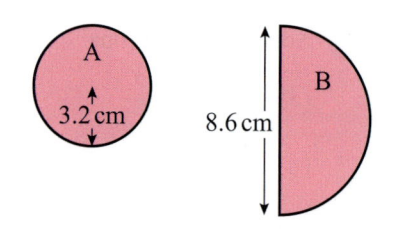

   3.2 cm   8.6 cm

14 *Construct* this triangle with a ruler and compasses only.
   Use a protractor to measure the size of $A\hat{B}C$.

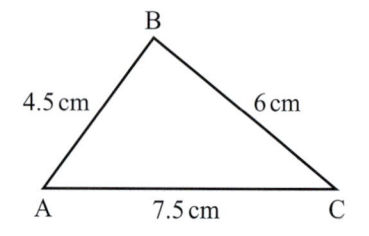

   4.5 cm, 6 cm, 7.5 cm

15 Copy and fill in the missing numbers.

   (a) 4.7 m = ☐ cm   (b) 63 g = ☐ kg
   (c) 4 feet = ☐ inches   (d) 360 m = ☐ km
   (e) 8 litres = ☐ ml   (f) 2 pounds = ☐ ounces
   (g) 45 mm = ☐ cm   (h) 5 yards = ☐ feet

Part two

1 The tenth number in the sequence 1, 4, 16, 64 ...... is 262 144.
  What is (a) the ninth number
          (b) the twelfth number?

2 Find the size of $B\hat{C}D$.

   25°, 118°

3 A car travels 10 miles on a litre of petrol and petrol costs 98p per litre.
  In six months the car is driven a total of 6500 miles. Find the cost of the petrol.

4 Solve the equations.
(a) $3y - 5 = 9$
(b) $4(2x + 3) = 52$
(c) $35 = 7(x - 4)$
(d) $5x + 2 = 3x + 20$
(e) $\dfrac{x + 2}{7} = 4$
(f) $3(2y - 1) = 3y + 24$

5 Mr Gibson, the famous balloonist, was at a height of 3.2 km when a fault developed and he started to descend at a speed of 10 m/s. How long does Mr Gibson have to fix the problem?

6 Lana is 5 feet 3 inches tall. Her sister Beth is 157 cm tall. Which sister is taller and by how much?

7 These nets form cubical dice. Opposite faces of a dice always add up to 7. Write down the value of a, b, c, d, e, and f so that opposite faces add up to 7.

8 A metal ingot weighing 58 kg is made into 20 000 buttons. What is the weight in grams of one button?

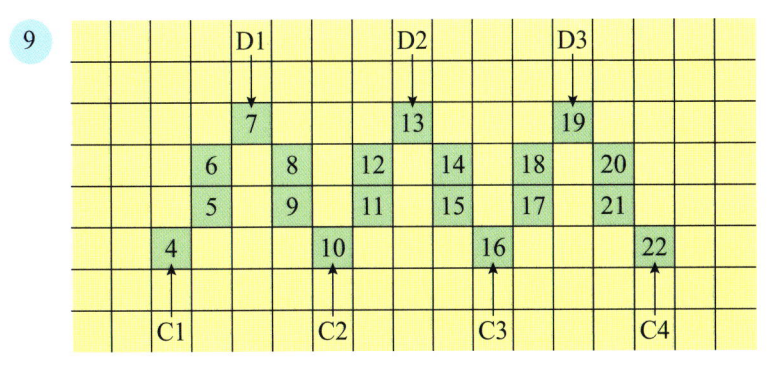

9

The numbers C1, C2, C3, … and D1, D2, D3, … form two sequences.
(a) Find C5 and D5.
(b) Use a rule to find C10 and D30.

10 (a) Use a ruler and compasses only to construct an equilateral triangle.
  (b) Construct the angle bisector of one of the angles.
  (c) Use a protractor to check that the angle bisector has made two angles each of 30°.

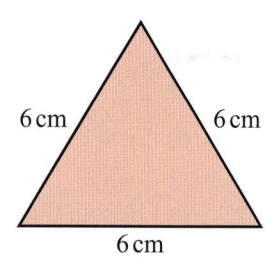

11 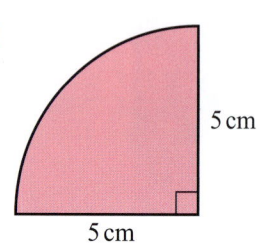 Cathy works out the perimeter of this shape as follows.

circumference = $\pi \times 5 = 15.7$ cm
curved edge = $15.7 \div 4 = 3.9$ cm
perimeter = $3.9 + 5 + 5 = 13.9$ cm

Explain clearly the mistake that Cathy has made.

12 Don has £5 more than Annie. Janine has £41 more than Annie. Janine has three times as much money as Don. Let Annie's money be x. Write down an equation involving x then solve it to find out how much money Annie has.

13 A shopkeeper buys coffee beans at £4.20 per kg and sells them at 95p per 100 g. How much profit does he make per kg?

14 The numbers 1 to 12 are arranged on the star so that the sum of the numbers along each line is the same.

Copy and complete the star.

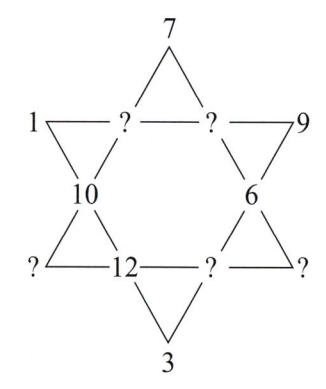

15 Find the size of angle x in each of the diagrams below.

(a)

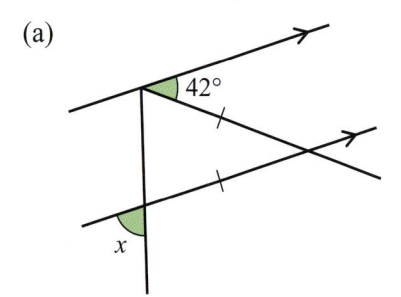

(b)

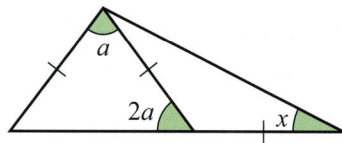

ANSWERS TO CHECK YOURSELF SECTIONS

Page 23 **Check yourself on sections 1.1 and 1.2**

1. (a) 8643   (b) 3468

2. (a) 439   (b) 2331   (c) 45   (d) 62   (e) 75   (f) 3306   (g) 26 each, 2 left over

3. (a) RELATION   (b)

	3.2	0.54	0.9	1.8
2.7	5.9	3.24	3.6	4.5
8.6	11.8	9.14	9.5	10.4
0.04	3.24	0.58	0.94	1.84
8	11.2	8.54	8.9	9.8

4. (a) 22.68   (b) 3.54   (c) 0.2   (d) 0.0401   (e) 72   (f) 53   (g) 1.96 m^2

Page 53 **Check yourself on units 1.3 and 1.4**

1. (a) 2   (b) 19   (c) 3   (d) 120   (e) $5 \times (4 - 1)^2$
2. (a) 6.05   (b) 3.6
3. (a) 15.18   (b) 622.008
4. (a) $n - 6$ (b) $5x - 8$ (c) $2w + 24$
5. (a) $2m + 9n$ (b) $7y$ (c) $4p + 6$ (d) $4xy + 4y$
   (e) $28mn$ (f) $32pqr$ (g) C and D
6. (a) 645   (b) 6   (c) 3
7. (a) $5x + 35$ (b) $np - 3n$ (c) $x^2 + 8x$ (d) $18x + 12$ (e) $11x + 27$
8. (a) □ = 8   (b) □ = 12, ○ = 3

Page 60 **Check yourself on section 1.5**

1. (a) -4 (b) -7 (c) -3 (d) -2

2. (a) -15 (b) 8   (c) -3 (d) 32

Page 91 Check Yourself on Sections 2.1 and 2.2

1. (a) $\dfrac{7}{42}$ (b) $\dfrac{28}{36}$ (c) $\dfrac{2}{3}$ (d) $\dfrac{49}{56}, \dfrac{63}{72}$ (e) B

2. (a) $\dfrac{29}{35}$ (b) $\dfrac{1}{12}$ (c) $2\dfrac{13}{40}$ (d) $3\dfrac{11}{12}$ (e) $2\dfrac{13}{40}$

3. (a) $\dfrac{27}{70}$ (b) $\dfrac{44}{45}$ (c) 2 (d) $1\dfrac{17}{25}$ (e) $1\dfrac{37}{40}$ cm²

4. 40%, 0.4, $\dfrac{2}{5}$;   75%, 0.75, $\dfrac{3}{4}$;   5%, 0.05, $\dfrac{1}{20}$;   45%, 0.45, $\dfrac{9}{20}$

Page 108 Check yourself on Units 2.3 and 2.4

1. P(−3, −2), Q(2, −1), R(−2, 1)
2. (a) (5, 3) (b) (7, 5) (c) (4, 3)
3. (a) (1, 4) (b) $x = 1$ (c) $y = 2$ (d) (3, 3)
4. (a) $y = x - 2$ (b) (i) $y = x + 3$ (ii) $y = 2x$ (c) P, R (d) 1, 3, 5
5. (a) 3 (b) $\dfrac{1}{4}$ (c) $\dfrac{2}{3}$ (d) $-\dfrac{3}{5}$

Page 134 Check yourself on sections 2.5 and 2.6

1. (a) 248 cm² (b) 115 cm² (c) 12 cm (d) 10.5 square units
2. (a) 120 cm² (b) 120 cm²
3. (a) 102° (b) 121° (c) 41°
4. (a) BÊF = 78°, FÊH = 102° (b) 61°
5. (a) 85° (b) 84°

Page 167 Check yourself on sections 3.1 and 3.2

1. (a) 53, 59 (b) 3 + 97, 11 + 89 (+ others)
2. (a) 24 (b) 15 (c) $3 \times 5 \times 7 \times 7$
3. (a) 108 (b) (i) 9 (ii) 189 (iii) 10
   (c) eg. 3, 4, 5 (d) 512
4. (a) 945 (b) 17 658 (c) 45 (d) 11 (e) 12.24, 13, 2.6
   (f) 40 (g) 30.1 cm²

Page 179 *Check Yourself on Section 3.3*

1. (a) 9 (b) 8.5 (c) 8 (d) 12

2. Warriors : mean = 23.8, range = 14 and Sabres : mean = 22.7, range = 12

3. (a) 3 (b) 2.6125 (c) 3

Page 209 *Check Yourself on Units 3.4 and 3.5*

1.

Stem	Leaf
3	1 3
4	4 5 5 8
5	2 2 5 7 7 7 9
6	3 4 4 5 8
7	3 6

Key: 5|7 means 57 years old

2. (a) Frequencies: 2, 5, 7, 4, 3

3. (a) 175 (b) 300 (c) 200

4. (a) White (b) (i) $\frac{7}{11}$ (ii) $\frac{3}{11}$ (iii) 0 (iv) $\frac{1}{11}$

5. (a) (10, 1) (10, 2) (10, 3) (10, 4) (10, 5) (10, 6) (20, 1) (20, 2) (20, 3) (20, 4) (20, 5) (20, 6) (30, 1) (30, 2) (30, 3) (30, 4) (30, 5) (30, 6)

(b) (i) $\frac{1}{18}$ (ii) $\frac{5}{9}$

Page 242 *Check Yourself on Sections 4.1 and 4.2*

1.

(a)	$\frac{2}{25}$	0.08	8%
(b)	$\frac{4}{5}$	0.8	80%
(c)	$\frac{9}{10}$	0.9	90%
(d)	$\frac{8}{25}$	0.32	32%
(e)	$\frac{18}{25}$	0.72	72%

2. (a) 40% (b) maths test

3. (a) £285 (b) £806.40

4. (a) $\frac{13}{22}$ (b) £61.32 (c) 150 g box

5. (a) 3:8 (b) 9 (c) £80

Page 253   Check Yourself on Sections 4.3 and 4.4

1. 5.3 cm or 5.4 cm   **2.** (a) 43°   (b) 49°

3. (a) trapezium   (b) square   (c) rhombus   (d) kite   (e) parallelogram

(f) Four equal sides, opposite sides are parallel, opposite angles are equal, two lines of symmetry, rotational symmetry order 2, diagonals perpendicular to each other, diagonals bisect each other.

(g) P, R   (h) 10   (i) This shape is a regular octagon

4. (a) 2   (b) 1

(c) The diagonal line of symmetry does not allow one half of the rectangle to fold exactly onto the other half of the rectangle.

Page 276   Check yourself on Sections 4.5, 4.6 and 4.7

1. (a) (i) $\binom{3}{2}$ (ii) $\binom{-2}{1}$ (iii) $\binom{0}{4}$

2. (a) 2   (b) 6   (c) 3   (d) 2   (e)

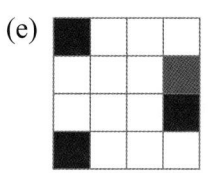

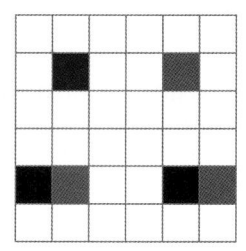

3. (a) (b) 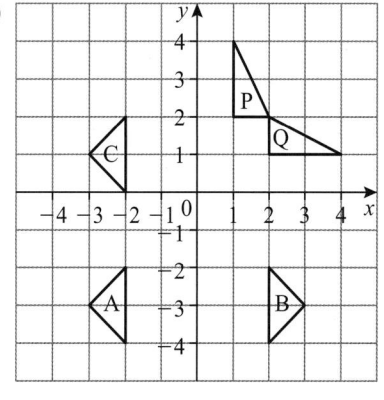   (c) $y = x$

4. (a) (b)

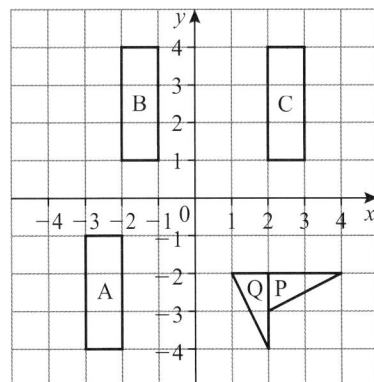

(c) 90° clockwise about (2, −2)

Page 309   Check yourself on Sections 5.1 and 5.2

1. (a) $2mn + m$ (b) 6 (c) $15mn$ (d) $21n - 35$ (e) 4

2. (a) 10 (b) 30 (c) $\frac{1}{5}$ (d) 7

3. (a) $3n + 9 = 10$ so $n = \frac{1}{3}$ (b) $5x + 50 = 180$ so $x = 26$. Angles are 36°, 77°, 67°

4. (a) 15°C (b) October (c) April and November
   (d) April, May (e) 21°C

5. 12.30

Page 327   Check yourself on Sections 5.3 and 5.4

1. (a) $2 \times 2 \times 7 \times 13$ (b) same answer $\frac{5}{12}$ (c) $\frac{3}{4}$ (d) 34
   (e) £1.61 (f) 15.15 (g) $1\frac{1}{2}$ hours (h) 56

2. (a) 0.18 (b) 0.084 (c) 32 000 (d) 680 (e) 43.2 (f) 0.0701

3. (a) 150 (b) 40 (c) 10 (d) £60

Page 339   Check yourself on Section 5.5

1. (a) $\frac{1}{4}$ (b) $\frac{3}{7}$ (c) $\frac{1}{6}$

Page 367 Check yourself on sections 6.1 and 6.2

1. (a) 7650 m (b) 40 cm (c) 7.5 litres

2. (a) 8 ounces (b) 22 pints (c) 6 feet

3. (a) 5 cm (b) £1.06

4. (a) P by 300 cm^2 (or 0.03 m^2) (b) 0.125 mm (c) 900

5. (a) 80° (b) 48° (c) 68°

6. 3.7 cm

Page 384 Check yourself on sections 6.3 and 6.4

1. (a) (i) 18.8 cm (ii) 13.2 m (iii) 28.3 cm

(b) (i) 28.3 cm^2 (ii) 13.9 m^2 (iii) 63.6 cm^2

(c) 77.0 cm^2

2. (a) 5 faces, 8 edges, 5 vertices (b) 7 faces, 15 edges, 10 vertices

3. (b) and (d)

Page 406 Check yourself on sections 6.5 and 6.6

1. (a) 9 (b) 56 (c) $\frac{5}{7}$ (d) $\frac{5}{6}$ (e) 9 (f) 6

2. (a) 7 (b) 9 (c) 7.5

3. (c) 2 times, add 6 (d) $g = 2b + 6$ (e) 43

INDEX

Addition   1, 12, 55, 75
Algebra   34, 287
Alternate angles   126, 360
Angles   122, 359
Area   111, 371
Averages   168, 174

Balance puzzles   49, 290
Bar charts   180
Bisectors (constructing)   362
Brackets   30, 46, 294, 387

Calculator   24
Circles   368
Comparing data   171
Constructing triangles   243
Coordinates   93
Corresponding angles   126, 360
Cross number puzzles   142, 281
Cube numbers   155

Decimals   11, 84, 163, 312, 314
Decimal places   320
Division   3, 17, 58, 80, 162

Equations   291, 385
Equations of lines   98, 100
Equilateral triangle   124
Equivalent fractions   74
Estimating   323
Expressions   35, 38

Factors   149, 310
Four colour theorem   146
Formulas   44, 288
Fractions   29, 74, 84, 312, 315

Gradient   103
Graphs   97, 102, 301
Grouped data   185

History of mathematics   72, 146, 219, 286, 348
Handling data   180

H.C.F.   152, 311
Hidden words   164

Imperial units   351
Improper fractions   77
Indices   27
Investigations   43, 69, 91, 122, 158, 253, 403
Isosceles triangle   124, 359

Kite   248

L.C.M.   152, 311
Long multiplication and division   6, 162, 313

Mean   168, 174
Median   168, 175
Mental arithmetic   70, 144, 218, 284, 347
Metric units   350
Mistakes (spot the)   33, 61, 110, 132, 166, 207, 240, 273, 307, 337, 382, 404
Mixed numbers   77
Mixed review   63, 138, 212, 279, 341, 408
Mode   169, 175
Multiples   149, 310
Multiplying   1, 14, 58, 78, 162
Multiplying brackets   46

nth term of sequence   396
Nets   378
Negative numbers   55

Order of operations   24
Operator squares   22
Ordering decimals   11
Outcomes (listing)   202

Parallel, perpendicular lines   126, 360, 362
Parallelogram   116, 248
Pascal's triangle   402
Percentages   84, 221, 312, 315

Pi   369
Pie charts   188
Place value   11
Polygons   249
Prime numbers   147, 150, 310
Probability   196, 328
Properties of numbers   147
Proportion   231
Protractor   123
Puzzles   67, 142, 216, 281, 345

Quadrilaterals   128, 248

Range   169
Ratio   231, 235, 316
Reflection   257, 260
Remainders   4
Rhombus   248
Roman numbers   348
Rotation   265
Rotational symmetry   258
Rounding   320

Satisfied numbers   157
Sequences   391
Significant figures   322
Speed   302
Square numbers   154
Stem and leaf diagrams   182
Substitution   44, 289
Subtraction   1, 55, 75
Symmetry   250

Terms   35, 41
Three dimensional object   376
Tile factory   273
Translation   255
Trapezium   116, 248
Travel graphs   302
Triangles   113, 124, 243
Two dimensional shapes   248

Venn diagram (L.C.M./H.C.F.)   153
Visualizing shapes   377